Thomas Jefferson's Granddaughter
in Queen Victoria's England

Thomas Jefferson's Granddaughter in Queen Victoria's England

The Travel Diary of Ellen Wayles Coolidge, 1838–1839

ANN LUCAS BIRLE &
LISA A. FRANCAVILLA

Editors

Massachusetts Historical Society, *Boston*

MONTICELLO
Thomas Jefferson Foundation, *Charlottesville*

DISTRIBUTED BY THE
University of Virginia Press, *Charlottesville*

© 2011 Massachusetts Historical Society
and the Thomas Jefferson Foundation, Inc.

Designed by Steve Dyer

LIBRARY OF CONGRESS CATALOGING-IN-PUBLICATION DATA
Coolidge, Ellen Wayles Randolph, 1796–1876.
Thomas Jefferson's granddaughter in Queen Victoria's England: the
travel diary of Ellen Wayles Coolidge, 1838–1839 / Ann Lucas Birle &
Lisa A. Francavilla, editors.
p. cm.
Includes bibliographical references and index.
ISBN 978-1-936520-02-2 (alk. paper)
1. Coolidge, Ellen Wayles Randolph, 1796–1876—Travel—Great
Britain. 2. Coolidge, Ellen Wayles Randolph, 1796–1876—Diaries.
3. Great Britain—Description and travel. I. Birle, Ann Lucas, 1964–
II. Francavilla, Lisa A., 1964– III. Massachusetts Historical Society.
IV. Thomas Jefferson Foundation. V. Title.
DA625.C775 2011
941.081092—dc23
[B]
2011040550
ISBN 978-1-936520-02-2

Dedicated to the memory of

GERALD MORGAN, JR.

CONTENTS

LIST OF ILLUSTRATIONS

PREFACE

Writing to his five-year-old granddaughter Ellen, Thomas Jefferson predicted that if she continued her rapid progress in learning to read and write, "you will become a learned lady and publish books yourself." Ellen Wayles Coolidge fulfilled her grandfather's promise of becoming a learned lady, but she never published her writings. Instead she preserved her letters and journals for her own reference and for her family. Together the Massachusetts Historical Society (MHS) and the Thomas Jefferson Foundation are pleased to bring Ellen Coolidge's London travel diary to the printed page for the first time.

In an era when many educated women living in elite households kept diaries, Ellen Coolidge's still stands apart, distinguished by her remarkable education and perspective. Corresponding regularly with her famous grandfather—even during his presidency—Ellen developed an exceptional aptitude for writing and observation. She also participated in what she called the "feast of reason" at Jefferson's Monticello, where she lived from the age of thirteen until her marriage at twenty-eight. Her diary makes clear that Jefferson was not the sole beneficiary of the intellectual and social riches he gathered around his mountaintop home.

When she married Bostonian Joseph Coolidge in 1825, Ellen left behind her life on a Virginia plantation for America's fourth largest city. Now a part of a prominent and prosperous mercantile family, she assumed the roles of wife and mother, including helpmate to a businessman with trade interests around the globe. Her journey to London, started in 1838, was her first outside of the United States.

When Ellen arrived in England, sixty-two years had passed since Jefferson wrote the Declaration of Independence, and a generation of Americans born as citizens of the United States had matured—and were venturing abroad. In her diary, Ellen defended Jefferson's view of democracy even as she acknowledged her appreciation of and affinity for England. Perhaps because of—or possibly in spite of—her grandfather's role as a leader of the Revolution, Ellen was accorded exceptional social access in London for an American, especially a woman. The result of this mix of access and perspective is a rare diary that excels in both style and substance. Equal parts travelogue and introspection, the diary conveys the sense of wonder that pervaded London in the summer of 1838, when a new queen made all things seem possible. As Ellen taps into her early education and love of art, memories unfold from her years at Monticello—stories that have never appeared elsewhere.

One hundred and seventy-three years after it was begun, Ellen Coolidge's diary will now reach a new audience, thanks to the stewardship and generosity of her family, the partnership between the Massachusetts Historical Society and the Thomas Jefferson Foundation at Monticello, and donors to both organizations on behalf of this project. We are grateful to all, starting with the four generations of Coolidge women who preserved the diary, and Ellen Coolidge's great-granddaughter Mary Churchill, who presented the manuscript to the Society in 1964. We would especially like to recognize the support of Mary and Gerald Morgan, Jr., Dr. Katherine and John Lastavica, Frank and M. L. Coolidge, J. Linzee and Elizabeth Coolidge, the Monticello Association, and the law firm of Ropes & Gray. We are grateful to Ellen Eddy Thorndike for her recent gift to Monticello of the Francis Alexander portrait of Ellen Wayles Coolidge, which graces the cover.

When Ellen's diary came to the MHS, it joined other family papers already given by her descendants. In 1898 Ellen and Joseph's son Thomas Jefferson Coolidge (1831–1920), who appears as a seven-year-old in Ellen's diary entries, presented the Society with a large number of Jefferson papers, initiating the Coolidge Collection of Thomas Jefferson Manuscripts. Ellen and Joseph's grandson Thomas Jefferson Coolidge (1863–1912), great-grandson, and great-great-grandson, all of the same name, continued to add to the collection, as have other family descendants, making the collection second in size only to that of the Library of Congress.

Thomas Jefferson's Monticello is one of the best documented plantations in the world, largely because of the Coolidge Collection at the MHS. The collection's drawings and manuscripts include thousands of pages of correspondence, almanacs, accounts, inventories, law treatises, and journals, including his garden and farm books. Collectively they document Jefferson's private life at Monticello and detail its architecture, landscape, slave community, and family life. They have also informed restoration, preservation, and interpretation decisions at Jefferson's iconic home.

This publication advances the educational missions of both institutions and offers readers a lively and authentic perspective on Thomas Jefferson, his world, and his legacy. We are grateful to Monticello research historian Ann Lucas Birle for recognizing the relevance of Ellen's diary when she first examined it in 1990, and to Lisa Francavilla, managing editor of *The Papers of Thomas Jefferson: Retirement Series*, sponsored by and housed at the Foundation, for lending her considerable expertise to the project. With the help of their colleagues, Ann and Lisa have amplified and contextualized a forgotten voice from a founding father's family, recorded at a critical and uncertain time in our nation's history, and restored to modern readers the all-important and oft missing female perspective.

Leslie Greene Bowman, *President* Dennis A. Fiori, *President*
Thomas Jefferson Foundation   *Massachusetts Historical Society*

INTRODUCTION

On 7 July 1838 Ellen Wayles Coolidge (fig. 13) arrived in London to find a city still celebrating the coronation of Queen Victoria. It was her first trip outside the United States, and her husband, Joseph Coolidge, Jr. (fig. 18), awaited her at Fenton's Hotel on St. James's Street.[1] With their five children safely in the care of relatives and boarding schools, the couple planned to explore London for six weeks before sailing to Canton, where Joseph had business to pursue. Their stay in London instead lasted nearly a year. Ellen began keeping a diary the day after her arrival, and she eventually filled four notebooks with her observations of the young queen and the crowded city, along with memories of her own family and youth. Covering topics that ranged from London's politics, smog, docks, and policemen to its museums, theaters, and unwavering social distinctions, Ellen's diary entries capture the essence of a nation on the brink of a new era. In her written words, we encounter the voice of an exceptional student of the world, a woman whose life and education began in Virginia under the care of her maternal grandfather, Thomas Jefferson (fig. 14).

Martha (fig. 15), Jefferson's eldest daughter, and her husband, a fellow Virginian named Thomas Mann Randolph (fig. 16), had twelve children; Ellen was their fourth.[2] In the fall of 1801, just a few weeks after her fifth birthday, she wrote her first letter, which was addressed to her grandfather, then president of the United States. It proves an assessment that Martha had shared with her father earlier that year: "Ellen is wonderfully apt."[3] As Ellen and Jefferson corresponded over the next eight years, the president of this young republic taught Ellen how to observe and how to write. "You have a thousand little things to tell me which I am fond to hear," he encouraged her.[4] Ellen's letters to her grandfather communicated in abundance the details of daily life at Monticello, Jefferson's plantation, and at her own home, Edgehill, three miles away across the

Rivanna River. She wrote accounts of bulbs sprouting and bantam chicks
hatching, reported her progress mastering foreign languages and books
of poetry, and kept her grandfather apprised of their family's health and
the remodeling under way at Monticello. Jefferson rewarded Ellen's epis-
tolary efforts with all the tools necessary to sustain a writer: volumes of
Shakespeare and Homer, pens that never needed mending, poems for her
scrapbook, reading assignments, and a writing desk of his own design,
made from wild cherry wood by John Hemmings, a joiner and a slave
at Monticello.[5]

In 1809, after Jefferson retired from the presidency, Ellen and her siblings came to live with him at Monticello (fig. 17). She was tutored by her
mother, who had been educated in Philadelphia and at a convent school
in Paris, and Monticello was her university. For the next sixteen years Ellen
lived and studied in Jefferson's "essay in architecture," an eleven thousand-
square-foot neoclassical home perched on the top of a mountain, the center of a seven thousand-acre tobacco and wheat plantation.[6] Monticello's
library contained the "choicest collections of books in the US," more than
six thousand volumes when Jefferson sold it to Congress in 1815, and its
scientific instruments were comparable to those at Harvard College.[7] The
entrance hall was a cabinet of curiosities, featuring artifacts from Lewis
and Clark's expedition, maps of the continents and Virginia, and fossil-
ized bones of the mammoth and mastodon, alongside paintings copied
after Leonardo da Vinci and Guido Reni, and a model of the pyramid
at Cheops—all items that Ellen and her siblings knew intimately. Ellen
was accomplished on the piano and harpsichord and had drawing lessons
with the artist Thomas Sully, one of several painters and sculptors who
came to Monticello to capture Jefferson's likeness.[8]

Around three times a year Jefferson, Ellen, and one of her sisters made
up a small traveling party that undertook the three-day journey to Poplar Forest, Jefferson's Bedford County plantation, where he had designed
and built an octagonal hermitage.[9] There they rejoiced in an intensity of
study that was impossible at the increasingly crowded Monticello. Jefferson deemed Ellen and her sister Cornelia "the severest of students." With
Jefferson's help, Ellen learned to read Greek, Latin, French, and Italian.
Writing to her mother in 1819, Ellen recalled the rigor of their life at
Poplar Forest: "every day for six weeks at a time I have devoted from seven
to eight hours to my latin. . . . [H]our after hour, I have poured over volumes of history. . . . I have often thought that the life of a student must be
the most innocent and happy in the world. . . . [I]f I had been a man with
the advantages of early education, I would have been just such a one, I

FIGURE 1. *Sally Cottrell Cole*, by
William Roads, ca. 1860–1875.
*(Courtesy of Special Collections,
University of Virginia Library.)*

think, but being a woman and not a rich woman, I must be content with peeping every now and then into a region too blissfull for my inhabitance."[10] Ellen's erudition and composure impressed Jefferson's physician, Thomas Watkin, who informed him that she was "so self confident, so charismatic, with a modest, yet somehow commanding presence, that I don't hesitate to say that but for the gender restrictions in place, if she were not a woman, and obliged to be content as a wife and mother, I believe she could have been president."[11]

Ellen and her sisters resented the intrusion that women's work made upon their studies, but Martha Jefferson Randolph was determined that her daughters would be better prepared than she had been for her role as plantation mistress.[12] Required to take turns supervising the Monticello household, each girl dreaded her turn "carrying the keys," a duty that included choosing menus, overseeing cleaning, providing access to locked cellars and cabinets, and directing the cooks, butlers, and attendants, all of whom were slaves.[13] In addition to learning how to manage a staff, from around the age of fourteen Ellen had her own lady's maid. Sally Cottrell (later Cole) (fig. 1), a slave girl who was about nine years old at the time, would remain in the position until Ellen married and moved north with her husband; over the years, Sally became known for her ability to refashion dresses for the cash-strapped Randolphs.[14]

Confident and outgoing, Ellen was an ideal emissary from Monticello. She traveled to Richmond, where her father lived from 1819 to 1822, when he was Virginia's governor; Baltimore; Washington, D.C.; and Philadelphia. She often sought out Jefferson's friends and had commissions from him to carry out, including the purchase of artwork. When Ellen was snubbed in Washington by Stratford Canning, the minister from Great Britain, Jefferson responded, "I [trust] I have still some old friends there who by their attention to you will prove that the friendships of those who love us as well as the enmities of those who hate, can descend from the fathers to the children of the 3rd and 4th-generation."[15] John Adams wrote Jefferson after meeting Ellen that she "deserves all the high praises I have constantly heard concerning her," an assessment her grandfather thought was "a certain passport to the good opinion of the world."[16]

Since Monticello became a popular destination for travelers when Jefferson was in retirement there, Ellen would not have needed to set foot outside Virginia to meet all manner of people. The world was literally coming to her door. Visitors stayed for weeks at a time, and Ellen recalled that "we had persons from abroad, from all the states of the Union, from every part of the State—men, women, and children. In short, almost every day, for at least eight months of the year, brought its contingent of guests. People of wealth, fashion, men in office, professional men, military and civil, lawyers, doctors, Protestant clergymen, Catholic priests, members of Congress, foreign ministers, missionaries, Indian agents, tourists, travellers, artists, strangers, friends."[17] Ellen alternately despised the intrusion and basked in the intellectual stimulation visitors provided. She found that at Monticello "the conversation I hear is completely the feast of reason."[18] Known for her ability as a conversationalist, Ellen was comfortable with topics ranging from philosophy, literature, and ancient history to botany, astronomy, and natural history.

Among the visitors to Monticello in 1824 was a twenty-five-year-old man from Boston, who arrived in May with a letter of introduction from Harvard professor George Ticknor.[19] Joseph Coolidge attended the Boston Latin School and graduated from Harvard in 1817, after which he spent three eventful years traveling through Italy, England, Ireland, and France. While on his Grand Tour he suffered a life-threatening bout with "thyphus fever," but Washington Irving, his friend and occasional traveling companion, nursed him back to health. He visited his favorite poet, Lord Byron, who was impressed by his American admirer, and collected books and fine art, including a bust of Lord Byron that he purchased in Rome from its sculptor, Bertel Thorvaldsen.[20] While abroad Coolidge learned of the death of Elizabeth Little, a young woman with whom he had hoped to share his future. Devastated, the twenty-one-year-old scion wrote to his father that he had "given up all thought of ever being other than I now am, a single man," and vowed to turn his attention to business.[21] His grandfather Joseph Coolidge also passed away while Coolidge was on his tour, leaving his youngest namesake with a successful business that he immediately drew upon to finance further travel.[22]

Born into Boston's merchant class, Joseph Coolidge, Jr., was the eldest son of Joseph and Elizabeth Bulfinch Coolidge. His father received his education at a French military academy and, because of his stature and deportment, was sometimes mistaken for the Marquis de Lafayette.[23] Back in Boston, Joseph Coolidge, Sr., built a life in the heart of the city's political and cultural activity. He was a member of the Massachusetts House of Representatives and a proponent of the introduction of railroads into the state. An active member of civic institutions such as the Overseers of the Poor, he helped establish the Massachusetts General Hospital. Coolidge joined the Massachusetts Historical Society in 1811 and was also active in the Boston Athenæum and the Horticultural Society.[24] His wife, Elizabeth Bulfinch Coolidge, was the sister of architect Charles Bulfinch, for whom Jefferson had arranged an architectural tour when both men were in Paris in the 1780s. Joseph and Elizabeth Coolidge lived in the Bulfinch homeplace on Bowdoin Square and raised their family in a city defined by Charles Bulfinch's neoclassical designs.[25]

Emerging into adulthood in a young nation at the same time, but still unknown to one another, Ellen Randolph and Joseph Coolidge, Jr., shared a general sense of dissatisfaction and a conviction that the conventional path of life would not be theirs. In the year before they met both expressed the belief that they were destined to remain unmarried, and each used the phrase "cui bono," which Ellen translated as "Of what use is all this?" to convey that sense of restlessness.[26] Nonetheless, by the end of Joseph's two-week stay at Monticello in the spring of 1824, it was clear that these two like-minded people had noticed one another. Where other suitors failed or even feared to venture, Joseph Coolidge succeeded. Writing to Jefferson in the fall, Joseph informed him that "during the fortnight which I passed so agreably in your family, the many valuable qualities of Miss Randolph made an impression upon me wh. at parting I did not attempt to conceal. I confessed to Mrs Randolph the interest her daughter had inspired." Joseph asked Jefferson's permission to return to Monticello, assuring him that Ellen was under no obligation and that "should she see fit to decline all connection but that of friendship I should think less well of myself, but not of her."[27] Jefferson gave Coolidge his unconditional blessing. "Nothing could be more welcome to me than the visit proposed, or it's object," Jefferson wrote. "[N]o two minds could be formed, better compounded to make each other happy."[28] He closed by mentioning that the Marquis de Lafayette would be visiting Charlottesville in November and invited Joseph to be his guest at the dinner that the University of Virginia would host in Lafayette's honor. On 4 November 1824 Joseph Coolidge watched the reunion of the heroes of the Revolution on Monticello's lawn, and the following night he was among the four hundred men who dined with the Frenchman and Jefferson in the university's unfinished Rotunda.[29]

In the midst of the fanfare surrounding Lafayette's visit, Joseph and Ellen became engaged. In the recollection of one of Ellen's cousins, the young couple setting out on a life together garners more attention than Lafayette and Jefferson:

> at the time of Genl. La Fayette's visit to Monticello (abt. the middle of November 1824) John Quincy Adams was President Elect. This festive occasion was graced by the presence of two lovers:—the lady, a member of Mr. Jefferson's family:—the gentleman, young, handsome, well educated, and recently returned from foreign travel—then a distinction—. She was preeminently endowed—with talent of the highest order,—culture, such as few women have the opportunity to attain,—the beauty which belongs to statuesque features, and eyes which the soul speaks from. She possessed as a crowning attraction the most varied power as a converser,—an attraction which, I have before mentioned, was greatly prized in those good old times. To lookers-on the byplay of this love affair between two handsome young people, made an interesting episode amid all the novel and exciting material which each day brought.[30]

On 27 May 1825, a half a year later, the Episcopal minister Frederick W. Hatch married Ellen Randolph and Joseph Coolidge in the parlor at Monticello. Jefferson himself wrote their marriage bond (fig. 2).

The couple remained at Monticello for three weeks before departing on their journey northward to Boston, where Ellen would reside with her new husband, but first they undertook a six-week tour of New England that covered one thousand miles.[31] Venturing farther from Virginia than she ever had before, Ellen was struck by the differences between the South and the North. She visited many of the same cities her grandfather had toured with James Madison, and she wrote to him that the world she

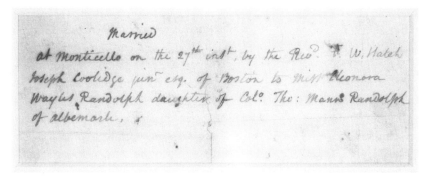

FIGURE 2. Marriage bond between Eleonora Wayles Randolph and Joseph Coolidge, Jr., in the hand of Thomas Jefferson, ca. 27 May 1825. (*Courtesy of Private Collection.*)

was seeing "has given me an idea of prosperity & improvement, such as I fear our Southern States cannot hope for, whilst the canker of slavery eats into their hearts & diseases the whole body by this ulcer at the core.... I should judge from appearances that they are at least a century in advance of us in all the arts & embellishments of life; & they are pressing forward in their course with zeal and activity which I think must ensure success."[32] Jefferson replied, "I have no doubt you will find also the state of society there more congenial with your mind, than the rustic scenes you have left: altho these do not want their points of endearment. Nay, one single circumstance changed, and their scale would hardly be the lightest. One fatal stain deforms what nature had bestowed on us of her fairest gifts."[33]

After traveling through upstate New York, Vermont, Connecticut, and Massachusetts, the exhausted couple arrived at Joseph's parents' home on Bowdoin Square. Ellen's homesickness was compounded by the fact that the ship carrying her belongings sank. She lost everything she had packed to bring from Monticello to Boston, including her prized writing desk. Jefferson shared his granddaughter's despair: "The documents of your childhood, your letters, correspondencies, notes, books, &c. &c., all gone! And your life cut in two, as it were, and a new one to begin, without any records of the former." As a replacement for all that Ellen had lost, Jefferson gave Joseph Coolidge the desk on which he had written the Declaration of Independence. "Mr. Coolidge must do me the favor of accepting this," Jefferson wrote. "Its imaginary value will increase with the years, and if he lives to my age, or another half century, he may see it carried in the procession of our nation's birthday, as the relics of the saints are in those of the church."[34] For Joseph Coolidge, who was sentimental and wealthy, it was perhaps far superior to a dowry, which neither Jefferson nor Ellen's father could supply. Ellen used the desk to compose her letters home.[35]

Ellen's correspondence highlighted the ways in which her life in Boston seemed so foreign to her—so different from what she had known in Virginia. She wrote her mother that she lived in "perpetual fear of violating some established rule, of sinning against the laws of propriety as they are understood here. . . . I am sure I often do or say things which I ought not, & it grieves me the more that Joseph . . . should now be evidently uneasy as to the impression I make upon his family & friends, & think it often necessary to check or advise me. . . . I weigh every word before I utter it, curb every sally of imagination, regulate my very countenance, & try to look, speak, walk, & sit just as I ought to do."[36] As much as she felt responsible for learning the mores of her northern home, she also encountered some very disappointing losses: the New England diet of fish, pudding, and potatoes paled in comparison to the French-influenced cuisine at Monticello, books were never spoken of, the climate was harsh, her toilette proved difficult to manage without a personal servant, and her grandfather was "utterly misunderstood."[37] Still Joseph held out hope for "making her something of a Yankee," and he promised her mother that Ellen's view of the North would improve once she saw the city's public buildings and made use of Harvard's library, cabinets of natural history, and scientific instruments.[38] Martha Randolph did what she could from afar to help her daughter acclimate to her new home. She gave Ellen a cookbook, *Le Cuisinier Royal,* annotated with five pages of notes and familiar recipes, and two fur capes that the explorer Meriwether Lewis had given Martha. The latter, she explained, would be valuable in the "tremendous winters of your new country."[39]

By November 1825 the couple had established themselves in a house on Sumner Street, directly behind the Massachusetts State House, on the fashionable side of Beacon Hill. Joseph Coolidge entered into a mercantile partnership with his cousin Thomas Bulfinch, and the following spring Ellen gave birth to their first child, a daughter they named Ellen Randolph Coolidge. Four months later Ellen and her sister Cornelia, who had come to help with the newborn, received word that their grandfather's health was failing. On 5 July 1826 Joseph Coolidge wrote to tell his brother-in-law that they would be leaving for Monticello as quickly as possible; they did not know that Jefferson had died the day before. Joseph's letter ended with the postscript, "The bells are now tolling for the decease of President Adams—he died yesterday, July 4th at Quincy."[40] Years later Ellen recalled

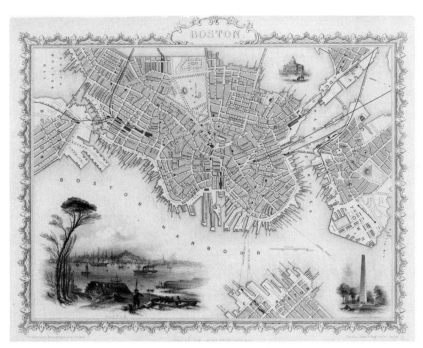

FIGURE 3. *Boston*, John Tallis & Company, 1838. *(Courtesy of the Norman B. Leventhal Map Center at the Boston Public Library.)*

arriving at Monticello after Jefferson's funeral had already been held. "I visited his grave," she wrote, "but the whole house at Monticello, with it's large apartments and lofty ceilings, appeared to me one vast monument. . . . After some weeks passed with my mother and sisters, for whose future fate I felt the most painful apprehension, I quitted the home of my youth never to return. I can never again feel a local attachment. As far as place is concerned I can never love again."[41]

For seven years after Jefferson's death the Coolidges were intimately involved in the settlement of his estate; Jefferson's debts had necessitated the sale of Monticello and its contents, including more than one hundred slaves.[42] In particular, the Coolidges managed the sale of Monticello's art collection. Joseph, who believed that the market in Boston offered the best prospects, arranged for Jefferson's art to be exhibited and sold first at the Boston Athenæum in 1828 and then at Harding's Gallery in 1833.[43] The insolvency of the estate also meant that Martha Randolph and her dependent children—seven in all, ranging from age eight to twenty-seven—were without a home. They stayed alternately with the Coolidges in Boston or with Ellen's married siblings in Virginia and Washington.

While Ellen mourned the loss of her grandfather and the breakup of the Monticello estate, her own family grew substantially. Over the course of six years she gave birth to six children, including a set of twins. Joseph may have entertained notions of his wife continuing her intellectual pursuits, but Ellen found herself confined to the nursery. Often during this time she wished for the assistance of Sally Cottrell from Monticello—rather than the insolent and unmanageable servants that Boston seemed to provide.[44] Visits from her Virginia family buoyed Ellen's spirits, particularly those from her mother, but she necessarily had in tow her two youngest—and most unruly—Septimia and George Wythe Randolph.[45] The two unmarried sisters who were closer to Ellen in age, Mary and Cornelia, were treasured companions and valuable nurses, and the Randolphs became part of Boston society, often spending months at a time living either with the Coolidges in the city or in rented quarters in the countryside in Cambridge.[46]

The growing family presented another challenge for Joseph Coolidge, who was mortified to find himself relying on his parents for financial support. He chose a remedy familiar to Boston's merchant elite: he joined the lucrative and sometimes perilous China trade.[47] In 1832, against his mother's wishes, Joseph went to work in Canton for Russell & Company, one of three Boston firms that maintained a branch office in China. His success there led to his travel to Bombay in 1833, where he took part in "the great trade in Opium & Cotton grown in that country and sent to China for sale on consignment." "My object," he wrote his parents in confidence, "is to become acquainted with the Native Merchants, and to take advantage of peculiarly favorable circumstances in securing a portion of this valuable trade to the House of Russell & Co." He carried with him "large funds & unqualified letters from Houqua, and the House."[48] In 1834 Joseph became a partner at Russell & Company, along with John Forbes and John Green, at the invitation of Augustine Heard (fig. 19), a retired shipmaster who was a senior partner with the firm. Heard left Canton after assembling this working partnership, returning to Boston and carrying out his promise to watch over the Coolidge family in Joseph's absence. He quickly became a favorite with Ellen, who hoped in vain that Heard might be a match for one of her unmarried sisters.

Heard helped manage even the smallest details of the Coolidge household, which in 1835 moved into the large house on Bowdoin Square that Joseph's grandfather had occupied. Ellen sent a measured description to her sister Virginia:

it is rather a gloomy situation on the north side of the hill and at a distance from the cheerful & more fashionable part of the town, but I prefer it greatly, notwithstanding these disadvantages, to any other house I could have commanded. All my early associations are in favor of space and I so much dislike the cramped and confined houses, with their narrow, dark entries and steep interminable stairs, which it is now the fashion to build in Boston that I rejoice in the prospect of elbow room for myself and play room for my children.[49]

The year following her move, Ellen sat for her first known portrait, done by the Boston artist Francis Alexander (fig. 13). In a letter to Heard, she expressed her worry about the outcome:

I wish the hundred dollars you will have to pay on Joseph's account for this ugly daub were appropriated to some better purpose. . . . [A]s far as I can see my presentiment on the subject is as gloomy as the ill-favored countenance which, I am told, is to be worked up into a resemblance of my own. I hope it will take a great deal of work to bring the likeness about, for a more faded, haggard and care-worn face I have seldom seen.[50]

While Ellen was often self-deprecating, especially in correspondence with her family and Heard, her description of Alexander's portrait hints at the growing feelings of despair and exhaustion that arose during Joseph's "dreaded" absences.

Ellen was awaiting her mother's return to Boston in 1836 after a summer spent at Edgehill when instead she received the news of her death.[51] It was a stunning loss, especially given that Joseph was away on business in China. Joseph was still absent when his own mother died the following February. He returned to Boston in October 1837 with the intent of moving himself and Ellen, if not the entire family, to London, where he would act as an agent for Russell & Company. But the economic panic in Europe and America, of which Joseph had been "wholly ignorant," caught him off guard and delayed his plans. By January 1838 Joseph had abandoned the idea of living in London and was instead planning on Ellen accompanying him to China after a brief stay in London to conduct business.

Ellen's joy at her husband's return was tempered by the news of the death of her younger brother Meriwether Lewis Randolph.[52] By this time Ellen was, in her sister Cornelia's words, "broken down" by Boston's climate and by "anxiety & fatigue."[53] Joseph wrote to his brother-in-law

Nicholas Trist that Ellen's "health of body and mind requires, absolutely, rest and change: she is feeble, thin, nervous and worn—the sea, and a new world, will do more for her than medicine."[54] On 24 March 1838 Joseph left for London ahead of Ellen, departing hastily and carrying with him the authorization from Augustine Heard to establish a new firm in the event of an emergency.[55]

Three months later Ellen Coolidge left the United States for the first time. When she departed, because she believed she would visit England briefly before moving on to reside in Canton, she had not equipped herself with some of the things that would benefit her on a longer stay, such as letters of introduction. Consequently, the types of activities she pursued while in London changed significantly during the course of the year she actually lived there. She began by visiting the sorts of popular sites that Joseph had seen on his Grand Tour, such as the Tower of London, the tunnel under the Thames, the British Museum, and St. Paul's Cathedral, often with guidebook in hand. Without the de rigueur letters, she had very limited social opportunities, so these public venues, frequented by unconnected travelers, filled her time in lieu of calls and events. In a stroke of good fortune, however, the American ambassador in London was Andrew Stevenson (fig. 27), an old friend of Ellen's from Virginia, and his wife, Sally Coles Stevenson (fig. 26), was Ellen's distant relative, born and raised in Albemarle County not far from Monticello. Through the Stevensons' influence the social possibilities available to the Coolidges broadened and multiplied. The Stevensons brought Ellen into contact with the circles of other Americans residing in London, which gradually opened out to the salons of English politicians, artists, writers, and aristocrats. Mrs. Stevenson was pleased to have "the advantage of introducing [*Ellen*] to these fastidious people as the grand daughter of our immortal Jefferson." She took pride in the fact that "Ellen has rather taken here. The desire to see Mr Jefferson's Granddaughter extends to all classes—torys & radicals & I whisper around, very like him—educated by him, &c, &c."[56]

By the spring of 1839 Ellen had left behind the life of a tourist. She found that her lack of a defined social set actually enabled her to move across the usual boundaries: "I am beginning to make acquaintance with persons, to see something of society, and as I am a stranger and belong to no particular set or circle, I have gained admittance to several, and can compare the different styles."[57] The Coolidges breakfasted with author and collector Samuel Rogers, attended the wedding of the Belgian ambassador to the daughter of an American financier, enjoyed fêtes at the Admiralty, and gained entry into artists' studios. They witnessed Queen

Victoria's opening of Parliament in February 1839, an event for which highly coveted cards of admittance were rarely obtained by Americans. Ellen became reacquainted with Harriet Martineau, whom she had met in Washington, D.C., and just as she finished reading Anna Jameson's newly published *Winter Studies and Summer Rambles in Canada*, Ellen met the author and went with her to call on the writer Joanna Baillie. Thomas Carlyle welcomed the Coolidges into his home on several occasions; after one such visit, they carried away manuscript pages of his *French Revolution* as a souvenir.

One of the most vibrant circles in which the Coolidges were active participants was that comprised of the upcoming "middle-class," or common, art collectors and the modern artists for whom they were patrons. Mrs. Stevenson introduced Ellen to art collector James Morrison, in whose company she visited auction rooms and private estates—and dined with the president of the Royal Academy of Art. It was likely Morrison who tried in vain to secure for Ellen an opportunity to visit the studio of J. M. W. Turner. The painter Charles Robert Leslie was more successful in his introductions, which gained the Coolidges admittance to the studios of brothers Alfred and John James Chalon and the home of collector Robert Vernon, who in turn introduced the Coolidges to the painters William Mulready and Edwin Landseer. Ellen paid two visits to the home of another collector, the retired coachmaker Benjamin Godfrey Windus, who owned more than two hundred watercolors and drawings by Turner. In fact, the opportunity to view art became one of Ellen's primary pursuits: in her diary she catalogues over four hundred works of art that she saw in more than forty public and private collections.

London was enamored of its young queen, whose image Ellen saw fashioned both in the public eye and in artists' studios. She was visiting the home and studio of the sculptor Sir Francis Chantrey when the clay model of his bust of Queen Victoria (fig. 31) was delivered—still wet—from the queen's sitting for the artist at Buckingham Palace. Ellen makes note of the shifting mood as the queen encountered her first scandal, what came to be known as the "Flora Hastings Affair," weaving together what she read in the daily papers with the accounts she heard in the salons.

Some of the current of British political debate was very familiar to Ellen, as her host country was then maneuvering in the wake of the 1833 Abolition of Slavery Act, which had brought emancipation to the fore. Unlike many of her English acquaintances, Ellen had an experience with slavery that was far from abstract. While she wonders at the "humbug" of Lord Sligo's display of the silver candelabrum that the emancipated slaves

FIGURE 4. Ellen Wayles
Randolph Coolidge, 1860s.
*(Courtesy of the Massachusetts
Historical Society.)*

in Jamaica had given him, Ellen comments that "though born & brought up in a Slave State I was early taught to abhor an odious system."[58] In this political atmosphere, Ellen found, to her delight, men and women who fondly recalled her grandfather and mother. She discovered that Harriet Grote was "a great admirer of my grandfather, which for me, like charity, covers a multitude of sins."[59] Lady Charlotte Lindsay, the daughter of Frederick North, Britain's prime minister during the American Revolution, became an unexpected friend and model. During Ellen's time in London Lady Charlotte was celebrated in the press and society for a letter she sent to her father's biographer in which she recounted her "impressions of my father's private life," including her family's rejoicing when North resigned as prime minister. Ellen invoked Lady Charlotte's example twenty years later when she, too, sought ways to work with a biographer and the press to illuminate Jefferson's character and repair his image by sharing her own anecdotes and observations.[60]

While she was abroad—and as busy as she became—Ellen still had frequent cause to turn her thoughts to her family and her Virginia home. Landscapes evoked memories of the Monticello mountaintop, and the smell of the tobacco warehouses reminded her of those she knew in Virginia. An imminent trip to Scotland precipitated her account of the Scotch tunes her grandfather sang while working in his study, and the

FIGURE 5. Thomas Jefferson
Coolidge, 1861. *(Courtesy of the
Massachusetts Historical Society.)*

hours spent looking at art reawakened the youthful love of painting she
had learned at Monticello. Certain social connections also prompted
reminiscences of her mother's schoolgirl friends from Paris, women who
had become intellectual icons in Martha Randolph's schooling of her
own children. But these memories are bittersweet, as Ellen transcribes
them in her diary, sharpening as they do the keenness with which she still
feels her mother's absence.

When Ellen was nineteen her mother had written, "<u>Ellen</u> fulfills the
promises of her childhood she is a nurse to me in sickness a friend and
companion in health and to her <u>grand Father</u> 'the immediate jewel of his
soul.'"[61] It was only after she had arrived in England and had the luxury
to reflect on her life that Ellen found herself assuming her mother's role
as matriarch while fully mourning her death, circumstances that transported her thoughts to Monticello and the lessons she had learned there.
In spite of tiring of the task of keeping a diary, Ellen continued the habits
of her youth by putting pen to paper to record news large and small for
those she held dear and from whom she was absent.

Ellen's journey to London marked the beginning of nearly a decade of
travel abroad for the Coolidge family. Ellen, Joseph, and Thomas Jefferson
Coolidge arrived back in the United States on 15 May 1839, and in a matter of weeks Ellen and Joseph departed again, this time sailing directly for

Canton. Chinese regulations required that Ellen live in the Portuguese settlement at Macao, and to her dismay she only saw Joseph intermittently during her eighteen month stay. Thomas Jefferson Coolidge and his three brothers also set sail in 1839—with Augustine Heard as their chaperone—but their destination was Geneva, where they enrolled at Alphonse Briquet's boarding school, a situation Ellen had arranged during her time in London. Ellen and her daughter later joined the four boys in Europe, and once Joseph Coolidge retired from the China trade in 1844 the entire family remained in Europe until 1847, when Joseph Randolph Coolidge and Thomas Jefferson Coolidge returned to study at Harvard; Algernon graduated from Harvard Medical School in 1854 and Sidney was granted an honorary master's from Harvard in 1857 for his work there in astronomy. By 1850 Ellen and Joseph were again in residence on Beacon Hill, at 12 Pemberton Square, and in the 1870s they settled into what would be their final home, at 184 Beacon Street in Boston's Back Bay.[62] By this time they had lost their son Sidney in the Civil War, but they had gained fifteen grandchildren.

In March 1876, in celebration of the centennial of the Declaration of Independence, Ellen Coolidge presented her grandson Thomas Jefferson Coolidge, Jr., with a copy of the Declaration, most likely an engraving, and an engraving of Thomas Jefferson's inaugural address, both of which she had found among Jefferson's papers.[63] Years later her grandson wrote,

> I remember my Grandmother, Mrs. Joseph Coolidge, who was especially kind and fond of me, perhaps on account of my holding the name of her greatly loved and respected grandfather, Mr. Jefferson. Her knowledge was so great and her memory so perfect that when any question arose, whether in history or in literature or about any other subject, if it could not be solved by reference to the encyclopedia, we would be sent to Grandmother Coolidge to get the information required, and it was seldom that she was not able at once to give it. Such another mind I have never known. In addition to showing this wonderful knowledge, which she had undoubtedly acquired by having lived for many years at Monticello and having often enjoyed the privilege of presiding at Mr. Jefferson's table surrounded by the many distinguished visitors constantly paying their respects to him, she had the charming faculty of endearing to herself her grandchildren and all others who surrounded her. She died April 21, 1876 and her loss was felt by all, young and old, and she continues to be referred to in the family as a splendid example of her generation.[64]

After Joseph Coolidge's death in 1879 his surviving children presented to the U.S. government the desk on which Jefferson wrote the Declaration of Independence—the same desk on which Ellen Coolidge composed her own correspondence. Today it remains one of the celebrated artifacts of the American Revolution, as well as a reminder of the lasting influence of a grandfather's affection.

The Diary and the Editorial Process

Ellen Wayles Coolidge wrote her travel diary in four thin notebooks, each covered in blue cloth and filled with lined paper, measuring about eight by ten inches. The first three notebooks are in good condition, with clean pages and sound bindings. The fourth notebook, made of lesser-quality materials, is more fragile, possibly from its exposure to sea air as Coolidge continued to make entries on her return trip home aboard the packet ship *Quebec*. Four generations of Coolidge women owned the diary; it passed from Ellen Coolidge to her daughter Ellen Coolidge Dwight and then to Dwight's niece Ellen Wayles Coolidge, who passed it to her niece Mary Barton Churchill. Mrs. Churchill deposited the diary at the Massachusetts Historical Society in 1964.

In this edition we have chosen to present all of Coolidge's entries as a continuous narrative, without highlighting the arbitrary breaks imposed by the individual notebooks. We have retained, however, the cumulative table of contents, with corresponding page numbers, which Coolidge made at the front of each notebook. While the diarist's topic headings have been transcribed exactly as she wrote them, we have replaced the page numbers with entry dates, which the reader can use to find her discussion of that topic. "Ellen Wayles Coolidge's Tables of Diary Contents" appears at the beginning of the diary transcription.

Coolidge wrote her diary with a very legible hand that required little conjecture on our part during the transcription process. Relying on notes in some cases, she composed her entries in cohesive narratives and paragraphs that rarely prompted her to change the text. Consequently, the manuscript contains very few corrections and changes. For the sake of readability and consistency we have chosen to incorporate Coolidge's rare revisions silently into the transcription, rather than marking her few emendations with distracting devices. Although Coolidge very consistently provided datelines for her diary entries, she sometimes began the text on a new line and sometimes ran it in with the dateline; these we have regularized, placing each date of composition at a standard location at the top of each diary entry.

Her spelling, punctuation, capitalization, and grammar have been retained. Like many nineteenth-century diarists, she employed dashes and spaces to signify a change of thought and, like her grandfather, preferred using "it's" rather than "its." Her use of underlining, abbreviations, and superscripted letters has also been preserved. Text notes appear for those few occasions where we have inserted punctuation or corrected spelling for the sake of clarity, and an ellipsis inside square brackets [...] indicates an illegible word or phrase. Within the editorial text, ellipses indicate omitted text and lower-case letters that have been altered to uppercase appear in square brackets. We hope that the editorial work recedes into the background and enables Ellen Coolidge's own voice to emerge.

ANN LUCAS BIRLE
Monticello, 2011

NOTES

1. Ellen Wayles Randolph Coolidge (1796–1876) and Joseph Coolidge (1798–1879).
2. The Randolphs' third child, also named Ellen Wayles, did not survive infancy.
3. Martha Jefferson Randolph to Thomas Jefferson, 31 Jan. 1801, in *PTJ*, 32:527.
4. Jefferson to Ellen Randolph Coolidge, 8 Feb. 1807, in Betts and Bear, *Family Letters*, 295.
5. Jefferson to Coolidge, 14 Mar. 1808, in Betts and Bear, *Family Letters*, 333–334; Coolidge to Henry Randall, 22 Feb. 1856, Ellen Coolidge Letterbook (ViU: Ellen Wayles Randolph Coolidge Correspondence). John Hemmings's last name reflects his spelling.
6. Jefferson to Benjamin Henry Latrobe, 10 Oct. 1809, in *PTJRS*, 1:595.
7. Jefferson to Samuel H. Smith, 8 May 1815 (DLC).
8. Coolidge to Martha Jefferson Randolph, 31 May 1820 (ViU: Ellen Wayles Randolph Coolidge Collection); Thomas Sully to Jefferson, 6 Apr. 1821 (DLC).
9. For details of Jefferson's journeys to Poplar Forest see "Route to Poplar Forest," *Thomas Jefferson Encyclopedia*, Monticello, Home of Thomas Jefferson, accessed 3 Feb. 2011, http://www.monticello.org/site/research-and-collections/tje. For Poplar Forest generally see S. Allen Chambers, Jr., *Poplar Forest and Thomas Jefferson* (1993).
10. Coolidge to Martha Jefferson Randolph, 18 July [1819] (ViU: Ellen Wayles Randolph Coolidge Correspondence).
11. Thomas Watkins to Jefferson, 9 Nov. 1823 (DLC).
12. Coolidge, diary, 11 Jan. 1839 (MHi: Ellen Wayles Randolph Coolidge diaries, 1838-1839).
13. Virginia J. Randolph Trist to Nicholas P. Trist, 2 Jan. 1823 (DLC: Nicholas Philip Trist Papers); Mary Randolph to Coolidge, 11–13 Sept. 1825 (ViU: Ellen Wayles Randolph Coolidge Correspondence). See also Elizabeth V. Chew,

"Carrying the Keys: Women and Housekeeping at Monticello," in *Dining at Monticello*, ed. Damon Lee Fowler (2005). For slavery at Monticello see Lucia Stanton, *Free Some Day: The African-American Families of Monticello* (2000).

14. Coolidge to Martha Jefferson Randolph, 26–27 June 1825 (ViU: Ellen Wayles Randolph Coolidge Correspondence).

15. Jefferson to Coolidge, 16 Jan. 1822 (N.J., private collection).

16. John Adams to Jefferson, 1 Dec. 1825, Jefferson to Adams, 18 Dec. 1825, in *The Adams-Jefferson Letters: The Complete Correspondence between Thomas Jefferson and Abigail and John Adams*, ed. Lester J. Cappon (1959), 2:611–613.

17. Henry S. Randall, *The Life of Thomas Jefferson* (1858), 3:330.

18. Coolidge to Martha Jefferson Randolph, 28 Jan. 1818 (ViU: Ellen Wayles Randolph Coolidge Correspondence).

19. Ticknor had been to Monticello in 1815 and there met Jefferson, Coolidge (then Ellen Randolph), and other family members. See Merrill D. Peterson, *Visitors to Monticello* (1989), 62–63.

20. Joseph Coolidge's bust of Byron is now at the Museum of Fine Arts, Boston, and his signed copy of *Marino Faliero, Doge Of Venice* is at the Boston Public Library. Ellen M. Oldham, "Lord Byron and Mr. Coolidge of Boston," *The Book Collector* 13 (1964): 211–213; Lord Byron to Thomas Moore, 5 July 1821, in *"Born for Opposition": Byron's Letters and Journals*, ed. Leslie A. Marchand (1978), 8:146; Joseph Coolidge, Jr., to Joseph Coolidge, ca. 22 Nov. 1820 (MHi: Joseph Coolidge Letters).

21. Elizabeth Little (1800–1820) was the daughter of Dr. Moses Little, a well-known physician in Salem, Massachusetts, and his wife, Elizabeth. Joseph Cogswell, who delivered the news personally to Joseph in Paris, described Little to Joseph's father as "the young lady, who was the chosen object of your son's highest earthly affections." James A. Emmerton, *Eighteenth-Century Baptisms in Salem, Massachusetts* (1886), 73; William W. Wellington, "Biographical Sketches of Deceased Members of the Obstetrical Society of Boston," *The Boston Medical and Surgical Journal* 105 (1881): 497; *New-England Galaxy* (Boston, Mass.), 17 Mar. 1820; Joseph Cogswell to Joseph Coolidge, 7 Apr. 1820, Joseph Coolidge, Jr., to Joseph Coolidge, June 1820 (MHi: Joseph Coolidge Letters).

22. Joseph Coolidge, Jr., to Joseph Coolidge, ca. 22 Nov. 1820 (MHi: Joseph Coolidge Letters).

23. Susan Bulfinch Lyman, "My Early Home, 2 April 1893" (MHi: Misc. Mss.).

24. [Robert C. Winthrop], "Memoir of Joseph Coolidge," *Proceedings of the Massachusetts Historical Society, 1835–1855*, 1st ser., vol. 2 (1880): 209–210.

25. Harold Kirker and James Kirker, *Bulfinch's Boston* (1964), 32–42, 76–81.

26. When Ellen was just nineteen Martha Jefferson Randolph despaired of her: "I think sometimes she will never marry and indeed after her sister's fate I almost wish she never may, her feelings are too acute for her own happiness." Ellen's sister Anne Cary Bankhead was at the time suffering in her marriage to Charles Lewis Bankhead, who was abusive and an alcoholic. Martha Jefferson Randolph to Elizabeth Trist, 31 May 1815 (ViHi: Elizabeth House Trist Papers); Coolidge to Nicholas P. Trist, 20 Jan. 1823 (DLC: Nicholas Philip

Trist Papers); Joseph Coolidge, Jr., to Joseph Coolidge, 21 Jan. 1824 (MHi: Joseph Coolidge Letters).

27. Joseph Coolidge, Jr., to Jefferson, 13 Oct. 1824 (MHi).

28. Jefferson to Joseph Coolidge, Jr., 24 Oct. 1824 (MHi).

29. Malone, *Jefferson and His Time*, 6:404–408.

30. Jane Blair Cary Smith, "The Carysbrook Memoir," ca. 1864, 69–78 (ViU: MSS 1378).

31. Their trip included a stop at Montpelier to visit James and Dolley Madison. Harold Jefferson Coolidge, "An American Wedding Journey in 1825," *Atlantic Monthly* 143 (1929): 354–366.

32. Coolidge to Jefferson, 1 Aug. 1825, in Betts and Bear, *Family Letters*, 454–457.

33. Jefferson to Coolidge, 27 Aug. 1825, in Betts and Bear, *Family Letters*, 457–458.

34. Jefferson to Coolidge, 14 Nov. 1825, in Betts and Bear, *Family Letters*, 460–462. Ellen's own copy of the same letter appears in her letterbook, pp. 68–70 (ViU: Ellen Wayles Randolph Coolidge Correspondence). Following Joseph Coolidge's death his four surviving children presented the desk to the U.S. government, and it is now in the National Museum of American History, Smithsonian Institution.

35. Coolidge to Martha Jefferson Randolph, 23 Jan. 1826 (ViU: Ellen Wayles Randolph Coolidge Correspondence).

36. Coolidge to Martha Jefferson Randolph, Aug. 1825 (ViU: Ellen Wayles Randolph Coolidge Correspondence). Cornelia Randolph described her bewilderment with the gradual change in service and attitude toward women on her first trip north to visit Ellen the following spring. From Washington on there was no one to get her a room or shield her from men. "I soon found that my being a woman was no sort of reason why the men should yield me a place at table or chair when I was standing." Cornelia J. Randolph to Virginia J. Trist, 16 Apr. 1826 (ViU: Jefferson, Randolph, and Trist Family Papers).

37. Coolidge to Henry Randall, 10 July 1853, Coolidge Letterbook (ViU: Ellen Wayles Randolph Coolidge Correspondence).

38. Joseph Coolidge to Martha Jefferson Randolph, 11 Nov. 1825 (ViU: Ellen Wayles Randolph Coolidge Correspondence).

39. Martha Jefferson Randolph to Coolidge, 26 Nov. 1825 (ViU: Ellen Wayles Randolph Coolidge Correspondence). Ellen's copy of Alexandre Viard's *Le Cuisinier Royal* (1817) is at the Boston Public Library.

40. Joseph Coolidge to Nicholas P. Trist, [5 July 1826] (ViU: Ellen Wayles Randolph Coolidge Correspondence).

41. Coolidge to Henry Randall, 16 May 1857, Coolidge Letterbook (ViU: Ellen Wayles Randolph Coolidge Correspondence).

42. Jefferson freed five slaves in his will and two slaves in his lifetime. Three other slaves left Jefferson's household with his tacit consent. See Stanton, *Free Some Day*.

43. *Catalogue of the Second Exhibition of Paintings, in the Athenaeum Gallery . . . Boston, May 1, 1828* (1828); *Catalogue of Valuable Oil Paintings . . . being the Collection of the Late President Jefferson. To be sold at Auction, on Friday, July 19,*

at *Mr. Harding's Gallery, School St.* (1833). Joseph was also instrumental in the 1829 sale of Jefferson's library, from which he and Ellen acquired books with "particular associations." After their deaths, the Coolidges' three thousand-volume library was given to Washington University in 1880 by their daughter and son-in-law, Ellen and Edmund Dwight. Within Washington University's library collection today there are more than eighty volumes that once belonged to Thomas Jefferson.

44. Coolidge to Virginia J. Trist, 9 May 1826 (ViU: Ellen Wayles Randolph Coolidge Correspondence); Coolidge to Jane N. Randolph, 26 Apr. 1835 (ViU: Edgehill-Randolph Papers).

45. Joseph wrote to his brother-in-law that, while he welcomed their mother-in-law, he was less enthusiastic about George and Septimia, fearing they would destroy or deface his new furnishings, disturb the tranquility of his home, and cause tension between himself, Ellen, and Martha Jefferson Randolph. "I dreaded their want of manners," he wrote, "their frequent bickerings, their absence of all subordination, and saw in the freedom wh. they had enjoyed, and which is not permitted to children of their age at the north, much annoyance. . . . [A]ll the difficulties wh. I had foreseen took place." He went on to say that the inconvenience was far outweighed by their accomplishment of removing Martha from Monticello, and that his house would always be open to her. He planned, though, to seek a place in the country for the summer. Joseph Coolidge to Nicholas P. Trist, 18 Apr. 1827 (DLC: Nicholas Philip Trist Papers).

46. Joseph Coolidge to Nicholas P. Trist, 1 June, 16 Oct. 1827 (DLC: Nicholas Philip Trist Papers).

47. During the Opium War Joseph Coolidge was seized by an angry mob and spent two nights in a Chinese prison. His subsequent claim for losses, including pain and suffering, met with disgust from members of the European community in Canton who saw the claim as inflated. Thomas N. Layton, *Voyage of the Frolic: New England Merchants and the Opium Trade* (1997), 34–36.

48. Layton, *Voyage of the* Frolic, 29; Joseph Coolidge, Jr., to Joseph and Elizabeth Coolidge, 30 June 1833 (MHi: Joseph Coolidge Letters).

49. Coolidge to Virginia J. Trist, 24 May 1835 (ViU: Ellen Wayles Randolph Coolidge Correspondence).

50. Coolidge to Augustine Heard, 8 Feb. 1836 (MH: Heard Family Papers).

51. Coolidge to Henry Randall, 2 Mar. 1856, Coolidge Letterbook (ViU: Ellen Wayles Randolph Coolidge Correspondence).

52. Meriwether Lewis Randolph (1810–1837) had ventured to settle land in Arkansas and died there of fever on 24 September 1837. Shackelford, *Descendants*, 2:122–127; Mary Randolph to Virginia J. Trist, 10 Nov. 1837 (NcU: Southern Historical Collection, Nicholas Philip Trist Papers). .

53. Cornelia Randolph to Nicholas P. Trist, 29 Mar. 1838 (NcU: Southern Historical Collection, Nicholas Philip Trist Papers).

54. Joseph Coolidge to Nicholas P. Trist, 6 Mar. 1838 (NcU: Southern Historical Collection, Nicholas Philip Trist Papers).

55. Cornelia Randolph to Nicholas P. Trist, 29 Mar. 1838 (NcU: Southern Historical Collection, Nicholas Philip Trist Papers). Coolidge was forced out of Russell & Company on his return to China in 1839. On 1 January 1840 he announced the formation of a new commercial house, Augustine Heard & Company. Layton, *Voyage of the* Frolic, 34–36. For Coolidge and Heard's partnership see Stephen Chapman Lockwood, *Augustine Heard and Company, 1858–1862* (1971), 3–19, and Thomas Franklin Waters, *Augustine Heard and His Friends* (1916), 33–48.

56. Sarah Coles Stevenson to Sarah Rutherford, 23 Feb. 1839 (NcD: Sarah Coles Stevenson Papers). The letters that Stevenson wrote from England to her sisters in Virginia are at Duke University. Selected letters have been edited by Edward Boykin in *Victoria, Albert, and Mrs. Stevenson* (1957).

57. Coolidge, diary, 2 Mar. 1839 (MHi: Ellen Wayles Randolph Coolidge diaries, 1838-1839).

58. Coolidge, diary, 24 Mar. 1839 (MHi: Ellen Wayles Randolph Coolidge diaries, 1838-1839).

59. Coolidge, diary, 30 Jan. 1839 (MHi: Ellen Wayles Randolph Coolidge diaries, 1838-1839).

60. Coolidge, diary, 24 Mar. 1839 (MHi: Ellen Wayles Randolph Coolidge diaries, 1838-1839). Ellen relied on the author Thomas Bulfinch, who was Joseph Coolidge's cousin and former business partner, to deflect criticism from Jefferson at the time of the publication of Henry Randall's three-volume *Life of Thomas Jefferson* (1858), for which Ellen had been a major source. Bulfinch's article in the July 1860 *North American Review* quoted Lady Charlotte's "charming letter," which bore the "impress of truth in every line." Bulfinch noted that "Lord North's antagonist, Mr. Jefferson, has been viewed with even more bitter feelings." Ellen apparently shared with Bulfinch her letterbook containing her correspondence with Henry Randall and others. She also directed that her husband share with Bulfinch the first page of her letter to Joseph in which she denies her grandfather's relationship with his slave Sally Hemings. [Thomas Bulfinch], "Jefferson's Private Character," *North American Review* 91 (1860): 107–118; Ellen Coolidge to Joseph Coolidge, 24 Oct. 1858, Coolidge Letterbook (ViU: Ellen Wayles Randolph Coolidge Correspondence).

61. Martha Jefferson Randolph to Elizabeth Trist, 31 May 1815 (ViHi: Elizabeth House Trist Papers).

62. Shackelford, *Descendants*, 1:94–99.

63. Ellen Coolidge to Thomas Jefferson Coolidge, Jr., 16 Mar. 1876 (Mass., private collection). The inaugural engraving remains in a private collection, but what Ellen referred to simply as a "Declaration of Independence" has not been located.

64. Thomas Jefferson Coolidge, Jr., unpublished autobiography, n.d. (Mass., private collection).

EDITORIAL ABBREVIATIONS

Short Title List

The following list indicates short titles for works cited frequently within this text and includes a URL for online works that the editors have cited.

Altick, *Shows of London*
    Richard D. Altick, *The Shows of London*, 1978

American Ancestors
American Ancestors, New England Historic Genealogical Society, http://
www.americanancestors.org

ANB
John A. Garrity and Mark C. Carnes, eds., *American National Biography*, 1999,
24 vols.

Ancestry.com
Ancestry.com, http://www.ancestry.com

Benezit, *Dictionary of Artists*
Emmanuel Bénézit and others, eds., French edition; Christopher John
Murray and others, eds., English version, *Dictionary of Artists*, 1999–2006, 14
vols.

Benson and Brett, *Letters of Queen Victoria*
Arthur Christopher Benson and Reginald Baliol Brett, eds., *The Letters of
Queen Victoria*, 1907, 3 vols.

Betts and Bear, *Family Letters*
Edwin Morris Betts and James Adam Bear, eds., *The Family Letters of Thomas
Jefferson*, 1966

Boykin, *Mrs. Stevenson*
Edward Boykin, *Victoria, Albert, and Mrs. Stevenson*, 1957

Brett, *Girlhood of Queen Victoria*
Reginald Baliol Brett, *The Girlhood of Queen Victoria: A Selection from Her
Majesty's Diaries between the Years 1832 and 1840*, 1912, 2 vols.

Burke and Burke, *Peerage and Baronetage*
Bernard Burke and Ashworth P. Burke, *A Genealogical and Heraldic History
of the Peerage and Baronetage, the Privy Council, Knightage, and Companionage*,
1914

Carlyle Letters
Charles Richard Sanders, Kenneth J. Fielding, Clyde De L. Ryals, Ian M.
Campbell, and others, eds., *The Collected Letters of Thomas and Jane Welsh
Carlyle*, 1970– , 33 vols.

Ian M. Campbell, Aileen Christianson, David R. Sorenson, and others,
eds., *The Carlyle Letters Online*, Duke University Press, http://carlyleletters.
dukejournals.org

Coolidge, *Autobiography*
Thomas Jefferson Coolidge, *The Autobiography of T. Jefferson Coolidge, 1831–
1920*, 1923

Curl, *Kensal Green Cemetery*
James Stevens Curl, *Kensal Green Cemetery: The Origins and Development of the
General Cemetery of All Souls, Kensal Green, London, 1824–2001*, 2001

DAB
Allen Johnson and Dumas Malone, eds., *Dictionary of American Biography*, 1928–1936, 20 vols.

Gray, *Daniel Webster in England*
Edward Gray, ed., *Daniel Webster in England: Journal of Harriette Story Paige, 1839*, 1917

Jameson, *Private Galleries*
Anna Jameson, *Companion to the Most Celebrated Private Galleries of Art in London*, 1844

Lockhart, *Life of Sir Walter Scott*
John Gibson Lockhart, *Memoirs of the Life of Sir Walter Scott, Bart.*, 1837

London Encyclopedia
Ben Weinreb and Christopher Hibbert, eds., *The London Encyclopedia*, 1983

London — World City
Celina Fox, ed., *London — World City, 1800–1840*, 1992

Macleod, *Art and the Victorian Middle Class*
Dianne Sachko Macleod, *Art and the Victorian Middle Class: Money and the Making of Cultural Identity*, 1996

Malone, *Jefferson and His Time*
Dumas Malone, *Jefferson and His Time*, 1948–1981, 6 vols.

Martineau, *Autobiography*
Harriet Martineau, *Autobiography*, ed. Linda H. Peterson, 2007

Martineau, *Biographical Sketches*
Harriet Martineau, *Biographical Sketches*, 1869

MB
James A. Bear, Jr., and Lucia C. Stanton, eds., *Jefferson's Memorandum Books: Accounts, with Legal Records and Miscellany, 1767–1826*, 1997

NPG.org
National Portrait Gallery, London, http://www.npg.org.uk/collections.php

ODNB
H. C. G. Matthew and Brian Harrison, eds., *Oxford Dictionary of National Biography*, 2004, 60 vols.

OED
James A. H. Murray, J. A. Simpson, E. S. C. Weiner, and others, eds., *The Oxford English Dictionary*, 2nd ed., 1989, 20 vols.

Old and New London
Walter Thornbury and Edward Walford, *Old and New London: A Narrative of Its History, Its People, and Its Places*, 1873–1878, 6 vols., http://www.british-history.ac.uk

Oxford Art Online
> Oxford Art Online, Oxford University Press, http://www.oxfordartonline.com

Oxford Reference Online
> Oxford Reference Online, Oxford University Press, http://www.oxfordreference.com

PTJ
> Julian P. Boyd, Charles T. Cullen, John Catanzariti, Barbara B. Oberg, and others, eds., *The Papers of Thomas Jefferson*, 1951– , 37 vols.

PTJRS
> J. Jefferson Looney and others, eds., *The Papers of Thomas Jefferson: Retirement Series*, 2004– , 7 vols.

Shackelford, *Descendants*
> George Green Shackelford, ed., *Collected Papers to Commemorate Fifty Years of the Monticello Association of the Descendants of Thomas Jefferson*, 1965–1984, 2 vols.

Sowerby
> E. Millicent Sowerby, comp., *Catalogue of the Library of Thomas Jefferson*, 1952–1959, 5 vols.

Stein, *Worlds*
> Susan R. Stein, *The Worlds of Thomas Jefferson at Monticello*, 1993

Survey of London
> Francis Henry Wollaston Sheppard, Hermione Hobhouse, John Greenacombe, and others, eds., *Survey of London*, 1894– , 47 vols., http://www.british-history.ac.uk

Tallis
> John Tallis, *London Street Views*, 1838–1840, repr. 2002

Timbs, *Curiosities*
> John Timbs, *Curiosities of London, exhibiting the most Rare and Remarkable Objects of Interest in the Metropolis*, 1867

TJF
> Denotes an item in the collection of the Thomas Jefferson Foundation, Inc.

Turner, *Dictionary of Art*
> Jane Turner, ed., *Dictionary of Art*, 1996– , 34 vols.

Waagen, *Works of Art*
> Gustav Waagen, *Works of Art and Artists in England*, 1838, 3 vols.

Wayland, *Andrew Stevenson*
> Francis Fry Wayland, *Andrew Stevenson: Democrat and Diplomat, 1785–1857*, 1949

Whinney, *Sculpture in Britain*
  Margaret Whinney, *Sculpture in Britain, 1530–1830*, 1964, repr. 1988

Zeigler, *Sixth Great Power*
  Philip Ziegler, *Sixth Great Power: Barings, 1762–1929*, 1988

Jefferson Family

Thomas Jefferson═Martha Wayles Skelton
(1743–1826)　　　(1748–1782)

   Martha Jefferson═Thomas Mann Randolph
   (1772–1836)　　　(1768–1828)

      Anne Cary Randolph═Charles Lewis Bankhead
      (1791–1826)　　　　(1788–1835)

      Thomas Jefferson Randolph═Jane Hollins Nicholas
      (1792–1875)　　　　　　　(1798–1871)

      Ellen Wayles Randolph
      (1794–1795)

      Ellen Wayles Randolph ══════════════ *m.* ══
      (1796–1876)　　　　　　　　　　　　　　　*(1825)*

      Cornelia Jefferson Randolph
      (1799–1871)

      Virginia Jefferson Randolph═Nicholas Philip Trist
      (1801–1882)　　　　　　　　(1800–1874)

      Mary Jefferson Randolph
      (1803–1876)

      James Madison Randolph
      (1806–1834)

      Benjamin Franklin Randolph═Sarah Champe Carter
      (1808–1871)　　　　　　　　(1810–1896)

      Meriwether Lewis Randolph═Elizabeth Martin
      (1810–1837)　　　　　　　(b. 1814)

      Septimia Anne Randolph═David Scott Meikleham
      (1814–1887)　　　　　　(1804–1849)

      George Wythe Randolph═Mary Elizabeth Adams Pope
      (1818–1867)　　　　　　(1830–1871)

Coolidge Family

Joseph Coolidge══Elizabeth Boyer
(1747–1820)   (1754–1786)

Joseph Coolidge══Elizabeth Bulfinch
(1773–1840)   (1777–1837)

Elizabeth Boyer Coolidge══Tasker Hazard Swett
(1797–1880)   (1795–1841)

Joseph Coolidge Jr.
(1798–1879)

Thomas Bulfinch Coolidge══Susan Elizabeth Goldsborough
(1802–1850)   (1806–1838)

Susan Apthorp Coolidge
d. young

Susan Bulfinch Coolidge══Joseph Lyman
(1812–1898)   (1812–1871)

Anna Coolidge
d. young

Anna Storer Coolidge══William Edgar Prince
(1819–1881)   (1816–1892)

Ellen Randolph Coolidge══Edmund Dwight
(1826–1894)   (1824–1900)

Elizabeth Bulfinch Coolidge
(1827–1832)

Joseph Randolph Coolidge══Julia Gardner
(1828–1925)   (1841–1921)

Algernon Sidney Coolidge══Mary Lowell
(1830–1912)   (1833–1915)

Philip Sidney Coolidge
(1830–1863)

Thomas Jefferson Coolidge══Mehitable Sullivan Appleton
(1831–1920)   (1831–1901)

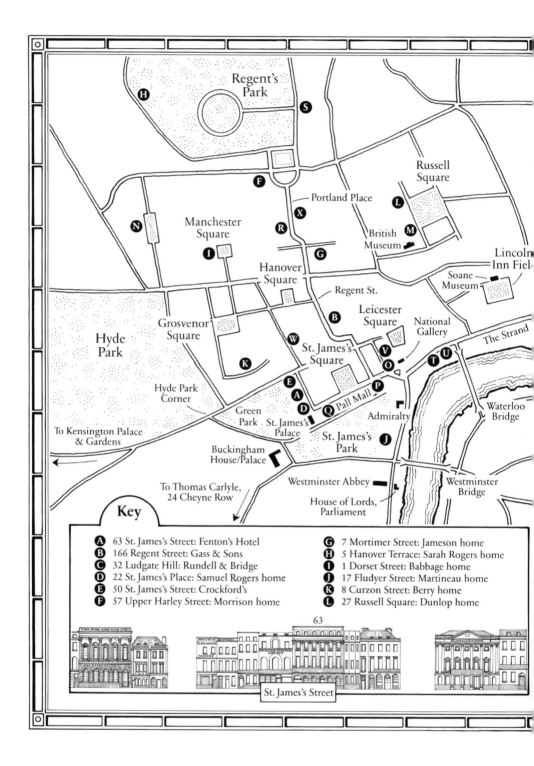

Regent's Park

Russell Square

Portland Place

Manchester Square

British Museum

Lincoln Inn Field

Soane Museum

Hanover Square

Regent St.

Leicester Square

National Gallery

The Strand

Grosvenor Square

Hyde Park

St. James's Square

Hyde Park Corner

Green Park

St. James's Palace

Pall Mall

Admiralty

Waterloo Bridge

To Kensington Palace & Gardens

St. James's Park

Buckingham House/Palace

To Thomas Carlyle, 24 Cheyne Row

Westminster Abbey

Westminster Bridge

House of Lords, Parliament

Key

- **A** 63 St. James's Street: Fenton's Hotel
- **B** 166 Regent Street: Gass & Sons
- **C** 32 Ludgate Hill: Rundell & Bridge
- **D** 22 St. James's Place: Samuel Rogers home
- **E** 50 St. James's Street: Crockford's
- **F** 57 Upper Harley Street: Morrison home
- **G** 7 Mortimer Street: Jameson home
- **H** 5 Hanover Terrace: Sarah Rogers home
- **I** 1 Dorset Street: Babbage home
- **J** 17 Fludyer Street: Martineau home
- **K** 8 Curzon Street: Berry home
- **L** 27 Russell Square: Dunlop home

63

St. James's Street

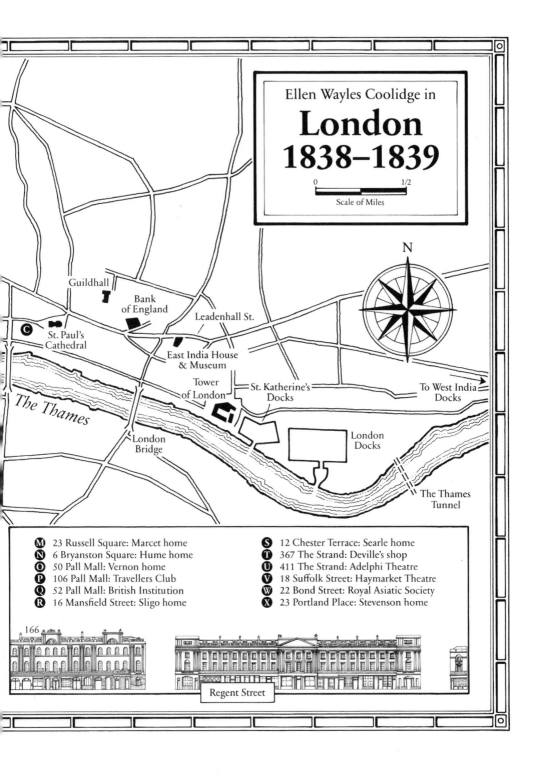

Ellen Wayles Coolidge in

London
1838–1839

0   1/2

Scale of Miles

N

Guildhall

Bank of England

Leadenhall St.

C

St. Paul's Cathedral

East India House & Museum

Tower of London

St. Katherine's Docks

To West India Docks

The Thames

London Bridge

London Docks

The Thames Tunnel

Ⓜ 23 Russell Square: Marcet home
Ⓝ 6 Bryanston Square: Hume home
Ⓞ 50 Pall Mall: Vernon home
Ⓟ 106 Pall Mall: Travellers Club
Ⓠ 52 Pall Mall: British Institution
Ⓡ 16 Mansfield Street: Sligo home

Ⓢ 12 Chester Terrace: Searle home
Ⓣ 367 The Strand: Deville's shop
Ⓤ 411 The Strand: Adelphi Theatre
Ⓥ 18 Suffolk Street: Haymarket Theatre
Ⓦ 22 Bond Street: Royal Asiatic Society
Ⓧ 23 Portland Place: Stevenson home

166

Regent Street

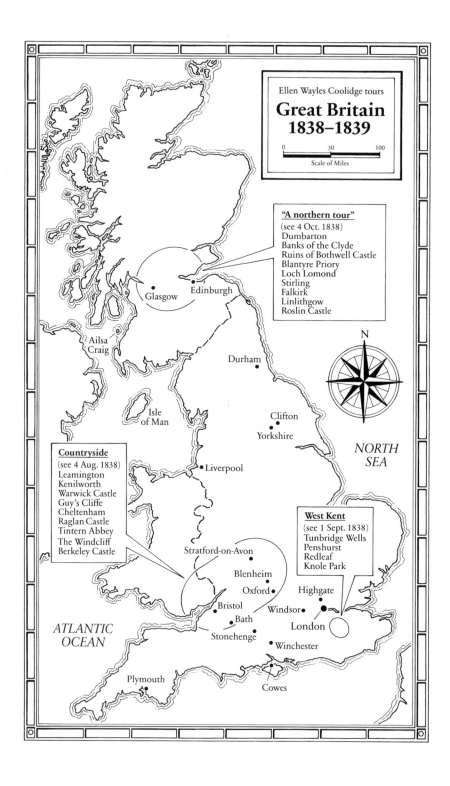

Ellen Wayles Coolidge tours

Great Britain 1838–1839

0   50   100
Scale of Miles

"A northern tour"
(see 4 Oct. 1838)
Dumbarton
Banks of the Clyde
Ruins of Bothwell Castle
Blantyre Priory
Loch Lomond
Stirling
Falkirk
Linlithgow
Roslin Castle

Glasgow   Edinburgh

Ailsa
Craig

Durham

Isle
of Man

Clifton

Yorkshire

N

NORTH
SEA

Countryside
(see 4 Aug. 1838)
Leamington
Kenilworth
Warwick Castle
Guy's Cliffe
Cheltenham
Raglan Castle
Tintern Abbey
The Windcliff
Berkeley Castle

Liverpool

West Kent
(see 1 Sept. 1838)
Tunbridge Wells
Penshurst
Redleaf
Knole Park

Stratford-on-Avon

Blenheim

Oxford

Highgate

Bristol   Windsor
Bath   London

Stonehenge

Winchester

ATLANTIC
OCEAN

Plymouth

Cowes

*The Travel Diary of
Ellen Wayles Coolidge,
1838–1839*

ELLEN WAYLES COOLIDGE'S
TABLES OF DIARY CONTENTS

VOLUME ONE

Passage to England from America.   *8 July 1838*
Isle of Wight & Portsmouth   *8 July 1838*
Journey to London. Fenton's Hotel.   *8 July 1838*
Shortsightedness. Lady's maid.   *8 July. 9 July 1838*
Drive in Hyde Park.   *11 July 1838*
English Hotel. Carriages   *12 July 1838*
The young Queen.   *11 July. 19 July. 15 Dec. 1838*
Regent's Park. Zoological gardens   *19 July 1838*
The City. Street Architecture. St. Paul's   *21 July 1838*
Chester Terrace. Wimbledon. Oriental Club.   *25 July. 27 July 1838*
Chauntrey's Studio. Italian Opera.   *27 July 1838*
English climate.   *31 July 1838*
Modern Artists at National Gallery.   *31 July 1838*
The Tower   *2 Aug. 1838*
Italian Opera. Fanny Elsler   *4 Aug. 1838*
My first excursion   *4 Aug. 1838*
Thames Tunnel.   *26 Aug. 1838*
Blackwall & White Bait   *26 Aug. 1838*
British Museum   *31 Aug. 1838*
My second Excursion. Tunbridge   *1 Sept. 1838*
Bank of England.   *24 Sept. 1838*
Preparations for Scotland.   *1 Oct. 1838*
Scotch music.   *1 Oct. 1838*
London in autumn.   *1 Oct. 1838*

Leave London for the north   *4 Oct. 1838*
Return to Fenton's Hotel   *13 Nov. 1838*
British Museum. Portland Vase.   *13 Nov. 1838*
Leave Fenton's   *26 Nov. 1838*
Jefferson at Highgate.   *4 Dec. 12 Dec. 13 Dec. 14 Dec. 16 Dec. 1838*
Adelaide Gallery. Parthenon.   *8 Dec. 1838*
Chimneys & windows. Lord Brougham.   *8 Dec. 1838*
Docks. Wine, silk, straw &c   *10 Dec. 1838*
Immensity of London.   *10 Dec. 1838*
Wine Vaults. Mahogany Logs.   *10 Dec. 1838*
Drury Lane & Van Amburgh.   *12 Dec. 1838*
Deville and Phrenology.   *13 Dec. 1838*
Leslie. Coronation picture.   *15 Dec. 1838*
Coronation ring   *15 Dec. 1838*
Carlyle's writings   *16 Dec. 1838*
Dulwich Gallery.   *18 Dec. 1838*
Murillo. Mrs Siddons   *18 Dec. 1838*
Josephine and Smith   *18 Dec. 1838*
Dinner at Mr Bates'   *20 Dec. 1838*
Poet Rogers   *20 Dec. 1838*
Lord Ashburton's House & pictures   *21 Dec. 1838*
Dinner in Spanish Place.   *22 Dec. 1838*
Old Indians. Mr Davis   *22 Dec. 1838*
English ignorance of America.   *22 Dec. 1838*
Mutual dislike   *22 Dec. 1838*
Rug Work.   *22 Dec. 1838*
Miss Sindry   *22 Dec. 1838*
Letter from Mrs J. Forbes.   *22 Dec. 1838*
Alice & Ellen Forbes.   *22 Dec. 1838*

VOLUME TWO

Party at Dr Boott's. Sons of Mrs Hemans.   *24 Dec. 1838*
Mrs Barbauld's "Charles." Mrs Bartley.   *24 Dec. 1838*
Foley Chapel. Dr Caunter. Clerk.   *24 Dec. 1838*
Text from Numbers.   *24 Dec. 1838*
Jefferson at Highgate   *24 Dec. 27 Dec. 1838. 2 Jan. 9 Jan. 1839*
Church of the Foundlings   *26 Dec. 1838*
Bad faces—degenerate race.   *26 Dec. 1838*
Covent Garden   *27 Dec. 1838*

Jane Shore. Christmas Pantomime   *27 Dec. 1838*
Bridgewater Gallery.   *27 Dec. 1838*
Messrs Rundell & Bridge.   *27 Dec. 1838*
Small value of the Crown Jewels.   *27 Dec. 1838*
Mr Hope's pictures & vases.   *28 Dec. 1838*
Blue Coat Boys.   *28 Dec. 1838*
Crockford's   *30 Dec. 1838*
Travellers Club.   *30 Dec. 1838*
Second Visit to Rundell & Bridge   *30 Dec. 1838*
Canon Riego & state of Spain.   *2 Jan. 1839*
Charles Sumner.   *2 Jan. 7 Jan. 14 Jan. 1839*
Carlyle.   *2 Jan. 1839*
His French Revolution   *2 Jan. 1839*
Crockford's likened to Pandemonium.   *2 Jan. 1839*
Angus Fletcher   *5 Jan. 1839*
Gibson's Psyche. Baillie's Eve.   *5 Jan. 1839*
Sam Slick.   *5 Jan. 12 Jan. 1839*
Chiswick.   *5 Jan. 1839*
L. E. L. Her death.   *5 Jan. 1839*
M^r & Mrs Stevenson at Windsor.   *7 Jan. 1839*
Lord Melbourne on Mr Jefferson.   *7 Jan. 1839*
Funeral in London.   *7 Jan. 1839*
Olympic Theatre.   *9 Jan. 1839*
Mme Vestris.   *9 Jan. 1839*
Mrs Annesley.   *9 Jan. 1839*
Dinner in Spanish place.   *10 Jan. 1839*
Mme Vestris again.   *10 Jan. 1839*
Military lady from India.   *10 Jan. 1839*
Manners of the English in America.   *10 Jan. 1839*
National Gallery.   *11 Jan. 16 Jan. 1839*
Resurrection of Lazarus.   *11 Jan. 1839*
Dinner at Mr Searle's. Female politicians   *11 Jan. 1839*
Mrs Annesley. My mother's early friends   *11 Jan. 1839*
My mother's early life.   *11 Jan. 1839*
The Abbaye Royal de Panthemont.   *11 Jan. 1839*
Haymarket Theatre.   *12 Jan. 1839*
Power the actor.   *12 Jan. 1839*
English & Americans.   *12 Jan. 1839*
Merchants in society.   *12 Jan. 1839*
Influence of Caste.   *12 Jan. 1839*

London smoke   *12 Jan. 1839*
Bavarian Chapel   *14 Jan. 1839*
Mr Livingstone from Paris   *14 Jan. 1839*
Mr Lane the Artist.   *15 Jan. 1839*
Sir Walter Scott's Diary.   *15 Jan. 1839*
French master   *15 Jan. 16 Jan. 1839*
National Gallery   *16 Jan. 1839*
Clapton & Mrs Glass.   *17 Jan. 1839*
Mrs Marx.   *17 Jan. 1839*
Lady Morgan   *17 Jan. 1839*
Charles Sumner.   *17 Jan. 1839*
Mrs Fletcher.   *18 Jan. 1839*
Professor T.   *18 Jan. 1839*
Mr Jefferson.   *18 Jan. 1839*
British Museum. Elgin Marbles   *19 Jan. 1839*
Adelphi Theatre.   *19 Jan. 1839*
Belgian Giant. Jem Crow.   *19 Jan. 1839*
Mrs Jamieson's book   *19 Jan. 1839*
Miss Martineau   *22 Jan. 1839*
Travellers in America   *22 Jan. 1839*
Leslie the painter   *27 Jan. 1839*
Anecdote of Queen Adelaide.   *27 Jan. 1839*
Artists' Club.   *27 Jan. 1839*
Water colour drawings   *27 Jan. 1839*
Lady Diana Rich.   *27 Jan. 1839*
Albert Chalon   *27 Jan. 1839*
Two pictures by Maes   *27 Jan. 1839*
Female politicians   *31 [30] Jan. 1839*
Abuses of democracy.   *31 [30] Jan. 1839*
M^r & Mrs Grote.   *31 [30] Jan. 1839*

VOLUME THREE

Wilkinson's Egypt.   *31 Jan. 1839*
Egyptian Saloon at the B.M.   *31 Jan. 1839*
Rogers the poet. His pictures.   *2 Feb. 1839*
The Strawberry girl.   *2 Feb. 1839*
Sir Walter Scott's first love.   *2 Feb. 1839*
Claude Lorraine   *2 Feb. 1839*
Gaspar Poussin.   *2 Feb. 1839*
French novels.   *4 Feb. 1839*

Volume Four

Visit to Mrs Marcet.   *11 Mar. 1839*
Mr Calhoun may come to England.   *15 Mar. 1839*
Radicalism   *15 Mar. 1839*
Rogers the poet.   *15 Mar. 28 Mar. 6 May 1839*
Charles Sumner   *15 Mar. 1839*
Turner the painter.   *15 Mar. 1839*
Dinner at Mr Mansfield's.   *15 Mar. 1839*
Sidney Smith   *15 Mar. 1839*
Mr Vernon & his pictures.   *15 Mar. 1839*
Landseer's High Life & Low Life.   *15 Mar. 1839*
Caricature by H. B.   *15 Mar. 1839*
Dinner at Miss Rogers'.   *15 Mar. 1839*
Luttrell. Mme V. d. W. & the Mansfields   *15 Mar. 1839*
Dinner at Mr Morrison's   *15 Mar. 1839*
Musical Matineé. Moscheles   *15 Mar. 1839*
Evening at Miss Berrys'   *18 Mar. 1839*
Sir Francis & Lady Chauntrey   *18 Mar. 1839*
English better than they seem.   *18 Mar. 1839*
Allan Cunningham & Robert Burns.   *18 Mar. 1839*
Christie's Auction Rooms. Rainy's rooms.   *18 Mar. 1839*
Buchanan's Rooms. Marshall Soult.   *18 Mar. 1839*
Evenings at Miss Martineau's & Mr Babbage's   *18 Mar. 1839*
Dress of French women   *18 Mar. 1839*
Sidney Smith preaches at St. Paul's   *18 Mar. 1839*
Dinner at Mr Grote's. Charles Austen.   *18 Mar. 1839*
Herald's Office. Guildhall   *21 Mar. 1839*
Visit to Miss Martineau. Her house.   *21 Mar. 1839*
Her opinion of the Queen, her
anecdotes of Lord Brougham   *21 Mar. 1839*
Queen & her ladies.   *21 Mar. 26 Mar. 1839*
First visit to Mr Sheepshanks.   *24 Mar. 1839*
East India Museum.   *24 Mar. 1839*
Lord Mayor's visit to the Queen   *24 Mar. 1839*
Party at Miss Berrys'. Distinguished persons.   *24 Mar. 1839*
Ball at Lady Sligo's   *24 Mar. 1839*
Visit to the Duke of Sussex.   *24 Mar. 1839*
Dinner in Spanish place.   *26 Mar. 1839*
Visit to Westminster Abbey.   *28 Mar. 1839*
Second visit to Mr Sheepshanks.   *28 Mar. 1839*

London. 8th July. 1838.

I began a journal at sea which my severe sufferings made me lay aside. It comprised only the events of a few days, the rest of the time being lost by incessant sickness. —

I sailed, in company with Mr & Mrs Aspinwall of N. York from New York, Wednesday 20th June. My daughter remains at Staten Island under Aunt Hackley's care, Randolph & Jefferson go to Edgehill, the Twins are with Mr Greene at Jamaica Plain. 'Twas with an aching heart I left my children, though I leave them in such good hands.

I sailed then in the packet ship Wellington, Capt. Chadwick, a good ship of 780 tons, with a good commander few persons in the cabin & none of them very disagreeable people. We had a good table and were well accommodated in all respects. We had fine weather favorable winds, made a grand run, taking in our Pilot about eighty miles from Cowes on the afternoon of July 6th (Friday.) On the morning of the 7th I went on deck — my sufferings during the whole voyage or nearly the whole voyage had been terrible — but I felt better & got on deck in time to see the Needles. Coasting along the northern side of the Isle of Wight we had a fine view of the country as far as Ryde. On the other side of the Strait the only object that attracted

First entry of Ellen Coolidge's travel diary, 8 July 1838.
Ellen Wayles Randolph Coolidge diaries, Massachusetts Historical Society.

London. 8th July. 1838.

I began a journal at Sea which my severe sufferings made me lay aside. It comprised only the events of a few days, the rest of the time being lost by incessant sickness.——

I sailed, in company with M^r & Mrs Aspinwall of N. York from New York, Wednesday 20th June. My daughter remains at Staten Island under Aunt Hackley's care, Randolph & Jefferson go to Edgehill, the Twins are with Mr Greene at Jamaica Plains. Twas with an aching heart I left my children, though I leave them in such good hands.

I sailed then in the packet ship Wellington, Capt. Chadwick, a good ship of 780 tons, with a good commander few persons in the cabin & none of them ^very^ disagreeable people. We had a good table and were well accommodated in all respects. We had fine weather, favorable winds, made a <u>grand</u> run, taking in our Pilot about eighty miles from Cowes on the afternoon of July 6th (Friday.) On the morning of the 7th I went on deck—my sufferings during the whole voyage or nearly the whole voyage had been terrible—but I felt better & got on deck in time to see the Needles. Coasting along the northern side of the Isle of Wight we had a fine view of the country as far as Ryde. On the other side of the strait the only object that attracted my attention was the gloomy old Penitentiary-looking place called Hurst Castle, where Charles 1st was for some time confined. The day was very fine, we saw every thing to the greatest advantage but it was not until we reached Cowes that I began to feel the charm of English landscape. Cowes is beautifully situated and I could not but remember that this was the only spot of British ground with which my dear mother was acquainted. She had lived several years in France, and on her return to her own country in September 1789, having sailed from Havre & passing near the Isle of Wight, her ship was becalmed & lay for several days at Cowes. She went on shore with my grandfather, was as much pleased as I have been with the rural & romantic scenery of Cowes, and very often spoke of it in after times to her children. With how much pleasure I should have written to her that I too had seen Cowes nearly half a century from the time of her visit! and two short years ago I might thus have written. But now alas!——

Near Cowes is the Gothic castle, modern Gothic, called Norris Castle, where I believe Queen Victoria passed some portion of her young life. I know not how much. This was my first view of a Castle—and whether owing to this circumstance, or whether Norris Castle is really a fine specimen of Modern Gothic, I cannot tell, but I admired it very much, and continued to look at it as long as it was visible. There it stood with it's round tower green with Ivy, it's massive walls of grey stone, it's lawns & woods bathed in the light of a July morning, and the waters of the Solent washing the rising ground on which it stands. Gothic Castles are familiar objects to English eyes, but Anglo-Americans hear of them, read of them, receive the imperfect impressions which drawings and paintings convey, and when the realities come before them then only know how far the truth excels the imagining—And yet I have only seen Norris Castle— How will it be when I am an older traveller?—

At Ryde we looked at the long pier and then took leave of the Wellington & her worthy Captain. We took boat for Portsmouth where, after getting an excellent breakfast at the George, fresh butter, good bread & the finest strawberries I ever ate. Mr Aspinwall secured seats in a fast coach and we proceaded to London.

Of Portsmouth we saw little or nothing. One general impression remains on my mind of extensive fortifications and a great military display of men and arms. We had no trouble at the Custom House where our luggage was barely glanced at. The Stewardess on board the Wellington had prepared me for this. "Dear me, Ma'am, said she, they do'nt trouble their heads about the United States. Nothing comes from there that they care about. If you were arriving from France now it would be another thing." This was not particularly flattering to my national vanity, but there was something comfortable in the fact that we were, by our very insignificance, spared the annoyance of a regular over-hauling of trunks, carpet bags &c. One gentleman only, our Presbyterian minister, was more strictly dealt with in consequence of his having a greater number of books,

newly printed & bound, than were thought necessary for his own edifica-
tion. The obnoxious volumes were weighed in the scale and found not
wanting but too heavy, and condemned accordingly. So many shillings
duty—twelve & sixpence I believe—for twenty three pounds weight of
American learning and literature—or it may be of divinity as the books
were the property of a divine.—At Portsmouth too we were initiated
into the mysteries of servants' fees—the innumerable shillings and pence
which form the privileges of place among English hirelings

The road from Portsmouth to London is called dull, but to my unpractised eyes the first twenty or thirty miles is through a country of surpassing
loveliness. England, beautiful England must be rich indeed in lawn and
grove and wood and hill if all that I saw yesterday can be slighted & lightly
spoken of. There were cottages with thatched roofs and latticed windows,
which like Castles I had read of & never seen. There were the green green
commons dotted with sheep; wild flowers of all hues embroidering the
fields—the beautiful scarlet poppy a weed, the purple heath, that poetic
flower, trampled under foot of man and beast, every breath of summer
air redolent of the fragrance which roses innumerable & woodbine, from
every cottage door and window, sent forth to greet us as we whirled too
rapidly by. I wish I could describe one particular scene of beauty to shew
that it is sober reality and not poetry which I am trying to write, but we
journied on with all the speed of English horses over English roads, and
the moving picture in it's varieties of loveliness could only produce the
general impression I now retain.

One thing charms me greatly already in England. It is the mingling of
the old & the new—all that is delightful to the imagination in the ancient
and the time-hallowed, with all that is gratifying to reason and a sense of
usefulness in modern improvements and inventions. Here are a people
not only in the highest state of civilization now, but who have been civilized for ages—not only great in the present, but great in the past, and I
hope to be great in the future.

The whole road from Portsmouth to London was full of interest to me.
At one time it wound round the edge of a deep black valley (black I believe
with furze killed in the severe frost of last winter) where a murder had
been committed and commemorated by an inscription. The spot indeed
looked wild and melancholy enough. In Guildford where we stopped to
dine, I saw from the window of the inn a very old and venerable church,
and we had, before arriving, passed the ruins of a chapel perched high
above the road. Ruins and old buildings are the greatest novelties to
me. I looked with wondering admiration, in the towns through which

we passed, at houses many of them probably as old as the discoveries of Columbus!

The approach to London disappointed me. The weather which had been exhibiting all the capricious beauty of an April day, now bright sunshine, now overcast, so that we had the charm of alternate lights and shadows on the landscape, settled into rain, and it was a damp and gloomy evening which brought us to Hyde Park Corner. The smell of smoke and the closeness and crowd of an immense city were a bad exchange for sweet odours and fresh airs—But I reached Fenton's Hotel, in St James' Street, where Mr Coolidge was waiting for me, and was glad to rest after all the various emotions of the day. Twenty four hours before I had been in the cabin of a packet ship, and in these last twenty four hours how much I had seemed to see, how much I had really felt! This is my first visit to England. My first experience of abroad.

My passage by sea & land from the Needles to London was too rapid for any thing like minute observation. I am but at the threshold of my travels. It remains to be seen whether I am capable of recording any thing but general observations. I mean if I can, to satisfy myself in this particular, and will keep a journal if I can. It is a habit of mine and not a good one perhaps, to trust very much to impressions. I am usually less struck with particulars than generals. My impressions are lively and have, for myself, the force of convictions, but I cannot always justify them to others who require the details on which they are or should be founded. The mind is so dependent on the body that perhaps another way I have of selecting a few prominent points & from them drawing general conclusions, may have originated in defective sight. I am very short-sighted, use glasses which are fatiguing to the eyes, & which I lay aside whenever I can. I dwell therefore only on those objects which most attract my attention. I see things in masses. Nature is for me, a painter who produces great effects with a few masterly strokes, broad and deep, mellow or bright, lights & shadows, darkness and day. Even the countenances of my friends are portraits done in the same style. I can seldom in remembering or describing them, go into any nice detail of form or colour, though I have a vivid impression of how they look. My standard of beauty is affected by this way of seeing or not seeing things—Other persons are often shocked by defects which I do not perceive and alive to beauties which I am sorry to lose. My tastes and pursuits are influenced by the same causes. I love flowers for their colours & their fragrance—I enjoy without knowing them—I can tell if they are beautiful and sweet, but I can neither class nor describe them nor remember their names—I could never be a florist even, to say nothing of botany. I am very much afraid that if called on, on my return home, to give an account of my travels I shall acquit myself as ill as did the three wise men who were permitted by Jupiter to visit the Moon. ——

William Henry ASPINWALL (1807–1875), merchant and partner in the firm Howland & Aspinwall, operated a fleet of ships active in world trade, including the *Rainbow* and the *Sea Witch*. Aspinwall chartered the Pacific Mail Steamship Company in 1848 and successfully lobbied the U.S. Congress and the government of New Grenada to build the Panama Railroad, completed in 1855. He married Anna Lloyd Breck in 1830 (*ANB*; *DAB*).

Coolidge's DAUGHTER was her eldest child, Ellen Randolph Coolidge (1826–1894). Educated in the United States and Geneva, Ellen was known within the family for her intellect. She married Edmund Dwight (1824–1900), a Harvard graduate and member of Boston's merchant elite. The Dwights had no children, and Ellen's health was often poor. The couple were active philanthropists and helped support their unmarried Randolph aunts in the 1860s. After Joseph Coolidge's death Edmund and Ellen Dwight donated Coolidge's library of about three thousand volumes, some of which had belonged to Thomas Jefferson, to Washington University in St. Louis. Edmund supported the Boston Public Library and donated over a thousand volumes to help establish its North End branch in 1895 (Shackelford, *Descendants*, 2:120–122; *Genealogy of Some of the Descendants of John Coollidge of Watertown, Mass., 1630* [1903], 26; Boston Public Library, *Forty-Fourth Annual Report 1895* [1896], 158; *Harvard Register* 1 [1880]: 168).

AUNT HACKLEY was Harriet Randolph Hackley (1783–1859), a sister of Coolidge's father. She was married to Richard Shippey Hackley (1770–1829), whom Jefferson appointed as a consular agent in Spain, and they had four children. Harriet Hackley, with her retinue of children and Spanish servants, was a frequent visitor to Monticello, and it was there that she gave birth to her third child. Coolidge had stayed with the Hackleys at their Richmond home and was fond of them, writing her mother that "Aunt H. treats me with a kindness truly maternal." Between 1818 and 1835 Hackley operated boarding schools for girls in Richmond and Norfolk, with a broad curriculum of academic classes as well as music, dancing, French and Spanish instruction, and painting and drawing. Ellen thought her aunt was "admirably calculated" to be a teacher and regretted that their family's constrained finances prevented her sister Virginia from attending. Randolph and Sidney Coolidge both stayed with Mrs. Hackley in 1850 while they worked as engineers in railroad construction (*U.S. Passport Applications, 1795–1905*, s.v. "Hackley, Richard S.," Ancestry.com; United States Federal Census, Seventh Census, 1850, Richmond, Virginia, s.v. "Hackley, Harriet," Ancestry.com; *Richmond Enquirer*, 11 Sept. 1829, 8 May 1835; *Fayetteville [N.C.] Observer*, 5 Dec. 1859; Coolidge to Martha Jefferson Randolph, 28 Jan. 1818, 31 May 1820 [ViU: Ellen Wayles Randolph Coolidge Correspondence]).

RANDOLPH, Joseph Randolph Coolidge (1828–1925), was educated in the United States in Boston and Virginia and abroad in Geneva, Vevey, and Dresden, where he attended the Royal Saxon Military Institute. He suffered hearing loss from a childhood illness and spent some of his time abroad seeking cures from physicians and recuperating in spas in Switzerland. He returned to the United States in 1847 and was in the first class of Harvard's Lawrence Scientific School, where he studied for two years. Coolidge worked briefly as a civil engineer, employed in laying out railroads in the South, including the Baltimore & Ohio and the Richmond & Danville lines. He left engineering to study law at Harvard, graduating in 1854, and was admitted to the Massachusetts bar in 1856. In 1860 Coolidge married Julia Gardner (1841–1921), daughter of a Boston shipping and real estate magnate, and the couple had five children. At the time of his death he was the oldest living Harvard alumnus (Shackelford, *Descendants*, 2:123–129; William Richard Cutter and William Frederick Adams, *Genealogical and Personal Memoirs Relating to the Families of the State of Massachusetts* [1910], 4:2144–2147; *Genealogy of Some of the Descendants of John Coollidge of Watertown, Mass., 1630, 26*; *Bellerive-Institution Sillig 1836–1892* [1892], 56; "Milestones: Nov. 23, 1925," *Time*, 23 Nov. 1925; Joseph Coolidge to Nicholas Philip Trist, 29 Dec. 1838 [NcU: Southern Historical Collection, Nicholas Philip Trist Papers]; Ellen Wayles Randolph Coolidge to Jane Nicholas Randolph, 17 May 1843 [ViU: Ellen Wayles Randolph Coolidge Correspondence]).

JEFFERSON, Thomas Jefferson Coolidge (1831–1920), was the youngest of the Coolidge children and the only one to join Ellen and Joseph during their London stay. He was educated at the Highgate Academy outside of London, in Geneva, and in Dresden at Blochman's School. Coolidge's *Autobiography* (1923) details his early years and the difficulty he had acclimating to the United States upon his return after ten years abroad. He graduated from Harvard in 1850 and pursued a career as a commission merchant. In 1852 he married Mehitable Sullivan Appleton (1831–1901), daughter of William Appleton, and they had four children. After the financial crisis of 1857 Coolidge became treasurer at one of his father-in-law's textile mills, and over the next half century he amassed substantial wealth through his successful management and investment. He was a director of the Merchants Bank, park commissioner for the City of Boston, a director of the Chicago, Burlington & Quincy Railroad, and president of the Atchison, Topeka & Santa Fe Railroad. Coolidge became U.S. minister to France (1892 to 1893) and served as a member of the Joint High Commission to settle disputes between Canada and the United States in 1898. His philanthropic interests were focused primarily on Harvard University and the Massachusetts Historical Society, and it was to the latter that he conveyed a sizable collection of Thomas Jefferson's papers in 1898 (*ANB*; *DAB*; Coolidge, *Autobiography*; Shackelford, *Descendants*, 2:140–150; *Genealogy of Some of the Descendants of John Coollidge of Watertown, Mass., 1630, 26, 28–29*).

EDGEHILL was the home of Ellen Coolidge's brother Thomas Jefferson Randolph (1792–1826) and his wife, Jane Hollins Nicholas Randolph (1798–1871). Jane, the daughter of Virginia governor Wilson Cary Nicholas, married Randolph in March 1815. The Randolphs had thirteen children, of whom nine daughters and three sons survived to adulthood.

Soon after his marriage Randolph took over the management of his grand-father's farms. After Jefferson's death Randolph became executor of his estate and struggled to pay its debts, selling Monticello, the slaves, and much of his grand-father's other possessions. In an effort to raise additional funds, Randolph, with the help of Jane, his mother, and his sisters, published the first collection of Jefferson's writings in 1829 and sold many of Jefferson's papers to the Library of Congress in 1848. Jane Randolph also founded the Edgehill School for Girls in 1829.

Randolph was a member of the Board of Visitors and later rector at the University of Virginia. He served in the Virginia House of Delegates and at the commencement of the Civil War was given a colonel's commission in the Confederate Army. In 1872 he was chairman of the National Democratic Convention. Once Monticello had been sold, Edgehill became a touchstone for the Randolph family, and Ellen often sent her children there to stay with their cousins and extended family. It was at Edgehill that Thomas Jefferson Coolidge attempted to ride his great-grandfather Jefferson's horse Eagle and also where he watched the unforgettable act of his uncle flogging a slave (*DAB*; *PTJRS*, 1:190–191n; Shackelford, *Descendants*, 1:76–88; Cynthia Miller Leonard, comp., *The General Assembly of Virginia, July 30, 1619–January 11, 1978: A Bicentennial Register of Members* [1978], 359–404; Coolidge, *Autobiography*, 3).

THE TWINS were Algernon Sidney Coolidge (1830–1912) and Philip Sidney Coolidge (1830–1863). Algernon was educated in Geneva and Vevey, and he earned his degree from Harvard Medical School in 1854. This same year he married Mary Lowell (1833–1915), granddaughter of textile magnate Francis Cabot Lowell, and they had five children. Algernon practiced as a surgeon and pathologist and during the Civil War served under contract to the Union Army. After the war Algernon was taken ill with what was diagnosed as a mild form of epilepsy, ultimately prompting his resignation from medicine. He spent the remainder of his life indulging his interests in horticulture, family history, and collecting rare printed works, most of which were donated to Harvard upon his death (Shackelford, *Descendants*, 2:134–139; Coolidge, *Autobiography*, 42; *Genealogy of Some of the Descendants of John Coollidge of Watertown, Mass., 1630*, 26–27).

Sidney received his early education in Boston and abroad, at Geneva, Vevey, and the Royal Military Institute at Dresden, from which he graduated in 1850. Unable to find a military commission either at home or abroad, he moved to Richmond, Virginia, in 1850, where he and his brother Randolph lived with their great-aunt Harriet Hackley, her son-in-law Andrew Talcott, and his family. Randolph and Sidney worked as engineers laying out the Richmond & Danville Railroad, a project that Talcott supervised. By 1853 Sidney had left the South for Boston and become associated with the Harvard Observatory, where he was a surveyor and astronomer, contributing observations and drawings to an ongoing study of Saturn. He was named assistant astronomer for the Japan Exploring Expedition to survey the North Pacific Ocean and the China Sea in 1853, and in

1855 he conducted a chronometric expedition to determine the latitude between Greenwich and Cambridge, Massachusetts, a task that required him to cross the Atlantic six times. In 1857 Harvard recognized Coolidge's years of devotion to the observatory with an honorary master's degree. In 1858 Coolidge again assisted Andrew Talcott, and while surveying for a railroad that would connect Vera Cruz and Mexico City, he was caught up in a civil war. Captured and imprisoned in Mexico, he was sentenced to execution, but an appeal to the Mexican ambassador in Washington, D.C., saved him. In 1861 Sidney received a commission as a major in the Union Army and died of wounds received at the Battle of Chickamauga in September 1863 (Coolidge, *Autobiography*, 42; Shackelford, *Descendants*, 2:130–133; Francis B. Heitman, *Historical Register and Dictionary of the United States Army* [1903], 1:325; *Genealogy of Some of the Descendants of John Coollidge of Watertown, Mass., 1630* [1903], 26; John Howard Brown, ed., *Lamb's Biographical Dictionary of the United States* [1900], 2:173; *Bellerive-Institution Sillig 1836–1892* [1892], 56, 62; United States Federal Census, Seventh Census, 1850, Richmond, Virginia, s.v. "Coolidge, Sidney," Ancestry.com; *Boston Daily Advertiser*, 2 Jan. 1864).

Charles W. GREENE (ca. 1782–1857) operated an academy for boys, with both day students and boarders, from the early 1820s until 1849. Greene's school was housed in Linden Hall, a 1755 house at the corner of Centre and Pond Streets in Jamaica Plain, a rural area southwest of Boston that was then part of the town of Roxbury. Greene was a member of the Harvard class of 1802 and author of *The Ready Multiplier* (1833) (Harriet Manning Whitcomb, *Annals and Reminiscences of Jamaica Plain* [1897], 11–12; Nathan Crosby, *Annual Obituary Notices of Eminent Persons* [1858], 164; "Family Boarding School for Boys," 1849, *American Broadsides and Ephemera, Series I, 1760–1900*, no. 7451, Archive of Americana; Coolidge to Virginia J. Randolph Trist, 8 Feb. 1837 [ViU: Ellen Wayles Randolph Coolidge Correspondence]).

Daniel CHADWICK (1795–1855), born in Lyme, Connecticut, began service as a packet captain in 1825 and had one of the longest records of continuous command. He was captain and part owner of the *Wellington* until 1845, when he turned the ship over to his brother and first mate, Charles. The *Wellington*, built in New York by Christian Bergh & Company, was launched in 1837 and featured seventeen state rooms, a "Ladies Cabin," and a large central dining space with sofas at each end (Nathan Reingold, ed., *Papers of Joseph Henry* [1979], 3:163–164, 185; Robert Greenhalgh Albion, *Square-Riggers on Schedule: The New York Sailing Packets to England, France, and the Cotton Ports* [1965], 161, 282, 333; Ship's Manifest for the *Wellington*, 15 Sept. 1838, 9 June 1845, Ancestry.com; *New York Morning Herald*, 17 Sept. 1838).

Charles I, king of England, was held at HURST CASTLE in 1647–1648, before his trial and subsequent execution for high treason in January 1649 (*ODNB*).

Coolidge's MOTHER was Martha Jefferson Randolph (1772–1836) (fig. 15), the eldest daughter of Thomas Jefferson (1743–1826) (fig. 14) and Martha Wayles Skelton Jefferson (1748–1782). In 1784 Martha accompanied Jefferson to France, where he negotiated commercial treaties and then served as minister pleni-potentiary. She attended school in Paris at the Abbaye Royale de Panthemont and returned home to America with her father and sister Mary Jefferson Eppes (1778–1804) via Le Havre and Cowes in 1789.

In 1790 Martha married Thomas Mann Randolph (1768–1828) (fig. 16), who had close ties to the Jefferson family and shared her father's interest in botany, experimental agriculture, and politics. The couple eventually settled in Albemarle County at Edgehill, a farm near Monticello, and had eleven children who survived to adulthood. Randolph served as a Virginia delegate, senator, governor, and congressman. His brief military career included service as a colonel during the War of 1812. During Jefferson's absences Randolph managed his farms, and Martha and their children joined her father at the President's House from 1802 to 1803 and from 1805 to 1806. After Jefferson retired in 1809, Martha and her family moved to Monticello, keeping it as their permanent residence until 1827 (*ANB*; *DAB*; *MB*, 1:560, 744–749; *PTJ*, 6:359–361, 14:356n, 16:189–191; *PTJRS*, 1:420n, 2:238n; Shackelford, *Descendants*, 1:45, 47, 50).

The medieval-style NORRIS CASTLE was built between 1799 and 1805 by James Wyatt (1746–1813). Queen Victoria visited there with her mother, the Duchess of Kent (1786–1861), in 1831 and 1833 (*ODNB*; David W. Lloyd and Nikolaus Pevsner, *The Buildings of England: The Isle of Wight* [2006], 195–196).

The GEORGE was best known as the inn from which Adm. Horatio Nelson departed for the Battle of Trafalgar in 1805 ("Old Portsmouth—Nelson Plaque," Memorials and Monuments in Portsmouth, accessed 20 Dec. 2010, http://www.memorials.inportsmouth.co.uk/old-portsmouth/nelson_plaque.htm).

The A3 follows the traditional ROAD FROM PORTSMOUTH TO LONDON, which passes the Devil's Punch Bowl in Hindhead, Surrey. There in 1786 an unknown sailor was robbed, beaten, and killed. Outraged locals erected the Sailor's Stone at the scene of the crime "in detestation of a barbarous murder committed here." The stone's INSCRIPTION lists the three men responsible and notes that they were hung in chains nearby as punishment for the deed. Charles Dickens was so struck by the story that he included it in the *Life and Adventures of Nicholas Nickleby* (1839) (Eric Parker, *Highways and Byways in Surrey* [1908], 147–148; William Hone, *The Table Book* [1828], 2:145–149; "Hindhead Commons and the Devil's Punch Bowl," National Trust, accessed 20 Dec. 2010, http://www.nationaltrust.org.uk).

FENTON'S HOTEL was located on the west side of St. James's Street, just two blocks from St. James's Palace. Francis Fenton and Henry Peto built the Palladian-style, four-story hotel in 1825, and F. H. Fenton, presumably Francis Fenton's son, operated the hotel during the Coolidges' stay. Fenton's Hotel offered fashionable lodging for foreign travelers, government officials, and visiting dignitaries. The exiled Louis Napoléon, later Napoléon III (1808–1873), and his entourage of seven stayed there from 25 October until 3 November 1838. John Tallis's *London Street Views* (fig. 6) shows the hotel among the neighboring clubs and residences on St. James's Street (Bryant Lillywhite, *London Coffee Houses* [1963], 206; *Survey of*

London, vols. 29 and 30 [1960], 459–471; *Morning Chronicle* [London], 26 Oct., 5 Nov. 1838; *Freeman's Journal and Daily Commercial Advertiser* [London], 31 Oct. 1838).

This fable associated with Linnaeus tells of seven (not three, as Coolidge recalled) WISE MEN from Greece who were permitted by Jupiter to visit the moon in order to document the flora and fauna and report their findings upon their return. Distracted by the hospitality that the inhabitants of the moon had shown them, the wise men returned to earth as ignorant as when they first set out (James Bolton, *Harmonia Ruralis; or, An Essay towards a Natural History of British Song Birds* [1830], 91–92; *The Classical Narrator: Consisting of Tales in Prose and Verse* [1823], 29–31).

Monday. 9th July.

I have been a day & a half in London and it will take me many days to recover from the effects of my voyage. I feel badly & look badly, thin, pale & sunburnt. Three large mirrors in our drawing room, & three more in my bed-chamber leave me no doubt on this subject. I cannot get away from my own image. and my costume is in keeping with my looks. A black travelling dress is hardly the thing for London but my luggage is all, save a carpet bag, aboard the Wellington which was expected last night and this morning is said not to have passed the Downs. I am worse off than Sterne with his six shirts and one pair of black satin unmentionables. My maid, the English lady's maid provided by the kind care of my husband, and whom I found waiting for me at Fenton's, bears the non-arrival of my trunks worse than I do. She is tired of the black travelling dress and keeps brushing my hair for want of something else to do. When I was a girl, living in Virginia, I had an excellent lady's maid who did every thing for me. When I married and went to New England where every lady is her own maid, and waits upon herself, and dresses her own hair, I felt as if I should never be able to perform such Herculean tasks. Thirteen years of persevering effort, however, made these things so easy to me that I fancied I should never desire to be waited on again, or have a hireling intruding her useless services on the independence & privacy of my toilette. But it was a mistaken thought. In five minutes I had relapsed into old habits— allowed my maid to undress and put me to bed the night of my arrival, and now cannot stick a pin or smooth a hair without her. Will it take me, when I return to Boston, another thirteen years, if I live so long, to learn to take care of myself again? Heaven forefend!

My sitting room is front, overlooking St James' St. and my eyes are constantly attracted by the curious variety of[1] carriages, coaches, coupés, barouches, broughams, britschkas, stanhopes, Tilburies, Dennets, Flys, Cabs (such they tell me are the names) to say nothing of vile hackney coaches, stage coaches carrying four inside and eleven outside passengers, waggons, carts and so on. The Cab Family is a numerous one, including many high-bred & low-bred specimens, as unlike each other as many other individuals grouped together by naturalists who understand their own reasons for doing so. A variety of Cab which it hurts my feelings to look at is an oblong packing box on wheels, the driver, or Cabman I suppose would be the English word, is perched on the top, the door behind, the occupants sit with their sides to the horse, and are jostled along looking like children in a Toss-about, of which machine I have only seen the picture in a Primer. St. James St. is wide & paved with what I supposed to be large bricks, but which are in fact, I am told, small oblong stones, looking very even and neat.

I am occupying rooms just vacated by Lady Alice Peale, sister-in-law, I believe to Sir Robert Peale. They are not elegant rooms though comfortable. The curtains, sofa, fauteuils & chairs of worsted damask—there are mahogany tables, white marble mantel pieces, Brussels carpets, gilt centre lamps and very large mirrors. But every thing is dingy with London smoke, and the walls papered, which strikes me unpleasantly accustomed as I am to the painted walls of Boston houses. We breakfast about ten and dine at seven, taking coffee immediately after and tea when we call for it—at any hour. Our breakfast consists of black tea, comme ça, butter la la—having no ice upon it; but delicious muffins, light, white, spongy just such as we had, in former days, at Monticello, when the cook happened to be sober. Such as I once heard a little boy desire his mother to "butter on the back, stick holes in with a fork, and squeeze down in the plate till the juice run out." Add to these, new-laid eggs with the date of their production written on them with a pencil, and very fine, large, ripe strawberries.

Our dinner is served on silver (plated?) dishes. We had, yesterday, first a soup, then fish with lobster sauce & potatos. Next came lamb, pigeons, green peas & again potatos—apparently as obligato here as in Boston. We had then an omelette with sugar and fresh cut lemons followed by Wiltshire and Stilton cheese & bread & butter. We have two waiters, and the master of the Hotel, Fenton, in shorts and black silk stockings, himself poured out the wine, which at my request, was Port.

There is a grand review to-day in Hyde Park which I am too unwell and weary to wish even to see. But the Horse Guards have just passed the window. Superb men on superb horses all black with white housings. Two officers of rank came a few moments after all scarlet & gold in an open Barouche, the box covered with scarlet & gold, the coachman and two footmen in scarlet & gold very fine & very gaudy, more like the figures on a Chinese Tea Chest than any thing else. The only persons I have seen since my arrival here are Mʳ Higginson, Mʳ, Mʳˢ, & Miss Bates, Dr Warren of Boston this morning, and just gone Dr Boott and his mother.——

Coolidge here refers to the first page of Laurence STERNE, *A Sentimental Journey through France and Italy* (1770), a two-volume work that was in Jefferson's library at Monticello. The UNMENTIONABLES were silk breeches (Sowerby, 4335).

Coolidge's LADY'S MAID was Sally Cottrell Cole (ca. 1800–1875), a slave in the Monticello household (fig. 1). Following Coolidge's marriage in May 1825, the new bride wrote to her mother that Joseph would sign a power of attorney allowing her brother Thomas Jefferson Randolph to "dispose of Sally and to protect her. Her own wishes you know my dear mother must direct the disposition that is made of her for I would not for the world that after living with me fifteen years any kind of violence should be done to her feelings. If she wishes to be sold let her chuse her own master, if to be hired she should have the same liberty or at least not be sent any where where she is unwilling to go." Sally was sold for four hundred dollars to Thomas Hewitt Key, a University of Virginia professor who intended ultimately to free her, and served as lady's maid to Sarah Troward Key and nurse to their infant daughter. Upon Key's resignation from the university, Sally worked for a brief time in the household of John Patten Emmett, another University of Virginia professor. By 1828 Sally was working on her own as a seamstress and nurse. She married Reuben Cole in 1846 and lived in Charlottesville, Virginia, until her death. The legal status of her freedom was still in question as late as 1850 (*ODNB*; Coolidge to Martha Jefferson Randolph, 26–27 June 1825, Cornelia J. Randolph to Coolidge, 13 July 1825, Virginia J. Randolph Trist to Coolidge, 4 Dec. 1825, Mary J. Randolph to Coolidge, 29 July 1827 [ViU: Ellen Wayles Randolph Coolidge Correspondence]; Documents in negotiation with Thomas H. Key, 21 July 1827 [DLC: Nicholas Philip Trist Papers]; Mary J. Randolph to Virginia J. Randolph Trist, 25 July 1831 [NcU: Southern Historical Collection, Nicholas Philip Trist Papers]; Marriage Contract between Sally Cottrell and Reuben Cole, 21 Nov. 1846, Albemarle County Deed Book, 44:400–401 [Albemarle County Courthouse, Charlottesville, Va.]; Eugene Davis to Thomas Key, Nov. 1850 [ViU: Papers of Eugene Davis, Mss. 2483-a]; Maplewood Cemetery, Charlottesville, Va.).

St. James's [ST. JAMES'] STREET, together with Piccadilly, Haymarket, and Pall Mall, surrounds St. James's Square and is only a short distance from Buckingham Palace and Hyde Park (fig. 20). It was one of the most fashionable residential neighborhoods in London through the middle of the nineteenth century (*Survey of London*, vols. 29 and 30 [1960], 459–471).

A TOSS-ABOUT was an early version of a Ferris wheel, with crisscrossed timbers supporting baskets in which small children could sit while the baskets rose and fell in a circular motion via a crank turned by an adult. An illustration, with accompanying story and rhyme, can be found in *Cobwebs to Catch Flies: or, Dialogues in Short Sentences, Adapted to Children from the age of three to eight years* (1783), by Mrs. Lovechild (Ellenor Fenn).

Alicia Jane Kennedy Peel [PEALE] (d. 1887) was married to Jonathan Peel (1799–1879), politician and soldier. Jonathan was also the younger brother of Sir Robert Peel (1788–1850), opposition leader, prime minister, and founder of the Metropolitan Police Force (*ODNB*).

FAUTEUIL: an armchair (*OED*).

The COOK may have been Peter Hemings (1770–after 1834), whose recipe for muffins Jefferson preferred, or possibly Edith Fossett (1787–1854), who trained and cooked at the President's House and became head cook at Monticello in 1809, after Peter Hemings departed. Coolidge requested the Monticello muffin recipe, among others, after her marriage and move to Boston (Damon Lee Fowler, ed., *Dining at Monticello* [2005], 42, 91, 93; Lucia Stanton, *Free Some Day: The African-American Families of Monticello* [2000], 60, 63–64, 80, 113, 129–131; Thomas Jefferson to Martha Jefferson Randolph, 2 Nov. 1802 [ViU: Thomas Jefferson Papers]; Coolidge to Randolph, 20 Nov. 1825 [ViU: Ellen Wayles Randolph Coolidge Correspondence]).

According to Monticello family tradition, the LITTLE BOY associated with these instructions is Coolidge's brother Benjamin Franklin Randolph (1808–1871), who gave these same directions to Dolley Payne Madison during one of James and Dolley Madison's frequent visits to Monticello. Randolph attended the University of Virginia and graduated with a degree in medicine in 1831. In 1834 he married Sally Champe Carter (ca. 1808–1896) of Redlands, an estate near Monticello, and the couple raised three children. Benjamin was a physician and farmer, served as a Virginia state senator from 1853 to 1856, and attended the Virginia Constitutional Convention in 1861 (Shackelford, *Descendants*, 1:114–121; Ellen Wayles Randolph Harrison and Martha Jefferson Trist Burke, "Monticello Child Life" [ViCMRL: unpublished manuscript, before 1915]).

Joshua BATES (1788–1864), merchant, banker, and philanthropist, was born in Weymouth, Massachusetts, but by this time he had been resident in London for more than twenty years. A senior partner in the firm Baring Brothers & Company, Bates was largely responsible for shifting his company's focus to the rapidly developing international trade, particularly with America and the Far East, and steering it safely through the Panics of 1837 and 1847 to become by midcentury the most powerful commercial house in the world. Bates married Lucretia Augustus Sturgis (d. 1863) in 1813, and they had two children, William Rufus Gray Bates (d. 1834) and Elizabeth Ann Sturgis Bates Van de Weyer (d. 1878). He was a substantial benefactor of the Boston Public Library (*DAB*; *ODNB*; Ziegler, *Sixth Great Power*, 112, 122–131, 143–160; Ralph Willard Hidy, *House of Baring in American Trade and Finance: English Merchant Bankers at Work, 1763–1861* [1949], 79–85, 205–238; Henry Wikoff, *Reminiscences of an Idler* [1880], 366–367; *Tribute of Boston Merchants to the Memory of Joshua Bates* [1864]; *Memorial of Joshua Bates, from the City of Boston* [1865]; *Gentleman's Magazine*, n.s., 13 [1874]: 109).

John Collins WARREN (1778–1856), surgeon and professor of anatomy and surgery at Harvard Medical School, was the Coolidges' family physician in Boston. In 1812 he cofounded what became the *New-England Journal of Medicine and Surgery* and gained fame as the first to perform surgery in a public demonstration of the use of ether anesthesia in 1846 (*ANB; DAB*; John C. Warren, *Etherization; with Surgical Remarks* [1848]; Coolidge to Martha Jefferson Randolph, 27 Feb., 23 Mar. 1826, 26 Apr., 21 June 1829, 14 Mar. 1830, Coolidge to Virginia J. Randolph Trist, 13 May 1837 [ViU: Ellen Wayles Randolph Coolidge Correspondence]; *Boston Daily Advertiser*, 6, 7, 8 May 1856; *Boston Daily Atlas*, 6 May 1856).

Francis BOOTT (1792–1863), physician and botanist, was born in Boston but resided in London from 1820. He was the son of Kirk Boott (1755–1817), founder of the industrial city of Lowell, Massachusetts, and Mary Love Boott (1766–1856). Mrs. Boott was the Coolidges' neighbor in Boston, living at 10 Bowdoin Square, where her husband had established a renowned garden and greenhouse. Francis Boott shared his family's interest in botany and is known for his thirty-year study of sedges, genus *Carex*, which resulted in a widely acclaimed multivolume work on more than six hundred species. His hospitality impressed Bostonian Ezra Stiles Gannett, who wrote of his 1836 visit to Boott, "'I give only one invitation,' said Dr. B. at dinner. 'Come at all times,—morning, noon, or night,—and use us as your friends. . . . He says that Boston has sent an influence across the ocean, which is felt in England, in the Establishment even. While English society indicates a higher refinement, there is an order of mind . . . existing in America, that cannot be found in England" (*ODNB*; Alan Emmet, *So Fine a Prospect: Historic New England Gardens* [1997], 34–46; William Channing Gannet, *Ezra Stiles Gannett, Unitarian Minister in Boston, 1824–1871* [1875], 159–160; *Proceedings of the American Academy of Arts and Sciences* 6 [1866]: 305–308).

1. Manuscript: "of of."

Wednesday. 11th July.

London is very full. The Coronation being just over and the town crowded with distinguished strangers. The young Queen is just now the Queen of Hearts—the "point de mise" for all eyes. I have had the good fortune to see her and the good taste to admire her—more honestly perhaps than a great many others, for I have nothing to gain by my admiration and it is very disinterested. Yesterday Mrs Bates called at Fenton's and proposed to me a drive in Hyde Park. The day was fine and I readily accepted the invitation. A drive in Hyde Park! and for me! I can scarcely believe it possible and feel inclined to doubt my own identity. That I, whose life for the last thirteen years has been so secluded, so domestic, shut up from the society even of Boston, living in my nursery and my morning wrapper—that I should be in England, in London, driving in Hyde Park. Am I really awake or only dreaming—but sleeping or waking, in the body or in the spirit, I went yesterday to Hyde Park and remained there from 5 till 7.A.M. In these two hours I certainly saw a great deal. Hyde Park itself, Kensington Gardens & Palace, the Queen, the Queen Dowager, the Countess of Jersey, the Countess of Blessington, the Count D'Orsey, Lady Aylesbury's equipage & the great Nassau Baloon, to say nothing of a crowd of shewy carriages & shewy people and a number of fine horses. The houses of the nobility, pointed out to me by Mrs Bates, on the way to Hyde Park, fell short in their external appearance, of my expectations. Their magnificence must all be within—And this I must now & always take upon trust, as it is little likely I shall ever prove it by my own eyes. We are in London without a solitary letter of introduction, and this by my own choice. I asked for none & would receive none. I desire to see as much as I can of the <u>country</u> in England, to visit the most remarkable spots, but for society, supposing it possible for me to gain admittance, stranger as I am, into what is really good, I have neither inclination nor spirits for it. I have lived too much at home, have become shy & somewhat unsocial. I wish to visit Parks & Picture Galleries—to extend my acquaintance with Nature & Art, but not with the motley mixture of nature & art called society.

Hyde Park at present does not, I am told, wear it's best looks. I should hope not—for the turf is dusty worn and down-trodden. Kensington Gardens, on the other hand, are beautifully fresh and green. The trees glorious in their verdure, & the turf delicious in it's soft & mossy pile I should say were I speaking of velvet—I was somewhat disappointed in the beauty of the women whom I saw in the Park. One hears so much & reads so much of English beauty! The women whom I met were either, many of them, fat and what Marryatt calls "fabsy" (a coarse word but what better can you expect from so coarse a man!) or where the fat was gone it seemed to have melted away irregularly leaving the face and neck unevenly furrowed. Their colouring too was somewhat coarse, natural colouring I mean for these ladies did not look painted. They were generally in demi-toilette and their dress had a somewhat tumbled and deranged look, as if they had been shopping all the morning & had gone through the wear & tear of that arduous operation. Some of them sat with their feet on the front seat of the Carriage, a little in the style of members of Congress, and were lounging on their cushions as they might have done on their couches at home. I do not pretend to say who these women were—perhaps not good specimens, but their equipages were shewy with full complements of servants.

The English carriages again are not what I expected to find them— They are less simple, less elegant, more gaudy & glaring. They are of every variety of form and colour, & the colours often ill-assorted. The harmony which should prevail between the body of the carriage, the linings, the hammock cloth & the liveries of the servants is too often neglected, and the effect is tawdry & bad. The plainest and handsomest carriages that I saw were those of the two Queens, and Lady Aylesbury's dark Britschka, with two bay horses & two outriders or grooms following behind dressed in plain colours & mounted likewise on bays.

Many of the carriages were drawn by horses of different colours, as a gray & a bay, a black & a roan, but matched perfectly in size, form & step. Miss Bates informs me that this just now is high fashion. There were many persons of both sexes on horseback. Englishmen and English women ride too well not to be above criticism. But the men have an easy, lounging way of sitting on their horses which I am not well enough acquainted with to like. The women have rather more of the somewhat stiff military air which I prefer. Count D'Orsay's graceful person reposed on his saddle as it might have done on a chair whilst his legs dangled lazily on each side. This successor to Brummel has an ultra look which I cannot reconcile with high breeding. His bearded throat and cheeks, his cravat of straw-colored silk, the general effect of his whole toilette & person is more, to my eye, that of a foreign adventurer than of an English gentleman. He was riding with what seemed to me an affectation of careless ease on a horse of most delicate and matchless proportions, by the side of an open carriage in which sat the once beautiful Countess of Blessington, now a fat, improper-looking old woman. Of Lady Jersey I caught only a glance. The Queen Dowager was bonnetted and veiled & muffled up, but the young Queen I looked at well. Her open carriage, drawn rapidly by four horses, passed Mrs Bates' where I was, four times in the Hyde Park round, and each time my eyes rested on the vision of a sweet, fair, modest yet frank face. I saw nothing I liked so well in Hyde Park. There is a prestige in this young royalty—this girl that holds the reins of empire over so many bearded men, such vast & powerful realms I cannot but fancy her some potent fairy in the disguise of a princess of eighteen.

On my return from my drive I found waiting for me at Fenton's, a letter from home. A charming piece of mosaic made up of the different handwriting of three of my children and two of my sisters. There were Ellen's fair unformed characters, Randolph's copy-book writing and dear Jefferson's printing with a pencil, with two kind postscripts from Mary & Septimia. Dear children, dear sisters—How much I prize your letter and love your precious selves.

The **YOUNG QUEEN** was Alexandrina Victoria (1819–1901), who became queen upon the death of her uncle William IV on 20 June 1837. Her coronation took place on 28 June 1838 (*ODNB*; Benson and Brett, *Letters of Queen Victoria*, 1:96, 153–160).

The **QUEEN DOWAGER** was Adelaide (1792–1849), widow of William IV and aunt of Queen Victoria (*ODNB*).

Sarah Sophia Child-Villiers, **COUNTESS OF JERSEY** (1785–1867), political hostess and heir to the Child's Bank fortune, was the wife of George Child-Villiers (1773–1859), fifth Earl of Jersey (*ODNB*).

Margaret Power Farmer Gardiner, the **COUNTESS OF BLESSINGTON** (1789–1849), an author renowned for her beauty and social prestige, married first Maurice St. Leger Farmer (d. 1817). Within months of Farmer's death she married Charles John Gardiner, second Viscount Mountjoy and first Earl of Blessington. Beginning in 1822 she maintained a lifelong relationship with Gédéon Gaspard Alfred de Grimaud, **COUNT D'ORSAY** (1801–1852), a French-born artist and sculptor (*ODNB*; Michael Sadleir, *Blessington–D'Orsay: A Masquerade* [1933]).

LADY AYLESBURY was Maria Elizabeth Tollemache Brudenell-Bruce, Marchioness of Ailesbury (1809–1893), second wife of Sir Charles Brudenell-Bruce, first Marquess of Ailesbury (1773–1856) (Edmund Lodge, *Peerage of the British Empire* [1843], 17; Edward Walford, *Hardwick's Annual Biography* [1857], 2–3).

The **NASSAU** balloon was the *Royal Vauxhall*, constructed by Charles Green (1785–1870) in 1836. Green subsequently renamed the balloon after a successful journey in which he, Robert Hollond (1808–1877), who financed the venture, and Thomas Monck Mason (1803–1889) ascended from Vauxhall Gardens on 7 November 1836 and descended the next morning at Weilburg in Nassau, Germany. During the Coolidges' stay Green and his balloon made numerous ascents and descents around the city of London (*ODNB*; *Times* [London], 9, 13 Aug., 11 Sept. 1838).

Frederick **MARRYAT** (1792–1848) was a naval officer and novelist (*ODNB*).

A **BRITSCHKA** was an open carriage with a folding hood and space for reclining (*OED*).

The socialite George Bryan **BRUMMELL** (1778–1840) was popularly known as Beau Brummell (*ODNB*).

Thursday. 12. July.

There is something in the quietness of an English Hotel that pleases me greatly. In the Astor House in New York there is an incessant clapping of doors, hurrying backwards & forwards of visiters, loud speaking &

calling, bad attendance, with a confused pell mell of servants, ringing of bells, running up & down stairs, with all sorts of bewildering movements & dissonant sounds. Here, at Fenton's, (which is to be sure a small place compared with the great democratic hotels of my own country) I never hear a door slam nor a person speak above their voice, nor have I seen anything like bustle since I have been in the house. My parlour, from being on the street, is rather noisy. There is an incessant rolling of carriages. It is not elegant for a lady to shew herself at the window, but I go to the window to see, not to be seen where no one knows me. These English carriages are certainly very gaudy, altogether too fine. One passed a little while ago with a bright yellow body, scarlet hammock cloth, footmen & coachman in white. On some you see a great deal of gilding or brass. One has just gone by, green body, grey hammock cloth with a crest worked in silver, & scarlet footmen. There goes another of a dark, modest colour on which is painted a great flaring coat of arms that looks like a huge dish of lobster salad, scarlet, white & green. I presume the very brilliant colours one sees on most of the equipages is less a matter of taste than of obedience to the laws of heraldry of azure, gules, or, argent, vert & sables.

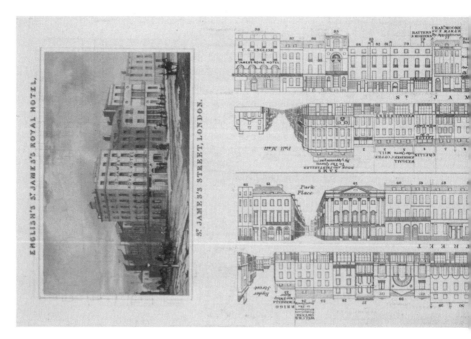

FIGURE 6. St. James's Street, *Tallis's London Street Views*, ca. 1838. Upon Ellen's arrival the Coolidges stayed in furnished rooms at Fenton's Hotel,

I had been hesitating what sort of carriage I should have for myself as Mr Coolidge leaves the choice to me. An important matter, as I can have but one, and not a dozen like some of the English women. My drive in Hyde Park decided me. I like a coupé best. I have a little of the Turkish feeling about women. I do not like a too ambitious display of the face or person, be they ever so lovely; far less if, as in many cases, they happen to be plain. I never particularly admired flaring bonnets, & I have a partiality for veils & shawls. In Hyde Park I observed ladies in open carriages, with sun, wind, dust & the eyes of the men assailing their faces & persons all at once, and they certainly looked less cool, neat, & quiet to say nothing more than others who were shaded without being concealed in vehicles of a less demonstrative character. The fair, young Queen is seen to best advantage in an open carriage, but then she is right to shew herself to her people, and they have a right to look upon her. This Virgin Mother, (may I use such words without ireverence, the feeling is reverential,!) of the Nations. But all women are not Queens and they had better not strive to become so.——

Mr Higginson went yesterday to Windsor & returned on an outside seat

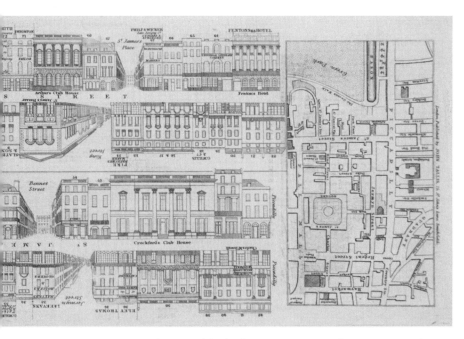

63 St. James's Street, just two blocks from St. James's Palace. *(Courtesy of the London Metropolitan Archives.)*

of a coach. He sat by the Coachman; close behind him were the Prince de Ligne & two of his attendants. There was a fête this day at Sion House at which the Queen was to be present, and all the dignataries, foreign & domestic, with whom London, so soon after the Coronation, swarms. As the coach rolled onward, towards the town, a great many splendid carriages of nobility & gentry & foreign ministers were rolling on in the opposite direction. Prince de Ligne, from his elevated position "on top the coach," smiled & bowed & received smiles & bows from the occupants of the gorgeous equipages. Nay when the coach stopped for a moment, his Highness disdained not to buy a pottle of raspberries from a little girl by the wayside, which his friends & himself ate with great satisfaction from the leaves in which the fruit was imbedded. Shakespere says all the world's a stage and all the men & women players—I do not know how this may be; but at present a great comedy is being played in London, in which the Queen & all the principal people are principal actors, where all who have any pretensions are ambitious to have their part, and many will come in on any terms rather than not come in at all. There is, besides the prominent characters, a numerous corps of inferior performers. And the relative value & position of all are as well appreciated by the great audience as if all really trod the boards of a painted theatre. I presume in the excitement of acting each one feels as if his role were a conspicuous one. Then what a train of scene shifters lamp-lighters & candle snuffers! What a "personnel" it must require where so much is to be done! What a magnificent shew is the result, and how glad I am to be where I can catch glimpses from time to time, even of the small details of what seems to me a great theatrical entertainment "où il y a beaucoup de spectacle." I come from a country where people are very fond of getting up exhibitions & of taking a personal part in them—But the stage is not so well adapted for effect & the costumes & scenery decidedly inferiour.

The ASTOR HOUSE was built at a cost of $400,000 by John Jacob Astor (1763–1848), fur trader and financier, and opened as the Park Hotel in 1836 (*ANB*; *DAB*).

The Coolidges purchased a "fashionable chariot," or COUPÉ, a short, four-wheeled, closed carriage with an inside seat for two or three passengers and an outside seat for the driver. Manufactured by G. C. Burnand of Bond Street, the carriage was drawn by two horses and outfitted "with town and travelling append-ages," which provided room for stowing luggage and seating to accommodate two servants. After their departure the carriage was advertised for sale by auction on 21 August 1839 as having been "lately on job to Mr. Coolidge, who only used it nine months" (*OED*; William Bridges Adams, *English Pleasure Carriages* [1837], 83–91, 220–225; *Morning Chronicle* [London], 21 Aug. 1839).

Eugene Lamoral, PRINCE DE LIGNE, d'Amblèse, and d'Epinoy (1804–1880), Belgian statesman, represented that country at Queen Victoria's coronation (*New York Times*, 22 May 1880).

Syon [SION] House was, and continues to be, the London residence of the dukes of Northumberland. The interior remodeling by famed Scottish architect Robert Adam (1728–1792) attracted visitors, including Coolidge's grandfather and John Adams, with his family, who visited the house together on 20 April 1786 (Bridget Cherry and Nikolaus Pevsner, *The Buildings of England: London 3: North West* [1991], 38; Susan Reynolds, ed., *History of the County of Middlesex* [1962], 3:97–100; *MB*, 1:622).

July 19th

I have just recovered from two days illness, & have had besides several days of close letter-writing.

I have been again to Hyde Park, where I got another sight of the young Queen which confirmed my previous favorable impressions. It is surprising what a feeling of loyalty women of all nations seem to have towards this sovereign of their own sex. We are so seldom called to fill high places that our hearts are stirred at once with pride & love when we see the destinies of a great people even nominally committed to hands like our own. And how much it says for that people, & for the Government they have worked out for themselves in a long process of time, that the machinery needs only the hand of a girl to direct it's movements,—so well arranged & manoeuvred are all it's springs & wheels—I hope that as new improvements are introduced into the body of the works, the forms may retain their grace & beauty. Long live all British Queens! And for that matter Kings too, if they will only consent to reign & not govern.

I have been twice to Regent's Park—a very beautiful place it is. Once I have visited the Zoological Gardens. I went to see the beasts, but I looked a good deal at the men & women of middling & lower rank who thronged the place. I was struck by an absence of comeliness in the women. I have yet to become acquainted with English beauty except by hearsay. The Nursery women and the tradesmen's wives at the Zoological Gardens were neither so well looking nor so neatly dressed as the same classes in America. There was much more of what might be called vulgarity in their general appearance—something that betokened a lower order of intellect and character.

I am charmed with the beauty of the Giraffes—a beauty so peculiar— The grace of their movements is also of it's own kind. They give one new ideas of what is graceful & beautiful, departing from all the old standards & conventions—Glimpses of new forms of creation. They might be creatures of another planet.

The Sirius is arrived and I have a letter from my dear daughter. One such letter revives my spirits often depressed by this absence from my children.

Coolidge suffered from ILLNESS for much of her sea voyage, the effects of which she continued to feel for several days after landing. The Coolidges' family physician, John Warren, also happened to be in London and visited her often during the first few weeks of her stay. When she had recovered enough from the seasickness, Dr. Warren vaccinated her and removed a mole from her left arm. Writing to a friend she declared that she bore the procedure "like a heroine" but that it left her arm bandaged, stiff, and sore so that she could "neither go to the opera, for which I have strength, nor dine out for which I have not inclination. Upon the whole then I can in no way make a mountain of this mole—What a detestable pun!" (Coolidge to Augustine Heard, 20 July 1838 [MH: Heard Family Papers]).

Portions of REGENT'S PARK were opened to the public two days a week beginning in 1835. The Zoological Gardens, opened there in 1828, were spectacularly popular and featured monkeys, bears, kangaroos, llamas, and zebras, among other animals. The Zoological Society added four giraffes to the collection in 1836, and they were housed in a pavilion (*London Encyclopedia*, s.v. "zoological gardens"; Timbs, *Curiosities*, 838–839).

The SIRIUS was built in Scotland by Robert Menzies and Son in 1837. A steamship originally intended for cross-channel trips between Cork and London, *Sirius* was chartered by the American Steam Navigation Company in 1838 to compete with Isambard Kingdom Brunel's *Great Western*, built in Bristol by William Patterson, in a race across the Atlantic. On its first voyage *Sirius* sailed from Cork on 4 April and arrived in New York on 22 April, one day before the *Great Western*, thus becoming the first steamship to make the transatlantic crossing (Lincoln P. Paine, *Ships of the World: An Historical Encyclopedia* [1997], 224–225, 476–477; *New York Morning Herald*, 24 Apr. 1838; *New-York Spectator*, 26 Apr. 1838).

Saturday 21. July.

My letters for the Great Western are gone, and I have now rather more leisure, but I have still many more letters to write before I can feel that I have done my duty by all my friends & best wishers.

Yesterday I went for the first time into the City—only as far as Bishops-gate St. but I saw St. Paul's and I passed Temple Bar, and thought I could form some idea of the immense concentration of life & labour called London. It was with some difficulty my coachman threaded his way through streets crowded with every sort of vehicle, whilst the living stream of men, women & children that passed in counter currents along the side walks filled me with a sort of awe, at the sight of so many human beings, with human passions & pursuits, yet driven on, as it seemed to me, by an unseen power. I could hardly reconcile with ideas of free-will such multitudes of creatures pouring along the same course. They appeared more like flocks or herds obeying the impulse of a voice & a hand from behind than thinking beings going on their own way, chusing their own path, impelled each one by individual motives & governed by their several & independent wills. Man seems a much more noble part of God's creation when you take him alone, weak as he is, than when taken in mass even with all the power which in mass, he wields. The single individual gains in the scale of humanity what he loses when he is merely considered as a part of a great whole. He ceases to be an atom.

This pouring crowd in the London streets saddened me with a feeling of the insignificance of individuals. I asked myself what might be the appearance of a great Ant Hill seen through a microscope of sufficient power. Would not these insects seem just as rationally busy in their several or collective pursuits, as the inhabitants of this great Metropolis streaming through it's innumerable streets and avenues? Has it not been shewn by Huber that Ants have a regular civil polity; that they are divided into Casts, have pastoral & military orders, keep what may be called their milch cows, make war upon other tribes, are kidnappers & slaveholders? But with them all is instinct, men are governed by reason. that is Ants are stationary, neither advance nor recede, whilst men are capable of both. Ants are the same now, no doubt, that they were in the commencement of their career—They were as wise & methodical as they are now. They are strict conservatives—I am something of a conservative myself in politics, that is I dislike innovation; yet change, the power of improvement, the restless desire for a better order of things is what distinguishes the man from the insect, since it shews the working within him of a principle of progress—a something always pressing forward, sometimes swept backward by the pressure of events, but whose tendency is onward onward still onward beyond the limits of his mortal life.——Such were some of the strange thoughts which distracted my attention from my immediate object, the pursuit of a Cashmere shawl.

In all my drives I have been struck with the truth of something I lately read in the Edinburgh Review. An article on Dr Waagen's book.—"Of the modern street architecture of London, with it's composition, ornaments and architectural decorations of pillars and pilasters . . . he thinks very poorly. The street architecture is condemned as destitute of those continuous simple main lines, indispensable to general effect in architecture, and to which all decoration must be subordinate. Farther, the decorations are introduced without regard to their own meaning, or the destination of the edifice; a fault particularly observable in the columns, which instead of being used as the supports of a wall, are frequently ranged before it."

Nothing seems to me more mistaken in architecture than useless columns, pillars out of place; but it is one of the commonest mistakes of false taste. In the United States many honest edifices are made simply ridiculous by such appendages. Here in London they stand every where like unprofitable servants, and these servants in livery. Hats of Acanthus leaves or volutes; their feet shod in Ionic pedestals or unshod after the Doric fashion—some short & stout, some tall & slender—some clad in plain clothes, some striped & grooved——

What gives London it's character of grandeur is it's immensity. Take from it it's vastness & not much would remain to boast of. But magnitude is in some things a chief element of the sublime and London is sublime from it's overpowering extent. There is, I suppose, nothing like it on earth. It is the Queen of Cities, the fitting capital of the greatest of nations.

The impression made on me by St. Paul's Church is some what akin to that produced by London itself. Vast, complicated, a grand whole, worthy of it's reputation, in spite of it's most anomalous architecture, it's "abnormities" as Dr Waagen would call them, & the general bad taste of the Monuments,—and in spite too of the dirt & disarray of all around. I felt as I looked at it that this was St. Paul's—the St. Paul's Cathedral of my expectations—that is when I looked at the interiour. And if this vast edifice only stood in a clear space the external effect might be similar to that produced within. But you are so pushed up against it, as it were, from without by contiguous buildings & narrow streets that the eye cannot embrace it as a whole.

The statue of Queen Anne, in front of the grand entrance, must be a likeness I think. It is by Francis Bird and gives you a good idea of a foolish woman, a Mrs Freeman in royal robes. The really glorious reign of "good Queen Anne" shews of how little importance it is for a British sovereign to be possessed of intellect. "Your Majesty is nothing but a piece of ceremony yourself" said I know not what minister to I know not what King, who objected to something as being nothing but a piece of ceremony.

From St. Paul's we turned our faces west-endwards, passed through the strand, over Waterloo Bridge, a noble work of hewn granite, & returned over Westminster Bridge, home.

The Thames as I saw it from Waterloo Bridge, looking downwards to London Bridge & St. Paul's Church, and upwards to Westminster Bridge & Abbey, seemed narrow & muddy & scarce worthy of it's great name and the works which cover it's banks.

Of Westminster Abbey I have as yet seen nothing but it's grim exteriour in which, however, there is something very imposing. They are just now tearing down the decorations which were introduced for the Coronation, & there is no admittance for visiters till these are removed.

My drives through London impress me with the perfection of the London police. Nothing could be more under the dominion of law & order than all that I saw yesterday. The press of carriages, of every descrip-tion, vehicles of every imaginable kind, was several times so great that my coachman was compelled to stop and wait several minutes together before I could pass. But there was no confusion, no forcing forwards, no shouting or swearing among coachmen & carters—each one waited quietly until his turn came & the consequence was that there was comparatively little delay. In any city of the United States under similar circumstances, there would have been shoving and pushing & bawling, vollies of oaths and perhaps an exchange of blows. It is true that in the cities of the Union one sees none of these blue-coated men with silver badges in their hats, so noiseless & quiet themselves, yet so powerful to enforce good order. They seem entirely civil too, but ubiquitous and despotic.

———Capt. Wormeley has just been in and talked among other things, of the United States and of my dear Grandfather. My earliest best friend, whom I look back to and remember as faultless in all the relations of domestic life. It warms my heart to hear him spoken of as he deserves to be spoken of. Capt. Wormeley called him the most remarkable man of his age, and I think he must hereafter be acknowledged as one of the great leaders of public opinion. No man of his times produced on his contem-poraries an effect so marked and so likely to be lasting. He was the Apostle of Liberty and of Reform, and however men may agree with or differ from him in the principles which he held, and acted upon through the whole of his public course, there is no denying that their influence has been immense, and must go on swelling like a great tide which will eventually overflow the lands. It may be like the overflow of the Nile, fertilizing all that it covers—or it may be a devastating flood. I hope that in doing all he could to throw power into the hands of the people he did not over-rate their fitness for self-government. He thought perhaps too well of his fellow-men, and if mischief should ensue from his too great confidence in them, the fault will be not in him but in them. If man requires to be bridled and bitted for his own good, then was my grandfather mistaken in his efforts to give him a blessing he is unworthy of and can only abuse.

Jean Pierre HUBER (1777–1840) was an entomologist and a member of the Physical and Natural History Society of Geneva. His work *Recherches sur les moeurs des fourmis indigènes* (1810) was translated from the French by James Rawlins Johnson and published in London as *The Natural History of Ants* (1820). The work covers social structure at length, including castes, warfare, kidnapping, and slavery.

Gustav Friedrich WAAGEN (1794–1868), museum director and art historian, frequently traveled from his native Germany to other European countries to study art, architecture, galleries, and museums, and his observations abroad and at home led to a number of significant publications. One of his most influential works, *Treasures of Art in Great Britain*, published in English in 1854 and 1857, catalogued for the first time two hundred of Britain's most significant art collections and is still relied upon to determine provenance and authenticity (*ODNB*; Turner, *Dictionary of Art*, 32:748).

The ARTICLE was a review of Waagen's *Works of Art and Artists in England* (1838), a compilation of letters and descriptive essays written during Waagen's first study tour to Britain in 1835 (*Edinburgh Review* 1 [July 1838]: 384–415).

Of London architecture Waagen writes that columns "are here ranged in numberless instances, as wholly UNPROFITABLE SERVANTS" (Waagen, *Works of Art*, 1:20).

The STATUE of Queen Anne (1665–1714) was completed by Francis Bird (1667–1731) in 1712 and stood before the western staircase to the cathedral (fig. 21). It was replaced with a replica in 1886, and the much-damaged original was moved to the private gardens of Augustus John Cuthbert Hare at Holmhurst (*ODNB*; *Times* [London], 19 Nov. 1920).

MRS FREEMAN IN ROYAL ROBES is a reference to Sarah Jenyns Churchill (1660–1744), Duchess of Marlborough. Friends since childhood, Queen Anne and the duchess used the "feigned names" of Mrs. Morley and Mrs. Freeman in their correspondence so as to "import nothing of distinction of rank between us" (*ODNB*; Sarah Jenyns Churchill and Nathaniel Hooke, *An Account of the Conduct of the Dowager Duchess of Marlborough, From her first coming to Court, to the Year 1710* [1742], 9–14).

The LONDON POLICE, or Metropolitan Police Force, began patroling the streets of London in September 1829. Initially resented and suspected, the three-thousand-strong force ultimately gained control of the streets and secured the confidence of the people (Phillip Thurmond Smith, *Policing Victorian London: Political Policing, Public Order, and the London Metropolitan Police* [1985], 15–60; David Ascoli, *The Queen's Peace: The Origins and Development of the Metropolitan Police, 1829–1979* [1979], xiii–xiv, 1–8, 65–87).

Ralph Randolph WORMELEY (1785–1852), rear admiral in the British navy, was born in Virginia but was taken to England as a young child and became a British citizen. He was a nephew to Edmund Randolph and a distant cousin to Thomas Jefferson, and therefore to Coolidge as well. He married Caroline Preble (1798–1872), daughter of Eben Preble, Boston merchant, in 1820, and they had four children: Mary Elizabeth Wormeley Latimer (1822–1904), James Preble Wormeley (1825–1851), Katherine Prescott Wormeley (1830–1908), and Ariana Randolph Wormeley Curtis (1834–1922). When the Wormeleys returned to America in 1848, they rotated their residence among homes in Washington, D.C.; Newport, Rhode Island; and Boston (*ANB*, s.v. "Wormeley, Katharine Prescott" and "Latimer, Elizabeth Wormeley"; *DAB*, s.v. "Wormeley, Katharine Prescott" and "Latimer, Mary Elizabeth Wormeley"; *Recollections of Ralph Randolph Wormeley, Written down by His Three Daughters* [1879]; George Henry Preble, *Genealogical Sketch of the First Three Generations of Prebles in America* [1868], 154–159).

Chester Terrace. Regent's Park. Wednesday. 25. July

We have left Fenton's Hotel, for the present, on the kindly urgent invitation of our friends, M^r & Mrs George Searle, and are staying with them at their house on Chester Terrace.

Regent's Park is the most beautiful if not the most fashionable part of London. High life has country seats of it's own or the command of those belonging to it's friends, and does not care for turf & trees in a city. We came here on Monday 23^d at six o'clock in time for dinner, and yesterday, tuesday, when I rose & looked from my window, I could scarcely believe that I was not in the country, so fresh & cool was the prospect before my eyes & so sweet the song of the early birds.

Last Sunday we passed the day at Wimbledon with M^r & Mrs Bates. They have a pretty cottage surrounded by pretty grounds. A lawn with clumps of trees, many of them American, & pastures of flowers. Beyond is a kitchen garden & a hay field. The grass newly mown gave out a delicious fragrance. It was all on a small scale but very very pleasant. It is only in England, I imagine, under it's weeping skies and with it's soft summer lights & shadows, that you can have such sweet little retirements from the busy world in it's immediate vicinity. In the arrangement of these cottage grounds I thought there was a great deal of taste. The trees were well distributed, so were the flower-beds, and there were vases filled with flowers, upon the lawn in the midst of the green sward a thing one rarely sees in America; I know not why, for the effect is very good. Among the American trees were superb locusts, a hickory tree of great size & beauty, and a Catalpa—Just such a one as grew under my window at Monticello. The summer of my marriage a robin frequented this tree, & long & sweetly he used to sing—and after my departure, my sisters told me, he continued his carol among the boughs when I was no longer there to hear him.

About three o'clock the carriage came round for a drive. Mrs Bates & myself occupied the back seat—Miss Bates and her betrothed, Mr Van de Weyer, the Belgian minister, were on the front making love very pleasantly in alternate french & english. This is (to be) one of those mixed marriages of love & of "convenance" which are perhaps the best of all. Mr Van de Weyer would never have proposed had not Miss Bates been an heiress, and would never have been accepted had he not been Belgian minister and, as such, a man of rank. One wants money, the other position, but they obtain their desires at no sacrifice of other feelings. They like each other very much indeed & look forward with great pleasure to passing their lives together. Mr Van der Weyer being himself a self-made man, or rather one who rose on the wave of the Belgian revolution, can never feel ashamed, as an English lord might do, of his wife's unfashionable connexions, and yet he will place her in a rank above the rank of lords—for diplomatic rank comes before all other. Nor is he at all likely to lose it, for the wheel with him is turning but to rise.

Mrs Bates dozed under her hat & feathers, the lovers were full of each other & of a blissful future. I alone had eyes for the scenery through which we passed. We drove through Richmond Park & to Richmond Hill. The view perhaps did not quite equal my expectations. I had heard & read so much of Richmond Hill! Mr Van der Weyer paused in his cooings to point out to me the spot where that crowned Bluebeard Henry 8th, waited, impatiently no doubt, for the signal which was to apprise him, (without a moment's delay, good news cannot travel too fast,) of the execution of Anna Boleyn, that her head had really fallen—that the slender neck was indeed separated from the ivory shoulders, and the royal coach might be prepared for another Bride.

We did not drive near the Royal Lodge. I thought of Jeanie Deans & of Queen Caroline. The creations of a genius like Walter Scott's are more real than realties where the mind is somewhat excited. I wanted to see the very spot where the interview, decisive of the fate of another creature frail & fair, of Effie Deans, had taken place, in the year of our Lord 17__.

Yesterday, Tuesday, 29th Mrs Searle & myself drove out together. We passed by several pleasant Squares & through handsome streets which she informed me all belonged to the terra incognita, the regions considered by the true West End, the inhabitants of Belgrave Square, St James' and other highly civilized districts, as undiscovered & remote, lying somewhere "between May Fair & Mesopotamia," inhabited by races of men of unknown habits & complexion.

To-day we are to visit the Oriental Club and Chauntrey's studio escorted by a gentleman who has kindly promised to introduce us to both.

George SEARLE (1788–1858), Boston merchant, and his wife, Susan C. Hooper Searle (ca. 1789–1843), were likely visiting George's brother, Thomas Searle (ca. 1796–1843), merchant and banker, and his British wife, Anne Noble Searle (ca. 1805–1841). After a brief partnership with Lewis Tappan, George Searle joined Thomas in a venture to import to the United States a variety of fine European goods and Saxony merino sheep. The brothers served as foreign wool agents and officers of the Nashua Manufacturing Company in New Hampshire. George Searle was a director of the Boston Bank, the Suffolk Insurance Company, and the National Insurance Company. The Thomas Searles lived at 12 CHESTER TERRACE, one of forty-two homes facing Regent's Park that were designed by John Nash and built by James Burton in 1825. It was here that their two sons Arthur (1837–1920) and George (1839–1918) were born (*ANB*, s.v. "Tappan, Lewis" and "Searle, Arthur"; *Survey of London*, vol. 19 [1938], 120–121; Henry S. Randall, "History and Characteristics of the Several Breeds of Sheep," *Transactions of the New-York State Agricultural Society* 1 [1842]: 313–314; *Boston Repertory*, 2 Mar. 1815; *Boston Gazette*, 23 Feb. 1818; *Boston Daily Advertiser*, 3 Nov. 1820, 27 Oct., 5 Dec. 1821, 30 Jan. 1823; *Independent Chronicle and Boston Patriot*, 14 June 1823, 9 Mar. 1825; *Boston Columbian Centinel*, 10 Nov. 1824; *Newburyport [Mass.] Herald*, 19 July 1825; *Boston Commercial Gazette*, 3 Oct. 1826; *Salem [Mass.] Gazette*, 12 June 1827; *Boston Directory* [1826, 1829, 1832]; *Essex County, Massachusetts Birth Records to 1850: Newburyport*, Ancestry.com; *London, England, Births and Baptisms, 1813–1906*, Ancestry.com; *Massachusetts Marriages, 1633–1850*, Ancestry.com; Register of Baptisms, Christ Church, Albany Street, London Metropolitan Archives, Ancestry.com; Ship's manifest for the *Philadelphia*, 26 May 1840, Ancestry.com; *Massachusetts Vital Records to 1850*, s.v. "Searle, Anne," American Ancestors).

The Bates owned a COTTAGE at Wimbledon, a suburb southwest of London, purchased in 1834, and a second home at 46 Portland Place, just to the south of Regent's Park (*ODNB*).

Coolidge's room at Monticello (fig. 17) was the only upstairs chamber on Monticello's west side and was known by the family as the "appendix." Located directly above Jefferson's cabinet, or study, the room has one WINDOW overlooking the south terrace. By late 1827 Monticello was empty, but the family occasionally ventured up the mountain to air the house and make sure it remained in good repair. Coolidge's sister Cornelia wrote to her after one such visit to say that "the ROBIN sung his sweetest song as he used to do the summer you were married & I sat in the hall a long time enjoying it & thinking of that time, with a mixture of pleasure & pain which I always feel here now" (Cornelia J. Randolph to Virginia J. Randolph Trist, 25 Oct. 1816 [NcU: Southern Historical Collection, Nicholas Philip Trist Papers]; Virginia J. Randolph Trist to Coolidge, 3 Sept. 1825, Cornelia J. Randolph to Coolidge, 18 May 1827 [ViU: Ellen Wayles Randolph Coolidge Correspondence]).

Jean Sylvain VAN DE WEYER (1802–1874), Belgian minister and author, studied law at the University of Louvain. Known as an energetic defender of public rights, particularly the protection of a free press, he openly supported those who spoke out against the Dutch monarchy and the forced union of Belgium and Holland. After Belgium won its independence from the Dutch in 1830, Van de Weyer became a member of the newly established National Congress, which determined that Belgium would become a constitutional monarchy. Leopold I of Saxe-Coburg-Gotha was elected king on 4 June 1831. Van de Weyer served as the Belgian envoy in London over the next eight years, throughout the negotiations with European powers that culminated in the Treaty of London, signed 19 April 1839, which recognized Belgium's independence and neutrality. He resided in England thereafter, continuing his career as Belgian minister for Leopold I and subsequently for Leopold II. He retired from politics in 1867 (George Edmundson, *History of Holland* [1922], 389–404; *Eminent Persons: Biographies Reprinted from "The Times"* [1892], 1:237–243; *Gentleman's Magazine*, n.s., 13 [1874]: 93–110).

The ROYAL LODGE, now known as White Lodge, is in Richmond Park and was the favored retreat of Queen Caroline, consort of George II. Sir Walter Scott used the lodge's gardens as a setting in his novel *The Heart of Midlothian* (1818). There, the protagonist, Jeanie Deans, is granted an audience with the queen, from whom she seeks a pardon for her sister Effie, who has been unjustly sentenced to death for infanticide.

Friday. 27 July

On Wednesday we went accompanied by Mr Ashburner, to the Oriental Club. He conducted us through all that part of the building open to strangers and explained to me the system of Club Life—a thing very perfect in it's way. Whether this way is as good in it's results as it is certainly well adapted to secure them, I do not pretend to say. A member of one of these well-arranged Clubs is so much better off without a home of his own than he can be with one, that domestic life, (which implies a certain amount of self-sacrifice and the endurance of a great many petty inconveniences,) must suffer immeasurably by comparison.

The rooms which I saw in the Oriental Club were.

1. A large, comfortable, well furnished drawing room—
2. A dining room where each member has his separate small table well provided with damask napkins, bright glass & neat china,—he orders what he pleases & every thing is furnished at the most reasonable prices.
3. A second dining room where small parties may dine together.
4. A Library—
5. A Map room, the walls hung with maps and the shelves covered with books of reference.
6. A Business room, furnished with writing apparatus, where persons having business with members of the Club can come & transact it without disturbing the rest of the company.
— Such were the rooms which I saw, and Mr Ashburner pointed out to me dressing rooms where the gentlemen of the Club might make their toilettes before going out to dine.

The kitchen is below having two staircases interlocking each other one for ascending, the other for descending, so as to prevent all confusion & collision among the waiters.

In an adjoining street a building was going up which was to consist of bedchambers & dressing rooms for the use of members of the Club, so that a man at a moderate expence, may find himself in possession of all the conveniences and even the luxuries of life, without the embarassment of domestic ties, without the plague of wife, mother, sister or home of his own. At his Club he has quiet, comfort, leisure, good eating, good drinking & if he loves literature, books, maps & silence. Truly this must be a paradise for cold hearts & good stomachs; all that, according to the frenchman's idea, is wanting to make a man happy.

From the Club we proceeded to Chauntrey's Studio, and, in the absence of the Sculptor, were admitted and conducted through all the rooms by a person who seemed a better sort of servant. Here we found, busts, statues, monuments, in clay, plaster, marble, finished, unfinished, just begun, in all the confusion which seemed to give us an insight into the Art itself, shewing the various works in their progress, from the first sketch to the completion. As far as I could trace this progress first came a drawing in broad outlines, then a small model, next a model of larger size, afterwards full size in clay, by which workmen, in the employ of the Artist, shape out the marble which afterwards receives it's finish from the master's own hand.

Chauntrey keeps plaster casts of all his own works, so that his studio, to a certain extent, gives you the opportunity of studying and comparing them. I had neither time nor critical ability for such an operation. I was sorry to find, however, that my general impression was disappointment, and a feeling that Chauntrey was not so great an artist as I had imagined him to be—Otherwise even my unlearned eyes & untaught feelings would have felt the power of his genius. But genius seemed to be just what was wanting. There is an absence of inspiration, of poetry, and, of course, the power to awaken in others those emotions which the Artist could hardly himself have known.

I do not like his attitudes, they often want grace & almost always repose. There is sometimes a straining after effect & then again the opposite extreme of a <u>too</u> <u>natural</u> stiffness and awkwardness. The busts I thought generally good & they are much the most pleasing of Chauntrey's works. The two statues of Watt and Grattan, although the latter especially be somewhat forced in the expression, are strongly marked and effective.

The monument, for two children in the Litchfield Cathedral which I had seen in an engraving and saw here in plaster, has something inexpressibly touching & a beautiful repose which in general is altogether wanting in Chauntrey's works even the monumental ones. In these there is sometimes in the countenances of the figures an unsettled expression which gives the idea of painful death. Of the equestrian statue of Sir Thomas Munroe I saw only a small model of the whole, and the legs and half the body of the horse in plaster, full size. These seemed to me clumsy & heavy as if belonging to a well-fed cart-horse. The smaller model interested me as shewing one of the ways in which an artist works. The figure of the man being naked, moulded thus to ensure anatomical precision, a wet cloth had then been thrown over it from which the drapery might be modelled with better effect.—— Among the busts which I particularly examined was one of the Duke of Wellington, another of Southey, and one, at which I looked with great interest, of Mrs Somerville. This truly remarkable woman has her eyes as near together as a monkey's. I am told by Mr Ashburner that the time she gives to study is from four o'clock in the morning until eight—four hours a day at all seasons, of severe application to severe studies. From eight o'clock till bedtime she employs herself as other rational women do, in domestic affairs, the society of her friends, general reading and recreation. Her husband I was very sorry to hear, is little better than good for nothing. There is a group representing Mrs Jordan, the mother of the Fitz Clarences, with two children. The attitude is one of maternal tenderness so pleasing in the expression that you are not disposed to quarrel with the execution. Mrs Jordan it seems was never married to any man. The real name of this celebrated person being Delia Bland. Chauntrey's monumental statues want both "the life and the death" which should characterize works of this sort, and for this I was prepared to a certain degree by what I had seen of his in the Cathedral of St. Paul's.

Thursday evening, 26. July, I went for the first time to the Opera and heard for the first time Italian music. The piece was the Somnambula, followed by one act of Romeo & Juliet. The performers Persiani Tamburini & Rubini in the first, Grisi & Persiani (Romeo & Juliet) in the second. I had heard the Somnambula, <u>done</u> into English; Wood, Mrs Wood, Brough & Mme Otto being the singers—I had listened with great pleasure, the voices being fine & the music Bellini's. Mrs Wood especially has natural powers of no common order. But Rubini, Tamburini, Grisi, Persiani! The world of song has opened upon me & I now know what music is! I went to the Opera feeling very feeble & unwell, expecting to hear Grisi & Lablache in a new Opera. I was much disappointed when I found that Lablache had a bad cold & could not sing, and that Grisi had "postponed her night," whilst the Somnambula, of which, sooth to say, I had become a little tired from hearing it, in it's English dress, repeatedly in Boston, was substituted for the promised novelty. I was near turning away from the door when this bad news was announced by hand bills, but we were there & Mr Coolidge advised me to go in. I was compelled to acknowledge that the body of the building was somewhat larger than the Tremont Theatre, but, en revanche, it was badly lighted and dark. The curtain rose upon my inward grumblings & again I could not deny that Her Majesty's Theatre had the advantage in scenery, dress & decoration over our own, but being disposed for fault-finding, I sulked on through two or three scenes, insisting that Persiani was not equal to Mrs Wood, and that Rubini's ugliness was unpardonable in spite of his voice. I cannot say how I became first conciliated, then interested, then wholly wrapped in forgetfulness of self, but I sat more than four hours unconscious of weakness or indisposition. At last however the pirouettes of the two Eslers & the gambados of Signor Guerra reminded me that I was becoming exhausted, and convinced me that astonishment and admiration both of which I certainly felt at their marvellous performances, are not as effectual stimulants to a weary body as the full sense of beauty which had supported me through the Opera—the first Italian music sung by Italians, (& such Italians,) that I had ever heard. And in what, independent of particular & individual voices, does the superiority of the Italians in the execution of their own music consist?—In taste, in expression, in the ease which made music seem a natural language, uttered as instinctively & with as little effort as words could have been. In Mrs Wood's acting there was a good deal of tragic power, so much that you sometimes forgot the music in the dramatic effect. With Grisi, Persiani, Rubini, Tambarini, all was music. They were inhabitants of another world where song was speech, and you seemed to be transported to that other world with them—so that for the moment you ceased to remember that the same passions could have found another utterance. The character of the Italian language no doubt contributes to this effect. The words melt into the music and the mingled stream of sense & sound flows on, and in the effect produced upon yourself, you cannot tell where thought ceases and sensation begins, for the mind and the senses are one. When Mrs Wood weeping over the faded flowers, says & sings "withered, past, just like his love" I understood her meaning, admired her fine voice & her pathetic representation of a very touching character—— But when Persiani sings,

> Passasti al par d'amore
> Che un giorno sol durò
> —and again
> Ma ravvivar l'amore
> Il pianto mio non può.—

I cannot attempt to describe what I thought or what I felt.—Wood's "False one I love thee still" had created a great sensation in Boston, was, at the theatre, rapturously encored again & again, and it seemed to me that I could not hear it too often. But Rubini's

> Ah perche non posso odiarti
> Infidel—

Not twenty four hours have passed since I heard it and I am in a state of bewilderment as I think of it.

Grisi took no part, of course, in the Somnambula. I only heard her deep, rich voice & saw the workings of her fine tragic countenance in the character of Romeo, & only one act of the piece was given. In the interval between this & the Somnambula I saw Fanny Elsler dance the Cachacha. She is a wonderful creature, light as a snow-flake, pliant as a flower stalk, sparkling and playful as moonbeams on the water. What must Taglioni be!!

George **ASHBURNER** (1810–1869), merchant and journalist, was in London at this time to negotiate for the establishment of a bank in Calcutta, where he represented Russell & Company and served as editor of the *Bombay Courier*. He was elected a member of the Oriental Club and the Royal Asiatic Society in 1837 (Stephen Wheeler, *Annals of the Oriental Club, 1824–1858* [1925]; *Pedigree of the Family of Ashburner* [1872], 5; *Calcutta Monthly Journal and General Register of Occurrences . . . for the Year 1837*, ser. 3, vol. 3, no. 26 [Jan. 1838]: 78; *Journal of the Royal Asiatic Society of Great Britain and Ireland* 4 [1837]: 51).

The ORIENTAL CLUB was founded in 1824 by Sir John Malcolm (1769–1833), administrator in India. To qualify for membership, a man had to be employed with the East India Company or another mercantile firm, or he had to have some role in the general administration of England's political and economic interests in the East. Initially established in rooms leased for the purpose at Lower Grosvenor Street, the Oriental Club engaged architects Benjamin Dean Wyatt (1775–1852) and Philip Wyatt (d. 1835) in 1827 to design a permanent residence at Hanover Square. The club remained there until relocating to Stratford House in Stratford Place in 1962, where it continues to operate today (*ODNB*; Wheeler, *Annals of the Oriental Club, 1824–1858*; Timbs, *Curiosities*, 253; "About and History of the Oriental Club," Oriental Club, accessed 20 Dec. 2010, http://www.orientalclub.org.uk).

Sir Francis Leggatt Chantrey [CHAUNTREY] (1781–1841), a self-taught sculptor, was known for the natural and original presentation of his subjects. His talent was sought after by sitters ranging from authors and men of science to military heroes and royalty. Chantrey's home and studio were located at 13 Eccleston Square in Belgravia, just opposite Eccleston Bridge and next to a creek that allowed for the easy barge delivery of marble to his doorstep. Chantrey's workshops came to cover twelve thousand square feet, including galleries and a bronze foundry. John Soane's last executed commission was the design of a domed, top-lit antechamber that linked Chantrey's drawing room to a sculpture gallery. Soane did the work in exchange for a marble bust that Chantrey created of the architect—a piece that Chantrey described as the best work he had ever done. The bust is still on display at the Soane Museum (*ODNB*; George Jones, *Sir Francis Chantrey, R.A.: Recollections of His Life, Practice, and Opinions* [1849]; Henry B. Wheatley, *London Past and Present: Its History, Associations, and Traditions* [1891], 152; Tate Gallery, *Within These Shores: A Selection of Works from the Chantrey Bequest* [1989]; Whinney, *Sculpture in Britain*, 399–425; Giles Walkley, *Artists' Houses in London, 1764–1914* [1994], 25–26; *Essays from "The London Times"* [1852], 274–285).

James WATT (1736–1819), engineer and inventor (*ODNB*).

Henry GRATTAN (ca. 1746–1820), politician (*ODNB*).

The TWO CHILDREN were Ellen Jane and Marianne Robinson (d. ca. 1815), daughters of Ellen Jane and the Reverend William Robinson (*ODNB*; Whinney, *Sculpture in Britain*, 402–403).

Robert SOUTHEY (1774–1843), author (*ODNB*).

Mary Fairfax Greig SOMERVILLE (1780–1872) was a scientist, mathematician, and author. Her second HUSBAND was William Somerville, a military surgeon whose poor health forced him to retire and relocate with his family to Italy in 1838 (*ODNB*).

Dorothy "Dora" Phillips (1761–1816), actress, performed under the name **MRS. JORDAN**, among others, and was one of numerous children born to Francis Bland and Grace Phillips. She was for many years the mistress of the Duke of Clarence, later William IV, and bore him ten children, all of whom carried the surname FitzClarence. The statue was commissioned by the king in 1831 and portrays Mrs. Jordan with two of their children, one an infant asleep in her arms, the other leaning upon her knee. Originally intended for placement as a memorial in Westminster Abbey, it was instead given to the Earl of Munster, the couple's eldest son (*ODNB*; Claire Tomalin, *Mrs. Jordan's Profession: The Story of a Great Actress and a Future King* [1994]; Clare Jerrold, *Story of Dorothy Jordan* [1969]; Whinney, *Sculpture in Britain*, 410).

La Sonnambula [**SOMNAMBULA**], an opera composed in 1831 by Vincenzo Bellini with words by Felice Romani, features a jealous woman whose former lover is betrothed to another. When she sleepwalks into a compromising situation, the spurned woman uses the occasion to attempt to win back her lover, ultimately to no avail.

The visiting Italian company at Her Majesty's Theatre, Haymarket, had planned to perform *Falstaff*, a new opera based on Shakespeare's *Merry Wives of Windsor*, but the illness of Luigi **LABLACHE**, who was to perform the lead, prompted a change of program. Fanny Tacchinardi **PERSIANI**, Antonio **TAMBURINI**, Giovanni Battista **RUBINI**, and Giulia **GRISI** were the performers Coolidge saw in London. Joseph and Mary Ann **WOOD**, William F. **BROUGH**, and Antoinette **OTTO** were those she had seen in Boston, probably during that company's second American tour, in 1835–1836, when they performed an English version of *La Sonnambula* to great acclaim (*ODNB*; Vera Brodsky Lawrence, ed., *Strong on Music: The New York Music Scene in the Days of George Templeton Strong* [1988], 1:36–38; Kurt Pahlen, *Great Singers from the Seventeenth Century to the Present Day* [1974], 137; *New Grove Dictionary of Opera* [1992], s.v. "Sonnambula, La"; *Times* [London], 26 July 1838).

Dancer Fransiska "Fanny" Elssler [**ELSLER**] (1810–1884) performed in Austria, Germany, France, England, and Russia, often with her sister Therese (ca. 1808–1878). Some of Fanny's signature roles included the leads in *Giselle*, *La Tarentule*, and *La Esméralda*, but she became known for the cachucha, a Spanish folk dance similar to the fandango. A professional rivalry existed between Fanny Elssler and her contemporary Marie **TAGLIONI** (1804–1884) (*ODNB*; Ivor Forbes Guest, *Fanny Elssler* [1970]).

July 31.

The last day of the month. We are still with Mrs Searle & she kindly urges us to remain until we leave London, which we propose to do very soon, on a little tour to see some of the remarkable places within easy reach. I do not know how long we shall remain in England. Our plans are very unsettled.

We have had for the last week variable weather but of different character from what would bear the same name in America. There are here no violent transitions from hot to cold, nor even from wet to dry, for the cool white light of an English sun seems obscured so easily, and the grey misty clouds in their turn melt & give way so readily to the first faint sunbeam, that the one state is always a preparation for the other, and the change not very great from the subdued brightness of what is called fair weather to the mist which presently dissolves into rain. I find walking in the Park about twelve o'clock is like walking out in early morning at home. There is no fierceness in the Sun, no glare, nothing of that insufferable brightness which makes an American midsummer noon too overpoweringly beautiful for mortal eyes to gaze on. The transparent atmosphere of a climate like ours, the splendour of our often cloudless sky are things to talk of and to admire, but like other glories these are sometimes more dazzling than our weak senses can well bear, and then the change from such radiance to it's opposite extreme must necessarily be violent. The weather in America, (the climate) has something of the character of the Ocean, beautiful and sublime as it is "calm or convulsed," but capricious and variable, having many moods of bright and sullen, smooth and stormy, essentially tyrannical, and often most unkind. In it's treatment of man we may carry out the parallel, referring to the well-known description of Byron. The American is shaken & spurned and sent shivering & perhaps howling, and often eventually "dashed to earth," when his "petty hope" of recovering from the shocks his weak frame has sustained, may haply lie in some foreign port or bay, where he goes for shelter.

America is not generally healthy and American women are essentially otherwise. This fact is too notorious for denial, & the cause, no doubt, lies partly in climate, & partly in our own ignorance. We do not know how to adapt ourselves to our circumstances.—

Saturday the 28th July, Mrs Searle & myself went to see the Exhibition of Pictures by modern artists, at the National Gallery. It was the last day of admittance, we were hurried and the place uncomfortably crowded. I confined my attention principally to Landseer's pictures of animals & Calcott's landscapes. I had never before seen any thing of Landseer's & was eager to make up for lost time. The pictures which I saw to best advantage were—

1. "The life's in the old dog yet."
2. "None but the brave deserve the Fair." Two stags fighting furiously

whilst a company of female deer look quietly on waiting to become the prize of the conqueror.

3. Her Majesty's favorite dogs & parrot. In this group a little black "King Charles" pleased me greatly and I thought the parrot excellent.

4. "A distinguished Member of the Humane Society"—being a large and beautiful Newfoundland Dog.

5. "Portraits of the Marquis of Stafford and the Lady Evelyn Gower." Two children. A boy lying on the ground looking at his sister, who is playing with a fawn, round whose neck she has tied a mantle having placed a crown of flowers on it's head. Two dogs "in attitudes" complete the group.

I was particularly pleased with the heads of Landseer's dogs. Calcott's landscapes are charming. There is a freshness & purity, a coolness and clearness in the colouring which distinguishes them from every thing else so that after examining one or two I found there was no mistaking the general character and that I could tell one of these pictures without referring to the Catalogue except for a confirmation of my "guess." Those which I looked at best, were

1. A scene on the Rhine

2. Cicero's Tomb near Mola di Gaeta.

3. Italian Composition from materials in the neighbourhood of Rome.

4. Dutch Boats leaving port in squally weather.

The other pictures which attracted my attention by different artists were.

1. Portrait of the Countess of Blessington by J. Wood—very beautiful and very unlike the fat, old Sultana whom I saw once in an open carriage in Hyde Park, and again at the Opera, making love to Count D'Orsay who sat in the same box, bearded like a Turk & looking as nonchalant— nothing wanting but the pipe.

2. Portrait of Her most gracious Majesty, Queen Victoria in her robes of State, by Hayter. She is seated on the throne and looks weary, as if she felt the weight of her robes if not of her Royalty.

3. Portrait of Rajah Ram Roy son of Ram Mohun Roy, by R. Evans. A fine looking young Barbarian.

4. Portrait of William 4th by Sir Martin Archer Shea. A corpulent old gentleman who looks as if he had been regularly made up to sit for his picture. An ignoble figure and an embarrassed countenance.

5. Portrait of His Grace the Duke of Hamilton & Brandon by H. W. Pickersgill. A personification of Aristrocracy, a figure made up of velvet, satin, ermine & ostrich feathers—be-plumed, be-puffed, be-slashed &

be-mantled but dignified withal, somewhat imposing and grand in it's stateliness.

6. Portrait of Daniel O'Connell. M. P. Sir David Wilkie. The O'Connell of Prince Puckler Muskau—the clever, underbred radical, whom it is impossible to mistake for a gentleman, let his tailor & his painter do what they may. The Duke and himself make a pleasant contrast.

7. Portrait of the Marchioness of Clanricarde, the daughter of Canning, by J. Lucas—Purely & coldly beautiful. The beauty of the Epic—see a classification of female beauty & hints on dress, by Diderot, in Grimm's Correspondence. Such an Epic as the Marchioness of Clanricarde, in whom no law is violated, so regularly & systematically perfect, might in her dress, have dispensed with the enormous <u>Bustle</u>, which forms an unsightly protuberance behind.

George Gordon Noel **BYRON** (1788–1824), sixth Baron Byron, poet. Coolidge was drawing particularly from verse 180 of Byron's "Childe Harold's Pilgrimage; A Romaunt" (1812), a work Byron composed during his travels across the Iberian Peninsula and the Levant (*ODNB*).

The **NATIONAL GALLERY** collection, housed since its opening in 1824 in four poorly lit rooms in the Angerstein Gallery on Pall Mall, grew tremendously in its first decade, and by 1832 plans were under way to construct a grand home for nation's museum. Designed by William Wilkins (1778–1839), the new gallery opened in Trafalgar Square in 1838. The exhibition Coolidge attended was a Royal Academy show, the second to be on display in the east wing of the National Gallery but the seventieth in the Academy's history. Queen Victoria opened the show on 4 May 1838 (*ODNB*; *Survey of London*, vol. 20 [1940], 15–18; *Morning Chronicle* [London], 5 May, 27, 28 July 1838).

The artist Sir Edwin Henry **LANDSEER** (1802–1873), knighted in 1850, was known for his genius in painting animals, especially in human situations. Highly successful and widely sought after both socially and professionally, Landseer remained popular through the end of his life, and his four bronze lions encircling Nelson's Column in Trafalgar Square are still a London landmark (*ODNB*; Richard Ormond, *Sir Edwin Landseer* [1981]; *Eminent Persons: Biographies Reprinted from "The Times"* [1892], 1:178–185; Allan Cunningham, *The Lives of the Most Eminent British Painters* [1880], 3:377–390).

The artist Sir Augustus Wall Callcott [**CALCOTT**] (1770–1844), knighted in 1837, was inspired in his youth by the book illustrations of Thomas Stothard (1755–1834) and entered the Royal Academy in 1797. Callcott began as a portraitist, then turned to painting landscapes at the beginning of the nineteenth century, working first in watercolors and later in oils. He was a contemporary of Joseph

Mallord William Turner (1775–1851), and the two artists' works were frequently compared to each other (*ODNB*; David Blayney Brown, *Augustus Wall Callcott* [1981]; Herbert Minton Cundall, *English Painters of the Georgian Era: Hogarth to Turner* [1876], 73–80).

Thursday. 2nd August.

Yesterday we visited the Tower. There is no place in England better worth seeing when we remember all that it's old grey walls have seen. An American should feel the influence of the grand recollections attached to the Tower of London even more than an Englishman. Our common origin connects <u>us</u> as nearly with the English of the times preceding the settlement of America, as the English of the present day themselves can be. We claim as ours all who lived before the time when our immediate ancestors sought a home in the new world. This would give us all that is most poetic & romantic, all that stirs the heart and excites the imagination in the history of the Tower. All the great & thrilling recollections, all the historic interest, the memories of feudalism, despotism, of the dark old times and the dawning of better days. We have with our English brethren common property in the legends, the traditions, the history of these "towers of Julius," or of William the Conqueror. We can gaze with the same feelings on the moat, the walls, the time-worn gates & vaulted gateways. We can remember as they do the men on whom those gates have closed, Wallace & Sir Thomas More, Raleigh & Our blood chills at the name of the Traitor's Gate & at the sight of the dark stones in the Court yard which mark the spot where fell the heads of Anne Boleyn & of Essex. We have all these memories belonging to the Tower of London entirely unvulgarized by more recent associations. We visit this remarkable spot fresh, unhackneyed, happy in our knowledge of the past, our ignorance of the present.

The Tower is a town in itself which covers more than twelve acres surrounded by a moat and wall. The moat is crossed by a bridge and you pass the wall under an arched gateway. Within are houses, streets and a population of men, women, children & soldiers amounting to nearly 14.000 souls. The Tower is now a regular shew place, to which you pay for admittance as to any other raree shew. You are received and courteously treated by Wardens or Yeomen in the costume of the age of Henry 8th, a sort of frock or shirt of scarlet cloth coming to the knee & trimmed with bands passing over the shoulders & down the seams, a girdle round the waist, a round hat with a flat crown decorated with bows of various coloured ribbons, and a sword in the hand. The Wardens have likewise badges on the breast & back, the Rose, Thistle & Shamrock in gold with the Queen's cipher. These men are old soldiers taken from various regiments to whom the place of Warden is given as a reward for good conduct. Visiters go in parties of twelve under the care of a Warden—to each party may be attached a limited number, (I believe two of each) of soldiers, police men or blue coat boys who enter as a privilege, gratis. Our Warden was a sturdy old fellow who had fought in Spain & at Waterloo.

The only places open for visiters are the Armories and the Strong Room where the Regalia are kept.

The armories are the Horse Armory, Queen Elizabeth's and the Grand Store House containing artillery & small arms.

The Horse Armory & Queen Elizabeth's Armory are within the White Tower, a large massive building, a sort of citadel or Keep rising high in the midst of the enclosure & surrounded by an open, paved space. There are four turrets at the four corners of the main tower.

The Horse Armory is a room one hundred & fifty feet long by thirty three wide. It contains a number of equestrian figures of English Kings and their attendant nobles, dressed, as well as their horses, in the armour belonging to the time in which they lived—in some cases the identical suits worn by the individuals themselves. Among these Edward 1st, Henry 8th, Robert Dudley Earl of Leicester, & Charles 1st wear their own armour.

In following the dates of these military & knightly accoutrements I remarked with some surprise, that the oldest in date, Edward 1st's is a coat of mail composed of iron rings, a sort of net work very flexible & apparently much more comfortable (if such a word can be applied to such a thing) and manageable, than the heavy plate armour of later times, covering back and breast, legs and arms with a load of steel (sometimes gilt, inlaid with gold or engraved,) enough, one would suppose, to weigh the wearer to the earth. The horses have iron petticoats that look like deep flounces, round their breasts and the lower parts of their bodies. I should like to know by what process of improvement these heavy sheets of metal were substituted for the easy, pliant coats of mail. The faces of these equestrian figures are of wax—very ugly and unnatural.

We had nothing to complain of in our guide, who repeated by rote a catalogue of the curiosities, except his hurrying us from room to room much too fast for any thing more than a hasty glance at the different objects. From the Horse Armoury we were bustled along to Queen Elizabeth's Armory, a room said to have been the prison room of Sir Walter Raleigh, and containing many things I should have liked much to examine had I been permitted to do so, but our Yeoman was impatient and strided on, calling on us to follow and explaining as he went, as rapidly as a schoolboy repeats his lesson. Among other things which I contrived to see because they were conspicuous or vehemently pointed out, were

1. Her Highness, Queen Elizabeth. A wax figure all petticoats and pearls, mounted on a cream-coloured horse led by a page, and appearing as when she went in procession to St. Paul's, to return thanks for her victory over the Spaniards.

2. A small room without light (or ventilation it seemed to me) except through the narrow door, dark, close & dungeon-like, I could scarcely breathe in it for one moment, said to have been Sir Walter Raleigh's sleeping chamber.

3. Windows which shew the thickness of the tower walls, more than fourteen feet.

4. Instruments of torture, said to have been taken from the Spaniards. The collar of torment a huge ring of iron of many pounds weight, thumb screws, and the cravat, a horrible looking engine by which an unhappy wretch, bent into a stooping posture, might have his neck, hands & feet confined in iron rings & locked together. Such inventions as these make me ready to believe that some men are a little lower than the devils!

5. A model in wood of the block & an axe of very clumsy form said (let who will believe,) to have been the very one with which Anne Boleyn & Essex had their heads stricken from their shoulders.

Against the walls were many specimens of obsolete armour, offensive & defensive, the names of which one meets with in ballads & novels particularly Walter Scott's. I should have liked much to examine them more particularly but our driver trotted us away from the White Tower, across a paved court (in which on our return, he pointed out to us the former site of the block, marked by a square of black stones,) to a long large building wherein is a storehouse full of cannons of all sizes, ages & materials & some naval curiosities, among others one of the guns of the Royal George, brought up with part of it's carriage or the frame in which it was set, after being fifty three years under water, all encrusted with shells & other things of the sea.

From this store house you ascend a wide staircase to a sight the grandest and most imposing of all. A room 345 feet in length, filled with small arms, guns, pistols, swords, bayonets &c &c for one hundred thousand men. These are either regularly stacked in the middle, or formed into columns, whilst ranged round the walls in the most rich & varied patterns, are arms of obsolete forms or such as are used by foreign nations, Russians, Austrians, Prussians or French. The Russian patterns seemed to me the most shewy & the most deadly, just as might be expected among a people imperfectly civilized. The love of destruction and of ostentation belongs to this stage of society when almost equal pleasure is taken in ornament and in bloodshed. Here too is a beautiful brass cannon of Italian workmanship, taken by Bonaparte from the Knights of Malta and by a British sea captain from Bonaparte, and here is a musket formerly the property of Tippoo Saib. "On a pillé partout" as the Mayor of London is said to have said to Marshall Soult, complimenting him on his universal genius for depredation. See that most pious & respectable sunday paper, the Age.

Having been allowed to remain in the Armory of small arms just long enough to see how much there was to see & how many things there were that we should have been delighted to see, had such been the will of our Commander in Chief, we were marched out. When we found ourselves, somewhat vexed & disappointed, in the open space before the door, we were asked whether we were willing to pay two shillings to see England's Regalia, valued at two millions. John Bull knows how to get in small ways the money which he spends in gross. After having been kept waiting a time as unreasonably long as the time during which we were allowed to examine the Regalia was unreasonably short, we were conducted into a strong cell, a sort of dungeon poorly lighted, where, in a stone recess barred with iron, like wild beasts in a Cage, were kept the Crowns, Sceptres, and Swords of state borne or worn on solemn occasions by the Sovereigns of Great Britain. Here likewise were various dishes, salt-cellars, flaggons and chalices of pure gold.

The old Hag wrinkled & doting, who inhabits, during a certain part of the twenty four hours, this dreary region, where precious things lie hidden as in their native mines & guarded by a Gnome, repeated in a sort of chant monotonous & rapid, the lesson from which we gathered what we could of the history of these insignia of royalty.

A crown worn by Edward the Confessor.   ?

A crown worn by Queen Elizabeth.

An ivory sceptre borne by Anne Boleyn, I presume as apocryphal as the Axe which cut off her head.

But then came the crown & sceptres of pretty Queen Victoria, modern & authentic. The Crown contains what seemed to my ignorant eyes "a sea of "red" light" in the form of a ruby and a heaven of blue, in a sapphire as large as one of Juno's eyes.

There was a gold salt-cellar as they called it in the form of the white tower itself, square with turrets that looked indeed like pepper boxes, massive and richly wrought said to have been presented to King William 3^d by some town or corporation, I forget what. A font of gold for royal christenings, two round dishes of the same precious metal, with various other utensils for shew or use of equal richness. We were warned to look rapidly and take in as much at once as our eyes would hold, for other eyes were waiting for the same sights, and the den was too small to hold many persons at once. We left the light of the Gems and Gold to return to the light of Heaven, our Warder led the way, pointing out to us as we went several traditionary spots; we repassed the Gateway, recrossed the Bridge & entered our carriage just as a drizly mist was turning into a rain.

We purpose to pay the Tower another visit and expect another six shillings in a second survey of the rooms. I do not much like this taking money at the door of such a place as the Tower. There is a sort of bathos in it; a fall from the high recollections with which one approaches the time-hallowed spot to this vulgar demand for shillings and pence before you are suffered to enter the Sanctuary. I would say to the Sovereign, were the Sovereign a man, what Sterne, when threatened with the seizure of his black satin breeches, said to the King of France, "It is not well Sire." Still less is it well this sordid grasping for pence under the sceptre of a fair, young girl. But poor Queen Victoria is no way accountable for it. I doubt if she knows of the existence of such an abuse and she certainly could not reform it if she would. I doubt if the Queen of England has ever visited the Tower of London or passed her royal feet over it's dusty threshold. What should Victoria do in the City? unless once in her life, to dine off of gold with the Lord Mayor, and think perchance of Whittington and his Cat.

The TOWER was, even in Coolidge's day, one of London's most popular attractions. Arthur Wellesley (1769–1852), first Duke of Wellington, army officer and prime minister, was appointed constable of the tower in December 1826. With security and the prevention of civil unrest uppermost in his mind, Wellington implemented severe restrictions on public visitation and access. Visitors purchased tickets for six shillings from the armory ticket office at the entrance gate and were guided by a warder [WARDEN] wearing the same uniform as the yeoman of the guard. Tours were given on the half hour between ten and four o'clock, groups were comprised of twelve people, and no more than one hundred visitors were allowed within the walls at any time (*ODNB*; Altick, *Shows of London*, 438–439, 446, 449–450; Timbs, *Curiosities*, 791–806; Joseph Wheeler, *Short History of the Tower of London, including a particular detail of its Interesting Curiosities* [1839]).

Whether the suits of armor were **THOSE WORN BY THE INDIVIDUALS THEM-SELVES** was a matter for debate. In 1825 Sir Samuel Rush Meyrick (1783–1848), prominent antiquary and historian, consulted on the rearrangement of the collection, which was as much made up of many separate pieces as it was of complete suits. The requirement that each suit be attributed to a great personage made Meyrick's task all the more difficult, especially since there was often no evidence to support a connection (*ODNB*; Altick, *Shows of London*, 439; *Old and New London*, 2:83).

The HMS **ROYAL GEORGE**, launched in 1756, was the first warship to exceed two thousand tons burden, and it saw action during the Seven Years' War and the American Revolutionary War. In August 1782 the ship was anchored at Spithead near Portsmouth to take on supplies and undergo minor repairs, in the midst of which the ship suddenly rolled over, filled with water, and sank, taking all aboard down with her, including 360 visiting women and children. In 1834 Charles Anthony Deane (1796–1848), diver and inventor of diving equipment, recovered thirty of the ship's guns, including the brass twenty-four-pounder that Coolidge noted (*ODNB*; Lincoln P. Paine, *Ships of the World: An Historical Encyclopedia* [1997], 439; Wheeler, *Short History of the Tower of London*, 21; "Loss of the HMS Royal George," Royal Naval Museum, accessed 20 Dec. 2010, http://www.royalnavalmuseum.org).

Napoléon Bonaparte's forces captured the brass **CANNON** at Malta, along with eight banners, in 1798. It was aboard the frigate *La Sensible* on its way to the French Directory when the HMS *Seahorse* captured it. Remarkably ornate, it features swaths of foliage, sunbursts, and two figures representing torch-bearing Furies that stretch the full length of the gun's carriage (*ODNB*; H. L. Blackmore, *Armouries of the Tower of London* [1976], 137, plates 24, 25; Wheeler, *Short History of the Tower of London*, 26).

Sultan Fateh Ali Tipu [**TIPPOO**] (ca. 1750–1799) was ruler of Mysore in the south of India. An innovative military leader, Tipu was the relentless enemy of the British East India Company and sought to drive the colonials out of India. He died during the course of the Fourth Mysore War when, outnumbered, his armies fought against a British force that was marching on the capital city of Seringapatam. The sword was one of several items belonging to Tipu that the British took after the fall (*ODNB*, s.v. "Wellesley, Arthur" and "Wellesley, Richard"; Maya Jasanoff, *Edge of Empire: Lives, Culture, and Conquest in the East, 1750–1850* [2005], 148, 152–154, 166–186).

Nicholas Jean de Dieu **SOULT** (1769–1851), duc de Dalmatia, French military leader and marshal of France, fought against and often eluded Arthur Wellesley, Duke of Wellington, during the Peninsular War, 1807–1813. In 1838 he was in London serving as French ambassador extraordinary, attending the coronation of Queen Victoria, and enjoying the hospitality of many of his former military rivals. When Soult visited the Tower of London on 16 July 1838, "every mark of respect was paid to the venerable Marshal," including a private tour, gun salutes, and a military band performance of the national anthem (Peter Hayman, *Soult: Napoleon's Maligned Marshal* [1990]; Owen Connelly, ed., *Historical Dictionary of Napoleonic France, 1799–1815* [1985], 385–388, 449–450; *Sunday Times* [London], 22 July 1838).

The AGE, a Tory weekly paper known for gossip and abusive personal remarks, was highly critical of the attention paid to Marshal Soult during his stay in London. Publisher Thomas Holt reminded readers that Soult enjoyed a "*peculiar* fame" that originated from his earlier career as an "'appropriator,' on a petty larceny scale" (Laurel Brake and Marysa Demoor, *Dictionary of Nineteenth-Century Journalism in Great Britain and Ireland* [2009], s.v. "Age"; *Age* [London], 15, 29 July 1838).

The six-shilling tickets allowed visitors access to the armories, but a viewing of the REGALIA required payment of an additional two shillings and a one-shilling gratuity to the attendant within the holding room (Wheeler, *Short History of the Tower of London*, 3–4).

The quotation "Sire, it is not well done" appears in the opening pages of Laurence STERNE'S *Sentimental Journey through France and Italy*.

The story of Dick WHITTINGTON and his cat tells of an orphan boy of humble origins who rose to political and financial prosperity in London, largely because of his rat-catching pet. The story was partly inspired by the life of Richard Whittington (ca. 1350–1423), merchant, moneylender, philanthropist, and four-time mayor of London (*ODNB*).

Saturday. 4ᵗʰ August.

We went on Thursday evening to the Opera & found the music admirable, as far as the execution went, but in itself less pleasing than before. The piece was La Gazza Ladra of Rossini. Grisi, Rubini, Tambarini & Lablache in the principal characters. Notwithstanding the "Di piacer" & other famous airs I cannot think Grisi's talents well employed in this Opera. She is too grand, too full of passion & high-toned tragedy for this part of a servant girl accused of stealing silver spoons. I wish I were a better judge of music that I might feel some confidence in my own opinions; but I am no judge, though I enjoy music greatly. That is some, not all. My ear is slow, and it takes me some time to get acquainted with an Opera or an air. I have never heard the Gazza Ladra before & for this reason, perhaps, I cannot appreciate it.

Fanny Elsler danced the Cachacha again, and afterwards a charming 'Pas de deux' with her sister. She has a good-humored countenance, beaming & joyous, but coquettish and of somewhat equivocal expression. Knowing nothing of what is said or thought of her I should take her for a frank hearted girl, full of fun and frolic & of morals not particularly severe.——

We left London on Sunday morning 5. August. Sunday travelling is permitted here though not altogether approved. Our movements are sufficiently uncertain to make us wish to save time, and as the weather was fine we took advantage of it and left London in a new & handsome hired carriage with post horses. My maid Smith, whom I find skilful, civil & attentive, accompanied us. I feel now as if I could not dispense with her services—A great change in a short time. We were absent just a fortnight or rather sixteen days, & returned to town & took up our quarters at Fenton's Hotel on Sunday 19th August. We had visited & seen Windsor, Oxford, Blenheim, Leamington, Kenilworth, Warwick Castle, Guy's Cliff, Stratford upon Avon, Cheltenham, Ragland Castle, the banks of the Wye, Tintern Abbey, the Windcliff, Berkeley Castle, Clifton, Bath, Salisbury plain, Stonehenge, Southampton, Netley Abbey and Winchester.——

(I am copying now only such of my notes as being written here & there & every where, and almost illegibly, I desire to bring together for my own amusement. It gives me pleasure to live out these days now long gone by. the few notes that remain of my little tour, a very happy sixteen days, are contained in small blank books & can be read as they are. I do not therefore except in part take the same trouble with them as with my early London notes.)[1]

LA GAZZA LADRA, *The Thieving Magpie*, was composed by Gioachino Rossini to a libretto by Giovanni Gherardini and was first performed in Milan in 1817. The story centers on Ninetta, a servant girl in the home of a prosperous farmer whose son Giannetto she hopes to marry. Ninetta is falsely accused of stealing a silver spoon and narrowly escapes execution. She sings the cavatina "DI PIACER mi balza il cor" to express her love for Giannetto, who is returning from the wars. The opera opened at Her Majesty's Theatre on 2 August 1838 (*New Grove Dictionary of Opera* [1992], s.v. "Gazza ladra, La"; *Times* [London], 1, 2 Aug. 1838).

1. Coolidge subsequently covered this notation with another piece of pencil-lined paper.

Saturday 26. August.

Mr Coolidge, Mrs Searle & myself visited the Thames Tunnel. I called in Regent's Park for Mrs Searle & we went by way of the New Road to Bishopsgate St. where Mr Coolidge joined us about half past three P.M. when we proceeded to the Tunnel.

After paying the usual fee we were admitted into the Shaft at Rother-hithe, a sort of well fifty feet in diameter, and, amid a din of machinery which almost stunned us, looked down into the abyss below, a depth I believe of sixty five feet, where shone a few glimmering gas lights, each one appearing a small distinct star just visible in the surrounding black-ness. The effect was all the better for this seeming darkness, but the shaft is in reality lighted at intervals all the way down, and we descended by a circular stairway, with occasional landing places, sufficiently wide and easy & light enough for all purposes of safety and convenience. In the centre of the outer shaft was a smaller one where stood a pump of great size, the working of which contributed not a little to the noise which had surprised me at my first entrance.

Notwithstanding the easiness of the way there was something trying to the nerves in the descent to what appeared the bowels of the earth, and it was with a feeling of awe if not of alarm that I slowly wound my way into the depth of this subterranean tower, which seemed a fit entrance to the lower regions, to the palace of Pluto or the abode of Hela; and indeed,

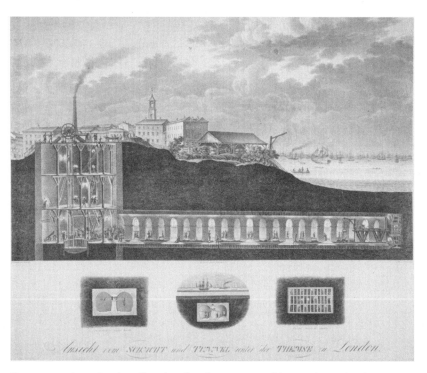

FIGURE 7. *Cross Section Showing the Thames Tunnel*, by Carl Friedrich Traut-mann after Bontsch, ca. 1835. *(Courtesy of the London Metropolitan Archives.)*

when having passed the last short reach of the staircase, the long vista of the Tunnel, with it's double arches lighted with gas, came suddenly into view, the effect was altogether grand and imposing.

The Tunnel has now reached a distance of 790 feet from the shaft of Rotherhithe towards Wapping, but visiters are not allowed to go within fifty yards or more of the farthest point, for fear of disturbing the workmen. It forms a sort of covered way under the bed of the Thames, 38 feet wide & 22 f. 6 inches in height, divided into two parallel roads by a very thick wall which is, however, cut into a succession of open arches affording easy communication from one to the other of these carriage ways. When completed there will be raised sidewalks for foot passengers on both sides of each road. At present only the left hand one is passable for visiters & the footway is complete on the sides next the Arcades only. The right hand road forms a kind of rail-way along which the waggons for conveying earth out of the Tunnel, pass & repass with a thundering noise on their way to & from the shaft, where, as they come full, to return empty, they are raised or lowered by machinery. The appearance of the Tunnel as you first see it is a succession of double horse shoe arches, something like the old Norman Arches, running away into the distance & forming a grand perspective as you look along the receding lines. The horse-shoe form is produced by a thickening of the middle wall at it's lower part & the sides of the Tunnel being excavated in the same semi-circular way they belly out like the mainsails of a man-of-war.

I walked heroically as far as the gate which bars the approach to visiters, and lingered enjoying the novelty of the scene all the more for the excitement of a vague feeling of uneasiness. I remembered, very distinctly, that the Thames with all it's shipping was rolling far over head, that perhaps at the very moment, men-of-war, merchant vessels and steamers were floating above. I thought of the enormous weight & the rapid-flow of the waters, of the advance tide sweeping in from the Ocean, and I almost expected each moment to hear the earthquake shock of collapsing walls, and see the solid mason work tremble & shake as I looked at it's massive arches. But no such convulsion of the elements ensued. Earth, air & water remained in their places. We walked out as we had walked in safe & well, and ascending the shaft to the light of day and to our carriage, proceeded very quietly to a place called Blackwall for the purpose of eating White Bait—a sudden transition from great things to small.

We found at Blackwall, where we were joined by Mr Searle, a good Hotel and an abundant supply of the fairy fish called Whitebait, too small, too delicately beautiful to be eaten. It is like feasting on Butterflies.

But they are Epicurean morsels notwithstanding. They are from one to three inches long, shine with a white light like beaten silver, are boneless, or their bones intangible as their scales are invisible, have little black eyes, and should be eaten tail, head, little black eyes & all, at one mouthful, hot from the frying pan, with no sauce but a fresh-cut lemon, and are food for an ancient Roman, equal I am sure to the brains of nightingales or the tongues of thrushes. And to think what numbers are swallowed by coarse throats down which a sturgeon cutlet or salt cod fish would pass just as readily. How many pearls are thrown to swine! Whitebait might be served up to the Water Gods.

From the windows of the Hotel we had a fine view of the Thames covered with vessels of every description. Opposite was a low, green, marshy looking place called the Isle of Dogs, formed by a great bend in the river which here appears to retrace it's steps and turn back as if loath to leave the Isle of Dogs.

I must not forget that Rotherhithe, pronounced, by the <u>natives</u> Redriff, is the birthplace of Capt. Lemuel Gulliver.

+ Our dinner at Blackwall did not consist entirely of Whitebait; there were substantials & sweets & a bottle of Champagne. When the time for departure arrived & the bill was called for, (it was not an extravagant one,) we discovered with some laughing dismay, that our purses were all nearly empty. I had a gold sovereign in mine, the rest of the party only a little silver in theirs. There was however no difficulty. We had come in a handsome carriage with servants, and the landlord was too experienced a man not to know with whom he had to deal. We returned to our Hotel and his pounds, shillings & pence were forthwith transmitted to him.

Construction on the THAMES TUNNEL, which would connect the docks at Rotherhithe and Wapping, began in March 1825, under the supervision of Sir Marc Isambard Brunel (1769–1849), civil engineer. Brunel's design for an innovative tunneling shield allowed a group of men working within a honeycomb-like structure to dig at the tunnel's wall while simultaneously reinforcing the tunnel with oak planks and bricks. From the beginning the project was fraught with setbacks that included ruptures, a gas explosion, disease, and worker discontent. In January 1828, when work had progressed well past the midway point, the tunnel ruptured yet again and water rushed in, flooding the space in fifteen minutes, killing two workmen, and propelling Brunel's son, Isambard Kingdom Brunel, upward through the access shaft. This disaster, combined with the depletion of the private funds raised to finance the project, brought work to a halt until 1835, when excavation recommenced. While under construction, the tunnel was open to the public every day except Sunday from nine in the morning until dusk. Visitors paid one shilling, then proceeded down a "commodious Staircase" to the gaslit archways below. At the time of Coolidge's visit, workers had come to within 130 feet of the low-water mark on the opposite shore. The tunnel was finally completed in December 1841 and opened to pedestrian traffic by Queen Victoria in late January 1843. A commercial failure, it was purchased by the East London Railway in 1865, which began using it for trains in 1869. It remains in use today as part of the London Overground System (*ODNB*; Richard Trench and Ellis Hillman, *London under London* [1985], 105–115; *Age* [London], 12 Aug. 1838; *Times* [London], 10 Sept. 1838; "The Thames Tunnel," The Brunel Museum, accessed 20 Dec. 2010, http://www.brunel-museum.org.uk/TheMuseum/ThamesTunnel).

WHITEBAIT refers to the small, silvery-white fry of various fishes, chiefly herring and sprat. Throughout the summer months, visitors to the riverside taverns at Greenwich and Blackwall consumed whitebait in "immense quantities." The fish were caught at high tide, dressed, dredged lightly in flour, and fried for no more than two minutes. At tableside they were dressed with cayenne pepper and a squeeze of lemon juice and then served up immediately with brown bread, butter, and iced champagne (*OED*; John Timbs, *Clubs and Club Life in London* [1908], 492–498).

According to the note "The Publisher to the Reader," included in the front matter to Swift's *Gulliver's Travels*, ROTHERHITHE, or Redriff, was Lemuel Gulliver's place of residence after he had completed his remarkable travels. Later, "growing weary of the concourse of curious people coming to him at his house," he relocated to Nottinghamshire, "his native country" (Jonathan Swift, *Gulliver's Travels into Several Remote Nations of the World* [London, 1834], 13–14).

Friday 31. August

I visited for the first time the British Museum. We entered the Hall and, ascending a staircase over which was a painted ceiling we passed on and merely walked through the rooms intending to return when more at leisure. I was disappointed in the Natural History rooms, particularly those devoted to Zoology. The stuffed specimens are in a bad state, dusty & dry-looking. The Giraffes particularly offended my sight. The living animals which I had lately seen in the Zoological Gardens with their large soft eyes, and the graceful movements of their long necks were too fresh in my recollection & I turned with disgust from the Mummies. The collection of Minerals I am told is fine—also of Shells—But it was not until descending the widest, easiest & most simply grand staircase I have ever seen, and entering the noble Library that I began to feel the spirit of the place and that I was really in the British Museum of which I had heard so much. This Library consists of one very long, wide, lofty room with galleries running all round. The Books arranged in two tiers or stories, accessible from the floor & from the galleries. They are in presses and protected by doors of brass network. These books formed the private collection of George 3^d and were presented to the nation by George 4th. Sir Joseph Banks bequeathed his library, in the same wise way, to the British Museum, which is also especially rich in M.S.S. Having walked once up & down the great length of this vast room, we re-ascended the grave staircase, repassed the Mineral Gallery which is hung with portraits, took another look at the long rows of dead beasts, birds & fish, which I longed to see, poor creatures! committed to decent graves, and went down the staircase with the painted ceiling to the Entrance Hall, where we received directions how to proceed in our search for the Elgin marbles.

We passed many rooms filled with antiquities, statues, vases, busts &c until, when we least expected it, we were checked in our career by the sight of two great Lions "couchant" in our path, and guarding the entrance of the Egyptian Saloon, as it is called, containing the monuments of Egyptian Art. I thought of the Lions in the Pilgrim's Progress that lay in the road to the House called Beautiful. Those Lions were chained, and ours were not to be wakened from a strong sleep of three thousand years, so we passed fearlessly on and found ourselves surrounded by genuine

FIGURE 8. *Interior View of the British Museum Showing Visitors in the Egyptian Room,* by William Radclyffe after B. Sly, ca. 1840. *(Courtesy of the London Metropolitan Archives.)*

antiquity, monuments which outdate the memory of man, his recorded histories, and remain the relics of ages known only by the stupendous ruins of former greatness. Here they are, colossal Heads, limbs of Giants carved in granite, statues of black basalt grotesque and uncouth, figures of birds & beasts, sepulchral vases, paintings from temples & tombs, and immense Sarcophagi which seemed formed to resist all force but that of the last trump, now broken open and despoiled, and lying here dark and massive and covered with hieroglyphics as unintelligible as the talismanic characters by which a wizard might strive to guard his own tomb from being rifled as these have been.

Time pressed however, we were much hurried, for we were on the eve of our departure for a second absence from London. We paused but a short time in the Egyptian Saloon where I looked particularly at the famous Rosetta Stone, — at two colossal heads one in red granite, found in ancient Thebes by Belzoni, the other taken from the Memnonium (also Thebes) wrought from a block of stone of two different colours and believed to be the head of Sesostris — At an arm of granite ten feet long belonging to the same statue with Belzoni's head, — at a double fist of enormous size found in the ruins of Memphis, and at a Sarcophagus of black marble entirely covered, within and without, with hieroglyphics.

Promising ourselves a longer look at all these treasures, we turned on our steps and entered a small room called the Phigalian Saloon which contains the Bas Reliefs from the temple of Apollo near Phigalia in Arcadia. They represent the battles of the Centaurs & Lapithæ, of the Greeks and Amazons and formed the frieze of the interiour of the Cella.

Passing on we at length found ourselves in the presence of the Elgin marbles, standing before the work of Phidias, the remains, how mutilated! of Art in it's highest form. My heart beat thick as I looked at the broken friezes, the headless trunks, the shattered groups, and asked myself, Are these the far-famed Elgin marbles? Was Grecian Art indeed so superiour to all that has come after it that these crushed fragments can exercise over the imagination an influence denied to all the efforts of modern genius, and satisfy those cravings for the Beautiful which modern art excites without the power to appease? ——

The **BRITISH MUSEUM** was established by an act of Parliament in 1753, following the death of Sir Hans Sloan (1660–1753), physician, president of the College of Physicians, and successor to Sir Isaac Newton as president of the Royal Society. During his lifetime Sloan amassed a large collection of botanical specimens, antiquities, coins, medals, botanical prints, art, and "artificial productions" from

Turkey, Persia, Japan, China, West Africa, Greenland, and the British colonies in America, as well as a sizable gathering of English materials spanning the nation's history from the medieval period through the Restoration. He bequeathed the entirety, including a library of more than ninety thousand volumes and catalogues, to the British government under the provision that the collection would be suitably housed and maintained for the use of the people. The collection was relocated to Montagu House in Bloomsbury on Great Russell Street, where it opened in 1759. The growth of the collection brought about the construction of several additions, designed by Sir Robert Smirke (1780–1867), that replaced all of Montagu House. Smirke's British Museum stands as one of the greatest examples of Greek Revival architecture in the country (*ODNB*; David M. Wilson, *British Museum* [2002], 11–25, 31–34, 58–75, 78, 94–98; Edward Miller, *That Noble Cabinet: A History of the British Museum* [1974], 19–45, 116–129).

The **BOOKS**, numbering more than sixty-five thousand volumes and pamphlets, were amassed by George III (1738–1820). In January 1823, George IV (1762–1830) informed the prime minister, Lord Liverpool, of his intention to present the king's library to the nation. A separate gallery was constructed within the British Museum and the collection was installed in late summer 1828, and supervised public access began in October 1829. Because of the overwhelming number of visitors, access to the collection ceased by the end of 1838 (*ODNB*; Philip R. Harris, *History of the British Museum Library, 1753–1973* [1998], 31–32, 56–60, 67–68).

SIR JOSEPH BANKS (1743–1820), naturalist and president of the Royal Society and the Society of Antiquaries, used his political and scientific connections to further the interests of the British Empire. He is perhaps best known for his botanical expedition aboard the *Endeavour*, from 1768 to 1771, with Capt. James Cook and British Museum librarian Daniel Solander (1733–1782). The voyage included lengthy visits to Tahiti, New Zealand, Australia, Batavia, and Java, and Banks returned to England with hundreds of specimens and drawings of the flora and fauna as well as detailed notes about the people and societies inhabiting those locales. Banks's vast collection of specimens, drawings, journals, and books, once housed in the informal research institute he created in his Soho Square home, was given to the British Museum after his death (*ODNB*; Neil Chambers, *Joseph Banks and the British Museum: The World of Collecting, 1770–1830* [2007]; Harold B. Carter, *Sir Joseph Banks, 1743–1820* [1988]; Andrea Wulf, *Brother Gardeners: Botany, Empire, and the Birth of an Obsession* [2008], 173–242).

Christian passes the chained **LIONS** before the palace, "the name whereof was *Beautiful*," in John Bunyan's *Pilgrim's Progress from This World, to That which is to come: Delivered under the Similitude of a Dream* (Cornhill, 1678; repr. 1875), pt. 1, p. 71.

The **ROSETTA STONE**, named for its place of discovery in Egypt, bears the text of the Memphis Decree, issued in 196 B.C., in three distinct forms: hieroglyphic and demotic scripts as well as a Greek translation. Since its rediscovery by a French soldier in 1799, the Rosetta Stone has enabled scholars to interpret early

Egyptian records. The Rosetta Stone and the FIST were two of the antiquities surrendered by the French to the English in 1801, and both were installed in the British Museum in 1802 (John D. Ray, *The Rosetta Stone and the Rebirth of Ancient Egypt* [2007]; Richard Parkinson, *Rosetta Stone* [2005]).

Giovanni Battista BELZONI (1778–1823), adventurer and Egyptologist, was born in Padua. A traveling stage performer and occasional amateur engineer, Belzoni began his career as an excavator of Egyptian antiquities in 1816, when he met Henry Salt (1780–1827), Britain's consul general in Egypt. Salt hired Belzoni to move the great granite head of Ramses II, which had fallen from its body in Thebes, to the Nile for eventual transport to the British Museum. Belzoni's subsequent discoveries included the temple at Abu Simbel; four tombs in the Valley of the Kings, including that of Seti I; and the entrance to the second pyramid at Giza. In England he met great success with the publication of a description of his experiences in Egypt and an exhibition of objects from the tomb of Seti I (*ODNB*; Stanley Mayes, *Great Belzoni: The Circus Strongman Who Discovered Egypt's Ancient Treasures* [2003]; Giovanni Battista Belzoni, *Narrative of the Operations and Recent Discoveries within the Pyramids, Temples, Tombs, and Excavations of Egypt and Nubia* [1820]).

The ELGIN MARBLES were comprised of sculptures and architectural fragments removed from the Acropolis in Athens by Thomas Bruce (1766–1841), seventh Earl of Elgin, ambassador to Constantinople. Elgin sold the entire collection to the British Parliament in 1816, which presented it to the British Museum (*ODNB*; Wilson, *British Museum*, 71–74).

+ *September 1st*

Mr Coolidge & myself with a Portuguese courier, Joseph di Ribera, whom he has taken into his service, and my maid Smith, went to Tunbridge Wells, where we remained a fortnight visiting Penshurst, Redleaf & Knole Park.

We returned to Fenton's Hotel, St. James St. on the 15th Sept.

JOSEPH DI RIBERA has not been identified.

TUNBRIDGE WELLS, approximately thirty miles southeast of London in West Kent, grew from a quiet village in the seventeenth century into one of England's most fashionable "watering places" by the 1830s. Its season generally extended from March through October (*Visitor's Guide to the Watering Places* [1841], 80–89; L. Fussell, *Journey round the Coast of Kent; containing Remarks on the Principal Objects . . . including Penshurst, and Tunbridge-Wells* [1818], 278–279, 286–288).

In a letter to a family friend, Coolidge wrote, "I find Tunbridge Wells so pleasant a place that I should prefer remaining altogether. I am in good lodgings, having a whole furnished house to myself, which is the way we do things in this civilised country, in front a beautiful hedge separating me from the street with fine turf & trees on my side, & back a charming flower garden full of bloom & fragrance. All the houses in the row being built on the same plan we have before us a long slip of grass & trees with the hedge extending beyonding them, & behind us nothing but flowers, turf & gravel walks. The only drawback to my satisfaction is that Joseph cannot be always with me. He returned to London yesterday and I do not expect him back again until tomorrow. I am drinking the waters which are chalybeate, but rely more on exercise in the open air & the very pure atmosphere of Tunbridge Wells for any benefit I am to derive from my stay here, than on any virtue in the Mineral Springs.... I will only add what I know you will be glad to hear that I am recovering my health & strength" (Coolidge to Augustine Heard, 6 Sept. 1838 [MH: Heard Family Papers]).

After returning to London, Coolidge wrote to her sister Virginia J. Randolph Trist, who was then in Havana, Cuba, and described her brief journies out of the city: "We have made one little tour through Berkshire, Wilts, Hunts Warwick & Gloucester, visited Oxford, Cheltenham Bristol & Bath, seen Kenilworth, Stratford upon Avon, the Banks of the Wye Salisbury & Winchester Cathedrals, and passed a fortnight at Tunbridge Wells in Kent. Every where the same beautiful highly cultivated country, every where parks & castles, gentlemen's seats, farm houses & pretty cottages, and no where the appearance of that misery among the working classes which is said to exist in so painful and dangerous a degree. I hope the accounts have been exaggerated for it seems strange that such extremes of poverty and suffering should either care or be able to conceal themselves. The distribution of property is most unequal no doubt, but let the radicals say what they will, the English are, I am sure, essentially a tory people, reverencing their church, proud of their aristocracy and confident in the superiority of themselves & their governments to all other nations and government upon earth. I saw at the village of Frant in Kent a little church which struck me as an Epitome of English law & manners, constitution & society. It was shewn to us with great pride and pleasure by an old verger or church officer of some kind. In the nave were wooden benches for the people, higher up comfortable seats for the gentry, occupying both side aisles in the chancel two rich pews, carpeted, cushioned, & lined with crimson cloth for the Marquis Camden & Earl of Abergavenny the two magnates of the neighbourhood, and just in front of the altar, between the pews of the lords, a high proud pulpit of carved oak with velvet hangings for the clergyman. It might seem invidious to remark that this pulpit by it's size & grandeur almost entirely obscured & concealed a window on which was traced the acts of the saviour & his apostles. From the top of the tower of this church was a most extensive view, but certainly the object which our guide pointed out to us with most eagerness was Lord Abergavenny's park covering several thousand acres of ground. I looked at it with great pleasure for it formed no painful contrast with other objects. The fields highly cultivated, snug farm houses & pretty villages told no tale of want or suffering.... There is a fashion of dressing children here which I think might suit your climate. Little boys wear short drawers coming only to the knee & the leg down to the shoe & sock is entirely naked; a short tunic also to the knee confined round the waist and a very broad trimmed straw hat completes the costume which is really picturesque. When the tunic is made, as it frequently is, of plaid the litt[le] fellows look like scotch highlanders with their naked knees as the trews are quite out of sight" (Coolidge to Virginia J. Randolph Trist, 28 Sept. 1838 [NcU: Southern Historical Collection, Nicholas Philip Trist Papers]).

Monday 24. September.

We went to see the Bank of England by invitation from the Governor, Mr Curtis. It rained violently but we nevertheless found a large party of ladies assembled, who conducted by Mr Curtis & Mr Oldham, went through different apartments containing the machinery for engraving banknotes & checks, for printing, binding &c. We were told that the process of engraving had been so much simplified by the aid of machinery, that what once occupied weeks was now accomplished in hours. This very morning a process had been gone through in one quarter of an hour which formerly required three weeks for it's completion. We examined one very perfect machine, small & of the nicest finish, the invention of Mr Oldham, for engraving the copperplates from which the notes were afterwards struck. This person, Mr Oldham, appeared very confident & sanguine in his expectations of farther improvement, and with some share of self-conceit, appeared to possess extraordinary genius and enthusiasm. I understand so little of the mechanical arts that an exhibition of machinery is in a great measure lost upon me. I am astonished at effects without being able to comprehend causes except in their most general principles. Details escape my unpractised mind and slow eyes. The whirl & noise confound & disturb me. I am stunned by the noise, & dazzled by the rapid motion, so that I carry away, in general, a confused impression of extraordinary works performed by unintelligible means.

If I remember right we were first shewn Mr Oldham's machine for engraving the copper plates, & one was engraved before our eyes. The different parts of the plate are done at different times, as, in this method of engraving, a very small surface can be operated upon at once. First I think all these parts, the vignettes, the words "Bank of England" in large characters &c &c are engraved by hand on blocks of soft steel which is afterwards annealed and hardened to the greatest possible degree. The first engraving is intaglio. Other blocks of soft steel are applied to these & by great force of pressure receive an impression which, of course, is in relief. These in their turn are hardened, and are then in a fit state for use in Mr Oldham's machine. The steel blocks are applied, one at a time, to the different parts of a copper plate just the size which the note is to be, and by powerful pressure the plate receives an intaglio impression from the raised figure on the steel. It took just twenty seconds to engrave on the copper the figure of Britannia on the corner of the plate, and not much longer for the words "Bank of England." I believe that the second set of steel blocks, those which have the figure in relief, are themselves stamped in this machine, and that nothing is done by hand but the first engraving.

We afterwards saw the machine by which the paper prepared for the notes is made wet. It seems that the pores of paper retain such a quantity of air that the operation of wetting it thoroughly is by no means an easy one. The notes, cut to a proper size and entirely blank, are put into a sort of box containing a somewhat complicated machinery. Air pumps worked from the top exhaust the air from the paper, whilst a communication with a reservoir below supplies water to take it's place.

The paper duly wetted is then put under press, the surplus moisture is expelled and the future notes come out soft, pliant and equally damp in all their parts. To avoid the danger of their becoming too dry, they are kept in a large box made of copper. Iron would rust and wood absorb the moisture, but copper preserves them for the longest space of time in a proper state.

We were then shewn the process of engraving the note from the copper plate. This was first rubbed with black or red ink, then the smooth surface carefully cleansed, leaving the ink only in the engraved lines. The note being then applied to the plate and passing through the press the impression was made in an instant. Indeed the astonishing rapidity with which every thing is done is startling to inexperienced eyes.

The notes are afterwards lettered and dated, and it is proposed before very long to have them signed by a process which will remove the necessity of a signature in the usual way. All is to be done by machinery. There was something in numbering the note which appeared exceedingly ingenious but which I could not at all understand.

It is no easy matter to understand any thing where there are several laughing, talking, flirting, fidgeting women, all eager to press forwards and to ask questions, not because they care to receive information but are merely anxious for the credit of appearing to do so. We had a large party and probably among them not more than two or three who really wished to understand what they saw. Some, and these were the best, in as much as they were the most sincere, looked as indifferent as they felt, & were only in the way so far as they increased the crowd. Others chose to shew off & be attended to, ask questions which proved that they had understood nothing they had seen or heard, and utter silly exclamations of senseless wonder or affected admiration. One lady made herself quite as conspicuous as she could have desired, although not exactly in the way she supposed and intended. She was pretty and apparently of some small importance at home from one or other of the many causes which confer petty importance. She talked of her residence at "the West End," of her being in town at "a season so unusual for her that she hardly knew when such a thing had happened before," of her fears for "her poor horses who were standing in the rain whilst she, thoughtless creature as she was, had neglected to order her coachman away." She overwhelmed the gentlemen with eager anxious questions to shew her love of knowledge, distorted her really pretty features by her violent efforts to look supremely intelligent & to throw dazzling brightness into her eyes, whilst every muscle of her face worked and quivered as she tried to see how animated & interested and intellectual she could force her countenance to seem. Poor lady, what pains she took to render herself ridiculous!

But we had better specimens of "inquiring minds" in two modest well-behaved girls daughters of Mr Curtis, and a lady-like person, easy & unaffected, a Miss Lee, with whom I had some conversation. We were shewn, through a window looking into a court, an apparatus for burning old Banknotes, which, as I think the same note is never issued twice, sometimes accumulate to an astonishing mass, amounting nominally to many millions of pounds sterling. We were also shewn a room where notes ready for circulation lay in piles on the shelves. Here no fire is ever admitted, or light except of the Sun. But what was better worth seeing than any amount of paper money was a barrow load of ingots, oblong masses of gold each weighing fifteen pounds & worth seven hundred sterling a piece. To get at these we descended some stairs, crossed a court and entered ground floor apartments of stone, fire proof and lighted only by lamps. Here were lying bars & boxes of silver, bags of Spanish dollars, masses of silver pure from alloy just as it came from the mines, and here were the barrows of gold, one of which alone contained the value of seventy thousand pounds sterling.

We returned across the Court under umbrellas as it rained bucketsfull, and after a two hours progress through the Bank were glad of a "déjeuné à la fourchette" which our hospitable host had provided for us. I looked at his good-humored face & wondered whether the story were true, (told me by my maid as she was dressing me to come out,) that Mr Curtis had twenty one children and kept seven nurses at once in his house. How can he look so cheerful with twenty one children and seven nurses! The story will not bear telling. Besides my Smith is as very a lady's maid as ever gossiped. With a little encouragement I should hear much more of my neighbours' affairs than I desire to know. She is fond of quoting her former mistress Lady Charlotte Guest—the wife I believe of a Welsh Iron-Lord. But she suits me well, being neat & civil & a very good hair-dresser, somewhat greedy of gain however & not unwilling to turn an honest penny.

The BANK OF ENGLAND has served as the British government's banker and debt manager since its founding in 1694. In 1734 the bank took up residence in its present location, fronting Threadneedle Street near the Royal Exchange, and gradually expanded until it occupied three acres at the time of Coolidge's visit. Sir John Soane (1753–1837), architect and surveyor to the bank from 1788 to 1833, gave the structure its neoclassical appearance (*ODNB*; H. V. Bowen, "The Bank of England during the Long Eighteenth Century, 1694–1820," in *Bank of England: Money, Power and Influence, 1694–1994*, ed. Richard Roberts and David Kynaston [1995], 1–18; Timbs, *Curiosities*, 27–31; "History," Bank of England, accessed 21 June 2011, http://www.bankofengland.co.uk/about/history).

Timothy Abraham CURTIS (1786–1857), second son of Sir William Curtis, was a merchant, banker, and investor, as well as a prominent member of the East India Company. First elected to the board of directors for the Bank of England in 1820, Curtis then served as deputy governor and finally as governor from 1837 to 1839. In addition to his positions in the Bank of England, he was involved in several other ventures, including mining in South America and investments in railroad and steamship firms, both in England and overseas. He married Margaret Harriet Green in 1809 (d. 1847) and had at least nine children by 1829 (*ODNB*, s.v. "Curtis, William"; Freda Harcourt, *Flagships of Imperialism: The P&O Company and the Politics of Empire from Its Origins to 1867* [2006], 43–66; Elizabeth Hennessy, "The Governors, Directors and Management of the Bank of England," in *Bank of England*, 187, 264; *Gentleman's Magazine* 99, pt. 1 [1829]: 274; Henry English, *General Guide to the Companies formed for working Foreign Mines* [1825], 10, 13; *Jurist* 11, pt. 2 [1848]: 34; Burke and Burke, *Peerage and Baronetage*, 556–557).

John OLDHAM (1779–1840), artist and inventor, was born in Dublin and apprenticed to an engraver. Oldham subsequently combined his artistic abilities with his interests in machines and in 1812 created a mechanism to number banknotes individually, thus helping prevent forgery. By 1814 he was employed as a full-time artist for the Bank of Ireland. From 1836 to 1840 Oldham worked for the Bank of England and continued refining his machines to increase note security and decrease expenses in manpower. The mechanisms Coolidge observed were in use from 1836 until after 1852 (*ODNB*; *Mechanics' Magazine, Museum, Register, Journal, and Gazette* 34 [1841]: 276).

Charlotte Elizabeth Bertie GUEST Schreiber (1812–1895), author, translator, and businesswoman, married the WELSH IRON LORD Josiah John Guest (1785–1852) in 1833 and moved to Dowlais House, located in the middle of the largest ironworks in the world. She promptly took an active role in the management of the ironworks, overseeing much of its correspondence and bookkeeping; she assumed complete control upon her husband's death (*ODNB*).

Monday 1ˢᵗ October.

I have been hoping for some time past to get away from London before the fine season was quite over. It is now decided that we go to Edinburgh. I am overjoyed at the thought. I shall see Scotland, I shall hear the "sweet Doric" of her spoken tongue, and in the home of Burns and Walter Scott do homage to the genius which has in my own distant country, so often warmed my heart and animated my fancy, kindled my imagination and moved my whole inward life. These illustrious men are gone, but their spirit still lingers, still glorifies the land which gave them birth. I have many early recollections connected with the name of Scotland. My father was educated there and retained to the last a kind memory of the years he had lived in Edinburgh. The professor Leslie who has since become so celebrated was engaged by my father as tutor for his father's children, & was sent or carried to the United States where he lived some time at Tuckahoe. I have often heard my aunt Randolph speak of him—that same aunt, Mʳˢ David Meade Randolph, who, during a summer passed in Newport, secured the services of Dr Channing, then only eighteen years old, as tutor for her own sons. He lived with them in Virginia I think two years. Leslie & Channing are distinguished names in very different ways, but none of their pupils, among my relations at least, became distinguished—

The music of Scotland may be almost called the national music of Virginia.—the simple, plaintive or sprightly airs which every body knows and every body sings are Scotch. We hear Scotch music in our nurseries when we are children. Scotch songs while away the hours of a girl at her needle, and with a simple accompaniment they enable her to cheer and soothe her father's evening hours. This music is natural, intelligible, comes home to every body's business & bosom, & supplies the place of that more refined and cultivated art which borrowed from Italy & Germany remains always an exotic. What mother lulls her child with an Italian air, or what father when resting after his days work, asks his daughter for a German song? A taste for foreign music, which when genuine is desirable & enviable, in America is too apt to be a thing of affectation & of cant.

My grandfather was a true lover of music—he enjoyed all that was good of it's kind—no one had a more true feeling for Italian music, but he likewise had a love of boyhood for the old Scotch songs. "The Lass of Patie's Mill," "The Broom of Cowdenows," "Robin Adair" & "Lochaber" were among his favorites—Among mine were "T'was within a mile of Edinbro' town," "Galla Water," "The yellow-haired laddie" "of a' the airts the wind can blow" & "Kinloch of Kinloch."

I shall be very glad to go to Scotland, very glad to leave London. September, a pleasant month almost every where else, is dismal here. The fogs are so thick that we see little more than across the street—the air is heavy, damp, smoky. The sun when visible at all is a dull, red ball; a slow, misty rain is the only change, from bad to worse, which the weather seems capable of, and this gives us streets reeking with black mud & exhalations rising from a wet and filthy earth. The smoke of a hundred thousand chimneys pays constant tribute to the dense cloud which always hangs over London, and fog, rain, smoke, black mud & heavy exhalations combine to make all below & all above equally insupportable. Let us get away as fast as we can.—

The West End is deserted by all that gave it life & brilliancy and this adds not a little to it's sombre aspect. So many houses shut up, so few carriages, so little passing. St. James' Street, the street of Club Houses, so near the purlieus of the Court, and which when I first arrived, literally swarmed with splendid equipages, is now dull, desolate and lonely. Every body gone. The Queen at Windsor, the Members of the two Houses of Parliament shooting partridges in the country, the nobility and gentry retired to their estates, strangers & foreigners making tours or visiting their friends in the country, every body glad to get away from London—dismal, dirty, gloomy London. Yet London in July & even in August, is a very pleasant place, the climate not disagreeable, and where there is a great deal to see and a good deal to be done.

Coolidge's **FATHER**, Thomas Mann Randolph, attended the University of Edinburgh from 1785 to 1788 (*ANB*; *DAB*; William H. Gaines, Jr., *Thomas Mann Randolph: Jefferson's Son-in-Law* [1966]).

John **LESLIE** (1766–1832), mathematician, natural philosopher, and author, began his studies at the University of St. Andrews in 1779 and entered the University of Edinburgh in 1785, where he knew Adam Smith. In early 1788 he met fellow student Thomas Mann Randolph, whom he briefly tutored in Scotland, until Randolph returned to Virginia, despite Leslie's protests that he should continue his education. Later that fall, on Randolph's request, Leslie traveled to Virginia to serve as a private tutor to Randolph and his brother William, but their studies were cut short by the death of Randolph's mother in the spring of 1789. Leslie returned to Scotland that June. He was elected chair of natural philosophy at the University of Edinburgh in 1819, a position he held until his death (*ODNB*; Gaines, *Thomas Mann Randolph*, 20–23; John Leslie to Thomas Mann Randolph, 12 May, 2 Aug. 1788, 16 June 1789 [ViU: Carr-Cary Papers]).

TUCKAHOE was the Randolph family's plantation near the James River in Goochland County, Virginia. Mary Jane Randolph Randolph (ca. 1763–1828), author of *The Virginia House-wife* (1824), was Coolidge's AUNT and her father's older sister. She was married to David Meade Randolph (ca. 1759–1830), a cousin, and lived in Richmond, where Coolidge and her sisters visited her, often staying for several weeks at a time to attend social events over the winter months (Gaines, *Thomas Mann Randolph*, 3–10; *Richmond Enquirer*, 29 Jan. 1828; *Richmond Commercial Compiler*, 28 Sept. 1830).

William Ellery CHANNING (1780–1842), Unitarian clergyman and author, was born in Newport, Rhode Island, and attended Harvard College, graduating at the head of his class in 1798. In that same year Channing accepted a position as private tutor for Coolidge's cousins in Richmond, but after a year and a half he returned north, where he studied divinity in preparation for a career in the church. In 1803 he was ordained and installed as minister in the Federal Street Church in Boston. He rejected the doctrine of original sin and was a firm believer in freedom of will and the importance of education and self-improvement, liberal ideas that were particularly appealing to a rising generation of New England intellectuals. Though never formally part of an abolitionist movement, Channing was a vocal opponent of slavery. His publications on that subject caused friction within his church and ultimately led to his resignation in 1840 (*ANB*; *DAB*).

Of her GRANDFATHER, Coolidge later wrote, "Mr Jefferson had a most decided taste for music and great natural dispositions for it. His ear was singularly correct and his voice, though he never sang except in the retirement of his own rooms, was sweet and clear and continued unbroken to a very late period of his life. My chamber at Monticello was over his, and I used not infrequently to hear him humming old tunes, generally Scotch songs but sometimes Italian airs or hymns. This was I think between whiles, in the intervals of his occupations. My mother inherited his taste & talent for music." Versions of several of the songs that Coolidge lists are in Monticello's music collection, on deposit in the Albert and Shirley Small Special Collections Library, University of Virginia (Helen Cripe, *Thomas Jefferson and Music*, rev. ed. [2009], 100–130; Ellen Coolidge, "Some remarks on the first chapters of Mr Randall's book which he sent me in MS. in 1853, & which I returned as I read them," 1853, Ellen Wayles Randolph Coolidge Letterbook, p. 37 [ViU: Edgehill-Randolph Papers]).

London. October 4th

We leave this great town to-day on a northern tour.

In a letter to her sister Mary J. Randolph, Coolidge described her journey through Scotland, including a visit to William Meikleham, a professor of natural history at the University of Glasgow. Meikleham's son David Scott Meikleham (1804–1849), a physician educated at Cambridge University, had married Coolidge's youngest sister, Septimia Ann Randolph (1814–1887), on 13 August 1838 at Edgehill.

In the letter to Mary, dated from late November, Coolidge recounted her trip in detail:

> I left London with Mr Coolidge early in October; one day brought us to Liverpool by the railroad, very much the finest work of the kind I ever saw. Indeed what characterises England is the perfection of the public works—whatever is done is done well, thoroughly, with every regard to excellence & none to expense. From Liverpool we went to Glasgow by the steam boat, but unfortunately our northern expedition was undertaken too late in the season, the weather was almost constantly bad which was the only drawback to the great pleasure of a six weeks tour. We passed the Isle of Man & Ailsa Craig in the night and sailed up the Clyde in a fog so thick as to render it's celebrated banks invisible. At Dumbarton, however, it cleared off a little, so that we saw the castle and rock and reached Glasgow late on Sunday. We staid here two days, & were hospitably entertained by the families of Professor Meikleham & Sir William Hooker. . . .
>
> Notwithstanding the kindness we received in Glasgow my impressions of the place are any thing but favorable—it is a large, dirty, noisy, vulgar, manufacturing town, constantly reeking with black smoke & at this season of the year with damp vapours. The inns are wretched, I saw no fine private houses and, from what I could learn from the Meiklehams and Hookers, the society with the exception of a very limited circle, is what might be expected among a people of money making manufacturers whose whole thoughts and powers turn in the one direction of gain. Indeed the banks of the "once romantic Clyde" are perfectly described by Campbell in his poem beginning "And call they this improvement?" But the banks of the Clyde, desecrated as they are and it's water polluted to the vile purposes of turning wheels & working machinery, are not all despoiled of their charms—We travelled, going & returning, nearly a whole day along them. The ruins of Bothwell Castle are among the most picturesque & interesting I have seen; they stand immediately on the Clyde overlooking a deep dell through which it flows—on the opposite side are the remains of Blantyre Priory. . . . The falls of Clyde, especially the one called the Cora Lynn, are of the most romantic beauty—We spent one day on Loch Lomond intending to cross on highland ponies from the head of the Lake to Loch Katrine & through the pass of the Trosacks to Stirling: This was rendered

impossible by the fury of the weather, which not only prevented our landing. but compelled us to keep below during the greater part of the day so that we only caught occasional glimpses of the scenery of Loch Lomond. What we did see however was all the finer for the effect of the storm. You know mountain scenery never shews to greater advantage than under the shifting shadows and flashing lights of a "bourasque." We passed half a day at Stirling. The view from the Castle is more like that from Monticello than any thing I have seen in my travels—not so fine, as far as the mere material objects go, but full of historic & poetic associations. There are the Grampian Hills, Ben Lomond, Ben Ledi, Ben venue, Ben voirlich, the Braes of Balquidder, the Links of Forth, the battle fields of Falkirk, Bannockburn & Sheriff Muir, all before your eyes, distant or near, whilst far away even the summit of Arthur's seat may be seen, in a very clear day, which we were so fortunate as to have. Leaving Stirling we passed through Falkirk & Linlithgow. . . .

We staid four days in Edinburgh, the most beautiful city I have ever seen. What with the natural advantages and the use which has been made of them there is nothing like it. The old town with it's grim castle towering high over the narrow, steep streets & houses, black with age, one story piled above another to the number of seven eight or nine, and the upper one of all frequently projecting beyond the others; then the names of the squares & streets rendered so familiar & so interesting by Sir W. Scott . . . the magnificent Frith of Forth spreading out like a vast lake, Calton Hill with it's numerous monuments, the new town with it's broad well paved streets, fine squares, handsome houses built of stone having in this the advantage over Philadelphia which it otherwise resembles—Altogether I have never seen a place which I thought at all equal to Edinburgh—The old University, where our father lived so many years, is gone and a new one built in it's place which I went to see. From Edinburgh we turned southwards & on our way visited the ruins of Roslin Castle & "the chapel proud where Roslin's chiefs uncoffined lie" & Hawthornden with it's remarkable caverns, travelled twenty miles along the borders of Gala Water, forded the Tweed (I have not forded a river before since I left Virginia,) spent several hours at Abbotsford, saw Melrose, not by moonlight but in the cold grey of a wintry morning & Dryburgh under a pelting shower, kept the Eildon Hills in sight for many miles of our road, gazed in passing on the hill of Cowdenknows & the tower of Smaylhome, crossed the T[weed] near it's junction with the Teviot. . . . At Berwick on Tweed we said goodby to Scotland, a beautiful country as far as I have seen of it, with a frank, hearty, hospitable people inhabiting it. I was much pleased with the Scots and received great kindness from them. They are far more amiable in manners than the English, more cordial & more courteous. Their language is what the Reviewer calls it "a sweet Doric," having nothing of the vulgarity of the Irish brogue & their voices are generally as clear as their countenances. I like every thing in Scotland but Glasgow. (Coolidge to Mary J. Randolph, 29 Nov. 1838 [NcU: Southern Historical Collection, Nicholas Philip Trist Papers]).

London Nov. 13.

Arrived at Fenton's Hotel St. James St. after visiting some parts of the north of England and south of Scotland.

I paid an early visit to the British Museum with M[r] I. I. Dixwell.

Portland Vase 9½ inches high—species of glass—Colour dark blue ground with white figures in bas relief.—Ancient Etruscan Vases. Roman lamps graceful forms but primitive construction—Mere receptacles for oil with a round hole or holes, for the wick to come through. I counted as many as twelve of these holes in one lamp.

Repository for wedgewood ware next door to the Pantheon—good imitations of antique vases—red figures not in relief, on a black ground. Shopkeeper's name Phillips. M[r] Dixwell bought a copy of the Portland Vase, white figures on a brown ground. Price 4 guineas.

John James DIXWELL (1806–1876), merchant and banker, was descended from the John Dixwell (ca. 1607–1688) who was one of three judges who conducted the trial of Charles I and signed the death warrant for his execution. John James Dixwell began his career as a clerk in the counting house of Boston merchant Thomas Wigglesworth in 1821 and served as that agency's supercargo on several voyages to Calcutta beginning in 1830. He was acquainted with Joseph Coolidge through their mutual friend and business associate Augustine Heard, and Dixwell's younger brother George (1814–1885) became an integral part of the new firm Augustine Heard & Company, of which Coolidge was partner. At the time of the Coolidges' visit, John Dixwell was making trips to London, Paris, and Geneva to introduce himself to European merchants and banking firms in preparation for the opening of his own office and import warehouse at Boston's India Wharf. Dixwell remained involved in the China trade, pursuing both his own investment interests and serving as a U.S. contact for Heard & Company, for nearly thirty years (*DAB*; Thomas N. Layton, *Voyage of the* Frolic: *New England Merchants and the Opium Trade* [1997], 31–44, 51–61; *Boston Daily Advertiser*, 20 Jan. 1877).

The PANTHEON, designed by James Wyatt, opened in 1772 on the south side of Oxford Street. It served as a place of entertainment for the upper classes during the winter social season, hosting assemblies, masquerade balls, plays, and concerts, one of which Thomas Jefferson attended on 23 March 1786. Although the Pantheon burned in 1792, it was rebuilt by 1795. Samuel and George Baker leased the property in 1833 and reopened it as the Pantheon Bazaar a year later, following an extensive reconstruction designed by architect Sydney Smirke (1798–1877) (*ODNB*; *Survey of London*, vols. 31 and 32 [1963], 268–283; *MB*, 1:615).

Jonathan and Jacob PHILLIPS, dealers in fine porcelain and glass, operated a large showroom at 358–359 Oxford Street, next to the Pantheon (Tallis, part 34; Henry-Kent Causton, *Kent's Original London Directory: 1816*, 260; B. Critchett, *Post-Office*

London Directory for 1836, 418; Frederic Kelly, *Post Office London Directory, 1841*, 514; John Linnell, *Mrs Phillips, Wife of the China Man, Oxford Street* [1814], Tate Museum, accessed 20 Dec. 2010, http://www.tate.org.uk/servlet/QuickSearch).

Monday Evening Nov. 26.

Left Fenton's Hotel, so far our abiding place, and a very comfortable one, in London, and went into furnished rooms, No 166 Regent St. Gass & Sons, Jewellers. Not particularly pleased with the appearance of things. Rooms small close & crowded — do not compare well with Fenton's.

David GASS, goldsmith, silversmith, and gunsmith, began business at 42 Oxford Street in 1834 and relocated to 166 REGENT STREET in 1836. Regent Street was built between 1817 and 1823 as part of the metropolitan improvements envisioned by architect John Nash. John Tallis described it in 1838 as a "noble street," with "palace-like shops, in whose broad showy windows are displayed articles of the most splendid description, such as the neighbouring world of wealth and fashion are daily in want of. . . . [I]t should be visited on a summer's day in the afternoon, when the splendid carriages, and elegantly attired pedestrians, evince the opulence and taste of our magnificent metropolis." The rooms above the shops were intended as exclusive bachelor lodgings (J. Mordaunt Crook, "Metropolitan Improvements: John Nash and the Picturesque," in *London — World City*, 77–96; Roy Porter, *London: A Social History* [1994], 126–130; Montague Howard, *Old London Silver: Its History, Its Makers, and Its Marks* [1903], 331; K. Baedeker, *London and Its Environs, Including Excursions . . . Handbook for Travellers* [1878], 18; William Robson, *Robson's London Directory, Street Key, and Conveyance List . . . for 1834*, 397; B. Critchett, *Post-Office London Directory for 1836*, 207; Frederic Kelly, *Post Office London Directory, 1841*, 400; Tallis, part 12).

Tuesday Dec. 4.

Carried my boy Jefferson, who had joined us under the care of Mr Heard at Durham, to Highgate, to the school of Mme Kieckhover highly recommended by Mr Bates. He wept & so did I. But I am sure it is for his good to get him to school and out of London.

Augustine HEARD (1785–1868), mariner and merchant, was born in Ipswich, Massachusetts; he was the son of John Heard, a prosperous ship owner and merchant trading in the West Indies and China (fig. 19). Heard began his career in 1803 with the leading Boston merchant Ebenezer Francis. He made his first voyage to Calcutta in 1805 and soon became one of the most prominent captains of the East India trade. Heard was highly regarded as a navigator, ship's master, and merchant. By 1829 he had made a sizable fortune and retired from the sea. He became a partner with the Boston firm Russell & Company and traveled on their business to Canton, where in 1833 he met Joseph Coolidge, then employed by the same firm. In late 1838 internal friction in Russell & Company threatened Heard's profits and challenged Joseph Coolidge's position as a partner, leading the two men to explore the possibility of establishing a new firm in 1839. With the assistance of Baring Brothers and other business contacts, both in London and in Boston, Heard and Coolidge formed Augustine Heard & Company in Canton, in operation by early 1840. The firm traded in teas, silks, opium, and various other commodities. Joseph Coolidge oversaw the Canton office while Heard remained in Boston. During Heard's absence Coolidge survived the Opium Wars and a succession of riots, during one of which he was imprisoned. Coolidge left the firm in 1844, returning home to Boston, and Heard followed shortly thereafter, leaving Heard & Company largely under the direction of his four nephews and George Basil Dixwell. Heard spent the remainder of his days living in the family home in Ipswich, monitoring the operations of his cotton mill in that town, maintaining his overseas business interests, and making occasional trips to Europe, but he never again returned to China.

Heard was intimately connected with the Coolidge family for many years, serving as friend, advisor, and confidant. During Joseph's absences it was Heard who helped Ellen Coolidge with the management of her household, and the two maintained a rich correspondence. When it became apparent that the Coolidges' stay abroad would be extended, Heard traveled to England in the fall of 1838, taking with him the Coolidges' youngest son, Thomas Jefferson Coolidge, to join his parents. Heard's services as shipboard guardian were called upon again in 1839 when he escorted all four Coolidge sons to Europe, where they attended school while their parents resided in China. Following her first meeting with Heard, Ellen Coolidge's sister Virginia wrote that she was "quite charmed that his personal appearance and manners should so perfectly suit the hero of my imagination. . . . There is repose, without dullness, and a frank cheerful manner." Ellen Coolidge was so taken with Heard that she tried twice, though unsuccessfully, to facilitate an attachment between him and, first, her sister Mary, then her sister Septimia. Heard never married (*DAB*; Coolidge, *Autobiography*, 3–4; Thomas N. Layton, *Voyage of the* Frolic: *New England Merchants and the Opium Trade* [1997]; Edward W. Hanson, *Heards of Ipswich, Massachusetts* [1986]; Thomas Franklin Waters, "Augustine Heard and His Friends," *Publications of the Ipswich Historical Society* 21 [1916]: 1–108; Coolidge to Martha Jefferson Randolph, 31 May 1833, 23 Jan., 19 Mar. 1834, Coolidge to Virginia J. Randolph Trist, 27 Sept. 1835, 10 May 1836 [ViU: Ellen Wayles Randolph Coolidge Correspondence]; Virginia Trist to Coolidge, [ca. 1835] [MH: Heard Family Papers]; Joseph Coolidge to Nicholas Philip Trist, 9 Feb., 6, 20 Mar. 1838, 5 June, 26 Sept. 1839 [NcU: Southern Historical Collection, Nicholas Philip Trist Papers]; "Augustine Heard (1785–1868)," Ipswich Historical Society and Museums, accessed 21 June 2011, http://www.ipswichmuseums.org).

George and Frances Kieckhöfer [**KIECKHOVER**] operated the Highgate Academy from 1829 until 1851; they instructed boys aged seven to twelve years following what was described as a "preparatory" curriculum. Reflecting on his early school days from 1836 to 1840, one former student remembered Mrs. Kieckhöfer as "a stately but kindly lady . . . presiding over an admirably-kept school," Mr. Kieckhöfer as a "jolly old German" known to the boys as "old Kick," and that as a student he was "tolerably happy and . . . picked up a fair grounding of education." The only "disagreeables" he recalled were the small playground and the lengthy country walks during the hot summers (Coolidge, *Autobiography*, 2; Edmund Hodgson Yates, *Edmund Yates: His Recollections and Experiences* [1884], 1:35–38; T. F. T. Baker and C. R. Elrington, eds., *History of the County of Middlesex* [1980], 6:189–199).

Wednesday. Dec. 5.

Mr Coolidge & Mr Heard visited my boy and brought me good accounts of him—much cheered by the news. Went to Clapton to see Mrs Glass who was ill in bed & not to be seen.

_____

John W. and Maria **GLASS** were the parents of Maria Glass Root (ca. 1819–1838). After a visit to her parents in London during the summer of 1838, Maria returned to America and married George Gabriel Root (1808–1864) on 30 October 1838 at the Staten Island home of Coolidge's aunt Harriet Hackley. Maria contracted scarlet fever and died suddenly six days later in Rochester, New York. George Root was a partner in the mercantile firm of Stuyvesant & Root in New York, but he was ruined not long after his young wife's death when the price of cotton plummeted (James Pierce Root, *Root Genealogical Records, 1600–1870. Comprising the General History of the Root and Roots Families in America* [1870], 261; Joseph A. Scoville, *The Old Merchants of New York City* [1885], 1:318–320; *New-York Spectator*, 7 June, 29 Oct. 1838; *Times* [London], 5 Dec. 1838).

Coolidge learned the cause of Mrs. Root's demise when she received a note from Maria's sister Ellen shortly after this attempted visit. In a letter to Virginia, Coolidge wrote, "I was much shocked also at hearing of Maria Glasses death. The last letter I got from Ellen, she was preparing with your daughter and Pat Hackleys to act as bridesmaids to Mrs Root. I was amused at the idea of such children being bridesmaids when I suddenly hear from the public papers and a note from Ellen Glass that the bride is dead" (Coolidge to Virginia J. Randolph Trist, 8 Dec. 1838 [NcU: Southern Historical Collection, Nicholas Philip Trist Papers]).

Friday. Dec. 7.

Dined with the Vaughns in Fenchurch St. Saw a large diamond ring sent to Mr Vaughn by the Emperor of Russia, and a rather curious piece of mechanism, an ivory head which may be separated from the neck by passing a small thin knife blade from back to front or vice versa, but not from side to side. Could not make it out.

William Vaughan [VAUGHN] (1752–1850), noted naval architect and author, was the driving force behind the creation of the West India and London docks. Born in London of an English father and American-born mother, Vaughan attended Warrington Academy under the care of Joseph Priestley, after which he entered his father's commercial business. His brothers Benjamin and John emigrated to America and were longtime correspondents of Coolidge's grandfather, sharing particularly an interest in science and invention. Jefferson's library contained several of William's publications. Energetic and extremely active, Vaughan was a fellow of the Royal Society, the Linnean Society, and the Royal Astronomical Society, and he was an honorary member of the Society of Civil Engineers. He was instrumental in the founding of London's first savings bank in 1827, was a member of numerous committees working for poor relief, and served for many years as governor of Christ's Hospital. When the Coolidges met with Vaughan in London, he had just begun his retirement. Vaughan never married but shared his home at 70 Fenchurch Street with extended family, where he died at the age of ninety-seven (*DNB*; *ODNB*; William Vaughan, *Tracts on Docks and Commerce, printed between the years 1793 and 1800, and now first collected; with an Introduction, Memoir, and Miscellaneous Pieces* [1839], 4–22; John H. Sheppard, *Reminiscences of the Vaughan Family, and more particularly of Benjamin Vaughan, LL.D.* [1865], 5, 26; *PTJ*, 23:99–100, 34:436n; *PTJRS*, 5:513–515; *Proceedings of the American Academy of Arts and Sciences* 2 [1852]: 231; American Philosophical Society, Minutes, 16 Apr. 1830, manuscript [APS]; John Quincy Adams, diary 29, 15 Sept. 1815, p. 320 [MHi: Adams Family Papers]; Sowerby, 1231, 3548, 3945; *Gentleman's Magazine*, n.s., 33 [1850]: 681).

In 1802, following a dinner party conversation between Vaughan and James Smirnove (ca. 1755–1840), chaplain of the Russian embassy in London, Vaughan received from Alexander I (1777–1825), EMPEROR OF RUSSIA, a "hydrographical plan of all the Russias, the rivers, and the canals, made and making, and the docks at Cronstadt." Vaughan returned his "grateful acknowledgments, through Mr. Smirnove, sending at the same time various plans of the docks then under formation in London, with hints on commerce, free trade, and the bonding system, to be presented to his Imperial Majesty." In late October 1803 Vaughan received from Alexander I, via Smirnove, a "valuable" DIAMOND RING as a token of gratitude (Vaughan, *Tracts on Docks and Commerce*, 40, 133; Transcript of Burials, All Souls Cemetery, Kensal Green, Kensington, 1840 Jan–1840 Dec., s.v. "Smirnove, James," p. 180, London Metropolitan Archives, Ancestry.com).

The CURIOUS PIECE OF MECHANISM Coolidge observed was likely a "paradoxical head," similar to a device created by Joseph Saxton (1799–1873). Saxton's version "consisted of the head and bust of a Turk," and when the blade of a small sword was passed through the neck, it appeared to sever the head "without disturbing the connection." The illusion was created by a sequence of catches that unlocked and locked in succession as the blade passed through them (Joseph Henry, "Memoir of Joseph Saxton, 1799–1873," *National Academy of Sciences, Biographical Memoirs* 1 [1877]: 287, 289–290, 294–295).

Saturday Dec. 8.

Visited the Adelaide Gallery with Mr Heard—impressions all confused from the multitude of objects. Looked at a model of the Parthenon & observed how it was lighted from above & of course without windows. For the first time remarked that windows are externally ugly things and injure the general effect of a building by breaking up the surface. Chimneys I have always detested as hideous things,—and yet without windows & chimneys our houses would be uninhabitable.—The ancients understood beauty—did they understand what we call comfort, or did they place the happiness of life in luxury and pleasure? In the gratification of their appetites, their passions, their tastes, and in the exercises of the intellect?——Saw in the Adelaide Gallery an electric eel of great size, and a marble head of Lord Brougham in a marble wig with marble curls. Looks like a Butcher's dog with a wig, on & reminded me of an anecdote of Garrick playing King Lear and laughing in the most pathetic scene, where he should have been weeping over the body of Cordelia, at the sight of a dog in the pit, upon whose head his fat, perspiring master had placed his wig to the great relief of his own shining & naked noddle.—— Dined the same day with Mrs Bates.

Popularly known as the **ADELAIDE GALLERY**, The National Gallery of Practical Science, Blending Instruction with Amusement was the creation of Jacob Perkins (1776–1849), an American-born engineer, engraver, and inventor. The gallery opened at the western end of the Strand in 1832 and featured a long, narrow room with both upper- and lower-level exhibition spaces. Visitors could observe a wide variety of mechanical instruments and demonstrations of new inventions, including a large steam-powered gun, models of trains and buildings, and a seventy-foot-long canal in which clockwork models of paddle-wheel steamships floated. The gallery also offered scientific lectures and an extensive collection of portraits, tapestries, and sculpture. The forty-inch-long **ELECTRIC EEL**, from South America, was said to have emitted "a most intense electric spark" (*DAB*; *ODNB*; Altick, *Shows of London*, 377–381; Timbs, *Curiosities*, 529).

Henry Peter **BROUGHAM** (1778–1868), first Baron Brougham and Vaux, was a statesman, philanthropist, and prolific legal and political writer; he cofounded the controversial yet widely popular *Edinburgh Review*. Brougham, a radical Whig politician, pursued a wide variety of interests, most notably reforms to Parliament and the constitution as well as to the laws governing divorce and property. He was a proponent of the expansion of public education and the abolition of slavery. Brougham's ambitions were often frustrated by his erratic behavior and inconsistencies in his political ideology and methodology. In the words of his contemporary Harriet Martineau, his "want of steadfastness" meant that in history there would "be forever—a blur where Brougham should have been" (*ODNB*; Trowbridge H. Ford, *Henry Brougham and His World: A Biography* [1995]; Martineau, *Biographical Sketches*, 392–402; *Gentleman's Magazine*, n.s., 1 [1868]: 121–124).

David GARRICK (1717–1779) was an actor, playwright, and longtime manager of the Theatre Royal, Drury Lane. His innovative and energetic style in both dramatic and comedic roles won him great acclaim, and his personal character earned him equally great respect. King Lear was considered one of Garrick's finest roles, and the ANECDOTE that Coolidge referred to was well known and published in a variety of works. It concerned a Whitechapel butcher who attended a performance of *King Lear* accompanied by his mastiff. The two were sitting beside one another on a bench in the center of the pit before the stage, the butcher leaning backward and the dog forward with his paws upon the railing. The butcher became overheated and momentarily placed his large powdered wig on the dog's head. The scene was too much for Garrick, who began to tremble and laugh. The actress portraying Cordelia then opened her eyes to learn what was disturbing the performance, saw the dog, and ran laughing from the stage (*ODNB*; Richard Ryan and François Joseph Talma, *Dramatic Table Talk; or Scenes Situations and Adventures, Serious and Comic, in Theatrical History and Biography* [1825], 1:101).

Sunday. Dec. 9th

Too cold and damp for church. Staid at home—

The approach of winter meant a return to the gloom Coolidge had come to know in Boston, which was far different from the winter climate of her native home. Complaining to her sister in a letter begun on 8 December but completed three days later, Coolidge wrote that her "letter has laid by until to day, dearest Virginia, when I resume it, trying to write in the twilight of an English noon, for it is as dark at twelve o'clock in London as at five A. M. in Virginia at this season. It is the great fault I find with the climate; the temperature is mild and uniform, no severe cold or heat, but after September the Sun is rarely visible or, if seen at all, shining with a light so weak and watery. . . . There is a feeling of distance from him, of a decrease in his size & the amount of light and warmth in his beams which you can only account for by supposing him removed some hundreds of millions of miles. The fogs of London are proverbial and I am told I have not yet seen one worth speaking of— yet I have seen the street lamps lighted at three o'clock in the afternoon repeatedly, and been compelled to lay down my pen or needlework for

want of light to get on. The mornings are so dark that there is no encouragement
to rise before nine, & break fast is seldom fairly over before ten" (Coolidge to
Virginia J. Randolph Trist, 8–11 Dec. 1838 [NcU: Southern Historical Collection,
Nicholas Philip Trist Papers]).

Monday. Dec. 10.

Visited the London Docks—St. Katherine's the London & the West
India.—Gave me the best idea I have yet had of the immense trade &
wealth of London. It is the heart of the civilized world & receives & pro-
pels the "vital fluid" which circulates through the whole body—And what
a throbbing heart it is, how full of life and motion! We visited the Warehouses where the cargoes of ships are stowed away on their arrival. One
room was filled with straw in bundles for bonnets, & with Leghorn braid
which coming in that form pays less duty than in the flat, & can be sewed
together in England. Another had raw silk in bales from Italy & Bengal
to be manufactured here; of this silk some was of a fine gold colour, the
rest a dirty white. I heard for the first time, that the silk produced in England is of inferiour quality to that of more southern climates, & that not
many worms are reared here as they find it better to import the silk itself.
It come in hanks and the thread is exquisitely fine.—One large room was
filled with bags of Cinnamon, another with Pimento or Allspice, and we
were told that in consequence of the disturbed state of the English West
Indies, the crops of this last spice were likely to fail, when the price would,
of course, rise.

The Wine Vaults at the London Docks are of immense size, arched
over & with groined ceilings, entirely dark & excessively damp, ventilated
by means of pipes & containing when I saw them, thousands of casks
of Sherry. Our party of four, were each provided with a lamp fastened
to a flat stick or handle. These we held above below to one side or the
other as we desired to explore around us. The casks were piled on each
other with open spaces or lanes between them. Against the walls were a
few lamps with concave reflectors, but we depended principally on those
which we held in our own hands. They shewed us the darkness visible of
the place, the groined roof almost dripping with moisture, cobwebs in
plenty, and the pillars which supported the ceiling and floor above. The
temperature of these vaults is, at this season, much warmer than that of
the external air. Above is a store house for Madeira, and there are large
vats in which pipes of different age and flavour can be mixed and mel-
lowed together. These huge vats go up from the floor to a sort of second

story whither we ascended & saw the manner in which the pipes discharged their contents into the mouth of the vat, four at a time. One of the vats was full, and the guide, to convince us of the fact, dipped his dirty hand into the wine. The mouth of the vat was large enough to receive the body of any individual chusing to die the death preferred by Clarence, the being drowned in wine. The duty upon all wine is about 5.s.6d. a gallon, except what is made at the Cape which being a British settlement, the product of it's vineyards is taxed in only about half the amount of duty on foreign wines.

The Tobacco Warehouse which we visited next, filled with hogsheads of tobacco, reminded me of home, my old home of Virginia, and Mr Vaughn informed me that quantities are still imported from the old State, exhausted as her soil has been by the culture, continued throughout so many years. Numerous boxes of Havana segars shewed the prevalence of a taste the most artificial that man has ever succeeded in engrafting upon his nature.——   The West India Docks, the largest of all, have two Basins, one of twenty four acres the other of about thirty.—these, with the buildings attached to them, are enclosed by a wall; the ships lie close to the Quai, and there are immense Warehouses containing numbers of hogsheads of sugar, rum &c &c. Formerly no products but those of the West Indies were admitted here, but this is no longer the case.—The rum is in a kind of cellar partly under and partly above ground; light is admitted through windows high above the floor, and, as no lamps or fire in any form is permitted within these walls, the persons who wish to examine the casks have what are called Reflectors, large flat pieces of wood covered with tin, and with handles by which they are held and turned to the light so as to reflect it upon the object to be examined. Besides Warehouses there are simple sheds, looking something like Market Houses open at the sides, which furnish sufficient protection for many articles and enable the ships to discharge their cargoes without exposing them to the weather. The climate of England is too wet and rainy not to make such a precaution desirable. I was much struck at the West India Docks by the immense size of the Mahogany logs exposed on the Wood Quai. One, measured by Mr Vaughn with his stick, was four feet in diameter. These logs when well-veined are of great value; one was landed, not long since, which from it's size and markings, was rated at upwards of £600.—The roof of one of the buildings or sheds at the West India Docks was pointed out to me as worthy of attention, being a frame work of iron covered with slate. Another, I think at the London Docks, consists of sheets of what Mr Vaughn called corrugated iron; iron crimped like a lady's frill by which it is enabled to support a greater weight.—Of the vast stores collected in the Magazines of these Docks a great part are for exportation not home consumption, being brought to London as the centre of the world's commerce, to be circulated thence through other countries.——

The "**LONDON DOCKS**" Coolidge refers to were maintained by several different dock companies that merchants formed at the beginning of the nineteenth century in an effort to protect their commercial interests. By the end of the eighteenth century, the volume of shipping in and out of London had increased tremendously. The Thames River was clogged with ships, particularly between July and November, making navigation hazardous and delay unavoidable. The merchants had access to three small wet docks, primarily intended for fitting out and repairing ships, but there were no secure docks or warehouses for commerce. Goods awaiting transport to commercial outlets were often stored on smaller boats and barges, leaving them vulnerable to theft. By the 1790s the losses were estimated as high as £500,000 a year.

The West India Dock Act of 1799 and the London Dock Act of 1800 enabled the West India Company and the London Company to build their own legal quays and bonded warehouses, surrounded by walls, and to create their own private police forces. The **WEST INDIA** Docks, comprised of a thirty-acre import dock and a twenty-four-acre export dock, opened in 1802 and 1805 respectively, and the twenty-acre **LONDON** Dock opened in 1805. William Vaughan was a proponent of both companies and served as one of the directors of the latter. **ST. KATHERINE'S** Dock Company came along in 1828, and the East India Docks, which had opened in 1806, ultimately joined with the West India Docks in 1838. When the Coolidges visited, the river region stretching between the Tower of London and Blackwall was bustling and competition between the dock companies was fierce.

The **WINE VAULTS** of the London Docks were located beneath quay level and covered approximately twenty-two acres. According to even the earliest accounts, George, Duke of **CLARENCE** (1449–1478), was executed in the Tower of London on 18 February 1478 for treason against his brother Edward IV by being drowned in a butt of malmsey wine.

In addition to warehouses, **SHEDS** were constructed to facilitate the sorting, grading, and occasionally storing of merchandise. Initially, all of the sheds were made of wood, but by the 1820s structures of cast iron, slate, and brick had supplanted several of their precursors. Flaps could cover the sides to protect goods from the weather. The mahogany shed for the East Wood Wharf [**QUAI**] was particularly innovative for its time; conceived and constructed specifically to support great weight, it allowed for the use of heavy machinery, including specially designed, hand-operated "overhead travelling cranes" used to lift and move the heavy mahogany logs, some of which weighed as much as five tons (*ODNB*; *Survey of London*, vols. 43 and 44 [1994], 247–268, 300–310, 575–585; *Old and New London*, 2:117–121; Theo Barker, "Dockland: Origins and Earlier History," and Malcolm Tucker, "Warehouses in Dockland," in *Dockland: An Illustrated Historical Survey of*

Life and Work in East London [1986], 14–19, 21–27; Joseph G. Broodbank, *History of the Port of London* [1921], 1:91–110, 113–120, 153–162, 207; Samuel Leigh, *Leigh's New Picture of London; or, a View of the Political, Religious, Medical, Literary, Municipal, Commercial, and Moral State of the British Metropolis* [1830], 84–90, 97–99).

Tuesday. Dec. 11.

Made some morning calls and passed the evening at home.

Coolidge's travels around town generally kept her within a few miles of their rooms, but occasionally she ventured farther. In a letter of this same date to her sister Virginia, Coolidge described her fascination with the city: "My time is dawdled away I scarcely know how, but most unprofitably and I fear nothing will remain hereafter of my London winter but a blank in my memory. I have visited most of the shew places, the Tower, the Tunnel, The Museum, the National Gallery, &c &c. but nothing surprises me so much as the immense size of of this mammoth town. Such a wilderness of streets & houses it is impossible to form an idea of, and no individual object produces any thing like the effect upon my imagination which I experience from simply driving for two or three hours through the crouded thoroughfares of this vast metrolpolis of the civilised world. You may go on & on, street after street, square after square succeed interminably. There seems no escape, you are beset with human habitations, you literally travel through regions covered with houses and swarmi[ng] with the population of two millions which are here condensed within a circumference of about thirty five miles, such being the limits of London. I went yesterday to see the Docks and passed through the city as it is called in distinction from the town or westend. I had frequently been in the city before to see St Paul's, the Tower, the Tunnel &c but never penetrated so far in it's unknown regions. We drove through Wapping & what is called Lime house & Poplar, & I gazed in awe and admiration at the outlandish inhabitants, the tribes of uncouth barbarians who people these remote districts. The city is crowded & close, & the streets generally narrow & almost impassable from the throngs of human beings & vehicles of all descriptions carriages, carts, wagons, cabs, vans, which are constantly pouring through them. The town or westend is more spacious & open with wider, clearer streets and numerous squares set in turf & trees which have been well called the lungs of London; but the caprices of fashion confine the residence of fashionable people to a few particular spots, selected it appears to me in a very arbitrary manner, whilst a great many pleasant situations are condemned as utterly vulgar. Regent's Park the most beautiful part of London is under the ban, and the 'pays inconnus' the unknown regions of Russell Square, (one of the largest & finest squares in the town,) are so utterly beyond the pale of civilisation that a coachman of any fashion will hesitate to acknowledge his acquaintance with the road which leads to them" (Coolidge to Virginia J. Randolph Trist, 8–11 Dec. 1838 [NcU: Southern Historical Collection, Nicholas Philip Trist Papers]).

Wednesday. Dec. 12.

Went to see my dear boy at Highgate and found him thin, pale & home-sick. Came home out of spirits & unhappy. Had an appointment for Drury Lane Theatre & went reluctantly. The house is large & beautiful, the scenery good, but the piece, the Opera of William Tell poor & poorly got up. Van Amburgh and his Lions a wonderful exhibition, came after the Opera. There were two cages into which Van Amburgh entered suc-cessively. These were occupied by Lions, Tigers and other feline animals. What a degrading passion is Fear! The man has played the tyrant with these lordly monsters until he has brought them into a state so abject as to be pitiable. The Lion sneaks and crouches, the Tigers fawn and flatter. But a day of retribution may come. This seems to me the type of despotic government. The people, the beasts have the real power but they are un-conscious of it. They are strong, fierce and ignorant as Van Amburgh's tigers, and like them kept in subjection by an inferiour force. They are governed by the eye and by the lash, unwitting of how small avail these would be against their teeth and claws. But as there are two kinds of supe-riority, one of mere brute force and the other moral, Van Amburgh pos-sesses the latter and awes his terrible slaves as much by the might of his look, the calm resolute, threatening expression of his fixed eye as by the dread of his whip. But let him take heed and beware of the first symptoms of revolt, of revolution. Lions and Tigers, set free, will shed as much blood as French Jacobins. How fortunate for America, North America, that this comparison holds good in no one point for her. Her people have never been a fierce or warlike race, her government never one of force.

The Theatre Royal, **DRURY LANE**, first opened in 1663 under a patent granted by Charles II. Between 1791 and 1794 Henry Holland (1754–1806) rebuilt Drury Lane, demolishing Christopher Wren's 1674 structure. Holland's theater, which burnt to the ground in February 1809, was replaced with a new, even grander structure designed by Benjamin Dean Wyatt and enhanced in 1822 by Samuel Beazley (1786–1851). This is the structure that Coolidge describes (*ODNB*; *Survey of London*, vol. 35 [1970], 30–39; Iain Mackintosh, "Departing Glories of the Brit-ish Theatre: Setting Suns over a Neo-Classical Landscape," in *London—World City*, 199–203).

Guillaume Tell [**WILLIAM TELL**], Gioachino Rossini's last opera, was to a libretto by Étienne de Jouy and Hippolyte-Louis-Florent Bis and was first performed at the Paris Opera in August 1829. Set in the fourteenth century and based on Friedrich von Schiller's play *Wilhelm Tell*, the opera presents the love story of Arnold, the son of the Swiss leader, and the Austrian princess Mathilde against the backdrop of Switzerland's struggle for independence from Austria. Rossini's opera opened at Drury Lane on 3 December, coincidentally the same night that Schiller's play was performed at Covent Garden (*New Grove Dictionary of Opera* [1992], s.v. "Guillaume Tell"; *Times* [London], 3, 23 Dec. 1838).

Isaac A. VAN AMBURGH (ca. 1811–1865), animal tamer and showman, was born in Fishkill, New York. In the early 1830s he was employed by the Zoological Institute in New York as "keeper of the lions," and he had begun performing with the animals by 1837. In the summer of 1838 Van Amburgh and his menagerie of lions, leopards, tigers, and other animals traveled to Europe and opened at Astley's Amphitheatre in London in late August; the "exhibition" became part of the program at Drury Lane a few months later. During his performance Van Amburgh entered a large cage where "he amused himself, his assistants, and the spectators, by causing the animals to jump on his back, apparently to attack him in the most ferocious manner, to simulate the most furious intentions, yet stop short in the climax of their fury, and become obedient to his voice and gestures." Van Amburgh also brought small children and lambs into the cages, thrust his head and arms into the animals' mouths, encouraged their roars and barks, and ended the program by feeding them fresh meat from a local butcher. Of his methods Van Amburgh explained, "they believe that I have power to tear every one of them in pieces if they do not act as I say. I tell them so, and have frequently enforced it with a heavy crow bar." Queen Victoria attended several of the Drury Lane performances, once going on stage to watch as the animals were fed. The queen commissioned a portrait by Sir Edwin Landseer that depicts Van Amburgh reclining in the center of a large cage next to a lamb and surrounded on all sides by his lounging felines. After his successful tour in England and France, Van Amburgh returned to America in 1845 and continued performing throughout the country before his sudden, but natural, death in Philadelphia (Van Amburgh and Company, *A Brief Biographical Sketch of I. A. Van Amburgh, and an Illustrated and Descriptive History of the Animals Contained in the Menagerie* [1860], 9–17; Brenda Assael, *The Circus and Victorian Society* [2005], 66–68; Nigel Rothfels, *Savages and Beasts: The Birth of the Modern Zoo* [2002], 158–160, 239; William Toynbee, ed., *Diaries of William Charles Macready, 1833–1851* [1912], 1:492–493; *New York Herald*, 28 Jan. 1837; *Times* [London], 24 Aug., 11, 19 Sept. 1838; *Daily National Intelligencer* [Washington, D.C.], 11 Oct. 1838; *Boston Daily Advertiser*, 2 Dec. 1865; Edwin Landseer, *Isaac van Amburgh and His Animals* [1839], Royal Collection, accessed 20 Dec. 2010, http://www.royalcollection.org.uk/eGallery/).

Thursday 13. December.

Went by previous agreement ^between ourselves^ to Deville. He examined Mr Coolidge's head and mine, and gave our characters in a manner that surprised me. He could not possibly have known any thing about us. We are two grains of sand in the vast desert of London, wafted thither by winds from a distance. Our names, our histories present and past, our position in society, our occupations and pursuits must have been as absolutely unknown to Deville when we entered his room, as had we been inhabitants of another planet. Being a shrewd man he might make some observations very rapidly & draw some conclusions, but none which could bring him near the point which he at once attained, in knowledge of our qualities moral & intellectual, by passing his hands a few times over our heads. We came in our own carriage from which he might derive some idea of our standing in the world. Dress, manners, countenance, tones of voice, modes of expression might throw some farther light upon what we were by fortune and education, but he laid his hands upon my head with a firm but gentle pressure and told me many of the secrets of my own character. My strength & my weakness, my dispositions, tastes and habits were laid down with extraordinary accuracy. It was the same with Mr C., though in a less remarkable degree.

Deville afterwards went round his rooms with us pointing out and explaining the plaster casts of heads (of which he has many hundreds,) and shewing the changes which take place in the form of the scull, even at advanced periods of life, when the individual makes a decided change in his habits and pursuits. Some parts expand, others recede, the forehead advances or retreats, the crown of the head looms large or small, rising or sinking, and that in a space of time proportionate to the efforts of the individual and the progress of his improvement moral or intellectual. On the other hand his deterioration, the increasing influence of his propensities, the diminished influence of his sentiments and of his intellect are marked on the skull with equal precision. Deville has as many as six casts taken from one head at different times of life and under differing circumstances. This change which takes place in the shape of the head rescues Phrenology from the charge of interfering with the free will of man; as it is not the skull that controuls the brain, but the operations of the brain which mould it's covering. The use of Phrenology is therefore to give us a clearer insight into our own characters. We may flatter and deceive ourselves in many ways, misunderstand our own motives, mistake our capacities and close our eyes to the evil effects of our tendencies and habits, but Phrenology sets them before us, shews in what degree our moral & intellectual faculties are losing power and preponderance, whilst the animal propensities are acquiring strength and development and threatening to overpower the better part of our nature. Phrenology is of importance in education as giving a key to the character of the child and enabling the parent or instructor to adopt the best means for counteracting the evil and carrying the good to perfection. It also shews what particular talents may be cultivated with success, and what deficiencies are likely to impede the progress if not altogether disappoint the efforts to attain excellence in a department for which there is no proper vocation. "Far be it from me," says Deville, "to assert that all tendencies may not be overcome and all deficiencies supplied by time and perseverance, or that any body may not become any thing; but much time & trouble may be saved by ascertaining what are the facilities and what the difficulties of the task." If one boy may acquire with ease in two years, what would occupy another, with pain and discouragement, six, it is surely worth while to direct their pursuits accordingly; and in the choice of a profession, to fix upon one for which the moral & intellectual qualities are well adapted, rather than another which perhaps requires exactly the powers possessed by the individual in an inferiour degree. Certainly, from what Deville told me of my own character, I should attach some importance to any advice he might give me touching the bringing up of a child, and I will, if I can, get him to examine my boy Jefferson's head. He has a very decided character of his own, which I have made my study, and if Deville's phrenological observations completed in five minutes, agree with what it has taken me seven years to ascertain, & that perhaps imperfectly, I shall at once be confirmed in my judgment with regard to my child and my faith in Phrenology.

Deville is an uneducated man speaking the Cockney dialect, transposing his vs, & ws, but very clear and sensible in conversation, giving a good account of his system and with less of cant or affectation than I have ever known in a phrenologist. He is small and looks like an operative, plain in appearance and with a benevolent countenance. Full of faith in his own art and discoursing upon it "con amore." He has a long room full of busts (many of them from the antique) and casts. These as I have said he likes to point out & explain, shewing the development of the organs and the changes wrought by time and circumstances, neglect or cultivation. Here he has a Malibran with the organs necessary for musical excellence developed in an extraordinary degree, forming an actual protuberance on the skull, and by her side the cast taken from a blind girl who had a positive dislike to music, an aversion to it's sounds, where there is a sensible depression in the same part of the head. Altogether I passed three hours very pleasantly at Deville's rooms. He is by trade a lampseller, and I believe a lampmaker and has a shop in the Strand. To reach his Museum of casts you have to pass through a room filled with lamps which, when he sells, he goes to your house and hangs himself.

The fault I found with Deville was that he seemed to want firmness in declaring the faults of a character. He rather indicates than insists upon, tells you what to guard against but uses no forcible language in describing your defects. Perhaps this may be explained by the fact that he seems to consider no propensity as evil in itself, and only to become evil by excess, by undue development. He says "the good God has made nothing bad"—we are only to take care that we make the proper use of his gifts both for ourselves and for those who depend upon us. My own character as given verbally by him and written down by Mr Coolidge, I must study a little. I think I shall find that although he considers my organization a good one there is quite enough of weakness and imperfection indicated if not enlarged upon. I have only to pursue the subject, see to what consequences these faults may lead, to what growth they have already attained, and I may discover that Mr Deville has not been so backward in telling me "mes verités" as I may have at first supposed. He told me too of a great many dispositions which it were a breach of trust not to cultivate; of powers of loving & doing good which it will be from my own supineness if they are not called into action. He put me on my honour where my virtures are concerned, and on my conscience with regard to my defects. At least this is the use I may make, if I please, of his words, his disclosures, and his admonitions.

_____

James DEVILLE (1777–1846) was a lampmaker, sculptor, and phrenologist who apprenticed with a plasterer and began creating plaster casts from John Flaxman's molds in his own shop in Soho. In the first decade of the nineteenth century, Deville began making lamps, and by 1816 he had begun building lamps for lighthouses. He became a member of the Institution of Civil Engineers, where he met founder Bryan Donkin (1768–1855), inventor and engineer. In 1817 Donkin approached Deville with the idea of creating phrenological postmortem casts to be used for the instruction and dissemination of that "new philosophy," but Deville did not develop a personal interest in phrenology until 1821. About this time he perfected a method for taking casts from living subjects and became an expert "head-reader," possessing "more quickness and tact as a manipulator" than anyone practicing at that time. His collection of casts and skulls numbered in the thousands and included artists, performers, authors, politicians, mathematicians, and scientists, as well as convicted criminals and the insane. He also tracked cranial changes over time, taking casts from the same individuals throughout life beginning in childhood. He lectured and published frequently, and his expertise in the subject generally compensated for his apparent lack of formal education. Very much sought after, particularly in the 1840s, Deville included among his clientele Harriet Martineau, Charles Bray, George Eliot, Richard Carlile, the Duke of Wellington, and Prince Albert. His shop was located at 367 The Strand (Roger Cooter,

The Cultural Meaning of Popular Science: Phrenology and the Organization of Consent in Nineteenth-Century Britain [1984], 208, 279-280; David de Giustino, *Conquest of Mind: Phrenology and Victorian Social Thought* [1975], 94–97; *Phrenological Journal of Science and Health* 92 [1891]: 109–112; *Phrenological Journal, and Magazine of Moral Science* 19 [1846]: 329–344; Frederic Kelly, *Post Office London Directory, 1843*, 159; J. Pigot & Company, *Pigot & Co.'s Directory of London for 1839*, 145).

Maria Felicia **MALIBRAN** (1808–1836), mezzo-soprano, was part of a celebrated musical dynasty. Malibran made her London debut in Gioachino Rossini's *Il Barbiere di Siviglia* in June 1825, and in October of that year she traveled to New York to introduce Italian opera to American audiences. Her extraordinary voice and passionate acting style made her an icon of the Romantic era. In September 1836, at the height of her career, she appeared at the Manchester festival but became seriously ill one night following her performance. Her husband, violinist Charles de Bériot (1802–1870), dismissed the three local doctors attending her and sent for Malibran's homeopathic doctor from London. Malibran died of unknown causes in her room at the Mosley Arms Hotel nine days later. Her husband permitted only a simple funeral, adamantly opposed a postmortem examination, and successfully fought for her exhumation and reinterment in Brussels several months later, all events that added to Malibran's mystique (*ODNB*; April FitzLyon, *Maria Malibran: Diva of the Romantic Age* [1987]; Howard Bushnell, *Maria Malibran: A Biography of the Singer* [1979]).

Two death masks were taken of Malibran, one by William Bally, sculptor and phrenologist, who used it together with sketches he made of her during her Manchester appearance to create a medallion portrait. This mask is held by the Henry Watson Music Library, Manchester Central Library. Malibran's husband made the other mask, which has been copied at least twice; Princeton University holds one copy, originally obtained by the collector Laurence Hutton and subsequently given to the university, and the Bibliothèque du Conservatoire royal de Bruxelles holds the other. It is unknown whether Deville's cast was a copy of one of these masks or another that he had made from Malibran in life, as he had occasionally done with other artists (*ODNB*; Cooter, *Cultural Meaning of Popular Science*, 274; Georg Kolbe and Margaret M. Green, *Undying Faces: A Collection of Death Masks* [1929], 98; Laurence Hutton, *Portraits in Plaster: From the Collection of Laurence Hutton* [1894], 53–54; *Musical Times* 50, no. 796 [1909]: 369; "Malibran, Maria Felicia, death mask," *Laurence Hutton Collection of Life and Death Masks (C0770): A Pictorial Guide by John Delaney* [2003], Department of Rare Books and Special Collections, Princeton University Library, accessed 21 June 2011, http://library.princeton.edu/libraries/firestone/rbsc/aids/C0770/l-o.html).

Friday. 14. Dec.

Yesterday after my visit to Deville, I dined with a pleasant pair, a brother and sister of the name of Robertson in Park Square. They are Scotch and the Scotch have more amiable manners than the English, more frank and cordial—they are not so terribly afraid of committing themselves. Mr Robertson has been in China. His sister, living in London, seems to sigh for Scotland. She remembers the heather.

To-day I have been to Clapton to see Maria Glass. Hers is a sad story. Poverty, disappointment and bereavement. Mr Heard has visited my boy whom he finds dissatisfied rather than unhappy. Poor, dear little fellow! I sent him yesterday a book of stories from antient history which I bought from Hursts, Corner of St. Paul's Church.

MR ROBERTSON and his sister have not been identified.

F. HURST was a bookseller and publisher at 5 St. Paul's Church Yard (Tallis, part 46).

Saturday. 15 Dec.

——We have been to-day at Leslie's house in Pine Apple Row. Being admitted to his painting room we saw the Coronation picture in a very unfinished state but promising well. The moment chosen is the taking of the Sacrament. The Queen, divested of her crown and ornaments, her dress concealed by an outer garment of pure white cambric over which is the Dalmatic robe of heavy embroidered satin almost an orange colour, is on her knees before the Primate, Archbishop of Canterbury, who holds in his hand, the consecrated elements. Eight young ladies of noble families, trainbearers, dressed alike, in white, form a group behind the Queen who is seen in profile, her young head bowed low & meekly down and her countenance noble and full of solemn thought, in fine contrast with the fair, girlish faces of her young attendants, who look pleased in their office & their conspicuous station and, devoid of all anxiety except the small care of performing a part in the pageant. The Mistress of the Robes, the Duchess of Sutherland, stands proud in velvet and ermine, Lord Palmerstone with the Sword of State has in Leslie's picture, a finer face than nature gave him—The Duke of Wellington is, as yet, merely sketched, the Duchess of Kent seated in the royal box, leans forward with an air of gratified pride tinged with care.

Leslie told us some anecdotes of the Coronation. The Ring made by the Court Jeweller was intended for the little finger; when it was to be put on the Archbishop insisted on pressing it upon the third finger for which it was manifestly too small. The consequence was pain and inconvenience to the Queen and difficulty in taking the ring off. It seems doubtful whether the Jeweller or the Primate were in the wrong. The expression in the Rubric is "the fourth finger," — The Archbishop counting from & including the thumb, & the Jeweller beginning with the fore finger, caused a diversity of opinion & it's unpleasant result. As the same artist had executed the coronation rings of George 4th & William 4th, he probably was in the right. In any case it was manifestly wrong to inflict a torture like the thumb screw on the sacred person of her little Majesty the very day of her coronation. ——

I have been suffering all day with feverish headache & shall go to bed early. Mr Coolidge dines at the Traveller's Club.

Charles Robert LESLIE (1794–1859), painter and author, was born in London to a Philadelphia clockmaker. When the family returned to Philadelphia in 1799, Leslie's education began at a school in New Jersey and continued at the University of Pennsylvania from 1804 to 1808. Leslie's talent became apparent during an internship with Philadelphia publisher Samuel T. Bradford of Bradford & Inskeep. Bradford, who was director of the Pennsylvania Academy of the Fine Arts, took a personal interest in cultivating Leslie as an artist. The academy hung some of Leslie's work in its 1811 exhibition, accepted him as a pupil, and facilitated his education in London. With a letter of introduction from portraitist Thomas Sully, Leslie arrived in London in 1811 to attend the Royal Academy under the instruction of Benjamin West, then its president. Leslie worked in portraiture, as well as in the literary and history genres, and at the urging of Washington Irving, he illustrated the *History of New York* and *The Sketch Book*. By 1820 Leslie's career was well underway and he determined to remain in London, a decision that he reaffirmed after a brief stint as a teacher of drawing at the Military Academy of West Point in the winter of 1833–1834. With the assistance of his patrons Henry Richard Fox, third Baron Holland, and Lady Holland, Leslie attended the coronation of Queen Victoria. He returned to his studio and immediately began his work entitled *Queen Victoria Receiving the Sacrament after the Coronation* (fig. 22) (*ANB*; *DAB*; *ODNB*; Charles Robert Leslie, *Autobiographical Recollections* [1860]; Allan Cunningham, *The Lives of the Most Eminent British Painters* [1880], 3:338–362; Henry Minton Cundall, *English Painters of the Georgian Era. Hogarth to Turner* [1876], 81–88).

William Howley (1766–1848) was ARCHBISHOP of Canterbury from 1828 until his death. The queen's EIGHT YOUNG LADIES were Lady Caroline Amelia Gordon-Lennox (1819–1890), Lady Adelaide Paget (1821–1890), Lady Mary Alethea Beatrix Talbot (1815–1858), Lady Francis Elizabeth Cowper (1820–1880), Lady Catherine Lucy Wilhelmina Stanhope (1819–1901), Lady Anne Wentworth Fitzwilliam (d. 1879), Lady Louisa Harriet Jenkinson (1815–1887), and Lady Mary Augusta Frederica Grimston (1820–1879). All were dressed in white satin with an overlay of silver tissue trimmed with pink roses and wore wreathes of pink roses in their hair. The DUCHESS OF SUTHERLAND was Harriet Elizabeth Georgiana Leveson-Gower (1806–1868). As mistress of the robes, the duchess served as head of the queen's female household. Coolidge misidentified Henry John Temple, Lord Palmerston (1784–1865); it was actually William Lamb, Lord Melborne (1779–1848), prime minister, who bore the SWORD OF STATE. The ruby RING, the *London Gazette* reported, was placed by the archbishop on "the fourth finger of the Queen's right hand," but Queen Victoria recorded the following in her journal: "The Archbishop had (most awkwardly) put the ring on the wrong finger, and the consequence was that I had the greatest difficulty to take it off again, which I at last did with great pain" (*ODNB*; Benson and Brett, *Letters of Queen Victoria*, 1:145–146, 153–160; *London Gazette*, supplement, 4 July 1838).

Sunday. 16. Dec.

Did not rise until nearly one o'clock having passed a bad night. Mr Sindry with his sister and his uncle Mr Davis called to see me. Mr C. went to Highgate to see our boy. He found him thin, hollow-eyed and with a subdued air. The child complains of no unkindness or neglect but seems to pine and droop. This must not be. There is something wrong in the atmosphere that he breathes. The natural state of a child is one of health and happiness, and discontent indicates disease of body or mind, or both. I have heard that the first going to school, the first absence from home with it's comforts and affections, is a severe trial. Perhaps this is what my poor little boy is now undergoing. His particular character probably makes him suffer even more than another might do. His aunt Mary, who has had him under her care during the summer and part of the autumn, and whose perception of character is singularly quick and her judgment very accurate, says in speaking of him—"I never saw any one who without being at all diffident, had such a dislike to new persons and new habits as he has—any thing like change is distasteful to him, and the transplanting him from his nursery in Bowdoin St. to Edgehill was a pretty severe trial to a child of his disposition. He did not take to any body though everybody was kind to him and inclined to pet him." —I sent him another book full of pictures of animals with what seemed to me a clear interesting account of each. But if at the end of another week he does not become more reconciled, I think we must make a change

Mr C. read aloud to Mr Heard and myself part of Carlyle's article (an old one) on Voltaire. Carlyle is an obscure writer—deep perhaps, but turbid. I grow old and lazy and averse to trouble and do not like to tax my powers of comprehension too heavily. I am apt to be suspicious too of an author who affects profundity and prefers obscurity. There are many fine striking thoughts in all of Carlyle's writings, and I get more and more reconciled to picking them out from the general mass which I leave to more patient scrutanizers. His late article on Lockhart's Life of Scott is the best thing of his that I have ever read. — I am writing this on monday morning whilst waiting for the carriage in which I am to go out.

John Francis DAVIS, first baronet (1795–1890), colonial governor and author, began his career with the East India Company in Canton in 1813 and by 1832 was that factory's president. In 1834 Davis was appointed Britain's superintendent of trade; he resigned less than a year later but took the role up again in 1844 and returned to Canton. Within two weeks of his return he was made governor and commander-in-chief of Hong Kong. The British entry into Canton, a condition of the 1842 Treaty of Nanking, had still not been granted by 1846, and hostilities between the residents of Hong Kong and the British merchants were escalating. Davis sent an armed force to capture some of the ports and factories, forcing imperial commissioner Qiying to capitulate by opening Canton, punishing those responsible for the aggression, and acknowledging Britain's right to construct warehouses. But Davis's heavy-handed style and resistance to the promotion of free trade resulted in political censure and his resignation. He returned to London in late 1847 and continued to publish works on China, as well as translations of Chinese poetry, literature, and plays. Oxford University awarded him the degree of Doctor of Civil Law in 1876, and Davis endowed a Chinese scholarship there the following year. He married first Emily Humfrays (d. 1866) and second Lucy Ellen Rocke (d. 1904), and the baronetcy passed to the son of his second marriage (*ODNB*; Burke and Burke, *Peerage and Baronetage*, 579–580; *Times* [London], 14 Nov. 1890).

Thomas CARLYLE'S review of *Mémoires sur Voltaire* was first published in the *Foreign Review, and Continental Miscellany* in 1829 and subsequently included in the second volume of his *Critical and Miscellaneous Essays*, published in Boston in 1838. Carlyle's review of John Gibson Lockhart's *Memoirs of the Life of Sir Walter Scott, Baronet* first appeared in the *London and Westminster Review* in January 1838 (pp. 293–345) and was included in volume 5 of his *Essays* in 1839.

Monday. Dec. 17.

Called on Miss Sindry, Miss Robertson, Mrs Searle, Mrs Atkinson, Mrs Stevenson, Mrs Bates, — of whom some were in & some out. In the evening Mr C. and Mr Higginson took turns to read aloud the first half of Miss Beecher's Letter on Abolitionism.——

Sarah Coles STEVENSON (1789–1848) (fig. 26) was born at Enniscorthy, the Coles' family estate in Albemarle County, Virginia, just a few miles from Monticello. The Coles were first cousins to Dolley Madison. Stevenson's brother Isaac (1780–1841) served as secretary to Thomas Jefferson during his presidency and remained a close friend throughout Jefferson's life. Her other brother, Edward (1786–1868), was James Madison's secretary and also corresponded with Jefferson, most notably in 1814 about a plan to eradicate slavery and his own immediate intentions to free his slaves.

Sally Coles married Andrew Stevenson (1784–1857) (fig. 27) in 1816, and Coolidge was well acquainted with the couple and knew of the tragic accidental death of the Stevensons' young daughter, their only child. Andrew Stevenson had been serving as the American minister to the Court of St. James's for two years by the time of the Coolidges' arrival, and Sally Stevenson was well established in London's literary, political, and artistic circles. She was a regular attendee at Queen Victoria's drawing room receptions and reported on her activities in over a hundred letters sent home during her five-year stay in England.

Sally Stevenson introduced the Coolidges into London society. In a letter to her niece Sarah Rutherford, Stevenson commented on her own sense of accomplishment at the success of Ellen Coolidge's reception: "Ellen has rather taken here. The desire to see Mr Jefferson's Granddaughter extends to all classes— torys & radicals & I whisper around, very like him—educated by him, &c, &c, She seems very grateful to me for the trouble I have taken for her, which has been—not a little—to get even Mr Jefferson's G.D. into society here, without any letters, or aid but what I have been able to give her, has been the means of taking me out much more than I should otherwise have gone. She goes to many of the places without Mr. Coolidge—& seems much at her ease, she has the repose of manner which is so English, & great self possession—with an air of modesty & sweetness. . . . [S]he comes to me for every thing, & I often laugh, & ask her how she thinks I have got on here without any one to tell me any thing—one of the strongest feelings of pleasure I have had in my success with Ellen is the assurance of my own strength—I feel now I can present whom I please, for many have said when I asked permission to present the granddaughter of Mr. J—'If she is your friend Mrs. S—that is sufficient.'"

Coolidge wrote to her sister Virginia, "if Mrs Stevenson was my own sister she could not be kinder or more solicitous to promote my comfort and enjoyment. . . . I really feel genuine gratitude to Mrs Stevenson for her attentions— I have no claim upon her and can in no way contribute to her well-being in England or else where, so that I give her credit for being actuated by no earthly motive but kind-heartedness and recollections of auld lang syne, when we were country neighbours and friends." The Stevensons returned to America in 1841, making their home at the Retreat, an estate near Richmond, Virginia (*ANB*; *DAB*; Boykin, *Mrs. Stevenson*; Wayland, *Andrew Stevenson*, 199–210; William B. Coles, *The Coles Family of Virginia: Its Numerous Connections, from the Emigration to America to the Year 1915* [1931], 123–141; *PTJRS*, 7:503–504, 702–704; Coolidge to Dolley Madison, ca. 30 Sept. 1822, in *The Dolley Madison Digital Edition*, ed. Holly Schulman [2009], The University of Virginia Press, accessed 20 Dec. 2010, http:// rotunda.upress.virginia.edu:8080/dmde/; Stevenson to Emily Coles Rutherford,

4 Feb., 8 Apr. 1839, Stevenson to Sarah Rutherford, 23 Feb. 1839 [NcD: Sarah Coles Stevenson Papers]; Coolidge to Virginia J. Randolph Trist, 14 Feb. 1839 [NcU: Southern Historical Collection, Nicholas Philip Trist Papers]; *Richmond Whig and Public Advertiser*, 4 Jan. 1848; J[ohn] Johns, *An Address Delivered in St. Paul's Church, Richmond, on the Fourth of January 1848, on the occasion of the Funeral of Mrs. Sarah Coles Stevenson, wife of the Hon. Andrew Stevenson* [1848]).

Catherine Esther Beecher (1800–1878) was an American author, educator, and reformer who published her LETTER ON ABOLITIONISM, otherwise entitled *An Essay on Slavery and Abolitionism, with reference to the Duty of American Females,* in 1837. Beecher advocated change away from "ornamental" female education, challenged the inaccessibility of higher education for women, and encouraged greater domestic influence and control for married women (*ANB; DAB*).

Tuesday. 18th

Just returned from the Dulwich Gallery. The day dark, cold and raw. My attention was turned principally to Murillo's paintings of which there are many. An exquisite Flower Girl, a true Spanish face, black eyes and most bewitching expression of youth, gaiety and archness. She offers her flowers (which are contained in one corner of her Scarf or Mantilla) with a look which no one could resist. The complexion is dark and mellow, the lips full and slightly apart with a smile, the cheeks also full, the whole person plump, the hands evidently those of one who does not sit with them gloved all day, but beautiful in the peasant style. I have never seen any thing of Murillo that I liked so much. There are also two groups of peasant boys by the same artist which I thought charming. One consists of two boys and a dog, the other two boys and a black man in the back ground. In the first, one of the boys is seated and looks up, (with a roguish smile which shews his teeth and a dimple,) at the other who has a mouth-ful of bread just bitten from a large piece in his hand.

An "Assumption of the Virgin" by Murillo, (the mother seated with the infant in her arms and two or three angels in the fore ground;) and a "Christ the good Shepherd," a beautiful boy with a flock of sheep, and with that peculiar countenance which Murillo always gives to the Saviour, are in this same collection. I staid but a short time as we went late and the Gallery closes at three, and I confined my attention to the Murillos—not so entirely however, as not to look long and earnestly at Sir Joshua Reynold's fine picture of Mrs Siddons in the character of the Tragic Muse. I observed also a piece by Gerard Dow, an old woman eating porridge, which I thought excellent. The ground is dark and the figure with it's tawny face and white cap, has something of the "fine golden hue" of Rembrandt's mother. Several coarse pieces by Rubens, and especially a beastly Sampson shorn by a Moll Brazen Dalilah, and Venus disgustingly fat made love to by a Mars with the air of a trooper, completed the dislike I have always felt for this gross and sensual painter. I have seen nothing by Rubens, except his "Daniel in the Lions' den," at Hamilton Palace, that gave me any feeling but disgust. — There is in the Dulwich Gallery, a portrait of William Linley by Lawrence which I like, and a young Samuel by Sir Joshua in which I was disappointed. ——

To-day my hair has been dressed by my new french maid, Josephine, who has lived three years with the Marchioness of Wellesley, which proves her to have some skill. Smith, my old English maid, a smooth, civil, dexterous rascal, whose manners are perfect in their respectful obsequiousness, goes away reluctantly after pillaging me for five months. She will not easily find such another "spoon" as I have been, and I shall know better hereafter than to be "done" as she has been "doing me" in regard to my money and her time, out of both which she has cheated me to her heart's content.

The Dulwich College Picture GALLERY was designed by Sir John Soane to house a collection of paintings donated to the college by Joseph Desenfans (1744–1807), art collector and dealer, and Sir Francis Bourgeois (1756–1811), artist. Gustav Waagen, who described the collection Coolidge saw, found the 355 paintings arranged well in five top-lit apartments, but he thought that the collection was highly overrated: "Much that is excellent is mixed with so much that is indifferent and quite worthless." Still Waagen found some works to praise, including one of Coolidge's favorites, the *Flower Girl* by Bartolomé Esteban MURILLO (ca. 1617–1682) (fig. 23). Waagen described it as "a choice example of the very peculiar contrasts and accords of colours, by which many of Murillo's pictures have such a magical effect" (*ODNB;* Waagen, *Works of Art*, 2:378–390).

Sir Joshua REYNOLDS (1723–1792), artist, favored classical poses and was one of the most sought-after portraitists of the eighteenth century. *The Tragic Muse* (1783–1784), his well-known allegorical portrait of the actress Sarah Kemble SIDDONS (1755–1831), depicts her seated upon a throne flanked by figures representing Pity and Terror (*ODNB;* Turner, *Dictionary of Art*, 26:270–282; Benezit, *Dictionary of Artists*, 11:946–949).

Gerard, or Gerrit, Dou [DOW] (1613–1675), an early student of Rembrandt, was admired for his use of color, balance of light and dark, attention to texture, and ability to capture daily life. Dulwich's *Old Woman Eating* was attributed to Dou until 1905 (Turner, *Dictionary of Art*, 9:192–195; Benezit, *Dictionary of Artists*, 4:1100–1103; Ronni Baer, Annetje Boersma, and Arthur K. Wheelock, *Gerrit Dou, 1613–1675: Master Painter in the Age of Rembrandt* [2000]).

Waagen also admired the portrait of **WILLIAM LINLEY** (1771–1835), author and composer, done by Sir Thomas **LAWRENCE** (1769–1830), writing, "it is so pleasing and refined in the simplicity of nature, so true in the colouring, so careful in the execution, that perhaps very few of his celebrated later pictures might bear a comparison with it" (*ODNB*; Waagen, *Works of Art*, 2:389–390).

JOSEPHINE DeVaux (b. ca. 1804), Coolidge's French maid, returned to America with the Coolidges and accompanied Ellen on her voyage to China in 1839 (Ship's Manifest for the *Quebec*, 15 May 1839, Ancestry.com; Coolidge to Augustine Heard, 5 Oct. 1839 [MH: Heard Family Papers]; Joseph Coolidge to Nicholas Philip Trist, 2 Apr. 1839 [NcU: Southern Historical Collection, Nicholas Philip Trist Papers]).

The **MARCHIONESS OF WELLESLEY** was Marianne Caton Patterson (d. 1853), granddaughter of Charles Carroll of Carrollton (1737–1832), longest-living signer of the United States Declaration of Independence. Her first husband, Baltimore merchant Robert Patterson, died before 1825; she later became the second wife of Richard Colley Wellesley (1760–1842), Marquess Wellesley, elder brother to the Duke of Wellington (*ANB*; *ODNB*; Ronald Hoffman, *Princes of Ireland, Planters of Maryland: A Carroll Saga, 1500–1783* [2000], 390; Thomas Meagher Field, *Unpublished Letters of Charles Carroll of Carrollton, and of His Father, Charles Carroll of Doughoregan* [1902], 197–210).

SPOON: slang or colloquialism for a shallow, simple, or foolish person (*OED*).

Thursday. 20ᵗʰ Dec.

Yesterday the 19ᵗʰ we dined at Mʳ Bates' with a party consisting of Sam Rogers the poet, his sister, Miss Rogers, Judge Haliburton better known as Sam Slick, the Mexican & Sardinian ministers, Mʳ Van der Weyer the Belgian minister, Mʳ Senior the political Economist, & Mʳ Tom Baring the Merchant. These with Miss Richards, Mʳ Coolidge & myself completed the number, making with Mʳ, Mʳˢ & Miss Bates, a party of fourteen.

Mʳ Rogers lead me to dinner—he grows old and sapless—withered in person and his conversation no longer equal in brilliancy to his reputation—his stories and bonmots are "passés" like himself. He says that Americans do wrong in devoting too much time to the country in England & too little to London—that London is better worth seeing than England—that it contains more objects of curiosity and interest. I could not agree with him and wondered at such opinions from a poet. Is Rogers a poet? I know that the Pleasures of Memory is written in rhyme, but is it poetry? I read it, or parts of it, in very early youth but have scarce looked in it since. I did not like it much then and doubt if I should like it better now, but I will send to the Library for it and see if it gives me a new impression. Miss Rogers is a plump, elderly lady in black. The Sardinian minister lively and chattering, the Mexican cold and taciturn, but he speaks no English which is a good reason for silence where neither the master nor mistress of the house speak french. Mr Senior has a voice like a pinched Rat. Judge Haliburton, a busy, American look. Staid till half past ten.

Samuel **ROGERS** (1763–1855), poet, banker, and art collector, initially intended to become a Presbyterian minister but instead entered into his father's banking business (fig. 9). Rogers developed a taste for poetry, favoring especially the works of Samuel Johnson and Thomas Gray, and began his own writing career with a few short essays published in the *Gentleman's Magazine*. The work most closely associated with Rogers was *The Pleasures of Memory*, a nostalgic exploration of places and people and the emotions that bind one to them. It first appeared in 1792 and by 1806 had gone through fifteen editions. Rogers's inheritance freed him for literary pursuits and socializing; he became famous for his success at both. Throughout his life his **SISTER** Sarah Rogers (ca. 1773–1855) was his favorite and frequent companion (*ODNB*; Richard Ellis Roberts, *Samuel Rogers and His Circle* [1910]; *Morning Chronicle* [London], 1 Feb., 19, 31 Dec. 1855; *Times* [London], 2 Feb., 19 Dec. 1855).

Thomas Chandler **HALIBURTON** (1796–1865), lawyer, judge, politician, and author, was born in Nova Scotia. Although he became a judge in Annapolis, Nova Scotia, he was best known for his satirical columns in the *Novascotian* newspaper, particularly *Recollections of Nova Scotia: The Clockmaker, or, The Sayings and Doings of Samuel Slick, of Slickville*, which first began appearing in the paper in 1835. Haliburton's character Sam Slick was an itinerant clock peddler who embodied the industrious, but vain and opportunistic, American. Slick's observations on "human natur," with every incident or conversation serving as a social or political commentary, were so popular that the anecdotes were extended and published in book form in Canada, America, and England. His visit to England in 1838 came at the height of his celebrity (*ODNB*; Richard A. Davies, *Inventing Sam Slick: A Biography of Thomas Chandler Haliburton* [2005], esp. 69–80; Richard A. Davies, ed., *The Letters of Thomas Chandler Haliburton* [1988], 86–90, 101–102).

The **MEXICAN** minister was Juan Nepomuceno Almonte (1803–1869). He served as aide-de-camp to Antonio López de Santa Anna and was with Santa Anna at the Battle of the Alamo when it fell to the Mexican Army on 6 March 1836. Taken prisoner following the Battle of San Jacinto on 21 April 1836, Almonte was incarcerated for a time on Galveston Island. He and Santa Anna met with Pres. Andrew Jackson over the course of several days in January 1837, after which both men were returned to Mexico. In March 1838 Almonte was appointed secretary of the Mexican legation in London, and in June 1839 he headed up the legation in Belgium. He was serving as Mexican minister plenipotentiary in Washington, D.C., from 1841 to 1845, under Pres. José Joaquin de Herrera, when diplomatic relations were broken in the prelude to the Mexican-American War; he returned to the United States as minister in 1853. Almonte was educated in New Orleans and spoke French (*Biographical Encyclopedia of Texas* [1880], 265–266; Jack Jackson, ed., and John Wheat, trans., *Almonte's Texas: Juan N. Almonte's 1834 Inspection, Secret Report and Role in the 1836 Campaign* [2003], 443; Albert A. Nofi, *The Alamo and the Texas War for Independence, September 30, 1835 to April 21, 1836* [1992], 79; Richard G. Santos, *Santa Anna's Campaign against Texas, 1835–1836* [1981], vii, 60–99).

Count Nomis de Pollon (ca. 1798–1846), SARDINIAN minister, first came to England in 1819 when serving as an attaché to the Sardinian embassy in London. He was chargé d'affaires to the Netherlands from 1834 to 1837, after which he returned to England as envoy extraordinary and minister plenipotentiary, a post he retained the remainder of his life (*Gentleman's Magazine*, n.s., 27 [1847]: 205; Charles Beavan, *Reports of Cases in Chancery, Argued and Determined in the Rolls Court* [1852], 14:441–444).

Nassau William SENIOR (1790–1864), lawyer and political economist, was educated at Oxford and was the first to hold the Drummond chair of political economy there. He published on law and political economy. Senior's interest in economy stemmed from his desire to examine the causes of poverty, and he was a member of royal commissions that evaluated the Poor Laws, working conditions in factories, and remedies for poverty including education (*ODNB*).

Thomas BARING (1799–1873), banker and politician, was the son of Sir Thomas Baring (1772–1848) and grandson of Sir Francis Baring (1740–1810), all of the merchant banking firm Baring Brothers. Under the leadership of the younger Thomas Baring and Joshua Bates, Baring Brothers became London's leading trade finance and merchant house. Thomas Baring was largely responsible for the administrative side of the firm and known for his integrity. He was a Tory, contrary to family tradition, and first entered the House of Commons in 1835, serving intermittently until his death. Baring was a fellow of the Royal Society and the Royal Geographical Society, a trustee of the National Gallery, and an avid art collector, favoring Dutch seventeenth-century works. He never married and his substantial estate was divided among his extended family members after his death (*ODNB*; Ziegler, *Sixth Great Power*, 112–185; *Times* [London], 20, 24 Nov., 24, 31 Dec. 1873).

Friday 21.

Yesterday the 20th M[r] C & myself, with M[r] Heard & M[r] Higginson went to Bath House to see Lord Ashburton's pictures. The family is absent but M[r] Tom Baring procured admittance for us & had the pictures uncovered. It is a very fine collection. The best Dutch pictures I have ever seen. Teniers, Cuyp, Wouvermans, A. Ostade, Berghem, Vandervelde &c. The pictures are generally small and mostly landscape with familiar figures of Boars, women old & young, children, cattle &c &c, but to this rule there are many exceptions. There is a Wolf hunt by Rubens, very large and the finest thing, except "Daniel in the Lions' Den" I have ever seen by that painter. Some fine heads by Rembrandt, a large Murillo representing some Saint, when a child, giving away his clothes to poor children, to one his coat, to another his waistcoat—he holds fast to his pantaloons as if to resist the temptation of parting with them too. A Herodias with the head of St. John by Titian, I admired greatly. The dead head with it's calm features, its ashy hue & dishevelled hair is in strong contrast with the female figure full of life and animal beauty, but the expression of whose countenance is a compound of cruelty & the love of pleasure—that of a remorseless wanton. The Saint is her victim but triumphs over her even in death—for what a contrast between the sublime composure in his face and the proud perturbation of hers!—There are some beautiful things by Ostade—1st. A saint reading on his knees, the life of the Virgin. 2nd. A large country scene, a cottage & peasants with various accessories of rural life; a cart and horse, domestic animals and implements &c &c. 3d. The interiour of a Cottage with children, one child in a go-cart, another turning his face from a window, through which he has been looking, towards a little girl evidently anxious to obtain the same position. 4th A woman at a rustic window, overhung with Ivy and having a fat Dutch child in her arms. 5th A woman drinking from a large glass whilst a man holds a candle from which a strong red light is thrown on her face and his.

Among those pictures which attracted my attention were a sea-piece by Backhuysen, two flower & fruit pieces by Van Huysum, a small landscape of Wouvermans with an exquisite clump of trees, and one or two works of Vandervelde & Berghem.

Lord Ashburton's house is a fine one. It consists of a central Hall, the whole height of the house lighted from above, with a Gallery running all round upon which the rooms of the second story open. This hall is parquetted in oak and you pass from it into the various apartments of the lower story. One suite of three rooms runs along the front of the house & has windows looking out upon a flower garden which is between the house and the street. (Piccadilly.) Beyond you see the Green Park & the Queen's Palace. To the left of the Hall is the great entrance from without with a broad flight of steps to the Court below, and on the right a door opens upon a grand stairway leading to the upper stories. The dining room & Library, or Lord Ashburton's study, occupy the side of the house opposite the three drawing rooms & on the other side of the great Hall. The offices are at the back of the house which opens upon a cross street, leaving the front unbroken. Upon my return to my lodgings I found

M^{rs} & Miss Glass who spent the day and dined with me. Mr Heard kindly went to Highgate to see my poor little boy whom he found better in looks and sprits. This news quite revived me.

I must not forget, among Lord Ashburton's pictures, two by my enemy Rubens in his usual gross style though on a small scale. The Rape of the Sabines and their intercession between their husbands and fathers.

Alexander Baring (1773–1848), first Baron ASHBURTON and son of Sir Francis Baring, was a banker and merchant. Thomas Baring, who conducted Coolidge through Bath House, was his nephew. Alexander Baring apprenticed with his father's firm Sir Francis Baring & Company and represented the firm's interests in the United States. There in 1798 he married Ann Louisa Bingham (d. 1848), daughter of U.S. senator William Bingham, a match that contributed significantly to Baring's wealth and produced nine children. In 1803 he concluded negotiations for the U.S. government's purchase of the Louisiana Territory, one of the most significant achievements of Thomas Jefferson's administration. Alexander Baring served in the House of Commons from 1806 until he was raised to the Lords as Baron Ashburton in 1835. In 1841 he served as British ambassador to the United States to negotiate with Daniel Webster the settlement of a boundary dispute between the United States and Canada.

Baring's other interests included acquiring land and estates, in addition to his London homes, and collecting art. He served as a trustee of both the National Gallery and the British Museum. BATH HOUSE, originally owned by William Pulteney (1684–1764), Earl of Bath, was at the west corner of Bolton Street, facing Piccadilly. Baring purchased the mansion in 1821, pulled down the structure, and rebuilt it in an unremarkable Georgian style that belied the opulence of its interior and his extensive collection of Dutch and Flemish masterpieces (*ODNB*; Burke and Burke, *Peerage and Baronetage*, 136; Ziegler, *Sixth Great Power*, 61–159; Arthur Irwin Dasent, *Piccadilly in Three Centuries, with Some Account of Berkeley Square and the Haymarket* [1920], 71–73, 78–79; Henry B. Wheatley, *London Past and Present: Its History, Associations, and Traditions* [1891], 123–124; Waagen, *Works of Art*, 2:265–286; Albert Gallatin to Thomas Jefferson, 31 Aug., 16 Sept. 1803 [DLC]).

Saturday. Dec. 22.

Dined yesterday at the house of Mr Davis, the uncle of M^r C's friend, Mr Sindry. A party of eighteen and a most luxurious dinner. Every thing in the shape of fish, flesh & fowl, puddings & pastry, jellies & creams, fruits fresh, dried & preserved, that money could purchase. An excellent cook had turned these good things to good account. There was old English abundance and good housekeeping, not exactly in accordance with modern ideas of taste and refinement, but excellent of it's kind. Engrafted upon the British stock was a scion of Orientalism. Mr Davis is an old Indian, so that we had not only Beef, pudding & mince pie but curry and Bengal rice. The company consisted of dowagers and men of business, merchants and what Miss Mitford calls West End Cockneys. There was but one young lady in the party, who dressed in a delicate robe of "bleu celeste," looked discontented and unhappy enough among the fat dames in black velvet. Poor girl, she was a pigeon among crows. Mr Davis I liked. He is hospitable, unpretending and kind, a little formal and exact, old-fashioned no doubt, but genuine of his sort.

Before dinner Mr Higginson being in conversation with one of the ladies who mistook him for an Englishman, she asked several questions about Mr C. & myself—our names—where we came from—was surprised to hear we were Americans, expecting probably to have seen Americans on all fours, or at least dressed in skins. "However," she exclaimed after a moment's reflection, "we are told that some of these people are very intelligent"—exactly as if she had been speaking of some newly discovered tribe of barbarians. ^If you except the best educated among^ the English, their ignorance of all that relates to America & Americans is ludicrous. In Tunbridge I was asked by a lady the wife of a Professor of languages, what language was spoken in the U.S. At Durham the daughter of a Prebendary, a person not otherwise deficient in intelligence or information, put questions to me shewing an unacquaintance with America, which had the question been of Africa, she would have been ashamed to acknowledge. I have no doubt that the travels of Denham & Clapperton & the Landers had made her more conversant with African affairs than with ours. At first, not comprehending the extent of her ignorance, and taking it for granted that she had general ideas of American history & geography, of the different nations by which the country had been colonised, & the sort of governments they had established, I answered as to the questions of a person possessed of leading facts. She evidently did not understand my answers—I explained; she was still embarassed, until at last, I found that she had confounded in inextricable confusion names, dates, races of men, every thing relating to the world discovered by Columbus. The Confederation of the States was a mystery to her, & Mexico & Canada were mixed up with British America & the Union. Mrs C. the wife of a clergyman and professor of mathematics at Durham, asked me if New York was in the United States, and if the President was the head of the Government like their King. Englishmen though not generally uninformed ^on these subjects^ to such an inconceivable degree as English women, are strangely without interest or accurate knowledge of what most concerns a nation sprung from the same stock with themselves, having the same laws, the same language and religion, and destined one day to become a powerful people. The English generally, as far as I can see, have an unfriendly feeling toward America, that is when they think of us at all. They despise us as semi-barbarians and dislike us as having successfully resisted themselves. Nor is this confined to any particular class of society—high & low seem to agree in misapprehension and distaste. Neither do we like them much better than they like us. There is no love lost between us. The interests of the two nations bind them together but it is not a union of affection. The Americans here, I am sorry to say, toady the English, flatter & court them, but inwardly they feel and resent their insolence, whilst the English barely tolerate & contemn them. Americans bringing good letters, find no difficulty in gaining admittance to good society, but they hardly form a part of it; they are passed from hand to hand and receive lip courtesy and, in some cases, obtain a sort of fashion, but it seems to me that after all, their position is a somewhat doubtful one, the mere result of accident and caprice & likely at any moment to be reversed.

But I am wandering far from my dinner in Spanish place, Manchester Square. After the ladies had retired to coffee in the drawing room their conversation turned upon the family affairs of themselves and of their neighbours, or upon the all engrossing topic of rugwork. There is a perfect mania among women of all ranks on the subject of this worsted embroidery. At Wentworth House we were shewn a set of chairs embroidered by the Grandmother of Lord Fitz William, and we were told that the ladies of the family were at work on another set. In Scotland a Scotch lady presented me with her work bag containing a pattern of the Royal Stewart plaid, with all it's colours, scarlet, blue, green, chocolate, yellow, white &c &c in small hanks of lamb's wool ready for the needle. In Durham, at Tunbridge Wells, at Leeds, I was called on to admire prodigies of industry in the way of this same worsted work. Here there are many fashionable shops in Regent St. & elsewhere expressly for the sale of materials and every lady prides herself on the quantity of canvas she covers with these needle paintings.

In Edinburgh I saw large pictures, that is some two feet square, copied in woollens by these ingenious artists. In London the number of flower-pieces is astonishing and some of them are really of great beauty.

Miss Sindry does rugwork, but she reads too, and has travelled and is pleasant in conversation; so no doubt are many others of these workers in lambs' wool, though it was not my fate to hear anything either pleasant or profitable from these with whom I now happened to be thrown, fat ladies in black, widows of old Indians, or wives of men good upon Change—better than in a drawing-room. We came away at half past ten. To-day, Dec. 22. is dark, dismal & gloomy even beyond the bond of an English December. N'importé—I have been writing about my yesterday's dinner, and shall drive this forenoon, wind & weather forbidding as they may.——

Mr Heard first & then Mr Higginson have been in bringing me news & letters from home, come by the Liverpool Steamer. A letter from Mrs Greene & others dictated by my darling Twins. Thank Heaven, they seem well & happy! Nothing from my daughter nor from my oldest boy—a drawback to my satisfaction. I have a letter from Mrs John Forbes. She has twin daughters born the middle of October, and calls one of them Ellen Randolph. I hope the name may be of good omen. But I distrust my own fortunes. They have been mingled with much that I would fain avert from the head of my little namesake.

> As half in shade and half in sun,
> The world upon it's path advances,
> May that side the light's upon
> Be all that e'er shall meet her glances.

Mary Russell **MITFORD** (1787–1855), novelist and dramatist, was the author of *Our Village: Sketches of Rural Character and Scenery* (1824–1832), a very successful multivolume work largely influenced by her life in the small village of Three Mile Cross, just south of Reading, Berkshire. Mitford used the term "cockney" in *Our Village* to refer to anyone who came to Three Mile Cross from London (*ODNB*).

Dixon **DENHAM** (1786–1828) and Hugh **CLAPPERTON** (1788–1827) set out in 1822 from Tripoli southward across the Sahara Desert to trace the course of the River Niger. The expedition never reached the Niger, but the men were the first Europeans to explore that southern interior region. In 1826 Denham published his *Narrative of Travels and Discoveries in Northern and Central Africa*. Fellow explorer Richard Lemon Lander (1804–1834) published *Records of Captain Clapperton's Last Expedition to Africa* in 1830. That same year Lander embarked on his own expedition with his brother John, and after returning to England **THE LANDERS** published their *Journal of an Expedition to Explore the Course and Termination of the Niger; with a Narrative of a Voyage down That River to Its Termination* in 1832 (*ODNB*).

WENTWORTH Woodhouse was the Yorkshire estate of Charles William Wentworth Fitzwilliam (1786–1857), third Earl Fitzwilliam in the peerage of Great Britain, fifth Earl Fitzwilliam in the peerage of Ireland. Its magnificent, six-hundred-foot-long east front was designed by Henry Flitcroft in the 1730s

(*ODNB*; Nikolaus Pevsner, *The Buildings of England: Yorkshire West Riding* [1967], 34–38, 47–53, 59, 61, 538–545).

Coolidge's reference to the GRANDMOTHER of the Earl Fitzwilliam may have been to the earl's paternal grandmother, Lady Anne (d. 1769), daughter of Thomas Watson-Wentworth, first Marquess of Rockingham, or to his maternal grandmother, Lady Caroline (d. 1760), Countess of Bessborough and daughter of William Cavendish, third Duke of Devonshire (*ODNB*; Burke and Burke, *Peerage and Baronetage*, 237, 792; *Gentleman's Magazine*, n.s., 26 [1833]: 365–367).

Sarah Hathaway FORBES (1813–1900) married John Murray Forbes (1813–1898), merchant, entrepreneur, and railroad developer, in 1834. Mrs. Forbes, herself a twin, gave birth to twins Alice and Ellen in November 1838. They were the first of Sarah Forbes's six children. The family lived in Boston, and Mr. Forbes was a former partner with Joseph Coolidge in Russell & Company, the two men having worked together in Canton (*ANB*; *DAB*; Sarah Forbes Hughes, ed., *Letters and Recollections of John Murray Forbes* [1899], 1:60–72, 110–111, 185; United States Federal Census, Seventh Census, 1850, town of Milton, Norfolk County, Massachusetts, s.v. "Forbes, John M.," Ancestry.com; *Boston Daily Advertiser*, 13 Oct. 1898; *Massachusetts Vital Records, 1841–1910*, s.v. "Forbes, Sarah," American Ancestors).

With HALF IN SHADE . . . MEET HER GLANCES Coolidge alters slightly four lines from Irish poet Thomas Moore's "Peace Be Around Thee" (Thomas Moore, *Melodies* [Philadelphia, 1821], 244).

London. December 1838.
Monday. 24. Dec.

On friday I succeeded in finding Mrs Osgood & paying my subscription to her book, which I have not read nor have the slightest intention of reading. To-day "Il fait un temps appeax," as Josephine informed me this morning—So dark that I can scarcely see to write, and raining. London is dismal in winter. I do not wonder that nobody "who is any body" remains here at this season, gloomy and dirty as the great city is—A "triste sejour" only fit for chimney sweepers.

Saturday evening we went to a party at Dr Boott's. I anticipated a dull evening and dull it was. There was music—good perhaps, but few persons listened to it, and many thought it a bore intereefering with conversation—Among the company were Judge Haliburton & two sons of Mrs Hemans, very ordinary young men in appearance, who receive a pension from the British Government because their mother was a good woman who wrote good verses. I wonder if the operatives from whose hard hands the money was wrung, ever read Mrs Hemans' poems. Had it been the mother herself however there might be an excuse, but really the sons should work for themselves.——There were also present two daughters of Charles Aiken—the "Charles" of Mrs Barbauld's Early Lessons, the best of books for young children. This "Charles" was, we are told, so over-educated by his excellent relatives, (Mrs Barbauld was his aunt and had no children of her own) that although a good and even a learned man, he is nervous, timid, and almost marred in the making, as other too elaborate works are apt to be. "Too much pains-taking" says Carlyle, "speaks disease in one's mind." In education it surely creates disease in the mind of the object on which it is expended. Another personage at Dr Boott's was Mrs Bartley the ci-devant actress—of whom says Lockhart in his life of Scott, "another graceful & intelligent performer in whom he (Sir Walter) took a special interest, and of whom he saw a great deal in his private circle, was Miss Smith afterwards Mrs Bartley." This was in the early part of the century, say 1808, thirty years ago. This lady was accompanied by her daughter. There were several other persons "of name" whose names I do not remember. Lions who did not roar.

Yesterday, Sunday 23^d, we went to Foley Chapel to hear the Revd Herbert Caunter, Editor of the Oriental Annual. We were in Mrs Bates' pew, very easy and private, allowing you to loll or sit as you please, but with it's curtains & cushions & chairs and private door of entrance, reminding one too much of a private box at the theatre. Opposite was the Duke of Richmond's pew, empty, as the family are out of town. Who would stay in town at the season if they could help themselves? The country in England is beautiful even in winter. Happy those who have country seats of their own, or invitations to other people's.—

Mrs Bates' pew is upstairs near the great window. The service was read not by Dr Caunter who had a cold, and most execrably read it was. The Clerk's nasal twang was even worse than usual. It is astonishing what a thing of custom the Clerk's voice is, or has become in English churches, I suppose by long usage. The responses are made in a tone between a whine and a howl to which custom has familiarised the people of the country, but which to foreigners and especially to Americans, is ludicrous & irreverent in the extreme. The sermon by Dr Caunter was a tolerable one and he reads well. This sermon was on the character of the Sabbath and the duty of observing it. Dr Caunter quoted, I hardly recollect apropos to what, a text from Numbers which, I know not why, exercises a strange influence over my imagination. It comes over me like a strain of solemn music wakening emotion rather than thought—vague, melancholy, touching & elevating. This text is from the prophecy of Balaam. "I shall see him but not now, I shall behold him but not nigh." At York

Minster, a very old MS. copy of the Old Testament, beautifully written on vellum, was shewn to me, and as it was opened before me, my eye rested upon this text & was rivetted as by a spell. There it was in large, open, steady characters, written with very black ink on smooth vellum—"I shall see him but not now—I shall behold him but not nigh."

The services being over I called on Mrs Searle, on Mrs Cryder, and then went to Highgate to see my dear Jefferson. I found him in better spirits and becoming reconciled to his school. The holidays have commenced & instead of twenty six boys to annoy him by their rudeness he has for a companions, one pretty little girl of nine years old, and her two brothers older & younger than herself, children of M^r Mc Lane of Canton, come to pass the holidays with M^r & Mrs Kieckhofer under whose care they are. Mr Coolidge & myself returning in our carriage, much satisfied with our visit, met Mr Heard on foot, walking to Highgate to see Jefferson. How kind and how like Mr Heard!

Frances Sargent Locke OSGOOD (1811–1850) was a Boston-born poet and editor who also published under the pen name Kate Carol. In 1835 she married the artist Samuel Stillman Osgood (1808–1885) and moved to London, where he continued to paint and she contributed to literary periodicals. In 1838 she published *A Wreath of Wild Flowers from New England*, a collection of poems and rhymes, with a "tragedy" entitled *Elfrida*. Her second BOOK, *The Casket of Fate*, appeared in 1839. Both works were favorably received and subsequently reissued in America. The Osgoods remained in England until 1839, when they returned to America and took up residence in New York City. There, counted among the New York literati, Osgood worked as an editor at the *Ladies' Companion* and published several additional volumes, including the popular *Poetry of Flowers and the Flowers of Poetry* (*ANB*; *DAB*; Benezit, *Dictionary of Artists*, 10:678; *New-York Daily Tribune*, 13, 14 May 1850; *New York Herald*, 13 May 1850).

Felicia Dorothea Browne HEMANS (1793–1835), poet, was born in Liverpool, moved with her family to Wales in 1800, and thereafter considered that place her home. She was liberally educated, read several languages, and studied the classics, music, and drawing. Her first book of poems, published in 1807, was well received, and her second garnered nearly one thousand subscribers before its appearance one year later. She married Alfred Hemans (b. 1781) in 1812, and they had five sons before separating in 1818. Hemans wrote prolifically, publishing collections of poetry, memorial and epic works, and narrative essays and poems for periodicals. In appreciation for Hemans's talents, Sir Robert Peel found clerkships for her SONS Henry William (1817–1871) and Charles Isidore (1817–1876), which they still held in 1850. Hemans was a favorite of Coolidge and her mother, Martha Jefferson Randolph, both of whom copied several of Hemans's poems into family commonplace books (*ODNB*; Emma Mason, *Women Poets of the Nineteenth*

Century [2006], 2–3, 17–48; *Gentleman's Magazine*, n.s., 34 [1850]: 212; Mary Elizabeth Cleland Randolph Eppes, Album of poems . . . 1820–29 [ViU: MSS 7443]; Album [ViU: Jefferson, Randolph, and Trist Family Papers]).

Anna Letitia Aikin BARBAULD (1743–1825), poet and essayist, began writing works in the 1760s that were highly regarded for their imaginative, contemplative themes. She married the Reverend Rochemont Barbauld (1749–1808) in 1774, and together they operated a school for boys in Palgrave, Suffolk, until 1785. Having no children of their own, they adopted Mrs. Barbauld's young nephew CHARLES Aikin [AIKEN] (1775–1847) in 1777, and shortly thereafter Mrs. Barbauld wrote *Lessons for Children* (1778–1779), specifically designed to help teach Charles and others of his age to read. The work was a collection of stories and conversations, with Charles often the main character, and used short sentences in "a clear and large type" because "they only, who have actually taught young children, can be sensible how necessary these assistances are." She followed *Lessons* with *Hymns in Prose for Children* (1781), a primer on religion. Both works were very popular, going through several printings in England and the United States throughout the nineteenth century. But Barbauld's interests extended beyond children's texts, and her associates included some of the most radical intellectuals of her time. Barbauld wrote pieces favoring the French Revolution, criticizing the British Parliament, and speaking out against slavery and the war with France. She also edited the correspondence of Samuel Richardson and compiled a literary anthology entitled *The Female Speaker* (1811). Charles Rochemont Aikin was educated at the University of Edinburgh, worked in London as a surgeon, and was a widely recognized expert on smallpox and the vaccination process for that disease; Jefferson owned his works on the topic. The TWO DAUGHTERS whom Coolidge saw with him on this evening were Susan, twenty-two, and Catherine, nineteen (*ODNB*; Sowerby, 955; Christening Records for Warrington, Lancaster, England, 1773–1775, s.v. "Aikin, Charles," Ancestry.com; Christening Records for St. Botolph, Bishopsgate, London, 1818–1819, s.v. "Aikin, Catherine," Ancestry.com; Census Returns of England and Wales, 1841, St. George, Bloomsbury, Middlesex, s.v. "Aikin, Charles," Ancestry.com; Register of Marriages, St. George, Bloomsbury, London Metropolitan Archives, s.v. "Aikin, Susan," Ancestry.com).

Thomas CARLYLE's observation that "Too much pains-taking speaks disease in one's mind" was from his review of John Gibson Lockhart's *Memoirs of the Life of Sir Walter Scott, Bart.* Carlyle's remark reflected on Scott's ability to produce novels quickly without laboring over them endlessly in pursuit of unobtainable perfection (*London and Westminster Review*, Jan. 1838, p. 338).

Sarah Smith BARTLEY (ca. 1783–1850), actress, enjoyed success primarily as a tragedian in Bath but also at Covent Garden and Drury Lane. She married fellow actor George Bartley (ca. 1782–1858), and they had a son and a DAUGHTER, Sophia Catherine Byng Bartley (b. ca. 1818). In November 1818 the Bartleys made a much-anticipated and highly successful American tour and returned home to London in 1820, after which Mrs. Bartley appeared on the stage only occasionally. LOCKHART's reference to Sir Walter Scott's opinion of Mrs. Bartley is in volume

3 of *Memoirs of the Life of Sir Walter Scott, Bart.* (*ODNB*; *London, England, Births and Baptisms, 1813–1906*, s.v. "Bartley, Sophia Catharine Byng," Ancestry.com; *New-York Evening Post*, 28 Oct. 1818, 3 Aug. 1820; *Boston Daily Advertiser*, 19 Nov. 1818; *Alexandria Gazette and Daily Advertiser*, 17 Mar. 1819).

John Hobart CAUNTER (1792–1851), author and clergyman, studied for the church at Peterhouse, Cambridge, after a brief military career in India. He was perpetual curate at St. Paul's CHAPEL, Foley Place, London, from 1825 to 1844, while also serving at Portland Chapel, London, from 1836 to 1843. Caunter wrote prolifically, publishing poems, novels, sermons and lectures, works of history, and, with artist William Daniell (1769–1837), seven volumes of *The Oriental Annual; or, Scenes in India* (1834–1840) (*ODNB*; *Gentleman's Magazine*, n.s., 37 [1852]: 627–628).

Charles Gordon-Lennox (1791–1860), fifth Duke of RICHMOND and Lennox, had been aide-de-camp and military secretary to the Duke of Wellington. He maintained extensive estates in England and Scotland, and with his wife, Caroline (1796–1874), daughter of Henry William Paget, first Marquess of Anglesey, had five sons and five daughters. When in London the family resided at 51 Portland Place (*ODNB*).

The PROPHECY OF BALAAM, "I shall see him, but not now; I shall behold him, but not nigh," is from the Bible, Num. 24:17.

Mary Wright Wetmore CRYDER (b. ca. 1808) was the wife of John Cryder (b. ca. 1796), American merchant and financier. In January 1836 Cryder joined James Morrison (1789–1857), merchant and politician, to form Morrison, Cryder & Company, a London mercantile banking firm that quickly rose to prominence and was, for a brief time, second only to Baring Brothers. Substantial losses in the late 1830s led to the dissolution of that partnership, and the Cryder family returned to America in 1840. In New York Cryder went into business with his brother-in-law William S. Wetmore (1801–1862), and their firm pursued mercantile interests in South America and China that ultimately earned Cryder a fortune (*ODNB*, s.v. "Morrison, James"; James Carnahan Wetmore, *The Wetmore Family of America, and Its Collateral Branches* [1861], 359, 363–364; *Vital Record of Rhode Island, 1636–1850*, s.v. "Cryder, John," American Ancestors; United States Federal Census, Eighth Census, 1860, Flushing, Queens, New York, s.v. "Cryder, John," Ancestry.com; Ship's Manifest for the *Railway*, 19 May 1830, Ship's Manifest for the *Mediator*, 28 Apr. 1840, Ancestry.com; *Baltimore Patriot*, 14 Oct. 1830; *Newport [R.I.] Daily News*, 23 June 1862).

MR MCLANE and his children have not been identified.

Dec. 26.

Yesterday, Christmas day, we went in the morning to the Church of the Foundlings where the music is good, the preaching "mediocre." The services were long and the execrable creed of St. Athanasius formed a part.

What an insult to God and Man the reciting of this blasphemous relic of barbarous ages!—There were present nearly two hundred children, boys and girls, ranged on each side of the Organ and Choristers—the boys to the right, as you looked at them from the body of the Church, the girls to the left. They were comfortably clad, the boys in dark coats & pantaloons, with red waistcoats and white collars,—the girls in a very old-fashioned & picturesque costume consisting of long-waisted gowns with short, plain sleeves, (over which the short sleeves of the chemise were neatly turned up) low in the neck with a sort of cambric tucker or frill, and a white apron with a bib or front-piece. Each little head was covered by a plain, high-crowned cap starched stiff, having a plaited frill, like the cap, of thick cambric. They were ranged according to their sizes and formed quite a pretty picture. Poor forlorn little creatures! Orphans and maintained by charity, I hope they are taken good care of! They look as if sufficient attention was paid to them, particularly the girls whose appearance is much more respectable and pleasing than that of the boys, I cannot understand why.

We went after the morning services were over, to see the children dine. In the first room, a very long table covered with a clean cloth, and with benches on each side, was appropriated to the girls, who each received, on a clean wooden platter, a large piece of baked plum-pudding. This constituted their Christmas dinner. They looked clean and healthy but grave beyond their years. This gravity may have been taught them as a lesson of propriety. In another room, at the opposite extremity of the building, the boys were served in the same manner, the puddings being placed at the head of the table and cut up by a woman belonging to the establishment. Grace was said by one of the larger children and their manners were entirely decorous. The appearance of the boys, however, was any thing but prepossessing. They had, on their faces, the stamp of low birth—the low birth which proceeds from a degraded stock, the human animal brutified by poverty & vice, degenerate in body and soul and perpetuating a degenerate race. These boys looked stupid and cross—ill shaped—and in all ways indicating a preponderance of the evil principle over the good. Whilst we were in the Church the carriage went on to Highgate and when we came out we found our dear boy come to pass his Christmas with us. It was a great pleasure to him and to me. We spent the evening at home and after our boy was gone to bed, Mr Coolidge read aloud to me from Lockhart's Life of Scott. I must not omit to say that this Christmas day was bright and clear, the Sun shining, which he had not done for a month before. To-day, the 26th, is again dark & sad, more so to me because I must take Jefferson home to his school. He has been talking to me incessantly so that I can hardly write, but his little dinner is over and the hour approaches when he must return to Highgate.

The CHURCH OF THE FOUNDLINGS was part of the Foundling Hospital established in 1739 by Thomas Coram (ca. 1668–1751), shipwright, sea captain, and philanthropist, for the "Maintenance and Education of Exposed and Deserted Young Children." Housed temporarily at Hatton Garden beginning in March 1741, the orphanage moved to Upper Guilford Street, the location Coolidge visited, in 1754; this structure was designed by architect Theodore Jacobsen (d. 1772). The large chapel featured an organ donated by George Frederic Handel, on which he frequently performed his *Messiah* oratorio as a fundraiser for the institution. Two long, three-story ranges containing dining rooms and dormitories flanked the chapel, forming a courtyard. The buildings Coolidge visited were demolished in 1926.

Infants and small children left with the Foundling Hospital were taught reading, writing, and arithmetic, as well as part-singing. After several years of instruction boys were apprenticed to the trades and girls were sent into domestic service. Once placed, their care, training, and behavior continued to be monitored by the board of governors. While the Foundling Hospital did receive some public grants, the majority of its support came from the wealthy and elite, many of whom provided a variety of professional services gratis and deemed election to the orphanage's board a mark of distinction. The Foundling Hospital moved to Berkhamsted in 1938 and closed in 1954, but the institution, now known as the Thomas Coram Foundation for Children, or simply the Coram Family, continues as one of the primary charitable organizations for children in Great Britain (*ODNB*; Bridget Cherry and Nikolaus Pevsner, *The Buildings of England: London 4: North* [1999], 27; Reginald Hugh Nichols and Francis Aslett Wray, *The History of the Foundling Hospital* [1935], 10–28, 36, 43, 48, 182, 199, 202, 233; *Survey of London*, vol. 24 [1952], 10–24; *Old and New London*, 5:356–368; "About Coram," Thomas Coram Foundation for Children, accessed 20 Dec. 2010, http://www.coram.org.uk/section/about).

Thursday. 27. Dec.

I carried my boy to Highgate yesterday, stopping at toy-shop by the way to get him a box of bricks, and whether he was comforted by the new toy, or rather that he is becoming reconciled to his school, we parted with less reluctance on his part than at first. He looked downcast but shed no tears. I believe he is getting used to a state of things painful whilst it was new, for he is too manly a boy to be much influenced by toys.

At night I went with M^r C Mr H. Mr Higginson & Mrs Wormeley & a party of children to the Covent Garden Theatre. The play was Jane Shore and cast with all the strength of the company. Gloster, Mr Vandenhoff, Hastings, McReady, Jane Shore, Helen Fawcett. It was a failure. Tame, cold and flat. There is nothing so tiresome as the expression of tragic passion in which you cannot sympathise. Smith's Theory of Moral Sentiment might be read with effect after such an evening as the last. I never looked with more utter indifference upon a representation of human suffering. The acting was "mediocre" but I cannot understand how Mrs Siddons even could make any thing great or eminently pathetic out of this play of Jane Shore. Yet this is said to have called forth some of her finest acting.

The attraction of the evening was understood to be a Christmas pantomime got up expressly for the season. The audience impatient for this pantomime behaved very tumultuously. I am sure Mrs Trollope never saw anything in the United States at all equal to the uproar of the pit and gallery at Covent Garden on this occasion. During the tragedy the voices of the actors were often entirely drowned in the clamour. There was some excuse for it when after the tragedy, we were kept waiting three quarters of an hour for the only part of the entertainment we cared to see. It came at last—a stupid sort of parody on the story of Fair Rosamond, in the worst possible taste, followed by a variety of antics and buffooneries performed by a clumsy Harlequin, a Columbine looking like a figure of painted pasteboard, a Clown too low for a Circus, and a Pantaloon worthy of the Clown. There was a great deal of scenery & machinery, more opening and shutting of trap doors, more would-be pageantry and vain pretension than I almost ever saw before, and less effect. The attempts at wit & satire utterly abortive, as they are wont to be in these "pieces de circonstance"[1] for which the English have no genius. I sat as long as I could and came away disgusted and exhausted, and wondering at the mis-placed patience of the audience in submitting to the Pantomime as much as I had wondered at their rudeness during the representation of the tragedy which was, after all, the more endurable exhibition of the two. The Queen,—among many other petty charges brought against her by her subjects who seem in a state of re-action after the burst of loyalty on her accession—the Queen is accused of liking no theatre but the Italian Opera. I honour her taste. Covent Garden Theatre is not, I think, so fine a building as Drury Lane, neither so large nor so elegant. Covent Garden & Drury Lane are names so well known in America, and are so thoroughly associated with the Drama, it's fashion & it's fame, that to have seen these two Theatres, to have been within their walls, is something to think of & talk of.

To-day, we have visited the Bridgewater Gallery, having obtained a special order through the interference of Mr Baring, this not being the season of exhibition. It is a noble collection—more pictures of the Italian masters than I have ever seen before. But I have a kindness for the Dutch masters after all, of which I am almost ashamed, seeing my great predilection for the romantic & poetic. I found myself in the presence of Sebastian del Piombo & Domenichino, of Carracci & Caravaggio, turning to look after Gerard Dow, Ostade, Cuyp, and above all Ruysdael, of whom there is one small piece in this Gallery which I could never tire of. It is a landscape with water and trees, one tree in particular hanging over the water and reflecting the light from it's white bark, in the same exquisite way, in which the same effect is produced, by the same master in a picture by Ruysdael which I saw in Mr Wells' collection at Redleaf. This of the Bridgewater Gallery is called in the Catalogue, from some figures at the entrance of the Forest employed in charring wood, the "Charcoal Burners." There is also a wild Calabrian landscape called "the Soothsayers" by Salvator Rosa, on which I looked with great devotion. I have a love of landscape extending from nature to art. Fine scenery either in itself or upon canvas gives me extraordinary pleasure, and this whether it be grand or simply beautiful—The Ocean, the Mountains, woods, rocks, cliffs, tumbling waters, groves, fields, meadows, streamlets, cottages, village churches, no matter what, provided it be good of it's kind & the objects singly picturesque, or grouped with effect.

I staid less than two hours in the Bridgewater Gallery. Among the pictures which I dwelt upon were,

1st   Titian's "Venus rising from the Sea," called by the French a Coquille because of a shell seen in the back ground. This Venus is a naked figure emerging from the waves which bathe her lower limbs & rise a little above the knee.

2nd   an exquisite head & bust of a female martyr by Domenichino.

3^d   Christ the good Shepherd—from Murrillo copied by Grimaux.

4th   A Holy Family by Raphael—the figures small—the Virgin full length, and looking down as only Raphael's Madonnas can look, upon her son who stands at her knee and receives the caresses of St John.

5.6.7. Holy families by Raphael, not in his best style I am told, but everything of Raphael's seems "best" to me

8th   An Assumption of the Virgin, who is represented standing on the crescent of the Moon.

were earrings of proportionate splendour.—Other necklaces scarcely inferiour to the first. We were introduced into a back room where pearls & jewelry of every description lay around in a rich profusion, and with an appearance of careless security, which dazzled my eyes & bewildered my mind. These pearl collars were worth from three hundred & fifty to four hundred guineas a piece. On a table in the centre of the room, were a number of morocco boxes lined with satin or velvet, echru, each one containing a set of precious stones. Emeralds, mixed with diamonds, rubies, sapphires, yellow, pink & violet topaz, amethysts of great size & brilliancy, all set in the richest & most costly manner. In one morocco box was a superb parure of emeralds & diamonds, wanting nothing but the bracelet which had been transferred to the possession of Miss Bates, at a cost of 750 guineas, a wedding present from her godfather, Mr John Baring. In a show glass on the right hand, were collars of pearl & various ornaments of precious stones in the form of crosses, stars &c. On the left hand, in presses with glass doors sliding back, were the large diamonds of which I have spoken, with diadems, combs & head ornaments "feronnieres" &c. One "feronniere" consisted of a small diamond Butterfly for the centre with chains to attach it to the temples. There were brooches in the form of Moths or large Butterflies, the bodies & wings of diamond, the spots on the wings of coloured stones, sapphires, emeralds, or rubies. The Opal flashed it's many colored rays in the bright company of other gems—I always liked this stone which seems to partake of the character of the pearl as well as of the diamond. Besides it is of good omen— it is said, among the Orientals, "to preserve its owner from disease & hence, in the East, is much used in the form of Amulets."[2] This I get from Lady Blessington's "Gems of Beauty for 1836." On the same authority I find that "it is reported of the Ruby by Baccius, Boetius & others that it keepeth the wearer from sorrow and danger." "The Sapphire" says Anselmus Boetius "procureth the wearer favour with princes." "Cardanus attributes to the Emerald great power in divination." Pearls "were considered by the Antients to be not only emblematic of purity but preservative of it." For the Topaz, "Cardanus relates wonders concerning the virtues of this stone in the cure of melancholy." "Andreas Baccius in his work entitled 'de natura Gemmarum' says that 'the Amethyst diminisheth sleep.'" "Epiphanius asserts that the Sardonyx causeth him that weareth it to be free from fear and nobly audacious." "Wurtzing states that the Aquamarine is useful in all diseases of the heart." "Rucus asserts in his history of precious stones that the Turquoise becomes pale & discoloured when the wearer is infirm or afflicted." Connoisseurs say that the "best method of judging of the water of a diamond is to examine it under the foliage of a thickly leaved tree."

So much for myledi Blessington's learning on the subject of Gems. Most of these treasures of Rundell & Bridge were with-in the reach of only the very rich, but, as one of the partners told me, they could en-able a lady to make a great shew at no great expence. They shewed me a diamond necklace and earrings consisting of not very large stones but so arranged as to produce the best effect. The necklace was composed of a number of pendents, somewhat wedge-shaped, hanging from a circle which clasped round the neck, and was a little in the style of the collars of shells worn by the South-Sea Islanders, the largest being in the middle. The price of the set was £1300.

But to describe the glories of these cases of Mount Caucasus, this palace of the Genii, or subterranean dwelling of magicians, the very treasure of Soliman, as the abode of Messrs Rundell & Bridge appeared to me, is past my power. Suffice it to say that the effect produced upon my imagination was such that I felt not the slightest desire to possess these gorgeous orna-ments. They were too far above any splendour of the toilette that I had ever come in contact with, to excite, in my mind, the smallest covetous-ness. I no more wished for them than I wish for the stars.

Wilt thou reach stars because they shine on thee?

From the Jewel department of the establishment we proceeded to an examination of the rooms which contained the silver & gold plate. Here the most elegant & costly articles had been ordered by the King of Hanover, the Queen's most unpopular but apparently wealthy uncle. Little Hanover, blessed with a Salic law, passed, at the death of the late King, under the dominion of his brother, said to be the worst prince of the

House of Hanover. For him Rundell & Bridge were producing their silver marvels. Candelabra & candlesticks in pairs—vases & table ornaments of the most exquisite workmanship. In a room above were two round dishes and a centre piece of silver gilt, to decorate a side board. Nothing could be richer.

The centre piece represents the shield of Achilles after the design of Flaxman. The figures are in relief and possess all the classic beauty which Flaxman, alone perhaps of modern artists, could have given them. Among other exquisite things was the Portland Vase, in silver, with it's beautiful and mysterious decoration of allegoric figures. I remember studying, when very young, an engraving of this Vase which made me familiar with it's general form and design.

I saw here various services of plate in which were introduced every variety of graceful & beautiful detail so as to give to those articles of daily use at a wealthy table a character of taste & elegance surpassing even the value of the material. It became, however, late and dark before we finished our examination. We were therefore politely invited to renew it at some early day, to which we gladly agreed,—I was surprised to hear from the person, (a partner of the firm) who had conducted us in our survey, that there were really no very fine stones in the Queen's Crown which I had seen and admired so much on my visit to the Tower. The Ruby which to me appeared so wonderful, has, it seems, little intrinsic value, though it derives a value of sentiment from a tradition that it once belonged to Edward the Black Prince. "I should be unwilling myself to give a hundred pounds for it," said the dealer in gems. The Sapphire is a much better stone.—From the City & Messʳˢ Rundell & Bridge we returned to Regent St. having accomplished much in one day.

The *Tragedy of* JANE SHORE, by Nicholas Rowe (1674–1718), was loosely based on the life of Elizabeth Shore, one of several mistresses to King Edward IV, and was first performed in 1714. Coolidge saw John M. VANDENHOFF (1790–1861) perform the role of the Duke of Gloster, William Charles Macready [MCREADY] (1793–1873) in the part of Lord Hastings, and Helen Faucit [FAWCETT] (1814–1898) in the role of Jane Shore. MacReady, who was also the manager of the Theatre Royal, Covent Garden from 1837 to 1839, noted in his diary for 26 December, "Acted Lord Hastings indifferently—my mind was on the pantomime." Of the PANTOMIME, entitled *Harlequin and Fair Rosamond; or, Old Dame Nature and the Fairy Art,* Macready wrote, "From the utter absence of arrangement on the part of Mr. Marshall, his clumsy attempt at contrivance, and the deficiency of his work, the pantomime completely failed. What will be the result I cannot guess—it will go near to ruin me. It is a terrible blow" (*ODNB;* William Toynbee, ed., *Diaries of William Charles Macready, 1833–1851* [1912], 1:484; Nicholas Rowe, *Jane Shore: A Tragedy* [1818]).

This was Adam Smith's THEORY OF MORAL SENTIMENTS (1759).

Englishwoman Frances TROLLOPE (1779–1863), author, lived in America from 1827 to 1831, recording her experiences and observations in a travel journal that she published upon her return to England. After attending a theatrical performance in Cincinnati, Trollope observed that "The bearing and attitudes of the men are perfectly indescribable. . . . The noises, too, were perpetual, and of the most unpleasant kind; the applause is expressed by cries and thumping with the feet, instead of clapping; and when a patriotic fit seized them, and 'Yankee Doodle' was called for, every man seemed to think his reputation as a citizen depended on the noise he made" (*ODNB*; Frances Trollope, *Domestic Manners of the Americans* [1832], 116–117).

The BRIDGEWATER GALLERY was in Bridgewater House on Cleveland Row, the private residence of Francis [formerly Leveson-Gower] Egerton (1800–1857), first Earl of Ellesmere. Following the death of his great-uncle Francis Egerton (1736–1803), third Duke of Bridgewater, and the subsequent death of his father, George Granville Leveson-Gower (1758–1833), the younger Leveson-Gower, a second son, assumed the surname of his great-uncle and inherited his properties, including Bridgewater House and an extensive collection of art. The gallery was normally only open to the public from May through July (*ODNB*; Jameson, *Private Galleries*, 77–163).

REDLEAF was the estate of William Wells (1768–1847), a retired shipbuilder and art collector who served as a trustee of the National Gallery and a director of the British Institution. At Redleaf Wells devoted his time to gardening, hunting, and building his collection, for which he favored works of old Dutch masters and his English contemporaries, including David Wilkie, John Constable, and Edwin Landseer, who was a close friend and frequent resident at Redleaf. Wells was particularly fond of Frederick Richard Lee's landscapes and over time purchased nearly fifty. Since Wells died without issue, his estate was inherited by his grandnephew, and the entire art collection was sold at Christie's in 1890 (*ODNB*; John Britton, *Descriptive Sketches of Tunbridge Wells and the Calverley Estate* [1832], 138).

The firm of RUNDELL & BRIDGE, founded in 1787 by master jeweler Philip Rundell (1746–1827) and John Bridge (1755–1834), operated just west of St. Paul's Cathedral at 32 Ludgate Hill. Granted a royal warrant in 1797, the firm served as the principal goldsmiths and jewelers to the royal family, and by 1804 it employed some of the finest talent and workshops in the city. Thomas Bigge (1766–1851), Rundell's nephew, joined the firm in 1808 and remained with it until its dissolution in 1845. When the Coolidges visited, the firm's partners included sons and nephews of Rundell, Bridge, and Bigge, and it may have been Thomas Bigge, the surviving senior partner, who met with the Coolidges and displayed the various pieces for their enjoyment (*ODNB*; Christopher Hartop, *Royal Goldsmiths: The Art of Rundell & Bridge, 1797–1843* [2005]; *Annual Biography and Obituary for the Year 1828*, 12 [1828]: 317–332; Anonymous, *Memoirs of the late Philip Rundell, Esq. Goldsmith and Jeweller . . . by a gentleman many years connected with the firm* [1827]).

FERONNIERE: a chain worn as an ornament encircling the head with a jewel at the center (*OED*).

Margaret Power Farmer Gardiner, Countess of **BLESSINGTON**, published *Gems of Beauty, Displayed in a Series of Twelve Highly Finished Engravings from Designs by E. T. Parris, Esq. with Fanciful Illustrations, in Verse*, in 1836. The work is a large folio portioned into twelve individual sections. Each section focuses on one gem, with an engraving depicting young women in various exotic or romantic settings, and is followed by a poem describing the attributes of the featured gem. Coolidge quoted from the comments included as notes in eleven of the twelve poems.

WILT THOU REACH STARS is from Shakespeare's *The Two Gentlemen of Verona*, act 1, scene 3.

The **KING OF HANOVER**, Ernest Augustus (1771–1851), fifth son of George III and Queen Charlotte, was referred to as the "Black Sheep" by members of the royal family. Made Duke of Cumberland in 1799, he followed a military career, was known for his imprudence and willful disregard of public opinion; he was even, on several occasions, suspected of plotting or committing murder. When William IV died in 1837, the **SALIC LAW** that prevents female dynastic succession prevailed in Hanover, and Cumberland became king (*ODNB*; *OED*).

The artist John **FLAXMAN** (1755–1826) was first educated in the Covent Garden shop of his father, John Flaxman (1726–1795), a sculptor. Flaxman's strengths tended toward the classical, allegorical, and poetic. His talents extended from decorative designs and reliefs to monuments and free-standing sculpture; he also did illustrations for works such as Homer's *Iliad* and *Odyssey* and Dante's *Divine Comedy*. Widely regarded as one of the most innovative and versatile artists of his time, he became the first professor of sculpture at the Royal Academy in 1810. The **SHIELD OF ACHILLES**, considered one of Rundell & Bridge's greatest achievements, was Flaxman's interpretation of Homer's description in the eighteenth book of the *Iliad*. In all, five shields were made, one for George IV's coronation banquet, now in the Royal Collection, and the others for members of the aristocracy. Each is of silver-gilt, measures thirty-five and a half inches in diameter, and weighs 669 ounces (*ODNB*; Hartop, *Royal Goldsmiths*, 105–108, 117, 154; John Flaxman, *Lectures on Sculpture . . . with a brief memoir of the author* [1829]; Philip Rundell, *The Shield of Achilles* [1821], Royal Collection, accessed 20 Dec. 2010, http://www.royalcollection.org.uk/eGallery/).

The silver-gilt copy of the **PORTLAND VASE**, the Roman vessel held by the British Museum since 1810, was reproduced by Rundell & Bridge to serve as a wine cooler and featured a watertight liner (Hartop, *Royal Goldsmiths*, 118, 154).

The **RUBY**, always associated with **EDWARD** of Woodstock (1330–1376), Prince of Wales and Aquitaine, is one of the oldest gems incorporated into the Imperial State Crown. The crown also includes the Second Star of Africa (the second largest stone cut from the Cullinan Diamond), the Stuart Sapphire, St. Edward's Sapphire, and Queen Elizabeth I's pearls. The Imperial State Crown is traditionally worn at the conclusion of the coronation service at Westminster Abbey and for the state opening of Parliament (*ODNB*; "The Crown Jewels," Official Website of the British Monarchy, accessed 26 July 2011, http://www.royal.gov.uk).

1. Closing quotation marks supplied.
2. Quotation marks supplied or altered for clarity in remainder of paragraph.

Friday. 28. Dec.

To-day we have visited Mr Hope's collection of vases & pictures in Duchess St. The house where these pictures are is built round a Quadrangle. a dreary, paved court. You enter a sort of hall on the ground floor, pass through a second hall and ascend a grand stair-case which conducts you to the shew rooms. Four of these are filled with antique Vases, mostly Etruscan, with red figures on a black ground, or vice versa, the black on the red. These vases, of every size and form, are many of them of great beauty. I believe the collection is considered the finest in England, and is still of much value, though not so much as it was some time since when such things were more rare.

The Vases are placed on shelves, and an iron railing runs before them, reaching high enough to prevent the curious spectator from handling these relics of ancient art, but not in the least degree obstructing his sight of them. Some few are in presses with glass doors. I looked long & admiringly, & marvelled in my own mind how things so apparently simple should excite such emotions so strong a sense of the beautiful.

From these rooms which are not very large, you pass into what is called the Picture Gallery. Here are principally the works of Italian Masters. There are four pictures close together by Guido. A Roman Daughter, a Lucretia, or what I took to be a Lucretia, a Cupid disarmed & bound, and a fourth of which I do not remember the subject.—A full length figure of the Saviour & the martyrdom of St. Sebastian are by Domenichino.—A large Raphael is the triumph of St. Michael the Archangel over Satan.—A Titian represents the Saviour, half-length, with a disciple or some other person who seems to be questioning him.—A wild landscape of rocks & mountains, with the figure of an old man suspended by his hands & feet with his face upwards, is marked Salvator Rosa. A charming picture by the same artist differs but little from the "Soothsayers" of the Bridgewater Gallery.——

There are Holy families by various Italian masters and a very large Venus & Adonis by Rubens. The Venus larger & fatter even than is wont with Rubens. The nymphs in the same style of Flemish beauty, and Adonis sprawling on his back, has the chest & limbs of a wrestler. A small landscape by the same painter, a cliff with a watchtower on which a red light is burning, overhanging the Sea, I admired much in spite of my general animosity against Rubens. From this Gallery we passed into a long room filled with statues, most of them if not all, I believe, antiques, A large marble vase, with figures in relief, occupied the middle of the room, and there were tripods and candelabra, and Egyptian figures in abundance.

Our next stage was the dining room. Here a marble mantel piece with a bust of one of the Hope family in the centre, was ornamented at the two ends by two horses heads as large as life. In the same room is a beautiful figure of a shepherd's boy seated on a fleece with his crook and dog, which Mr Coolidge thinks he once saw in Italy, and believes to be by Thorwaldson.

We passed through many rooms variously furnished & adorned, all however in "deshabille" as this is not the shew season, and it is only through the interest of Mr Baring that we obtain admittance at all. One room was filled with Egyptian, another with Indian curiosities & relics, vases, obelisks, candelabra, figures of men or beasts, pictures of Mosques &c. &c. In other rooms were Chinese Jars & such like orientalisms, but we reached at last a large apartment hung almost entirely with paintings by Dutch masters. Game and domestic animals, dogs, swans, peacocks &c by Weenix. Fruit and Flower pieces by Van Huysom and Van Os. Peasants, boors, soldiers, women and children by Teniers & Ostade. Landscapes by Ruysdael, Cuyp and Wouvermanns. Seapieces by Vandervelde and Backhuysen. Dutch ladies in satin & velvet, Musicians &c by Miens. Cattle pieces by Paul Potter. The walls of this room were not only covered but there was a sort of stand going it's whole length, leaving only space to pass easily round, the top covered with vases and small figures in marble and bronze, and the sides hung with paintings so as almost to double the number which the room could otherwise have contained. From hence we returned to the great staircase, and after stopping to look at a portrait of Hope, the author of Anastasius, arrayed in Turkish costume, we paid our fee of half a guinea to the housekeeper and left this temple of taste and the arts. This residence of an English ^untitled^ gentleman. Yet I had heard so much of Mr Hope and Mr Hope's house, of his fastidious taste, his high fashion, his elegant wife, become since his death Viscountess Beresford, that what I saw hardly equalled my expectations. There are surely a great many beautiful & curious things collected together between these four walls—Vases, pictures, statues, antiques, articles of virtu, but the whole has the air of a magazine, a storehouse, a ~~fancy~~ Bazaar, rather than a dwelling house, a home where a family live and move, having their wants, their occupations and their habits. There is more than the coldness & dampness & formal arrangement of a townhouse shut up, under the care of servants, during the dead season; but perhaps, light & warmth & dress & company might put life where it seems most wanting. The rooms did not strike me as particularly well proportioned, nor finished with much effect. The floors are parquetted, the ceilings painted, the furniture generally after the antique. I believe that Mr Hope wrote a book upon furniture, which procured for him the "soubriquet" of Furniture Hope.

From Duchess St. where I parted with Mr Coolidge, Mr Heard & Mr Higginson, I took my way alone to call on Miss Sindry Mrs Bates, Mrs Searle & Mrs Wormeley. On my way to Mrs W. Mrs Searle being with me, I was struck by the appearance of a small company, six or eight children in a most peculiar costume, long, blue gowns falling from their necks to their heels, with girdles round their waists, gaiters on their feet & ankles, their heads bare & closely shorn. They looked like miniature monks. They were, as Mrs Searle informed me, Bluecoat Boys—belonging to the school where Coleridge & Lamb were educated. Mrs Searle told me farther that this uncouth and antiquated dress, comprehending pantaloons of buckskin, leather breeches in short, was worn by these charity boys at all seasons, no change being permitted from the old, established laws of the foundation—and that summer & winter, they go with their cloth gowns and leathern under clothes, and with their heads bare, through cold & heat, sunshine and storm.—Surely this cannot be. Mrs Searle must be mistaken.—I reached home about 4. P.M. have dined (at 6. P.M.) and am now writing by candle-light. Mr C. has gone with Mr Heard to see Power the actor in some one of his droll characters.

———————————————————————————————————

Thomas **HOPE** (1769–1831), art collector, author, and designer, was the son of John Hope (1737–1784), a wealthy Dutch banker in the Amsterdam-based firm of Hope & Company. Thomas Hope studied classical civilization and as a young man spent eight years traveling around the Mediterranean, sketching and collecting antiquities. In 1795 Hope relocated to London and was soon recognized as a scholar, connoisseur, and patron of the arts. His membership in several of the most prestigious institutions provided him with the opportunity to influence modern design and taste. His Duchess Street mansion, designed by

Robert Adam but altered greatly from the original, first opened to select ticket-holding visitors in 1804. The rooms and galleries within the mansion contained furniture of Hope's design made by skilled craftsmen he chose personally, more than 1,500 vases, ancient and contemporary sculpture, and numerous works of art, particularly of the Renaissance and Baroque periods. In 1807 Hope published *Household Furniture and Interior Decoration*, a work that included line drawings of the interior spaces of the Duchess Street mansion and schematic drawings and measurements of the furnishings. From 1787 through 1817 Hope made several European tours, collecting as he traveled, and during one trip to Rome, he met the young sculptor Bertel Thorvaldsen [THORWALDSON] (ca. 1770–1844). Hope owned eleven works by Thorvaldsen, including the *Shepherd Boy* (1817) that Joseph Coolidge may indeed have seen during his own European tour in the early 1820s. Hope's ELEGANT WIFE, Louisa Beresford Hope (d. 1851), married William Carr Beresford (1768–1854), a cousin, in November 1832. At her death Hope's extensive collection was distributed between two other family homes, and the Duchess Street mansion was demolished (*ODNB*; Turner, *Dictionary of Art*, 14:744–745, 30:763–766; Ziegler, *Sixth Great Power*, 70–72; *Gentleman's Magazine*, n.s., 101 [1831]: 368–370; *Times* [London], 4 Feb. 1831).

The BLUECOAT BOYS were residents and students at Christ's Hospital, a school for children of indigent parents. The clothing, little modified since the school's sixteenth-century founding, consisted of "a long blue coat, reaching to the ancles, and girt about the waist with a leathern girdle; a yellow cassock or petticoat . . . and stockings of yellow worsted. A pair of white bands about the neck . . . and the black cap, upon the smallness of which the boys now pride themselves as a peculiar distinction of the school." In order to facilitate the growth of Britain's commercial interests, many of the boys were apprenticed to merchants in the British colonies in America, in the Caribbean, or on board merchant trading vessels, and girls were sent to serve as domestics in the homes of colonial elites (Peter Wilson Coldham, *Child Apprentices in America, from Christ's Hospital, London, 1617–1778* [1990]; G. A. T. Allan, *Christ's Hospital* [1984]; William Trollope, *A History of the Royal Foundation of Christ's Hospital* [1834], 50).

Samuel Taylor COLERIDGE (1772–1834) and Charles LAMB (1775–1834) were both students at Christ's Hospital from about 1782 until the early 1790s and became lifelong friends. Their experiences at the school are reflected in some of the poetry, stories, and reminiscences they subsequently published (*ODNB*).

Tyrone (William Grattan) POWER (1797–1841), actor, was born in Ireland and, though striking in appearance, met with only a lukewarm reception in his earliest attempts on stage. Beginning in 1824, however, he achieved success for his comic portrayal of Irishmen, and from that point on, he limited himself to those. His energetic portrayals of "blundering, good-natured, and eccentric Irish characters" were popular in the London and Dublin theaters and met with moderate success in America. He made his last performance at New York's Park Theatre on 9 March 1841; departing America two days later on the steamship *President*, he was lost at sea when the ship foundered in the mid-Atlantic (*ODNB*; *Boston Daily Atlas*, 13 Mar. 1841; *New-Hampshire Sentinel*, 28 Apr. 1841; *Daily National Intelligencer* [Washington, D.C.], 2 Apr. 1845).

Sunday. 30. December.

yesterday we visited Crockford's, the Traveller's Club, and for the second time Rundell & Bridge. We obtained access to the Pandemonium of St. James St. by means of a card from one of Crockford's sons procured by Mr Baring. Verily like it's great prototype in the regions below this palace of Devils is a goodly building. The exteriour is sufficiently modest, but within the amount of gilding might satisfy the taste of Mammon. I must get the Paradise Lost and read Milton's description of the real Pandemonium. I have a vivid impression but no distinct recollection of it's gorgeous glories.

You enter Crockford's from St. James' St. To the right as you enter, is the Coffee room, where fires were burning in two grates and several tables spread about the room. On the left is the reading room, maps hang against the wall, and newspapers and reviews lie upon the tables. In neither of these rooms is there any shew or finery. Their character is of warmth, comfort and pleasant employment. Refreshment for the body, recreation for the mind. The furniture is not particularly elegant, the carpets faded and all a little worn. Between the Coffee & the reading rooms there is a passage way from which you ascend a few broad steps & find yourself in a Hall lighted from above. Here the walls are marble, and a magnificent staircase, with a balustrade of bronze and gilding, leads to the upper story. The staircase lands on a corridor the ceiling of which is supported by marble columns with gilt bases and capitals. From the corridor you enter the principal apartments. First a saloon, a large room with three windows on the street. Between the windows and on the opposite side of the room, are looking glasses of great size and beauty, four in number. Over the doors are paintings done on the walls or perhaps inserted, representing, apparently, sporting scenes, hunting, hawking &c. but the day being dark, I saw these pictures indistinctly. The house is at present undergoing some repairs, the velvet curtains had been taken from the windows, and the rich carpets from the floors, so that the apartments were not in their glory. What I saw of the furniture consisted of marble tables on gilt stands and chairs of silk & gold, card tables carved & gilt, and rich chandeliers. In the saloon the walls & ceiling were adorned with much gilding and a huge gilt chandelier hung in the midst.

From the Saloon you pass into a smaller room also decorated with gilding and mirrors, gold and glass. Two doors, besides the one from the Saloon, open from the smaller room. The one to the right leads to an elegant supper-room, whilst just before you, at the extremity of the suite of apartments, lies the fatal hazard-room, the Sanctum of this diabolic temple. It's walls are papered in chocolate and gold in a rich and rare pattern, and two doors open from it into bathing rooms. A chill came over me as I looked round and thought of the amount of human suffering, of misery, despair & ruin that these walls of chocolate and gold had looked upon. No dungeon, no torture chamber has probably witnessed such agonies. The worst that man can do to man is less than what he inflicts upon himself. Are there evil spirits who are permitted to walk the world & whisper into men's ears and tempt them to perdition? Are such bad influences within the scheme of Providence?

> Death, darkness, danger, are our natural lot;
> And evil spirits <u>may</u> our walk attend
> For aught the wisest know or comprehend—

The very bath rooms connected with the Hazard room could tell their tale of fevered wretches, hot, weary, worn & miserable, seeking refreshment, bodily relief, after nights & perhaps days of mad exitement. In D'Israeli's "Young Duke," (a book I am told of little worth as a picture of ^high^ society,) there is a gambling scene where the hero remains, if I remember right, fortyeight or more hours, given up to the fiend by whom he is possessed, sits knee-deep in torn cards, scarcely tastes food, sleeps not at all, and rises having lost a hundred thousand pounds, half a million of dollars,—a vast fortune in America.

Seeing the Unholy of Unholies we returned to the Corridor and visited two cardrooms at it's farther extremity. The walls of one of these were hung with blue satin. Going down stairs we remarked in the marble-coated wall, and opening on one of the landing places, a private door which leads to the private apartments of the High Priest of the Infernal Temple, Crockford himself. This man, (God made him and therefore let him pass for a man.) this man has a daughter married to a Clergyman!! Was it on the same principle that the "Old woman of Berkeley," who anointed herself with the fat of babes, made her son a monk and her daughter a nun, to stand between her and the fires of Hell? And does Crockford expect by the intercession of the Church, to elude the summons of <u>his</u> master? When the roll call sounds for the evil ones of the earth, if the evil are those who do evil, I doubt whether any valid excuse can be found for this great

Captain of the host. I quitted his abode with mingled feelings of pain and gratified curiosity. During my stay within these rich apartments I wondered whether my eyes had not been rubbed with the fairy ointment of which Sir Walter Scott tells in one of his works, and by means of which the dark, damp, unwholesome caves of Elves are made to appear stately halls & splendid chambers.

My next visit was to the Traveller's Club in Pall Mall. To get an idea of the perfection to which comfort has been carried in England, it is necessary to see the interiour of a Club House. The neatness, order and admirable arrangement of these establishments is marvellous. Never were means better adapted to ends. No where does the spirit of system which pervades English life shew itself to greater advantage. The only objection that can be made to these Clubs is on the ground of their moral influence. They must interfere with domestic life, weaning the husband from his home, and diminishing the inducements to marriage. Single men may live with so much ease & elegance at comparitively small cost, and with no cares of a family, that they have every motive to remain single, whilst married men are tempted by the superiour luxuries of a Club establishment to desert their own less desirable abodes; or if they remain at home it is with a discontented and repining spirit. They are ill content to share the narrow quarters & homely meal of the wife and children.

We walked through the Coffee room where several tables were spread with neatness & elegance. In the library we found books, (not a great many as the Traveller's library is small,) maps, periodical publications &c &c. with many armchairs & tables. In the reading room were newspapers and ottomans. There are sitting rooms, dressing rooms, bathing rooms. A man may do any thing at his club but sleep, and be better served than at his own house. The Club Houses are large, well-furnished, well-warmed, well-lighted, well-provided in all ways. There are books, society, conversation, good servants, good wines, and as simple or as recherché a dinner, excellent in it's kind, as a man's taste or purse may decree. It seems to me that to make a person perfectly happy in Club life there are no requisites but those of the french philosopher, a good stomach and a cold heart. There is every thing for bodily comfort and much for intellectual gratification. Nothing for the affections. Yet here I speak like a woman, who considers the affections inseparably connected with her own sex. A man may have his friendships warm & disinterested, without being either a husband or a father.

From the Travellers we went to Rundell & Bridge to finish our examination of the treasures contained in a homely shop on Ludgate Hill, far exceeding those of palaces. I looked again at diamonds, rubies, emeralds, sapphires, opals & other forms of petrified light, but this time our principal object was the plate. The Vases, cups, dishes, candlesticks &c &c at Rundell & Bridges, setting aside the value of the material, are beautiful as works of art. The designs are graceful, fanciful, tasteful & elegant in the extreme. The workmanship is I suppose, equal to anything in the world. The figures chased on the different pieces of plate are often from the antique, often the designs of the best artists, and the form of each article is generally such as to captivate the eye and the imagination. We were told that gold plate, as it is usually called, means silver gilt—that with the exception of very few articles, not even Royalty itself required all gold. Gold is not only, according to the English standard, worth sixteen times as much as silver, but it is, owing to it's greater softness, so much more difficult in the workmanship, as to be seldom called for in plate. Not even the Marquis of Westminster, with his thousand pounds a day, cares to pay for it. I cannot particularise what I saw in the plate of Rundell & Bridge. All the most beautiful forms of Nature & of Poetry, as far as these last are tangible, seemed to have been put in requisition. Nymphs, Goddesses, Graces, Loves in all the variety of exquisite attitude, supported fruit-baskets, desert-dishes, candelabra & ornamental vases. There were Swans with arching necks, serpents turning in graceful folds, Rams with "wreathed horns superb," Goats with shaggy beards, birds with long legs, necks & bills, such as Herons, Storks & Cranes,—to say nothing of flowers, leaves & vines, the Grape with it's tendrils & clusters, the Ivy, with berry and leaf, the Oak leaf & acorn, the Rose & it's bud, the olive & it's fruit—Cups, Goblets, Ewers, Candlesticks, Inkstands, Bowls, every description of article useful & ornamental, were upheld, or entwined, or over-arched & over-shadowed, by all manner of bending & wreathing standing & falling, stooping or lying, erect or prone, creeping, clinging, winding, waving, curling, grasping, complex or simply beautiful forms of life, animal & vegetable, which the taste of the designer and the skill of the workman had combined to call into new life, the life of art.

The frosted and chased works of silver & silver gilt, are executed, as we were told, only by the most patient, careful, ingenious & experienced of the operatives in the employ of the great Jewellers. Hence the immense cost of the workmanship. I shall remember my two visits to Messrs Rundell & Bridge as among things well-worth remembering.

I returned home, Mr Coolidge going in another direction, by way of the Pantheon Bazaar. Capt. Wormeley dined with us. John Glass was to have come but declined on the plea of another engagement. ——

———————————————————————————————————

At the time of the Coolidges' visit, CROCKFORD'S was the most fashionable club in London. It was owned by William Crockford (ca. 1776–1844), a fishmonger's son who built a small fortune on gambling at hazard, cribbage, and horseracing, and used the proceeds to open his own lavish gaming club at 50 St. James's Street. Crockford commissioned architect Benjamin Dean Wyatt, and although the exterior was simply done, it was here that Wyatt introduced his "Louis Quatorze" style, featuring an expansive use of gilt and mirrors and launching a new fashion for extravagant interior design. The club, already proclaimed as the "Pandemonium in St. James's," opened its doors on 2 January 1828; the clientele was determined by Crockford's personal invitation. Membership, which cost thirty pounds per year, was limited to between 1,000 and 1,200 of the wealthiest of Britain's male society, but ambassadors and "foreigners of distinction" were welcomed gratis. In the elegant dining room gentlemen enjoyed the finest in French cuisine, paired with wine from Crockford's generous cellar, for modest prices, but while in the gaming room members indulged at no additional cost (*ODNB*; Henry Blyth, *Hell and Hazard or William Crockford versus the Gentlemen of England* [1969], esp. 88–116; John Timbs, *Clubs and Club Life in London* [1908], 240–244; *Bentley's Miscellany* 17 [1845]: 142–155, 251–264; *Gentleman's Magazine*, n.s., 22 [1844]: 103–104; *Times* [London], 1 Jan. 1828).

DEATH, DARKNESS . . . KNOW OR COMPREHEND is from William Wordsworth's "Apology," first published in 1822 in his *Ecclesiastical Sketches, in a Series of Sonnets* (reprinted in the first American edition of *The Poetical Works of William Wordsworth* [New Haven, 1836], 173).

In book 4 of Benjamin DISRAELI'S *Young Duke: "A Moral Tale, Though Gay"* (1831), the hero, George Augustus Frederick, Duke of St. James, is gradually drawn into the world of gambling through a series of visits to the false and scheming Baron De Berghem's gaming room. The young duke grows tired of small gains and losses, and the baron, sensing this, invites him to come to a more private session, along with a few other select men, the following evening. Over the course of two days in which the men play and dine, the duke's appetite dwindles along with his fortune, and at the end he has lost £100,000. But more than the money lost, he has lost his youth and beauty to his "dissipated career" and sees himself as a disgrace to his ancestors and in danger of becoming one of the "unhallowed things that were around him" (Benjamin Disraeli, *Young Duke: "A Moral Tale, Though Gay"* [London, 1831], 3:73–74).

The OLD WOMAN OF BERKELEY, a ballad "showing how an old Woman rode double, and who rode before her," was written by Robert Southey and relates the story of one who was unable to escape, even in death, the consequences of a wicked and sinful life (Robert Southey, *Poems* [Bristol, 1799], 149–160).

The FAIRY OINTMENT is a reference to Sir Walter Scott's "Introduction to the Tale of Tamlane. On the fairies of popular superstition," printed in volume 2 of *Minstrelsy of the Scottish Border* (London, 1802).

The TRAVELLERS CLUB was founded on 5 May 1819 in order "to form a point of re-union for gentlemen who had travelled abroad; and to afford them the opportunity of inviting, as Honorary Visitors, the principal members of all the foreign missions and travellers of distinction." Temporarily housed first at 12 Waterloo Place, then moved to 49 Pall Mall, members of the club formed a committee and conducted one of the first design competitions held by a London club, soliciting plans from a select group of architects for a new permanent location. Charles Barry (1795–1860), the chosen architect, recreated the elegance of the Italian Renaissance, inspired by his own recent travels and studies in Italy, achieving one of his first masterpieces of architectural design. In 1832 the Travellers Club opened its doors at 106 Pall Mall, where it continues today (*ODNB*; *Survey of London*, vols. 29 and 30 [1960], 399–408; Timbs, *Clubs and Club Life*, 198–201).

Robert Grosvenor (1767–1845), first Marquess of WESTMINSTER (*ODNB*).

Monday. 31. December

the last day of the year. The Sun shines and the air is mild. Yesterday, Dec. 30. Capt. Wormeley dined with us again & Col. Gamble with him.——

John Grattan GAMBLE (ca. 1779–1852), son of American Revolutionary War veteran Robert Gamble, had started his career as a merchant in Richmond and became director of the Farmers' Bank in that city. During the War of 1812 Gamble was a lieutenant in the Richmond Light Infantry Blues, part of the corps of Virginia Militia under Coolidge's father, Thomas Mann Randolph. By the end of 1827 Gamble and his family had relocated to Tallahassee, Florida, where he held large tracts of land and planted cotton, tobacco, and sugarcane. With Coolidge's uncle Thomas Eston Randolph and her cousin Francis Eppes, Gamble served as trustee to the fledgling University of Florida. In 1838 Gamble was the first president of the Union Bank of Florida and sold Union Bank bonds to European firms, including nearly one thousand while he was visiting London (*PTJRS*, 6:305; Herbert A. Johnson, Charles T. Cullen, Charles F. Hobson, et al., eds., *Papers of John Marshall* [1974–2006], 3:121; Michael G. Schene, "Middle Florida Entrepreneurs," *Florida Historical Quarterly* 54 [1975]: 61–73; Clarence E. Carter and John Porter Bloom, eds., *Territorial Papers of the United States* [1934–1975], 25:109–111, 267–268; "Richmond Light Infantry Blues, of Richmond, Virginia," *Huddy and Duval's U.S. Military Magazine* 3 [1841]: 28; United States Federal Census, Seventh Census, 1850, 8th Division, Leon County, Florida, s.v. "Gamble, John G.," Ancestry. com; *Richmond Enquirer*, 10 May 1805; *New-York Spectator*, 18 Apr. 1839; *Richmond Daily Dispatch*, 26 Oct. 1852).

London. January. 1839.
Wednesday. 2nd

Yesterday, New Year's day, we gave our french servants, Joseph and Josephine, leave and money to go to Drury Lane, where they saw Van Amburgh & his Lions, followed by a Christmas Pantomime. I asked Josephine, on her return late at night, whilst she was arranging my hair, what she had seen—She answered that the "bêtes" came first and afterwards "la betise"—the Pantomine,—of which she spoke with true french disgust for the clumsiness of English attempts at pleasantry.

On this same day, tuesday, Mr Heard went to Highgate to see Jefferson and carry him his New Year's presents, a book from himself and one from me. He found him well in health, but in spirit subdued and restrained. I am not satisfied with his situation. I wish I knew what it were best to do. London & Regent St. is no place for my boy, nor does the school at Highgate come up to my expectations.

Our New Year's dinner was taken with Capt. & Mrs Wormeley. Here we met the Canon Riego, brother to the murdered patriot of that name. He is living in poverty and obscurity—an old and broken-down man, swarthy & meagre, but fire-eyed & apparently unquenched in spirit. He speaks English grammatically but with a bad accent. This first of January was the anniversary of the day when, nineteen years ago, his brother rose in rebellion to set in blood.

The Canon spoke in few words, but with concentrated bitterness, of the present disastrous state of Spain, and of the idle yet cruel curiosity with which the rest of the world looked on upon the bloody "spectacle" of butchery which is being enacted, as it were, for their amusement. "My countrymen murder each other," he said, "to fill your newspapers; your pampered and luxurious state of society takes pleasure in such excitement." I felt sorry to think indeed how little sympathy exists in the sufferings of the Spaniards, and how true it is that their murderous contests form a sort of gladiatorial exhibition at which the civilized world, the Romans of the day, gaze without horror. This Canon Riego, would, it is said, have been Archbishop of Toledo but for the change of times and his own downfall and exile. He speaks in the highest terms of Mr Prescott's book which he considers one of the best works on Spanish History ever written.

We came home at 10. P.M. I began to read Sam Slick, borrowed from Mrs Wormeley & to be kept only two days. At half past eleven, just as I was preparing for bed, or rather to leave the drawing-room, Mr Sumner came in & staid till half past one. He had been dining out, as he does every day, but to-day with some choice spirits. He has got into the best society of London and England—not only Lords & Ladies, but statesmen, authors, wits & scholars. Mr Sumner's anecdotes of persons he sees and things he hears make me regret that Mr Coolidge & myself brought no letters, and that we know nobody. Charles Sumner is a lawyer, clever in his profession, simple in his manners, and independent in his speech—He gives his own opinions freely but respects those of others—is entirely <u>national</u>, a true son of Uncle Sam, who neither disclaims his pedigree nor boasts of it—two rocks on one of which Americans in this country, are, in conversation, almost sure to run. He is tall and rather <u>not ill</u> then positively well-looking, sufficiently well-bred but neither high-bred nor pretending to it.—dresses like a gentleman but has no air of fashion. He is in short a <u>right</u> clever, sensible, respectable young man who has had a run in the best circles of England, passes his time in the best company, and has been visiting from one nobleman and gentleman's house to another through the autumn and winter.

He speaks with great admiration of three <u>old</u> ladies with whom he has become acquainted, Mrs Joanna Baillie, Mrs Basil Montagu, and the mother of Lord Brougham. He tells us that in England, Carlyle is little known and his writings, comparatively speaking, little read. The United States is the field of his popularity. His history of the French revolution fell dead-born from the English press, he has received for it here, not one shilling, but fifty pounds sterling have been sent him from the U.S. the profits of an edition published in Boston for his benefit. It seems that the "snatchy" style in which it appears at present written, was, to a certain extent, the result as much of accident as of intention. The book was originally more in the narrative form, but the MS. having been entrusted to a friend was, through his carelessness, and the act of some mischievous children or ignorant servant, torn, burnt and reduced to a fragmentary state, out of which the author, dismayed and bewildered by his misfortune, restored it from memory, hastily, impatiently, almost unwillingly, jotting down his thoughts as they rose or were recalled, and getting through with his task under the excitement of a vexed spirit and a sore heart. The result has been the wonderful work on the French Revolution, a sort of Arabesque painting, from which some turn with displeasure on which others gaze with avidity, and which none can contemplate with indifference. It is but just to that friend of Mr Carlyle, under whose careless guardianship the accident happened, to say that he was greatly grieved, and desired to make at least every pecuniary compensation in his power, offering as large a sum as would have been given for the copy-right by any London pub-

lisher, which the author declined receiving. Mr Sumner, after much such
pleasant talk left us at half past one o'clock in the morning, which did not
prevent my giving a few moments more to Sam Slick.

This morning I opened a copy of Milton's "Paradise Lost" left here by
Mr Higginson. I found the description of Pandemonium which haunted
me, in vague recollection, during my visit to Crockford's. I thought of it
whilst within those unsanctified walls, surrounded by painting, carving
& gilding, columns with gilt capitals & bases, mirrors, lamps, candelabra,
chairs & couches of silk & gold &c—and when we entered the Hazard
room—where, during the season, only those persons are admitted who
play, no simple spectator being allowed to witness the proceedings of
the "secret conclave" who set their all on the cast of a die. The saloon
may be crowded, but when once the doors of the Sanctum are closed,
and Crockford has taken his seat, there is no interruption permitted and
no admittance for the uninitiated.

> (Pandemonium, the high capital of Satan & his Peers.)
> And here let those,
> Who boast in mortal things, and wondering tell
> Of Babel and the works of Memphian Kings
> Learn how their greatest monuments of fame—
> ——and art are easily outdone
> By spirits reprobate—
> ——out of the earth a fabric huge
> Rose like an exhalation—
> Built like a temple where pilasters round
> Were set, and Doric pillars overlaid
> With golden architrave; nor did these want
> Cornice or frieze with bossy sculptures graven;
> The roof was fretted gold.—
> ——from the arched roof,
> Pendent by subtle magic, many a row
> Of starry lamps and blazing cressets, fed
> With raptha and asphaltus, yielded light
> As from a sky.——all access was thronged—
> ——but chief the spacious hall,
> Of that infernal court——far within
> The great Seraphic lords and cherubim
> In close recess and secret conclave sat—

I do not mean to say that Crockford's Club House vies, as a building,
with Babel or the works of Memphian Kings, nor that Crockford himself

ranks among the great Seraphic lords, even of the lower regions—I presume that Satan & his peers are not only lords but gentlemen, which Mr Crockford certainly is not. But there is a great deal of glare & shew, "pillars overlaid with golden architrave," "cornice with sculptures graven," "starry lamps & blazing cressets," and sufficiently "spacious halls," and certainly one "close recess" where deeds of darkness, worthy of devils, are daily & nightly done.

The Wormeleys were longtime friends of the CANON RIEGO, Miguel del Riego y Nuñez (ca. 1780–1844), who left Spain for England in March 1823 in the company of his ill sister-in-law, Maria Teresa (ca. 1800–1824). His BROTHER, Rafael del Riego y Nuñez (1785–1823), led a military insurrection in 1820 that turned into a liberal revolution to force Ferdinand VII to acknowledge and support the 1812 constitution he had thrown aside several years earlier. The revolution to form a constitutional monarchy lacked sufficient support from the Spanish people and raised the ire of the Holy Alliance. France dispatched an army to restore Ferdinand VII's absolute power, and Rafael del Riego was captured after Cadiz fell to the French. He was tried for treason in Madrid and hung in November 1823. The British newspapers followed the course of the revolution, printing numerous accounts of "the brave and virtuous" Riego and his "Exaltados," detailing Ferdinand's "machinations," expressing disdain and outrage at France for her interference, and publishing memorials and odes to Riego after his execution. The death of Ferdinand VII in 1833 was followed by seven years of war between factions who supported Don Carlos and the defenders of the throne of Queen Isabella, causing the DISASTROUS STATE of Spain (Raymond Carr, ed., *Spain: A History* [2000], 202, 294; Raymond Carr, *Spain, 1808–1975* [1982], 127–141, 155; Elizabeth Wormeley Latimer, *Spain in the Nineteenth Century* [1897], 131, 139–144; Thomas Crofton Croker and Thomas Francis Dillon Croker, *A Walk from London to Fulham* [1860], 96–99; Francis Lieber, ed., *Encyclopædia Americana* [1832], 11:37; Census Returns of England and Wales, 1841, St. Pancras, Middlesex, s.v. "Del Rago, Miguel," Ancestry.com; *Gentleman's Magazine*, n.s., 27 [1847]: 103; *Examiner* [London], 17 Mar. 1822; *Morning Chronicle* [London], 9 Aug. 1822, 26 Sept., 4, 28 Oct., 15, 20 Nov. 1823).

William Hickling PRESCOTT (1796–1859), historian and author, was the grandson of William Prescott (1726–1795), who commanded the American soldiers at the Battle of Bunker Hill in 1775. The younger Prescott's three-volume work *History of the Reign of Ferdinand and Isabella, the Catholic* (1838), based on ten years of research using books and manuscripts previously unavailable in America, was an international triumph (*ANB; DAB*).

Charles SUMNER (1811–1874), lawyer, politician, and reformer, arrived in England a month before the Coolidges. He had spent the previous five months in France, the starting point of his European tour. Sumner graduated in 1833 from

Harvard Law School, where he was mentored by Joseph Story. After three years of practice Sumner convinced Judge Story, among others, to finance a trip abroad for the purpose of "obtaining a knowledge of languages, of observing the manners customs & institutions of other people than my own," and for legal studies in France, England, and Germany. Sumner's ties with Story and other prominent American legal and literary figures guaranteed his success. Within weeks of his arrival in London he was welcomed into its legal circles and was able to observe proceedings in the Common Pleas and Queen's Bench. Soon a favorite among the political, literary, and aristocratic sets, he achieved a social status far beyond his own expectations, even attending the coronation of Queen Victoria. After his return to Boston in 1840, Sumner focused his energies on prison and educational reform and worked against the spread of slavery. He was elected to the U.S. Senate in 1851, where he fought for the repeal of the Fugitive Slave Act and argued vehemently against the expansion of slavery into the recently acquired western territories. In 1856 he delivered an antislavery oration that so offended South Carolina congressman Preston Brooks that he attacked Sumner in the Senate chamber, beating him severely with his cane. Sumner continued to speak out against slavery, and he worked during the Civil War to convince President Lincoln to put an end to the institution. Sumner was acquainted with the Coolidges from their shared social circles in Boston, as was his brother George, and he thought Ellen Coolidge possessed "a fine intelligence." The two occasionally exchanged books and discussed the merits of various political, historical, and literary publications (*ANB; DAB*; Anne-Marie Taylor, *Young Charles Sumner and the Legacy of the American Enlightenment, 1811–1851* [2001], 88–125; Charles Sumner to Joseph Story, 13 July 1837, Sumner to George Sumner, 14 Apr., 13–14 June 1848, 18 Mar. 1850, in *The Selected Letters of Charles Sumner*, ed. Beverly Wilson Palmer [1990], 1:27–28, 219–222, 230–232, 287–289; Charles Sumner to George Sumner, 1 June 1838, Sumner to Joseph Story, 14, 27 June, 12 July 1838, in *Memoir and Letters of Charles Sumner*, ed. Edward L. Pierce [1877], 1:312, 315–317, 321–325, 329–338).

Anna Dorothea Benson Skepper was the third wife of Basil MONTAGU (1770–1851), noted author and legal reformer. Eleanor Syme Brougham (1750–1839) was Lord Brougham's MOTHER (*ODNB*, s.v. "Montagu, Basil" and "Brougham, Henry Peter").

In early 1835 Thomas CARLYLE had completed the first volume of his history of the French Revolution and passed the manuscript to his good friend John Stuart Mill for his comments. On the evening of 6 March, Mill arrived at the Carlyles' home, "the very picture of despair" and "in a state not unlike insanity," to tell Carlyle that the manuscript had been "utterly destroyed." The work, which had consumed more than five months of Carlyle's time, a servant mistook for waste paper and threw into the fire. Writing to his publisher the next day Carlyle described the "accident," omitting the details to protect Mill, and explained that the publication would be delayed. He reassured Mill that he was not giving up and had ordered more paper and books, convinced that the work could go on. Mill promptly gave Carlyle two hundred pounds, twice what Carlyle said his labor and materials were worth, and helped procure the additional books Carlyle wanted for research. *The French Revolution* was published in 1837. In his review Mill wrote, "This is not so much a history as an epic poem; and notwithstanding, or even in consequence of this, the truest of histories." It has become a classic work on the subject (*ODNB*; John D. Rosenberg, introduction to Thomas Carlyle, *The French Revolution: A History* [2002], xix; Thomas Carlyle to James Fraser, 7 Mar. 1835, Carlyle to John Stuart Mill, 7, 9 13, 17 Mar. 1835, Carlyle to John A. Carlyle, 23 Mar. 1835, Carlyle to Margaret A. Carlyle, 25 Mar. 1835, in *Carlyle Letters*, 8:66–87).

Coolidge's DESCRIPTION OF PANDEMONIUM comes from John Milton, *Paradise Lost*, bk. 1, lines 692–795.

Thursday. 3ᵈ January.

Yesterday, Wednesday, we dined in Fenchurch St. Mʳˢ & Miss Richards of the party. Fenchurch St. is in the heart of the City. A weary way to go for a dinner. It is possible to be too hospitable & err by compelling people to receive too much. Luckily the night was starlight. The day had been fine and I had taken advantage of it to walk in Gordon Square with Mʳˢ Wormeley. Every one knows that between the town & the city of London, the residences of the gentry & of the cockneys, there is a large space, comprised no doubt within the limits of the town, but having a character of it's own, inhabited by the unfashionable classes of society, the respectables, the professionals, the intermediates, people very often of substance but never of rank. Here are streets & pleasant squares & often large houses. Among fashionables it goes by the name of the Terra Incognita and is said to lie somewhere between Mayfair & Mesopotamia.

Saturday. 5ᵗʰ January.

Thursday was an uneventful day. I called in Dean St. where I saw Angus Fletcher and spoke to him of a packet, containing Sargeant's "Temperance Tales" and Miss Beecher's "Letter on Slavery" which I wished to send to his mother in Edinburgh. He shewed me some casts. One a bust of Mʳˢ Hemans in which the profile is finer than the full face—Also a charming head of Psyche, a cast from Gibson. Psyche is represented as a very young girl with a modest and timid expression, the eyes cast down, the whole head bending a little forward. The bosom that of fourteen years, just beginning to swell. An Eve by Baillie is a small, naked figure but not in the slightest degree indelicate—so much is modesty a thing of expression. This naked Eve looks far more like a virtuous woman than does many a lady draped from throat to toe—

I passed the evening in reading Sam Slick of which I finished the first volume. Is it strange that the Yankee character (and under the general name of Yankee, Europeans include all Americans,) should be held in contempt when such representations of it are before the public and in high favour for their wit and cleverness? Sam Slick, for example, is full of shrewd sense & practical wisdom. He is kind-hearted, good-tempered, cheerful and even, to a certain extent, liberal, willing to give and to do good to his neighbour. Yet what a genu-ine rascal he is after all. What a low-bred, conceited knave! How full of craft & trickery! What a lying, cheating, swindling, peddling, impudent scoundrel! What gentleman could tolerate the companionship of such a fellow as Sam Slick with all his sagacity, gaiety and wit? The language is the slang introduced by Major Downing, less pure & characteristic but a good imitation of the original. There is too much of Sam Slick—he is, after all, a long-winded, prosy fellow who talks at times a good deal of nonsense and dull nonsense, but there is in this book much knowledge of "human natur" in some of it's modifications, and a quick eye for effects with no great depth of penetration into causes. There are home truths and quaint expressions which, arrest the attention though they do not dwell in the memory. "This is what I call independence" says old Slick to his son, slapping his pockets well filled with gold American Eagles, "line the pockets and the spirit will be free." And again whenever Sam Slick hears cant he suspects hypocrisy—"A long face" he says, he has generally found to cover "a long conscience." He describes the blank expression which succeeds a look of covert triumph, upon some unexpected disclosure or announcement, as "rubbin the writin" out of a man's face &c &c.

Yesterday, Friday 4th Jan. Mr Coolidge & myself went to Chiswick a villa belonging to the Duke of Devonshire, on the banks of the Thames, a few miles from London. The day was cold and dark and the season winter, the house out of order and undergoing a cleansing process, furniture all covered up, many of the pictures taken down, and every thing in disarray, yet I can conceive that under more pleasant circumstances, it must be a charming spot. The grounds looked beautifully even in this depth of winter, the grass still green and fresh, the dark foliage of evergreen trees, cedars and I believe yews, relieved upon a grey sky, and the murmur of waters always pleasant to the ear, made a most pleasant change from the mud and filth and smoke and noise, of dirty, dark London. The house is old having been built by the Earl of Burlington more than a hundred years ago. The plan was originally after one of Palladio's, a celebrated though small building at Vicenza, but being found deficient in accommodation has been altered and added to, until little, I should think, of the original character can remain. It consists now of a centre building with wings. You enter from the front portico, by a somewhat narrow vestibule, into a circular Hall hung with pictures. Back of the Hall comes what is called the Gallery, three rooms opening into each other much gilt and ornamented. A portion of this gilding has not been re-newed since the house was built and is still in good preservation. In the gallery are paintings & statues. On each side of the Hall are parlours & bed-rooms with dressing rooms. So far for the main body of the building. There are two wings. In one is the dining & other living rooms, on the other the private apartments of the Duke. The whole house is strangely cut up—there are more dressing rooms & minute bedchambers, closets & recesses than I ever before saw crowded together. It would be the place of all others for a good game of Hide & Seek. The walls in general are papered in fantastic french patterns, some however, of the shew rooms are painted & gilt. There is a profusion of gilding about the ceilings, and the whole finish is what I take to be the french taste of the last Century. Still the effect is, to me at least, pleasing. There is a great deal of elegance and a most gentlemanly or aristocratic air throughout the whole establishment. By no possibility could you mistake this villa or chateau for the residence of a "parvenu," of a rich cit or enriched manufacturer. Even with small rooms, papered walls, chintz furniture and attic chambers, there is an in-describable something which only pervades the dwellings of gentlemen titled or untitled. Two of the chambers at Chiswick have an interest for all the civilised world, for in these chambers died Fox, Charles James Fox, and Canning! The room where Fox breathed his last is one belonging to the original building and has a window looking towards the river. You pass from the Hall into the righthand Saloon, from which opens a bed-chamber hung with Gobelins tapestry and known by the name of the Tapestry Chamber. Here expired one of the greatest of England's great Statesmen. The bed on which he died has been removed to the Duke's own chamber, & the Tapestry room serves as a dressing room to an inner chamber, formerly a dressing room now a bedchamber; the two apart-ments having changed uses since the time when Fox occupied them.

The room in which Canning died is upstairs in the new part of the building, and the same bed remains on which he lay during his last illness and from which he never rose. The chamber itself is on the same side of the house with that of Fox. All the windows of all the apartments look out upon gardens and pleasure grounds and the upper windows command a view of the Thames. There is no Library properly so called at Chiswick, but book shelves & books in every room of the house. [*Floorplan*] The paintings are some of them fine, but many have been taken down and others are in a bad light. I remarked a Susanna & the Elders by Paul Veronese in which the great depth and harmony of colouring was delightful to the eye. I never saw so mellow a painting, one in which there were so few abrupt transitions from colour to colour or light to shade.

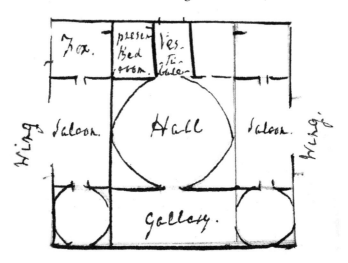

I was also attracted by a landscape of Salvator Rosa and some fine heads of old men by Rembrandt. There was a beautiful head of a saint or a Magdalen, and a group of two figures representing Painting and Design, by Guido. I hope to pay another visit to Chiswick. If it has so great a charm even at this ungenial season, what must it be in Spring, Summer or Autumn.

I thought the servants I saw at Eton Hall the best bred I had seen in England. The civilest and most obliging house-keeper is unquestionably at Chiswick. We returned to town in time to rest and dress for dinner, and I passed the evening in writing to Mrs Forbes.

To-day, 5th January, I have brought my boy from Highgate to pass some days in town. — Angus Fletcher called and brought me his sister's novel of "Concealment." He tells me that the husband of L.E.L. the particulars of whose tragical death are filling the newspapers, is a man of most ferocious temper. In this case his wife could do nothing better than die, and her friends should bless the happy accident, if accident it were, of a few drops too many of Prussic acid. She a woman of keen feeling and he (McLean) a savage! It is one of those situations in which no hope remains, there is nothing left for the wife but death or madness, and for the husband but corroding remorse here, or retribution hereafter.

ANGUS FLETCHER (1799–1862), sculptor, occupied a studio at 91 Dean Street from 1838 to 1839. He came to London from Edinburgh in 1824 to take up residence with Allan Cunningham (1784–1842) and work in the studio of Francis Leggatt Chantrey, for whom Cunningham was a secretary. The following year Fletcher studied in Rome, after which he lived in a studio created for him within Millburn Tower, the home of longtime family friends Sir Robert Liston (1742–1836) and his wife, Henrietta (1751–1828). It was in this studio that Felicia **HEMANS** sat for her bust in 1829. Referring to the work as her "*effigy*," Hemans wrote, "it is so very graceful that I cannot but accuse the artist of flattery, the only fault he has given me any reason to find." Fletcher's **MOTHER** was the poet Elizabeth (Eliza) Dawson Fletcher (1770–1858), a favored hostess among the artistic and literary circles, both in Edinburgh and the Lake District, where she relocated in 1839 (*ODNB*, s.v. "Fletcher, Archibald," "Fletcher, Elizabeth," "Liston, Sir Robert," and "Chantrey, Sir Francis Leggatt"; "Dean Street Area: Portland Estate: Dean Street," *Survey of London*, vols. 33 and 34 [1966], 128–141; Mary Fletcher Richardson, ed., *Autobiography of Mrs. Fletcher with Letters and other Family Memorials* [1875], 66, 79, 165, 182, 201; Henry F. Chorley, *Memorials of Mrs. Hemans, with illustrations of Her Literary Character* [1836], 153; *Times* [London], 11 Mar. 1862; *Caledonian Mercury* [Edinburgh], 13 Mar. 1862).

Lucius Manlius **SARGEANT** (1786–1867) was an energetic writer and speaker who advocated against the use of alcohol. His *Temperance Tales* first appeared individually between 1833 and 1843, bearing titles such as "My Mother's Gold Ring," "I Am Afraid There Is a God!" and "What a Curse: or, Johnny Hodges, the Blacksmith," often followed by the phrase "founded on fact." The tracts were published collectively in two volumes in 1848 (*DAB*).

MAJOR DOWNING was the fictional, comic creation of Maine newspaperman Seba Smith (1792–1868). In 1830 Smith founded the *Portland Courier*, a political paper in which his first letters under the name of "Jack Downing" appeared. Rendered in a Yankee dialect, Downing's naïve rustic letters to the *Courier* poked fun at politics. The character of Jack Downing was an instant national success. In 1833 Smith compiled the works into *The Life and Writings of Major Jack Downing, of Downingville, Away Down East in the State of Maine*, "written by himself" with the promise to "tell folks more about politics, and how to get offices, than ever they knew before in all their lives; and what is the best ont, it will be pretty likely to get me in to be President" (*ANB*; *DAB*).

CHISWICK was the seat of William George Spencer Cavendish (1790–1858), sixth Duke of Devonshire; he was the grandson of its architect, Richard Boyle (1694–1753), third Earl of Burlington and fourth Earl of Cork. Chiswick House, located near the Thames River to the west of London, was built between 1725 and 1729 in a style largely influenced by Burlington's study of the architecture of Andrea Palladio (1508–1580), especially his Villa Rotunda at Vicenza. The interior ornamentation, as well as much of the landscaping, was created by Burlington's friend William Kent (ca. 1686–1748), with subsequent landscaping by Lancelot "Capability" Brown (ca. 1716–1783) and expansion of the residence under the care of James Wyatt. Coolidge's grandfather did not share her appreciation for Chiswick. Thomas Jefferson visited in April 1786, paid the servants for his entry, and noted later, "The Octagonal dome has an ill effect, both within and without; the garden shews still too much of art; an obelisk of very ill effect. Another in the middle of a pond useless" (*ODNB*; Thomas Francis Timothy Baker, ed., *A History of the County of Middlesex* [1982], 7:74–78; *MB*, 1:617; *PTJ*, 9:369).

Charles James **FOX** (1749–1806), Whig politician and close friend of Devonshire's mother, Georgiana Spencer Cavendish (1757–1806), Duchess of Devonshire, was a critic of Britain's policies in the colonies prior to the American Revolution. An advocate for the recognition of American independence as early as 1776, Fox believed Britain would ultimately lose after a long and costly war. When Fox became ill in December 1805, Devonshire's father, William Cavendish (1748–1811), loaned him Chiswick for the period of his illness, which ended in death on 13 September 1806 (*ODNB*).

An abbreviation of citizen, **CIT** is usually applied contemptuously to a tradesman or shopkeeper to distinguish him from a gentleman (*OED*).

George **CANNING** (1770–1827), foreign secretary and prime minister, caught a cold while waiting for the funeral of the Duke of York in January 1827. He never fully recovered and was very ill by the end of July. The Duke of Devonshire loaned him the use of Chiswick to recuperate, but he finally succumbed to an inflammation of the lungs and liver on 8 August 1827 (*ODNB*).

Eaton, or **ETON**, Hall was one of several expansive estates held by Robert Grosvenor (1767–1845), first Marquess of Westminster, located near Eccleston, Cheshire. Architect William Porden (ca. 1755–1822) reconstructed the estates from 1803 to 1812, and his assistant Benjamin Gummow added wings from 1823 to 1825. At the time of Coolidge's visit Eaton Hall was on its way to becoming the largest and costliest Gothic Revival mansion in England (*ODNB*; Nikolaus Pevsner and Edward Hubbard, *The Buildings of England: Cheshire* [1971], 207–213; "The Administration of the Estate 1785–1899: The Free Estate, 1808–45," *Survey of London*, vol. 39 [1977], 43–47).

Mary Fletcher Richardson (1802–1880) was the author of **CONCEALMENT**: *A Novel*, published in London in 1821. In 1847 she married Sir John Richardson (1787–1865), physician, naturalist, and explorer, knighted in 1846 (*ODNB*; Richardson, ed., *Autobiography of Mrs. Fletcher*, 237).

L.E.L. was Letitia Elizabeth Landon (1802–1838), a poet and author whose first works began appearing under her initials in the *Literary Gazette* in 1820. The mystery of her identity contributed to the success of her poems and novels in England and America. Known to be a single woman living independently, Landon incurred speculation about her virtue. Though linked romantically to several men, Landon did not marry until 1838. In June of that year she wed George Maclean (1801–1847), then governor of the British post at Cape Coast, west Africa. Landon arrived at her new home in mid August but died two months later from an accidental overdose of hydrocyanic, or PRUSSIC, acid. News of her death filled the British and American papers for several days, and friends authorized the printing of Landon's cheerful letters to them and published their own memorials of her to refute insinuations that her death was a suicide (*ODNB; Morning Chronicle* [London], 3, 9 Jan. 1839; *Times* [London], 1, 2, 4, 7, 9, 10, 12 Jan. 1839).

Monday. 7th January.

Yesterday was a dark, turbid day. I staid at home and wrote a long letter to Mrs Gorham. Sunday in London is perfectly quiet. The stillness of the streets is remarkable, and more striking from the contrast with the six week days which are noisy & bustling enough. Capt. Wormeley called and Mr Coolidge walked out with him. They called on Mrs Searle who had been dining at Mrs Atkinson's. She there met Mr Charles Sumner whom she thought much elated by his success in fashionable society and very full of conceit.

In the evening after seeing my boy in bed I went to pass an hour with Mrs Stevenson. I found Mr S. & herself alone. She gave me an account of their visit to Windsor. They arrived at the Castle at half past five P.M. were received by some members of the household and ushered into their own apartments, which consisted of two handsome drawing rooms & two bedchambers with dressing rooms. Having rested and changed their dresses Mrs Stevenson was conducted by Miss Murray, one of the maids of honour, to the drawing room, where in about fifteen minutes, the Queen made her appearance very elegant and gracious. She welcomed Mrs Stevenson to Windsor and offered her hand to be respectfully touched not shaken. Who ever heard of shaking hands with a Queen! It was signified to Mr Stevenson that he was expected to lead her Majesty to dinner. He did so, and was seated by her, the Duchess of Kent being on his other hand. A high post of honour between an illustrious pair. Before the conclusion of the dinner the Queen's health was drunk, all standing but herself. Presently her Majesty rose and left the room followed by the ladies. She tarried a while in the drawing room and then retired to her private apartments all being at liberty to do the same. After some time the company re-assembled, card tables were laid at one of which the Duchess of Kent seated herself, Mrs Stevenson was invited to play chess with Miss Murray, and the Queen took her place on a sofa with Lord Melbourne at her side and a small lap dog between them, whose pretty ears her Majesty amused herself by pulling whilst she conversed with Lord Melbourne, calling him by the familiar name of <u>Melly</u>. After an evening of elegant formality, the party broke up. Mrs Stevenson was suffering from a very bad cold and the Queen sent a kind message to say that she must take care of her cough and not trouble herself to come out to breakfast, with some other gracious expressions of interest, very commendable and of course very commonplace. In the morning however, Mrs Stevenson perhaps moved by curiosity, was ready for breakfast. The Marchioness of Tavistock did the honours of this informal repast, at which the Queen never appears, nor yet does her Majesty lunch in public—It must be a blessed relief this little interval of rest from state and representation.

After breakfast M^r & Mrs Stevenson were conducted over the Castle through the private apartments, the plate-room &c &c. Luncheon succeeded, the Queen then appeared equipped for riding. Mr Stevenson was invited to accompany her, whilst Mrs Stevenson with the Ladies Tavistock & Albemarle in a carriage visited Virginia Water. The Queen rides well and went farther & faster than altogether suited a middle aged gentleman of diplomatic habits, whose excursions from Portland place to the Foreign Office, are generally made in an easy chariot. Another toilette and another dinner followed the out-door exercise. The Queen this day wore the Order of the Garter and a suit of magnificent pearls "as large," says Mrs Stevenson, "as gooseberries." During dinner Lord Melbourne addressed Mr Stevenson. "I believe" said his Lordship, "that Jefferson is a great name on the other side of the Atlantic, is it not?"[1] "It is my Lord." "His principles being democratic makes him popular among a democratic people; he is not one of my favorites. I consider Hamilton as your great man." "Of course your Lordship would prefer a man who desired a Presidency for life and a septennial Congress &c. &c. &c.[2]

My grandfather can never be a favorite with the few, being himself the friend of the many. There is a perpetual opposition between the rich and the poor which makes an advocate for the one always appear an opponent of the other; but this is temporary; posterity, although divided into the same classes, judges with less "esprit de corps" the actions of past times, and tardy justice is done, even by the priviledged classes, to the merit and the memory of their adversaries. Even English Lords of the present day reserve all their acrimony for contemporary republicans & reformers. They are willing to commend those of past ages. Their own honours and emoluments are secure from Cincinnatus or the Gracchi, & Publicola cannot interfere with their titles or next roles. The hatreds of an Aristocracy are like those of a Priesthood directed against the living or the recently dead, for their privileges are endangered by none other.

The last day of M^r & Mrs Stevenson's stay at Windsor they were present at a Stag hunt and returned in the afternoon to London.

I have just seen a funeral pass down Regent St. A Hearse with four black horses, crowned with immense plumes of black Ostrich feathers— Mourning coaches, mourners &c followed. The effect to me was not solemn but burlesque. I do not like it. It is making a Puppet shew of Death. These parade funerals, the Hearse & it's plumes, the hired mourners with their crape bands & faces of assumed grief, are out of character with the times. It is the pageantry of a past age, a mere antiquated sham, with nothing real about it but it's absurdity. The plumed Hearse is like an Owl flying abroad in daylight. Is it by perseverance in such senseless customs, (that is customs which whatever sense they may originally have had, have lost it now,) that stanch conservatives hope to stay the tide of innovation?

Margaret GORHAM (ca. 1792–before 1850) was the wife of Benjamin Gorham (1775–1855), lawyer and U.S. senator from Massachusetts. Her friendship with Coolidge spanned three generations, as she knew Coolidge's mother and was remembered fondly by Thomas Jefferson Coolidge for easing his return to the United States in 1847, when he entered Harvard (*Biographical Directory of the United States Congress, 1774 to Present*, s.v. "Gorham, Benjamin," accessed 2 Dec. 2010, http://bioguide.congress.gov/; Timothy Kenslea, *The Sedgwicks in Love: Courtship, Engagement, and Marriage in the Early Republic* [2006], 103–108, 199; Coolidge, *Autobiography*, 7–8; United States Federal Census, Seventh Census, 1850, Boston Ward 7, Suffolk, Massachusetts, s.v. "Gorham, Benjamin," Ancestry.com; Coolidge to Martha Jefferson Randolph, 7 Aug. 1831, 31 May 1833, Coolidge to Virginia J. Randolph Trist, 22 Feb. 1837 [ViU: Ellen Wayles Randolph Coolidge Correspondence]; *Daily National Intelligencer* [Washington, D.C.], 30 Nov. 1829; *Boston Daily Atlas*, 6 Oct. 1855).

Coolidge was undoubtedly anxious to hear the Stevensons' ACCOUNT OF THEIR VISIT TO WINDSOR. Upon first learning of the Stevensons' invitation in early December 1838, Coolidge wrote to her sister Virginia expressing her concerns: "The Stevensons are sufficiently kind & attentive to us; I wish they were better calculated to do honour to the intelligence and refinement of their country, but they are 'old Virginny' to the very uncouthest vulgarisms of pronunciation & manners. They are just now invited to Windsor, on a visit to the Queen, and will display their accomplishments on a more distinguished stage than has hitherto been allowed them. Oh that they may not say 'charmber' & 'yarnder' & 'mighty good,' but they will, they surely will! and he will wink at the Queen and she will giggle & twitch & fidget just as you may perhaps remember she used to do twenty years ago" (Coolidge to Virginia J. Randolph Trist, 8–11 Dec. 1838 [NcU: Southern Historical Collection, Nicholas Philip Trist Papers]).

Amelia Matilda **MURRAY** (1795–1884), author and philanthropist, was the daughter of Lord George Murray and Anne Charlotte Grant, a lady-in-waiting to the daughters of George III. Murray became maid of honor to Victoria in 1837 and remained part of the royal household, including service as a woman of the bedchamber, until 1853. In 1854 she traveled to the United States (*ODNB*).

Anna Maria Stanhope Russell, Marchioness of **TAVISTOCK** (ca. 1783–1857), was woman of the bedchamber to Queen Victoria from 1837 to 1841, the same position her mother held in Queen Charlotte's household. Her father was Charles Stanhope, aide-de-camp to the commander of the British forces in the northern campaigns of the American Revolutionary War and governor of Windsor Castle from 1812 until 1829 (*ODNB*; Burke and Burke, *Peerage and Baronetage*, 216, 960–961; *Gentleman's Magazine*, n.s., 3 [1857]: 230).

Susan Trotter Keppel, Lady **ALBEMARLE** (d. 1885), was the wife of George Thomas Keppel (1799–1891), sixth Earl of Albemarle (*ODNB*).

VIRGINIA WATER, the 150-acre lake that lies on the southern edge of Windsor Great Park, was at this time the largest man-made lake in the United Kingdom. It was surrounded by woodlands with artificial cascades and picturesque temples and ruins. There Mrs. Stevenson, Lady Tavistock, and Lady Albemarle visited "the pavilion built by the luxurious George IV" while Andrew Stevenson went horseback riding with the queen. Mrs. Stevenson recalled that the queen rode a "beautiful Arabian" twenty miles in two hours, leaving the ambassador "groaning and twisting for a week after" (Jane Roberts, *Royal Landscape: The Gardens and Parks of Windsor* [1997], 391–461; Boykin, *Mrs. Stevenson*, 117; "Virginia Water," The Royal Landscape, The Crown Estate, accessed 5 Dec. 2010, http://www.theroyal-landscape.co.uk).

THE ORDER OF THE GARTER is the highest and oldest British Order of Chivalry, created by Edward III in 1348. Queen Victoria was then Sovereign of the Order, which recognizes twenty-five knights for service to their country. The ensigns of the Order were a "surcoat, garter, mantle, hood, George, collar, cap, and feathers. . . . The garter is of blue velvet, bordered with gold. The George is the figure of St. George on horseback, in armour, encountering a dragon with a tilting spear." St. George's Chapel, Windsor, is the spiritual home of the order (William Courthope, ed., *Debrett's Complete Peerage of the United Kingdom of Great Britain and Ireland* [1838], 773; "Order of the Garter," Official Website of the British Monarchy, accessed 6 Dec. 2010, http://www.royal.gov.uk/MonarchUK/Honours/OrderoftheGarter/OrderoftheGarter.aspx).

Coolidge would have been familiar with her grandfather's opinions of Alexander **HAMILTON** and some of the details of the long-standing conflict between them.

Jefferson asserted that Hamilton objected to the Constitution because it lacked "a king and house of lords" and that Hamilton wanted a large central government with supreme power over states. Jefferson accused Hamilton of using his position as secretary of the treasury to manipulate the legislative branch of the government and to force his own agenda rather than working for the benefit of the people (Stanley Elkins and Eric McKitrick, *The Age of Federalism* [1993], 285–292; Malone, *Jefferson and His Time*, 3:65–67, 245–260; *PTJ*, 24:351–360, 28:475–477, 539–541).

1. Omitted opening quotation marks editorially supplied.
2. This last comment is most likely Coolidge's own.

Wednesday 9th January.

Monday evening we went to the Olympic Theatre to see Mme Vestris. Her quarrel with the Yankees makes her just now, a Lion. She is received all the better by the English public. The longer I stay in this country the more aware I become of the ill-feeling towards the United States. Madame played in a sort of farce got up on the story of Blue Beard, in which the scenery & dresses are "bien magnifiques" as Josephine would say. The Olympic is a beautiful little theatre all painting and gilding and looking like a large "bonbonière," the scenery is shewy, the dresses rich, the acting good, both Farren & Mrs Nisbett play there, and with such an "entourage"[1] I was curious to see how Mme Vestris would acquit herself. She is a very noted person, and I wished to judge if possible by my own eyes of those merits which counterbalance her immense demerits. She is a courtezan for whom many have ruined themselves in fortune & reputation, (she can boast, I am told, of more than one illustrious or distinguished lover who has thought no price too high to pay for her meretricious smiles,) and whom in the decline of her years and the wane of her attractions, a young man of respectable connexions & of some talent & education, has been base enough to marry, thus voluntarily submitting to the greatest earthly degradation an honest man can bow beneath, the sharing his name & fortunes with an infamous woman. And if Mme Vestris has not taken her husband's name because of the wider notoriety of her own, the greater shame to him—She is shameless.

We got a box close to the stage, for I was most desirous to get a near view of the Circe who has transformed so many of the nobler sex into what I will not say. I fixed an eager expectant look upon the stage, upon the vacant space soon to be illuminated by the presence of one so dangerously bright. In a few moments the graceful form would glide before my eyes and my ears would be filled with the voice of the Syren. I had not long to wait. But what was my astonishment, my absolute dismay, when, amid plaudits long & loud expressive of enthusiastic welcome and intense admiration, then came trippingly & mincingly forward, an old battered, painted, disreputable-looking jade, with glassy leering eyes, discoloured teeth, cheeks daubed with rouge beyond even the modesty of art a neck and bosom made up of putty, white lead and wrinkles, and a form which whatever may have been it's original proportions has now shared the general wreck. Such is now Mme Vestris. We were placed too near for scenic illusion. We saw her in her miserable decay. Farther off, patched & plastered & painted as she is, our eyes might have been deceived. She sang, and her voice is still good though occasionally hoarse. Her acting is pretty, and may have been graceful whilst grace was still an ingredient in her composition, but this great charm has fled with the others. Whatever there was of fascination in the looks or movements of this woman is gone. Nothing remains but unseemly ruin. Her young & no doubt loving husband, Mr Charles Matthews, looked well and played well in the farce of Patter versus Clatter.

Yesterday Tuesday 8th (how the days fly and how soon I shall be preparing for my Indian voyage!) I carried my dear boy back to Highgate. He had been passing two happy days at home, for a child's home is with his mother wherever she may be. Mr Child and Mr Heard dined with us, and at half past eight, Mr Coolidge and myself drove to Somerset St. Portman Sq. to spend the evening with Mrs Annesley. She is the widow of a younger brother of that Miss Annesley, a daughter of Lord Valencia, with whom my mother became acquainted in a french convent of Paris, the Abbaye Royal de Panthemont, where they were both educated. My dear mother retained always a warm affection for her old school and for many of her school fellows. I had heard her speak of them so often that some of their names had become household words. I do not remember that Miss Annesley was one whom she liked best, but she must have liked her, or my impressions would not be so favorable as they are. I find Mrs Annesley, who is a friend of Mrs Searle, and her sister Miss Ainsworth well-bred & intelligent. Both Tory in their politics, as it seems to me a great many of the most respectable of the English are.

To-day there is a slight coating of snow on the ground, but the Sun shines and the air is of a pleasant bracing coolness. I have walked out with Mr Heard, called on Mrs Hillard, and paid an enormous price to Atkinson for a few brushes some soap & Cologne water. Just double what the same articles, the indispensables of the toilette, would have cost in Boston.

Lucia Elizabeth Bartolozzi VESTRIS Mathews (1797–1856), actress, singer, and theater manager, was born in London to Italian and French parents. She married first Armand Vestris (1787–1825), lead dancer and ballet master of the King's Theatre, and debuted under the name of Madame Vestris in 1815. Beginning in 1816 she traveled, studied, and probably performed in Paris and Naples; she returned to London in 1819, where she was engaged at Drury Lane. Though audiences applauded her mezzo-soprano voice, she was unable to compete with the great operatic performers of her day. Instead, she built her career on her beauty, exhibiting her much-admired figure by daringly appearing in several breeches roles; she also engaged in a string of relationships that sometimes supported, and other times threatened, her lavish lifestyle, all of which made her a popular topic for gossip and speculation. She leased the OLYMPIC THEATRE, located at Drury Lane and Wych Street, from 1830 through 1839, redesigning it to create an intimate and elegant setting that offered only light musical pieces and farce, all of which brought great success when larger, more traditional houses were suffering.

Vestris hired Charles James Mathews [MATTHEWS] (1803–1878) in late 1835 to work as both an actor and a writer, and they first performed together in January 1836. The pair quickly developed an easy rapport both onstage and off. In the summer of 1838 they undertook bookings for theaters in New York, Boston, Baltimore, and several other American cities, and in mid July they were quickly and quietly married just days before their departure on board the *Great Western*. The visit was highly anticipated from New York to New Orleans, but accounts of a series of social missteps quickly turned Americans against the couple. A London *Times* story describing how their hasty marriage took place so as to avoid offending "the sterner morals of 'brother Jonathan'" (a popular British personification of the United States) was picked up by American papers, some of whom took it as "a sneer" and others, as a compliment. Stories circulated that in Saratoga Springs and again in Poughkeepsie Mathews had allowed their five servants to dine in the dining rooms and subsequently responded to complaints by insisting "that he had a right to do as he pleased in a republican government," an assertion that was interpreted by Americans as another insult, for "in England servants do not sit and dine with their masters and mistresses, any more than they do in America." One newspaper noted that "thousands are anxious to see Mr. Matthews, but the feeling will not be maintained unless he contradicts or satisfactorily explains the matter."

In a farewell speech given at New York's Park Theatre in November 1838, Mathews described the couple's anticipation of an enjoyable and profitable tour and their genuine desire to see the country and to please their American audiences. According to Mathews their efforts had all been confounded by the unrelenting gossip of the press. He insisted that the story about Saratoga Springs could not be true because the couple had never been there. He concluded with the announcement that the entire experience had not only hurt his wife deeply, but it had also made her very ill. The couple was newly returned to London when the Coolidges saw them at the Olympic in **PATTER VERSUS CLATTER**, a popular comedic musical that Mathews wrote in 1838 (*ODNB*; Charles Dickens, ed., *The Life of Charles James Mathews* [1879], 2:83–87, 279–283; *Bristol Mercury*, 28 July 1838; *Freeman's Journal and Daily Commercial Advertiser* [Dublin], 3 Oct., 5 Dec. 1838; *Morning Chronicle* [London], 1 Oct., 7, 26 Nov. 1838; *Times* [London], 19 July 1838; *New Orleans Daily Picayune*, 24 Aug., 30 Sept., 16 Nov. 1838, 2 Jan. 1839; *Pennsylvania Inquirer and Daily Courier* [Philadelphia], 21 Nov. 1838; *Portsmouth [N.H.] Journal of Literature and Politics*, 25 Aug. 1838, 12 Jan. 1839; *Rhode-Island Republican* [Newport], 8 Aug. 1838; *Salem [Mass.] Gazette*, 14 Aug. 1838; *Daily National Intelligencer* [Washington, D.C.], 16, 27 Nov. 1838).

William **FARREN** (1786–1861), actor and theater manager, was a popular performer of comedic and character roles. He was part of Vestris's company at the Olympic and later Covent Garden. Farren performed at the Haymarket Theatre and the New Strand before assuming management at the Olympic, where he remained nearly to the end of his career in 1855. His performances were described as nuanced, sophisticated, and even exquisite (*ODNB*).

Louisa Cranstoun Macnamara **NISBETT** Boothby (1812–1858) was considered one of the most appealing actresses of the London theater. Her second marriage, to Sir William Boothby (d. 1846), baronet, of Ashbourne Hall, made her Lady Boothby (*ODNB*).

Sarah Ainsworth **ANNESLEY** (d. 1861) was the widow of Henry Arthur Annesley (1792–1818), fifth son of Arthur Annesley (ca. 1744–1816), first Earl of Mountnorris and eighth Viscount **VALENTIA** (L. G. Pine, ed., *Burke's Genealogical and Heraldic History of the Peerage, Baronetage and Knightage* [1956], 2200–2201).

Juliana Lucy **ANNESLEY** (ca. 1773–1833) was the eldest daughter of Arthur Annesley. Fourteen-year-old Martha Jefferson met Annesley at the Parisian convent school of the Abbaye Royale de Panthemont in 1786. On a list of schoolmates Martha drew up about that same time, she placed "XXX" beside Annesley's name, marking her as a particular favorite and one with whom she had exchanged locks of hair. Annesley was lively, intelligent, and humorous, and wrote to her "dear Jeffy" about their fellow students, their studies, and the rules of the Abbaye. The pair was occasionally allowed to go on outings together, including at least one carriage ride in the company of Martha's father. Teasingly affectionate toward Martha, Annesley boasted "I am the strongest girl in the world. . . . I believe you one of the best—I am certain I shall never find myself mistaken." Annesley left the Abbaye for London in 1788, and in July 1789 she married John Maxwell (ca. 1768–1838), fifth Baron Farnham, a representative peer and privy counsellor for Ireland and colonel of the Cavan militia (*Burke's Peerage* [1956], 2200; *Gentleman's Magazine* 103 [1833]: 557; *Gentleman's Magazine*, n.s., 10 [1838]: 546; Thomas Jefferson to Martha Jefferson, 6 July 1787, in *PTJ*, 15:638; "Martha Jefferson's List of Schoolmates at the Abbaye Royale de Panthemont, Paris, ca. 1786" [Thomas

Jefferson Foundation, Inc., on deposit at ViU: Mss 5385-i]; Juliana Annesley to Martha Jefferson, 20, 27 Apr. 1786, ca. 1788 [transcripts at ViU: Edgehill-Randolph Papers]; *Examiner* [London], 30 Sept. 1838).

James **ATKINSON** (ca. 1783–1853) and his partner Edward Atkinson were perfumers with a shop on Old Bond Street at the corner of Burlington Gardens, just off Piccadilly (Henry Buckler, *Central Criminal Court. Minutes of Evidence* [1837], 924; *Gentleman's Magazine*, n.s., 40 [1853]: 213).

1. Single quotation mark at beginning of word in manuscript.

Thursday. 10. Jan.

Yesterday we dined at No. 2. Spanish Place, Manchester Sq. at the house of a gentleman formerly a merchant in India. The dinner was sumptuous. We had every thing of the best. The company consisted principally of persons connected with Indian affairs. There was the sprightly wife of a British Officer returned to England for her health, (she is as round and plump as a Quail) whilst her husband, a Major in the Cavalry, remains at Guzzerat. She has been eighteen months in Europe fattening & recovering her good looks, whilst the Major grows more meagre & more bilious at "a frontier station in the Upper Provinces." This Indian lady reminds me by her shape and by her incessant clack of a Guinea hen. She should have been a frenchwoman, only that with her animation and her volubility, she has neither the courtesy nor the "tournure" of female France. She talks on all subjects fluently & sufficiently well, decides every point with the tone of a master, submits to no contradiction, resents a shadow of dissent, and becomes rude the moment she is opposed. She is just the sort of person that I could not possibly get along with, and finding my stock of patience evaporating very rapidly, and my good-humour "oozing out at my fingers' ends," I turned away from the discussion of subjects literary, scientific, dramatic & fashionable, in all of which the Indian lady found herself perfectly at home, to talk rugwork with a respectable single woman. From my universal genius, the Guinea Hen, I had however received some account of Mme Vestris which explained the secret of her fascinations. She is a woman of talent, accomplished in the extreme, speaks almost every modern language of Europe with equal ease and elegance, is musical and a musician, is a good actress and dresses exquisitely. On this last point I demurred. Her dress, when I saw her, was less tasteful and becoming than that of any one of her companions on the stage. I received a sharp answer from the "hen Major" as Miss Mitford would surely have called her, who told me with a look of virtuous indignation, that Mme Vestris employed the same dress-maker with herself, the very french woman, Mme Girardot, who "made the gown that I have on," casting a downward look of complacency upon the black satin which certainly displayed her bosom as large as life. From this argument there was no appeal. I could not tell the lady I saw nothing particularly admirable in her dress, and therefore subscribed tacitly to the perfection of Mme Vestris's. Charles Matthews it seems has lost cast in a great degree by his connexion with the Venus of the Olympic. He was in really good company & encouraged & patronised by many eminent persons, partly for his father's sake, and partly from the promise of his own talent, when this disreputable marriage made his friends fall off and his patrons in society turn away. Mrs B. (the Indian) thinks that poor, pretty Mme Vestris was brutally treated by the Yankees. I have not taken the trouble to inquire into the merits of the case, but as the English who go to the United States are apt to be insolent in their intercourse with a people whom they consider little better than Hottentots or Yahars, and seldom fail to render themselves unbearable by their impertinence, I think it more than probable that the Vestris & Matthews brought upon themselves whatever inhospitability they may have to complain of. Mrs B. says, No.—impossible—that they went full of hope and expectation and anxiety to please, that Mme Vestris made the most splendid additions to her wardrobe, bought dozens & dozens of white satin shoes with which to tread the American boards &c &c. I could only repeat that I knew no particulars, nor could explain why the white satin shoes had failed in their effect. One good idea on the subject of the toilette I did receive from the champion of Mme Vestris, that she, Mme Vestris, never allowed a dress to be altered, if it did not fit to a hair when it came home, it was thrown back upon the hands of the dress-maker who furnished both materials and work. Were this rule generally observed how much more care would be taken by these manglers of silk & muslin.

I must not forget to remember as a counterbalance to the impertinence of the pretty Anglo-Indian, that I was seated at dinner, by one of the finest specimens of an old Englishman that I have seen in the country. A man with a fine bald head and a benevolent countenance, manners frank, quiet and kind, and conversation sensible, liberal & unpretending. His ideas seemed to me accurate and shewing much observation & information, his expression of them was simple and clear, and in all that he said and looked there was the same general character of good sense and bonhommie. Mr Coolidge afterwards told me that when the ladies had left the table, the old gentleman having been pressed into a political discussion, bore his part with the same temperate spirit & sound judgment that marked all his sayings and doings, and by the touchstone of his good sense & good temper, shewed the base quality of much argument that certain declaimers were trying to pass for gold. I think this gentleman's name was Rutt—not a very aristocratic one, and he may be one of those persons who as Sir Jacob says in the "Woman of the World," are said to come from nothing because they only come from honest parents and a good education.

This morning I have been running over a few chapters of the 2nd vol. of Sam Slick. He is an odious fellow this peddling Yankee, vulgar, conceited, a consummate knave, and tiresome in his impertinences. Sam is evidently an advocate for a strong-handed government as men who ramble much over the world are apt to become. There is in decided measures, a saving of time and trouble which makes a favorable impression upon a traveller. He has few sympathies with the people among whom he happens to be, and the oppression of any particular act of so called justice is not so apparent to him as it's vigour and promptitude. Such things must visit a man at his own hearth, must be brought home to his own business & bosom, before he appreciates the importance of the maxim that it is better to allow ten offenders to escape than one innocent man to suffer unjustly. But I am treating Sam Slick as if he were a bona fide travelling Clockmaker, and paying a great compliment to the book and to it's author, Judge Haliburton, by reasoning upon the character & opinions of the hero as if he were a responsible person.

Mr Heard has called to accompany me to the National Gallery. He was kind enough to visit my boy yesterday and has brought me good accounts of him.

The GENTLEMAN residing at 2 Spanish Place has not been identified.

Gujarat [GUZZERAT], in western India, had been under British control since the end of the Second Anglo-Maratha War in 1805 (*ODNB*, s.v. "Wellesley, Arthur").

OOZING OUT AT MY FINGERS' ENDS is a reference to the cowardly character Bob Acres of Richard Brinsley Sheridan's play *The Rivals* (1775).

Madame Girard [GIRARDOT] was a milliner at 36 Newman Street (J. Pigot & Company, *Pigot & Co.'s Directory of London for 1839*, 162).

John Towill RUTT (1760–1841), politician and author, was the son of George Rutt, merchant. He was an intimate friend to Joseph Priestley and Gilbert Wakefield, a member of the Society for Constitutional Information, a founding member of the Society of the Friends of the People, and an advocate for social reform. Rutt published a varied collection of works that included a selection of poems; another of prayers, psalms, and hymns; and several articles in the *Monthly Repository*, the *Christian Reformer*, and the *Encyclopædia Metropolitana*. He also served as editor and compiler of the works of other writers, including the twenty-five-volume *Theological and Miscellaneous Works of Dr. Priestley* (1817–1831) and *The Life, Journals, and Correspondence of Samuel Pepys* (1841). Of decided political and religious opinions, Rutt nevertheless had a reputation as a man of "great courtesy and presence of mind . . . not ambitious to eclipse others, but to draw them forth, and diffuse animation and good humour throughout all the proceedings" (*ODNB*; *Gentleman's Magazine*, n.s., 25 [1841]: 437–438).

The character **SIR JACOB** Harford is speaking of himself in Catherine Grace Frances Gore's novel *The Woman of the World* (1838).

Friday. 11. January.

Yesterday I passed an hour & a half at the National Gallery. I have been there repeatedly before but I am just now beginning to see clearly & understand understandingly. Hitherto my mind has been confused and my eyes dazzled by a multitude of objects which I am learning to separate & reduce to their several individualities. My impressions are becoming distinct. Yesterday there was a fine light for the pictures and especially for those in the large end room. I seated myself opposite the great picture of the Gallery, the "Resurrection of Lazarus," by Sebastian del Piombo, with the aid of Michael Angelo. This, Dr Waagen considers the best picture of the Italian school in England. I have just come into possession of Dr Waagen's book, which I had in my hands for a short time last summer, but it is only now that I have secured a copy of my own. I visited the rich collections of Chatsworth, the Bridgewater Gallery, the Dulwich Gallery, Lord Ashburton's, Mr Hope's & Chiswick without guide or even Catalogue. The consequence was that being ignorant of art, having a limited time for examination, and with no companion who understood things much better than myself, I gained few ideas and perhaps none that were accurate. I experienced most varying emotions, brought away delightful impressions and not many distinct images. I shall now study Dr Waagen and try to associate his criticism with my recollections. But to return to the National Gallery and the "Resurrection of Lazarus."—Cardinal Giulio de Medici, afterwards Pope Clement 7th, whilst he was Archbishop of Narbonne, caused two pictures to be painted for the Cathedral of that City. One was the Transfiguration by Raphael, the other the Raising of Lazarus by Sebastian del Piombo. To this picture Michael Angelo furnished perhaps the whole composition, but <u>certainly</u>, say the Connoisseurs, the figure of Lazarus could have been drawn by no hand but that of Michael Angelo, the painting being by S. del P. who excelled in colouring. The picture remained in Narbonne until purchased by the Regent, Philip of Orleans, for the sum of 24.000 francs. From the Orleans Collection, sold by Egalité, it passed into the hands of Mr Angerstein who paid for it 35.00 guineas. He refused to part with it to Mr Beckford for 20.000 pounds sterling. At Mr Angerstein's death, his whole collection of pictures, thirty eight in number, was purchased by the nation for £56.000. and formed the foundation of the National Gallery.

Knowing the high reputation of this great picture, I have been sorry and mortified not to feel more admiration in looking at it. Yesterday the light was very favorable, and I began, for the first time to acknowledge it's merits. I account for my previous disappointment in this way. The Scripture account of the miracle which restored Lazarus to his family is one of the most beautiful & touching things on record. Save only the impatient, and in our translation the coarse expression of the impetuous Martha, there is not an image but of tenderness, love and pity. The mind dwells on the Saviour as he stands supreme, conscious of his own power, with unlimited faith and trust in God, yet with a heart full to overflowing with compassion and deep affection. He weeps over his friends, even at the moment when by an exertion of miraculous power, he is about to restore to them that object of their love for whom they have shed so many bitter tears. Then the sisters of Lazarus, their faith, their submission, their tenderness—the whole picture is so exquisite that we forget every thing but it's moral & spiritual beauty—the dead man four days buried, the grave, the shroud, the ghastly images of disease and death do not come before our eyes, and therefore, I think it was that I was shocked not pleased by the dark, unearthly figure, grim from the tomb, his head still bound about with the napkin, his feet fettered by the grave clothes, a heavy shadow over his face, whilst his eye gleams wildly with returning life, and his whole body and limbs are of the wan and ghastly hue of a four days burial. I had never dwelt upon the necessity of such appearances, and when it was forced upon me I turned away almost with a shudder. Little by little the judgment corrects the errors of the imagination, and I am now awakening to the truth, the justness of the representation which the combined genius of two great artists has given of this great subject. I will return to the Gallery and study it till farther—I will say to myself, this is the death from which we have been rescued, this is the grave over which faith is victorious.

The other pictures which I looked at with most interest were,

1st   The vision of St. Jerome by Parmegiano painted in the year 1527. "This," says Waagen, "was probably the picture over which the painter was so absorbed in his work that he did not know any thing of the taking of Rome by the troops of the Constable de Bourbon, till some German soldiers entered his work room with a view to plunder, but were so astonished at the sight of the picture, that they themselves protected the artist against the ill behaviour of other soldiers. Parmegiano was at this time only twenty four years old. This picture is 11 feet 6 inches high, by 4 feet 11 inches in width, and consists of four figures, the Virgin in glory with her son, a child of a few years old, whilst St. John, a full grown, vigorous, young man, in a somewhat constrained attitude, is in the fore ground, and St. Jerome, the figure ungracefully foreshortened, is asleep on the ground. The effect, notwithstanding these blemishes, is noble in the extreme.

2nd   The "Ecce Homo" by Correggio, of which Waagen says that it is one of the best pictures done by this artist.

3.   "The Education of Cupid"—Corregio three figures. Mercury, Cupid & a Venus with wings.

4.   Correggio. A small Madonna & child.   La Vierge au Panier

5.   Ganymede borne away by the Eagle. (Octagonal)   Titian

6.   Bacchus & Ariadne with Bacchantes & Satyrs.   Titian

7.   Venus & Adonis (which Waagen pronounces to be   Titian
     a school copy.)

8.   Christ among the Doctors (Injured by   Leonardo da Vinci
     injudicious repairs.) Waagen considers this
     a work of Bernardino del Luini

9.   Cardinal Hippolito de Medici & Sebastian   Sebastian del Piombo
     del Piombo. (Portraits)

10. French portrait (a saint) Colossal &   Sebastian del Piombo
     beautiful   This is called a portrait of Julia
     Gonzaga, but Waagen doubts.

11. Consecration of St. Nicholas—Very large   Paul Veronese

12. Pope Julius 2nd (Waagen calls it a school copy)   Raphael

13. La Madonna del Gatto   Baroccio

14. Virgin & Child, St. Joseph, the Holy Ghost,   Murillo
     the Father, angels—

15. Susanna & the Elders. (Waagen doubts if it be   Ludovico Caracci
     really by—)

16. Embarkation of the Queen of Sheba. Exquisite   Claude Lorraine

17. Narcissus—Still water, rocks & trees—   Claude

18. Embarkation of St Ursula & the Eleven thousand Virgins	Claude
19. Sinon brought before Priam	Claude
20. Cephalus & Procris	Claude
21. Italian Seaport at Sunset	Claude
22. Isaac & Rebecca—not noticed by Waagen	Claude

All these works of Claude are beautiful[1] as landscapes—the figures comparatively unimportant, give names to the pieces.

I went home from the National Gallery and dressed to dine with Mrs Searle. Among the company I found Mrs Annesley & Miss Ainsworth. The toryism of the English women, especially such as consider toryism as a mark of Caste, amuses me by it's unreasoning violence. What a pity that women will meddle with politicks, for they will not take the trouble to understand any of the great questions   I am a bit of a Conservative myself, yet I feel that this is a matter of taste & feeling rather than of principle. It is no great matter, after all, in the present times, what a woman's politicks are. She may make herself impertinent & disagreeable, by an unfeminine display of her prejudices in such matters, but scarcely dangerous. I must say however that the ladies who talk radicalism render themselves more than ridiculous,—absolutely disgusting—There is a something in the boldness & bravado of this party singularly unpleasant in a woman. The petulance and namby pamby of tory ladies is a thousand times more lady-like.——Upon the whole it is a pity,

——when charming women
Talk of what they do not understand.

Female writers even on political economy are very apt to be made tools of by men to serve party purposes. Witness Lord Brougham & Miss Martineau. Women are too imaginative and emotional for subjects which admit of neither fancy nor feeling, and they are moreover, as a general rule, far more rational in action than in discourse. I heard from Mrs Annesley what interested me far more than her politicks—some account of the lives and fortunes of some of my mother's old friends in Paris & the Abbaie Royal de Panthemont.

Miss Annesley became Lady Farnham; Lady Elizabeth Tufton is living & unmarried; Lady Caroline Tufton married Mr Barham and is dead—killed about three years ago, coming home alone in the dusk, knocked down in crossing a street—what an extraordinary death for a woman of rank & fortune! ^How singular that she should have been out, at that hour, in the streets of London, alone and on foot.^ I suppose that ladies of great wealth & high station take the same pleasure in descending a little from both, that little girls do in playing washerwoman, or making believe scour or scrub. Lady Caroline Tufton was an intimate friend of my mother who spoke of her as a most amiable & excellent person, less beautiful than Lady Elizabeth but far more attractive & agreeable. They were the nieces of the Duke of Dorset who was English Ambassador in Paris at the time my grandfather was American Minister there.

I take great interest in all details relating to my dear mother's early friends. She remembered her residence in France as the brightest part of a life much shaded & saddened by care & sorrows. Her girlhood was however a very happy one. She went abroad when only twelve years old, & was placed for education in the convent, the Abbaie de Panthemont, where she remained four years. Then, from sixteen to seventeen years old, she lived in her father's house in Paris, and went freely into society both French & English.

Her recollections of the Convent were in the highest degree pleasant & favorable. She always spoke with the greatest approbation of the system of education pursued there—of the attention paid to the morals and manners of the girls, and of the care which was taken to train them to habits of neatness, modesty and scrupulous regard to purity and propriety. The superintendants were watchful to prevent any species of indecorum. Lessons of truth, justice, charity, & piety a little too Roman Catholic in it's complexion, were sedulously taught, and many of the pupils profited in no small degree, by the great moral advantages which they enjoyed. They were instructed in all elegant accomplishments by the best masters in Paris, and the useful branches of education, arithmetic, geography, history and modern languages were taught with the utmost care. House-wifery indeed, and needle-work, formed no part of the educational system of Panthemont, for the élèves, being in general daughters of wealthy & considerable persons, were considered as above the necessity of attention to such homely matters. An omission which my mother, destined to become wife, mother and mistress in a Virginia family, afterwards felt severely, having to acquire with painful conscientiousness, a knowledge of many matters certainly not taught in the Abbaye Royal de Panthemont, Faubourg Saint-Germain, Paris.—

If I could take my mother, however, as a sample of convent education I should say that, in most respects, it formed a beau-ideal of moral & intellectual training. But this would not be fair, for she was a person richly & rarely endowed by Nature with talents of a superiour order, a temper of unrivalled sweetness and cheerfulness, and a heart overflowing with all warm & good affections. But she certainly did honour to the schooling of Panthemont. She was graceful in figure and movement, an accomplished musician, well acquainted with several modern languages, well grounded in all the solid branches of a woman's education, save only the arts of housewifery, to which she afterwards attained with pain & difficulty, by untiring perseverance, so soon as she was placed in a situation which rendered a knowledge of them essential for the comfort of others. After living and moving for one year in the gay circles of Paris, she accompanied her father on his return to the U.S. in 1789, married very soon and settled down in the country in Virginia. And there certainly could not be well imagined a greater contrast than between her single and her married life! But she bore the change with true female heroism, which is made up of resistance to small evils and cheerful courage and patient endurance under domestic grievances. And she had too her full share of heavier calamities. Not only petty trials but great ones. She was equal to all. Yet she seemed born not only to bless but to shine. She was not only excellent, but captivating to all who came within the sphere of her manifold attractions. And she is gone, with her deep affections, her high principles, her generous & magnanimous temper, her widely diffused benevolence, her sound judgment and glowing imagination, her highly cultivated understanding and fascinating manners! She has passed away and the world has not known her. She has left no memorial but in the recollection of her friends & the hearts of her children, and they will soon disappear as she has done. A few short years and perhaps all record, all remembrance of her name, her qualities will be gone, lost like so much else of what is best worth preserving. It may be told for a while in the neighbourhood of her and her father's home, that a daughter of Thomas Jefferson sleeps by his side in that neglected burying ground at Monticello, but of who or what she was, otherwise than the daughter of a well known statesman & great political leader, no tradition will, after one generation remain, and by and by, perhaps, the very fact be forgotten that she lies near him, on the same spot where her only sister preceded her, and whither her mother had gone many years before! But I can never think, speak, or write of my mother without forgetting, for the time, all other things. It is of some of her early friends that I was talking with Mrs Annesley.

Miss Annesley was a beautiful & very proud girl, a granddaughter by the mother's side, of Lord Lyttelton. The Ladies Elizabeth & Caroline Tufton my mother reckoned among her most pleasant associates. For a while after she parted from them some intercourse was maintained across the Atlantic, but family cares & more engrossing affections soon interfered to put an end to it. Their uncle, the Duke of Dorset, was an amiable & gentlemanly man, with none of the "Morgue" or reserve of his countrymen. His acquaintance with my grandfather ^with whom his diplomatic functions brought him into contact^ was of a pleasant & cordial description. I have often heard my mother say that during the time that she was abroad, notwithstanding the recent war between England & America, the still excited feeling on the subject of the American Revolution, and the fact that my grandfather had been an active promoter of what the English called Rebellion, and was even the author of the Declaration of Independence, that she had personally never experienced anything like unkindness or coldness on the part of the English whom she met in Paris. She was received into their society, invited to their parties, and treated with uniform courtesy & attention. In one instance only had she found herself an object of prejudice or neglect from the fact of her being an American. The person who condescended to remember against a young girl the sins of her country, was Lady Radnor, the wife or mother I know not which, of that Lord Radnor who had served against the Rebels. Among the persons who were in Paris during the time that my mother was there were the celebrated Dutchess of Devonshire & her successor Lady Elizabeth Foster, the Countess now Countess Duchess of Sutherland, Mr Coutts the Banker with his vulgar, old wife, Maria Cosway the engraver, & others of less note. All these are now dead, except the Countess Duchess of Sutherland, of whom I often hear Mrs Stevenson speak, and whose castle of Dunrobin I should dearly like to see. When on a visit of curiosity to Knowle Park the old Housekeeper pointed out to me the portraits of the Duke of Dorset, his Duchess & his son afterwards killed by a fall from his horse, I felt a degree of interest which I could hardly have anticipated, simply from the fact that I had heard my mother speak of the Duke, an unmarried man when she knew him, and had seen her wear an enamelled ring which he had given to her as a young girl and the friend of his nieces.

My mother was fond of telling us stories of her school-days & of her subsequent residence, (one short happy year,) in her father's house in Paris. Should I ever go thither I will seek out the site of this house, and that of the Convent of Panthemont. The Convent was in the Faubourg St. Germain. If the buildings no longer remain I should like the see the place where they stood.

How well I remember the two Abbesses who reigned at Panthemont whilst my mother was there. One a kind, good-hearted, venerable woman but so old, & latterly so almost doting, that she was necessarily superseded by her chosen successor, a dignified & Queen-like person, at whose table mamma dined during the last year of her residence in the Convent. The dinner hour was one o'clock, whereas at the school table it was 11. A.M.!!   I was likewise familiarly acquainted with many of the ladylike & aristocratic Nuns, who received I think, the title of Madame, and with several of the good lay sisters who took care of & waited on the girls. One of them, a kind, rough, half scolding, half laughing, honest, sort of good fellow, called by the young ladies Papa, was always a special favorite of theirs & mine. Then came the pupils themselves, French, English, West Indian & Anglo American (of these last I believe there were only about three,) how I entered into their characters, habits, studies, sports & adventures! The history of their convent lives furnished my mother with an ample fund of anecdote and illustration for the pleasure & profit of her own children, and her recollections were so vivid and her manner of narrating so lively & delightful that we hung upon her words and listened eagerly to her stories. The English Misses and French Mademoiselles became to us objects of emulation or warning as effectually as if they had been placed bodily before our eyes and observation. The industry of one, the sweet temper and obliging disposition of another, the firmness and high principle of a third, the good breeding of a fourth used to stimulate our ambition to be industrious, kind, honorable, true, polite as they were—whilst on the other hand, Miss such a one was idle and dirty (dreadful to say), Mademoiselle Une Telle was selfish & greedy, and we should have blushed to resemble persons so disagreeable & disgusting.

Children are much moved by examples. If you draw objects of comparison from their contemporaries and companions you cultivate an evil spirit of uncharitableness, and encourage a habit of evil speaking, on the one hand, or you run the risk of exciting envious feelings on the other. Children do not like to hear their friends praised at their own expence, and unfortunately they do not dislike to hear their companions disparaged. For this reason it is better to offer to their imitation fictitious characters to which their entire imaginations give reality & effect. Such tales as Miss Edgeworth's are, I think, invaluable in the education of children & young people. Beginning with "Early Lessons" and going up through the "Parents' Assistant" and "Moral Tales" to the crowning climax of "Tales of Fashionable Life," these most entertaining volumes form a body of practical morality in a very captivating form. My mother's tales of her Convent school combined for us, all the interest of fiction with the force of truth. The facts were undoubted and the persons so far removed from us by time and distance that although we had, as it were, an intimate personal acquaintance with them, we could have no feelings personal to ourselves when they were held up before us as patterns and warnings. We were certainly educated with great care & wisdom, and if my mother's children were not as good as she was, it was no fault of hers, but partly our own, and partly Nature's.

I have let my pen run away with me, but why should I not dwell upon recollections which no time can efface, recollections of my early years and of my mother's love, as well as upon those late impressions which I wish to rescue from their own evanescence. When at some future day, (should future days lie before me, my life may be even now bounded to a span,) I may chance to glance over this idle record of idle hours, how natural it will appear to me that the acquaintance of a person who, like Mrs Annesley, could speak to me of my mother's old school fellows & friends, should turn my thoughts to them and to her.

The first volume of Gustav **WAAGEN'S BOOK** *Works of Art and Artists in England* (1838) contains a description of his visit to the National Gallery (Waagen, *Works of Art*, 1:183–242).

John Julius **ANGERSTEIN** (ca. 1732–1823) was an insurance broker and art patron whose business dealings enabled him to build a remarkable collection of thirty-eight works, including *The Raising of Lazarus* by Sebastian del Piambo (fig. 24) and masterpieces by Michelangelo, Raphael, Titian, Claude, Poussin, Correggio, Rembrandt, and Rubens. The British government purchased his collection in 1824 (*ODNB*; John Young, *A Catalogue of the Celebrated Collection of Pictures of the Late John Julius Angerstein, Esq.* [1823]).

WHEN CHARMING WOMEN ... DO NOT UNDERSTAND is taken from the poem "The Charming Woman" (1835), by Helen Selina Hay Blackwood (1807–1867), Lady Dufferin and Claneboye. Blackwood was the granddaughter of author Richard Brinsley Sheridan (1751–1816) and the sister of author Caroline Norton. "The Charming Woman" was "set to music and circulated around English drawing rooms, where it was enthusiastically sung after dinner for years." The *Court Journal* recommended it "to ladies who love a laugh" (*ODNB*; Kathleen Hickok, *Representations of Women: Nineteenth-Century British Women's Poetry* [1984], 68; *Court Journal: Court Circular and Fashionable Gazette* 7 [1835]: 780).

ELIZABETH TUFTON (ca. 1768–1849) was the daughter of Sackville Tufton (1733–1786), eighth Earl of Thanet. She never married, and at her death, just three months after that of her childless brother, Henry Tufton (1775–1849), eleventh Earl of Thanet, the Tufton line became extinct. Elizabeth and her sister **CAROLINE** (d. 1832) corresponded with Martha for at least two years, beginning with their return to London in 1789. The sisters enquired after her welfare, expressed regret at their separation from her, and sent news and gossip from London society. In 1792 Caroline married Member of Parliament Joseph Foster-Barham (1760–1832), who possessed estates in Pembrokeshire and a fashionable London home on Queen Anne Street. Lady Barham was "generally regarded as one of the leaders of the *beau monde*," and her sudden and violent death came as a great shock to London society. Just weeks after the death of her husband, Lady Barham was crossing Margaret Street when a cab driven by a sixteen-year-old boy "drove furiously round the corner, and one of the shafts coming against her before she could get out of the way, knocked her to the ground." Lady Barham suffered a broken arm, multiple broken ribs, and lacerated lungs that caused her death shortly thereafter. The coroner's inquest returned a verdict of "Manslaughter against Henry Bartholomew," the owner of the cab, with a "deodand of £50 on the cab and horse" and the reasoning that "the jury have levied this fine to mark their sense of the great impropriety of inexperienced boys being entrusted with the management of a horse, and endangering the lives of the public." The boy was tried and acquitted (*ODNB*; Bernard Burke, *Genealogical and Heraldic History of the Landed Gentry of Great Britain and Ireland* [1875], 55; Caroline Tufton to Martha Jefferson, 2 May, 9 Aug. 1789, Caroline Tufton to Martha Jefferson Randolph, 21 Mar. 1791, Elizabeth Tufton to Martha Jefferson, 13 Aug., 2, 18, 24 Sept., 23 Oct., 19 Dec. 1789, 1 Feb. 1790, Elizabeth Tufton to Martha Jefferson Randolph, 21 Mar. 1790 [transcripts at ViU: Edgehill-Randolph Papers]; *Gentleman's Magazine* 102 [1832]: 573; *Gentleman's Magazine*, n.s., 32 [1849]: 201, 555).

John Frederick Sackville (1745–1799), third DUKE OF DORSET, was uncle to the Tufton sisters, the daughters of Dorset's sister Mary Sackville Tufton (1746–1778). Dorset served as ambassador to France from December 1783 until his recall in 1789. Jefferson considered him honest and amiable but recognized that Dorset did not have the confidence of the British court. Although Dorset's political activities were unremarkable, his numerous philanderings became noteworthy, including a lengthy relationship with Georgiana Spencer Cavendish, DUCHESS OF DEVONSHIRE. The Tufton sisters were very fond of their uncle and were often in his company. Just before the trio's departure from Paris, he sent Martha a blue enamel RING, bearing the phrase "J'Aime et J'Espere" and engraved inside with "Martha Jefferson 1788"; he enclosed the gift in a note expressing his wish that she wear it always. The ring is part of the Thomas Jefferson Foundation's collection (*ODNB*; Amanda Foreman, *Georgiana, Duchess of Devonshire* [1998], esp. 178, 196–198, 233, 242–243; *PTJ*, 12:39–40, 16:384–385; Caroline Tufton to Martha Jefferson, ca. Aug. 1789 [transcript at ViU: Edgehill-Randolph Papers]; TJF Accession 1962-1-63).

Juliana Annesley was granddaughter to Sir George Lyttelton (1709–1773), first Baron LYTTELTON, by his daughter Lucy (d. 1783) (Burke and Burke, *Peerage and Baronetage*, 467–468; L. G. Pine, ed., *Burke's Genealogical and Heraldic History of the Peerage, Baronetage and Knightage* [1956], 2200).

Anne Duncombe Pleydell-Bouverie (1759–1829), **LADY RADNOR**, was the wife of Jacob Pleydell-Bouverie (1750–1828), second Earl of Radnor, Lord Lieutenant of Berkshire, and colonel of the Berkshire militia. They married in 1777. In actuality, he did not serve directly against the "Rebels," and he often voted against Lord North in the House of Commons before succeeding to the title in 1776. In 1778 he opposed the continuation of the war with the American colonies. Coolidge's confusion about Lady Radnor's relationship may stem from the fact that her mother, Anne Hales Duncombe (d. 1795), was the third wife of the first Earl of Radnor, William Bouverie (1725–1776), who was Jacob's father; this complication made Lady Radnor stepsister to her husband (*ODNB*; Ronald K. Huch, *The Radical Lord Radnor: The Public Life of Viscount Folkstone, Third Earl of Radnor, 1779–1869* [1977], 5–7; Emma Elizabeth Thoyts Cope, *History of the Royal Berkshire Militia* [1897], 309; James E. Doyle, *The Official Baronetage of England* [1886], 94–96; Edmund Lodge, *The Peerage of the British Empire* [1856], 455; *Gentleman's Magazine* 98 [1828]: 268; George Washington to Jacob Pleydell-Bouverie, 8 July 1797, in *The Papers of George Washington*, retirement series, ed. W. W. Abbot, Dorothy Twohig, Philander D. Chase, et al., 1:242–243).

The Duchess Georgiana's **SUCCESSOR**, Lady Elizabeth Christiana Hervey Foster (1757–1824), married William Cavendish, fifth Duke of Devonshire in 1809, after cohabiting with him and his first wife since 1782 and bearing the duke two illegitimate children (*ODNB*; Foreman, *Georgiana, Duchess of Devonshire*).

Thomas **COUTTS** (1735–1822), banker, owed his great success to his discretion and his keen business practices. The Duchess Georgiana, a reckless gambler, was one of his clients. Susannah Starkie (d. 1815), whom Coutts had met while she was serving as nurse to his niece, was his first wife (*ODNB*).

Maria Louisa Catherine Cecilia Hadfield **COSWAY** (1760–1838), artist and educator, was the wife of Richard Cosway (ca. 1742–1821), renowned portraitist and miniaturist. The couple were among the most fashionable of London society and entertained frequently at Schomberg House, their home on Pall Mall. In 1786 they traveled to Paris, where Maria Cosway was introduced to Coolidge's grandfather by the artist John Trumbull. There, Cosway and Jefferson formed an intimate friendship, spending much time together and corresponding frequently. One of Jefferson's most extraordinary letters, and the closest document to a love letter that exists within his extensive correspondence, was written to Maria Cosway after she and her husband departed Paris in October 1786. In it Jefferson employed the literary device of a dialogue between the head and the heart. Jefferson's heart felt that their departure made him "the most wretched of all earthly beings," reliving their days of friendship and toying with the notion that the Cosways might visit America. His head reasoned that these were nonsensical ideas and that being carried away by such passions would only lead to disappointment and pain. After Jefferson's return to America, his correspondence with Cosway continued for some time, dwindled, then was resumed during Jefferson's retirement. At Monticello, Jefferson kept an engraving of Maria Cosway by

Francesco Bartolozzi, after a portrait by Richard Cosway (*ODNB*; *PTJ*, 10:443–455; Stein, *Worlds*, 176).

At Knole [**KNOWLE**] House Coolidge could have seen portraits of the duke by Thomas Gainsborough and Joshua Reynolds; portraits of Arabella Diana Sackville (1769–1825), Duchess of Dorset, by Elisabeth Vigée-LeBrun and John Hoppner; and a portrait of their son George John Frederick Sackville (1793–1815), fourth Duke of Dorset, by George Sanders (Lionel Sackville West, *Knole House: Its State Rooms, Pictures and Antiquities* [1906], 58–59, 66–73).

The first of the **TWO ABBESSES** was Madame de Béthisy de Mézières, abbess from 1743 until 1790, at whose table Martha **DINED**, and the second was Sister Jeanne-Louise de Stendt de Taubenheim, the school's maîtresse des pensionaires, who was likely the one referred to as "papa" (Martha Jefferson to Thomas Jefferson, 8, 25 Mar., 9 Apr., 27 May 1787, Thomas Jefferson to Martha Jefferson, 28 Mar. 1787, in Betts and Bear, *Family Letters*, 32–38, 42).

Maria **EDGEWORTH** (1768–1849) was an author whose works were particularly favored by Coolidge and her sisters when they were girls at Monticello. Jefferson, who believed that all of Edgeworth's books were good, obtained new publications as soon as they were available in America. He passed them along to Martha Jefferson Randolph for review, and then the girls would draw lots and "she who drew the longest straw had the first reading of the book—the next longest straw entitled the drawer to the second reading—the shortest to the last reading, and the ownership of the book" (*ODNB*; *PTJRS*, 3:122–123, 623, 633–635; Thomas Jefferson to Nathaniel Burwell, 14 Mar. 1818 [MoSHi: R. R. Hutchinson Papers]; Virginia J. Randolph Trist to Nicholas Philip Trist, 26 May 1839, in Henry S. Randall, *The Life of Thomas Jefferson* [1858], 3:349–350).

1. Manuscript: "beatiful."

Saturday. 12. January.

Another week come to it's end. Time travels in a Locomotive. Not that he appears, as he goes, to move so fast, but that he so soon reaches his Saturday stages and finishes his week's journey. So on the actual railroad, hours hang heavily and yet how soon the journey is over. Yesterday the day being dark & rainy I staid at home till six o'clock & then went with Mr C. to 26. Pall Mall, to dine with our friends Messrs Heard & Higginson. At nine we all went to the Haymarket Theatre, the first time I have ever been. The pit is almost a square with rounded corners, the boxes seeming to run in straight lines to the point where they turn round the corners of the pit. There is a good deal of painting and gilding and attempt at shew, but it has after all rather a cheap look, with neither the size & splendour of Drury Lane & Covent Garden nor the good taste of the Olympic. I saw Power in

"O Flanagan & the Fairies," & in the "Irish Lion." He plays low characters very well, but I do not like low characters, and a drunken Irishman on the stage is the next most disagreeable thing to a drunken Irishman off of it.

To-day I have made half a dozen calls, left a card for Mrs Annesley, and for pretty Miss Low, whose french maid told me that Mademoiselle was in bed with a cold. To night Mr Coolidge has a party of gentlemen to dine—I shall take some soup and a cup of coffee in my chamber and go early to bed. I write whilst waiting for my light dinner. Next week I shall be more quiet & at home. We have no invitation a head, having refused one from a wealthy tea-broker living in the purlieus of Berkley Square. I presume something in the Longman Tompkinson style. I am not in the circles here to which I think I might have obtained an introduction had I brought proper letters—or any letters, for I had not one. My situation is an anomalous one. My husband in character, manners, education, appearance, is a gentleman, but he is a merchant. A merchant in the U.S. ranks with the best, but in England it is not so. They may say what they will of the British merchant; high as the name is made to sound abroad, they may be men of wealth, integrity, resource & have great things in their power, but at home, in the land enriched by their commerce & dependent on their intelligence and activity, they are not gentlemen nor are their wives ladies. They sometimes purchase by their gold a painful admittance into fashionable society, but they are made to pay for it by a thousand vexations & mortifications. Perhaps that by the laws of true courtesy, an individual in a foreign country, should be judged by the customs of his own, and should not be excluded from the privileges to which he is entitled at home, by any arbitrary distinctions of another state of society. In such case I might here ask and obtain an introduction into the best company. But I certainly have made no such demand, and have no right to complain of not enjoying what I have never sought. Good society in England may be haughty & exclusive even towards strangers I know nothing to the contrary. On the other hand the English nobility and gentry may be equally hospitable and courteous. I have no means of judging. I have more than once regretted having come to England unprovided with any passport to their notice. Still more unwise was it to neglect the means of introduction to the literary portion of the community. I must say that considering how little we have done to secure attention or kindness we have been, on the whole, kindly treated. Wherever we have brought forward the shadow of a claim it has been readily admitted. Not that the English have friendly feelings towards Americans. I think the contrary very evident. But the educated classes at least, do not visit upon individuals their dislike for the nation. Witness the attentions paid to N.P. Willis, for which he made an ungentlemanly return, and to Charles Sumner, who is now in the full tide of success. It is seldom, however, that Americans in England strike the right medium in their intercourse with the English. They are either too supple or too stiff, they flatter or they bully, and John Bull despises both. He likes neither toadyism nor rampant republicanism—and he is in the right.

Good society in England, guards with jealous care, the barriers which separate the different ranks. Perhaps I should say that all ranks are pervaded by the same spirit in this respect. It is the spirit of caste, very powerful throughout society. It divides and subdivides, and is apt to introduce restlessness & uneasiness every where. Every individual seems anxious to rise into the rank just above him, whilst he is equally anxious to keep down those who are just below. All seem grasping upwards with their hands & kicking downwards with their feet. But this applies only to their own countrymen—towards foreigners this jealousy probably does not exist & better feelings come in.

When I left the United States my health and spirits were bad. I was in deep mourning, and separated from all my children. I was moreover, as I still am alas! looking forward to continued separation from them. Not only I felt no desire to seek the acquaintance of strangers, but an absolute reluctance to encountering it. In leaving Boston I asked for no letters & declined those which were offered to me. In coming hither I desired to see England but not the English. My imagination, in spite of the sadness of my heart, warmed towards all that I pictured to myself of antiquity, historical association, poetry, romance & beauty in the works of nature and of art. I longed for old Castles and parks, ancient Cathedrals, village churches, cottages with thatched roofs & woodbine against the latticed windows, for woods, groves, fields, hedges, for the ivy & the heather, the primrose, the cowslip, the nightingale & the lark. I had heard so much, & read so much, & thought & dreamed so much of all these things! And I have travelled through England, or some beautiful parts of it, with infinite pleasure, disappointed in nothing, enjoying every thing, but here in London, in spite of the Tower and the Thames, the British Museum & National Gallery, the Picture Galleries, Rundell & Bridge the Theatres, & Crockford's, I am beginning to weary of nothing but sights, and to wish that I had made some preparation and taken some pains to secure for myself acquaintance with persons, and introduction into society. But perhaps it is as well as it is. Mr Coolidge is here on business. We are not to remain long, and in all that concerns comfort I am perfectly well off, whilst we have a few friends, principally Americans, whose company always gives me pleasure.

Our rooms in Regent St. which I thought at first a very poor exchange for Fenton's, improve on acquaintance & are really convenient & comfortable. I have an excellent carriage, horses & coachman, entirely at my command, and my french maid, Josephine, is accomplished in her art. I hear regularly from home and my dear little Jefferson is within an easy drive. Then I have choice of books, & have just finished Sam Slick. This picture, as it professes to be, of American life and manners, is calculated to bring the Yankees in greater disrepute than ever, yet without professing dislike, and according a sort of ironical praise. With much good sense & some sound views, it is full of prejudice, error & misrepresentation.

The weather is gloomy, dark & mild. I suffer less from cold in a London January than I have habitually done in a Boston May. The inconveniences of the season here are darkness and dirt. I suffer at noonday for want of light, and the dampness of the air combining with the coal smoke, forms a filthy deposit on every thing within and without. A white kid glove is soiled in one wearing for every touch on table, chair, book or desk is pollution. Stockings are unclean at the end of an hour, and in ten minutes a white handkerchief looks like a dirty duster. French collars must go to the Blanchisseuse far too often for their good, and silk gowns, which cannot be washed, are soon defaced, unless their colour is too dark to shew the dirt, and then you have the uncomfortable feeling that it is always about you. The hair is kept clean by a great deal of brushing & the hands by a great deal of washing. No wonder that an English dressing room is rich in basins & ewers of every description, that water and fresh towels are given without stint, that Atkinson makes a fortune by soap, cologne water & pastes for the skin—No wonder that for all outer garments "les couleurs les plus foncées," as my maid calls them, should be most in fashion.

The character **LONGMAN TOMPKINSON** is a wealthy manufacturer from Stoke Park in Catherine Gore's *The Woman of the World*. Although his looms have earned him "mansions in Buckinghamshire and Carlton Terrace, his plate, equipages, parliamentary interest and promise of a baronety," his wealth cannot gain the respect of the nobility (Gore, *The Woman of the World* [1838], 66–67).

MISS LOW has not been identified.

Nathaniel Parker **WILLIS** (1806–1867), journalist, poet, and editor, was engaged by the *New York Mirror* and sent abroad in 1831 as a foreign correspondent. Willis toured Europe and arrived in England in 1834. Handsome, elegant, and charming, he entered London society with assurance and his company was much sought after. His London friends and acquaintances were angered, however, by the lack of discretion exhibited in the letters he published in America, many of which quoted private conversations and correspondence. Willis's articles for the *Mirror*, known as "Pencillings by the Way," were published in a book of the same title in 1835 (*ANB*; *DAB*).

14. Jan.

Yesterday, Sunday 13. January, we went to the Bavarian Chapel to hear the music which is good. I never heard the "Adeste Fideles" so well sung. This was a favorite of my dear mother's and I thought of her when the full tones of the Choristers' voices swelled on my ears. The words were of course given in the latin which was not unfamiliar to me although I followed them involuntarily in English.

> Hither ye faithful, haste with songs of triumph,
> To Bethlehem haste the Lord of Life to meet
> To you this day is born a Prince and Saviour,
> Oh come and let us worship at his feet.
> Verite adoremus Dominum

After the service was over I took a short drive and returned home, where I met Mr Bates come to call upon me. We talked of Paris where I much wish to go, and then of my voyage to China. Mr Bates told me they would send out their ship Adelaide, which has the best accommodations for passengers, on purpose that we might go in her, should we decide to go by the Cape of Good Hope rather than by the overland route. Of course I did not understand this very kind offer as meant to convey the idea that the Messrs Baring, Brothers & Co. would send a ship to China on purpose to oblige Mr Coolidge & myself, but simply that the Adelaide should go in preference to another to give us the advantage of her superiour accommodations.

Just before dinner Mr Sumner came in. He had been dining (the day before?) with Lord Durham, with a regular radical party including Sir William Molesworth & Harriet Martineau. He had also been at a party at Miss Martineau's own house where he met among other distinguished individuals, Rogers the poet. A strange guest it seams to me, under the roof of a female radical—But I suppose Mr Rogers goes every where.

After dinner Mr C. & myself passed a couple of hours in Portland Place with M^r & Mrs Stevenson. I talked with her about old times and old friends far away whilst the gentlemen discussed the political relations of America & England. Mrs Stevenson wants me to go with her to see Mrs Grote, the blue stocking wife of an eminent Radical, Lady Morgan & Miss Joanna Baillie. I am willing, they are all Lions in their way, Miss Baillie the only Royal one. (We were to have commenced this hunt to-day (14th Jan.) but it rains and Mrs Stevenson's health is too delicate to bear any exposure.) Whilst we were still in Portland Place Mr Livingstone came in. He is fresh from Paris. The capital of fashion, he says, is under a cloud from sympathy in the affliction of the King & Queen & Royal Family caused by the illness & death of the Princess Mary Dutchess of Wirtemberg. This only means I suppose that the gay City has thrown an elegant veil of black blonde over her rouged face, whilst her eyes still sparkle & her lips smile under the half sentimental & half coquettish shade of lace. I have no doubt that the Princess Mary is regretted, for she was young and lovely and good, but the French know so well how to associate graceful grief with present enjoyment! Charming Paris! Shall I really leave Europe without once breathing the intoxicating gas of your atmosphere!

We returned home a little after ten and found Mr Heard. Mr Higginson failed to call, and as he leaves London to-day, happy man, for Paris! I shall not see him before his departure.

The rain continues,—I fear I must stay at home all day.

———

The **BAVARIAN CHAPEL**, on Warwick Road in Westminster, was known for the "beauty of its choral services." The Roman Catholic chapel was supported by the electors of Bavaria and built in 1790 on the site of the Bavarian embassy chapel, which had been damaged, but not destroyed, in the 1780 anti-Catholic Gordon Riots. Italian architect Joseph Bonomi (1739–1808) created a deliberately subdued façade that allowed the chapel to blend in with other small-scale public buildings (*Survey of London*, vols. 31 and 32 [1963], 167–173; *Old and New London*, 4:235–246; Timbs, *Curiosities*, 229; *London as It Is To-day: Where to Go and What to See during the Great Exhibition* [1851], 74).

John George Lambton (1792–1840), first Earl of **DURHAM**, was a politician whose temper and proposals for drastic parliamentary reforms earned him the nickname Radical Jack (*ODNB*; Leonard Cooper, *Radical Jack: The Life of John George Lambton* [1959]).

SIR WILLIAM MOLESWORTH (1810–1855), eighth baronet, was a politician and reformer who advocated the radical transformation of Britain's institutions, including the abolition of the House of Lords (*ODNB*; Alison Adburgham, *A Radical Aristocrat: The Rt. Hon. Sir William Molesworth, Bart., PC, MP, of Pencarrow and His Wife Andalusia* [1990]).

The DEATH of Princess Marie (ca. 1813–1839), Duchess of Würtemburg, followed an extended illness and was a painful blow to her family, including her young cousin Queen Victoria (Benson and Brett, *Letters of Queen Victoria*, 1:182; *Times* [London], 12 Jan. 1839; *Examiner* [London], 13 Jan. 1839).

Tuesday. 15. January.

Half of January gone already! I went out yesterday, after all, and in defiance of weather, almost the only way to go out at all in such a climate as this. Mr C. & myself called at the house of a Mr Lane, an artist, who lives beyond the Regent's Park on the Regent's Canal. He draws in chalk, exquisitely as far as execution goes, but I think he exaggerates expression. His heads all want repose & have a theatrical air. Perhaps he depraves his taste by making too many sketches of theatrical characters—his room is hung with them. There is a likeness of Ellen Tree beautifully done, but the one I liked best was a head which he was drawing on stone, of a certain Miss Philips. He desired us to call in Bond St. at Mitchell's, to see the best finished of his works, his portrait of the Queen. We found this a little constrained both in attitude & expression, looking too much as if she were playing Queen for the purpose of being painted. Mr Lane told us that she desired to have as grave a face as possible, and the mouth entirely closed, which is not natural, as from the confirmation of her upper jaw, her lips are always slightly apart. The result of this struggle between nature and art is a compressed upper lip in the portrait, and altogether an artificial expression. The execution, as far as mere manual skill can go, is fine. The artist is a man of pleasing manners & gentle demeanour, but I doubt if he is the man to take my portrait. I am too far from handsome for him. It will require a freer and more manly touch for a face like mine. They tell me it has character if not beauty, and this is just what Mr Lane cannot give. We dined at home and Mr Heard passed the evening with us. Mr Coolidge read aloud from Lockhart's Life of Scott, part of Sir Walter's Diary, where he describes his feelings on finding that his ruin was impending & finally accomplished. It is rather too evident, I think, that he anticipated the publication of this diary. There is something somewhat studied in his "abandon." Like Caesar he composes his drapery before he falls. He wishes too much for sympathy & admiration in his downfall.

This morning, 15. January, the Sun shines—a sight good for "sair e'en." I was interrupted in my writing by a french master who has given me one lesson & is to come three times a week—"Never too old to learn," says the proverb. I am to go out with Mrs Stevenson to-day to pay some visits.

———4. P.M. The ladies, all but one, were out. I have heard from my little Jefferson who is well.

The sculptor and lithographer Richard James LANE (1800–1872) was known for his portraiture. He began exhibiting at the Royal Academy in 1824 and was elected an associate in 1827. Ten years later he was appointed lithographer to Queen Victoria, whose portrait he first made when she was ten years old. Lane's 1837 portrait of the queen was displayed at the shop of theater manager, bookseller, and publisher John MITCHELL, at 33 Old Bond Street (*ODNB*; Turner, *Dictionary of Art*, 18:727–728; Benezit, *Dictionary of Artists*, 8:404; Tallis, part 7; Richard Lane, *Queen Victoria* [1837], NPG.org).

Eleanora (Ellen) TREE (1805–1880) was a celebrated dramatic actress who performed widely in Britain. She traveled to America in 1836 for engagements in New York, Boston, and New Orleans and returned triumphantly in 1839. She married Charles Kean in 1842 and from that point performed primarily with him under the name of Mrs. Charles Kean. Lane created several works that featured Tree throughout her career (*ODNB*; Richard Lane, *Eleanora Tree Kean* [various dates], NPG.org).

Wednesday. 16. January.

Have taken another lesson in french. Agreeably surprised to find that my master commends my pronunciation—says I only want practice. At twelve o'clock paid another visit to the National Gallery—Looked long and earnestly at Titian's "Ecce Homo," at the fainting head of the Virgin, and am becoming more & more alive to the beauty of the work. I gave another fifteen minutes to Correggio's "Education of Cupid" & his "Vierge au Panier." I also looked at his two studies of heads which I am not yet able to appreciate. Titian's "Ganymede" fixed my attention for long—So did the Claudes and two noble landscapes of Gaspar Poussin, the "Land storm"[1] and the "Sacrifice of Isaac." Both Claude & Poussin, frenchmen by birth, were painters of the Italian school, and educated at Rome where they executed their works. Claude's landscapes, says Waagen, remind one of the Islands of the West described by Homer in the Odyssey. Poussin excels in storms, in clouded skies, in dark masses of forest—he is grave, melancholy & sometimes sublime, as Claude is cheerful and often glowingly beautiful. A landscape by Poussin (Gaspar) in the second room of the Gallery, gives a storm with Eneas & Dido driven into a cave. This has darkened much with age as Gaspar Poussin's pictures are apt to do. His figures, though often admirably done, are mere accessories in his pieces & serve to give them their names. After looking again at the "Resurrection of Lazarus" at the Holy Families of Parmeggiano & Murillo, which, however unequal in merit, are placed exactly opposite to each other, and at the "Madonna del Gatto," I took my leave, rejoicing to think that I could come again. The pictures which I dwelt upon to-day were Gaspar Poussin's Land Storm, his "Sacrifice of Isaac" & his "Dido & Eneas"[2]— "Mercury & the Woodman," a landscape by Salvator Rosa "Venus attired by the Graces," very large, by Guido—Portrait of a Jew by Rembrandt— "Christ lamented by the Angels"—small, by Guercino "Ermenia with the Shepherds"—marked Annibal Carracci—Waagen says Domenichino.—

Gaspard Dughet (1615–1675), artist, was born in Rome of French parents. He was sometimes known as Gaspard, or Gaspar, POUSSIN, a conflation of his name and that of his brother-in-law Nicolas Poussin (1594–1665) (Turner, *Dictionary of Art*, 9:375–378; Benezit, *Dictionary of Artists*, 4:1296–1298, 11:300–304).

1. Omitted closing quotation marks editorially supplied.
2. Omitted closing quotation marks editorially supplied.

Thursday 17 January.

To day I have been to Clapton to see M[rs] Glass with whom I sat an hour. She has received letters from Staten Island as late as 23 Dec.—Her son James writes that they had heard lately from Norfolk, that Aunt Hackley & her party, (consisting of her daughter and mine & their governess Miss Inglis) were well. This is later news than I have received. I was beginning to feel restless at not hearing from my Ellen. My dear children! I cannot trust myself to write about the absent ones. My tears would drop upon my paper—they are even now swelling to my eyes. And when I remember[1] that I may perhaps find it necessary to send my youngest boy back to the United States, and thus be separated from all my children, the thought "unmans" me—makes me weaker, even than a woman should be, when supported by a consciousness of doing her duty.

The country looked beautifully though it is the 17th of Jan.—dead winter—the fields were green, the Sun shining,—there seems to be already a promise of Spring. When I returned home there was still an hour of light, and I was looking over some tradesmen's bills, when I was surprised by an unexpected visit. The day before yesterday I went out with M[rs] Stevenson. We called at several houses where I was not acquainted, and where Mrs Stevenson left cards and I did not. Among these was Lady Morgan's. But there was a certain Mrs Marx, the rich widow of a German Jew, whose brother had many years ago established himself in Richmond, Virginia, & made a large fortune there. In my girlish days I was well acquainted with the family of this gentleman   His sister Miss Henrietta Marx, an old maid when I knew her, was a very clever & accomplished woman, and so fond of me that when she died, the family sent me various pieces of her work and other little memorials which I much valued. The daughters of this Mr Marx were clever too, and handsome & amiable. They were and deserved to be, in the best society in the little town where they lived—and an excellent society there was, in my young days at least, in little Richmond. Under these circumstances when Mrs S. stopped at the door of Mrs Marx and found her at home, I determined to go in & be introduced to this relation of my old friends. We were very cordially received and I found the lady & her daughter entirely willing to talk of their American relations who are amply possessed of both merit & money. Mrs Marx proposed that Mrs Stevenson and myself should pass an evening with her, and promised to invite some <u>Lions</u> to meet us, such as Sir Edward Lytton Bulwer, Campbell the poet and Lady Morgan. I was pleased at the thought of seeing such famous folk and willingly agreed to come and look at them—More than this I did not wish. Bulwer, I am told, is an insolent coxcomb, Lady Morgan fat & affected, and Campbell a sot! Nevertheless it is pleasant to see either <u>shew</u> people or things. They all rank as sights. I expected neither courtesy, refinement or good morals in Van Amburgh's lions, yet I was curious to visit them.

To-day, whilst sorting my bills, I heard a rap. Immediately after my french servant, Joseph, announced Mrs Marx. I received her at the door of the drawing room. She was followed by another lady whom she presented as Lady Morgan—a fat, round, red-faced little old woman, with twinkling eyes, and who waddles like a duck,—I was so much amused at this sudden apparition of Glorvina advanced in years and decidedly corpulent, that I could scarcely command my countenance to receive her with the honour due to her. She is just such a figure of an old Irishwoman as you would expect to find sitting under a hedge, with a red cloak, and a short pipe in her mouth—a sort of Goody Grope. Her conversation, however, was animated and pleasant; the matter perhaps being of less value than the manner, but the whole decidedly amusing. She spoke of Charles Sumner, whose success in society here, she says, is altogether unprecedented <u>for an American</u>. These people speak of us as if we were altogether low caste—they forget that they have been themselves, and to their great disgust, called a nation of shopkeepers. Lady Morgan will not read Sam Slick. She hears it is a very clever book, but she cannot forgive the Tory principles of the author—toryism in an American is too unnatural, too hateful. I represented that Judge Haliburton, as a British American, a British subject, had good right to be as tory as he pleased—that colonists & provincials were apt to be extra-loyal, exaggerating the fashion of their politics as of their dress. Lady Morgan seemed not to have been aware of the fact that the Judge had nothing to do with the United States but to misrepresent the character of the Government and of the people. I asked why Lady Morgan herself had never honoured us with a visit. To which she replied in the true spirit of a book-maker—"O your country has been gleaned, there is nothing left for me to pick up." She spoke of Miss Martineau and of the rough manner in which she had been handled by Judge Haliburton, but gave her credit for writing with honest intentions. I doubted the fact. I placed no faith in Miss Martineau. "Well," said Lady Morgan, "I am not acquainted with her, I have no reason to like her, for she speaks very ill of me, but I can sympathise with any woman reviled and abused as she has been. I know what it is to be reviled." Lady Morgan is evidently proud of this very circumstance as indicating her importance, and alludes as often to her persecution by the Quarterly Review as Cobbett used to allude to his imprisonment in Newgate. Both considered themselves as martyrs to their principles and exulted in the malice & hatred of their enemies. Lady Morgan is evidently very vain, and very proud of the social position she conceives herself to have achieved. There is a good deal of the "parvenue" in the funny little woman. Soon after she had taken her departure with Mrs Marx, Mr Coolidge came in. He had been to Highgate & brought good accounts of our boy. After dinner Mr Heard & himself went to the theatre.

Mrs. MARX was the widow of George Marx, partner with Philip Gowan in a mercantile and banking firm in London. George Marx was the BROTHER of Richmond merchant and financier Joseph Marx (ca. 1771–1840), with whom Coolidge was acquainted; his DAUGHTERS Adeline, Judith, and Louisa had occasionally attended parties and balls in Richmond with Coolidge prior to her marriage. Joseph Marx was born in Hanover, Germany, but was living in Richmond by 1791, along with his mother and three sisters, including HENRIETTA. Marx amassed a sizable fortune through his import-export business, banking interests, and speculation in western lands, including a purchase of Arkansas lands through Coolidge's brother Meriwether Lewis Randolph in 1836. Thomas Jefferson knew Joseph Marx as a business associate. Marx facilitated the purchase of books in London for Jefferson

FIGURE 17. *View of the West Front of Monticello and Garden*, by Jane Braddick Peticolas, 1825. This watercolor of Monticello was painted for Ellen by her friend Jane Braddick Peticolas, a Richmond, Virginia, artist. Coolidge's siblings Mary, Cornelia, and George Wythe Randolph are shown on the lawn, while an unidentified artist sketches the scene. (*Courtesy of Monticello / Thomas Jefferson Foundation, Inc.*)

FIGURE 15. *Martha Jefferson Randolph*, by Thomas Sully, 1836. Ellen was still mourning her mother's 1836 death when she arrived in London, and her diary became a repository of the anecdotes and details that in the past she would have shared with her mother. *(Courtesy of Monticello/Thomas Jefferson Foundation, Inc.)*

FIGURE 16. *Thomas Mann Randolph, Jr.*, by unidentified artist, 1919. Ellen's father shared Thomas Jefferson's interest in botany, experimental agriculture, and politics. He had been educated in Edinburgh from 1785 to 1788, managed Monticello's farms during Jefferson's absences, and served as a Virginia delegate, senator, governor, and congressman. *(Courtesy of the Collection of the University of Virginia.)*

FIGURE 14. *Thomas Jefferson*, by Gilbert Stuart, 1805. Gilbert Stuart made this portrait during Thomas Jefferson's presidency, just a few months before Ellen and her family spent the winter with Jefferson in the President's House. Ellen considered it "an incomparable portrait, and the only likeness I think that gives a good idea of the original." *(Courtesy of the Harvard Art Museum, Fogg Art Museum.)*

FIGURE 13. *Ellen W. Randolph Coolidge*, by Francis Alexander, 1836. Ellen Coolidge, who was thirty-nine when she sat for this portrait by Boston artist Francis Alexander, worried whether the artist would be able to transform her "faded, haggard and care-worn face" into a presentable likeness. Two years later Joseph Coolidge's concern for his wife's "health of body and mind" prompted him to bring her to London, where he hoped that "the sea, and a new world, will do more for her than medicine." (*Courtesy of Ellen Eddy Thorndike and Monticello / Thomas Jefferson Foundation, Inc.*)

FIGURE 18. *Joseph Coolidge,* by Jean Baptiste Duchesne, 1820. Joseph Coolidge was on his European Grand Tour when the French artist Jean Baptiste Duchesne made this miniature. Duchesne also painted Napoléon Bonaparte and members of the British royal family, including Queen Victoria. A lock of hair is enclosed in the back of the miniature's frame. *(Courtesy of Private Collection.)*

FIGURE 19. *Augustine Heard,* by unknown artist, ca. 1820–1825. Joseph's business partner Augustine Heard was a valued friend of the Coolidge family. He joined Ellen and Joseph in London in December 1838 and brought with him the Coolidges' youngest child, seven-year-old Thomas Jefferson Coolidge. *(Courtesy of the Ipswich Museum.)*

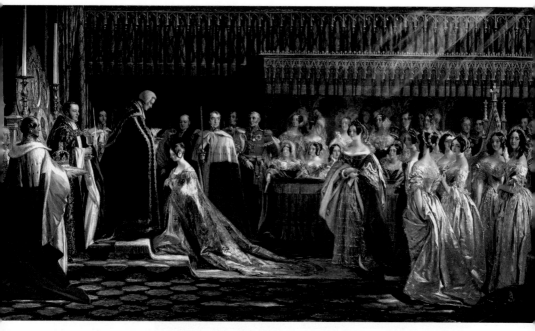

FIGURE 22. *Queen Victoria Receiving the Sacrament at Her Coronation*, by Charles Robert Leslie, 1838–1839. Ellen arrived in London after Queen Victoria's coronation, when the city and its many visitors were still celebrating the event. Charles Robert Leslie, whose art education began in Philadelphia, attended the coronation and immediately began this painting, which the Coolidges saw in progress when they visited the artist's studio in December 1838. *(The Royal Collection © 2010 Her Majesty Queen Elizabeth II.)*

FIGURE 20 (OPPOSITE, ABOVE). *View through Grosvenor Gate to Wilton Place, Hyde Park*, by Rudolph Ackermann after E. L., 1839. Ellen Coolidge rode through Hyde Park between five and seven o'clock in the morning, when spectators on horseback and in elaborate carriages gathered to watch as the newly crowned queen circled the Hyde Park round in an open carriage. *(Courtesy of the London Metropolitan Archives.)*

FIGURE 21 (OPPOSITE, BELOW). *St. Paul's Cathedral with the Lord Mayor's Procession*, by David Roberts, 1836. Ellen's visits to London's center frequently included St. Paul's Cathedral, where she heard the Reverend Sydney Smith preach. *(Courtesy of the London Metropolitan Archives.)*

FIGURE 23. *The Flower Girl*, by Bartolomé Estéban Murrillo, ca. 1660–1665. This Spanish painting was Ellen's favorite at the Dulwich Picture Gallery. *(By Permission of the Trustees of Dulwich Picture Gallery.)*

FIGURE 24 (OPPOSITE, ABOVE). *The Raising of Lazarus*, by Sebastiano del Piombo, ca. 1517–1519. Ellen's intensive study of this work at the National Gallery, aided by the writings of art historian Gustav Waagen, was a turning point for her understanding and appreciation of art. *(© National Gallery, London / Art Resources, NY.)*

FIGURE 25 (OPPOSITE, BELOW). *A Woman Scraping Parsnips, with a Child Standing by Her*, by Nicolaes Maes, 1655. Harriet Leslie, wife of the painter Charles Robert Leslie, recommended that Ellen find this painting by Maes when she visited the National Gallery, and it became a touchstone on her visits there. *(© National Gallery, London / Art Resources, NY.)*

FIGURE 28. *The House of Lords, Her Majesty Opening the Session of Parliament,* by Henry Melville, ca. 1840, after Thomas Hosmer Shepherd. Ellen attended Queen Victoria's 1839 opening of Parliament and may well be depicted in this view of the event. She observed the ceremony from a crowded window well. *(Courtesy of Private Collection / The Stapleton Collection / The Bridgeman Art Library.)*

FIGURE 26 (OPPOSITE, ABOVE). *Sarah Coles Stevenson,* by George Peter Alexander Healy, ca. 1839. Sarah (Sally) Coles Stevenson had known Coolidge since the two were young girls growing up just a few miles apart in Albemarle County, Virginia. Residing in London in the 1830s with her husband, Andrew Stevenson, she took pride in her ability to introduce Thomas Jefferson's granddaughter into the highest levels of London society. *(Courtesy of the Virginia Historical Society.)*

FIGURE 27 (OPPOSITE, BELOW). *Andrew Stevenson,* by Cephas Thompson, 1810. Andrew Stevenson, a native of Virginia and acquaintance of Ellen's, served as the American minister to Great Britain from 1836 to 1841. He provided the Coolidges with highly coveted tickets to the queen's 1839 opening of Parliament. *(Courtesy of the Collection of the University of Virginia.)*

FIGURE 29. *The Great Hall, Christ's Hospital*, by George Hawkins, 1830. The Coolidges attended one of the "Suppings in Public" held each Sunday in Lent at Christ's Hospital, a school for the children of indigent parents. Students there were known as "bluecoat boys" for their uniform, which was little modified since the school's sixteenth-century founding. *(Courtesy of the London Metropolitan Archives.)*

FIGURE 30. *The Library at Tottenham, the Seat of B.G. Windus, Esq.*, by John Scarlett Davis, 1835. In February 1839 the Coolidges viewed the art on display in the library of collector B. G. Windus, including more than two hundred watercolors by J. M. W. Turner. (© *The Trustees of the British Museum / Art Resource, NY.*)

FIGURE 31. *Queen Victoria*, by Sir Francis Chantrey, 1839. Ellen was visiting
Sir Francis Chantrey's studio in March 1838 when a clay model of this bust of
the queen arrived, still wet, from her sitting at nearby Buckingham Palace.
(The Royal Collection © 2010 Her Majesty Queen Elizabeth II.)

FIGURE 32. *John Sheepshanks at His Residence in Old Bond Street*, by William Mulready, 1832–1834. In March 1839 the Coolidges dined at the home of art patron John Sheepshanks, who collected modern British paintings and commissioned their engraving. Sheepshanks arranged for the Coolidges to visit the studios of artists William Mulready, who painted this portrait of Sheepshanks and his housekeeper, and Edwin Landseer. *(Courtesy of the Victoria and Albert Museum.)*

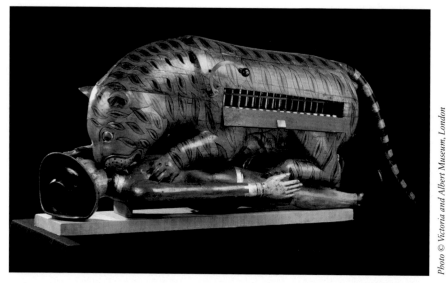

FIGURE 33. *Tippoo's Tiger*, emblematic organ made in India for Sultan Fateh Ali Tipu, 1790. After the capture of Seringapatam, India, British soldiers took this life-sized mechanical organ from the palace of Sultan Fateh Ali Tipu. The mechanism became a favorite among visitors to the museum of the East India House, where Ellen saw it in March 1839. (*Courtesy of the Victoria and Albert Museum.*)

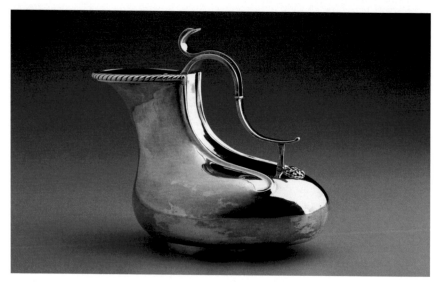

FIGURE 34. Silver Askos, Simmons and Alexander, ca. 1801. This silver askos, known fondly as "the duck" at Monticello, had served as a chocolate pot when Ellen was a child. Its design was based on a wooden model Jefferson commissioned in 1787 from a Roman ewer excavated at Nîmes, France. Ellen's mother gave it to Joseph years later. (*Courtesy of Monticello / Thomas Jefferson Foundation, Inc.*)

through his brother George's firm, and he acted as a liaison in Jefferson's 1819 bond agreement with Wilson Cary Nicholas, which ultimately ended with Nicholas's default and Jefferson's assumption of a twenty thousand dollar debt. In 1824 Marx advanced to Jefferson and the other members of the fledgling University of Virginia Board of Visitors two bills of exchange, drawn on his brother's firm of Gowan and Marx. These funds enabled Jefferson's agent Francis Walker Gilmer (1790–1826) to travel to England in order to procure books, instruments, and professors for the new university (*ANB*; *DAB*; Jacob Rader Marcus, *United States Jewry, 1776–1985* [1989–1993], 1:149–151, 718; Myron Berman, *Richmond's Jewry, 1769–1976* [1979], 70–72, 109; Virginius Dabney, *Richmond: The Story of a City* [1976], 83; Philip Alexander Bruce, *History of the University of Virginia, 1819–1919* [1920], 1:356–359; W. Asbury Christian, *Richmond: Her Past and Present* [1912], 83; Cornelia J. Randolph to Virginia J. Randolph Trist, 14 Dec. 1817, Martha Jefferson Randolph to Trist, 13 Dec. 1820 [NcU: Southern Historical Society, Nicholas Philip Trist Papers]; Meriwether Lewis Randolph, Deed for Purchase of Arkansas Lands, 4 Nov. 1836 [Vi: Randolph Family Papers]; for purchases, see Joseph Marx to Thomas Jefferson, 8 Dec. 1817, 3 July 1820, Jefferson to Marx, 8 July 1820 [DLC], and Bernard Peyton to Jefferson, 26 Oct., 2 Nov. 1820, Richard Rush to Jefferson, 11 Dec. 1820 [MHi]; for Nicholas bonds, see Wilson Cary Nicholas to Jefferson, 17 Aug. 1819, Marx to Jefferson, 2, 27 Sept. 1819, Jefferson to Marx, 20 Sept. 1820 [DLC], and Jefferson to Nicholas, 24 Aug. 1819, Jefferson to J. B. Dandridge, 31 Aug. 1819, Dandridge to Jefferson, 4 Oct. 1819 [MHi]; for Gilmer and the University of Virginia, see Gilmer, Receipt to Alexander Garrett, 30 Apr. 1824, Gilmer, Report to the Rector and Board of Visitors of the University of Virginia, 25 Jan. 1825 [ViU: Thomas Jefferson Papers]; *Richmond Whig and Public Advertiser*, 14 July 1840).

Edward George Earle Lytton **BULWER** (1803–1873), first Baron Lytton, was an author and politician whose prolific literary works and tumultuous marriage kept him in the public eye (*ODNB*).

Thomas **CAMPBELL** (1777–1844), poet, was the author of *Pleasures of Hope* (1799), *Gertrude of Wyoming* (1809), and *Theodric* (1824), among various other works, including biographies of Sarah Siddons (1834) and Petrarch (1841) (*ODNB*).

Sydney Owenson Morgan (ca. 1776–1859), **LADY MORGAN**, was an Irish novelist who had moved to London two years prior to meeting Coolidge. Her works often contained thinly veiled criticisms of the English, praised her Irish countrymen and -women, and generally featured heroines modeled after herself. **GLORVINA** was the name of the female heroine in Morgan's most famous novel, *The Wild Irish Girl* (1806), and it was also the name by which the author soon became known, particularly within literary circles. Morgan wrote prolifically and her writings attracted praise as well as criticism, which she perceived as **PERSECUTION**. She never hesitated to confront her critics by authoring refutations or sometimes incorporating satirical characterizations of them in her compositions. Her appearance was remarkable because she suffered from a slight deformation to the spine and face—one eye being larger than the other—and was scarcely above four feet tall (*ODNB*; Lionel Stevenson, *The Wild Irish Girl: The Life of Sydney Owenson, Lady Morgan (1776–1859)* [1936]).

GOODY GROPE, so called because she spent much time "groping in old castles and in moats" looking for a lost treasure, was a character in "The Orphans," featured in Maria Edgeworth's *The Parent's Assistant, or Stories for Children* (1796). Edgeworth describes Goody Grope as an old woman in ragged clothes, with a broken tobacco pipe in her mouth, who hobbled about "leaning on a crab stick."

William COBBETT (1763–1835) was an English political author, editor, and agriculturalist who spent more than five years in Philadelphia but returned to England in 1800 after losing a libel suit brought against him by Benjamin Rush (1746–1813). Jefferson, who possessed some of Cobbett's works, wrote, "he is the only man in England who seems to know any thing about us: but his prophecies, like those of Cassandra, are fated not to be believed." From 1810 to 1812 Cobbett was imprisoned in Newgate for criticizing the British government's flogging of militiamen at Ely (*ANB*; *ODNB*; *PTJRS*, 5:384; Sowerby, 1429, 3222, 3223, 3420).

1. Manuscript: "rememember."

Friday. 18. January.

A fine day as yesterday was. My french master has been in. I have just finished "Concealment," a novel by Miss Fletcher of Edinburgh, lent me by her brother. Her mother, Mrs Fletcher, whom I knew in Edinburgh, is a person of superiour character and talent. I found her much interested in all benevolent plans and schemes for the good of mankind. She asked about Temperance societies in the U.S. and we discussed the prospects of Abolitionism. I have lately sent her the Temperance Tales of Mr Sargent, & Miss Beecher's very sensible and judicious letter on the conduct of the Abolitionists in America. She told me that Mr Ticknor of Boston had spoken to her in the highest terms of her daughter's book, and declared his intention of causing it to be republished in the United States. I doubt it's success. This book has good sense & good feeling but is rather prosy & dull. I do not know what I shall say about it to Mr Fletcher.

I was sorry to hear from other sources that Mr Ticknor has been speaking harshly & disrespectfully of my grandfather. This was wrong and ungrateful. I hope that I may have been misinformed. Mr Ticknor came to Monticello many many years ago, a young man with letters from I know not whom. He was most kindly received & treated with courtesy & regard. He remained several days & left us professing entire satisfaction at the hospitality he had met with, and great personal regard for Mr Jefferson who had shewn him every attention and who gave him let-

ters to many of his old friends in Europe. Mr Ticknor was then preparing
to go abroad, and during his absence he wrote frequently very pleasant &
affectionate letters to my grandfather. After his return he continued the
correspondence, and when he had been a year or two married, he came to
Monticello again, in 1824, bringing his young wife with him. They were
received with the utmost cordiality and we parted excellent friends —
and Mr Ticknor continued to write letters addressed to my grandfather
full, I may say, of devotion & admiration. It would be easy no doubt to
find these letters among Mr Jefferson's papers, as also others written by
Mr Ticknor's father & mother, I think, one or both, during the first absence
of their son in Europe, expressive of gratitude for the kindness, for the fa-
vors he had received from my grandfather. Every man's political opinions
are his own. I blame no one for disapproving the democratic tendency of
Mr Jefferson's, but for any one who knew him as a man, had corresponded
with him as a friend, and who had enjoyed the hospitality of his roof, and
seen him in family life, for any such person to speak against him in the
way that Mr Ticknor is reported to have done, argues something essentially perverse or wilfully false.——The last day that I dined at Mr Searle's
he said to me "I was all my early life forming a wrong opinion of M^r
Jefferson which all my maturer years have been enabling me to correct."
This will be the case with all fair & candid men who take into review the
whole course of Mr Jefferson's public life. He was always so evidently acting upon principle, upon strong conviction, that no just man who takes
pains to follow & understand his political career can ever accuse him of
sinning against his own principles or abjuring his own faith. There was a
firmness of purpose, an energy of action, an undeviating pursuit of whatever object he wished to accomplish or believed to be right, that commanded the devotion of his friends, and excited the hatred of his enemies
in an almost equal degree. But these days of political excitement are now
so long gone by, that, even the persons whose political creed differs most
widely from Mr Jefferson's, should be able & willing to do justice to his
motives. His ~~political~~ opinions were, perhaps, as they often are, the result
of temperament. His bodily constitution was healthy & vigorous; his affections warm, his temper cheerful & sanguine in a remarkable degree, his
intellect powerful, his character one of extraordinary force & energy. He
lived in exciting times when the past was in battle array against the present and the future, and it was to be decided whether old habits and abuses
or new claims & aspirations were to regulate the destinies of nations. He
threw himself on the generous & hopeful side. He was the friend of the
many. His confidence in the powers & virtues of man was unlimited. He

believed that the people every where wanted nothing but knowledge to make them capable of self-government, and knowledge might and should be placed within their reach. Whether in judging other men too much after his own proportions he was right or wrong remains to be proved. If not deceived, by his own ardent and generous nature, in his estimate of his kind, if men are what he believed them to be, then will his name descend to posterity one of the brightest on the records of history. If, on the contrary, the melancholy fact should be too clearly proved that human nature is too wicked or too weak to be trusted, that liberty must degenerate into anarchy, and that man can only be protected by force from the consequences of his own folly, even then the just and impartial will give Mr Jefferson credit for his generous intentions and only mourn that his great powers should have been wasted in a hopeless cause, and his name abused by those who have perverted his principles. His domestic character was the most perfect I have ever known. After many years, and much experience of the qualities necessary to make the happiness of family life, I am but the more confirmed in my opinion that these were possessed by my grandfather in a greater degree than I have found in any other individual. If devoted attachment on the part of all his household, — children, grandchildren, servants, dependants of every sort, and the warm affection and unqualified admiration of friends and neighbours be any test of domestic and social excellence, then was Mr Jefferson equalled by few, surpassed by none in all the virtues that command reverence and love.

As it turned out, *Concealment: A Novel* was REPUBLISHED in Philadelphia in 1839, and Ticknor sent to Mrs. Fletcher a note along with two copies explaining that "he had no hand in it," and he informed the press in Boston to stop its work when he came across the Philadelphia edition. The novel was not very well received. About the Philadelphia edition, the reviewer in *Burton's Gentleman's Magazine* quipped, "if the booksellers had indulged in the concealment of the novel, the injured public would have been saved the infliction of considerable twaddle. We pity the poor creature, who, on a rainy day, has no other book at hand than this same novel of 'Concealment'!" (Mary Fletcher Richardson, ed., *Autobiography of Mrs. Fletcher with Letters and Other Family Memorials* [1875], 237; *Burton's Gentleman's Magazine* 4 [1839]: 112).

George TICKNOR (1791–1871), educator and author, first visited Jefferson at Monticello in February 1815, carrying with him letters of introduction from Jefferson's longtime friends John Adams and Caspar Wistar. Ticknor remained among the family for several days, held lengthy conversations with Jefferson about his impending journey to Europe, and perused the expansive library that, having just been sold to the United States, was soon to make its way to the

Library of Congress. Ticknor enjoyed the hospitality of Jefferson's table and family, noting particularly that the ladies of the home, including nineteen-year-old Ellen, were "accustomed to join in the conversation, however high the topic may be." Ticknor departed for Europe in April 1815 with several letters of introduction from Jefferson, a list of books to purchase on Jefferson's behalf, and Jefferson's letters to several acquaintances in Europe. After four years of study in Europe Ticknor returned to Boston in the summer of 1819 and became a professor at Harvard University, where he remained until his return to Europe in 1835. By late 1838 Ticknor was back in Boston and immersed in researching and writing his *History of Spanish Literature* (1849), drawn primarily from his own fourteen-thousand-volume personal library. In his later years Ticknor was instrumental in the establishment of the Boston Public Library, for which he traveled to Europe to purchase books and to which he donated and bequeathed portions of his own collection.

For eleven years Jefferson corresponded with George Ticknor, and Ticknor's parents were deeply honored by and grateful for the interest the former president took in their son. Jefferson took an interest in Ticknor's travels and education, and by 1817 he was discussing with Ticknor his ideas for establishing a university. As Jefferson's plans for what would become the University of Virginia progressed, he and Ticknor exchanged thoughts about curriculum and the names of European scholars for professorships, and Jefferson sent ground plans in order to give Ticknor "some idea of it's distribn & conveniences." Ticknor also wrote Jefferson about his dismay at the manner in which Harvard University was functioning and his ideas for reform, many of which echoed Jefferson's own for the University of Virginia, including the creation of departments and a system that allowed students to choose their own fields of instruction. In mid December 1824 Ticknor, with his wife, Anna Eliot Ticknor, and their young daughter, again visited Monticello, and Ticknor rode down the mountain with Jefferson to visit the new university. He observed that the eighty-two-year-old Jefferson was "very little altered from what he was ten years ago, very active, lively, and happy, riding from ten to fifteen miles every day, and talking without the least restraint, very pleasantly, upon all subjects."

It was Ticknor's letter of introduction that accompanied Joseph Coolidge on his first visit to Monticello in May 1824. Ticknor described Coolidge as "a young gentleman of Education & Fortune, a native of this town, who is well known to all of us for his amiable & excellent character and who, by a residency of several years in Europe, has recently completed the course of instruction he had so well begun at home. . . . I am sure he goes to visit you with feelings of respect which will render him sincerely sensible of the obligations your protection & regard will impose on him." It was during this visit that Joseph Coolidge and Ellen Wayles Randolph first formed the attachment that would lead to their marriage one year later (*ANB*; *DAB*; George S. Hillard and Anna Ticknor, eds., *Life, Letters, and Journals of George Ticknor* [1909], 1:34–38, 348–349; Herbert B. Adams, *Thomas Jefferson and the University of Virginia* [1888], in Contributions to American Educational History, no. 2, 122–129; John Adams to Thomas Jefferson, 20 Dec. 1814, Caspar

Wistar to Thomas Jefferson, [received 4 Feb. 1815], George Ticknor to Thomas Jefferson, 14 Oct. 1815, 15 Mar. 1816, 14 Aug. 1817, 10 Aug. 1818, 27 May 1819, 10 Feb. 1820, 1 Sept. 1821, 25 Dec. 1823, 27 Mar. 1824, Thomas Jefferson to George Ticknor, 24 Dec. 1819, 16 July 1823 [DLC]; George Ticknor to Thomas Jefferson, 6, 21 Mar. 1815, 13 Feb. 1819, Elisha Ticknor to Thomas Jefferson, 7 Aug. 1815, Elizabeth Ticknor to Thomas Jefferson, 10 Sept. 1816, Thomas Jefferson to George Ticknor, 16 Aug. 1815, 25 Nov. 1817 [MHi]; *Boston Daily Advertiser*, 27 Jan. 1871; *New York Times*, 27 Jan. 1871).

Saturday. 19. January.

Rain, rain, rain, nothing but rain. Yesterday I went to the British Museum and staid an hour and a half in the Elgin Saloon confining my attention solely to the fragments from the Parthenon. These consist 1st of the Frieze which ran round the Cella on the outside and where was represented in Bas Relief the Panathenæa, or festival celebrated every five years in honour of Minerva. 2nd, fifteen Metopes, with a cast of the 16th, from the southside of the Temple, in alto relievo. 3^{d}, the Statues, or their mutilated remains, from the Eastern pediment representing the birth of Minerva, (the figures of Jupiter & Minerva both wanting) and from the Western pediment on which was represented the contest between Minerva & Neptune for the honour of giving a name to the city of Athens. A fragment of the head of Minerva and a portion of the breast with the upper part of the torso of Neptune are all that remain of these principal figures, and when we remember that these statues of the pediment were probably the work of Phidias himself, we cannot regret too deeply the parts that are gone, nor rejoice too greatly in those that we still possess, mutilated though they be.

I am profoundly interested in all that I see in this Elgin Saloon. Yesterday I began at the beginning of the Frieze and examined every part. It is sadly broken and defaced; some parts are lost and supplied by plaster casts, but the remains are exquisite. The figures in low relief of men & horses & victims for the altar, all mutilated, some headless, others trunkless, now a body without limbs, then limbs without a body, but all how perfect of their kind! The men finely formed and in attitudes admirably graceful, yet so natural that you can imagine them in no others which would appear more easy & unconstrained. The horses worthy of their riders, and in their fine proportions affording a contrast with those of the Oxen or Bullocks equally as good after their own sort. Is there less beauty now than there was in former days among the Greeks, or are artists less skilful in the imitation of beauty? Is it Nature or Art whose works have degenerated? We certainly see nothing modern equal to these adorable fragments of the antique.——

The figures in the frieze are in very low relief and no where detached from the ground, whilst those in the Metopes, in alto-relievo, stand out almost entirely, and seem attached only on one side to the ground. The eastern part of the Frieze representing the festival of the Panathenæa, was on the principal front of the Temple, and has figures of Gods seated, women bearing gifts, and men presiding over the ceremonies; whilst on the north, south and west is represented the procession of horsemen, chariots, animals for sacrifice & their attendants, coming up on each side towards the principal figures, the Gods, occupying the centre of the Eastern Front.

The Metopes give the battles between the Centaurs and the Greeks and to me are less beautiful than the Frieze. The relief is so very high that it seems as if it might be better to have the figures altogether detached. But I have no doubt that they are just as they should be. They were not meant to be looked at in the Elgin Saloon, face to face, but to be seen at a great height where they doubtless produced a great effect.

The figures of the pediments are frightfully mutilated. The most perfect are, a Theseus who has lost his feet, his hands, his nose, and the back of his head; Ceres & Persephone & the Group of the Fates, headless trunks and broken in parts of their bodies and limbs; a figure of the Ilyssus, and another of Isis. The arm of Hyperion and the heads of his horses at one extremity of the Eastern pediment, and a horse belonging to the Car of Night at the other end, are in tolerable preservation. These statues being intended to fill a triangular pediment, were arranged with regard to the frame in which they were set, so that the heads of the horses of Hyperion are just emerging from the Ocean at one end, and the figures that succeed, recline, sit, or stand as they were placed nearer to the centre where the height was greatest. Of the statue of Minerva taken from the Western pediment, part of the head remains, the forehead and brows, with the hollows of the eyes which were probably filled up with some coloured material. The Helmet was of bronze, and the holes by which it was fastened to the head, I believe, still remain, but I did not see them.

In the evening we went to the Adelphi, a mean, vulgar-looking theatre, with tawdry, tinsel decorations. — Here we saw the Belgian Giant said to be the largest man alive. He is eight feet high, well-proportioned and might be called comely, but he is to my eyes a disagreeable object. He seems a sort of unnatural creation and made me think of Frankenstein. After the piece in which he played the part of a Saracen Giant, came the renowned Jem Crow. Rice does the negro pretty well. He has the laugh, the loud "gaffaw" to perfection, and so the movement in dancing,—as far as the straight limbs and small feet of the Caucasian race can imitate a motion peculiar to the crooked shin and broad flat foot, with the heel projecting almost as far behind as the instep does in front. The negroes dance in perfect time to the music, and in this respect, Jem Crow is a good representative of his black brethren. The performance was greeted with rapturous applause, and Rice was compelled to go again & again through his dance, till he became nearly exhausted and had to beg for mercy. There was some contrast between a morning passed with the Gods and Heroes of Greece, and an evening with Belgian Giants, niggers and Jem Crow. But variety is charming.

To-day having been one of close rain I have staid at home, paid the bills and settled the accounts of the week, reprimanded the cook for adding (at our last small dinner party) several dishes, without orders, "de sa façon," gave audience and part of his wages to the coachman, who wanted "a little money" if my ladyship would be pleased to be so good, did part of a flower in my tapestry work, read a few pages in Lady Morgan's "Life & Times of Salvator Rosa," received several gentlemen visiters, dressed for dinner, dined, heard Mr Coolidge read aloud the first fifty pages of Mrs Jamieson's new book upon Canada, and now, having written my day's experiences, am going to take up my french and prepare for a visit from my master. Mr Coolidge has gone out and I am alone & at leisure. This is the last day of the week, and to-morrow, Sunday, I shall not want the company of Grammars & Dictionaries.

The ADELPHI Theatre, 411 The Strand, was extensively renovated before the 1 October 1838 opening of the season. The London *Times* reported that the "ceiling is heightened and made into the form of a dome, and the whole of the boxes, proscenium &c., decorated, painted, and gilded with great taste." Adaptations of Charles Dickens's *Nicholas Nickleby* and *Oliver Twist* contributed to the season's critical and financial success, but novelty acts such as the Bayaderes, a troupe of eight Indian dancers, were more exciting to the press and the public (Alicia Kae Koger, "The 1838–1839 Season," in *The Adelphi Theatre, 1806–1900: A Calendar of Performances*, ed. Alfred L. Nelson and Gilbert B. Cross [1998], accessed 4 July 2011, http://www.emich.edu/public/english/adelphi_calendar/hst1838.htm; Timbs, *Curiosities*, 780; *Morning Chronicle* [London], 2 Oct. 1838; *Times* [London], 2 Oct. 1838).

Jean Antoine Joseph Bihin (b. 1807) stood seven feet eight inches tall and was known as the BELGIAN GIANT. Bihin debuted on the London stage on 31 December 1838 at the Adelphi in the role of Al Heireb in the *Giant of Palestine*. The play, loosely based on the epic poem *Jerusalem Delivered* by Italian poet Torquanto Tasso (1544–1595), was primarily a vehicle for displays of the giant's strength. Bihin weighed 320 pounds and the circumference of his chest was four feet two inches. He toured America first in 1840, performing as a vocalist and actor but also exhibiting feats of strength such as holding three men at arm's length. Later Bihin worked for P. T. Barnum (P. T. Barnum, *The Life of P. T. Barnum* [1888], 71; Benson J. Lossing, *History of New York City* [1884], 2:520; *American Phrenological Journal* 5 [1843]: 451; "The Theatres, Concerts, &c.," *Aldine Magazine*, 5 Jan. 1839; *Hudson River Chronicle* [Sing-Sing, N.Y.], 24 Mar. 1840; *Charleston [S.C.] Southern Patriot*, 28 Mar. 1840).

The New York actor Thomas Dartmouth RICE (1808–1860) created the character of Jim Crow, whose comic song and dance launched a minstrel sensation in America and Great Britain, catapulting Rice to fame. Rice based his blackface routine on the song and dance of an African-American man he observed in Louisville, Kentucky, in 1828. The song was published the following year and was immediately popular in America and England. Rice adapted the lyrics to suit his venue, but the chorus of "Jim Crow" remained the same: "First on de heel tap, den on de toe, / Ebery time I wheel about I jump Jim Crow. / Wheel about and turn about and do jis so, / And ebery time I wheel about I jump Jim Crow." In 1832 Rice performed "Jim Crow" in New York, Philadelphia, Boston, and Washington, D.C., with phenomenal success. London audiences were equally enthusiastic when Rice introduced his act there in 1836. Coolidge's friend Sally Coles Stevenson, wife of the American minister, wrote of dancing "Jim Crow," among other children's games, on Christmas Eve in 1837. Rice wrote numerous plays for the Jim Crow character, including the one that Coolidge saw, called "Jim Crow in His New Place," which premiered at the Adelphi on 31 December 1838 and ran through 16 February 1839. The London *Era* observed, "Mr. Rice, the 'Jim Crow,' is come over to visit his father-in-law, and 'turn about' upon his old stage of the Adelphi, and is again delighting crowded audiences with his vagaries."

Jim Crow and Thomas Rice were celebrated by nineteenth-century audiences, but by the twentieth-century the term came to describe repressive laws in the American South that denied African Americans equal rights (*ANB*; *DAB*; Nelson and Cross, *The Adelphi Theatre, 1806–1900: A Calendar of Performances*; W. T. Lhamon, Jr., *Jump Jim Crow: Lost Plays, Lyrics, and Street Prose* [2003], 61–65, 93–102, 301–313; Boykin, *Mrs. Stevenson*, 117; *Era* [London], 16 Dec. 1838).

Anna Brownell Murphy Jameson [JAMIESON] (1794–1860) was the author of numerous works. Her fifth book, *Winter Studies and Summer Rambles in Canada*, was published just three months before the Coolidges began reading it. "Winter Studies" describes her impressions of Toronto and its society, while "Summer Rambles" is a lively travelogue of her tour through the southwestern part of the province, including Niagara. Critics praised Jameson's descriptive writing, congratulating her for the honesty of her reaction to Niagara Falls, but questioned the motives of her work. Jameson compared the lot of the European and the "savage woman" and found the latter in some cases occupying a more honored position. This assertion led some critics to charge that her purpose was to "disturb the mutual existing relations between man and womankind." The success of *Winter Studies and Summer Rambles* secured Jameson's literary reputation and furthered her writing on women's issues. She focused her attention for the next twenty years on the history of art, writing the *Handbook to the Public Galleries of Art in or Near London* (1840), *Companion to the Private Galleries of Art in London* (1844), and *Sacred and Legendary Art* (1848), her most influential work (*DCB*; *ODNB*; Clara Thomas, *Love and Work Enough: The Life of Anna Jameson* [1967], 138–143; Gerardine Macpherson, *Memoirs of the Life of Anna Jameson* [1878]; Martineau, *Biographical Sketches*, 113–120).

Monday. 21. Jan.

Rain, rain, rain, rain but the weather as mild and dark as an April night in Virginia. Yesterday Mr Coolidge & myself went to Highgate to see our little son, whom, thank heaven, we found well. I have gone on with Mrs Jamieson's book, "Winter studies & Summer rambles." The studies are German and there is much desultory criticism. The rambles I have seen nothing of as yet, but an account of her visit to Niagara. She declares herself to have been greatly disappointed!!! Yet her description of the falls, as seen in winter, is graphic & interesting. Surely she must desire to gain celebrity as "the person who does not admire the Cataract of Niagara." But there is sometimes a sensation of coldness and bewilderment when one sees for the first time, any remarkable object after long and anxious expectation. When our wishes have run high and our imagination been greatly excited. It is not disappointment but a want of comprehension, an uncertainty of impression,—the power of appreciation seems benumbed. I was a woman grown when I first saw the Ocean and my feelings were of stupefaction. It took me some time to wake up to the full sense of what I saw. So in my visit to the Natural Bridge. I had been all my life hearing of it, longing for it—my expectations were wrought up to the highest pitch, and when on a bright summer morning, after having crossed the Blue Ridge on horseback the day before, I found myself in presence of this great work of Nature's Architecture, I felt cold and confused and unable to reply to the questions of my companions, or to define my own sensations   It was by degrees that I became sensible to the full beauty and solemnity of the object before me. I remained for three hours intent upon it, and the longer I looked the more difficult I found it to tear myself away, and I believe I should have remained till nightfall but for the better regulated memories of my friends, to whom the prospect of a ride of some miles through a mountain country, after dark, was not particularly pleasant.

In August 1817 Coolidge traveled from her grandfather's retreat, Poplar Forest in Bedford County, to see **NATURAL BRIDGE**, in Rockbridge County, Virginia. She was accompanied by her sister Cornelia Randolph and Jefferson, who had owned the bridge and its surrounding 157-acre tract since 1774. Coolidge described their journey to her mother as "a complete chapter of accidents." One of their horses broke through a decayed bridge and became stuck, their lodging at Greenlee's Landing on the James River in Rockbridge County was filthy, and Coolidge developed a cold that kept her awake all night. Still, she wrote, "I cannot however regret my trip for the wonder and delight I experienced at the sight of the bridge, (which surely deserves the name of the 'most sublime of Nature's works') was greater than I can describe." The travelers had reason to fear a latenight return. Cornelia reported that along the way they had "made a great many enquiries about bears, wolves, panthers, & rattle snakes & found they were nearly exterminated. . . . [W]e heard tho that a bear had eaten a child sometime before we were there & that wolves were frequently heard howling in the mountains." Aside from encountering another broken bridge, their return to Poplar Forest was uneventful.

Natural Bridge was ever-present at Monticello, where Jefferson displayed William Roberts's painting of the bridge in the dining room alongside two engravings of Niagara Falls made after paintings by John Vanderlyn. Jefferson first saw the bridge in 1767, when he sketched it and recorded its dimensions on the inside back cover of his Memorandum Book. This formed the basis of his description, from which Coolidge quoted in the letter to her mother, in *Notes on the State of Virginia* (1787): "It is impossible for the emotions, arising from the sublime, to be felt beyond what they are here: so beautiful an arch, so elevated, so light, and springing, as it were, up to heaven, the rapture of the Spectator is really indiscribable!" (*MB*, 1:38–39; Stein, *Worlds*, 188–191; Thomas Jefferson, *Notes on the State of Virginia*, ed. William Peden [1955], 24–25; Cornelia J. Randolph to Virginia J. Randolph Trist, 17, 30 Aug. 1817, Cornelia J. Randolph to Virginia J. Randolph Trist and Mary Elizabeth Randolph Eppes, 24 Sept. 1817 [NcU: Southern Historical Collection, Nicholas Philip Trist Papers]; Coolidge to Martha Jefferson Randolph, 18 Aug. [1817] [ViU: Ellen Wayles Randolph Coolidge Correspondence]).

Tuesday. 22 January.

A fine bright day. We took tea last evening with Mrs Hillard. Mrs Osgood the poetess being of the party. Both these ladies are intimate with Miss Martineau. Miss Martineau is surprised and <u>hurt</u> that Americans coming to England do not call upon her! What <u>are</u> her claims upon American gratitude and respect? She comes to our country and flings through it, every where hospitably entertained, almost every where kindly and cordially welcomed. She is loud, noisy, disputatious and dogmatic, amazes the gentlemen, shocks the ladies, offends all, save only a clique of her own friends, to some of whom she pays obsequious court, whilst from some others she exacts obsequious homage. She meddles every where, in every thing, thrusts herself into public assemblies and into private families, lays down the law in religion and politics, and admits of no appeal, in small things or in great, from her own decisions. Moreover she has a most unhappy knack of inflaming people's minds wherever they are most inflammable. She aggravates dislikes, stimulates the violence of party spirit, irritates one portion of the community against the other, cries Havoc and lets slip the dogs of war, urging them forward with voice and lash, and seeming to take equal pleasure in the bay of a bloodhound or the yelping of a cur. Any thing to promote the great object of strife and confusion. Having made herself as disagreeable and her hosts as uncomfortable as she well could during her visit, she comes home and writes a book in which she denounces all parties and all persons, save her select few, of whom her praise is as extravagant as her dispraise of all others is absurd. She calls our ministers of religion time-servers, our lawyers tories, and our women drunkards, and then she is surprised to find that she has given offence. Verily Miss Martineau you are a most unsophisticated innocent! Lord Brougham we are told, after drinking two bottles of wine, says that you are "a d—d ass." What an ungrateful man! after making a tool of you to serve his own particular purposes so long as you were a popular writer, now that he is out of office and you out of fashion, to bestow upon you a name so opprobrious and so unjust! For an Ass you are not, but a clever, ingenious, vain, restless and extravagant woman, with no object in life but the advancement of your own glory.

I hear that two of Miss Martineau's particular friends, Dr & Mrs Follen are expected in England. He is a worthy German, a man of intellect and of learning but thoroughly German. He is not, I take it, a person to underestimate his own merit, yet I think he must feel that it is "tant sait peu" over-rated by his devoted Miss Martineau, when she says, as we are told she does, that "Dr Follen is the most valuable present ever made by the Old World to the New." Now considering that the old world has given us our language, laws, literature, arts, religion & civilization, this seems to me "un peu fort," as my french master would say and I think the excellent Dr Follen would himself subscribe to my opinion.—It may be noted that Miss Martineau's particular animosities in many instances may be traced to private pique. She has a great hatred to Boston. It is well known that she gave offence to the Bostonians upon her first arrival, shocked their ideas of womanly propriety, and was treated with entire neglect by the educated & wealthy, except in a very few instances, where there was previous private friendship, or by such persons as had received special letters in her behalf which they felt bound to respect. She has reviled Gov. Everett. He did not invite her to stay at his house, after receiving a broad hint (she was in the habit of giving such hints) that the invitation would be acceptable and accepted. She is abusive of Mr Sprague, or rather her criticisms of one of his speeches have all the violence of personal dislike. He knew her in Washington, was disgusted by her manner and manners, thought her homely in person, and altogether unfeminine & unpleasant. The consequence was that he withheld the attentions amounting to homage, which she certainly did receive from a great many persons in Washington. When a "distinguished stranger" arrives at the "head quarters" of our Government, where, for part of the year, there are persons assembled from all parts of the country, there is apt to be a disgraceful competition of parties to see who can secure the new arrival, attack the individual, endoctrinate him or her with their own political views & personal prejudices, and purchase by flattery and obsequiousness the present influence and future good word of a new ally   I was in Washington when Miss Martineau arrived there and I witnessed and blushed at the extravagant court paid, even by many of our public men, to this clever & bold-faced woman who, it was conjectured, would "write a book." Can we wonder that books of travels in America contain so much harsh censure, so many misrepresentations, false statements, and even such an amount of personal invective & calumny? These are but the reflections of our own passions & hatreds. A stranger arrives, it is known or suspected that he means to observe and publish his observations. His observations! Mistaken man or woman! His or her book receives it's tone, it's colouring from the party politics, individual prejudices, private resentments or public disappointments of the persons who lay hold of him and get possession of his ear. These combined with his own particular & private grievances of stage coach and steamboat, bad inns, bad fare, bad attendance, weather too hot or too cold, too wet or too dry, rough roads, the absence of his accustomed comforts and the presence of unaccustomed small annoyance, the ill humour, the indigestion, the irritability consequent on petty discomforts, make up those descriptions of men and manners in America, which the world is every day receiving as genuine accounts of things as they are. These books of travels are often marked by the overweening self-conceit of the authors. No wonder. The writers are frequently persons of no great importance at home, who see themselves suddenly made of much importance abroad; who are taught to believe that much depends on the oracles they are about to deliver, and who utter them accordingly with all possible pomp, and pride in their own sagacity and authority. This overweening attention to strangers in the United States, is every way productive of evil effects. They learn to resent as an insult the absence of these excessive civilities, when, as sometimes happens, they are omitted. Witness Miss Martineau's rage against Boston, Gov. Everett & Mr Sprague.

There is however, one other way of explaining the too frequent virulence of English travellers against America. Their books sell all the better. John Bull <u>does</u> like to hear his rebellious children well abused. The old wound still rankles—the old grudge remains.

Harriet **MARTINEAU** (1802–1876) was born in Norwich to Thomas Martineau, a cloth manufacturer, and his wife, Elizabeth. The sixth of eight children, Martineau was schooled largely at home and interested in serious discussions of politics and religion. Her progressive deafness was virtually complete by the age of twenty, and the ear tube (later a trumpet) she employed was often described as a daunting device. Writing proved to be a welcome respite as well as a financial necessity following the loss of Martineau's brother, father, and fiancé, and the failure of the family business. Initially a Unitarian, she first published in the Unitarian *Monthly Repository*, whose editor—W. J. Fox—would secure her entrée into London's intellectual circles. It was Fox who encouraged Martineau to begin work on *Illustrations of Political Economy*, a series of twenty-three tales published monthly starting in 1832 that made her famous almost overnight. Martineau rapidly followed with four more volumes and essays in the *Westminster Review*. Seeking relief from constant deadlines, Martineau traveled to the United States in August 1834 accompanied by Louisa Jeffrey, a young Unitarian woman, and there she observed the creation of a new society.

For two years Martineau traveled from the Great Lakes to Charleston, with stops at every major city in between. She made no secret of her opposition to slavery, complaining that in Charlottesville "the evil influences of slavery have entered in to taint the work of the great champion of freedom. . . . [T]he eyes of the world will be fixed on Jefferson's University during the impending conflict between slaveholders and freemen." In Boston Martineau aligned herself with the radical abolitionist William Lloyd Garrison and met Maria Weston Chapman (1806–1885), who would become her literary executor and first biographer. Author Margaret Bayard Smith described Martineau's reception in Washington: "As I had always understood she was of the Liberal if not radical party, the advocate of the poor and of the working-class, I did not anticipate the reception she has met with from our dignitaries and fashionables. But the English minister was the first to wait on her, introduced her into the Senate, to the President. . . . She has literally been overwhelmed with company. I have been told that the day after her arrival near 600 persons called, (an exaggeration I suppose) but the number was immense." Smith observed that many who came to see Martineau had not read her writing and that "the gentlemen laugh at a woman's writing on political economy. Not one of them has the least idea of the nature of her work." Coolidge and her mother, Martha Randolph, first met Martineau in 1835 at a small dinner party hosted in Washington by Smith, their longtime friend. Smith wanted Martineau to see "the daughter of Jefferson to advantage"; however, Mrs. Randolph was so unsettled by Martineau's ear trumpet that "the very touch of the Tube put all her ideas to flight."

After returning to London Martineau published *Society in America* (1837), a two-volume work. The following year she further mined her American voyage in two publications, *Retrospect of Western Travel* and *How to Observe: Morals and Manners*. She produced her only large-scale novel, *Deerbrook*, in 1839, after which her health declined and she was bedridden. Still Martineau pursued philanthropic and literary causes and captured her experience in *Life in the Sick Room* (1844). She caused a stir when she claimed that she was cured through mesmerism, after which she completed an extensive tour of Egypt and the Near East in 1846–1847 and published *Eastern Life: Present and Past* (1848). Her *Autobiography* (1877) reveals the depth of her commitment to the abolition movement as well as women's rights and is recognized as one of the best self-studies of the century. She maintained a lively correspondence up until her death at her Ambleside home, the Knoll, in 1876 (*DAB*, s.v. "Chapman, Maria Weston"; *ODNB*; Margaret Bayard Smith, *The First Forty Years of Washington Society*, ed. Gaillard Hunt [1906], 355–356, 363; Harriet Martineau, *Retrospect of Western Travel* [1838; repr. 1942], 1:205; Lucia Stanton, "Looking for Liberty: Thomas Jefferson and the British Lions," *Eighteenth-Century Studies* 26 [1993]: 665–666; Coolidge to Henry Randall, 19 July 1853, Ellen Coolidge Letterbook [ViU: Ellen Wayles Randolph Coolidge Correspondence]).

The German poet Karl (Charles) T. C. FOLLEN (1796–1840) emigrated to the United States in 1824 and, aided by letters of introduction from the Marquis de Lafayette, established himself in Massachusetts society. George Ticknor arranged for Follen to join Harvard's faculty as professor of German language and literature, but his appointment was revoked in 1835 largely because of Follen's strong abolitionist views. He was outspoken in his support of the Ladies' Anti-Slavery societies and considered radical, though Harriet Martineau asserted that he was neither "blood-thirsty" nor "fanatical." After Harvard, Follen became an ordained Unitarian minister, but his extreme antislavery views alienated his congregations, and he considered returning to Germany. He remained in the United States, however, and was hired by a Lexington, Massachusetts, congregation. He was married to the socially prominent Eliza Lee Cabot (1787–1860), author of children's books and the introduction to the American edition of Harriet Martineau's *Life in the Sick Room* (1844). The Follens had one son, Charles Follen (1830–1872), who graduated from Harvard and was also an active abolitionist. Harriet Martineau credited the Follens for the introduction of the German Christmas tree into the

United States and immortalized young "Charley" in her description of the family's celebration. En route to the dedication of his new parish church Follen died in a steamboat accident (*DAB*; Martineau, *Autobiography*, 343; Martineau, *Retrospect of Western Travel*, 2:178–179; Harriet Martineau, *The Martyr Age of the United States* [1839], 55; Eliza Lee Cabot Follen, *The Works of Charles Follen, with a Memoir of His Life* [1842], 1:380–387; Thomas S. Hansen, "Charles Follen: Brief Life of a Vigorous Reformer: 1796–1840," *Harvard Magazine* [2002], 38, accessed 20 Dec. 2010, http://harvardmagazine.com/2002/09/charles-follen.html).

The renowned orator Edward EVERETT (1794–1865), governor of Massachusetts from 1836 to 1840, was an ordained Unitarian minister, succeeded Andrew Stevenson as minister plenipotentiary to Great Britain, served in Congress, and was president of Harvard University. During Everett's tenure as professor of Greek literature at Harvard, he corresponded with Jefferson on subjects ranging from European diplomacy to details of Greek grammar, of which he sent Jefferson several volumes. It was Everett who delivered the Boston eulogy for Jefferson and John Adams, who both died on 4 July 1826. Martineau had nothing but contempt for Everett, whose transition from scholar to politician she viewed as regrettable and whose motives she questioned. "Edward Everett," Martineau wrote, "the man of letters *par excellence*, burning incense to the south, and insulting the Abolitionists while they were few and weak. . . . I early saw in him the completest illustration I met with of the influences of republican life upon a man of powers without principle, and of knowledge without wisdom" (*ANB*; *DAB*; Martineau, *Autobiography*, 372; Edward Everett, *An Address Delivered at Charlestown August 1, 1826, in Commemoration of John Adams and Thomas Jefferson* [1826]; Thomas Jefferson to Edward Everett, 24 Feb. 1823 [MHi: Edward Everett Papers]).

Peleg SPRAGUE (1793–1880), senator, lawyer, and judge from Maine, roused Harriet Martineau's indignation with his speech at the anniversary festival of Forefather's Day at Plymouth in 1835. Martineau recalled that "The orator of the occasion was Senator Sprague, whom I had known well at Washington. He took particular pains to have me seated where I could hear him well; and then he fixed his eye on me, as if addressing to me particularly the absurd abuse of England which occupied much of his address, and some remarks which were unmistakably intended for my correction" (*DNB*; Martineau, *Autobiography*, 358–359).

Wednesday 23ᵈ January.

A bright day. Yesterday two letters came from my dear Ellen, my daughter. One to her father, one to myself—full of interest they were. She tells me of her studies, her progress in french, her health, that she has grown taller, and a thousand little details that none but a mother could appreciate. God bless my child! My prayer should be that of Nemorin in Estelle with now the change of one word—"Faites que j'aime la vertu autant

que j'aime mes enfants." Formerly I took it word for word, as uttered by
Nemorin at the tomb of his mother. "Faites que j'aime la vertu autant que
j'aime ma mere."

Coolidge here quotes not from ESTELLE but *Galatée* (1783), a similar pastoral
work from the same French author, Jean-Pierre-Claris de Florian (1755–1794).
Martha Jefferson Randolph received a copy of *Galatée* when she was a student in
Paris, and it is now in the collection of the Thomas Jefferson Foundation (*New
Oxford Companion to Literature in French* [1995], 317; Jean-Pierre-Claris de Florian,
Oeuvres de M. de Florian: Estelle et Galatée [1805], 1:108; TJF Accession 1927-74-5).

Sunday. 27. January.

I have been busy and unwell since my last entry and am now feeble &
somewhat low spirited.

Wednesday evening, 23 Jan, we passed pleasantly with M^r & Mrs Leslie,
who live on the Edgeware road, Pine Apple place. Cherubina would say
there is a green and yellow melancholy in the name, but certainly not
extending, as far as we could see, beyond the name, and if the domestic
life of the accomplished artist and his amiable wife be not all "couleur
de rose" it seems at least very pleasantly tinged with that colour They
are not rich, I presume, and they have a family of six children, but the
three little ones whom we saw at the tea-table, seemed healthy, happy
and well-behaved, and the parents fond of the children and of each other.
Mr Leslie's conversation is pleasant, turning principally on art and artists.
He spoke in terms of high admiration of Hogarth, and told a story of
the pious Queen Dowager, a propos to another great artist, Wilkie, which
amused us a good deal. It was simply that she would not allow the "Penny
Wedding" to hang in one of the Royal Palaces, because among the figures
there is one of a man kissing a girl which the good Queen considered an
immoral exhibition.

I was greatly delighted with a portfolio of watercolour drawings exhibited by Mr Leslie for our amusement. These charming sketches were
made by the two Chalons, Stanfield, Uwins, Landseer & Leslie himself
under the following circumstances. During the London season, a society
consisting of about eight artists meet once a week or once a fortnight, at
each other's houses, when a subject is proposed, I believe by the master
of the house, which, all the necessary materials being provided before

hand, each man treats after his own manner. He completes his sketch in three or four hours and it becomes the property of the host, under the condition that it is never to be given away. A very necessary precaution. The drawings which we saw had thus come into Mr Leslie's possession, and he gave me to understand that they were selected from a number less successful. I was astonished to find how rich and elaborate many of these hasty productions were; how many figures there were, and how much finish, not of minute touches, but in all that was necessary to give character and expression.

The subjects that interested me most were the following

The Salute—The Vale of Tempe—An Adventure—Peril—Scenes from the 3^d Canto of Don Juan—The escape of Rassales with Imlac, Nekayah & Pekuah from the Happy Valley—Lady Diana Rich terrified whilst walking in the Gardens of Holland House by an apparition of herself.—

As each artist works in his own style, persons acquainted with the style would recognize the hand. In Stanfield's pieces the figures are entirely subordinate to the landscape, and the Sea and ships are introduced wherever they can be. Stanfield's "Salute" is between two ships, whilst another artist makes it military, bringing in a figure of the Duke of Wellington—One of the Chalons personifies the "Salute" in the celebrated kiss given by an Italian lady to Milton in his sleep.

In "Peril," Stanfield has a shipwrecked sea-boy clinging to a rock, with a boiling sea below and a stormy heaven above, the foundering vessel seen in the distance. Chalons had drawn with great spirit, a female somnambulist, a beautiful figure in white, walking, at a giddy height, on the top of a parapet. Another artist represents "Peril" by a woman gazing with rapt attention on the moon, whilst a serpent approaches unheeded. Stanfield's Rasselas is an Abyssinian or Egyptian landscape, with palm trees, temples, pyramids, the figures small and mere accessories, whilst in the same subject treated by the two Chalons, in two different designs, they introduce the Prince, his sister, her attendant and the Philosopher, making every thing else subordinate to their graceful & beautiful figures.

The story of Lady Diana Rich gives Stanfield an opportunity to make a fine drawing of Holland House and it's gardens, where two little female figures scarcely attract any attention. The two Chalons (I did not distinguish between these two though their styles are no doubt very different,) treat the subject in quite another way, and I think one much better than the other. The story is, that this young lady walking alone in the grounds of Holland House, in a distant and solitary spot, was astonished by the sudden apparition of a figure exactly resembling her own, which seemed approaching towards her. Struck with sudden terror she turned and fled. The mysterious resemblance pursued so as to keep close behind, till Lady Diana reached and entered the house in a paroxysm of wild dread. She was immediately seized with fever and died in a week from the day on which she had seen the apparition. One of the Chalons represents her rushing down a flight of garden steps, but looking back with a countenance of horror at a tall figure in white which follows at some distance behind. The other artist of the same name, and I thought his effort much the most successful, has taken the moment when Lady Diana, exhausted by terror and her rapid flight, and ready to sink upon the earth, has reached the house and rests upon the balustrade of a grand marble staircase which she is about to ascend. Her dress is black, long and graceful, flowing to her feet, her arms and bosom bare. She gives one backward glance of agony towards the tall, fine figure in a black flowing robe, with arms and bosom bare, slowly and solemnly approaching the place where she stands— herself yet not herself—the form, features and dress identical with her own, yet the whole veiled in a sort of misty indistinctness and with a calm and grave expression, forming a marked contrast with the well-defined outlines and the agitated manner of the living, breathing, terrified girl clinging almost convulsively to the stairway balustrade for support.

There were but few of Leslie's own. One a Don Quixotte defying the Lion, another a scene from the Tempest, and Mrs Leslie complained that he took no pains in getting them mounted and in setting them off to the best advantage as he did those of his brother artists.

Of the two Chalons, J.J. Chalon is a landscape painter and Albert a portrait painter in water colours, but only two of these sketches in which the difference was very apparent was in the Vale of Tempe, where J.J. Chalon had given a landscape without figures, and Albert had introduced a naked Venus and half a dozen Cupids.

Mrs Leslie recommended me on my next visit to the National Gallery to look at two Dutch pictures, a woman scraping a carrot watched in her operations by a child, and a fat Dutch baby rocked in a wicker work cradle by an elder sister. Both by Maes. We remained with these amiable persons until ten o'clock. We talked among other things about Miss Leslie the artist's sister in America, who has written some clever tales. The first series of "Pencil Sketches" has some graphic details & a good deal of the "couleur locale," particularly as regards the middling classes of American society.

Thursday 24th January I went to Albert Chalons rooms where I saw some of his finished drawings. A beautiful full-length of the Duchess of Sutherland and a group of three sisters whose names I do not remember.

His terms are high. Sixty guineas for a full-length and thirty for a half length figure. He excels in the details of drapery, laces, velvets, fans &c &c. No lady's finery is thrown away in her portrait. I said to him "I should be afraid to sit to you, Mr Chalon, I am not handsome enough—all your subjects seem to be beauties." "Ah," said he, "you need not fear. A great deal of such beauty is in the artist's eye."

From Chalon's rooms I went to the National Gallery and after looking first at my own favorites I made a point of finding out the two dutch pictures spoken of by Mrs Leslie. I thought them admirable. One is a woman seated with a basket of carrots by her side and a colander at her feet, into which she throws those which she has prepared for use. She is in the act of scraping one of these carrots, whilst a little girl looks on with a countenance of intense interest which seems to say, "Shall I ever be so happy as to be allowed to scrape a carrot?" Those who know any thing of children, of their eager desire to do what they see others do, of the peculiar interest which little girls in particular take in household affairs, and their early anxiety to be initiated into the operations of domestic economy, will understand the whole spirit of truth in this truly dutch picture. The companion is a girl permitted to rock the baby's cradle with the baby in it. What a countenance of pride and joy and hope fulfilled! In these two pictures we have humanity under two aspects, operated upon by two powerful agents, excited ambition in the girl aspiring to the time when she may scrape a carrot, gratified desire in the one who is permitted to rock a cradle.

On Friday 25 Jan. Mrs Stevenson & myself went to Hampton to see Miss Baillie who, unfortunately for us, was out. I returned by Highgate and passed ten minutes with Jefferson. That night I went ill to bed with headach, and am just now tolerably well again.

Charles Robert LESLIE married the Londoner Harriet Honor Stone (1799–1879) in 1825, and together they had six children in ten years: Robert Charles Leslie (1826–1901), Harriet Jane Leslie (b. 1828), Caroline Anna Leslie (1829–1859), Bradford Leslie (b. 1831), Mary Leslie (b. 1833), and George Dunlop Leslie (1835–1921). Both George and Robert went on to become painters. Leslie and his family took up residence at 12 Pine Apple Place upon their return to London in 1834 after his short-lived appointment as drawing instructor at West Point Military Academy in New York.

Leslie's technique and scale were inspired by the English painter and engraver William HOGARTH (1697–1764), who was known for his detailed depictions of what he termed "modern moral subjects" such as *A Rake's Progress*. Leslie's patron George Wyndham, third Earl of Egremont, who commissioned the famed *Sancho Panza and the Duchess*, described Leslie as the "Hogarth of elegant life" (*ODNB*;

Tom Taylor, ed., *Autobiographical Recollections by the Late Charles Robert Leslie, R.A.* [1860], 2:196, 315).

In 1808 the Swiss brothers Alfred Edward CHALON (1780–1860) and John James Chalon (1778–1854) founded the Society for the Study of Epic and Pastoral Design, later known as the Chalon Sketching Society. Members included Leslie; Clarkson STANFIELD (1793–1867), known for his landscapes; and Thomas UWINS (1782–1857), who became keeper of the National Gallery. In the beginning membership was restricted to eight artists and the host was allowed to invite one visitor, as Leslie had apparently done with Edwin LANDSEER. Uwins described the Society's arrangements in his memoir: "They met at each other's houses weekly during the season, in rotation, the host of the evening being also president, and giving out the subject to be treated after tea and coffee. At eight o'clock they commenced operations and at ten sat down to supper. . . . [A]fter supper the drawings were collected by the president, and put up separately for each member to criticise, and this was done with more candour and judgment than is usually found in professional critics. The drawings remained the property of the president of the evening." Themes included classical literature, history, and poetry, and the resulting sketches tended to be romantic. The society survived more than forty years, with Queen Victoria choosing the themes of "Desire" and "Elevation" for their work in 1842. Alfred Chalon attended the society 971 times, and at his death it was estimated that he owned more than two thousand sketches made by the group (*ODNB*; *Grove Art Online*, s.v. "Chalon," "Stanfield, Clarkson," "Uwins, Thomas," Oxford Art Online; Giles Walkley, *Artists' Houses in London, 1764–1914* [1994], 194–196; Richard Ormond, "'The Sketching Society' at the Victoria and Albert Museum," *Burlington Magazine* 113 [1971]: 169–170; *Gentleman's Magazine*, n.s., 10 [1861]: 101–103, 193; Sarah Uwins, *A Memoir of Thomas Uwins* [1858], 1:163–164).

LADY DIANA RICH (d. 1658) was the daughter of Henry Rich, first Earl of Holland (ca. 1590–1649), for whom Holland House was named. Lord Holland was beheaded, and it was said that his ghost also roamed Holland House (*ODNB*, s.v. "Rich, Henry"; *Old and New London*, 5:161–177; thePeerage.com: A Genealogical Survey of the Peerage of Britain As Well As the Royal Families of Europe, comp. Darryl Lundy, s.v. "Rich, Lady Diana," accessed 6 July 2011, http://www.thepeerage.com/p6786.htm).

Dutch painter Nicolaes MAES (1634–1693) studied with Rembrandt but developed his own style with genre paintings such as *A Woman Scraping Parsnips, with a Child Standing by Her* (1655) (fig. 25) and *A Little Girl Rocking a Cradle* (ca. 1655). Both paintings have been at the National Gallery since their bequest in 1838. Waagen, commenting on a similar work by Maes in the Bridgewater Gallery, noted that "more attention has lately been paid to the merit of pictures of this kind, by this scholar of Rembrandt, so that they are now much esteemed in England. They generally represent quiet domestic scenes, and are distinguished by great clearness and warmth of the light and shade, which is always very effective" (Waagen, *Works of Art*, 2:65; Nicolaes Maes, *A Woman Scraping Parsnips, with a Child Standing by Her* [1655], and Maes, *A Little Girl Rocking a Cradle* [ca. 1655], National Gallery of Art, accessed 20 Dec. 2010, http://www.nationalgallery.org. uk/paintings/).

Alfred [**ALBERT**] **CHALON** was the first artist to portray Queen Victoria in her robes of state and was appointed the queen's painter in watercolor. Waagen noted that "among the portrait painters, A. E. Chalon is above all in fashion. By a tasteful composition, a certain lightness and elegance in the design, a delicate harmony in the colouring . . . he charms every body, and causes them to forget the often indifferent drawing, the great superficialness, the affectation of many attitudes." The *Monthly Chronicle* considered Chalon "without a rival—without an equal in his own department; that of conventional elegance and artificial grace. . . . The Duchess of Sutherland is supremely elegant and duchess-like." Chalon's minia-tures were beautifully detailed and captured the elaborate dress of his subjects, many of whom were actresses. His response to the queen when asked whether he was worried about the invention of photography is often repeated: "Ah non, Madame, photography can't flatter" (*ODNB*; *Gentleman's Magazine*, n.s., 10 [1861]: 101–103; Waagen, *Works of Art*, 2:153; *Monthly Chronicle* 1 [1838]: 355).

Wednesday. 31. [30] January—

the last day of the month I do not know how it is that doing so little I have so little time to do any thing in. It is a problem I cannot solve.

On Sunday, feeling somewhat feeble from my late indisposition, I went with Mrs Stevenson, by appointment, to call on Mrs Grote, wife of the radical member of parliament, and herself a politician of no common vigour and zeal. I do not admire female politicians. My ideas on that sub-ject have not kept pace with the march of intellect. My Grandfather used to tell me that it was one of the privileges of my sex to be exempt from the necessity of taking active part in the violence & turbulence of party politics. Of course if a woman thinks at all she must have an opinion, and I am myself "tant sait peu" conservative in my ideas. Perhaps because, in my country, all the tendencies are towards an abuse of the opposite prin-ciples. Putting domestic slavery out of the question, it has never been my lot to see any thing like oppression of the many by the few. My sympathies have never been excited on the popular side, because with us the people have all the power. Property, if not equally divided, is accumulated by no arbitrary law in the hands of a few. The spirit of caste, where it exists at all, is perpetually shifting it's ground. There is perpetual movement every where. We are in a state of constant revolution. All the evils that I see, arise from too much liberty and not too little. The violence, the vulgarity of Democracy is always before my eyes. Were it otherwise my feelings would be different, because no one can feel greater indignation than I do at a tale of injustice or oppression, or a more deep and solemn reverence for the inalienable rights of man.——But to return to my radical Mrs Grote, she is a tall, masculine looking woman, with a countenance full of intelligence & independence, decided in her manner and tone and altogether a favorable specimen of her kind. Perhaps Mrs Grote might be Mme Roland in Mme Roland's place. Mr Grote is milder and more <u>gentlemanly</u> than his wife, and is said to be much under her influence, and much indebted to her superiour vigour of character if not of intellect. He is called, in a spirit of prophesy, the Wilberforce of the vote by ballot—A measure of reform which he seems pledged to carry through, if his concentrated powers and perseverance can possibly accomplish it.

From Mr Grote's house, 3. Eccleston St. we drove to the door of the Countess Duchess of Sutherland. Mrs Stevenson who had been always very kindly treated by this aged and great lady wished to inquire after her health. She had been seriously ill for several days, but ~~to-day~~ was now, we were told by a servant at the door, very much better. This morning's paper announces her death!

The same day, Sunday, we dined with Mrs Stevenson and passed a pleasant evening. Monday, Mrs Glass dined with us. M^{r} & Mrs Grote left their cards as did M^{r} & Mrs Morrison with an invitation to pass this (Wednesday) evening at their house.—Tuesday Mr Coolidge & myself called on Mrs Stewart a Scotch lady who visited me some time ago, and on Mrs Mill the wife of an old friend of his in India.

——I have made a mistake in my date and gained a day. This is the 30th & not the 31st of the month which ends on thursday, to-morrow. To-day is the coldest I have felt in England, there is a slight sprinkling of snow on the ground, and for the first time, I, this morning, wished for a fire in my bed-chamber. The cold, however, is not severe enough to be unpleasant, and I go now to prepare for a sortie into the open air.

Harriet Lewin **GROTE** (1792–1878) was at the height of her involvement and influence in politics at the end of the 1830s, a time she later described to Harriet Martineau as "a pregnant decade, if ever there was one." Her husband was the historian and politician George Grote (1794–1871), an intellectual who admired the radical views of Jeremy Bentham and James Mill. George Grote became a member of Parliament for the City of London after the passage of the 1832 Reform Bill and was widely regarded as the leader of the radicals. He advocated popular democracy and called for greatly extended suffrage, a secret ballot, and frequent elections to Parliament. There was disagreement between the Grotes on the agressive tactics proposed by some radicals, with George Grote advocating a more moderate position than his wife, prompting the observation that she was "more of a man, but not a better man than her husband." Even though the approach favored by Harriet failed and the radicals in Parliament disbanded, Mrs. Grote was acknowledged to have been a significant player. The editor of the *Examiner* referred to "Mrs. Grote's little party," while Richard Cobden observed, "Had she been a man, she would have been the leader of a party."

The Grotes were friends of the Stevensons, and Andrew Stevenson shared with them stories of his time as Speaker of the House of Representatives. Harriet Grote recalled that "American politics had for many years occupied Grote's attention, and engaged his sympathy. He was a great admirer of the 'Federalist,' the pages of which, he always declared, revealed the highest qualities of philosophical statesmanship. I may here add that Grote was ever ready to accept the society of well-educated Americans, with some of whom both he and I contracted in bygone years ties of personal friendship." On the eve of his departure from England in 1841, Stevenson presented Grote with a portrait of Thomas Jefferson that he described as a head done in crayon. Stevenson wrote that it was "done from life, by one of his accomplished grand-daughters, and it hung in my house for many years. It is quite simple and plain, but I hope not too much so, to have a place in your library. I present it to you with the greatest pleasure, because I know no one who understands and appreciates his principles and character better. I hope it may prove acceptable. Rely on it, my dear sir, he was one of the noblest and purest patriots that ever lived, and emphatically the apostle of liberty. I beg its acceptance moreover, as a token of my esteem and regard." Harriet Grote noted that "the picture occupied a conspicuous place in the Historian's library ever afterwards." Its present location is unknown.

George Grote left Parliament in 1841 and devoted his attention to scholarship, producing his monumental, twelve-volume *History of Greece* (1846–1856), which was regarded as the standard text on the subject for more than half a century. He wrote on philosophy and served as a trustee of the British Museum. At the University College, London, for which he was one of the founders, he acted as president of the council and he was vice-chancellor of the University of London (*ODNB*, s.v. "Grote, Harriet" and "Grote, George"; Harriet Grote, *The Personal Life of George Grote* [1873], 122–123).

Marie-Jeanne ROLAND (1754–1793) authored key documents for her husband, Jean-Marie Roland, during his term as Louis XVI's minister of the interior, including a letter of protest to the king that spurred the French public toward revolution. Her behind-the-scenes power over her husband's office resulted in a campaign of slander and persecution that ended with Mme. Roland's imprisonment on charges of treason and her execution by guillotine (*Encyclopedia of the Enlightenment* [2004], s.v. "Roland, Marie-Jeanne," by Mary Seidman, Oxford Reference Online).

Elizabeth Leveson-Gower, the COUNTESS DUCHESS OF SUTHERLAND (1765–1839), died on 29 January 1839, two days after Coolidge and Stevenson called at her Hamilton Place home (*Examiner* [London], 3 Feb. 1839; Testament Inventory of Elizabeth Duchess Countess of Sutherland, s.v. "Sutherland, Elizabeth," ScotlandsPeople: Connecting Generations, accessed 4 May 2010, http://www.scotlandspeople.gov.uk/).

James MORRISON (1789–1857), member of Parliament, merchant banker, and patron of the arts, was the wealthiest commoner in nineteenth-century Britain. Orphaned at fourteen, Morrison began his career as a shopman in the wholesale haberdashery firm Todd & Company, where he became a senior partner and met his wife, Mary Anne Todd (ca. 1795–1887), daughter of the owner, John Todd. Mrs. Stevenson counted the couple among her earliest and best acquaintances in London. She wrote that "It seems to me as if Heaven had inspired the hearts of these strangers in a strange land with such very kindly feelings towards us," adding that Mr. Morrison had "strong prejudices in favour of us Americans." Morrison heavily invested in American interests through his merchant bank, Morrison, Cryder & Company. In 1836 he estimated his worth at over £1 million (*ODNB*; Boykin, *Mrs. Stevenson*, 29; Caroline Dakers, "James Morrison (1789–1857), 'Napoleon of Shopkeepers,' Millionaire Haberdasher, Modern Entrepreneur," in *Fashion and Modernity*, ed. Christopher Breward and Caroline Evans [2005], 17-32; Caroline Dakers, "'A Casket to Enclose Pictorial Gems,'" *Apollo* 159 [2004]: 29–35).

Thursday. Jan. 31

The day I have gained by a mistake of dates I have lost almost entirely—dawdled away. But I have had a succession of callers, all gentlemen and this pleads some excuse.

Yesterday I went to the British Museum and devoted myself to the Egyptian Saloon. To-day I have been turning over the leaves of Wilkinson's book upon Egypt. It is full of vignettes, sketches from Egyptian tombs and temples. The lives of civilized people in all ages of the world seem embellished by the same amusements. Here are a party of ladies evidently discussing the merits of their ornaments, pointing to their earrings and gesticulating with the animation due to such a subject. There is a gentleman "taken home royal," by two servants. I was amused by a few words from Wilkinson on the use of the Bastinado among the ancient Egyptians, and the great reverence with which, to this day, the Stick is regarded by their descendants or their successors in the Valley of the Nile. They look upon it as the most efficient means of Government, and the Moslems have a saying or proverb, that "the Stick was sent from heaven a blessing from God."

When I went yesterday to see the Egyptian Saloon I took with me a catalogue, and a volume of Waagen's book, that, as I should not have time for every thing I might look at what was best worth seeing.

1st   The head of the Pharaoh Rhamses the Great, or Sesostris. No.19. Catalogue. Waagen calls this the gem of the collection The block of stone from which it is cut is of two colours, the upper part as far as the chin, "a quartrose mass of a red colour, the lower a blackish sienite." The whole is about nine feet high, and part of the bust and part of one arm remain. The face is in excellent preservation, the features full & somewhat thick & blunt, but the expression mild & pleasing, and the whole not unlike some good-natured, agreeable faces that one meets with now. There is nothing at all of the negro visible in this head. The lips are thick but not more so than those of an Austrian Princess. The nose a little swollen and slightly depressed at the tip, much such a nose as one sees in a fat face of the present day. The forehead is good. This colossal head comes from the Memnonium at Thebes, and was presented by Mr Salt.

2nd   A statue of Pharaoh Phthahmenoph, the son of Rhamses the Great, "admirably executed in red granite," says Waagen, "in which there appears a strong resemblance to his father which indicates that both are portraits." This statue, No. 6. Catalogue, is altogether on a smaller scale than that of Sesostris, but the likeness is visible; the forehead of Phthahmenoph, however, recedes much more than that of Rhamses the Great.

3d   A colossal head in red granite—about nine feet from the top of the headdress, found in ancient Thebes by Belzoni. A far less pleasing face than that of Sesostris, just opposite, but the workmanship very remarkable. One ear which remains Waagen likens in it's execution to a Cameo. The features are more heavy and puffed than those of Sesostris, and the expression by no means so good.

4th   An arm ten feet long belonging to the same statue. Waagen praises this as indicting a knowledge of sinew and muscle not often seen in Egyptian sculpture. No. 18. Catalogue. All these remains of Egyptian art indicate an early and imperfect state of art, and were also made to be seen from a distance. They seem heavy masses, grand in the design and in the development as far as it goes, finished off too externally and polished with care, so that the first idea and the last touches are equally fine in their way, but it appears as if there was an intermediate stage, a something between the general conception & the superficial execution, which has been left out & is missing.

5th   A doubled fist, No 9. found in the ruins of Memphis, five feet long There is a good deal of character in this fist.

6th   A Colossal Ram's Head. No. 7. formerly belonging to a Sphynx. Very grand.

7th   A column of grey granite not mentioned by Waagen. No. 64. very perfect, the shaft in four pieces, the capital entire,—shaft ribbed rather than fluted, the swell advancing thus. The very lowest part of the shaft is contracted as the stalk of a plant might be by a thread or cord tied tightly round it. The whole thing looks like an immense Cactus.

8th   The celebrated Rosetta stone. No. 24. with it's three inscriptions, one in hyerogliphics, another in the ancient Egyptian language & character, and the third in Greek. They record the services of Ptolemy 5th, and are wonderfully distinct & clear, the characters scarcely at all defaced though the stone is broken and part of it gone. It is of sienite & was found at Rosetta.

9th   A colossal Scarabæus about five feet long brought from Constantinople. No 74. It formed part of the Elgin collection and is of admirable execution. The colour, the polish, the attitude, every thing is so true that I almost feared the gigantic beetle might crawl. It's long legs seem ready to move.

10.   Two immense Sarcophagi, one, No 10, of Brescia brought from Alexandria, the other No. 23, black granite from Grand Cairo, called by the Turks there the "Lovers' Fountain." It had been used as a cistern. Both of these are covered inside and out with hyerogliphics

11.   An immense Sarcophagus of grey stone with it's cover. No. 32. discovered at Thebes at the bottom of an excavation 130 feet deep covered inside & out with sculptures and hyerogliphics. This is the Sarcophagus of an Egyptian Queen, and has a female figure engraved on the bottom and another on the inside of the top.

12.   Two Lions of red granite, Nos 1. & 34, presented by Lord Prudhoe. These Waagen pronounces "perfect models of architectonic sculpture," and they certainly produce a fine affect. The same critic observes that though the forms are simplified very much, "every thing is retained which expresses the grandeur of the Lion." They are at the entry of the Saloon, one on each side of the way.

Besides these principal objects I noticed many mutilated groups and single statues, hawk-headed sphynxes, painted figures, bodies without heads, heads without bodies, architectural remains of friezes, painted walls &c—many interesting and curious relics. On my return home, the weather being very cold and the streets slippery, I decided to give up my evening party at Mrs Morrison's, spare my servants, my horses and myself, and stay comfortably at home—which I did. Mr Coolidge shewed me a polite note from Mr Rogers (the poet) giving us the entrée to his picture gallery. To-day it is snowing in good earnest.—

¼ past 4. P.M. I have been out in spite of the weather & called on Mrs Stevenson, & on Mrs Morrison who tells me she had a large "little party" last night notwithstanding the cold. Mr John Van Buren has called since my return and given me an amusing account of his travels in Scotland and of his visit to the Earl of Selkirk—a nobleman of rather uncouth aspect whom I had the pleasure of entertaining at my own house in Bowdoin St, some year or two ago. He arrived in Boston consigned to the care of Mr Frank Shaw, who brought him to a small party, really a small party, I had collected I almost forget on what occasion—I believe for the friends of my sister Septimia. I remember his criticising my pronunciation of the word Loch, and giving it himself with a strong guttural which could only have issued from a Scotch throat.

The EGYPTIAN SALOON (fig. 8) was installed in 1834 in the neoclassical addition to the British Museum designed by architect Robert Smirke. In spite of the new setting, the British Museum continued to present its Egyptian antiquities in a traditional picturesque arrangement dictated in part by an artifact's size, which led to misperceptions regarding its importance. This was in contrast to contemporary Egyptian galleries at Munich's Glyptothek and the Louvre, where objects were arranged chronologically or contextually according to themes (Stephanie Moser, *Wondrous Curiosities: Ancient Egypt at the British Museum* [2006], 148–157).

John Gardner WILKINSON'S BOOK UPON EGYPT, based on his twelve-year survey of ancient sites, was the first work of its type to describe the daily lives of ancient Egyptians. Wilkinson described and illustrated the punishments inflicted by the bastinado in the second of three volumes (*ODNB*; John Gardner Wilkinson, *Manners and Customs of the Ancient Egyptians* [1837], 2:40–44).

The CATALOGUE that Coolidge carried with her was the *Synopsis of the Contents of the British Museum* (1838). WAAGEN described the gallery of "Egyptian Antiquities" in the first volume of his 1838 *Works of Art and Artists in England*.

JOHN VAN BUREN (1810–1866), lawyer and politician, was the son of Pres. Martin Van Buren. He first made his mark on English society in 1831, when he accompanied his father to England to serve as attaché to the American mission. His quick wit and engaging manner made him a favorite at court and earned him the nickname "Prince John" in the American Whig press. The Senate's failure to confirm his father's appointment as minister cut short his first English stay, but he returned in 1838 in time to crowd into the carriage carrying Mr. and Mrs. Stevenson to Princess Victoria's coronation, at which Van Buren expected—but did not receive—a front row seat. That affront aside, Sally Coles Stevenson wrote that "he has enjoyed advantages no other person could as the son of the President of the United States." Van Buren, like the Coolidges, was the beneficiary of the Stevensons' introductions into society. Mrs. Stevenson noted that "Mr. Van Buren and Ellen Coolidge literally live here & come in upon me at all times & all hours." Van Buren's provoking character was a challenge for Mrs. Stevenson, who observed that he "resembles his Father in using his fellow men as a ladder upon which to mount & when he is up, kicks it down, & without any scruples of conscience denies he has had any aid." Despite her frustration with his arrogance, she liked Van Buren very much, remarking to her sisters that "there is such a mixture of good with all his faults that I regard him very kindly, & besides he is so amazing."

After the coronation Van Buren left London for a tour through Ireland and Scotland that ultimately lasted until the end of the year. He boarded the *Liverpool* on 20 October 1838 bound for New York only to return to Cork after his ship was plagued by bad weather and ran low on fuel. A month later Van Buren was still in Ireland "feasting & enjoying the hospitalities of the good people of the Emerald Isle, his health quite returned" (*ANB*; *DAB*; Boykin, *Mrs. Stevenson*, 144, 146, 162, 198, 200, 212–213; *Freeman's Journal and Daily Commercial Advertiser* [Dublin], 3 Sept. 1838; *Examiner* [London], 21 Oct. 1838; *Champion and Weekly Herald* [London], 4 Nov. 1838).

Dunbar James Douglas, sixth EARL OF SELKIRK (1809–1885), Scottish peer from 1830 to 1885, was the only son of Thomas Douglas, fifth Earl of Selkirk (1771–1820), founder of the Red River Colony in what is now Manitoba, Canada. The earl arrived in New York in October 1835 en route to Canada, where the following year his family transferred the colony, also known as Assiniboia, to the Hudson Bay Company (*DCB*; *ODNB*; Ship's Manifest for the *North America*, 30 Oct. 1835, Ancestry.com; *Glasgow Herald*, 13 Apr. 1885).

Francis George SHAW (1809-1882) studied briefly at Harvard before joining the merchant firm owned by his father, Robert Shaw (1776–1853), for whom Joseph Coolidge had also worked early in his career. Frank Shaw was a social reformer who married the abolitionist Sarah Blake Sturgis and settled near the utopian community Brook Farm in West Roxbury, Massachusetts. Their only son, Robert Gould Shaw (1837–1863), served as colonel of the Massachusetts Fifty-Fourth, the Union army's first African American regiment in the Civil War. Frank Shaw's sister Anna Blake Shaw (b. 1817) was friends with Coolidge's sister SEPTIMIA (*ANB*; Russell Duncan, ed., *Blue-Eyed Child of Fortune: The Civil War Letters of Colonel Robert Gould Shaw* [1992], 2–3, 106; "Deaths, Francis George Shaw," *New England Historical and Genealogical Register* 37 [1883]: 116; Coolidge to Martha Jefferson Randolph, 4 Apr. 1832, Coolidge to Virginia J. Randolph Trist, 27 Sept. 1835 [ViU: Ellen Wayles Randolph Coolidge Correspondence]).

Saturday. 2. February.

Yesterday we availed ourselves of the permission we had received to visit the house of Mr Rogers the poet, and inspect his valuable collection of pictures. The house is in St. James Place with it's back windows opening towards the Park. Here every thing indicates that the owner is a man of taste, of fortune and a lover of ease and comfort: you pass through a Hall, from whence a staircase ascends to the second story, and enter the dining room, a large, low room with a bow at the farther end and three windows down to the floor, opening upon a small, pleasant garden, from which there is access to the park. The dining room is the perfection of comfort and, notwithstanding it's low ceiling and it's somewhat faded and worn furniture, has a character of elegance from the beauty of the paintings which decorate the walls, and the many gems of art, ancient and modern, which are tastefully arranged around. At the upper end of this room an antique marble vase sculptured in bas-relief, stands upon a piece of furniture made of mahogany and brass, a singular looking thing somewhat of an obelisk form, but of which the carved work at top was done by the hand of Chauntrey, more than thirty years ago, he being then in the employment of a cabinetmaker as a carver in wood.

There are many Etruscan vases in different parts of the room and still more in the rooms above, with candelabra, fragments of ancient sculpture &c A good fire was burning in the dining room, there were tables, easy chairs, writing apparatus, books, every thing necessary for literary recreation and the pleasant and profitable employment of time; but withal an air of bachelor precision in the arrangements, whether for rest or light labour, which shewed nothing of the carelessness of genius, and something of the formality of one who does every thing, even to the making of poetry, by rule. I am sure that Mr Rogers always mends his pen, or at least takes care to have a good one, squares his paper, and sees that the articles on his table are all in their proper places, before he begins to compose.— On the mantel piece are two beautiful busts, children's heads in marble, which gave rise to a somewhat profane jest from a clergyman, from the Revd Sidney Smith of witty celebrity. At a dinner party in this room someone enquired who these children were. "Do not tell," said the clerical wag, affecting to lower his voice, "but they are by different mothers."—Another time the question was asked whether Rogers wrote with facility. "By no means," answered the same Sidney Smith, "when he is going to make verses, the knocker is tied up, the street strown with straw, and if any one inquires how Mr Rogers is, they are told, "as well as can be expected."

The pictures in the dining room are

1st An exquisite little Claude, scarcely larger than an enamelled brooch of the present fashionable proportions, a clump of trees, water upon which the shadows fall with a coolness & freshness that none but the inhabitant of a southern climate could have expressed in painting, &

a Shepherd seated on the ground with his goats & kids browsing & capering round him.

2nd A small picture of Christ on the Mount of Olives, by Raphael, in his earlier style whilst still in the trammels of his master Pietro Perugino.

3^{d} A Virgin & child & group of saints, small, by L. Caracci.

4th Original sketch by Tintoretto of his martyrdom of St. Mark.

5th The original and well finished sketch by Titian representing the glorification of the Emperor Charles 5th. He is kneeling in the clouds with his crown at his knee. Above are two persons of the Trinity, the Father & the Son surrounded by the heavenly host, and below are Noah, Moses and other Bible and patriarchal characters. The great picture of which this is a sketch, known by the name "La Gloria de Tiziano," was painted by command of Philip 2nd, for the church of the Convent where Charles 5th died, and is now at the Escurial.

6th An Ecce Homo, a Christ crowned with thorns by Guido.—

7th A Madonna del Gatto, similar to the one at the National Gallery and like that marked with the name of Barocci.

8th The good Samaritan by Giacomo Bassano. Why are there dogs in this picture, and is it because there are dogs that Waagen calls it "the Rich Man and Lazarus?" The dogs have their noses to the earth as if, perhaps, picking up crumbs. But the figures, a healthy looking traveller supporting a naked, wounded, fainting man, whilst, in the back ground, a priest or Levite seems to be hastening onward, cannot be mistaken for Dives and Lazarus.—

Above stairs in Mr Rogers' house, are three rooms in a suite. A well furnished drawing room, over the dining room, with a gilt ceiling and the walls hung with plain crimson silk. This makes an excellent ground for pictures in gilt frames. The carpet is of crimson Brussels, (the one in the dining room is a heavy Turkey,) and three large windows open over the garden. A number of fine pictures, antique vases, sculptures &c make of this drawing room a "perfection of a place" where one might linger & loiter & forget the passage of time. An anti-room connects the drawing room with a small library well furnished with books, and having it's due proportion of pictures and vases, besides two framed drawings by Michael Angelo and Raphael, and other objects of greater or less interest. These three rooms, with the landing place of the stairs upon which the ante-room opens, give the size of this small but elegant and luxurious English-gentleman's house, in London. The pictures are, I believe, all good, none poor, and many very excellent. Those which I remember best are as follows,

1ˢᵗ   A most beautiful Titian—Christ appearing to Mary Magdalen—two figures about one third the size of life. The Saviour has in one hand a gardiner's tool, whilst with the other he holds back his drapery from the touch of Mary Magdalen on her knees with her hand extended towards him.

2ⁿᵈ   A Christ leaning and falling under the weight of his cross—a moderate size—by Andrea Sacchi.

3ᵈ   A portrait of Rembrandt by himself. I should like to see it by the side of his mother, also by his own hand—a beautiful thing in the collection at Redleaf.

4ᵗʰ   A free copy by Rubens of a picture by Montegna. Part of a triumphal procession in which there are victims, rams & bulls, dressed for sacrifice, with elephants & other wild beasts, altogether spirited & animated, colouring very rich—One of the things by Rubens which has pleased me best—I am not in general an admirer of his pictures.

There are four pictures by Sir Joshua Reynolds. A girl with a bird which I thought affected & did not like. A Cupid & Psyche well spoken of by Waagen but to me not pleasing. A Puck or Robin Goodfellow, charming, worthy of the Midsummer Night's Dream. The fantastic elf is represented as a fat child with a large head, long ears and a countenance of the most exquisite fun and drollery. His eyes twinkle as you look at them; he sits on a large round mushroom, a good deal in the attitude of an infant Bacchus, his legs stuck out & his arms extended, grasping in one hand a bunch of flowers, the very ones with which he has been doing so much mischief, and so tormenting the Fairy Queen and the Athenian lovers. In the back ground are Titania and Bottom. But the best picture by Sir Joshua Reynolds that I ever saw is in this collection. The Strawberry Girl, a bewitching little creature who, with her hands folded, her basket of strawberries under her arm, a handkerchief tied round her head, and dressed in a child's frock of simple white, looks full in your face with a pair of dark eyes, that have a sort of fascination in them, and attract and fix your own so that you can hardly turn them away.

Two other pictures in this collection attracted my attention. A small Murillo, St. Joseph and the infant Jesus, a dark, mellow, Spanish looking painting of great beauty, and a Holy Family by Correggio, having much something of the character of the "Vierge au Panier" at the National Gallery.

The Mantel piece in the drawing room is of white marble—two bas-reliefs by Flaxman, a Muse and ^the Goddess^ Mnemosyne, decorate the slab, and two small figures of Cupid & Psyche, by the same artist, stand at

the two corners. On the other side of the room is a low book-press or chif-
fonier painted by Stodthard, with subjects from Chaucer's Canterbury
pilgrims, Scenes from Shakespeare or rather representing characters from
Shakespeare, and one scene, I think, from the Arabian Tales.

The drawing by Raphael, in the Library, represents the entombment
of Christ, is done with a pen, and was purchased by Mr Rogers for £120.

Among the vases one very low and flat, standing under a glass, particularly caught my eye. The figures are yellow on a dark ground. Some
of these vases have dark figures on a red or yellow ground. They are numerous, of most graceful forms, and with that indescribable charm of
the antique, which it seems impossible to transfer to any thing modern.
A small, bronze candelabrum is noticed & commended by Waagen, a female figure seated with a crown in her hands, and supporting on her head
a socket which rises tall and straight like the thick jointed stalk of a plant.

From this temple of elegance, comfort and the arts, I went leaving my
companions at the door, to see Mrs Stevenson. I found her with a visiter, a
spirited, animated scotch lady, Lady Elizabeth Hope Vere. She talked sen-
sibly and agreeably about Scotland and the embodied genius of Scotland,
Sir Walter Scott. I was curious to hear something of his first love, his earliest and best affection, but could obtain little information on this subject.
Lady Elizabeth thought that the lady's name was Skene, and spoke of her
as a distinguished and lovely woman, married to a man whom she was
said to regard with indifference if not dislike, Sir William Forbes, a rich
Banker, with whom she had lived a few discontented years and then died,
leaving several children of whom the present Sir John Forbes, is one. —

Mr Coolidge and myself dined with Mr Heard and returned home at
nine o'clock. Mr Sumner came in at past eleven o'clock, after I had retired
for the night, so that Mr C. alone had the benefit of the midnight visit.
To-day I have had an interview with my french master, and afterwards run
over some pages of Lady Morgan's Salvator Rosa. I found some mention
of my favorite Claude. He was the son of a pastry cook and pronounced
by his father too stupid ever to bake a pie. When in the zenith of his fame
as a painter, his prices were so enormous that only crowned heads could
purchase his works, which they were glad to monopolise. His original
name was Claude Gelée to which Lorraine was afterwards affixed according to prevailing custom. Gaspar Poussin was one of his elèves, having
previously studied in the school of Nicholas Poussin from whom he took
the name of Poussin.

At three o'clock I went to Highgate and brought home my boy to spend
to-morrow with his father and myself. Whilst my french maid, Josephine,

a most accomplished person in her line, was dressing my hair, I turned over the third volume of Mrs Jamieson's Canada, where I noticed the following remark. "While among the Indians, I often had occasion to observe that what we call the antique and the ideal is merely free, unstudied nature. Since my return from Canada I have seen some sketches made by Mr Harvey when in Ireland—figures of the Cork and Kerry girls, folded in their large blue cloaks; and I remember, on opening the book, I took them for drawings after the antique—figures brought from Herculaneum or Pompeii or some newly discovered Greek temple.—"

The principal rooms belonging to **MR ROGERS** at 22 St. James's Place overlooked Green **PARK** and featured his remarkable art collection. "In his house," Waagen enthused, "you are everywhere surrounded and excited with the higher productions of art. In truth, one knows not whether more to admire the diversity or the purity of his taste." Anna Jameson marveled at Rogers's ability to collect and harmoniously display works of various styles, periods, and emotions, likening it to the brilliant circle over which Rogers presided socially. Rogers's achievement was all the more impressive for the relatively modest scale of his 1803 four-story townhouse, designed by the architect James Wyatt with interior ornamentation by John Flaxman and Thomas Stothard. After his death Rogers's library and art collection were sold over a nineteen-day period at Christie's. Rogers bequeathed three of his paintings to the National Gallery, of which he was a trustee (*ODNB*; Macleod, *Art and the Victorian Middle Class*, 28, 38, 468; *Survey of London*, vols. 29 and 30 [1960], 511–541; *Catalogue of the Celebrated Collection of Works of Art and Vertû Comprising . . . the Property of the Late Samuel Rogers, Esq., Sold by Messrs. Christie and Manson* [1856]; Jameson, *Private Galleries*, 383–413; Waagen, *Works of Art*, 2:132–146).

Charles Mottram's engraving after John Doyle's painting *Samuel Rogers at His Breakfast Table* (ca. 1823) shows Rogers in his **DINING ROOM** in an imaginary gathering of the artists, literati, and politicians who frequented his breakfasts. The pedestal by Chantrey [**CHAUNTREY**] that Coolidge described appears in the lower left corner of the image (fig. 9) (Jameson, *Private Galleries*, 411; Charles Mottram, *Samuel Rogers at His Breakfast Table* [ca. 1823], Tate Collection, accessed 6 July 2011, http://www.tate.org.uk/collection).

The wry and profane observations of **SYDNEY SMITH** (1771–1845) contrasted with the fiery sermons he delivered from St. Paul's Cathedral, where he was canon. His "bon mots" became part of the London vernacular and endure in his writings and memoirs. Smith was one of the founders of the *Edinburgh Review*, enjoyed the patronage of Henry Richard and Elizabeth Fox (Lord and Lady Holland), and befriended Charles Dickens, who named his seventh child after Smith. With his wife, Catharine Amelia Pybus (1768–1852), Smith had five children. Though he considered America culturally immature, Smith enjoyed the company of Americans such as George Ticknor, Daniel Webster, and Charles Sumner. To Sumner he wrote in 1838, "I have a great admiration of America, and have met with a great number of agreeable, enlightened Americans. There is something in the honesty, simplicity and manliness of your countrymen which pleases me very much."

In January 1810 Jefferson received a copy of Smith's *Letters on the Subject of the Catholics*, written under the pseudonym Peter Plymley, as a gift from Thomas Ritchie, editor of the *Richmond Enquirer*. In thanking Ritchie, Jefferson called Smith's work a "treat," saying that he had "never read a richer compound of logic & ridicule" (*ODNB*; Peter Virgin, *Sydney Smith* [1994], 242–249; Sydney Smith, *Sermons Preached at St. Paul's Cathedral, the Foundling Hospital, and Several Churches in London* [1846]; *PTJRS*, 2:161; Sowerby, 3385; Sydney Smith to Charles Sumner, 16 Aug. 1838, as cited in Alan Bell, *Sydney Smith* [1980], 209).

Waagen's catalog of Rogers's collection only listed Giacomo Bassano's *The Rich Man and Lazarus*, but at the time of Coolidge's visit Rogers also owned Bassano's painting of the **GOOD SAMARITAN** (Jameson, *Private Galleries*, 391–392; Waagen, *Works of Art*, 2:139).

Waagen wrote that the "free and graceful design" of this Italian **CANDELABRUM** belonged "to the period when art was in its perfection" (Waagen, *Works of Art*, 2:144).

Mrs. Stevenson first encountered **LADY ELIZABETH HOPE-VERE** (ca. 1794–1868), daughter of George Hay, Marquess of Tweeddale, and wife of James Joseph Hope-Vere, the previous fall. Stevenson described Hope-Vere as "a very intelligent high bred woman" with "the most insatiable fondness for telling ghost-stories or tales of chivalry & romance, she is a Scotch woman, & lived near the great Magician [*Sir Walter Scott*], so that his mantle may have fallen upon her."

Hope-Vere misidentified Scott's first love as Jane Forbes **SKENE** (1787–1862). Williamina Belsches Stuart (1777–1810) was Scott's first love, and in 1797 she married the weathly Scottish banker Sir William Forbes, baronet (1773–1828), ending Scott's four-year-long courtship. Though disappointed, Scott remained Forbes's friend and confidant. Scott's chief biographer, son-in-law John Lockhart, ranked Forbes as "a gentleman of the highest character . . . who lived to act the part of a most generous friend to his early rival" (*ODNB*; Boykin, *Mrs. Stevenson*, 187; Lockhart, *Life of Sir Walter Scott*, 1:165).

Monday. 4th Feb.

Yesterday was a damp unpleasant day, and to-day which promised well in the beginning, is now over-cast. I have just parted with my son, who has been with me since saturday and returns to his school at Highgate. This morning brought my french master, who found fault with my <u>french composition</u>. It was too ambitiously written—I had forgotten that I was but a novice in writing french and should not aspire to any thing beyond the merest commonplace. I tried too high a flight and my waxen wings gave way. I have finished Mrs Jamieson's book on Canada. It is pleasantly written has some interesting details of the North American Indians, and good descriptions of American Lake scenery. I have likewise read a little french novel called "Edouard" by the author of Ourika. This lady who writes with taste and feeling, is so destitute of accurate knowledge that she makes her hero, in a voyage from L'Orient in France to Baltimore in the United States, pass through the tropical seas. America is still to her that vague, mysterious country of "Les Indes" which she has read of in novels.

Claire Lechat de Kersaint, duchesse de Duras (1778–1828), was the author of OURIKA (1824) and *Édouard* (1825). Both novels originate in stories Duras told at gatherings of her prestigious French salon, and each explores the prejudices of class and race common to the salon world. *Ourika*, loosely based on an actual late-eighteenth-century episode, tells of a Senegalese girl rescued from slavery and raised by an aristocratic Frenchwoman yet ultimately rejected by French society. The novel's immediate popularity led to translations and an adaptation for the theater. *Édouard* follows the son of a laborer as he falls in love with an aristocrat's daughter and abandons hope of their alliance (Peter France, ed., *The New Oxford Companion to Literature in French* [1995], 265; Doris Y. Kadish and Françoise Massardier-Kenney, eds., *Translating Slavery: Gender and Race in French Women's Writing, 1783–1823* [1994], 185–193).

Wednesday. 6. February.

Yesterday was a busy day with me. In the morning Mr C. & myself received a note from Mr Stevenson and two cards of admittance to the House of Lords. The Queen was to go in state to open Parliament and the ceremonies were expected to be brilliant and imposing. They would be very curious & interesting to persons, like ourselves, who had never witnessed any thing of the kind before. There was a great demand for tickets and difficulty in obtaining them. Mrs Stevenson anxious that I should see the shew, had requested Mr Stevenson to write to Lord Willoughby for them. This he had accordingly done and they had been sent only on the morning of the day; rather late for my convenience as I had made no preparation for going and it was necessary to go in full dress. I hesitated between my desire to be present at such a scene, and alarm at the thought of so much hurry and trouble. Curiosity prevailed. Then it was such a privilege to go! I knew that Mrs M. was dying for a ticket which she could not obtain. Miss B. wrote me a note of congratulation on my good fortune. Mr D. & Miss S. desired exceedingly to be present but the thing was impossible.

How could I resist the temptation of seeing what so many persons desired in vain to see. So that roused from the torpor of indolence which so often makes me feel that "le jeu ne vaut pas la chandelle," I exerted myself to be dressed. Bare arms, bare neck, a black satin dress made by Mrs Murray and trailing gloriously upon the ground; my hair arranged by Mrs Stevenson's maid with her lady's plumes (five tall ostrich feathers) and pearls, a feronnière with a diamond frontlet, and a necklace with a diamond clasp; wrapped in an elegant white Indian shawl of my own, my looking-glass assured me that I was presentable even in the House of Lords. Mr Coolidge and myself entered our carriage at a quarter past twelve. Long, however, before we reached our destination we were forced to take our place in a line of carriages, of formidable length before us and which was constantly lengthening in the rear. Carriage after carriage of those in front, deposited it's occupants, and slowly, surely our own drew up to fill each vacant space as it occurred. There was no hurry, no confusion, the street on both sides bordered with police-men who kept all things and persons in exact order. Thousands of spectators were assembled but every thing was conducted peacefully and properly. Presently our carriage stopped before the door of the House of Lords. We entered together, and after traversing some passage and stair-ways, we passed through the Royal Gallery to the door of the "Salle de Spectacle." Here we were compelled to part. Mr Coolidge's ticket was for the Royal Gallery, Morning dress, and carried him no farther. I entered the Hall alone but with no feeling of embarrassment. I was a stranger—no one was watching for or looking at me. There was no one to whom my good or ill appearance was a matter of the smallest moment. There were no eyes sharpened by friendship or malice to note whether my entrée were graceful or awkward. Those who looked at all looked with utter indifference. They were thinking only of themselves, their friends or their enemies. The coat of darkness worn by Jack the Giant Killer, had it covered my satin, cashmere and pearls, could scarce have made my 'incognita' more complete. The man in waiting by whatever name he may be known, performed his mechanical duty. He looked at my ticket which was for the Strangers' Gallery, informed me that all there was full, but that he could find me standing room in a window in the body of the House. Standing room for one who can no more stand than an empty sack!—Who sinks into a seat as if volition were out of the question, and the law of gravity the only moving power! Standing room were words of direful import to ears like mine, but I determined to trust to chance, and took my place accordingly, in the recess of a window, behind a row of ladies seated comfortably on a cushioned form. Chance did not stand my friend, and it was to Courtesy that I was indebted for a place on that very cushioned form, the ladies pressing more closely together and inviting me to be seated among them. Gratefully I accepted the offer and found a commodious resting place, rather farther than I liked from the throne and the door of entrance, but far better than, coming so late, I had any right to expect. I believe I was the last lady under the rank of a peeress, who obtained a seat at all. It was now past one—the Queen not expected until two, and I had time to look round and observe. The room was full or filling fast. There were Peers in their robes of scarlet, gold and ermine; Peeresses in velvet, satin, plumes & diamonds; Judges in flowing wigs; Ambassadors of various nations in various rich dresses with stars, ribbons and orders innumerable; ladies not "milédis" with tickets of admission, dressed some tastefully, others in bad taste; looking, some, like ladies of Nature's making, and others as if they could be made ladies by no process of Fortune.

In about an hour and a half the firing of cannon and the "fanfare" of trumpets announced the arrival of the Queen. Her Majesty having passed through the Royal Gallery, in full sight of the ticket holders, entered the Hall. She wore her full robes of state with the crown on her head, and was preceded, accompanied or followed, by members of the Royal Family, great Officers of state, Ladies in waiting, military men, mace-bearers &c &c. Such a gorgeous display of diamonds, gold, scarlet, purple, stars, crosses, ribands, plumes, velvet & ermine of course I had never witnessed. The Queen having seated herself upon the throne, with Lord Melville on one side, bearing the sword of state, and Lord Shaftesbury on the other with the cap of maintenance, remained for a few moments quiet & calm and apparently as much at her ease as if in her own chamber. In the mean while the "Gentlemen of the House of Commons" having been summoned, made their entry by a side door, into a place partitioned off for them, a sort of pen, at the other end of the Hall and opposite the throne. They came in awkwardly, stumbling & almost tumbling over each other, very much as sheep do when driven for the night into their fold. Some little time elapsed before order could become the order of the day, but silence at length prevailed until broken by the silver tones of the young Queen. She read her "speech from the throne," the string of commonplaces prepared for the occasion, and which, I presume, was all sufficient for the purpose it was meant to serve, heads of chapters for future development in parliamentary debate, a cautious text for long commentaries. The Queen's reading was remarkably correct and exact. Her voice clear, well sustained and never faltering nor failing for an instant. Her articulation distinct, her manner calm, self-possessed and dignified. She emphasized her words and sentences enough to give them their full meaning and their relations to each other, but in no instance so as to bring some subjects into bolder relief and throw others comparatively into the shade. She gave nothing to the speech, by accent, tone or manner, which it did not inherently possess, treating as I have said the matters which it discussed with strict impartiality, and the absence of all preference for one over the other. This no doubt was just as it should be, and the Queen had probably repeated her lesson in private more than once before committing it to the public ear. The ceremony over Her Majesty rose slowly and composedly and retired from the Hall, speaking as she passed, I think to the Duke of Cambridge. Her manner, movements and carriage were all worthy of her position, but her want of height is a misfortune in a Queen. She is altogether too short for Royalty. When she entered the Hall with her large and somewhat clumsy crown, which upon that little head and above that childish face, is singularly unbecoming, [...] ^it seemed out of proportion with her petite figure;^ the white plumes of the ladies in attendance waved high above the symbol of power and royalty, which ^in itself^ produced an effect not unlike that of the bearskin cap worn by a dragoon. Were the Queen six inches taller the moral effect of her presence would be altogether greater. How willingly would I give her Majesty the six inches in which she is deficient; thus raising her to "a just stature," and bringing me down no lower than my pretensions.

The Queen gone, the crowd was long in dispersing, and even when the Hall and Royal Gallery were cleared, the stairs and entries were filled with persons waiting for their carriages to draw up to the door. Name after name was shouted out as each successive carriage stopped the way. Each one in their turn—no confusion, no disorder, and after a reasonable delay I found myself safe on my way home again.

I know not why, but the scene I had so recently witnessed seemed to me to have no more character of reality than had I seen it on the stage. It was a shew, a theatrical pageant, not a sober and serious ceremony by which a great people ushered in their national councils—those deliberations and debates which almost decide the fate of the world. That young girl with a crown on her head, that sword of state and cap of maintenance, those gowns and wigs, all that scarlet and gold, did they belong to the realm of fact & not of fiction?—Perhaps to feel as one should feel on such occasions, it is necessary to have been born and brought up where they are of frequent occurrence and associated with ideas of reality, of power and of dignity. An American coming from a land so matter-of-fact as ours, where so little is given to the imagination or senses, finds it difficult to regard this pageantry except as a mere shew—just as a protestant regards the ceremonies of the Roman Catholic religion. I am by no means sure that we have not made a great mistake in simplifying and vulgarizing the forms of our Government too much. We have destroyed too entirely the "prestige" which is so often the foundation of respect.

Another circumstance prevented my receiving a full impression from the glories of the day. The great glories were wanting. The distinguished men whom I hoped to see were absent. The Duke of Wellington kept away—Lord Brougham staid growling in his own kennel. To be sure My Lord Viscount Melbourne was present—"Gros et gras, le teint frais et la bouche vermeille—Le pauvre homme."—and the Royal Duke of Cambridge with the paunch if not the wit of Falstaff, was making himself agreeable to the ladies.—Another drawback to my complete satisfaction was the somewhat soiled finery of the ladies. In spite of the brilliant general effect, when you came to examine a little closely you became aware that many plumes were soiled, and that the blonde and silk looked somewhat dingy, as if with the smoke & wear & tear of the last season. There were diamonds however and fine ones, and in one instance at least, they glittered on the person of a woman who though a peeress, should not have insulted by her impure presence the ceremonial state of a Maiden Queen. She occupied a conspicuous position in the ranks of the noble ladies, but I was afterwards told, that her life had been an infamous one. She was present in right of a coronet which an Earl had not been ashamed to bind on her dishonoured brow. Aristocracy of England—ancient & time-hallowed institution, take care what you do, for the times are dangerous, and the spirits of cavil and of doubt are walking widely abroad!

Apropos to faded finery the robes of the Peers were in many cases somewhat the worse for wear, the scarlet passé, the gold tarnished, and the ermine no longer spotless. But this I am told is all as it should be. It is somewhat a point of pride with the Lords that their robes should be shabby. It shews that their titles are not of new creation. The robe is a sort of cloak or loose gown thrown over the shoulders, and capable I should think of being gracefully worn, but the Peers manage it awkwardly, dragging it up, or letting it trail on the ground, twitching it now to one side, now to the other, in great apparent disrespect for so honorable a garment.

Wednesday. 6. February.

I went to a small party at Mrs Morrison's where I met Sir Francis & Lady Chauntrey. He is a fat apoplectic looking man, stout & corpulent, but with a fine bald head. She feeble ^in health^ and uninteresting, as is often the case with the wives of distinguished men. Perhaps she might improve upon acquaintance, but she seems now somewhat puffed up in spirit by her husband's honours. He is a self-made man and a man cannot be expected to make himself and his wife too. They have no children and I have heard an amusing story bearing upon this fact. His next heirs are some country relations who are proud to pay him an occasional visit in town where he lives in a good house, in good style, having made a fortune as well as a name and a title for himself. Once on a time then, the country relations came, the parents bringing their children to visit Sir Francis and Lady Chauntrey. One of the little ones, "un enfant terrible," after surveying all the wonders of the drawing room, the carpets, curtains, mirrors, french clock, vases, candelabra &c &c, being particularly struck with some articles more shewy than the rest, exclaimed, with childish greediness and in a loud voice—"Mother are these fine things all to belong to us?" The consternation of the mother at this indiscreet allusion to her expectations, may well be imagined.

Strangers were required to present **CARDS OF ADMITTANCE** in order to attend the opening of Parliament. These were obtained from the office of the Lord Great Chamberlain, Peter Robert Drummond-Burrell, Baron **WILLOUGHBY** de Eresby (1782–1865). As the hereditary officer of state responsible for all arrangements surrounding the 5 February 1839 opening of Parliament, Lord Willoughby issued 300 tickets for the House of Peers and 420 for the Royal Gallery, noting in his Minute Book that "the House was exceedingly full & the attendance of Peers numerous" (Lord Great Chamberlain's Minute Book for the Reign of Queen Victoria, 5 Feb. 1839 [Parliamentary Archives–LGC/3/6]; *London Gazette*, supplement, 4 Feb. 1839).

Mrs. Stevenson wrote her sister, "Mrs Coolidge here to dress to go to Parliament—I have just put all my finery upon her & she looks very well." A portrait of Stevenson by the American artist John Goffe Rand (1801–1873) captured her **FULL DRESS** complete with ostrich feathers and ferronnière. Rand exhibited Stevenson's portrait at the Royal Academy in 1840 and kept the original, now unlocated, for himself. He painted another portrait, presumably a copy, for Stevenson. This copy was apparently destroyed by fire shortly after its publication in Edward Boykin's *Victoria, Albert, and Mrs. Stevenson*, where it was erroneously attributed to George Peter Alexander Healy (1813–1894). Rand's portrait inspired the Boston-born Healy to request that Stevenson sit for him, and her four sittings resulted in the portrait that is illustrated as figure 26 (*Grove Art Online*, "Healy, George Peter Alexander," Oxford Art Online; Virginius Hall, Jr., *Portraits in the Collection of the Virginia Historical Society* [1981], 232; Algernon Graves, *The Royal Academy of Arts* [1906], 6:234; Stevenson to [Emily] Coles Rutherford, 5 Feb. 1839 [NcD:Sarah Coles Stevenson Papers]).

MRS. M was Mary Anne Todd Morrison, MISS B. was Elizabeth Ann Sturgis Bates, MR D. was John Francis Davis, and his niece MISS S. was Miss Sindry.

LE JEU NE VAUT PAS LA CHANDELLE: "the play is not worth the candle," an allusion to the habit of paying a host for the cost of the candles used in a night of card playing.

In a series of popular English folktales dating from the early eighteenth century, JACK THE GIANT KILLER employed a coat of darkness to render himself invisible (*A Dictionary of English Folklore* [2000], s.v. "Jack the Giant-Killer," Oxford Reference Online).

PEERS wore robes ornamented according to their aristocratic rank: baron, viscount, earl, marquess, or duke. Thomas Hosmer Shepherd's (1793–1864) painting of the very scene Coolidge described, *House of Lords. Her Majesty Opening the Session of Parliament*, later engraved by Henry Melville, captured the splendor of the robes, the ladies' ostrich feathers, and the crowded window wells (fig. 28) (*ODNB*; William J. Thoms, *The Book of the Court* [1838], 89–150).

Coolidge misidentified Sir Robert Dundas, second Viscount MELVILLE (1771–1851), as the bearer of the sword of state when in fact it was carried by Lord Melbourne (*ODNB*; *London Gazette*, 8 Feb. 1839).

The queen's SPEECH FROM THE THRONE marked the official opening of the second session of the thirteenth Parliament. Charles Sumner was dazzled by the ceremony and Victoria's performance, noting, "I think I have never heard any thing better read in my life than was her speech." Mrs. Stevenson described the queen's VOICE at her first opening of Parliament in 1837 as being "as sweet as a Virginia nightingale's" (Boykin, *Mrs. Stevenson*, 107; Edward L. Pierce, ed., *Memoir and Letters of Charles Sumner* [1877], 2:60; *Hansard's Parliamentary Debates* [1839], 45:2–6).

Prince Adolphus Frederick, first DUKE OF CAMBRIDGE (1774–1850), was the seventh and reputedly favorite son of George III and Queen Charlotte. He was also the viceroy of Hanover from 1816 to 1837. Courteous and sensitive to the arts and music, Cambridge was popular at court and, unlike his brothers, unburdened by debt or scandals in his private life. The affable Cambridge stood next to Mrs. Stevenson at Queen Victoria's opening of Parliament on 20 November 1837 and immediately engaged her in conversation. Mrs. Stevenson remarked upon their meeting to her sister, writing, "Royal persons dispense with introductions" (*ODNB*; Boykin, *Mrs. Stevenson*, 103).

Queen Victoria's PETITE FIGURE, standing four feet eleven inches, was a source of distress to the monarch and a popular topic of conversation. "Everybody grows but me," she complained to Lord Melbourne, to which he laughed and replied, "I think you are grown." King Leopold reassured her that "she shone more by her virtues than by her tallness." Ellen Coolidge was five feet six inches tall (*ODNB*; Christopher Hibbert, *Queen Victoria: A Personal History* [2000], 61; Brett, *Girlhood of Queen Victoria*, 1:299; *U.S. Passport Applications, 1795–1905*, 5 Oct. 1841, s.v. "Coolidge, Ellen W.," Ancestry.com).

GROS ET GRAS ... LE PAUVRE HOMME is from Molière's *Tartuffe*, act 1, scene 4.

It was at the Morrisons' townhouse that Coolidge first met sculptor Francis Leggatt Chantrey [CHAUNTREY] and his wife Mary Anne Wale Chantrey (1787–1875). Chantrey was known and highly regarded in Boston, where his full-length, marble statue of George Washington [1826] is displayed in the Doric Hall at the Massachusetts State House. Joseph Coolidge remarked on the statue's installation to his brother-in-law in November 1827: "The beautiful statue of Washington, by Chantry is just arrived, and placed on its pedestal" (*ODNB*; Ilene D. Lieberman, "Sir Francis Chantrey's Monument to George Washington: Sculpture and Patronage in Post-Revolutionary America," *Art Bulletin* 71 [1989]: 254–268; Joseph Coolidge to Nicholas P. Trist, 5 Nov. 1827 [DLC: Nicholas Philip Trist Papers]).

Saturday. 9*th* February.

I have seen more of high life in England since last monday, than, considering my want of letters of introduction, I had any right to expect. I have recorded my visit to the House of Lords on tuesday. On Thursday evening I went, by invitation from Lady Minto with Mrs Stevenson to a soirée at the Admiralty. I was glad of an opportunity to see something of the English Aristocracy which one hears and reads so much about. I should have been sorry to leave England without a nearer view of this essential part of the community. At the opening of Parliament I had seen them as at the theatre—Now face to face. There were present on this occasion many titled persons. We had the Countess Sebastiani the french Ambassadress, Baroness B. & her Baron, Danish dignitaries, & Count Pollen the Sardinian Minister, but these were not the people I desired to see. It was to the native nobility, the "genuine Lords, Britannia's issue" to whom I desired to say with Gray's Bard, "All Hail." Of these come first on my list, Lord Minto himself, dark and grave, his Countess fair & comely, the mother of ten children, and still looking young & fresh, with a neck plump and white, a forehead unbroken by wrinkles, and cheeks as full and delicately rounded as those of her girlish daughters. Three of these young ladies were present, one quite a child, all dressed with extreme simplicity and perfect taste, in white muslin frocks with black ribbons, the whole fashionable world being in demi-mourning for the french Princess Mary, Duchess of Wirtemburg.

The Marchioness of Sligo is another of these fine preservations, such as one sees in this climate so favorable to beauty. A woman with grown daughters, (two of Lady Sligo's were at her side,) little touched by years, blooming, fair, still essentially young, and if not beautiful, very pleasing in appearance. I can, since I have seen these matrons, better understand the hitherto inexplicable declaration, that "a man may not marry his grand-mother."—Lady Langdale not so handsome as some others, is vivacious and courteous—Lady Brougham, the wife of the ci-devant Lord Chancellor, has a worn look. She would make, (in the well known H. B. caricature of the Wolf and the Lamb, where Lord Brougham looks so wolfish,) not the Lamb, her lamb-days are long over, but a respectable ewe. She is utterly without the "air noble."—Mr Abercrombie, the Speaker of the House of Commons was present with Mrs Abercrombie. Mr Baron Parke with Lady Parke; Lady Charlotte Lindesay, a daughter of Lord North, spoken of in Lady Charlotte Bury's book of the Court of George 4th, whatever her other merits may be, is certainly neither young nor handsome. I presume her charm lies in her conversational power; she was always surrounded by what seemed an interested & admiring group of gentlemen.

The apperance of the company was certainly superiour to any thing I have yet seen in England. The ladies better-looking and better bred—the gentlemen more gentlemanly; but there is among the English, I presume always, a certain degree of stiffness, even in their intercourse with each other, an air of restraint, an absence of ease and joyousness. This belongs to the race and runs in the blood. I have remarked it in those whom I have seen in America—the same almost wherever I have been in England, and here I found lords & ladies afflicted with the national disease. Their gaiety does not seem to be spontaneous, their mirth does not set easily upon them, and their laughter is too much from the teeth outward.

Mary Brydone, **LADY MINTO** (1786–1853), was married to Gilbert Elliot Murray Kynynmound, Lord Minto (1782–1859), first lord of the Admiralty. Following an appointment as ambassador to Berlin, Lord Minto presided over the Royal Navy from 1835 until 1841. Among their daughters likely to be present at the Admiralty that evening were Elizabeth Amelia Jane (ca. 1823–1892) and Frances Anna Maria (ca. 1820–1898). Their eldest daughter, Mary-Eliza Elliot, had married Ralph Abercromby (1803–1865) the previous September. Abercromby was the son of James Abercromby [**ABERCROMBIE**] (1776–1858) and Mary Anne Leigh Abercromby, Baron and Baronness Dunfermline; the baron was also at that time the Speaker of the House of Commons (*ODNB*, s.v. "Abercromby, James" and "Elliot Murray Kynymound, Gilbert"; *Annual Register or a View of the History and Politics of the Year 1859* 101 [1860]: 459–461; *Gentleman's Magazine*, n.s., 7 [1859]: 306).

The **COUNTESS SEBASTIANI**, wife of the French ambassador Count Horace François Bastien Sébastiani (1771–1851), was Aglaé Angélique Gabrielle de Gramont (d. 1842) (Abraham Kriegel, ed., *Holland House Diaries, 1831–1840* [1977],

427; R. R. Madden, *Literary Life and Correspondence of the Countess of Blessington* [1855], 2:473–474; *Gentleman's Magazine*, n.s., 36 [1851]: 537–538).

BARON Adolf Frederik Blome (1798–1875) was minister plenipotentiary from Denmark from 1832 to 1841. Franciska Juliane Friederike Reventlow (1803–1856) was his wife (Svend Cedergreen Bech, ed., *Dansk Biografisk Leksikon* [1979]).

Thomas **GRAY'S** "The Bard: A Pindaric Ode" includes the line "All-hail, ye genuine kings, Britannia's issue, hail!"

Lady Hester Catharine de Burgh, **MARCHIONESS OF SLIGO** (1800–1878), and Howe Peter Browne, Marquess of Sligo (1788–1845), were the parents of six sons and eight daughters. Their eldest daughters were Louisa Catharine Browne (ca. 1816–1891) and Elizabeth Browne (*Gentleman's Magazine*, n.s., 23 [1845]: 423).

LADY LANGDALE, Jane Elizabeth Harley Bickersteth (1796–1872), was the daughter of the Earl of Oxford. She married Henry Bickersteth (1783–1851), Baron Langdale, who was master of the rolls in 1839 (*ODNB*; Thomas Duffus Hardy, "Memoirs of the Right Honble. Henry Lord Langdale," *Law Review and Quarterly Journal of British and Foreign Jurisprudence* 17 [1853]: 10; *Belfast News-Letter*, 9 Sept. 1872).

Mary Ann Spalding (1785–1865), Baroness **BROUGHAM** and Vaux, was sickly and reclusive; she gradually succumbed to a mental breakdown in the 1840s. Henry Brougham was her second husband (*ODNB*; George Edward Cokayne, *Complete Peerage of England, Scotland, Ireland, Great Britain and the United Kingdom*, ed. Vicary Gibbs [1912], 2:342; *Daily Post* [Birmingham], 14 Jan. 1865).

The painter and printmaker John Doyle (1797–1868) used the cipher **H. B.** for his satirical caricatures of English politicians. The London *Times* described his adaptation of William Mulready's painting **THE WOLF AND THE LAMB** as "an altered parody upon the picture of Mulready, 'The Wolf and the Lamb,' in which Lord Brougham is the wolf, Lord Melbourne the lamb, and her Majesty the young lady screaming for that assistance which the old widow woman (who is a *fac simile* of the Duke of Wellington) is rushing to afford" (*Grove Art Online*, s.v. "Mulready, William," Oxford Art Online; John Doyle, "The Wolf & the Lamb a Parody on Mr Mulready's Highly Popular Picture" [1838], ref. no. mudyx6a, British Cartoon Archive, University of Kent, accessed 6 July 2011, http://www.cartoons.ac.uk; *Times* [London], 8 Mar. 1838).

James **PARKE** (1782–1868) and Cecilia Arabella Frances Barlow (ca. 1794–1879) were Baron and Baroness Wensleydale (*ODNB*; George Edward Cokayne, *Complete Peerage of England, Scotland, Ireland, Great Britain and the United Kingdom* [1898], 8:94–95).

Lady Charlotte North Lindsay [**LINDESAY**] (1770–1849), daughter of Lord North, had been lady-in-waiting to Queen Caroline and testified on her behalf in her 1820 adultery trial. According to the queen, Lady Lindsay was in charge of her "soul and body, which she always do well, and she is very witty, and amuses me"

(*ODNB*, s.v. "North, Frederick"; Roger Fulford, *The Trial of Queen Caroline* [1968], 139; Lady Charlotte Campbell Bury, ed., *Diary Illustrative of the Times of George the Fourth* [1839], 4:88).

Sunday 10. February.

A fine spring-like day. I have walked as far as St. James' Park and back again, & feel all the better for it. On friday the 8th I walked to the British Museum, ordering the carriage to follow. My particular object was the Etruscan room, to reach which I passed through the Egyptian Saloon, where I gave another look to my friends the Pharaohs, and examined more particularly the frescos illustrative of the domestic habits of the Egyptians. From the saloon we entered a wide passage way and ascended a staircase of five flights, ninety steps in all, the widest and easiest of staircases. Here we found a suite of rooms lighted from above, the last of which, before coming to the medal room, is the Etruscan room. In presses with glass doors, going all round the room, are contained innumerable vases of every form and size. They have generally dark grounds, the figures upon them being reddish yellow; or the order of colours is reversed, and there are dark figures on a lighter ground. Some are tall, others quite flat, they are with or without handles, but various as the forms may be, the universal character is grace and beauty. What an extraordinary people were the ancients! Their whole souls seem to have been filled with images of beauty. From the statues of their Gods down to the humblest of their household utensils, they did nothing but produce and re-produce forms of beauty. I delight to visit this Museum of Antiquities. My imagination seems to dilate, and I feel as if breathing a purer atmosphere, and the dark, cold room grows warm and bright with the sunlight which still lingers around these relics of a glorious past. As I returned to the carriage, passing, on my way, through the rooms below, I lingered at every step, attracted now by a mutilated group, now by a single figure, a bust, a torso, some new object which arrested my attention in spite of myself. When in the last room I seated myself to wait till the carriage could be called, my eye became fixed on the head of a young Hercules crowned with poplar leaves, which for it's attire, it's air, it's indescribable grace, would have been the master-piece of a modern artist, though here perhaps overlooked in a crowd of master-pieces. Another bust, that of a woman, nymph or goddess, in a very perfect state of preservation, and which appeared to me of exquisite loveliness, I could not even find on the printed catalogue.

Saturday. 9th February. M[r] C. & myself went to a party at M[r] Grote's, where we found, amongst other persons, Mrs Austen the translator of Prince Puckler Muskau's letters, Mrs Jamieson, Miss Martineau, Mr Hume, Mr Charles Buller, Mr Charles Austen & Mr Joseph Park—all more or less distinguished in the literary or political world. Mrs Austen has a fine intellectual face, though in person she is I fear rather stout for symmetry. Mrs Jamieson did not strike me as prepossessing either in person or manner. She was badly dressed and looked what in common parlance might be called "out of sorts." Miss Martineau sat on her sofa with an ear trumpet in one hand and a man in the other. I do not know who the victim was, but listening to her tirades he probably wished himself as deaf as she is. Such a specimen as this "deaf woman of Norwich" is enough to bring female authorship into disrepute. If women in turning bookmakers and politicians, must lose all that is attractive in appearance and feminine in character they had better embroider muslin and copy music.

Mrs Grote I liked better than on my first visit. She seemed less masculine, more gentle and kind. She treated me with genuine hospitality, remembered that I was a stranger, knowing no one. She took pains to introduce agreeable persons to me, such as Mr Buller and Mr Parke, the first of whom being newly returned from the United States, could talk to me of home, and the second, Mr Parke, married to an American wife may be supposed to have some sympathy with Americans. I passed the evening pleasantly, in conversation with sensible men, but it seems to me that in England just now, if not always, politics is as much the order of the day, in the drawing room and the boudoir as it can be in Parliament. Every one talks politics. It mingles in the conversation of women who are not enthusiasts like Mrs Grote, nor political economists like Miss Martineau. It falls from rosy as well as from bearded lips, and was poured into my feminine ears by such men as Mr Parke & Mr Buller.—Mr Buller praised America and Americans, but a slight touch of "badinage" in his manner more than in his words made me somewhat distrustful. Mr Parke was more downright in his tone and more qualified in his commendations. Of course I put more faith in what he said. Another gentleman with whom I conversed was Mr Evans. He told me he had been defending Mr Calhoun against Miss Martineau. I did not hesitate to say that I thought the lady's animosity against slave-holders had become a monomania, and that her judgment was not to be relied on in any thing that related to them. Mr Evans seemed entirely to agree with me.

———————————————————————————————————

The author Sarah Taylor Austin [AUSTEN] (1793–1867) was celebrated for her translations, which included the 1832 *Tour in England, Ireland and France* by

German nobleman Hermann von Pückler-Muskau. Austin's correspondence with Pückler-Muskau revealed the depth of her despair in her marriage to the lawyer and professor John Austin (1790–1859), who battled depression throughout his life. The Austins had recently returned to London from Malta, where John directed a commission for reforming the legal system and Sarah had opened new schools and nursed the sick during a cholera epidemic. As her husband's career faltered, Sarah Austin supported their family with her writing and translating. The couple lived in Dresden and Paris, where Sarah befriended Guizot, head of Louis Philippe's government, and translated his writings, including *Democracy in France* (1849). Sydney Smith, Anna Jameson, and Jane Carlyle were among Sarah's friends and admirers, as was Thomas Carlyle, who praised her as "literally the best of all womankind" (*ODNB*; Thomas Carlyle to Sarah Austin, 13 June 1833, in *Carlyle Letters*, 6:400).

Anna Jameson [**JAMIESON**] returned to England from Canada in 1838 following a legal separation from her husband, Robert Jameson. Her book *Winter Studies and Summer Rambles in Canada* (1838) had rendered her a minor celebrity. "At this moment I have fame and praise," she wrote, "for my name is in every newspaper" (Gerardine Macpherson, *Memoirs of the Life of Anna Jameson* [1878], 151–152).

The Scottish radical Joseph **HUME** (1777–1855) as a member of Parliament supported the 1832 Reform Act and advocated for religious tolerance. After his death in 1855 the *Gentleman's Magazine* pronounced him "one of the most powerful, and at the same time one of the most practical, of reformers in a reforming age" (*ODNB*; *Gentleman's Magazine*, n.s., 43 [1855]: 416–419).

CHARLES BULLER (1806–1848), chief secretary to Lord Durham, had just returned from a tour of Canada, a mission that resulted in Lord Durham's 1839 "Report on the Affairs of British North America," which recommended the unification of Upper and Lower Canada (*ODNB*).

Joseph Parkes [**PARK**] (1796–1865), was a legal reformer and utilitarian. Parkes came to London from Birmingham in 1833 to serve as secretary to the commission on municipal corporations. The following year he was among the founders of the Westminster Reform Club and worked with Brougham toward the 1835 passage of the Municipal Corporations Act. He was a follower of George Grote's "philosophical radicals" and admired the American political system. Parkes brought with him to London his American wife, Elizabeth Rayner Priestley, who was the granddaughter of theologian Joseph Priestley, Jefferson's friend and advisor, and their two young children. Parkes's daughter Elizabeth Rayner Parkes (1829–1925) became an advocate for women and was the mother of poet and author Hilaire Pierre René Belloc (1870–1953) (*ODNB*, s.v. "Belloc, Hilaire Pierre René," "Parkes, Elizabeth Rayner," "Parkes, Joseph," "Priestley, Joseph").

DEAF WOMAN OF NORWICH is a reference to Lord Brougham's defense of Martineau's attempt to publish *Illustrations of Political Economy*, which was turned down by the Society for the Diffusion of Useful Knowledge. Brougham wrote to an acquaintance that a "deaf woman from Norwich was doing more good than any man in the country" (Martineau, *Autobiography*, 148).

George de Lacy EVANS (1787–1870), member of Parliament for Rye and West-minster (*ODNB*).

South Carolina senator and former vice president JOHN C. CALHOUN (1782–1850) was outspoken in his support of slaveholders' and states' rights. Calhoun wrote that abolition "strikes directly and fatally, not only at our prosperity, but our existence as a people." His theory of nullification laid the constitutional ground-work for secession (*ANB*; *DAB*; *Niles' Weekly Register* 50 [1836]: 432).

Tuesday. 12 February.

Engagements begin to multiply. Saturday I was at Mrs Grote's, Sunday at Mrs Stevenson's to tea, Monday I dined with her—but I must take things in order——

Wednesday 13. February.

I had written so far yesterday when I was interrupted and laid down my pen. I now resume. Sunday evening I took tea with M^rsStevenson, and she proposed to me to accompany Mrs Jamieson and herself, the next day, to Hampstead, to call upon Miss Joanna Baillie. I asked nothing better and it was decided that we were to go in my carriage. I was to go first for Mrs Stevenson and we were then to take up Mrs Jamieson at No. 7. Mortimer St. Accordingly on Monday morning I proceeded to Portland Place where I found Mrs Stevenson too unwell to leave her house. Much disappointed I went, by her request, to make our excuses to Mrs Jamieson. [...] She came down all prepared for the little expedition. She had written to Miss Baillie to inform her of the proposed visit, and was of opinion that we had better go even without Mrs Stevenson. To this I readily agreed and we departed together. We were an hour on the road, owing to their coachman taking a round-about way, and if I have said or thought any thing against Mrs Jamieson I here retract it. I found her unpretending in manner, agreeable in conversation and as little as possible blue. There was good sense and good feeling in all she said. We spoke of the United States where she has been, and where she has friends. She declared her determination to write no book about the Americans. She had been kindly received, hospita-bly entertained, had warm personal friends among them—people whom she loved and valued—but still she had seen things of which she could not approve. Were she to write she must tell the whole truth. There was much to praise and to admire in the United States, but there were some things to blame. The task of critic and censor was one which she had no wish to undertake. With regard to her remaining in America, a suggestion which had been made to her, she could not say that she did not find England a better residence for her than the United States would be. Even in the matter of personal comfort, there were many little things, conveniences of various sorts to which she had been always accustomed at home, which had become almost necessaries, which in the United States she was compelled to do without. She found living at Hotels expensive and disagreeable, and American boarding houses most unpleasant residences. There were no furnished rooms to be had, as in England, where it was possible to live at once economically and privately. Every thing was too public and every thing too dear. There were still other reasons for her preference of her own country over ours, putting home and its affections & it's associations out of the question. She had a love of art, a taste for the works of art, for which in America there were no means of gratification. She had many other tastes formed in an old country which could not be satisfied in a new one. I was obliged to acknowledge that her reasons were cogent, and although I had begun by telling her I thought she had better come and live with us on our side of the water, I ended by feeling that she is better where she is. When afterwards I spoke of the delight with which I visited picture galleries and passed hours in the Gallery of Antiquities at the British Museum, her eye brightened, she put her hand on my arm and said, "Now you understand why I must remain in Europe. The pleasures you describe I cannot dispense with, and these I cannot find in the United States."   Poor woman, I hear that her marriage has proved a very unhappy one, that her husband is a man with whom it is utterly impossible for any decent woman to live, and she, perhaps fortunately for herself, has no children.

On our arrival at Hampstead we found Mrs Joanna & her sister Mrs Agnes waiting to receive us. Miss Baillie is a small, thin & very aged lady, I know not how far past eighty, with her gray hair under a neat cap, her small hands encased in black gloves, and her little person in a black silk dress. Her whole appearance some what starched and prim perhaps, but simple and unaffected. Her manner seemed to me a little cold, not as if she knew or shrunk from me as an individual, but merely as looking on me as one of a tribe of sight-seers & lion-hunters to whom she was reconciled by habit but whom she could not be expected to view with any particular favor. I spoke of M^r & Mrs Norton whose acquaintance she acknowledged but not warmly—of Dr Channing who had just sent her his last work, on Self-Culture, whom she knew only as an author. Her reception of Mrs Jamieson was affectionate & flattering. She spoke to her as to a personal friend as well as to a successful writer. It was most pleasant to witness this interview between two literary celebrities (not of equal note) for there seemed, on both sides, a good deal of genuine feeling—on Mrs Jamieson's admiration & veneration mingled with love, and on Miss Baillie's affectionate approbation. Mrs Jamieson had brought a portfolio of her own drawings, sketches in lead pencil made in Canada, on purpose to shew them to Miss Baillie, and the conversation between these ladies was altogether indicative of mutual regard. In the mean time Miss Agnes talked with me. She is a dear, old lady, quite easy & friendly in her manners from the consciousness of not being a Lion. I had not come to look at her, nor was she set up to be looked at, she could therefore afford to be cordial and kind. She spoke of M^r & Mrs Norton, asked questions about Dr Channing, talked of England & of the United States and entertained me very agreeably. Presently Miss Joanna turned to me and somewhat stiffly though not ungently, entered into conversation with me. Knowing her great friendship for Sir Walter Scott I asked her some questions about his first love, Miss Skene, and remarked that I could find no one who seemed to know anything about her. Miss Baillie believed there was not much to be known. She thought that perhaps Mr Lockhart had thrown an air of romance over this part of Sir Walter's life somewhat more than the occasion required—that Sir Walter himself, in his old age may have remembered the feelings of his youth as more vivid than they really had been, and that he was more in love with the image conjured up by his imagination than he had ever been with the original. Miss Baillie declared herself not at all sentimental, nor apt to attach great importance to such stories of romance in real life, and said she believed Sir Walter to have been more attached to his own wife than he ever had been to any one else. This surprised me not a little as I had supposed Lady Scott to be any thing rather than loveable.

Miss Baillie is a single woman and a Scotchwoman, and may have to a certain extent the characteristics of her class and country. But she is a remarkable person, and seems to have in addition to her peculiar superiority, all the good sense & acuteness of North Britain. She speaks with a decided accent though not a disagreeable one. I have never seen a poetess who appeared to me to have so little of the poetic temperament. Warmhearted I have no doubt she is, and clear-headed, and troubled, in actual life at least, with no thick-coming fancies as other women of genius sometimes are. She inspires respect at first sight from the decorum and dignity of her manner, and there is something admirable in her simplicity and absence of pretension, when one remembers her great reputation, and the place she occupies in the literary world.

Mrs Joanna Baillie, or Miss Baillie as she seems to be indifferently called, lives in a small house at Hampstead with her sister Mrs Agnes. We found the venerable pair seated in a lower room looking as old as the Fates and nearly as busily employed. The furniture of the room consisted of a table covered with books, a few chairs and other necessary articles—nothing could be plainer or more simple than the whole establishment. We remained about an hour and came away, each satisfied, though in a different way, with the result of the visit. Our drive home was rendered very pleasant to me by Mrs Jamieson's conversation. We spoke among other persons of Lady Byron. I told her my impression that she was a narrow-minded bigot who had driven her half-mad husband wholly mad by her pious persecution, and disgusted him with religion by forcing it upon him in it's most unbearable forms, or rather disguises of cant and intolerance. Mrs Jamieson knows Lady Byron well and exclaimed against such a misapprehension of her character. She describes her as mild, benevolent and charitable—pious without a touch of bigotry; indeed very liberal in her religious views, agreeing with Joanna Baillie and with Dr Channing!

Mrs Jamieson has never, in all her intercourse with Lady Byron, heard her utter a syllable of complaint against her husband, or a word in exculpation of her own conduct—But she looks, moves and acts like a person whose existence has been blighted, over whom some withering influence has passed and left her [. . .] heart-stricken and hopeless. She has been exposed to bitter censure, to scoffing and to reproach. She has been accused of the hardest unkindness towards her husband, of the most unforgiving and most unloving spirit in all her dealings with him. She has borne all in silence, never coming forward to reply or to recriminate, except in one instance, and that in defence of her mother. Mrs Jamieson's idea is that Lord Byron rendered himself intolerable to her by no single act of atrocity, but by a series of injuries and insults, and by inflicting upon her an amount of mental torture which it became at last impossible to endure and live.

I put Mrs Jamieson down somewhere near Regent's Park where she wished to make a call, and came home much pleased with the way in which my morning had been spent. The day was closed by a dinner at Mrs Stevenson's. Our company consisted principally of the Mansfield family. Mr Mansfield, Mrs Mansfield (a Baltimore lady long resident in

England, a daughter of Gen. Smith,) their son and two daughters. Pleasant people all.

Poet and playwright JOANNA BAILLIE (1762–1851) was a literary lion by the time of Coolidge's visit. Baillie began her career as a writer with *Plays on the Passions* (1798–1812), a series based on the passions of the mind—love, hatred, ambition, fear–with each being the subject of a tragedy and a comedy. First published anonymously, the plays generated much interest and controversy. A second volume in 1802 appeared under Baillie's name, as did the third and final installment in 1812. Baillie went on to write a tragedy, a religious pamphlet, and three volumes of *Miscellaneous Plays* (1836), the publication of which critics compared to discovering a work by Shakespeare or an unknown novel by Sir Walter Scott. Modest and pragmatic, Baillie relished the opportunity to support fellow writers, especially women such as Anna Jameson, to whom she had been introduced by Lady Byron. Baillie praised Jameson's most recent work in a letter to George Ticknor written the month after Coolidge's visit: "What a clever pleasant book Mr[s] Jameson has made of her winter studies & summer Rambles in Canada; particularly the last part of it. As I am not a german scholar nor very conversant in works of art, I cannot well appreciate the winter studies as they deserve. She is a very agreeable, amusing woman in herself, and has deservedly become a popular writer in this country, where popular books & popular writers abound."

Joanna never married, and her sister, AGNES Baillie (1760-1861), was her constant companion. For fifty years the women received luminaries from the art and literary worlds at Bolton House, the early-eighteenth-century brick terrace house they shared in Hampstead, four miles north of London. In a letter to Mary Berry, Baillie wrote that "I naturally take more interest in all who come from America, because I think they take interest in me." Still Coolidge sensed Joanna Baillie's wariness of visitors, which Baillie described to Walter Scott in March 1826: "Travellers are the most selfish & the most impudent of human beings; and that you should have been their prey to such a degree provokes me, so that I must per force give some vent to my humour. It is a curious coincidence that we should learn a few weeks since that the ex-president of Congress, the celebrated Jefferson has applied to that Council for leave to dispose of all that remains of his once great property by lottery, and one of the principle reasons given for this is the great concourse of Travellers who went to visit him &c &c" (*ODNB*; Nikolaus Pevsner and Bridget Cherry, *The Buildings of England: London 4: North* [1999], 222; Clara Thomas, *Love and Work Enough: The Life of Anna Jameson* [1967], 91; *Old and New London*, 5:462–472; Joanna Baillie to Walter Scott, 27 Mar. 1826, Baillie to Mary Berry, 8 July 1833, Baillie to George Ticknor, 29 Mar. 1839, in *The Collected Letters of Joanna Baillie*, ed. Judith Bailey Slagle [1999], 1:171–174, 434–435, 2:1077).

Sally Coles STEVENSON visited Joanna Baillie several times, and the author found her "very conversable & agreeable" (Joanna Baillie to Catharine Norton, 27 Apr. 1841, in *Collected Letters of Joanna Baillie*, 2:957).

The biblical scholar Andrews NORTON (1786–1853) was a dominant figure at the new Harvard Divinity School, and his *Statement of Reasons for Not Believing the Doctrines of Trinitarians* (1819) became a Unitarian classic. He was best known as the author of *The Evidences of the Genuineness of the Gospels* (1837–1844), one of the earliest critical studies of the Bible published in America. He was married to Catharine Eliot, daughter of prominent Boston merchant Samuel Eliot, and lived in Cambridge, Massachusetts. In his correspondence with Joanna Baillie, which began in 1827 and lasted nearly twenty-five years, Norton posed literary and religious topics, expressed a desire to help her publish her works in the United States, and introduced her to a new circle of American intellectuals, including his brother-in-law George Ticknor. When Baillie's works were published in Philadelphia in 1832, Norton sent a copy to the author, which she saw as proof of her status in the United States: "I received not long since a present from Dr Andrews Norton of Boston of all my works printed in one thick volume like a dictionary with the pages divided into columns. This surely looks as if I were popular in that country, and I am right proud of my book, tho' it is as ugly a thing to look at on the outside as ever lay upon a table."

Norton frequently sent Baillie works by American authors, including his own 1834 review of Thomas Hamilton's *Men and Manners in America* (1833), in which he suggested that Hamilton ought to be pilloried for repeating what he considered to be the unsubstantiated allegation that "a daughter of Mr. Jefferson by a slave was publicly sold as a slave at New Orleans." Norton wrote that he had always been "politically connected with the party in opposition to Mr. Jefferson," and that there were many stories to his disadvantage, "some true, it is likely, and some false; but this story ... is, intrinsically, all but absolutely incredible." In thanking Norton for sending the review Baillie wrote, "I am particularly glad that you have in so strong a manner contradicted that vile story of Mr Jefferson, and God forbid that Hamilton should be able to prove the truth of it; yet I make no doubt he received it from what he conceived to be perfectly good authority, and deserves the shame of public refutation & reproof rather than the punishment you have pointed out for him" (*ANB*; *DAB*; Judith Bailey Slagle, *Joanna Baillie: A Literary Life* [2002], 237–239; Andrews Norton, "Men and Manners in America. By the Author of 'Cyril Thornton,'" *Select Journal of Foreign Periodical Literature* 3 [1834]: 99; Joanna Baillie to Mary Berry, 8 July 1833, Baillie to Andrews Norton, 4 Apr. 1834, in *Collected Letters of Joanna Baillie*, 1:173–174, 2:929–930).

William Ellery Channing's address on SELF-CULTURE, published in Boston in 1838, called for the full development of the potential of every human being. Baillie was an outspoken admirer of Channing, and their correspondence kept him informed of the literary news in Britain including the success of his work there (Channing, *Self-Culture: An Address Introductory to the Franklin Lectures, Delivered at Boston, September 1838* [1838]; Slagle, ed., *Collected Letters of Joanna Baillie*, 1:35–36).

Anna Jameson and her DRAWINGS impressed the ethnographer Henry Schoolcraft, superintendent of Indian affairs for Michigan, whose family hosted Jameson.

He recalled that "she is, herself, an eminent landscape painter, or rather sketcher in crayon, and had her portfolio ever in hand. She did not hesitate freely to walk out to prominent points, of which the island has many, to complete her sketches. . . . [S]he also stepped out on the piazza and saw the wild Indians dancing; she evidently looked on with the eye of a Claude Lorraine or Michael Angelo." A collection of sixty-six drawings by Jameson, illustrating her tour in Canada and the United States, are in Special Collections at the Toronto Reference Library (*DAB*; Capturing Canada on Paper and Canvas, Toronto Public Library, accessed 6 July 2011, http://ve.torontopubliclibrary.ca; Thomas, *Love and Work Enough*, 224; Henry R. Schoolcraft, *Personal Memoirs of a Residence of Thirty Years with the Indian Tribes on the American Frontiers* [1851], 561–562).

Anne Isabella Noel, LADY BYRON (1792–1860), married Lord Byron in 1815 after rejecting his first proposal, only to discover that he was in love with his half-sister Augusta Leigh. Shortly after their only child was born in 1816, Lady Byron returned to her parents' home, never to reconcile with Lord Byron, and steadfastly maintained her silence regarding their relationship despite vigorous public debate on the subject. Harriet Martineau eulogized Lady Byron, who established the Ealing Grove School for the underprivileged, observing that "While everybody assumes to know Lady Byron's history, none but her intimate friends seem to have any notion of her character" (*ODNB*; Martineau, *Biographical Sketches*, 282).

John Edward MANSFIELD (1777–1841) was married to Mary Buchanan Smith Mansfield (1788–1868), the daughter of SAMUEL SMITH (1752–1839), U.S. senator from Maryland during Jefferson's administration and general of the Maryland militia in the War of 1812. The Mansfields maintained residences at 51 Grosvenor Street, London, and Diggeswell House, Hertfordshire, where the Stevensons spent a fortnight experiencing "Christmas gambles in the country." The couple had seven sons and three daughters (*ANB*; *DAB*; *ODNB*, s.v. "Mansfield, William Rose"; *Survey of London* [1980], 40:44–57; Boykin, *Mrs. Stevenson*, 113–118; *Gentleman's Magazine*, n.s., 16 [1841]: 217; *Pall Mall Gazette* [London], 17 Nov. 1868).

Thursday 14. February.

I am getting tired of my diary. I began it partly because, with a <u>leaky</u> memory like mine, I could not hope to retain ideas or impressions unless I made some record of them, and partly because I thought that my sisters would desire to know all my <u>experiences</u>, however insignificant they may be.

On Tuesday the 12th, Shrove Tuesday when all good people eat pancakes, was married, at St. George's Church, Hanover Square, his Excellency Mr Van de Weyer, Belgian Ambassador, to Miss Bates, daughter of Mr Bates, of the house of Baring, Brothers & Co. Mr Coolidge and myself had been invited but we had "politely declined"—On monday we dined with Mrs Stevenson, and the "marriage in high life" which was to take place next day was a principal subject of discussion. The Mansfields were amazed that I should lose such an opportunity of witnessing such a ceremony, and seeing such a company as would be there assembled. Mrs Stevenson told me she had a message from Mrs Bates to Mr Coolidge & myself to say that we must certainly retract our refusal, but what weighed a great deal more with us was, that Mr Bates himself, whom we hold in great regard, had expressed a decided wish for our company. Then the invitation was a compliment which after all it would be somewhat ungracious to decline. Accordingly when on monday night, after returning from Mrs Stevenson's I was undressing for bed, I told my french maid, Josephine, that if I only had a proper bonnet & collar I would go to the wedding. Great is the zeal of a french woman where dress and company are concerned. Josephine rose by times next morning went to a country-woman of her own, secured her services, and before twelve o'clock, a beautiful white hat, made from the foundation & trimmed for the occasion, rich with Ostrich plumes, was ready for my wearing, and on my toilette table lay a french collar bordered with Mechlin lace. In five minutes more I was equipped and in the carriage. We drove to the Church, were rather late for the ceremony which was nearly over, but were present at the signing of the marriage contract or certificate of marriage, and were gratified by a sight, in the Vestry room, of Mr Van de Weyer's "distinguished friends."—The Bride has youth and money, is good-looking without being beautiful, and has quiet, composed manners. The Bridegroom brings rank (diplomatic rank,) if not birth, court-favour, and I believe a good deal of literary attainment. He was, I am told, the son of a bookseller. I understand he stands well in his profession as a diplomatist and politician. He is of insignificant appearance and has a touch of the "parvenu" in his manners. He is thirty six, she eighteen, but old of her years, and very ambitious of distinction in society; an advantage which, so far, she has not enjoyed, her father being a merchant, and her mother intensely vulgar. As may be inferred the "distinguished friends" were all Mr Van der Weyers, as he already enjoys, in virtue of his office, the social position to which he raises his now-made Ambassadress. She looked very well in her white satin and mechlin, and behaved with the most perfect self-possession, notwithstanding the presence of the great people.

There were present the old Count Sebastiani, still redolent of the days of Napoleon; his insolent Countess who entered the Church, as some one said, looking as if she meant to walk over bride and bridegroom, and whom I afterwards saw at the dejeuné in Portland Place, tossing her head and sniffing the air as if terrified at breathing the same atmosphere with plebeians. She was dressed in a flowered lilac silk, and though equally destitute of youth and beauty, made a better appearance than she had done at Lord Minto's, where her black gown and heavy black plumes made me turn away from her as if she had been a hearse. She had an ill-omened look which at a party is particularly unpleasant.

Count Pollen, the lively, chattering envoy from Sardinia was likewise of the wedding party, with an old grey-headed Baron from Belgium. Lord Holland was here supported on two crutches, accompanied by his son Col. Fox, born before the marriage of his father & mother, and himself married to an illegitimate daughter of the late King. Bar sinister on both sides. Lord Lansdowne and the courtly Lord Palmerstone likewise paid Mr Van der Weyer the compliment of signing his certificate. The poet Rogers with his sister and M^r & Mrs Senior represented the worlds of poetry & political economy. The Marchioness of Wellesley, once the beautiful Mrs Patterson of Baltimore, grown old & red-faced—Mr Spring Rice, the worst dressed man in the room—Mr Sumner, to whom the equivocal compliment is often paid of being the least of an American of all Americans, helped to fill the little vestry room which was somewhat crowded but not uncomfortably. The ceremonies being over the party adjourned to Mr Bates' house in Portland Place, to a dejeuné furnished by Gunter, and not dear at a guinea a head, which as Mrs Bates afterwards informed me, was her bargain with him. She is a managing woman Mrs Bates and likes to do her own work. The number of gay equipages, the crowd collected in the street both before the Church and in front of the house, the presence of police officers, liveried servants and other attendants usual on such occasions, gave a character of bustle, animation & importance to the whole scene, no doubt very satisfactory to it's chief actors. All persons within the drawing rooms appeared to be thinking some of themselves, others of the shew as a shew—the Lords & Ladies were perhaps wondering at their own condescension—the untitled guests discussing the breakfast and the bride—the newly wedded pair anticipating their bridal tour and hurrying their preparations for departure—Mrs Bates fluttered with pleasure and excitement and exulting in her noble guests—Mr Bates alone seemed to be thinking of his daughter, nothing but his daughter, all other feelings merged in one, and his manner had the simplicity & self-possession which resulted partly from character, & partly from the presence of one engrossing idea. No persons behave so well in trying situations, as those who lose all thought of self.

These "dejeunés à la fourchette" are incongruous things; the permitted anomalies in eating & drinking & dressing are extraordinary; the tables are covered with breakfast, luncheon, dinner & supper all at once. I took a cup of tea and a glass of Champagne, a sandwich & some jelly. One of my neighbours feasted on lobster salad, another took ice-cream, a third cold chicken and Madeira. The dress, the toilette is neither morning, dinner, nor evening. There were no frock coats among the gentlemen, and the ladies were in velvet, light silks &c with bonnets, shawls or mantles. The company broke up about two o'clock. M^r & Madame Van der Weyer went off in a carriage & four, with man & maid in the rumble, and the guests dispersed in various directions. Mrs Stevenson & myself took a drive in Hyde Park and it was four o'clock before I got home.

In the course of the morning at Mr Bates' Mr Coolidge & myself had received an invitation from the poet Rogers to breakfast at his house on saturday. I had been introduced to Lord Palmerston who spoke to me courteously of my grandfather. I was throughout very well amused & entertained, and I felt well pleased that I had made the effort to go. I am beginning now to see something of persons as well as things.

Wednesday. 13th was Ash Wednesday. Shrove tuesday good christians were expected to feast on pancakes. Ash Wednesday they are required to fast on saltfish. We had it for dinner according to English custom, but we had soup, and tongue, and chicken, and pudding, besides.

Mrs Stevenson & myself did not neglect to call [. . .] Wednesday morning on Mrs Bates. We found the bereaved mother, between two & three o'clock, enjoying a substantial luncheon of hot cutlets & coffee & surrounded by piles of wedding cake.— M^rs & Miss Wormeley came to see me in the morning.

Thursday the 14th I walked with Mr Heard to the British Institute to see the exhibition of modern paintings. These were done by Turner, Calcott or Leslie, one only by Etty, and two by Edwin Landseer. I came away weary, blinded, dazzled by the glare of gaudy colours; blue, green, red, yellow of the brightest, the most flaring, such as one sees in a bed of tulips, or in a lady's worsted work. My eyes ached as if I had been looking through a prism, and I entered the National Gallery for a few moments to refresh my sight and my mind with better things. With what deep, calm delight I looked long and earnestly on the works of the great masters of this glorious Art. Rubens, with whose fat women and snub-nosed children I have so often quarrelled, Rubens was here with his exuberant imagination, and his colouring so rich yet so deep and mellow, like that with which an American autumn paints an American Forest towards the close of the season, when the glowing scarlet & the shining yellow are subdued into the general masses of crimson and of golden brown—the rich, warm tone which precedes the Quaker simplicity and russet gravity of the last mournful days, when winter is at hand, and the trees are about to be despoiled even of their faded honours and left utterly stripped and bare. Certainly for a full enjoyment of the National Gallery there cannot be a better preparation than a previous visit to the British Institute with it's modern artists. I felt as if I had never before done justice to the real masters. Sebastian del Piombo, painting whilst Michael Angelo guided his hand—Titian, Correggio, Claude, Gaspar Poussin, Annibale Carracci, I walked from one to the other, and when weary, seated myself before a landscape by Rubens, with a small Teniers on one side, and my little Dutch girl watching her mother scrape a carrot, by Maes, immediately above. I was obliged to go all too soon. From the National Gallery I went to see my kind friend Mrs Stevenson, who is always doing all she can to promote my pleasures. I sat some time with her and was by her presented to two of her morning visiters, Lady Sherburne and her daughter the Honorable Miss Dutton. With the young lady I had some conversation. It turned upon the announcement in the Morning Post of a "Marriage in High Life," to which Miss Dutton looked as if she longed to add "below stairs." She tossed and supposed it was the old story of "rank exchanged for money," and thought it a good thing for "this Miss Sturges" that M. Van der Weyer himself was a self-made man. Miss Bates' name was given in the paper as Elizabeth Ann Sturges, daughter of Joshua Bates Esq.

From Mrs Stevenson's I went to Mrs Searle's. We did some shopping and driving together, after which I returned home. A letter from my dear boy Randolph, in Virginia, with a long and kind one from his good aunt, which I found on my table, filled my heart with better thoughts and happier feelings than any thing in the great city of London can do.

Caroline Lucy Scott's 1828 novel *A MARRIAGE IN HIGH LIFE* explores the relationship between a pious middle-class wife and her aristocratic husband (*ODNB*).

Lord Holland's eldest son, Charles Richard **FOX** (1796–1873), was born eight months before his parents married. Fox served first in the navy but later joined the army, where he became a colonel in 1837 and general in 1863. He married Mary FitzClarence (1798–1864), daughter of William IV and actress Dorothy Phillips (Dorothy Jordan), in 1824 (*ODNB*).

Henry Petty Fitzmaurice (1780–1863), **LORD LANSDOWNE**, was an influential member of the Whig Party and Lord Holland's first cousin. He served as lord president of the Privy Council from 1830 to 1834, from 1835 to 1841, and finally from 1846 to his retirement in 1852 (*ODNB*).

Irishman Thomas **SPRING RICE** (1790–1866) was then chancellor of the exchequer, a post he withdrew from later that year, admitting his own inadequacy (*ODNB*).

The **GUNTER** family of confectioners were well known for producing sumptuous receptions for members of the royal family and aristocracy. The Gunter name came to be synonymous with an extravagant scale of dining. Robert Gunter (1783–1852), who inherited the business from his father, James, studied confectionery in Paris and operated a fashionable shop in Berkeley Square. Shortly after the Van de Weyer and Bates wedding, Gunter catered the wedding of the son of the Duke of Wellington and Lady Elizabeth Hay, for which he produced a wedding cake weighing over one hundred pounds, decorated with bouquets of orange blossoms and white roses, surrounded by baskets of sugar work filled with orange flowers and tied with satin (*ODNB*; *Morning Chronicle* [London], 22 June 1838; *Chartist* [London], 21 Apr. 1839).

Miss **WORMELEY** was most likely Mary Elizabeth Wormeley, who married Randolph Brandt Latimer of Baltimore (*ANB*; *DAB*).

Founded in 1805, the British Institution for Promoting the Fine Arts in the United Kingdom [**BRITISH INSTITUTE**] was located in the Pall Mall building that formerly held John Boydell's Shakespeare Gallery. The institute hosted two annual shows: a spring show for living artists and a summer show of ancient masters. At the exhibition Coolidge attended there were 437 paintings and 10 sculptures displayed in three lofty galleries lit by skylights (*Survey of London*, vols. 29 and 30 [1960], 325–338; Thomas Smith, *Recollections of the British Institution for Promoting the Fine Arts in the United Kingdom* [1860], 19–20, 105–106; Waagen, *Works of Art*, 1:156–159).

Anne Constance **DUTTON** (1816–1858) was the daughter of John (1779–1862) and Mary Legge Dutton (d. 1858), Lord and Lady Sherborne [**SHERBURNE**]. Mrs. Stevenson first met the "sensible, gentle, well bred" Lady Sherborne during an 1837 visit to Holkham Hall, the grand Palladian estate of Thomas Coke, Lord Leicester, in Norfolk. Lady Sherborne rescued Stevenson when she became lost in Holkham's cold rooms and subsequently initiated her into the social world of the country house. Stevenson described Lady Sherborne's daughter as "rather pretty—well educated and sensible, but prides herself upon her English reserve—and her knowledge of phrenology." The Sherbornes were among the select recipients of the sensational Pippin apples the Stevensons imported from Albemarle County, Virginia, and presented to Queen Victoria in 1838 (*ODNB*; Boykin, *Mrs. Stevenson*, 89, 95, 123; thePeerage.com: A Genealogical Survey of the Peerage of Britain As Well As the Royal Families of Europe, comp. Darryl Lundy, s.v. "Sherborne, John Dutton, 2nd Baron," accessed 25 July 2011, http://www.thepeerage .com/p2935.htm).

The much-anticipated **MARRIAGE** between Jean Sylvain Van de Weyer and Elizabeth Bates had been a source of discussion since the previous fall. Queen Victoria recorded in her diary a conversation she had with Lord Palmerston in September 1838: "We spoke of Van de Weyer's marriage to a Miss Bates, a great match in point of money, which Lord Palmerston said was a great thing." The *Age* characterized Van de Weyer as "a lucky dog. . . . No doubt the *reasons* for his marriage may be traced to the *Stock Exchange*" (Brett, *Girlhood of Queen Victoria*, 2:13; *Age* [London], 17 Feb. 1839, quoted in *Benjamin Disraeli Letters*, ed. J. A. W. Gunn [1987], 3:157).

Sunday 17. February.

We have a clear cold morning with a bright sun, the season beginning to look towards March. Mr Coolidge & Mr Heard are gone to Windsor, and I am quite alone and free to go on with my history of last week. Let me recapitulate. Sunday last I took tea with Mrs Stevenson. Monday, I went with Mrs Jamieson to see Mrs Joanna Baillie—Tuesday, the marriage of Miss Bates. Wednesday, "Merchede de Cendres"—Thursday, the British Institute—Friday 15th, we dined with M^r & Mrs Searle, sensible & excellent people whose society I always enjoy, and in whose house I am always at home. In the morning I had received a long visit from Mr Charles Sumner. He had been (I suppose the day before) dining with Mrs Norton of poetic name, and fame somewhat tarnished, whom he describes as beautiful & fascinating almost beyond any thing he has seen in England. He confirmed the story I had heard of the very disrespectful way in which Lord Brougham speaks of Miss Martineau. He himself heard Lord B. say seated at a dinner table, between two ladies, that Miss Martineau was "a d–d ass!" What should we, semi-barbarians of America, think of a distinguished man, calling himself a gentleman, who should use such language in speaking of any woman, in the presence of ladies? Surely it must have been <u>after dinner</u> and after some bottles of wine, but Mr Sumner said nothing of the sort. I mentioned to him a story which I heard some time ago of a breach of faith in Lord Brougham, and which is, to say the least, well authenticated & probable. It was a propos to the breaking up of the Cabinet in King William's time. Lord Melbourne had been all day at Brighton, and arrived very late & very much exhausted with fatigue, at Lord Holland's house in South St. He had been expected there to dinner, and several members of the Cabinet and Lord Brougham were still with Lord Holland. Lord Melbourne announced the fact that the Ministry was <u>out</u>, but begged that the secret might be kept until the next day. This being agreed on he retired for rest to his own house, whilst Lord Brougham drove rapidly to the offices of two of the principal newspapers and caused to be inserted, in one a short notice, in the other a long paragraph, announcing the downfall of the ministers. The few lines, published perhaps in the Times, were to this effect— "The Ministers are kicked out; the Queen has done it." The consequence was that the first news which many members of the Cabinet received of their disgrace was from the public prints, and one who had neglected to look at his newspaper, (and this for an Englishman, Englishmen live by bread and their newspapers, is the least probable part of the story,) became informed of the fact of his dismissal from a person in an Omnibus, who having read <u>his</u> paper, knew more of the gentleman's predicament, though unacquainted with his person, than he did himself.

Mr Sumner and myself talked of home and of the things we should feel most in returning to our old modes of life. He will have much to regret in the way of personal friendships formed in England, and the choice society into which he has obtained admission. I shall lose but little in either of these ways—what I shall sigh for are first, the ease and comfort of English home life—the spirit of system of order and method which prevails in every thing—the goodness of the servants who are respectful, well-trained, acquainted with their business, and, as far as I can see, treated upon the whole, with more uniform <u>civility</u> by their masters than our domestics, (help as they ridiculously call themselves,) are, in our free country where the name of master is unknown. On the other hand it seems to me that English servants, the good ones I mean, with less absurd pride than ours, have far more genuine self-respect.

Secondly, what I greatly like is the privacy with which one lives in a huge place like London—the absence of domiciliary visits, of domestic or rather neighbourly "espionage," the presence of which is so intolerable in Boston, where your neighbours or townspeople know so much more of your affairs than you know yourself, and discuss them so freely with such lively embellishments and kitchen-maid refinements.

Thirdly the number of interesting topics of conversation always afloat which prevents any one subject from being hunted down, torn to pieces, and then cooked in every variety of form, served up at every table, hot, cold, hashed, cut and come again, until one sickens at the thought and turns pale at the very mention. I would not have been in Boston this winter, to hear the discussions on the subject of Miss Harriet Sumner's marriage with Mr Nathan Appleton, not for the full amount of the bridal presents, diamonds, cashmeres, Brussels veils, blonde lace and Genoa velvets. Miss Bates' marriage will cause the transfer of as many hundred thousands of pounds as it is probable Mr Nathan Appleton has of dollars, (though I know not how rich a man he may be,) and yet notwithstanding the good will of the Americans here to make the most of so interesting a topic, there are so many other things to think & talk about, that we have escaped any thing like a surfeit.

Fourthly, what I shall miss, O how much, are the objects of art, the picture Galleries, the Claudes, the Correggios, the Murillos—the gallery of antiquities at the British Museum, the Elgin marbles, the Egyptian Saloon—and such houses as Mr Rogers where I breakfasted yesterday—a house where refined society, intellectual conversation, literature & the fine arts combine their attractions.

But after all home is still home, wherever & whatever it be, and mine is a home to love and be proud of. I must be thankful for it's numerous blessings and not look too closely at the evils which accompany them. This is really what I have been doing here; keeping my eyes fixed on the bright side of things. Why not do the same in my own land? We may certainly be a great deal more selfishly happy abroad than at home, in England than in America. Here, as strangers, we have nothing to do but enjoy the much there is to enjoy, without too curious inquiry into things which do not immediately concern us. In London, with money, it is possible to secure a degree of ease, comfort and an absence of domestic annoyances which in America, no money can purchase. Out of London, in the country, even moderate means will effect the same purpose. Yet the English themselves are perhaps a discontented people. The spirit of Caste seems to me to embitter ^& even to degrade^ their lives. All ranks are tormented with the desire to rise higher, not so much in solid advantages as in social position. In America when disturbed by petty annoyances, discomforts abroad and vexations within doors, we should feel (if we can) that these things are trifles in comparison with that general good which is secured by our institutions, and by our natural and political advantages—by a state of society where every man may rise to the level of his talents & his merits, where no one is oppressed by the iron yoke of Caste, and your position among your fellows does not depend upon accidental circumstances, and where if many rise higher than their deserts, few are kept far below them.   But what a tirade I have been indulging in. Mrs Stevenson had written to me to beg that I would call for her that we might make some visits together. This I accordingly did, and on my return with her I found a card, which had been lying twenty four hours at her house, for a saturday evening party at Mr Babbages'. For this civility as for most of those which I have received, I am indebted to Mrs Stevenson's friendship.

Saturday, yesterday morning, Mr Coolidge and myself went at half past ten, to breakfast with Mr Rogers. He has a most pleasant house, a charming collection of pictures, and (retracting what I thought & said of him after our dinner at Mr Bates') I should say he was a delightful old man, could we only feel secure of that benevolence which shews itself in his countenance and even in some of his actions, but is, we are told, sadly belied by the caustic severity of his words. He has the reputation of sparing neither friend nor foe in the pungency of his satire—of saying the bitterest things whilst he looks the kindest. He is certainly a remarkable man if it is only from the circumstance of his having been intimately associated with so many remarkable men, statesmen, philosophers, poets, artists. He was the friend of Sheridan, Fox, Byron, Scott, Flaxman &c &c &c. I suppose the small elegant rooms of his small house, dining-room, drawing-room & library, have witnessed the "reunions" of as many scholars, wits & wise men, as have met together in any private house in England during the same space of time. These walls have echoed as many brilliant conversations, and had ears for as much wit and repartee, anecdote, discussion, & grave or lively dissertation, & for the display of as [. . .] much varied

FIGURE 9. *Samuel Rogers at His Breakfast Table*, by Charles Mottram after John Doyle, ca. 1823. The engraving shows the author and collector in his dining room in an imaginary gathering of the artists, literati, and politicians who frequented his breakfasts. (© *Tate, London, 2010.*)

talent applied to social purposes as any in the three kingdoms. Rogers himself has wealth, taste, a love of art, talks as well as any man in England, is social, hospitable, gives most "recherchès" dinners, most exquisite little breakfasts, and considered as a man of "fashion and fortune," a poet & a wit, holds just now a place & a character unique of their kind. I did not like him at all at Mr Bates', he probably felt out of his element; and I distrust him now, but he should be seen at his own house, surrounded by all that harmonizes with himself, to be seen to the best advantage. The picture needs it's frame. In Portland Place I thought him far-fetched in his witticisms and constrained in his whole bearing. He was only out of place. I thought then that he had grown old in spirit as in flesh, that his blood had stagnated in his veins, but it flowed freely when he found himself at home. My impressions had been changing in the interval between the Bates dinner and this breakfast in St. James' Place. His polite note admitting us to see his pictures, the few words which passed between us at the wedding, his invitation to this very breakfast, had all shewn him to me in a point of view far more amiable than the one in which I first saw him, and his manners now easy, polite & gentlemanly, his conversation lively, graceful & refined, completed my change of opinion as far, at least, as regards his being eminently agreeable. In fact I now admire him so much that I should be very glad to esteem him more, and to get rid of the idea that he is hard, malicious and treacherous. Mrs Stevenson is a person of lively wit herself, and being very well acquainted with him, she bantered him a little on his reputation for ^a habit of^ satirical remark on the characters & manners of his friends. He answered pleasantly yet seriously, disclaimed altogether the charges brought against him, and told Mrs Stevenson that if she could hear & know every word he had ever spoken of her she would like him better than she does now. This may be, but I am obstinate in my doubts.

Upon our first arrival we were ushered into the drawing room, and I amused myself in listening, occasionally volunteering a remark which was always well received, or in looking at my friends among the pictures, especially Puck & the Strawberry Girl, and the triumphal procession with the figures of elephants. When breakfast was ready we descended to the dining room where a round table was spread for seven, one place remaining vacant. The breakfast consisted of varieties of bread, white rolls, rusk, hot muffins and a good brown loaf, pounded chicken & ham, fresh butter in very small pats & a great many in one dish, coffee, tea, and after all, ice-cream. Finger bowls, as after dinner, closed the ceremonies of the repast. Mr Rogers & Mrs Stevenson were on one side of the table and I just opposite, so that when I was not looking at the poet, I could see beyond him an exquisite little picture by Claude, which had won my heart when I saw it on my first visit to the house.

Breakfast being over we returned up stairs & went into the library where we were shewn ^an^ autograph of Washington, and letters written to Rogers by Fox, Sheridan, Byron & Scott. Sheridan's was dated in May, (he died the 7th of the following July,) and contained an urgent request for the loan of one hundred & fifty pounds. Were Rogers a man of high & generous feeling could he expose this letter, as a curiosity, to indifferent eyes? Sheridan was his friend.—I asked myself the question.—There were several letters from Byron. One from Venice, a reply to one from Rogers asking him, Lord Byron, if he were about to wed the Adriatic. His Lordship answers that if the Adriatic would take his wife he would marry the Adriatic in her place—that he had had wife enough, and so on. Poor Lady Byron! I had forgotten this letter which Mr Rogers tells me was published in Moore's Life of Byron.

We remained till about twelve, after receiving an invitiation from Miss Rogers to breakfast with her, at her house in Regent's Park, on tuesday 19th. Mr Coolidge had been talking with this lady and found her pleasant in conversation. I had passed two hours very agreeably. Mr Rogers & Mrs Stevenson were the principal speakers and I must say that I thought my countrywoman acquitted herself extremely well. She is not a woman of much early education. She lived in the country in Virginia, & her parents were excellent old-fashioned people, wealthy, hospitable, but not over-burthened with literary attainment. Mrs Stevenson has a great deal of native intelligence, is quick witted, lively, frank & courageous—not bold or unfeminine, but with the fullest self-possession and afraid of nobody. She is as much liked in England as Mr Stevenson is <u>not</u>. She has a warm heart & feelings as quick as her wit. She has no mean power of repartee, and too kind a temper ever to say an unpleasant thing. Upon the whole she is an amiable & estimable person.

The author Caroline Elizabeth Sarah **NORTON** (1808–1877), granddaughter of dramatist Richard Brinsley Sheridan, was known for her beauty, quick wit, and flirtatiousness. The disastrous state of her marriage to George Chapple Norton (1800–1875), whose personality and tory politics were the opposite of her own, became common knowledge with the widely publicized 1836 adultery trial against Lord Melbourne, which was quickly dismissed. Mrs. Norton sought Melbourne's influence to secure an appointment for her husband, but theirs was apparently a platonic relationship. To supplement the family income Mrs. Norton became a writer. Her first work, *The Sorrows of Rosalie* (1829), traced the downfall of a seduced and abandoned woman, while *A Voice from the Factories* (1836) departed from the romantic genre and addressed the plight of working-class children. Her marriage provided the material for her first anonymously published novels; *The Wife* and *Woman's Reward* (1835), issued together, dealt with the theme of women's powerlessness in marriage. Charles Sumner thought her one of the "brightest intellects" he had ever met and also "grossly slandered" for the freedom of her associations with men. After the Nortons' marriage effectively ended in 1835, George Norton took custody of the couple's three children, leading Caroline to campaign for the legal rights of mothers and to publish a pamphlet on the subject in 1837, *Observations on the Natural Claim of the Mother to the Custody of Her Infant Children*. Her efforts led to the passage of the 1839 Infant Custody Act, unprecedented in English law as a challenge to the patriarchal structure. The act gave custody of children under seven to the mother on the condition that she had not been proven in court to have committed adultery (*ODNB*; Charles Sumner to George S. Hillard, 16 Feb. 1839, in *Memoir and Letters of Charles Sumner*, ed. Edward L. Pierce [1877], 2:62).

LORD BROUGHAM'S penchant for intrigue and control in the months leading up to William IV's dissolution of Melbourne's Whig ministry in November 1834 effectively ended his political career. The story of the cabinet's breakup, widely publicized by the *Times* and the *Morning Chronicle*, played upon Queen Adelaide's tory sympathies and her supposed influence: "We have no authority for the important statement which follows, but we have every reason to believe that it is perfectly true. We give it, without any comment or amplification, in the very words of the communication, which reached us at a late hour last night, or, rather, at an early hour this morning:—'The King has taken the opportunity of Lord Spencer's death to turn out the Ministry; and there is every reason to believe that the Duke of Wellington has been sent for. The Queen has done it all.'" This last phrase was posted throughout London. Enumerating his reasons for abandoning Brougham, Melbourne wrote, "You worked, as I believe, with the press in a manner unbecoming the dignity of your station." Following his dismissal Brougham's behavior continued to be erratic, and he was known for his strange dress and inappropriate manners, especially with women (*ODNB*; Asa Briggs, *Age of Improvement* [1959], 272; William White, *Notes and Queries* [1875], 87; Spencer Walpole, *History of England* [1890], 3:480; *Times* [London], 15 Nov. 1834).

Harriet Coffin SUMNER (1802–1867), Charles Sumner's cousin, married textile entrepreneur Nathan Appleton (1779–1861) on 8 January 1839. Appleton was one of the founders of the industrial city of Lowell, Massachusetts, and served in the Massachusetts House of Representatives. Upon his return to Boston in 1840 Sumner visited the Appletons on a regular basis. In 1852 the Coolidges' youngest son, Jefferson, married Appleton's cousin Mehitable Sullivan Appleton (*DAB*; Anne-Marie Taylor, *Young Charles Sumner and the Legacy of the American Enlightenment, 1811-1851* [2001], 128; Shackelford, *Descendants*, 2:141).

EXQUISITE LITTLE PICTURE: Coolidge is paraphrasing Waagen's description of Claude Lorrain's *The Mill*, an octagonal landscape measuring twelve by eighteen inches, which Rogers purchased from Benjamin West in 1831 (Jameson, *Private Galleries* [1844], 393; Waagen, *Works of Art*, 2:139).

Deep in debt, **SHERIDAN** wrote to Samuel Rogers in 1815 that he was "undone and broken-hearted" and that "£150 could remove all difficulties" (*ODNB*).

Lord **BYRON** wrote to Rogers from Venice on 3 March 1818, "I have not as you say 'taken to wife the *Adriatic*' but if the Adriatic will take my wife—I shall be very glad to marry her instead;—in the mean time I have had wife enough as the Grammar has it '*taedet vitae pertaesum est conjugii*' [*life is boring, marriage utterly so*] however the last part of this exquisite quotation only is applicable to my case—I like life very well in my own way" (Thomas Moore, ed., *The Works of Lord Byron: With His Letters and Journals, and His Life* [1832], 4:89; Leslie A. Marchand, ed., "*The flesh is frail*": *Byron's Letters and Journals* [1976], 6:16).

Monday. 18. February.

Dark & gloomy enough, but I shall go out & leave some cards for Mr Coolidge. This is a very convenient fashion for gentlemen who can visit by proxy, and not inconvenient for ladies, who can, as well as not, drop their husbands cards even in houses where they are themselves admitted. Since the party at Mr Babbage's several cards have been left for us. My old acquaintance Lord Selkirk, who I think must look very much like his namesake Alexander of Juan-Fernandez memory, M^r & Miss Rogers, and M^r, M^rs & Miss Hallam.

Saturday morning we breakfasted with Mr Rogers and Saturday evening at half past nine, went to Mr Babbage's house in Dorset St. Manchester Sq. Here was a gathering of the elect, a "re-union" of literary & scientific men, artists, authors, celebrities of both sexes. Those who like myself had no claim of learning or letters for admittance into so choice an assembly, could only rejoice in the opportunity of seeing so many Lions in one cage. We had, Mr Babbage himself the inventor of the famous calculating machine, Mr Hallam, the author of the "Middle Ages," the Revd Mr Whewell, whose Bridgewater Treatise I had read in the U.S. and whose Architectural Notes on German Churches I have been studying this summer, a propos to my recent acquaintance with English Cathedrals; Mr Morier, whose Hadji Baba in Persia & England, I have cried & laughed over; Judge Haliburton, alias Sam Slick; Mr Rogers, the poet of Memory & of Italy; Mr Hume, the political calculator; Mr Grote, the friend of the Ballot & of Dugald Stewart; Mr Taylor, the author of Philip Van Artevelde; Mr Justice Maule, who possessed of talents, knowledge, every thing which fits him to do honour to the place he holds, might have remained a sim-

ple barrister for all his life, had he not <u>bought</u> himself into Parliament—
he gave two thousand pounds for a seat in the House of Commons, and
a seat upon the Bench soon paid him his money with interest. This is the
way they manage things in England it appears. Then came Sir Francis
Chauntrey; Sir David Wilkie; Turner, a very favorite painter here though
rather slightingly mentioned by Dr Waagen, who allows him great talent
it is true, but reproves him for the abuse of it; Sir Charles & Lady Morgan;
Mrs Austen, whose translation of the Letters of a German Prince (Puckler-
Muskau) the best translation ever made into the English language, has
put her on a footing with original writers; Miss Martineau, to whom there
is no denying the praise of talent, though accompanied by self-conceit
& prejudice—such was the character of the company. There were a few
titled persons present, among whom I heard the name of Lady Anna
Maria Donkin, sister of the Earl of Minto, and the Earl of Selkirk, whose
family history connects him with the more famous Paul Jones, who was
the son of a gardener in the service of Lord Selkirk's father. The Americans
of the party were M^r & Mrs Stevenson, Mr John Van Buren, Mr Charles
Sumner, Mr C. & myself. It was a pleasure to me to see so many persons
whose names I had seen in print, and the assembly of the evening was
literally what Carlyle calls "that crowning phenomenon, and summary of
modern civilisation, a soirée of Lions."[1] There were no doubt "many blue
men and women, dear Mrs Rigmaroles, great Mr Rigmaroles" in this company of distinguished persons—many "pewter tankards scoured bright"
and mistaken by "dim-eyed animals" like myself, for "solar luminaries,"
but there were also some rightful objects of that hero worship which even
Carlyle applauds. "Veneration of great men is perennial in the nature of
man; this in all times, especially in these, is one of the blessedest facts
predicable of him."

The rooms, after a while, became crowded and warm, and I went below
with Mrs Stevenson to get a cup of tea. Refreshments of various kinds were
served up on tables behind which servants were stationed to attend upon
the guests; there was tea, coffee, lemonade, wine, fruit, cake, thin bread &
butter, and I believe sandwiches. Enough of every thing and good, but no
affectation of style or shew. Returning up stairs I encountered Miss Rogers
whom I like better & better. She is not only a sensible but a good-natured
person. Now good nature is not a common virtue among the English. If
they happen to possess they are ashamed to acknowledge it, and when you
do find it, it has the charm of rarity. I was presented to some few persons,
exchanged a few words with M^r & Mrs Hallam, Mr Whewell & Judge Haliburton, & held something approaching to a conversation with Mr Morier

& Mr Babbage—but as to becoming acquainted with any one in such a crowd, and where all talk is necessarily desultory, I do not understand the possibility of it. Miss Martineau whom I knew in America, says, I am told, that she should be pleased to renew the acquaintance. If so let her make the first advance. She is on her own ground now and I am the stranger. I certainly shall not do homage to her. Lady Morgan was rather cold. One of my friends told me that I had committed an unpardonable mistake in speaking to her of any thing but herself & her own writings. That Glorvina expected to hear of nothing but her own perfections, and that when I talked to her on other subjects I had shewn a want of taste & feeling, at which she was naturally disgusted. Alas!—The little Goody was dressed in scarlet velvet with a black hat & feathers and a band of small diamonds over her brow, but the Irish witch prevails over all her finery. Mr Babbage invited us to join his saturday evening parties whenever we were not otherwise engaged—a permission of which we shall gladly avail ourselves.

ALEXANDER SELKIRK (1676–1721), the earl's namesake, was cast away for more than four years on the South Pacific island Juan Fernandez off the coast of Chile. When Selkirk was discovered by two Bristol privateers in February 1709, he was clothed in goat skins and described as looking wilder than the skins' first owners. Selkirk was the probable inspiration for Daniel Defoe's *Robinson Crusoe* (ODNB).

Charles BABBAGE (1791–1871), mathematician, inventor, and author, lived at 1 Dorset Street, Manchester Square, Marylebone. There he displayed his "Difference Engine no. 1," the first known automatic calculator, and hosted gatherings of London's scientific, artistic, and social elite. Harriet Martineau recalled that "all were eager to go to his glorious soirées; and I always thought he appeared to great advantage as a host. His patience in explaining his machine in those days was really exemplary." Mary Lloyd, Babbage's friend and frequent guest, wrote that he began his gatherings as a way of allowing his infirm mother the opportunity to meet some of the "remarkable characters" that he knew. "The rooms were ordinary rooms," Lloyd wrote, "with folding doors, not large or handsomely furnished. The model of 'the calculating machine' was on a stand in the middle of one room; and in the other was the celebrated Automaton figure, called 'the Silver Lady.' . . . [T]his figure moved her arms and head most gracefully, and even moved her eyes, and almost smiled, as if she was amused with your astonishment."

Babbage recalled his amusement in watching the guests at one of his receptions attending to his two attractions: "A gay but by no means unintellectual crowd surrounded the automaton. In the adjacent room the Difference Engine stood nearly deserted: two foreigners alone worshipped at that altar. One of them, but just landed from the United States, was engaged in explaining to a learned professor from Holland what he had himself in the morning gathered from its constructor. . . . My acute and valued friend, the late Lord Langdale, who had been observing the varying changes of my own countenance, as it glanced from one room to the other, now asked me, 'What new mischief are you meditating?'—'Look,' said I, 'in that further room—England. Look again at this—two Foreigners'" (*ODNB*; Ian Brunskill, ed., *Great Victorian Lives* [2007], 88–92; Martineau, *Autobiography*, 271; Mary Lloyd, *Sunny Memories* [1880], 57–59; Charles Babbage, *Passages from the Life of a Philosopher* [1864], 426–427).

Henry **HALLAM** (1777–1859) was best known for his 1818 two-volume *View of the State of Europe during the Middle Ages*. With his wife, Julia Maria Elton (1783–1840), Hallam had eleven children, but only one daughter, Julia Maria Frances Hallam (1818–1888), survived him (*ODNB*; Jack Kolb, ed., *Letters of Arthur Hallam* [1981], 42).

The Anglican priest William **WHEWELL** (1794–1866) first published *Architectural Notes on German Churches, with Remarks on the Origin of Gothic Architecture* anonymously in 1830, though the 1835 edition bore his name. He also authored the third Bridgewater Treatise, *Astronomy and General Physics Considered with Reference to Natural Theology* (1833), one of eight treatises funded by the bequest of Francis Egerton, Earl of Bridgewater. Whewell's work, which was the most popular of the series and remained in print until 1864, suggested that the relationship of the sun and earth were oriented for the benefit of living things (*ODNB*).

James Justinian **MORIER'S** (1782–1849) diplomatic service in Persia inspired his humorous and popular novel *The Adventures of Hajji Baba, of Ispahan*, published in 1824 (*ODNB*).

DUGALD STEWART (1753–1828) was one of the most able disciples of the Scottish "common-sense" philosophy, and the influence of his writings and teaching extended to America. Jefferson met Stewart in Paris in 1788 and later nominated him for membership in the American Philosophical Society. When faced with engaging professors for the new University of Virginia in 1824, Jefferson called on Stewart, invoking the memory of their time in Paris, when "we saw together Louis XVI. led in triumph by his people thro' the streets of his capital" (*ODNB*; *PTJ*, 13:242, 29:415; Thomas Jefferson to Dugald Stewart, 26 Apr. 1824 [MHi]).

HENRY TAYLOR (1800–1886), public servant and poet, gained immediate fame with the 1834 publication of the historical drama *Philip Van Artevelde*, a two-part play that traced the rise and fall of the popular fourteenth-century Flemish leader. Taylor's preface to the play is still recognized as an important document in Victorian poetry, as it called for a shift in poetic taste away from the excesses of the school of Byron and Percy Shelley toward a more restrained and reasoned style (*ODNB*; *Victorian Poets before 1850*, s.v. "Taylor, Henry," by Lawrence Poston, Dictionary of Literary Biography, vol. 32 [1984], Gale Literary Databases, accessed 20 Dec. 2010, http://go.galegroup.com/).

Beginning in January 1839 it was rumored that William Henry **MAULE** (1788–1858) would succeed Baron Bolland as baron of the exchequer. Maule was named to that post in March of that year. He had earned a considerable amount of money when he became counsel to the Bank of England in 1835, a position that aided his winning the Carlow borough in 1837 as a Liberal member of Parliament (*ODNB*).

Joseph Mallord William TURNER (1775–1851), elected the youngest member of the Royal Academy of Arts at age twenty-six, was the defining British artist of his era. Inspired by the works of seventeenth-century painters Gaspar Poussin and Claude Lorrain, Turner elevated the status of landscape painting. His watercolor and oil paintings were characterized by their brilliant colors and broad range of subject matter, from seascapes to literary, classical, and contemporary events. While Waagen acknowledged Turner's "great talent" and "remarkably bold and spirited" pictures, he complained that in works such as *The Burning of the Houses of Lords and Commons, 16th October, 1834* there was "such a looseness of treatment, such a total want of truth, as I had never before met with. He has here succeeded in combining a crude, painted medley, with a general foggy appearance." Later Waagen admitted that on his first visit to England he knew very little about Turner and offered a glowing reassessment of his work, declaring him the Byron of landscape painters (*ODNB*; *Grove Art Online*, s.v. "Turner, Joseph Mallord William," Oxford Art Online; Ian Warrell and Franklin Kelly, eds., *J. M. W. Turner* [2007]; Gustav Waagen, *Treasures of Art in Great Britain* [1854], 1:383–384; Waagen, *Works of Art*, 2:152).

Anna Maria Elliot DONKIN (1785–1855) was the second wife of Rufane Shaw Donkin (1773–1841), author, Whig member of Parliament, and army officer who served in the West Indies and India (*ODNB*).

Early biographers erroneously linked Paul Jones (d. 1767), father of John PAUL JONES (1747–1792), to the estate of the fourth Earl of Selkirk at St. Mary's Isle, Kirkudbright, Scotland, when in fact he was a gardener at the nearby estate Arbigland, which belonged to William Kraik. The confusion may have arisen because of the younger Jones's failed 1778 attempt to kidnap the Earl of Selkirk from his Scottish home (*ODNB*; Samuel Eliot Morison, *John Paul Jones: A Sailor's Biography* [1999], 489–490).

1. From this point to end of paragraph, Coolidge quoted and paraphrased lines from Thomas Carlyle's review of Lockhart's *Memoirs of the Life of Sir Walter Scott* (*London and Westminster Review*, Jan. 1838, pp. 294–295).

Thursday 21. February.

Time flies. My last date was the 18th. I resume. I had got no farther than Saturday night & Mr Babbage's. Tuesday we breakfasted with Miss Rogers, who lives 5. Hanover Terrace, Regent's Park. a pleasant house in a pleasant situation, not fashionable but something better. Miss Rogers has some fine pictures. Among others a small & beautiful Rubens, and a Teniers wild & fantastic in the extreme; the subject a witch entering the infernal regions to collect herbs for her diabolic purposes. She has past the cave-like portal, through which light from the upper world is streaming, enough to shew the wierd forms which crowd the vestibule of Hell. On one side Cerberus chained springs angrily towards the Sorceress, on the other imps of various fantastic shapes draw back from the presence of one whose power they have felt and tremble at. It is altogether a wild, strange story most forcibly told. Beyond even Retsch's imaginings. Sancho conversing with the Duchess by Leslie, hangs over the mantel-piece of a small room where are none but English masters. A little girl dressing herself in her mother's cap by Sir Joshua Reynolds much faded but having a good deal of the peculiar charm which Sir Joshua almost always gives to his children. The original of the Canterbury Pilgrims by Stothard, scenes from the Arabian Tales by the same artist, and many others which I had not time to look at.

Miss Rogers does the honours of her house easily & hospitably. She is ready in conversation and not without some share of her brother's vivacity and sportive wit. The poet himself was one of the breakfast party and made the life of it. He has the most astonishing skill & facility in the somewhat difficult art of small talk. He is called ugly but it is impossible to think him so when listening to him. You remember his ugliness in his absence but forget it in his presence. Mr Rogers cannot be called a man of genius. He is not a poet. There is good sense, good feeling & good taste in his writings, there is measure always & sometimes rhyme, but all these together do not constitute poetry, and poetry is just the one thing wanting in his graceful pages. He is a man of varied information and of exquisite taste; taste that peculiar gift, that sixth sense, a talent apart from all other talents and alone capable of appreciating all, Mr Rogers does possess to a delightful extent. He surrounds himself with an atmosphere of taste, and every thing he touches seems to come into the right form & colour & place, and harmonize with a general character of order & refinement. He is really, in his way, so admirable & so unique that I am very sorry to believe him "false and hollow." Malice and insincerity are not only morally wrong but they are sins against good taste. There is something contrary to all our ideas of the beautiful in ~~false~~ ^social^ treachery & in ill-nature. Yet one fault Mr Rogers certainly has which opens the door to many others. He is intensely vain; and though too much a man of the world to shew his vanity offensively, it betrays itself occasionally in very slight but unmistakeable ways. I take it he is a man who would never pardon the slightest slight or faintest shadow of a shade of neglect. He is probably rendered a little more susceptible by the fact that his birth & business do not place him exactly in the position which he holds in the best society.

I have spoken of his powers of conversation. He is one of the best talkers in England, yet it is difficult to give any samples by which a person who has never heard him, might judge of this peculiar talent of his. It would be next to impossible to do it justice. Readiness & apropos are among the great charms of what he says. He always seems to bring out the right thing at the right time, to give the best turn to the idea and the best form to the expression.

Our party broke up reluctantly at twelve o'clock. The morning had passed most pleasantly. Mr Coolidge & myself drove as far as Chelsea to see Carlyle, the Carlyle, the author of so many strange things, books, articles in Reviews, and that "crowning Phenomenon" of all, "the History of the French Revolution." Mr Coolidge had visited him before and made an appointment for me to go too. We found him in a small house & with all appearance of limited means. But Carlyle, upon the whole, comes up to the idea I had formed of him, perhaps nearer than any distinguished man I have seen in England. He is more strongly characterised as a person apart from the crowd, with the stamp of the mint fresh upon him, the coin not worn by constant attrition with others. He has individuality, that attribute which men in society seem so anxious to get rid of. Yet he does not seem odd, or excentric, or ultra. He is only a distinct existence, a man with his own views, opinions, feelings, which he expresses freely, with earnestness and with great power.

The persons, on the other hand, whom I meet in society have all, more or less, the same style of manners and ^of^ dress, and their ordinary conversation is pitched nearly in the same key. They vary because Nature has put it out of their power to conform in all things to a given standard, but they vary as little as they can. This, in general society, produces a certain amount of insipidity, a want of heartiness, or earnestness, of any sort of warmth or glow. At "Babbage's Menagerie," as Lady Anna Maria Donkin calls his saturday evening parties, where so many political, literary, scientific & artistic characters assemble, I should say that the distinguishing mark was want of all character for good or evil. This is, I suppose, unavoidable, at least to a certain extent. If each individual carried into the company of others too much of his individual self there might be many petty shocks & some rude collisions. Yet it seems a pity that Babbage, Hallam, Whewell, Wilkie &c &c should move about requiring, as Mr Morier said, to have labels pinned to their backs, in order to tell one from another. Yet it is better to have them simply ticketed with their names than be obliged to add as Mr William Coke did when he rode a vicious mare, "she kicks," which might be the case were these gentlemen to come into society without leaving their individualities behind. Of one thing I am sure however, that Carlyle could no more lay aside <u>his</u> than he could change the colour of his eyes. He is Scotch and speaks in a broad Scotch accent, has the complexion and the high cheek bones of his countrymen, and, in his way, the mixture of simplicity & sagacity that so often distinguishes them. But what strikes me most is the good faith and deep earnestness of his character as it shews itself in his conversation. He seems to feel always full of his subject, as if it were worth his whole attention, and this adds much to the force of all that he says. Mrs Carlyle is also Scotch, speaks in the Doric tones of her country which to me are never unpleasant, and sometimes, as in her case, peculiarly sweet. She was quietly at work in her little parlour when we arrived, but laid aside her needle to summon her husband, and then to join calmly and with intelligent interest, in the conversation. Her aged mother seated in an easy chair by the fire, netting not knitting what seemed to be the border of a cap, completed a most pleasing family group, and when I spoke of narrow means as evident in Mr Carlyle's establishment, I meant merely the absence of wealth, for in all that I saw there, there was neatness and comfort. We learnt in the course of conversation that Carlyle is employed in writing a life of Cromwell, and we came away with an understanding that we are to pass an evening of next week with these new friends of ours, as I desire to call the Carlyles.

The evening of this day, tuesday, I went with Mrs Stevenson to a small party at the house of a friend of hers where we heard some good music, and where I saw three little boys, the sons of the Turkish Ambassador, who, with their interpreter, had been invited to pass the evening. They were apparently from six to twelve years old, with dark complexions and full black eyes. Their dress was European, a cloth tunic & trowsers, but they wore the caps of their country, tall cylinders of red cloth with a plume, black or dark blue, hanging from the back part of the crown and almost touching their shoulders behind. On the top of the crown, which was flat, there was a star of precious stones, diamonds & emeralds. The Interpreter told us that they were the children of different mothers. They were not greatly alike, but one of them, the eldest and finest looking, had to me a most touching resemblance to my own dear boy, Algernon.

Wednesday 20. February, we dined with Mrs Mansfield. She is a Baltimore lady who ^married an English gentleman &^ has been living twenty eight years in England. Mr Mansfield has a good fortune and they are in good society. The company consisted of Sir Rufane & Lady Anna Maria Donkin, Lady Charlotte Lindsay, Mr Morier, Mr Lockhart, Mr Childers a member of parliament, and two or three other gentlemen whose names

I did not hear. Lady Charlotte Lindsay, married to a son of the Earl of Balcarras, is a widow, the daughter of Lord North, the old enemy of our country, but she seems to bear no malice against us, and was kind & attentive to me. She is old, singularly ugly, but exceedingly intelligent, animated and amusing in conversation. Lady Anna Maria Donkin, the sister of Lord Minto, is also clever and says very good things. I sat at table between Mr Morier, (Hadji Baba) and Sir Rufane Donkin.—Sir Rufane is a whig member of parliament, fully imbued with whiggism. This "juste milieu" between Toryism & radicalism calls itself moderate & wise. The theory is perhaps both. The practice not always either. "The Whigs," says Mr Rogers, "are like the Bats in the fable, disclaimed equally by Birds & Mice." I pleased Lady Charlotte Lindsay by comparing them to Martin in Swift's "Tale of a Tub," the Tories being my Lord Peter with his three hats, the Radicals, Jack who cut & slashed & tore until the garment (the Constitution) was all in tatters. But Sir Rufane, whig though he be, has a good deal of the good old English gentleman in his composition, if character may be judged by manners and tone of coversation. Mr Morier is a fat, florid, comfortable-looking person, perfectly well characterised in that sketch in Fraser's Magazine, where, as a "fire-worshipper," he is standing with his back to the grate & the tails of his coat drawn away, so as to give his person the full benefit of the genial element. He talks pleasantly and is without affectation or pretension, forming a complete contrast with Lockhart who sits curling his lip, and affecting the extreme fastidiousness which I believe, was some time ago, a fashion among aristocrats of talent and has now fallen to their apes. It did very well in it's novelty, and no doubt imposed upon the crowd, but the day has past, and it is now, I should think, as "mauvais ton" as it is ridiculous. After dinner I had some further conversation with Mr Morier whom I liked better and better.

I had been struck at dinner by something that Sir Rufane said to me. He spoke of the necessity in parliament, of yielding to the clamours of the public, or certain portions of it, and of adopting measures, from time to time, of more than doubtful wisdom, solely to silence or satisfy the noisy crew out of doors. "Oh, for example," said he, "what terrible people are the Saints, and how much we are compelled to do, against our better judgments, to put an end to the outcries of these over-righteous." He left on my mind the impression that the Saints very often did more mischief than the sinners. Upon the whole my dinner was a pleasant one.

George Ticknor described Sarah Rogers's **HOUSE** in 1838 as "a sort of imitation—and not a bad one either—of her brother's on St. James's." Her collection was catalogued by Waagen and Anna Jameson (Macleod, *Art and the Victorian Middle Class*, 468–469; Peter W. Clayden, *Rogers and His Contemporaries* [1889], 2:165; Gustav Waagen, *Treasures of Art in Great Britain* [1854], 2:266–271; Jameson, *Private Galleries*, 412–413).

Thomas CARLYLE (1795–1881) received a visit from Joseph Coolidge and Charles Sumner on 4 February 1839, interrupting the author as he wrote a letter to his brother and leading him to complain about the Americans "clattering . . . above an hour; till my nerves are all in a flutter." Carlyle and Sumner never warmed to one another, but Joseph Coolidge made a more favorable impression. Carlyle described him to Ralph Waldo Emerson as a "Boston man of clear iron visage and character." On this first visit Coolidge left with Carlyle a review of Emerson's "Divinity School Address" from the 27 August 1838 *Boston Daily Advertiser*. Carlyle himself returned the review, along with a copy of the address, to Charles Sumner and expressed his regret at not knowing the Coolidges' address so that he might call on them personally. Carlyle wrote Coolidge with an invitation to visit, specifically addressing it "to <u>you</u> not to Sumner! There is a choice in men and Americans: all men are not equally washy and dreary and benevolent—thank Heaven!" After Sumner left London Carlyle informed Emerson that "Popular Sumner is off to Italy, the most popular of men,—inoffensive, like a worn six-pence that has no physiognomy left. We preferred Coolidge to him in this circle; a square-cut iron man, yet with clear symptoms of a heart in him" (Thomas Carlyle to John Carlyle, 4 Feb. 1839, Carlyle to Ralph Waldo Emerson, 8 Feb. 1839, Carlyle to Charles Sumner, 14 Feb. 1839, Carlyle to [Joseph Coolidge], [late Feb.–early Mar.?] 1839, Carlyle to Emerson, 13 Apr. 1839, in *Carlyle Letters*, 11:16, 24, 30, 37, 79–82).

London's luminaries flocked to then unfashionable Chelsea for the society of Carlyle and his wife, Jane Welsh Carlyle (1801–1866), who presided over their salon. At the time of the Coolidges' visit, Jane Carlyle's MOTHER, Grace Welsh (1782–1842), had just begun a two-month stay. The Carlyles chose their three-story brick terrace house at 24 Cheyne Row, built in 1708, for its spaciousness rather than its style, and they lived the remainder of their lives in what Carlyle called their "eminent" and "antique" home (*ODNB*; Robin Fedden and Rosemary Joekes, *The National Trust Guide*, 3rd ed. [1984], 76–77; *Carlyle Letters*, 11:xiii–xiv).

Coolidge was not alone in her fascination with the children of TURKISH AMBASSADOR Mustapha Reschid Pasha (ca. 1800–1858). After the diplomat left London in March 1839, where he had been lobbying for support in the war with Egypt, he continued his mission in Paris. Benjamin Disraeli described seeing him there "with two little sons about 6 & 8 years of age in costume whose diamond tassels to their red caps & large melancholy eyes captivated the ladies." The names of the ambassador's younger children are unknown, but an elder son, Mehemet Djemil Pasha (b. 1823), went on to become minister of foreign affairs and ambassador to Paris. Arakel Dadian was INTERPRETER for the Turkish embassy in London (Pierre Larousse, *Grand Dictionnaire Universal du XIXe siecle* [1875], s.v. "Réchid-Pacha, (Moustapha)"; J. A. W. Gunn, ed., *Benjamin Disraeli Letters* [1982],

4:69–70; *Morning Chronicle* [London], 23 Aug. 1838, 28 Jan. 1839; *Freeman's Journal and Daily Commercial Advertiser* [Dublin], 13 Mar. 1839).

LADY CHARLOTTE LINDSAY married the Honarable John Lindsay (d. 1826) in 1800 (*ODNB*).

The moral of Aesop's FABLE "The Bat, the Birds, and the Beasts" is "he that is neither one thing nor the other has no friends."

Jonathan SWIFT'S 1704 religious satire, *A Tale of a Tub*, is the story of three brothers—Martin (Martin Luther), Peter (Saint Peter), and Jack (John Calvin)—who represent the major branches of western Christianity. Each brother inherits a coat from their father that will last a lifetime if never altered. Peter embellishes his coat and wears three hats at once. Martin and Jack also trim their coats according to fashion but later think better of it. Martin successfully restores his coat to its original appearance, but Jack tears at the added trimmings so violently that he destroys the coat itself.

FRASER'S MAGAZINE published Daniel Maclise's portrait of James Justinian Morier warming himself at the fire grate in its February 1833 issue (Daniel Maclise, *James Justinian Morier* [1833], NPG.org).

Saturday. 23. February.

I go on from Wednesday 20th. Thursday 21st I called by appointment on Miss Rogers. We were to go to Highgate together, I to see my boy, and she to visit the son of a friend absent in the East Indies. Whilst she was getting ready I took another look at her pictures. The Rubens is full of spirit and life—the subject is the breaking down of a bridge over which a body of soldiers on horseback are rapidly advancing. The scene of confusion is perfectly expressed—the horses some rolling and floundering in the stream under or over their riders, others just coming headlong down, others rearing & falling back upon their haunches striving to avoid the catastrophe though evidently in vain—the men in different attitudes of pain, terror, and the struggle for life or death, all in the free flowing lines which characterise the hand of Rubens, and with his rich, harmonious coloring. It is a gem this picture, and serves as a "pendant" to "the Sorceress" by Teniers, which Sir Thomas Lawrence said should be covered three times thick with guineas to pay for it at any thing like it's worth. Miss Rogers has also a Titian, a Holy Family, in which is introduced a portrait of Charles 5th as one of the Magi, kneeling before the Mother & Child, in slashed doublet, ruff and pointed beard, like a proper Spanish gentleman.

Our drive to Highgate was very pleasant. Miss Rogers converses very well, sustaining her own part in the conversation and expecting you to do the same, being at once a good talker and a good listener. I asked many questions about the eminent men, her brother's friends, whom she had known in his society. Her account of Sir Walter Scott interested me particularly. She described him as simple in manners, almost rustic, but self-possessed and manly—wanting refinement however ^in his tastes^ and being too jovial and rather too much of a boon companion to relish the quiet elegance of Mr Rogers' dinners. Sir Walter liked a glass of hot whisky punch and a bottle song, catch, glee or chorus, and the absence of these good things made the entertainment dull. He certainly, in some of his novels, gives a peculiar zest to his descriptions of such scenes, as if he understood and enjoyed them. Miss Rogers disapproves of that part of his Diary in which he speaks of his wife after her death, as a person whose counsels had assisted to guide him; his "thirty years companion and friend." Lady Scott's habits were sufficiently notorious to give such expressions a doubtful character, as if publication had been anticipated and prepared for. (I heard in Scotland that she was often seen intoxicated at the theatre and in other public places.) None of Sir Walter's children appear to have inherited his talents. Mrs Lockhart was amiable & of pleasing manners, but not particularly clever. Anne Scott was of striking appearance, having black eyes and a quantity of black hair which gave her a foreign and somewhat decided air. The present Sir Walter was presented, at nineteen years old, by his father to Mr Rogers, with some such words as these—"This is my son, who can read & write I believe, but I know that he can back a horse as well as any man in England." Charles Scott, the second son, has bad eyes and is somewhat deaf, so as to shew to great disadvantage, at least in society. These anecdotes brought to my mind that theory, I do not know how old it may be, but brought forward by Dr Rush of Philadelphia, which traces talent in a man to his mother, as if intellect were transmitted through the female, and was an entail passing from the woman to her son.

Sir Walter Scott, according to Miss Rogers, had in his character & manner the repose & simplicity which belong of right to a strong man. Little people are apt to bluster & fidget—not so the morally or intellectually large. Miss Rogers described an interview at her brother's house between Walter Scott and "American Cooper" as Carlyle calls him. They both happened to come in about the same time. Cooper was agitated, restless & perturbed, evidently jealous and uncertain what course to pursue, whilst Scott was calm as usual, frank, at his ease, and entirely himself, shewing no symptoms of consciousness that he had a character to support, and a rival! to encounter. Cooper is undoubtedly clever but vain, nervous & "on dit," ill-tempered. Miss Rogers speaks, as every one seems to do, in terms of the highest praise of Mrs Joanna Baillie.

When arrived at Highgate, Miss Rogers mentioned what I had forgotten, that Bacon died here. I heard also that the house in which Oliver Cromwell lived is still standing, and not far distant from Mrs Kieckhoefer's school—the school itself being in a house believed to be one wing of an old palace of the Earl of Leicester, Queen Elizabeth's favorite.

Our return home was pleasant, and after putting my companion down at her own house, I left cards for Mrs Hallam, Mrs Hume & Mrs Mansfield. In the evening, having received an invitation to Lady Minto's, I went & met Mrs Stevenson, by appointment there. Mr Coolidge did not care to go. The rooms were crowded with brilliant company—there were many fine looking elderly ladies and some beautiful young ones. Lady Minto herself, considering that she is the mother of ten children, wears glasses, & walks with a sort of crutch, is wonderfully fair & fresh. She is I presume, near-sighted and her glasses are not spectacles, and her lameness proceeds from recent illness. Spite of all she is a most distinguished-looking person. The ladies were generally elegantly dressed in velvet, mechlin lace and pearls or diamonds. The dress of the better sort of people here, the ladies I mean, is at once rich & simple, being of the most costly materials but with little trimming & no excess of ornament. There is certainly more beauty, grace and good breeding in the high circles than in any below them. The company I see at Lord Minto's is more elegant & more refined than what I have seen at less distinguished houses. This probably arises from the ease & security which acknowledged high position must always give. People are not obliged to fight for their places, and there is no temptation to fawn on the one hand, nor to flout on the other. On this occasion I heard a long list of names belonging to the peerage and the gentry. I recognized some persons whom I had seen before, others were strangers to me. I was introduced to Lord Landsdowne and had some conversation with him. He spoke of my grandfather, Mr Jefferson, and in high terms. What pleasure this always gives me! How I rejoice when I find justice done to him who was one of the noblest of his kind!

Lady Charlotte Lindsay was present, as sprightly, agreeable and ugly as ever. She is certainly the most quizzical looking person I ever saw, with one eye always winking, and more "nods and becks and wreathed smiles" than would set up half a dozen young coquettes. She seems much in request among gentlemen and ladies from her entertaining powers which are great. I am sure this daughter of Lord North must have been the one pointed out to him at the theatre, when he was asked by a foreigner, who that very ugly woman was. Sir Rufane & Lady Anna Maria Donkin were of the company, to my great satisfaction, as they are very kind and polite to me. I saw the nodding plumes on Mme Sebastiani's hearse-like head, and the diamonds glittering on another witch-like foreign woman whose name I could not hear. Next morning the Post gave a long list of Illustrissimos who had graced the soirée at the Admiralty, and this was read with avidity by a Lord-loving public.

Friday was a dull rainy day. I was somewhat surprised at receiving an affectionate note from Miss Martineau, enclosing her card, claiming me as an old acquaintance, astonished to hear that I was in England and had been in the same room with herself without her knowing it. Why did I not come up and shake hands with her as she would have done with me in any part of the world?

I was somewhat at a loss to know what it was best for me to do. I do not like Miss Martineau, nor do I think well of her, but this is merely from her conduct in society and her writings. I have never had any personal difficulty of any kind with her, and as she has now made such advances to me as cannot be rejected without my dislike assuming a personal character, I believe my right course will be to treat her as one lady should treat another under ordinary circumstances. I am not Quixotte enough to tilt with every one of whom I do not think particularly well, and I am on visiting terms with many persons whom I esteem less than I do Miss Martineau. "Nous verrons."

Miss Martineaus's note was brought me by Mr Adam, whose family I knew in Boston. He is here on the hopeless errand of trying to interest the East India Directors in the welfare of their native subjects, to direct their attention to the education of the Hindoo children, to the improvement of the people of India—As if the merchants of Leadenhall Street cared that their slaves should know anything but the necessity of obedience! Mr Coolidge read aloud a quotation from Lord Thurlow. "Bodies corporate have neither bodies to be kicked nor souls to be damned." What hold can any one have upon such an anomalous existence and what fear of consequences in this world or retribution in the next can have any hold upon it? Mr Adam is moreover too much of an enthusiast to make much impression upon matter-of-fact people who always distrust enthusiasm. He makes his object too much a thing of heart, and though an honest & well-meaning man he perhaps lacks discretion.

Jefferson's good friend **BENJAMIN RUSH** argued in his 1787 "Thoughts upon Female Education" for an American system of education distinct from that of

Great Britain. "Children would discover the marks of maternal prudence and wisdom in every station of life," Rush wrote, citing among others the example of Edward VI, who "inherited those great and excellent qualities which made him the delight of the age in which he lived, from his mother, lady Jane Seymour" (Benjamin Rush, *Essays, Literary, Moral and Philosophical*, 2nd ed. [1806], 88–89).

American author James Fenimore COOPER (1789–1851) recalled an awkward dinner with Scott at Rogers's table on 17 April 1828: "There is something too gladiatorial about such dinners, to render them easy or entertaining. As a homage to Scott it was well enough, but it wanted the *abandon* necessary to true enjoyment" (James Fenimore Cooper, *Gleanings in Europe, England*, ed. James P. Elliott [1837], 2:19).

NODS AND BECKS AND WREATHED SMILES is from John Milton's "L'Allegro" (1645).

The Scottish-born WILLIAM ADAM (1796–1881) arrived in India in 1818 as a Baptist missionary but soon resigned and became a founder of the Calcutta Unitarian Society. For twenty years he worked in India as a linguist, a biblical scholar, and the commissioner of vernacular education, authoring *Reports on Vernacular Education in Bengal and Behar* (1838) and *The Law and Custom of Slavery in British India* (1840). Adam's wife and family left Calcutta for Boston in 1834, where Adam joined them briefly in 1838 before sailing to London to help form the British India Society. Upon his return to Boston in 1839 he accepted the position of professor of Oriental literature at Harvard, a post he held for just one year (Clare Taylor, *British and American Abolitionists* [1974], 86; Louis Ruchames, ed., *The Letters of William Lloyd Garrison* [1971], 2:654–657; *Dictionary of Unitarian and Universalist Biography*, s.v. "Adam, William," by Andrew Hill, Unitarian Universalist Historical Society, accessed 20 Dec. 2010, http://www25.uua.org/uuhs/duub/articles/williamadam.html).

Monday. 25. February.

Sunshine & showers—April weather in February. Have received letters from home—one from my dear Randolph.

Sunday I accompanied Mrs Bates to the Cemetery on the Harrow road, called I believe Kensall Green. It is a pleasant morning drive from the West End, is well situated and commands a fine view. Except that it wants that air of seclusion which one likes in a place of tombs, and which it would be hopeless to look for within five miles of London, this spot seems well adapted to it's purpose. At present however, it looks too new. The trees are but lately planted and have no height or size beyond mere shrubs, but the turf is green and fresh, the gravel roads & paths smooth and dry and, even at this early season, the crocus & snowdrop are blooming within the small enclosures which surround some of the monuments. This new Cemetery is already well peopled and three funerals, one of a child, arrived whilst we were there. Many of the monuments are simple, & there are rows of headstones, flat tomb-stones, urns, small obelisks & the like. But others stand aloof from their humble fellows & look purse-proud & ostentatious. Two of the most presumptuous of these exclusive tombs, as elaborate as bad taste can make them, are, first, the family monument of the Ducrows, (Circus riders I believe they are or were) in the Egyptian style, guarded by an immense Sphynx on each side of the door—second, a tomb erected in honour of a Quack doctor whose murders became so manifold as to attract attention and create scandal. A Grecian temple encloses, as in a cage, a statue of Hygeia with a serpent in her hands, whilst an inscription on a pedestal below entreats that the stranger who respects the repose of the dead, will read without comment the name of John St John Long. Such tombs as these are in the style & taste of the villas which one sees in the neighbourhood of London. The Cockney whether from the City or the West End, the Ostro or the Visigoth, builds a villa for his living body near the high road, & another for his dead body in some conspicuous Cemetery.

FIGURE 10. "The General Cemetery, Kensal Green," from *The Mirror of Literature, Amusement, and Instruction*, 28 Apr. 1838. (*Courtesy of Harvard College Library, Widener Library.*)

Here, at Kensall Green, lie the remains of the only son of Mr Bates, killed in a shooting party by the accidental going off of a gun. The Monument is an obelisk of white marble on a square pedestal, simple and with a simple inscription. I am very sorry that I did not know until after I had left the place, that Mrs Lockhart, the daughter of Walter Scott, lies buried here. I should surely have sought for her tomb.

When Mrs Bates & myself left the Cemetery we took our way home through Hyde Park, which begins to fill even as early as February when a fine days calls out the Butterflies.

Count D'Orsay was making himself conspicuous by his dress and equipage, as he does whenever and wherever he shews himself. It was nearly five when I reached home, and I had then to dress & dine and be at Christ's Hospital by half past six. It was one of the days when the Blue Coat boys eat in public, and we had tickets of admittance to the Governor's seats. We went accordingly, Mr Coolidge & myself, taking Jefferson with us, and calling for Mr Adam. My interest in the Blue Coat boys was first excited by Lamb's writings, and the appearance of these miniature monks as they walk the streets, with a grave air, in the dress of the sixteenth Century, is well calculated to awaken curiousity in a stranger.   Through the kindness of a most kind family, that of Mr William Vaughan, from whom we have received numerous civilities, we were, after some hinderance from the crowd, inducted into good seats, from which we had a view of the fine old Hall, and of the boys in their long blue gowns, open in front & shewing what looked like a yellow petticoat beneath.

The ceremonies began with a lesson from the New Testament read (from a pulpit placed at one side,) by one of the elder boys; next came prayers & a hymn. The boys, except those who were in the Organ Gallery just opposite to us, were seated with their backs turned to the long tables covered with clean cloths, at which they afterwards supped. The religious services being over, they took their seats at table and we descended to get a clearer view of their operations. Each boy had a large piece of white bread with a small pat of nice-looking butter upon it. There were little wooden pails filled with water or small beer from which they drank as they pleased. A comfortable meal eaten in a comfortable manner. The tables were lighted by candles placed at intervals, whilst a number of chandeliers hung from the ceiling & being lighted up, when seen from the street, through the great Gothic windows, produced the effect of an illumination. Supper being over the boys stood whilst an anthem was sung, and then began the procession and the salute given to the Lord Mayor. This dignitary in his scarlet robe, with his mace-bearer in attendance, occupied a large seat just below the Gallery, whither we had returned & from whence we enjoyed a full view of his person and that of Lord Morpeth who sat at his right hand. In front of the Mayor's chair, inlaid in the floor, was a long narrow plate of brass to mark the line beyond which it was not necessary for the boys to pass. They came up in procession, two and two, and having "toed the brass line" made profound bows to the Mayor, approaching & wheeling off in couples, except a few who advanced singly. These were large boys with baskets on their backs, or small ones with candles in their hands; for I should have said that as soon as supper was over, the tables were cleared, the table-cloths rolled up, the knives, forks &c put into large baskets, the candlesticks brought together, and all these things taken up by a certain number of boys appointed to the service of carrying them from the Hall. Thus the procession advanced, first several couples empty-handed, then a single large boy with one of the great baskets on his back which rather interfered with the gracefulness of his bow, then boys in couples carrying table cloths, trenchers &c, then a small boy with a candlestick & candle in each hand, next one of the matrons in attendance upon the boys, afterwards a renewal of the same order, until the seven or eight hundred boys with baskets, table-cloths, trenchers, wooden pails, candlesticks &c &c &c, had all made their bows and filed off marching with their burdens out of the room. His Worship the Mayor made a slight inclination of his head to each pair or single boy as they advanced & retired. More of a bow could scarcely be expected when we remember that it was to be repeated upwards of four hundred times. I should have had the rheumatism in my neck for a week after such an infliction. It was altogether a curious & interesting scene. There was the grand old Hall with it's Gothic ceiling & a row of immense windows on one side, whilst the other was adorned by a picture of mammoth proportions, the largest piece of painted canvas I have ever seen, but what the subject of the painting was, I could not make out, as the great size of the Hall rendered it gloomy in spite of the many lights. I saw heads & bodies & limbs confusedly, looking liking a painted procession, but nothing distinctly. Within the Hall I had seen from seven to eight hundred boys clothed in a peculiar but not unpicturesque dress, decent in their appearance, orderly in their manners, sober in their movements, evidently under close discipline, but with no external evidence of undue strictness in that discipline, apparently well-fed, and as the New Englanders say, "well cared for." These boys are mostly the children of respectable parents, many of them sons of clergymen. This charitable institution dates from the time of Edward 6th, and still receives munificent donations from private liberality. It has a sort of branch school in Hertfordshire, making the whole number of individuals who receive the benefits of a very thorough education, from a thousand to eleven hundred. They are taught good Greek, Latin & Mathematics, & have sent forth such men as Charles Lamb & Samuel Taylor Coleridge. What antiquated notions the majority may imbibe, what ideas of the 16th Century, I do not know, but it is a noble charity and carries a most imposing face. We did not get home until nine o'clock.—I must say that I thought Lord Morpeth ugly, awkward & most unaristocratic in his appearance.

The General Cemetery of All Souls, Kensal [**KENSALL**] Green, consecrated in 1833, was inspired by the garden-style Parisian cemetery Père-Lachaise and was the first of its type on the outskirts of London. Established by the joint-stock General Cemetery Company, Kensal Green consisted of landscaped grounds dotted with stylish tombs and monuments that were by design a vast improvement over the scandalous burial conditions within London's city limits. Though still new at the time of Coolidge's visit, the cemetery had a celebrity status, which was confirmed with the 1843 burial of George III's son Augustus Frederick, the Duke of Sussex (1773–1843) (Curl, *Kensal Green Cemetery*, 2–20, 103–106; Roy Porter, *London: A Social History* [1994], 273; Michael Leapman, ed., *The Book of London* [1989], 134) .

Equestrian showman Andrew **DUCROW** (1793–1842) staged legendary productions such as *The Battle of Waterloo* and was known for circling an arena on horseback while posing as classical statuary. His flamboyant shows were patronized by the royal family and drew crowds at Astley's Amphitheatre. Ducrow's graecoegyptian mausoleum at Kensal Green (fig. 10) was the work of stage designer George Danson (1799–1881). It had been erected for the burial of Ducrow's first wife, Margaret Griffith (d. 1836), and Ducrow was buried there as well in 1842, following a spectacular funeral (*ODNB*; Curl, *Kensal Green Cemetery*, 105, 189-190).

Sculptor Robert Sievier (1794–1865) designed the Greek temple memorializing **JOHN ST. JOHN LONG** (1798–1834) (fig. 10), a quack who remained popular in spite of two well-publicized malpractice trials. He was acquitted in one case but found guilty of manslaughter in the death of a second patient whom he had treated with a lotion intended to cure consumption. Sievier was also buried at Kensal Green (*ODNB*; Curl, *Kensal Green Cemetery*, 103–105, 191) .

Joshua Bates's **ONLY SON** was William Rufus Gray Bates, named in honor of the Boston merchant for whom his father once worked. Five years before Coolidge's visit, he was killed instantly when the gun slung over a friend's back accidentally discharged. Mrs. Stevenson, who had also lost a child, commiserated with the family, noting that "they have not recovered & probably never will from the shock." In August 1839 Mrs. Bates also took Daniel Webster, who was visiting London, to see her son's grave (*ODNB*; Boykin, *Mrs. Stevenson*, 19–20; Gray, *Daniel Webster in England*, 169; "Melancholy Accident," *Ipswich [Mass.] Journal*, 3 Jan. 1835).

"Suppings in Public" were held at CHRIST'S HOSPITAL each Sunday of Lent, with visitors admitted by ticket. Originally housed in the defunct Greyfriars monastery on Newgate Street, the school was largely rebuilt under the supervision of architect Christopher Wren following London's 1660 fire. The "old" hall in which Coolidge observed the boys dining was in fact the newest part of the building, having been built between 1825 and 1829 to the Tudor designs of John Shaw. The Great Hall (fig. 29) measured 187 feet long, 51 feet wide, and 47 feet high, and it was lit by nine enormous windows. Opposite these hung a painting over 160 feet long and 16 feet high by the Italian painter Antonio Verrio; it depicted the founding of the Royal Mathematical School at Christ's Hospital (John Summerson, *Georgian London*, rev. ed., ed. Howard Colvin [2003], 272–273; Augustus J. C. Hare, *Walks in London* [1878], 162–166; Timbs, *Curiosities*, 95–101; Thomas H. Shepherd and James Elmes, *London and Its Environs in the Nineteenth Century* [1829; repr. 1968], 120–122).

Samuel Wilson (ca. 1792–1881) was then LORD MAYOR, the annually elected head of the City of London Corporation. Among the other offices and ceremonial responsibilities that he performed, the lord mayor reviewed students at Christ's Hospital several times throughout the year, and he received them at the Mansion House, his residence, the Tuesday of Easter week, when he presented each with a new sixpence. A colonel in the Royal London Militia, Wilson had also been sheriff and an alderman prior to his election as lord mayor (William Trollope, *A History of the Royal Foundation of Christ's Hospital* [1834], 105–112; *Pall Mall Gazette* [London], 9 July 1881; "The Lord Mayor of the City of London," City of London, accessed 20 Dec. 2010, http://www.cityoflondon.gov.uk)

LORD MORPETH was George William Frederick Howard (1802–1864), a member of the Privy Council and chief secretary for Ireland (*ODNB*).

Tuesday. 26. February.

Another bright day. The Morning Post tells of some new H. B. caricatures. In one, called the Somnambulist, Lord Glenelg asleep, is walking out of the Colonial office with a <u>flat</u> candlestick in his hand. The downfall, or retirement, or whatever it may be called, of Lord Glenelg, has been of late, much the subject of conversation. I heard it discussed at Mr Mansfield's when some rather biting things were said of his Lordship, who was spoken of as an elderly young man, always half in love but never enough so to marry; a lazy, sleepy, torpid "parvenu;" a new made peer, no nobleman &c, clever & good-natured no doubt, a man of talent but inefficient. It was ridiculous to talk of such a person as Keeper of the Privy Seal. This office indeed puts a man upon the shelf, but it is a high shelf, and has always been appropriated to men of real rank, noblemen of old family, not lords of three years standing like Charles Grant. I have sent for the caricature, the Somnambulist, which acquires an interest in my eyes from it's connection in my mind with this conversation.

Yesterday we went to Tottenham Green to the house of a Mr Windus, Benjamin Godfrey Windus, the owner of a very fine collection of water colour drawings which we were desirous of seeing. We found a small but very pretty house, called by it's owner a Cottage, well-fitted up and furnished almost richly. We entered a small Hall having on the left hand a dining room, on the right two drawing-rooms and a library. The drawing-rooms were ornamented with large mirrors in antique frames finely carved & gilt. The chairs were likewise gilt & covered with rich figured silk. They were very ancient french chairs, said to have come originally from Versailles but entirely "refaites." There were sofas and ottomans in abundance, tables of different sizes and all the furniture necessary for elegance & convenience. The windows at the back of the house consisted of two panes of plate glass, so large that the lower part of the window was formed by one entire plate, the upper & lesser light being another of smaller dimensions. These windows opened upon a smooth lawn, even at this season beautifully green and with early flowers in bloom. The Library, from the chair-board up was hung with crimson silk, which forms the best relief for paintings in gilt frames. Below were many books in rich bindings. A large double window, opening like a door, each panel consisting of a single pane of plate glass, opened upon the lawn. All these rooms were hung with drawings in water colours. The Library was appropriated entirely to Turner, the favorite artist of Mr Windus, who possesses more of his drawings than any other individual has been able to collect. As many as the walls will hold are richly framed, and there are portfolios full of others for which no other place can be found. These are all landscapes in Turner's peculiar style. Various views taken in England, Scotland, or on the Continent—One of Windsor, & another of Richmond ^in Yorkshire^ particularly pleased me, perhaps because they were comparatively familiar scenes. The coast & sea views are fine, and Mr Windus possesses all the original drawings from which were taken the illustrations of Scott's works in the great edition published by Cadell. Cadell paid Turner at the rate of twenty five guineas a piece for these drawings which he afterwards sold to Mr Windus for what price I did not hear. There are sixty four of them, all small and none of them framed. Turner is said to be very rich and very excentric; somewhat rough and dogged in manner, and of a temper so strangely jealous, where his art is concerned, that he never allows any one to see him at work—as if a talent like his was a thing to be stolen. This mania goes so far that some people affirm that he will never handle a pencil nor draw a line in presence of a second person, and that having once been seen at work upon one of his pieces, he had rubbed out all that was already done and begun afresh. "Rum critturs is women," says one of the respectable characters in the Pickwick papers. "Rum critturs is artists," say I.——

In the drawing rooms are other water colours by Turner, and in the dining room by Westall, Stephanoff, & Cattermole. I do not believe that there is an oil-painting in the house. There are portfolios full of the finest engravings which we hope to examine another time as Mr Windus kindly invites us to return. One visit is nothing for such a collection—It is a bare reading of heads of chapters. Mr Windus has just given 1500 guineas for the original drawings of Sir David Wilkie, the studies from which he has developed his pictures, his first ideas & "premières ebauches." The engravings which one sees in Annuals and illustrated works in general give a very poor idea of the drawings from which they are taken. None of the Artists however suffer as much from engraving as Westall. I had conceived a dislike for him from what I had seen of him in Annuals &c, where his men & women all stare with wide open eyes. I thought he had no way of expressing passion or feeling but by these Owl eyes. Since I have seen his drawings I think very differently of him.

After remaining two hours at Tottenham Green we returned to London where I proceeded to pay some visits. Miss Martineau had written a note and sent her card—Mrs Abercrombie, Mrs Grote & Lady Charlotte Lindsay had called & left theirs. I returned all these courtesies, finding no one at home but Lady Charlotte Lindsay, with whom I had some very pleasant conversation. She is certainly a most agreeable person.

Charles Grant, LORD GLENELG (1778–1866), had just resigned his post as Melbourne's secretary of state for the colonies and refused the offer of the Privy Seal. Grant had once fallen asleep at the end of a cabinet dinner, and John Doyle's cartoon "The Somnambulist," published 25 February 1839, was one example of the public lampooning that episode inspired (*ODNB*; John Doyle, "The Somnambulist" [1839], ref. no. mudyx6f, British Cartoon Archive, University of Kent, accessed 7 July 2011, http://www.cartoons.ac.uk).

BENJAMIN GODFREY WINDUS (1790–1867) was born into a wealthy family of coachbuilders and briefly practiced the trade himself. He also owned medicine warehouses, where he manufactured Windus's Pills, and extensive rental property. After receiving an inheritance from his father in 1832, Windus began buying art in earnest, particularly the works of the modern British artists Thomas Stothard, David Wilkie, and J. M. W. Turner. Windus drew the ire of some artists with his introduction to the art world of the mercantile tactic of "cornering the market." He bought 650 drawings by Wilkie and held them until just after the artist's death, when he sold select items at substantial profit. Windus highly prized his collection of over 200 watercolors and drawings by Turner and constructed a library without windows at his Tottenham Green home for their display. He further protected Turner's delicate watercolor washes from natural light by glazing each framed piece, while unframed works were kept in portfolios or cabinets or mounted in albums, all of which are visible in an 1835 watercolor of Windus's library by John Scarlett Davis (fig. 30). John Ruskin studied Turner's paintings in this room and credited access to Windus's collection with enabling him to write the first volume of *Modern Painters* (1843) (*ODNB*; Celina Fox, *London—World City, 1800—1840* [1992], 354, 358; Macleod, *Art and the Victorian Middle Class*, 41–43, 487–488; John Scarlett Davis, *The Library at Tottenham, the Seat of B. G. Windus, Esq.* [1835], British Museum, accessed 20 Dec. 2010, http://www.britishmuseum.org).

The Scottish publisher Robert **CADELL** (1788–1849) urged Sir Walter Scott to engage Turner as the illustrator for the new twelve-volume edition of his *Poetical Works* (1834), writing, "With his pencil I shall insure the subscription of 8000— without, not 3000." Turner's prolific engravings in the 1830s spread his fame to Europe and the United States. He provided illustrations for the twenty-eight-volume edition of Scott's *Prose Works* (1833–1835), the writings of Samuel Rogers and Lord Byron, his own *Rivers of France* series, and *Landscape Illustrations of the Bible* (1834–1836) (*ODNB*; *Grove Art Online*, s.v. "Turner, Joseph Mallord William," Oxford Art Online).

The statement "Rum creeters [**CRITTURS**] is women" sums up the "dirty-faced man's" assessment of the odd behavior of a handmaid at the Peacock Hotel in Charles Dickens's first novel, *The Posthumous Papers of the Pickwick Club*, published serially by Chapman and Hall from 1836 to 1837.

Richard **WESTALL** (1765–1836) exhibited at both the Royal Academy and the British Institution, but his primary expertise was book illustration, including the fifth edition of Samuel Rogers's *The Pleasures of Memory* (1793). Francis Philip **STEPHANOFF** (ca. 1789–1860) painted in both oil and watercolor, with subjects ranging from Shakespeare to historical and domestic scenes. He contributed watercolor costume portraits to George Nayler's *The History of the Coronation of George IV* (1824–1839) as well as producing illustrations for annuals. George **CATTERMOLE** (1800–1868) was known for his historical watercolor paintings that recreated medieval, Elizabethan, and seventeenth-century scenes. He illustrated some of the novels of his friend Charles Dickens, including *Barnaby Rudge* (1841) and *The Old Curiosity Shop* (1840–1841) (*ODNB*; *Grove Art Online*, s.v. "Westall, Richard" "Stephanoff, Francis Philip," "Cattermole, George," Oxford Art Online).

Wednesday. 27. February.

A day of showers & sunshine. I have been to see Mrs Stevenson and left a card for Miss Rogers. Yesterday I went to the National Gallery and paid particular attention to the pictures of Rubens whom I every day admire more & more. My first impressions of this master were those of disgust. I could not bear his great masses of women, and his children looking like pug-dogs. I thought him gross & sensual. Little by little I became aware, first of the richness of his colouring, then of the boldness of his touch and the fertility of his imagination. I shall end by becoming a complete convert. Those of his pictures which I particularly looked at yesterday were in the middle room. The Allegory of Peace & War was painted for Charles 1st & is a large picture, more than nine feet wide & six feet high. Peace is a fat woman in a disagreeable attitude, then there is a black Minerva & a filthy Satyr, all the characteristic coarseness of Rubens, yet the painting seems to me admirable and some of the heads exquisite. There is a little girl with golden hair & large dark eyes from whom I could scarcely tear myself away. Miss Rogers was at the Gallery & I talked with her about Mr Windus. This man with his love of art & his fine collection of pictures, is a retired coachmaker, who having made a fortune, chuses to indulge his taste and spend his money in a way it is impossible not to admire. In what country except England are such things done by such people? There is at Cambridge Port, near Boston, a leather dresser named Douce, who plies his trade & buys books & pictures—But I know no other instance of the sort. I believe that here there is more than one Mr Windus.

Thomas Dowse [DOUCE] (1772–1856) was a tanner and leather dresser in Cambridgeport, Massachusetts. Dowse's book collecting began early in his life, and he slowly amassed an impressive library of English literature, travel accounts, history, and biography, including a 1787 edition of Jefferson's *Notes on the State of Virginia*. His library and art collection were well known within Boston's intellectual circles. In an 1831 lecture Congressman Edward Everett described Dowse's collection as "a treasure of taste and knowledge, not surpassed, if equaled, by anything of its kind in the country. . . . What is more important than having the books, their proprietor is well acquainted with their contents." Just months before his death, Dowse donated his 4,665-volume library to the Massachusetts Historical Society in Boston, though he was never a member. The Dowse Library was installed in the Society's Tremont Street headquarters in 1857 and moved to the Society's present Boylston Street location in 1899 (Louis Leonard Tucker, *Massachusetts Historical Society: A Bicentennial History, 1791–1991* [1995], 80–90; *Catalogue of the Private*

Library of Thomas Dowse, of Cambridge, Mass. [1870], esp. 102; Edward Everett, *Eulogy on Thomas Dowse, Cambridgeport, Boston* [1859]; "Thomas Dowse," *American Journal of Education* 3 [1857]: 284–288).

Saturday. 2ⁿᵈ March.

A soft, hazy day—the sun shining with a mild light. I drove to Regent's Park, got out of the carriage & walked from Gloucester Gate to the Zoological Gardens and back. The weather enchanting—early Spring with birds singing, the trees beginning to bud, and the turf which has been green through the winter, now of the freshest emerald. The time of our departure is close at hand and I feel more sad than I could have supposed possible at the thought of leaving England. It is a beautiful country & a glorious country. There is so much to admire that I can never lose the impression I have received during my eight months stay. How sorry I am to go away just as the Spring is coming on, the only season I have seen nothing of in England. I shall return to America without having heard the nightingale sing, or breathed the odour of the Cowslip & the Primrose, those flowers celebrated by so many poets, and by a favorite author of mine, Miss Mitford, in her charming prose pastorals. I have already seen the Snowdrop blooming in the open air & bouquets of fragrant violets are offered to me whenever I go out—the purple violet, "dim, but sweeter than the lids of Juno's eyes, or Cytherea's breath." There is another circumstance that redoubles my regret at going away just now. I am beginning to make acquaintance with persons, to see something of society, and as I am a stranger and belong to no particular set or circle, I have gained admittance to several, and can compare the different styles.

On thursday 28 Feb. we went to the Carlyles at Chelsea, where we found a dozen or fifteen persons assembled. As I wished to hear Mʳ Carlyle <u>talk</u> I was sorry to see so many people. But for this disappointment the evening wore agreeably away. Miss Martineau <u>crossed the room</u> to renew her acquaintance with me. She talked freely & frankly as if nothing had happened to interrupt our amicable relations, nor has there ever been any personal "refroidissement," and there is no reason why I should not be civil to her. She has acted a treacherous part by poor Dʳ Gannett & Miss Tuckerman, the daughter of an excellent father, but I cannot fight the battles of all my countrymen, so shall let these things pass. She talked of matters & things in general, domestic service, maids of all work, Dʳ Follen & his son Charley, the new poor law, Switzerland, Miss Sedgwick, but I do not remember that she introduced Shakespeare or the musical glasses. She does not like Miss Leslie's writings of which she knows but little, but when I said I thought the "Pencil Sketches" gave a good idea of what might be called vulgar high life in America she answered quickly "O if it is so you should not acknowledge it for your country's credit." It is true nevertheless that the pictures of Miss Leslie have all the homely fidelity of the dutch school. She does not give you the kitchen with it's pots & pans—but the parlours of boarding houses, the interiour of second-rate ^country^ lodgings; the dress & manners of rich & vulgar parvenus, and the small details of household miseries from which scarcely any rank is exempt, are very life-like under Miss Leslie's treatment. Her negro portraits, or rather sketches & silhouettes, are amusingly like the originals.

Among the company at Mr Carlyle's were Mrs Reeve the sister of Mrs Austen, & M^r & Miss Wilson. With Miss Wilson I formed a pleasant acquaintance. She talks well without pedantry or affectation, & with intelligence & information. We got upon the subject of pictures & I asked what strange perversion of public taste had ever brought West into favour or fashion. She answered quickly "Do us at least the justice to acknowledge that it is a fashion which has passed away."

To-day, Saturday, we have cards from M^r & Mrs Carlyle, & M^r & Miss Wilson.

———————————————————————————————

"dim, but sweeter . . . CYTHEREA'S BREATH," is from William Shakespeare's *The Winter's Tale*, act 4, scene 4.

Unitarian pastor Ezra Stiles GANNETT (1801–1871), the Boston colleague of Dr. William Ellery Channing, was one of the organizers of Harriet Martineau's trip to the United States. He hosted Martineau during a portion of her tumultuous visit to Boston, and it was in his home on 30 December 1835 that she first met the abolitionist William Lloyd Garrison, editor of the *Liberator*. Anti-abolitionist fervor was at its peak in the city that fall, and on 21 October 1835 Garrison was dragged through Boston's streets by an angry mob, narrowly escaping tar and feathers. Martineau, unaware of Garrison's plight, had remarked on the unusual crowd that day to a fellow traveler who "condescended to explain it by the pressure near the post-office on foreign post day!" The October meeting of the Boston Female Anti-Slavery Society, which had sparked the mob violence Martineau witnessed, was continued on 18 November 1835, and it was here amidst protesters pelting windows with mud that Martineau first publicly supported the American abolitionist movement. After her declaration of support Martineau was shunned socially and threatened bodily. Gannett suffered a nervous breakdown and left Boston in 1836 on doctor's orders to travel through Europe to restore his health. His trip began and ended in London, where his 1838 sermons produced "a great sensation in the

London pulpits," drawing crowds and the following of Lady Byron and Joanna Baillie. Gannett visited Martineau in London and found her "in her little parlor surrounded by her comforts, with her pile of American books in the corner. Her own book is half-written. She speaks of it as an easy and delightful employment, and says nothing has yet been written so favorable to the Americans as this work will be" (*DAB*; Martineau, *Autobiography*, 345–358; Wendell P. Garrison and Francis J. Garrison, *William Lloyd Garrison, 1805–1879* [1885], 2:69; William Channing Gannett, *Ezra Stiles Gannett, Unitarian Minister in Boston, 1824–1871: A Memoir* [1875], 173–177; Stephen Bloore, "Miss Martineau Speaks Out," *New England Quarterly* 9 [1936]: 414; Deborah Logan, ed., *The Collected Letters of Harriet Martineau* [2007], 1:208–210).

Jane TUCKERMAN was the daughter of Boston merchant Gustavus Tuckerman (1785–1860). She came to see Martineau at the home of her Boston host, James Walker, in early December 1835, the morning that news of Martineau's attendance at the Anti-Slavery Society was published in local papers. Walker had attempted to shield Martineau from the provocative reports by burning the morning's paper. Martineau recalled in her autobiography that Tuckerman was "evidently full of something that she was eager to say. With a solemn countenance of condolence she presently told me that she had never seen Dr. Channing so full of concern as on that day, on the appearance of a most painful article in the 'Daily Advertiser;' and she proceeded to magnify the misfortune in a way which astonished me." Channing's apparent response was echoed throughout Boston, where those who had attended the meeting feared for Martineau's well-being and their own. Thomas Carlyle, who met Tuckerman in 1840, wrote of her to Emerson: "we did not know what to make of the bright Miss Tuckerman here; she fell in love with my Wife,—the *contrary*, I doubt, with me: my hard realism jarred upon her beautiful rosepink dreams" (Martineau, *Autobiography*, 351–352; Bloore, "Miss Martineau Speaks Out," 408–416; Thomas Carlyle to Ralph Waldo Emerson, 2 July 1840, in *Carlyle Letters*, 12:182–186).

Eliza LESLIE (1787–1858), sister of artist Charles Robert Leslie, was the Philadelphia-born author of *Pencil Sketches: or, Outlines of Character and Manners* (1833–1837). Leslie's stories satirized pretension and were filled with the dialect and mannerisms of sharp-witted heroines, sensible men, and their servants (*ANB*; *DAB*).

Susan Taylor REEVE (1788–1853) was the sister of author Sarah Austin and widow of physician Henry Reeve (1780–1814). Their only surviving child, Henry (1813–1895), translated his friend Alexis de Tocqueville's *De la démocratie en Amérique* (1835) into English and became editor of the *Edinburgh Review* (*ODNB*, s.v. "Reeve, Henry").

Thomas WILSON (d. 1872) and his sister Jane Wilson (1790–1890) had known the Carlyles since 1835. Thomas Carlyle considered them "'quality people'. . . of good endowment every way" (Thomas Carlyle to John Carlyle, 15 June 1835, in *Carlyle Letters*, 8:151).

Benjamin **WEST** (1738–1820), the American-born painter, was a mentor for artists such as John Trumbull, Gilbert Stuart, and Mather Brown. Coolidge had first-
hand knowledge of West's paintings. After Jefferson's death she held back from
public sale in Boston a watercolor drawing by West that had hung at Monticello,
The Fright of Astyanax, for fear that it would be "sacrificed" at auction as had other
pieces from his collection (Stein, *Worlds,* 150; Coolidge to Martha Jefferson Randolph, 21 July 1833 [ViU: Ellen Wayles Randolph Coolidge Correspondence]).

Sunday. 3ᵈ March.

An invitation to dine with the Miss Berrys on tuesday just brought in—
But I am only as far as thursday 27ᵗʰ, at Mʳ Carlyle's. Friday I made some
calls on Mʳˢ Wormeley & others & brought Mʳ Coolidge home from Bishopsgate St. I never go into the City, as I have said before, without thinking of an Ant Hill as it might be seen through a powerful microscope.
The coming & going, the running hither & thither, the haste, the press,
the eager pursuit of some unseen object must be about the same, & the
people seem busy, quick, active & eager as the insects. There is too much
life & motion to look like the result of reason, the promptings of instinct
seem more competent to produce such an effect. On our way home we
called at Edwards' & saw some of his matchless dressing cases. One for the
small price of 300 guineas was a chef-d'ouevre.

Friday evening we had two engagements, for the Miss Berrys & Mʳˢ
Grote. I had heard much of the Miss Berrys, belles of the last Century,
venerable remains of the days of Horace Walpole, who lead hospitable
& pleasant lives, receiving their friends cheerily, and seeing the best company of the nineteenth as they had done of the eighteenth century. I was
certainly greatly surprised when upon being presented to them, instead
of figures from the Pyramids, antiquities from the British Museum, two
fine fresh-looking women, richly & tastefully dressed in the best modern
fashion, answered to the name of Berry pronounced by Mʳˢ Stevenson.
One of them, the elder sister, may be called decidedly handsome, and
both are high-bred & singularly courteous in manner. I have heard that
the handsome sister received an offer from Horace Walpole, and might
now, had she so pleased, have been Countess of Orford & mistress of all
the Bric-a-brac at Strawberry Hill. She was a young girl at the time and he
an old man, but he has been dead upwards of forty years, and we are not
told how long before his death the gallant old gentleman made his proposals. Miss Berry is certainly an extraordinary person, fair, gay, graceful &
"distinguée," a lovely woman who saw Horace Walpole sighing at her feet,
as she now sees paying respectful homage to her attractions, Luttrell the

modern wit, Prince Czartorisky once King elect of Poland, and Mountstuart Elphinstone, the wisest of Brahmins, the most pure-hearted & right-minded of men. These three gentlemen & some others had been dining with the Miss Berrys the evening that we were there. As dress is always a matter of importance with women I paid particular attention to theirs. Dark velvet, long sleeves, & their necks entirely covered, caps without flowers or feathers, short full curls, and no ornaments but a rich bracelet on one arm, and a delicate one on the other, (according to the prevailing fashion,) and waist buckles of gold. Two finer specimens of what amiable old women may be in this happy land where female beauty belongs to that family of flowers called "immortelles," could no where be found. — If during the early part of my stay in England, I was disappointed in the beauty of the women, it was because I looked for it too much among the young. Now the daughters seem to me less lovely than the mothers, and even grandmothers sometimes bear away the palm. Elsewhere you often hear it said of a fair young girl that she is not so handsome as her mother was at her age. Here you may say she is not so handsome as her mother is now, but perhaps she may become so if she lives to be as old. Happy land where a woman's person improves with her mind, so that at a certain age, she combines the hightest attractions of both, and is at the zenith of her intelligence and of her beauty at one & the same moment! In America women have beauty in their youth and cultivated understandings when beauty & youth are in the wane. At sixteen you must pardon their insipidity in favor of their good looks, and at thirty you must accept their good sense & their good manners as a compensation for faces somewhat faded, and figures that have lost their graceful outlines.

We spent a very pleasant evening, I becoming more & more fascinated with Miss Berry & ceasing to wonder at the odd fashion which once prevailed ^(& perhaps still prevails)^ in England of young men falling in love with old women. George 4th was a man of taste. "Fat, fair & forty" presents no pleasant image to an American imagination, but a fair, fresh & plump English woman of forty, with her fine person & fine manners, is certainly a very attractive creature. Miss Berry must be seventy, at least. — Several persons came in during the evening, some in full dress, on their way to a party given by Lady Antrobus at which the Duke of Cambridge was to be present. "I hope he may not be drunk to night," said one. "He was very much so at the last party," added another. Mr Sumner has since told me that he had seen this uncle of the Queen's so much intoxicated after a dinner party, as to walk sidewise. Among the persons who called on their way to Lady Antrobus was Lady Charlotte Lindsay, whose appearance was hailed almost with a scream by her familiar friends on account of her unusual magnificence. She wore a white-watered silk with a quantity of blonde lace about the neck & throat, and a white hat with two long curling ostrich feathers. Being short & short-necked, she seemed muffled up in her finery, but she bore the bantering of her friends with perfect good humour, and made herself, as she always does, eminently agreeable. One lady in a velvet dress & with a diamond feronnière, was introduced to me as Lady Hislop. She is, I believe, a relation of Lord Minto. We went late to Mrs Grote's, found her suffering with headache & soon came away—

This morning the papers allude to a disagreement between the Queen & her mother, the Duchess of Kent. There is, no doubt, a great deal of "tracasserie" at the Palace, & there are many scandalous stories afloat about maids of honour. One lady in the service of the Duchess of Kent, Lady Flora Hastings, whose reputation had been assailed, it seems unjustly, wrote to her brother to claim his protection. His courage & decision is said to have restored his sister to the confidence of the Queen. On receiving her letter he hastened to London, sought an interview with Lord Melbourne and requested through him, an interview with Her Majesty. The old gallant tried to turn the matter into pleasantry, as if the reputation of a woman was a thing to be pleasant about. He represented that it would be an awkward subject to discuss with the young Queen &c &c. Lord Hastings was not to be put off by ill-timed "badinage" or weak reasonings, and demanded, as a right, an interview with his Sovereign which resulted "on dit" in the exculpation of Lady Flora. This is one side of the story. How many more it may have there is no saying. Many persons are mixed up in the disgraceful tale. Lady Tavistock, the Queen's physician, Sir James Clarke, and others.——There are many rumours afloat concerning the Queen's manners to her attendants which are said to be harsh & imperious. Miss Spring Rice has been ordered to her chamber for some small offence, and a friend who undertook to excuse her, was sent off to share her disgrace. It is difficult to know what to believe, but it is better perhaps, that the Queen should err, if she must err, on the side of too much decision than too little. Weakness is always miserable but especially so in a sovereign, even in a constitutional sovereign who, having little power to do good, may always do harm. "Point de faiblesse," the motto on Mrs Carlyle's seal would do well for Royalty. It is so much easier to curb an impatient spirit than to excite a sluggish or strengthen a weak one, that I had rather the young Victoria boxed her courtier's ears like Queen Elizabeth, than allowed them to take advantage of her indolent good-nature. The most serious charge brought against the Queen is of want of respect

LADY FLORA HASTINGS (1806–1839) had been brought into the Duchess of Kent's service in 1834 as a lady of the bedchamber with the intent of providing companionship for Princess Victoria and lessening the influence of Baroness Lehzen. Over time Victoria viewed Lady Hastings as an "amazing *spy*" and thought it "very disagreeable having her in the house." Hastings became allied with John Conroy (1786–1854), the duchess's comptroller and Victoria's avowed enemy. Conroy and the duchess had managed Victoria's youth through their Kensington System, a strict set of rules guiding the princess's education and upbringing designed to isolate her from her royal family and render her dependent on Conroy. The queen despised Conroy for his attempts to control her and his domination of her mother's household.

In January 1839, after celebrating the Christmas holidays in Scotland, Lady Hastings shared a carriage ride to London with her friend Conroy. Shortly after arriving at Buckingham Palace, Hastings complained of abdominal pain and swelling and consulted the Scottish royal physician, James Clark [CLARKE] (1788–1870), who suspected that Hastings was pregnant. Queen Victoria, apprised of the events, speculated in her diary that Lady Flora was "*with child!!*" and that the father was Conroy, "the Monster and demon Incarnate." The Duchess of Kent held firm in her belief in Hastings's innocence and released Clark as her physician; on behalf of the queen's household, Lady Tavistock demanded action from Lord Melbourne. What had been a private matter became the first public scandal of Queen Victoria's reign.

On 2 March 1839 Charles Greville, then clerk of the Privy Council, observed in his journal that "the whole town has been engrossed for some days with a scandalous story at Court. . . . [T]he whole proceeding is looked upon by society at large as to the last degree disgusting and disgraceful." The *Times* defended the queen; the *Morning Post* condemned her. Meanwhile Hastings submitted to a medical examination that established her virginity and continued to appear in public to dispel rumors of her pregnancy, but by June 1839 she was confined to her bed. There Victoria visited her on 26 June and found her "as thin as anybody can be who is still alive." Nine days later Hastings died and her postmortem revealed that she had been suffering from a liver tumor for several months.

Flora Hastings haunted Queen Victoria's dreams and brought about political upheaval in what came to be known as the Bedchamber Crisis. Tories seized upon the episode as an opportunity to question the queen's advisors, and the Hastings family published correspondence that showed the queen, her ladies, and Melbourne in an unfavorable light. Following Melbourne's resignation in May 1839, the queen refused to part with the Whig ladies of the bedchamber, as the incoming Robert Peel requested. The ensuing stalemate between the queen and Peel prevented him from forming a ministry and resulted in Melbourne's return to office (*ODNB*; Charles C. F. Greville, *The Greville Memoirs (Second Part): A Journal of the Reign of Queen Victoria, from 1837 to 1852*, ed. Henry Reeve [1885], 1:149, 150; Christopher Hibbert, *Queen Victoria: A Personal History* [2000], 76–84; Monica Charlot, *Victoria: The Young Queen* [1991], 129–147; Cecil Woodham-Smith, *Queen Victoria: Her Life and Times* [1972], 1:162–169; Elizabeth Longford, *Queen Victoria:*

Born to Succeed [1964], 446; R. F. Spall, "The Bedchamber Crisis and the Hastings Scandal: Morals, Politics, and the Press at the Beginning of Victoria's Reign," *Canadian Journal of History* 22 [1987]: 19–39; *Morning Post* [London], 5, 25 Mar. 1839).

Flora Hastings's **BROTHER** was George Augustus Francis Rawdon Hastings, second Marquess of Hastings (1808–1844) (*ODNB*, s.v. "Hastings, Barbara Rawdon" and "Hastings, Flora").

Mary Alicia Perry **SPRING RICE** (1812–1875), the eldest daughter of Thomas Spring Rice, served as Princess Victoria's maid of honor (Brett, *Girlhood of Queen Victoria*, 1:211–212; Sidney Lee, *Queen Victoria: A Biography* [1904], 63).

POINT DE FAIBLESSE, "no weakness," was the motto on Jane Carlyle's signet ring (Martineau, *Autobiography*, 292; Jane Carlyle to John Sterling, 30 Sept. 1837, in *Carlyle Letters*, 9:323).

Monday 4th March.

A great day every four years in America—here this year at least, a bright one, the Sun shining & blue sky visible—I am going again to Tottenham Green & shall call for Miss Rogers to go with me.

More talk about the Queen & her Court. Another version of the story of Lady Flora Hastings, who is now said not to have sent for her brother until after she had succeeded in justifying herself. Lord Hastings insisted on an interview with the Queen that he might, if possible, induce her to dismiss two of her ladies whom he accused of slandering his sister. In this form of the story Lord Hastings is hot-headed & obstinate, Lord Melbourne wise & judicious. "You may" said he to the angry brother, "insist, as a peer, on an interview with the Queen, but you cannot compel her Majesty to open her mouth in reply, or to comply with your demands." It is evident that the little sovereign is not considered as wanting in pluck. The Duchess of Kent is said to have written to the Duke of Wellington, (the brave & loyal old Tory!) on the subject of her own relations with the Queen her daughter, and that the Duke wrote in reply "in times like these Royalty cannot be too cautious."—The whole medley of small talk & court scandal, coming to my ears in various ways, brings to my mind the polite conversation of Lady Blarney. "Sir Tomkinson drawing his sword" &c &c.

But under all this upper froth is there not something brewing which may have fearful mischief in it? I am told that the disorganizing principle is deeply at work in England—that the fiends of revolution are abroad, as yet walking in disguise but biding their time—that all this idle talk & these stories about the Queen & her attendants, her ministers & her ladies,

are symptoms of growing disaffection & disloyalty, of increasing disrespect for the Government & for the privileged classes. And yet it seams to
me that whilst the great agricultural interest goes with the Crown and the
British Constitution, whilst the army, the navy, the clergy, the aristocracy,
the gentry, almost all the men of property & education the merchants the
tradespeople, the servants, a numerous band, the small shopkeepers &
more classes of society than I can enumerate are attached to the existing
order of things & loyal to their sovereign, there can be no danger of revolution. The Pyramid of law & order will stand too firmly on it's base to
heed the assaults made upon it's sides. Cabinet Ministers may be foolish
& perverse—Court ladies may squabble & calumnate each other, a great
deal of nonsense may be talked, many silly things done, and many serious
evils cry aloud for reform, which they will ultimately though gradually
obtain, yet the fabric of the Constitution will endure in spite of all. Surely
demagogues, radicals & agitaters, cotton spinners and manufacturers of
Birmingham, Leeds & Manchester, malcontents & disorganizers cannot
be more than a match for the Kingdom of Great Britain!——

EVERY FOUR YEARS America inaugurated its incoming president on 4 March
until the event was moved to its present 20 January date by the Twentieth Amend-
ment in 1933. Jefferson's 1801 inauguration was the first to take place in the new
capital of Washington, D.C. Four years later Jefferson paused amid "the pressure
of the day" of his second inauguration to write to Coolidge, enclosing poems
for her scrapbook with his letter. After her grandfather's death Coolidge found
"among some of his old papers" an engraving of the text of his first inaugural
address, which she gave to her grandson Thomas Jefferson Coolidge (1863–1912)
on the occasion of his birthday during the centennial year of 1876 (Akhil Amar,
America's Constitution: A Biography [2005], 428–430; Malone, *Jefferson and His
Time*, 5:17–20; Coolidge to Thomas Jefferson Coolidge, 16 Mar. 1876, and engraving [private collection, Mass.]; Jefferson to Coolidge, 4 Mar. 1805, in *Family Letters*,
ed. Betts and Bear, 268–269; Jefferson, First Inaugural Address, 4 Mar. 1801, in *PTJ*,
33:134–152).

LADY BLARNEY and Sir Tomkyn were characters in Oliver Goldsmith's *The Vicar
of Wakefield* (1766).

Tuesday 5. March.

Cold, dark, gloomy, thermometer down at 34°. I have just come from seeing Sir John Soane's Museum. 13 Lincoln's Inn Fields. It is very rich in
quantity & some of the articles are curious & valuable. The house itself
is intricate & endless in it's divisions. It has as many cells as a piece of

honeycomb, & some of them not a great deal larger than those made by the Bees. There are a few rooms of good size & the rest are closets & passage ways, going in & out & up & down in labyrinthian confusion. We entered first the Library consisting of two rooms with painted ceilings. In the back room were two large pictures opposite each other. One by Sir Joshua Reynolds, called "The Snake in the Grass," represents Love untying the girdle of Beauty, a very modest picture in spite of name & subject, a little faded as Sir Joshua's pictures are wont to be. The other by Sir Thomas Lawrence is the likeness of Sir John Soane himself. In the front room was a large Library table. Upon this table Mr Baillie, the Curator, whom we found a very pleasant & polite person, spread open for our inspection, several rare & curious books which he took from the shelves.

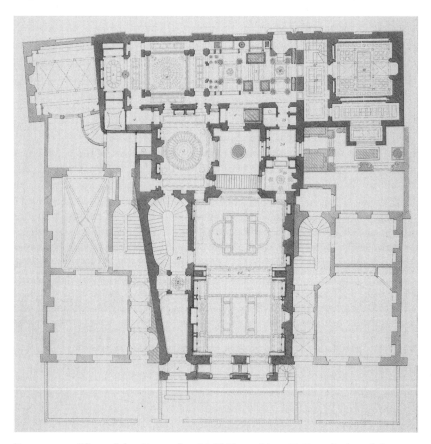

Figure 11. Plan of the Ground or Hall Floor, Plate II, *Description of the House and Museum . . . of Sir John Soane*, 1835. *(Courtesy of Special Collections, University of Virginia Library.)*

The first edition of Shakespeare's "Comedies, Histories & Tragedies," in folio, two columns on a page. A very large folio edition of Josephus, black letter on parchment, with gorgeous illuminations such as were in fashion 300 years ago. The last & large edition of Palladio in grand folio, & several other such like literary curiosities. Here in this Library, were some Etruscan Vases, one of great size called the Cawdor Vase, from having once belonged to the Earl of Cawdor. A Roman Ewer shaped somewhat like a Duck, reminded me of a silver vase now in our possession the model of which my grandfather found at Nismes. A Chopine or measure of white earthen ware, with the date of 1593, had a portrait of Queen Elizabeth in relief upon one of it's sides. The awkward shape, that of a common pint pot, the coarse material & the overdone ornament of raised work, shewed the state of the arts at that time. A half civilized people will be deficient in taste & skill and fond of shew.

From the Library we passed through a maze of small rooms. Among other things I noted a head of John Kemble, fine, but the lower part of the face rather heavy for beauty. But what chiefly arrested my attention was a cast from a monument, the original of which is to be seen at Ashbourne in Derbyshire, & was executed by Banks. I had heard of this most touching & tender tribute offered to the memory of an only & darling child, by Sir Brooke & Lady Boothby, and been told indeed that Chauntrey had borrowed from this work the idea of his celebrated monument to two children in the Cathedral of Litchfield. Nothing can be more beautiful than it is even in a plaster cast. A little girl of six years old lies in an easy, graceful & perfectly natural attitude on a mattress, her head supported by a pillow. This charming head, with the full eye over which the lid gently closes, ready to open at the first sound of a well-known voice, lips slightly parted, the cheeks full & rounded, tell of the beautiful life not death. "The child is not dead but sleepeth." That light sleep too so easily chased away! What agony to a parent's heart to look & feel that it is a sleep which, in this world, knows no waking!

On the original monument is the following inscription.

> To Penelope, Only child of Sir Brooke and Dame Susanna Boothby.
> Born April 11. 1785. Died March 13. 1791.
>> She was in form and intellect most exquisite.
>> The unfortunate Parents ventured their all
>> On this frail bark, and the wreck was total.

In this Museum are many original pictures by Hogarth once I believe, the property of Garrick. One series is called the Election, another the Rake's Progress. The more I see of Hogarth's works the more convinced

I am that Lamb in his "Essay on the Genius of Hogarth," has done him no more than justice. In looking at the Rake's Progress I was particularly struck with the great truth of what Lamb says that it is altogether a mistake to class Hogarth among comic painters. There is a tale of folly, vice & misery told in this series of pictures, which belongs to deep tragedy, though not the tragedy of Kings & Queens & Heroes in gorgeous trappings & flowing robes, with bowls & daggers, blocks & axes, but of common life which has more of reality in it than the sceptred & sworded miseries of the throne, the castle or the camp. I was also reminded of what Lamb says of the beauty by which Hogarth always softens his worst scenes—sometimes merely physical, at others moral, & then again both. In this Rake's Progress, for example, there is great moral beauty in the principal female character. You see her in the first picture, betrayed, abandoned, consigned to ruin and shame. Her seducer, a foolish, vain, not originally wicked young man, who, just come into a great inheritance by the death of a miserly father, & surrounded by fawners & flatterers, tries to make her amends by an offer of that gold which he finds so powerful in it's effects upon himself & others. He wishes to buy off her sense of misery & disgrace, and pay in pounds, shillings & pence, for the tears he is causing her to shed.—In the second picture where he is in a company of greedy harpies preying upon him, she does not appear—nor in the third where he is sinking, drunk, upon the bosom of a prostitute. But in the fourth where fortune begins to frown & he to feel the effects of his own follies, where he is seized by bailiffs, she, the true-hearted, is again at his side. In the fifth where he marries a rich hag to replenish his coffers with her spoils, she is again absent, and in the sixth, where we find him at the gaming table, she is still away. But in the 7th where he is in jail, and in the 8th where he is in the Madhouse, she is present heart-stricken at his misery, and trying to soothe his madness. It is very long since I read Lamb's Essay, and I forget whether this beautiful tribute to the truth and tenderness of a woman's heart is pointed out by him and merely revived in my own recollection by the sight of the pictures, or whether it exists so forcibly in the painted Drama as to be visible at once to every eye.

There are several pictures by Calcott, an oil painting of Turner's, a drawing of Canaletti's on which I looked with pleasure, also models in cork of the temples of Pæstum & the town of Pompeii; and others, very beautful, in plaster, of many ancient buildings and especially of the Portico of Diocletian. There were ancient Vases of marble with figures in bas relief, casts from antiques &c &, but perhaps, among these things, what I looked at with most interest was an Egyptian Sarcophagus of Alabaster, covered with hyeroglyphics, the one found by Belzoni in the tomb which he discovered, brought to England by him & offered for sale to the British Museum. The Institution happened at the moment to be afflicted with a fit of economy and declined the purchase, which was made by Sir John Soane for the sum of two thousand pounds sterling. This Sarcophagus is translucent and a lamp placed within it shines through the sides with a dull red light. It is probably between 3000 & 4000 years old and inclines to an oval or coffin shape. There is a figure engraved on the bottom with the hands & arms pinioned to the sides in the Egyptian fashion, & the eye in full on a profile face, which is likewise characteristic of the Egyptian style.

Architect JOHN SOANE's (1753–1837) eclectic collection of architectural drawings, models, building fragments, paintings, sculpture, books, and antiquities was intended first to instruct his sons and later his students at the Royal Academy. His collections were displayed in three adjoining houses at 12, 13, and 14 Lincoln's Inn Fields, remodeled to create a "succession of those fanciful effects which constitute the poetry of architecture." Soane's museum demonstrated his belief in the "union and close connexion between Painting, Sculpture, and Architecture, —Music and Poetry." So that his arrangement of the collection would be preserved, Soane authored the catalogue *Description of the House and Museum on the North Side of Lincoln's Inn Fields* (1835) and negotiated an act of Parliament enabling his house and office to become England's first architectural museum (fig. 11) (*ODNB*; Susan Feinberg Millenson, *Sir John Soane's Museum* [1987]).

George Bailey [BAILLIE] (1792–1860), Soane's former architecture student and assistant, became the museum's first curator following Soane's death in 1837, a position he held until his death. That year's *Architectural Magazine* deemed the curator's position "one of the most honorable and important situations in the profession" (Millenson, *Soane's Museum*, 149; Howard Colvin, *Biographical Dictionary of British Architects, 1600–1840* [2008]).

The first folio of SHAKESPEARE's *Comedies, Histories, & Tragedies* (1623) was Soane's greatest literary treasure (Eileen Harris and Nicholas Savage, *Hooked on Books: The Library of Sir John Soane Architect, 1753–1837* [2004], 8, 29).

Flavius JOSEPHUS (ca. 37–100 A.D.) was the Jewish priest and historian who became a Roman citizen. His writings documented Jewish history, including the 70 A.D. fall of Jerusalem. The book in Soane's collection is the second volume of a ca. 1480 French translation of Josephus's works, which contained the latter part of his *Antiquities* and *De Bello Judaico* and was illuminated by a Flemish artist (Sir John Soane's Museum Concise Catalogue of Drawings, p. 84, entry for vol. 135, accessed 8 July 2011, http://www.soane.org.uk/concise_catalogue/).

The DUCK was a silver askos used at Monticello as a chocolate pot (fig. 34). It was made in 1801 by the Philadelphia silversmiths Anthony Simmons and Samuel Alexander based on a wooden model Jefferson commissioned in 1787 from a Roman ewer excavated at Nîmes, France. Jefferson intended, though never gave, a model of the askos as a gift for the French architect Charles-Louis Clérisseau in appreciation of his assistance in preparing drawings and a model of the Maison Carrée for Jefferson's design of the Virginia State Capitol. Martha Jefferson Randolph inherited the askos and bequeathed it to Joseph Coolidge; both the askos and its model, which Jefferson gave to the artist Thomas Sully, are in the Thomas Jefferson Foundation's collection (*MB*, 2:1046; Stein, *Worlds*, 328–329; *PTJ*, 15:xxx-xxxii, 172–173; Joseph Coolidge to Nicholas P. Trist, 5 Jan. 1827 [DLC: Nicholas Philip Trist Papers]; TJF Accession 1957–29 and 1974–20).

Sculptor Thomas BANKS (1735–1805) immortalized Penelope Boothby (1785–1791) in his most famous work, a 1793 marble monument that has been called "perhaps the first truly Romantic work by an English sculptor." Banks's daughter presented the plaster model of this work to John Soane in 1830. Coolidge's reaction to the model was no doubt influenced by her own loss of a daughter, Elizabeth Bulfinch Coolidge (1827–1832), who died of scarlet fever. Joseph Coolidge informed his brother-in-law on the day of her death, "My little Bessie is dead! . . . Ellen is almost broken hearted, and so is Yrs. J. C jr" (Peter Thornton and Helen Dorey, *A Miscellany of Objects from Sir John Soane's Museum* [1992], 61; Shackelford, *Descendants*, 2:120; Whinney, *Sculpture in Britain*, 328–329; Joseph Coolidge to Nicholas P. Trist, 9 June 1832 [NcU: Southern Historical Collection, Nicholas Philip Trist Papers]; Joseph Coolidge to Martha Jefferson Randolph, 11 June 1832 [ViU: Ellen Wayles Randolph Coolidge Correspondence]).

THE CHILD IS NOT DEAD BUT SLEEPETH is from the Bible, Mark 5:39.

Charles Lamb's ESSAY "On the Genius and Character of Hogarth" was published in the *Reflector* in 1811.

The alabaster SARCOPHAGUS of the Egyptian pharaoh Seti I (ca. 1300 B.C.), excavated in 1817 by the Italian Giovanni Belzoni, was the focal point of Soane's museum. Belzoni described it as "not having its equal in the world, and being such as we had no idea could exist. It is a sarcophagus of the finest oriental alabaster, nine feet five inches long, and three feet seven inches wide. Its thickness is only two inches; and it is transparent, when a light is placed inside of it. It is minutely sculptured within and without with several hundred figures, which do not exceed two inches in height, and represent, as I suppose, the whole of the funeral procession and ceremonies relating to the deceased. . . . [N]othing has been brought into Europe from Egypt that can be compared with it." Its legendary acquisition was cause for a three-night, illuminated celebration in March 1825 (Thornton and Dorey, *Miscellany of Objects*, 59; Giovanni Belzoni, *Narrative of the Operations and Recent Discoveries within the Pyramids, Temples, Tombs, and Excavations of Egypt and Nubia* [1820], ix, 236).

Wednesday. 6. March.

A day of snow, a regular storm. I have been out however & left cards for Mme Van de Weyer. We dined with the Stewarts in Portman Square—I go back to the Museum of Sir John Soane to say that it is in Lincoln's Inn fields, where Lord Russell was executed. We are just reading a life of Lady Russell by Miss Berry at whose house we dined the day of our visit to the Museum. The party, besides the Miss Berrys, consisted of Lady Charlotte Lindsay, Lady Hyslop, Mr Taylor (Philip Von Artevelde) Mr Lewis, Mr Foley Wilmot formerly in America, & some others. The conversation at table was animated & distinguished by that <u>tone of good society</u> which is in itself a charm. The one who said the least was Mr Taylor. He sat either lost in meditation on his own perfections, or chewing the cud of sweet & bitter fancy over the memory of his unfortunate loves. I had heard a story of his being jilted by a Miss Spring Rice, daughter of the Chancellor of the Exchequer. Not the homely one who waits upon the Queen and is "on dit" occasionally snubbed by her Royal mistress, but a younger & prettier sister. The <u>dinner talk</u> turned upon different subjects, all touched lightly & never discussed. Discussion is never more out of place than at a dinner party of gentlemen & ladies. It is not so easy however for me to record what the rest of the company said as what Mr Taylor did not say. I might as well, like the projector in Laputa, undertake to bottle sunbeams from cucumbers, as try to preserve the spirit of such conversation as I heard at Miss Berry's, especially as there was present no professed wit whose good sayings were prepared to be repeated. We had, on leaving the drawing for the dining room, no marshalling of the guests according to strict forms of etiquette as is usual in England. I fancy the Miss Berrys have lived too much on the Continent of Europe, & in France especially, to pay much attention to these English observances. On this occasion Miss Berry having given her arm to Mr Coolidge, & desired some gentleman, I forget who, to take Lady Charlotte Lindsay, whose age, independent of her rank, entitled her to this distinction, left Lady Hyslop & myself to accept the arms that were offered to us and sit just where we pleased at table. After dinner other company dropped in, but I must not forget that, when the ladies retired from the dining room, we had still another version of the story of Lady Flora Hastings and more "scandal about Queen Elizabeth," who is said to quarrel with her mother and treat her ladies in a very imperious manner. The last edition of Lady Flora's story, a very sad one, shews her conduct under trying circumstances to have been wise & good-tempered. She neither raged nor fainted when she heard the scandalous reports that had got abroad to the blighting of her good name. She shewed no weakness, no violence, but went calmly to work, adopted the best means for refuting the slander, & has, I hope, completely succeeded in doing so. Sir James Clarke, the Queen's ignorant physician, seems to be the individual upon whom shame should rest. Want of skill in his profession & indelicacy in his conduct are the least charges that can be brought against him. He is already dismissed from attendance on the Duchess of Kent, and why he should still be retained in the Queen's service is rather unaccountable. I do not like the looks of this Sir James Clarke whom I met at Mme Van der Weyer's wedding. He has a long-eared Spaniel countenance which is much against him. Among the guests who came in to Miss Berry's in the evening, were the Polish Prince Czartorisky, and the clerical wit, Sidney Smith. A little party collected round the tea-table in one corner of the drawing room, where a gay, sparkling sort of tea-table talk was carried on with much spirit — Sidney Smith, Lady Charlotte Lindsay & Lady Hyslop giving & taking many good-natured raps, & Miss Berry contributing her full share to the animation of the scene. I listened with great pleasure & amusement, although want of familiarity with the subjects of conversation generally prevented me from joining in it, though whenever I ventured a remark it was well received. This sort of conversation requires the "sleight of hand" which practice gives, besides natural readiness and acquaintance with the topics of the day.

The Miss Berrys, like a good many other clever single women in England lead most pleasant & rational lives; in their case however, I should think rather more french than English. They collect around them a distinguished society, men & women of rank and literature, without parade, or gêne of any kind except so far as the laws of good breeding require. About the commencement of the season properly so called, when night is turned into day, horses driven to death, and the madness of Crockford's & Almack's, of balls beginning at midnight, & breakfasts at six in the afternoon have succeeded to rational society & moderate amusement, these two sisters retire into the country and pass the season of long, bright days, of rural beauty & country pleasures where only they can be found or enjoyed. Thus they wisely distribute their amusements throughout the year and take advantage of the good things of life each in it's own season.

Miss Berry edited the works of Mme du Deffand, (the great friend of Horace Walpole to whom her best letters are addressed,) and is likewise an authoress in her own right. She has written a comparative view of

"Society in England & France" and the life of Lady Russell which I am trying to read in the midst of my now very numerous engagements.

This was Coolidge's first social call to Elizabeth Bates VAN DE WEYER since the latter's 12 February 1839 wedding to the Belgian ambassador.

William Russell (1639–1683), LORD RUSSELL, son of William Russell, first Duke of Bedford (1616–1700), and Anne Carr (1615–1684), was an ally of Whig leader Anthony Ashley Cooper, first Earl of Shaftesbury. Russell's political and personal life were characterized by his recklessness, and he feared Charles II's government favored France, Catholicism, and absolute power. In response to the Popish Plot, in which Catholics were allegedly conspiring to assassinate Charles II and elevate his Catholic brother James, the Duke of York, to the throne, Russell and Shaftesbury sought to prevent James's succession through a series of exclusion bills. Following the failure of these measures, Russell became a visible friend of radical Whigs, engaged in secret meetings, and was arrested and sent to the Tower on charges of conspiring to kill the king in a scheme known as the Rye House Plot.

After a trial on 13 July 1683 Russell was declared guilty of high treason. He was sentenced to death the following day and for the next week kept a journal at the request of his wife, Rachel Russell (ca. 1637–1723), who helped him write out copies of his scaffold speech. Refusing the blindfold, Russell was beheaded in Lincoln's Inn Fields on 21 July, and onlookers dipped their handkerchiefs in his blood. In his speech, which was immediately and widely distributed, Russell declared his innocence and allegiance to true English liberties and religion. His martyr status was sealed with the success of the 1688 revolution, and during King William III and Queen Mary II's reign Lady Russell enjoyed a renewed social and political position as the "grande dame" of the Whigs. Over the centuries, biographical sketches such as Mary Berry's *Some Account of the Life of Rachael Wriothesley Lady Russell* (1819) inspired admiration for Lady Russell's piety, devotion to her husband, and strength in the face of tragedy (*ODNB*, s.v. "Russell, Rachel," "Russell, William," "Rye House plotters").

This was George Cornewall LEWIS (1806–1863), later editor of the *Edinburgh Review*, whose wife, Theresa Lewis, edited Mary Berry's journals and correspondence (*ODNB*).

Charles FOLEY WILMOT (ca. 1799–1852) accompanied Stratford Canning to Washington, D.C., in 1820, serving as secretary during Canning's three-year appointment as minister plenipotentiary from Great Britain (*ODNB*, s.v. "Canning, Stratford"; *Gentleman's Magazine*, n.s., 37 [1852]: 532; *New York Mercantile Advertiser*, 26 Sept. 1820; *Daily National Intelligencer* [Washington, D.C.], 27 June 1823).

Theodosia SPRING RICE (1817–1891) and Henry Taylor broke their engagement on account of Taylor's alleged religious unorthodoxy, but the two eventually married on 17 October 1839 (Edmund Lodge, *Peerage and Baronetage* [1877], 422; *Victorian Poets before 1850*, s.v. "Taylor, Henry," by Lawrence Poston, Dictionary of

Literary Biography, vol. 32 [1984], Gale Literary Databases, accessed 20 Dec. 2010, http://go.galegroup.com/)

Among the inane scientific experiments Lemuel Gulliver observed on the island of Laputa was the attempt to extract SUNBEAMS FROM CUCUMBERS, which had been ongoing for eight years (Jonathan Swift, *Gulliver's Travels into several Remote Nations of the World* [London, 1834], 205).

Mary BERRY edited the selected correspondence of Marie de Vichy Chamrond, marquise du Deffand (1697–1780), which included letters to Voltaire and many of the most important figures of the French Enlightenment. Du Deffand offered news of politics, court gossip, and literature to correspondents in France and abroad, where her witty letters were often read aloud at social gatherings and copied to be shared with others. Mary Berry's 1810 edition of the letters caused a sensation, and Napoléon Bonaparte carried the four volumes on his Russian campaign. Berry's edition contains only a portion of the eight hundred letters du Deffand wrote to the English novelist Horace Walpole, a figure with whom she became obsessed in the last fifteen years of her life (*ODNB*; Samia I. Spencer, ed., *Writers of the French Enlightenment I*, s.v. "Du Deffand, Marie," Dictionary of Literary Biography, vol. 313 [2005], Gale Literary Databases, accessed 20 Dec. 2010, http://go.galegroup.com; Mary Berry, *Letters of the Marquise du Deffand to the Hon. Horace Walpole . . . to Which Are Added Letters of Madame du Deffand to Voltaire, From the Year 1759 to the Year 1775* [1810]).

Thursday. 7th March.

Cold, gloomy, cheerless. Winter come back again. March is a detestable month in all the countries & climates that I have any acquaintance with. In Virginia it is a return of winter, February being mild with many pleasant days & March a howling, tomahawking savage. In New England the whole spring is so miserable from March to June, so cold & homicidal that it is difficult to say which month is worst & whether March enjoys there the bad eminence belonging to it elsewhere. Bryant has written some beautiful lines on this "wild stormy month." He is not the first poet who has prostituted his Muse in praise of tyrants. Of March he says—And in thy reign of blast and storm,

<blockquote>Smiles many a long, bright, sunny day—</blockquote>

The worst of tyrants have their moments of good humour, and in history a wicked reign often precedes a good one, as that of March precedes the arrival of April, Prairiale, the month of meadows, green grass & singing birds, a pleasant month every where but in New England.

I have omitted to speak of my second visit to Tottenham Green, to the house of Mr Windus, whither I was accompanied 4th March by Miss

Rogers, always a pleasant companion, sensible, well-bred & well-informed. Another amiable & apparently happy single woman. In England their name is Legion. I saw, on this second visit, a number of drawings by Stothard & Westall. The original drawings, in Indian ink, touched up with chalk, by Stothard for the illustration of Cadell's 8o. edition of Robinson Crusoe were among these—also a beautiful drawing, by Westall, to illustrate Milton's "Penseroso."

We walked in the grounds where, to my great delight, I saw, blooming in the open air, the Primrose, of which I have read so much. Mrs Windus not only gathered a number of them for me, but made her gardener transplant two bunches into pots, which I have now on the mantelpiece of the room where I am writing. I was struck with the good sense & good taste which Miss Rogers shewed in her manners to these worthy people, M^r & Mrs Windus. The spirit of caste prevails in such an intolerable degree among the English, and they are so dreadfully afraid of committing themselves with their inferiours, that I had taken care to inform Miss Rogers who Mr Windus was; a retired coachmaker, who having made a fortune by the mechanic arts, was enjoying it by gratifying a taste for the fine arts. She behaved with entire courtesy however, to M^r & Mrs Windus, praised their pictures, their house, their neat & well-kept grounds, and invited them to call and see her collection of paintings at her house in Regent's Park, giving her card by way of address. All this was done kindly, without affection & was evidently very gratifying to our hosts.

William Cullen **BRYANT**'s (1794–1878) poem "March" was first published in the *United States Literary Gazette* (1824) and was included in his *Poems* (1832), the London edition of which was edited by Washington Irving and dedicated to Samuel Rogers.

M^RS **WINDUS** was Margaret Armiger (d. 1842), Benjamin Godfrey Windus's second wife (*ODNB*, s.v. "Windus, Benjamin Godfrey").

Friday 8th March.

Cold, dark, dismal; the worst weather I have seen in England has been this week. Wednesday 6th after dining with the Stewarts in Portman Square, we went for an hour to the Dunlops in Russell Sq. These excellent people are just returned from Brighton. I found with them M^r & Mrs Long, old acquaintances from Virginia. Mr Long, an Englishman, had been a professor in the Charlottesville University—the pretty widow of a Western Judge who had been shot in a duel, won the heart of the learned man and he made her his wife, notwithstanding the encumbrance of two little daughters, whom he is said to treat with great kindness. I knew them both before their marriage but have never seen them since.——I was much amused by a small comic exhibition with which we were favored by one of the company. An Orange with a face cut on the side, dressed in a napkin which fell over the head & wrist of the exhibiter, was made to turn & gesticulate in the character of an old woman on board ship for the first time. A dialogue was carried on between the Captain of the ship & herself, & you heard alternately the bluff, rough voice of the sailor & the cracked & treble squeak of the crone, whilst the fingers concealed under the napkin, turned & twisted the orange head in the most natural way imaginable. The farce concluded with a fit of sea-sickness on the part of the old woman, & left us in convulsions of laughter which a more refined exhibition would have failed to call forth.

Yesterday, Thursday, I called on Mrs Grote, found her at home & had a long conversation with her. She is sensible & manly, has read a great deal & stored her mind with ideas, but her manliness is somewhat too masculine & her learning tinged with pedantry. She is too bold and too blue. She is however, a great admirer of my grandfather, which for me, like charity, covers a multitude of sins, far more than could be found in Mrs Grote. I asked her what articles she had written for the Westminster Review, knowing her, in former days, to have been a contributor, and she lent me several volumes of the Review containing her own & Mr Grote's pieces which I am now reading.

We had on this same day, several gentlemen to dine with us, friends of Mr Coolidge. After breakfast to-day, I read one of Mrs Grote's articles in the W. R. It is on the Military Profession & is of old date, as far back as 1827. There are some very good things in it, although the views are tinged no doubt, with party feeling. One remark I will transcribe because I thought it just & concise. Speaking of the false excitement which the rulers of a people often create in the minds of the people, to serve purposes of their own, she says, "It is the perfection of the science of misrule to make the misgoverned co-operate in the work, by perverting their ideas of what is praiseworthy or blameable."

At eleven o'clock I walked with Mr Bowman to the rooms of the Asiatic Society in Bond St. They are small, crowded, & contain not much that has interest for me. There are arms of various sorts, swords, matchlocks, spears, bows & arrows, Malay creeses &c &c, things which I do not understand, and which I look at as I should at the tools in a Butcher's shop. The pride & circumstance of glorious war exercise but little influence over

my imagination. There were some things at which I looked more earnestly. A model of the Car of Juggernaut, a picture of the transformations
of Vishnu, another of the Shah of Persia holding his Court, and a small
alabaster painted figure, the Chinese emblem of Perfect Happiness. Here
were superstition, despotism & sensuality, the characteristics of Asiatic
nations. The Car of Juggernaut is a sort of tent or pavilion, curtained with
crimson, resting on a stage supported by rude columns, & the whole upon
a number of clumsy wheels. Three hideous idols, seated on a couch, are
seen through the curtains of the tent, numerous distorted figures & faces
are carved on the columns or grin from between them—other misshapen
wretches stand upon the stage without the pavilion. Four rudely sculptured figures of horses just in front, have their fore feet in the air, & are fastened by their backs to the Car, far above the wheels.—those murderous
wheels under which the frantic votaries of the God throw themselves to
be crushed in honour of Juggernaut! ^So much for Priestcraft!^ Of all the
disguises which the power of evil, he who is a Liar & the father of Liars,
has chosen to assume since the beginning of his reign upon earth, none
has ever accorded so well with his own character, as when he has wrapped
himself in the garments of a high priest, whether that priest be Caiphas,
or a minister of Juggernaut, or Moloch, or a Chief Inquisitor in Spain.

The Chinese emblem of perfect Happiness is the figure of an old man,
disgusting, bloated, swollen, seated on the ground, with a paunch which
rests upon the earth, his breast & arms like pillows, a double chin, hanging cheeks, laughing, twinkling half-closed eyes, & a "bouche vermeille"
like Tartuffe or Lord Melbourne. The pictures of the transformations
of Vishnu all seemed to have some reference to the effects of a general
Deluge. The God is first half fish, then resting on a turtle, an amphibious
animal, then destroying wild beasts, the earth being not yet habitable for
man, then instructing men in various arts of clearing forests, tilling the
earth &c &c—The Shah of Persia, the "Shadow of God upon the Earth"
(there is something equally blasphemous & sublime in this Persian name
of honour,) is represented seated on his throne, his long black beard descending to his girdle, upon his arms the two diamonds called the Sea
of Light & the Mountain of Splendour, whilst his courtiers robed & tur-
baned, are in long rows on the right & left. To make all intelligible there
is a written or printed explanation.

Returning from the Asiatic Rooms I dressed myself & made some calls
on Mrs Stevenson ^M^rs Vail^, Mrs Wormeley, Mrs Stewart & the Misses
Berry, being driven away from this last house by an obstinate fit of cough-
ing which could not be checked—This is a new trouble for me & cannot

be of long duration, though I have been suffering from it already an unusually long time for one whose lungs are made of India Rubber.

James DUNLOP (1769–1841), who lived at 27 Russell Square, was a third-generation Scottish tobacco merchant with strong ties to Virginia. Dunlop conducted his business in both London and Virginia, where he owned tobacco plantations in Chesterfield County. His wife, Nancy Gilliam Duncan, was a native of that state, the daughter of tobacco trader Charles Duncan and Jennie Gilliam of Blandford. The Dunlops' London home welcomed those with connections to America, including the artist Charles Robert Leslie, for whom Dunlop was an important friend and patron. Dunlop commissioned from Leslie *Sir Roger de Coverley Going to Church* (1819), a work that helped launch Leslie's London career. Leslie traveled with the Dunlops, attempted in vain to find a publisher for Dunlop's history of American painters, and named his son in Dunlop's honor. The artist Thomas Lawrence lived near the Dunlops at 65 Russell Square and produced a full-length portrait of the couple (ca. 1825) that is now in the collection of the Worcester Art Museum in Massachusetts (*ODNB*, s.v. "Leslie, Charles Robert"; Tom Taylor, ed., *Autobiographical Recollections by the Late Charles Robert Leslie, R.A.* [1860], 1:213, 297–299, 334, 357–359; Curl, *Kensal Green Cemetery*, 194; Kenneth Garlick, *Sir Thomas Lawrence: A Complete Catalogue of the Oil Paintings* [1989], 181, plate 74; "Personal Notices from the Virginia Gazette," *William and Mary Quarterly* 9 [1901]: 240; *Bailie* [Glasgow], exhibition supplement, 4 July 1888; *Old and New London*, 4:564–565).

George LONG (1800–1879) was recruited from England in 1824 by Francis Walker Gilmer, acting on behalf of Jefferson and the Board of Visitors, to serve as the first professor of ancient and modern languages at the newly formed University of Virginia. Upon his arrival in Charlottesville, Long walked to Monticello to meet Jefferson, who was surprised by his youth. He became a frequent visitor to Monticello, dining there and staying overnight, and he was well known by Jefferson's grandchildren. On one of Long's visits Jefferson showed him the original draft of the Declaration of Independence and described the story of the American Revolution. To Joseph Coolidge's dismay, Long acquired two works of art from Monticello after Jefferson's death: a print of Zenobia, which Long insisted on keeping, and an engraving of Alexander von Humboldt, which he considered selling to Joseph's brother-in-law Nicholas Trist. Long returned to England in 1828, accompanied by his new wife, Harriet Gray Selden (d. 1841), the widow of Lt.-Col. Joseph Selden, an Arkansas supreme court judge (*ODNB*; Merrill Peterson, ed., *Visitors to Monticello* [1989], 100–103; Malone, *Jefferson and His Time*, 6:409–410, 465–469; Philip Alexander Bruce, *History of the University of Virginia, 1819–1919* [1920], 2:1–9; Joseph Coolidge to Nicholas P. Trist, [2 June] 1827 [DLC: Nicholas Philip Trist Papers]).

Harriet Grote's essay on the MILITARY PROFESSION was published in the *Westminster Review* 7 (1827): 484–505.

The Royal ASIATIC SOCIETY, then located at 22 Bond Street, was founded in 1823 and remains an active research center for the study of Asian culture. Mr. [BOWMAN] has not been identified (*ODNB*; *Old and New London*, 4:291–314; "About Us," Royal Asiatic Society of Great Britain and Ireland, accessed 8 July 2011, http://royalasiaticsociety.org).

Mʀˢ VAIL was Emilie Lawrencine Salles Vail (ca. 1815–1860), the wife of Aaron Vail (1796–1878), who served in the American legation at London from 1831 to 1836. Vail was the son of the New York merchant Aaron Vail and his French wife, Elizabeth Dubois. The elder Vail was an American commercial agent at Lorient, France, during Jefferson's presidency, and the family visited Monticello on several occasions. During one visit after Coolidge had married and moved to Boston, Aaron Vail painted a picture of Monticello with the intent of sending it to Coolidge. Vail was well received in London and on good terms with statesmen such as Palmerston and Wellington. Sometime between 1831 and 1836 Princess Victoria requested from Vail an autograph of Jefferson, and Jefferson's son-in-law Nicholas Trist conveyed the message to Martha Randolph. She apparently chose to send the 28 November 1783 letter from her father in which he outlines what he recommends as a proper "distribution of your time" between practicing music, dancing, drawing, writing letters, reading French, and reading English.

With Andrew Stevenson's confirmation as minister in 1836, Vail briefly returned to the role of secretary, and he and his wife, whom he married in 1835, welcomed the Stevensons to London. Mrs. Stevenson commented that "Mr. & Mrs. Vail have been very kind to us. I shall never cease to think of their kindness with the deepest gratitude. They have been of infinite use to us. We take their house, servants & equipage untill we can find a house & carriage we like better." Vail returned to the United States and continued his life as a diplomat in the Department of State and abroad in Canada and Spain (*DAB*; *PTJ*, 6:359–361, 25:622; Boykin, *Mrs. Stevenson*, 17–18; Sarah N. Randolph, *Domestic Life of Thomas Jefferson* [1871], 68–69; Coolidge to Martha Jefferson Randolph, 14 Dec. 1821, Martha Jefferson Randolph to Coolidge, 1 Sept. 1825, Virginia J. Randolph Trist to Coolidge, 3 Sept. 1825 [ViU: Ellen Wayles Randolph Coolidge Correspondence]; Coolidge to Nicholas P. Trist, 3 May 1823 [DLC: Nicholas Philip Trist Papers]; *Examiner* [London], 30 Aug. 1835; "Aaron Vail (1796-1878)," object no. 1968.34, Henry Luce III Center for the Study of American Culture, New-York Historical Society, accessed 8 July 2011, http://emuseum.nyhistory.org).

Sunday. 10ᵗʰ March.

Dismal dismal weather—been snowing again and the sky looks like lead—very cold too, colder than any part of January. Friday night I was seized with violent pain in my back & kept my bed till two o'clock Saturday. On this day we had a dinner engagement at Mʳ Hume's in Bryanston Square, & I did all I could to get well enough to go. By means, in great part, of Josephine's good nursing, I succeeded, & at seven o'clock we drove to the house of the Great Radical. I found him a frank, good humoured man, civil & not over refined—I should say very <u>American</u> in his ways. This sounds like treason, but it is true that, although we have in the U.S. as refined people as any where in the world, yet refinement is not the general character of our society. Mrs Hume made a pleasant impression upon me. She is small, not elegant or fashionable, but she is something that is becoming rare now-a-days—she is feminine. In the present time when the women all aspire to be men, it is something to find woman-liness & gentleness—and one is willing to compound for a good deal in favour of these lovely qualities—for lovely they are in spite of all that the Amazons can say. I discovered quite accidentally, several little family habits which speak well for the family affections. Mr Hume, during the session of Parliament, is busy all day and out till late at night. He comes home between one & two o'clock, weary of course, and probably needing refreshment in body & mind. His wife sits up for him, is ready to wel-come him, to give him his cup of tea, and tell him the small family news, to talk to him of their children, and, to use her own expression, "gossip a little" before retiring to rest, which they both do, in defiance of fash-ion, in the same room. Some of their servants have been with them ever since their marriage, now twenty three years ago. One man who was Mr Hume's servant before his marriage, and a housekeeper who came with Mrs Hume from her father's house & has never left her. The daughters are fresh, modest-looking girls, & were dressed with the most becoming sim-plicity, with manners as simple as their dress, respectful to their parents, affectionate to each other & courteous to strangers. When we first arrived the younger members of the family, who had dined hours before, were seated in one of the parlours, whilst the elder sister who is "out," was with her mother in the other room, assisting to receive & entertain the guests. The young people were all evidently & in the best sense of the word, <u>at home</u>. English girls, generally, dress with more taste than we see among young people in America. White muslin frocks, & ribbon sashes, instead of silks, laces, gauzes, &c &c in which our juvenile belles delight to deck themselves. The trinkets worn by girls here are few & simple. Only mar-ried women wear expensive jewelry. I am told that I can form no idea of the richness of the ^ladies'^ toilette from anything I have seen, as they do not display their magnificence till after Easter. Such is the custom. During the early part of a London winter there are but few persons belonging to good society in town, & those few go out but little; of course there is not much dress. Parliament opens in February. The town meanwhile, has been slowly mustering it's legions. On the opening of Parliament the ladies come out very fine, but their finery is of the last season & somewhat the worse for wear. Nothing new is yet to be seen. Parties begin and velvets & diamonds appear in abundance, & as these are things which <u>endure</u>, the diamonds always, the velvets for several years, the ladies make a great figure in them. This is the stage at which I have arrived in my experience of such matters. But they tell me I have as yet seen nothing. During the Easter Holidays every body retires to the country. The holidays over, the <u>Season</u> begins in good earnest, and then the ladies shine forth in all their splendour. This is the time for the "grande toilette," for the display of the utmost magnificence, and, in this rich country, female extravagance in dress almost exceeds belief. The Duchess of Sutherland stands pre-eminent for the immense sums which she lavishes on her person. Her dress upon the day that the young Queen, after her accession, dined in the city, was literally covered with diamonds. The effect was such as to throw the sovereign into the shade, as far as could be done by superiour magnificence of attire. This was displeasing to the Queen, who expressed her disapprobation. It was surely bad taste in the Duchess, putting loyalty out of the question. It is also whispered that the Duchess of Sutherland flourishing pocket handkerchiefs worth fifty guineas a piece, her Majesty remarked that <u>she</u> found handkerchiefs at ten guineas good enough for <u>her</u>.

Joseph **HUME** was married to Maria Burnley Hume (b. 1786), the daughter of a merchant, with whom he had three sons and four daughters. Their youngest daughter, Mary Catherine Hume-Rothery (1824–1885), was an author and medical reformer (*ODNB*, s.v. "Hume, Joseph" and "Hume-Rothery, Mary Catherine").

Monday 11. March.

Another cold, raw day, although the morning promised better things. Yesterday I called, by appointment, on Mrs Marcet the authoress.

Jane Haldimand **MARCET** (1769–1858), daughter of Swiss merchant and banker Anthony Haldimand, was the London-born author of *Conversations on Chemistry* (1805). Formatted as a series of dialogues between a mother and her children, the elementary science textbook presents complex concepts written, in her words, for the female sex. This volume became influential in Europe and America, where it was widely adopted as a textbook in female academies. Jefferson acquired the 1807 edition of Marcet's work in 1809, and it is now at the Library of Congress. At her home in Russell Square Marcet received the leading scientists of the day, and she continued to update her chemistry volume for most of her life. Following the same format, Marcet went on to produce *Conversations on Natural Philosophy* (1819), *Conversations on Vegetable Physiology* (1829), and *Conversations on Political Economy* (1816), a work that inspired Harriet Martineau's writing (*ODNB*; Sowerby, 837).

London.
Monday. 11. March. 1839.

I am compelled to have recourse to Chinese paper & close lines————

On this day I called on Mrs Marcet, by appointment, to obtain some information on the subject of schools in Geneva. We have some thought of sending our sons to the "Pension" of Messrs Humbert & Briquet.—Mrs Marcet is of English birth but I believe of Swiss descent. Her name was Huldemand & her husband, Dr Marcet, a Genevese physician, the friend of Sir Samuel Romilly, to whose son Mrs Marcet's daughter is I believe nöot very long since married. Mrs Marcet is a widow & has, besides her house in London, a country seat on the shore of Lake Leman, where she passes a good deal of time. Her eldest son has adopted his father's country, is Professor in the Geneva College & married to a Genevese lady.

I owe my introduction to Mrs Marcet to Mr Sumner. I found her an elderly woman with great benevolence of countenance & manner. She answered my questions freely & fully, and promised to write to her son in Geneva for farther particulars. This was a kindness I had no right to ask or expect, but which I did not hesitate to accept.

Mrs Marcet speaks favorably of Geneva, it's schools, it's modes of life & it's general intelligence & respectability. Were any thing to prevent my accompanying my husband to China I would take my children, go to Geneva & remain till his return. It is comparatively a cheap place. It is possible to live there with a family ^decently^ for £500. about $2500. a year, and for £1000 or $5000. very comfortably & pleasantly. I think it better, if our sons are to be deprived of their father's care, that they should be educated, at least during their early years, out of America, where the democratic spirit pervades our very schools & boys are apt to be lawless.   Thermometer this week as low as 18° of Fahrenheit.

CHINESE PAPER & CLOSE LINES refers to the quality and format of Coolidge's fourth diary notebook, which begins with this entry.

From 1839 to 1844 Coolidge's four sons, Randolph, Algernon, Sidney, and Thomas Jefferson Coolidge, were enrolled in the cosmopolitan boarding school run by Alphonse **BRIQUET** (1809–ca. 1880) at 97 Chemin Gourgas in the Geneva, Switzerland, district of Plainpalais. Augustine Heard accompanied the boys to Geneva in 1839 as their parents were en route to Canton. Thomas Jefferson Coolidge recalled Briquet's establishment with fondness: "here I remained five years—I think as happy years as I have ever enjoyed, but I did not know it. I learned French and acquired all the elements of arithmetic, geography, history, and French literature. When I left at thirteen years of age, I knew as much in many of those things as I ever did. . . . M. Briquet loved me and praised me, and good Madame Briquet took as good care of my body as he did of my mind. The only interesting feature of the school was the journeys on foot with knapsack on our backs, that we took every August through the Swiss mountains. The first few days we dragged ourselves along footsore and cut by the straps of the knapsack, but very soon we did our twenty miles a day with pleasure. In this way I wandered through almost all the passes of Switzerland and saw the Jungfrau and Mont Blanc. Of course, boys of twelve could not ascend mountains, but one would be surprised to find what the school did accomplish." On a return trip to Europe from 1865 to 1868 Thomas Jefferson Coolidge visited his former schoolmaster, finding Briquet and his wife looking "as young as I recollected them twenty-five years before." Among the Americans who studied at Briquet's school were the architect Richard Morris Hunt and his brother William; it was at Briquet's that Hunt began his architectural education in 1844 (*ANB*, s.v. "Hunt, Richard Morris"; Gabriel Mützenberg, *Education et Instruction à Genève autour de 1830* [1974], 220; Coolidge, *Autobiography*, 3–5, 58, 63; *Guide du Voyageur à Genève* [1836], 48).

SAMUEL ROMILLY (1757–1818), lawyer and politician, was particularly interested in the reform of criminal law. His son Edward Romilly (1802–1870) married Sophia Marcet (1809–1877) in 1830. Jane Marcet lived with Sophia and Edward Romilly in her later years and died at their home in 1858 (*ODNB*, s.v. "Romilly, Samuel" and "Marcet, Jane"; Joseph Jackson Howard, ed., *Miscellanea Genealogica et Heraldica* [1884], 4:370; Martineau, *Biographical Sketches*, 76).

Friday 15. March.

A day of rain. Capt. Wormeley comes in with a story that Mr Calhoun is coming to England to settle our differences with France & England. The silly Bantam-Cock like conduct of the Governor of Maine, his call or crow of defiance, is equally absurd & unconstitutional, and Mr Calhoun, the author of Nullification, is to explain away the logical deductions from his own doctrines. He is a brilliant if not a solid man, has great personal courage, courtesy of manner, vivacity of intellect and command of good English. He can harangue John Bull & Lewis Baboon fearlessly, civilly and in all probablity, without being sneered at in English society for bad grammar or bad pronunciation. I think that Mr Stevenson must feel mortified at the supposed necessity for such a coadjutor. He will be virtually superseded if not in the forms of his office, at least in it's spirit. He must play second fiddle, & he is a proud, vain man.

Capt. Wormeley seems this morning in a perfect fever of radicalism. He has probably received some small slight—has been omitted in an invitation extended to persons one round higher up on the fashionable ladder. It is such petty grievances as these that urge men on. It is astonishing how much real oppression they will bear if you leave them the consolations of vanity. I do not pretend to say that there is not a great deal to reform in the state of things in England, but if unequal laws, unjust distributions of property, the sins of Church & State, corruption, abuses, starvation & nakendness, are collecting materials for explosion, the insolence of the Aristocracy & the petty mortifications of self-love will fire the train. There are Radicals no doubt, made so by a sense of injustice, & indignation against what they think a violation of the rights of Man—there are others urged on by Ambition, restlessness, love of change or wild & distempered imaginations, but there are many Radicals of the bitterest or most fiery, principally instigated by vanity, wounded pride, a desire for petty distinctions & mortification at petty neglects.—Capt. Wormeley is really a lover of his kind, a good but wrong-headed man, and a very vain one, so that he is a triple radical; a warm heart, a light head & an irritable temperament combining to make him so.

From the days of ancient Rome to the times of modern France—since the change effected in the government of Rome by consular honours paid to the husband of one woman and denied to the husband of another, to the affront offered to Madame Roland by a purse-proud farmer general, mortified vanity & indignation against social distinctions of rank have had their full share in reformations & revolutions.

——Rogers the poet does not gain ground on better acquaintance. His cold sneers & his habit of "médisance" become more offensive—his apparent benevolence & "bonhommie" fade as you approach nearer to him. I have heard him ridicule in their absence, persons to whom present, he paid the most cordial attentions. He deceives by expressions of regard to your face which he belies behind your back. He is occasionally capable of small impertinences, the surest mark of a morally small mind. He affected the other day in presence of several Americans, to confound the names of Van Buren & Van Amburgh. He spoke of Van Buren's exhibitions, his appearance on the stage &c repeating the name, which is that of a President of the United States, oftener than was necessary, in order it seemed to me to render it's introduction more ridiculous. Mrs Stevenson at last interrupted him—"I think Mr Rogers that you <u>mispronounce</u> that name;" upon which he affected to correct himself and explain. Bad taste if nothing else.

Mr Sumner spent last evening with us—that is came in at eleven and staid until half past one. His conversation is sensible & pleasant.

I hear now that what I heard of Turner the painter, his excessive jealousy, his unwillingness to let any one see him at work, is all a mistake. How strange such contradictory reports about an individual not in public life! To the contrary his friends say that he sends his pictures to the Exhibition of the R.A. in an unfinished state and works them out after they are in place. He sometimes rubs in his colours with a finger & thumb instead of a brush. These colours, too glaring in the first instance, are said to soften down with age. He is aware of the change that time produces in his pictures and pleases himself in the anticipation of it, as he works for the future rather than the present. A gentleman who owns a water-colour drawing done by Turner many years ago, just at the time when he adopted his present brilliant style, tells me that the artist often comes to look with satisfaction, at the mellowing of the colours and the general softening down of the glowing tints. He has at his own house, two large oil paintings which he is indignant with the public for not appreciating. He threatens to use one of them as a winding sheet, & cause himself when he dies, to be rolled in the canvas and buried with his favorite and neglected masterpieces.——

Since writing the above I have received a proof of Turner's brusque and disobliging temper. A gentleman, a friend of mine & of his, applied to him for permission to visit his rooms and shew me his pictures. He received an abrupt refusal—softened to a certain extent, by a sort of excuse,—He was preparing a picture for the approaching exhibition and could not be disturbed by visiters.

Since the date of my last regular entries (for these are mere notes,) I have done a good deal. On Monday morning I called on Mrs Hume & to return a visit from Lady Hislop, and in the evening dined with Mrs Mansfield. Our party consisted of Lady Hislop herself, a gay, animated & sparkling person, the Rev^d wit Sidney Smith & Mrs Smith, (who I observe is always spoken to as Mrs Sidney, to avoid I suppose, the obnoxious name of Smith,) Mr Charles Romilly, secretary to the Speaker, & some other persons, like ourselves, of less note. The conversation at table was animated, the wit of Sidney Smith being, of course, the vivifying principle. We heard from him that Macauley, Tom Macauley as he is called in society, has undertaken to finish the history of England begun by Sir James Mackintosh.

Many good things were said during dinner, which like the flavour of the meats & wines, were enjoyed at the moment, left a pleasant impression, but no lasting recollection. One charm of this light, graceful & agreeable talk is perhaps it's evanescence. Like a perfume it evaporates as you inhale it. The best talkers seldom, in general society, say anything to be specially remembered. To get their truly good things you must, I suspect, have them "en petit comité." Sidney Smith, as I hear him, pleases by a gay, easy & amusing tone & style of conversation, rather than by distinct witticisms or striking "bon mots."

From Mrs Mansfield's we went to a party at Mrs Stevenson's. Here I met Mrs Marx, a friend of Lady Morgan's, and heard from her that my offence against this my-ladyed "parvenue" was the not having immediately returned her visit. She is probably implacable & I am certainly not inconsolable.

Tuesday. March 12. we went with Leslie's card as our passport, to see a collection of paintings done by modern artists, almost entirely English, at the house of a Mr Vernon in Pall Mall. This house occupies the ground once filled by the dwelling place of the renowned Nell Gwyn. Mr Vernon is another instance of a fortune made by hard & homely industry & spent in the encouragement and enjoyment of the arts. He was keeper of a Livery Stable and now inhabits a house sufficiently large, well furnished, containing all possible appliances for comfort, and hung with pictures by Wilkie, Landseer, Leslie, Newton, Uwins, Callcott, Eastlake, Stanfield, Smarte, Smirke &c &.—The pictures at which I looked particularly were—1st Crossing the Ford. Gainsborough. 2. High-bred & Low-bred the Hound & the Butcher's Dog. Landseer. Inimitable. The aristocratic bearing of the high-bred Gentleman's dog, his slender head, lambent eye, clean limbs and general air of patrician birth & breeding are in admirable contrast with the heavy, stupid, currish expression of his low-lived rival. The Butcher's dog has one eye half closed and his tongue partly out, his legs are crooked, his body bloated, his skin apparently diseased, his countenance full of vulgar ferocity & stupid spitefulness. The use which H.B. has made of these two pictures in the same frame, in his well-known caricature of O. Connell & Sir Francis Burdett is the happiest possible. The fierce & vulgar demagogue on the one hand, and the high-spirited English gentleman on the other, could not be thrown into better approximation & opposition.

3^d   A Highland Piper & Scotch dogs. Landseer.
4th   A Dutch girl. Stewart Newton. 5th Sterne & the Grisette. Stuart Newton.

6th   Uncle Toby & the Widow Wadman. Leslie. 7th Crossing a stream. Calcott.

8th   The peep of day Boy. Sir David Wilkie. An Irish scene. A man asleep with his head on his wife's lap, a naked infant by his side, upon whose little body one hand is resting whilst on the other arm lies the loaded musquet.

9th   Portrait of a lady, dark browed & beautiful. Rippengail.

10.   Portrait of a Jew. Rippengail. 11th Landing of William the Conqueror. Turner.

12.   Clarissa Harlowe on her knees at prayer. Charles Landseer.

13th   A girl, her head fantastically dressed——

14.   Female head with white drapery.——

There was apparently a fine collection of pictures besides busts & statues in marble. There were paintings by Sir Peter Lely & Sir Godfrey Kneller—A group in marble by Gibson representing Hylas carried off by the nymphs—a Bust of Milton by Bailly—also, by the same artist, a beautiful female head taken from his own Eve—An antique, a statue of Venus rising from the waves wringing the water from her hair, and many other works of art which a bad headache prevented me from enjoying as I should otherwise have done.

Among the articles of furniture were several Buhl tables & cabinets. One inlaid in brass & tortoise shell, another in brass, ebony, mother of pearl & coral.——On the same day, tuesday, we dined & spent the evening with Miss Rogers. Our party included the poet, Mr Lyell the Geologist & his pretty wife, Mr Luttrell the conversationist, Mrs Stevenson & some others. Mr Luttrell has an easy flow of table talk, less elaborate than the colloqueal effusions of Mr Rogers which are finished off & polished like his writings. Mr Luttrell's good sayings are more spontaneous & more like the growth of the soil. Miss Rogers improves on acquaintance as much as her brother does not. I like her better & better. In the evening other company came in. M. & Mme Van der Weyer, & M^{rs} & Miss Mansfield among the number. Mr Van der Weyer does not please me. He is evidently a man of moderate abilities & great pretensions. Madame was beautifully dressed, as she always is, & towards me delightfully gracious, at which I smiled, understanding as I did, the wherefore— that her manner to me might be in marked contrast to her treatment of the Mansfields, with whom she played off the great lady, the haughty Ambassadress. When she was insignificant Miss Bates, the Mansfields, some steps higher up the ladder of fashion, huffed her, & ridiculed her mother, (no wonder,) Now the tables are turned.

Mr Luttrell said at dinner, that the only thing in England of which the supply was never equal to the demand, was Humbug.

Wednesday 13. March, I lay in bed with headach until luncheon time, when I took a cup of tea and then rose & dressed for a dinner at Mr Morrison's. He is a very wealthy merchant whose house is in Upper Harley St. He is also the present owner of Fonthill. Our dinner party included Sir Martin Archer Shee, President of the Royal Academy & Eastlake the painter. Mr Morrison loves pictures & old china, Buhl tables & gold plate. His house is richly furnished, a little too much crowded perhaps, with articles of taste and virtù. There are too many china vases & bronze statuettes, too many miniatures & carvings in ivory, too much of knickknackery on the tables and mantel pieces. But opulence shews itself likewise in the more comfortable forms of luxurious furniture, a "cordon-bleu" in the kitchen, and well trained servants M^r & Mrs Morrison are hospitable & attentive to their guests, which I am old-fashioned enough to like.

Thursday 14th March, we went to a concert at the Queen's Concert Rooms in Hanover Square. The third and last of the "Matineés" of Moscheles. His performance on the piano is admirable. What I particularly like is the absence of exaggeration and of the ambitious desire of display. To me it seems that in all the fine arts, there is a certain spirit of repose necessary to high excellence. Violent efforts after effect, even where there is skill to carry them through, always fail to satisfy or to convince. An artist in the enthusiasm of his art, should forget that he has hearers or spectators, and a certain subdued tone, the character of power submitting to the laws of good taste, and ever alive to the sense of beauty, appears to me the perfection of excellence.

In February 1839 the **GOVERNOR OF MAINE**, John Fairfield (1797–1847), sent militia to occupy a disputed portion of territory between Maine and New Brunswick along the Aroostook River valley, part of a bloodless conflict known as the Aroostook War. On 3 March 1839 Pres. Martin Van Buren approved an act of Congress that authorized him to employ military and naval forces to resist Great Britain and vested in him the discretionary power to appoint a special envoy to London to settle the boundary question, much to Andrew Stevenson's disappointment. Though John Calhoun was named as that envoy in both American and British papers, ultimately no special envoy was sent. While Stevenson worked with diplomatic dispatches in London, Gen. Winfield Scott calmed tensions in the region. Stevenson hoped to see the matter put to rest during his tenure, but it was his successor, Daniel Webster, who negotiated the 1842 Ashburton-Webster Treaty that defined the disputed border with Canada. The lands south of the Saint

John River valley, including the Aroostook River, became part of Maine (*ANB*; *DAB*; *Oxford Companion to Canadian History* [2004], s.v. "Aroostook War," Oxford Reference Online; Wayland, *Andrew Stevenson*, 144–147; *Morning Chronicle* [London], 15 Mar. 1839; *Freeman's Journal and Daily Commercial Advertiser* [Dublin], 27 Mar. 1839).

J. M. W. **TURNER** exhibited five works at the Royal Academy's spring show, which opened on 3 May 1839, including *The Fighting Temeraire Tugged to Her Last Berth to Be Broken Up, 1838*, the work he called "my Darling" and that came to define the era. His rendering depicted the once-glorious ship from Nelson's victory at the Battle of Trafalgar in 1805, stripped of its sails and guns and being led to the scrapyard. The image stirred the nation's heightened sentiments at the time of Victoria's accession and became one of Turner's most famous works. It was among the pieces he bequeathed to the National Gallery (*ODNB*; *Grove Art Online*, s.v. "Turner, Joseph Mallord William," Oxford Art Online; A. J. Findberg, *The Life of J. M. W. Turner, R.A.* [1961], 502; *Morning Chronicle* [London], 4 May 1839; J. M. W. Turner, *The Fighting Temeraire Tugged to Her Last Berth to Be Broken Up, 1838* [1839], National Gallery, accessed 20 Dec. 2010, http://www.nationalgallery.org.uk/paintings/).

CHARLES ROMILLY (1808–1887) was then secretary to James Abercromby, Speaker of the House of Commons, and went on to become clerk of the Crown in chancery (*ODNB*, s.v. "Abercromby, James"; *Gentleman's Magazine*, n.s., 3 [1867]: 682; *Annual Register: A Review of Public Events at Home and Abroad, for the Year 1887* [1888], 148).

Thomas Babington **MACAULAY** (1800–1859) had just returned from a tour in Italy in February 1839 and immediately begun work on the first of three volumes of *The History of England* (1848–1861). At his disposal were the papers that James Mackintosh had gathered for his unfinished work on the history of the Revolution of 1688, intended as a companion to Mackintosh's *History of England from the Earliest Times to the Final Establishment of the Reformation* (1830). Macaulay's work also drew on popular literature of the time, and its narrative style gave it wide appeal (*ODNB*).

Robert **VERNON** (ca. 1774–1849), who owned a townhouse at 50 Pall Mall as well as a country house in Berkshire, amassed a fortune by expanding his father's carriage rental business and investing in real estate. His father left him a collection of old master paintings to which Vernon began adding modern British artists by 1820, commissioning and buying art directly from the artists. Together with Chantrey and Turner, Vernon had in 1830 begun making plans for bequests of galleries and monies for the benefit of artists. He formed his collection with the purpose of donating a survey of British art to the National Gallery and allowed the trustees to select what they wished from it. Vernon donated 157 paintings and 8 sculptures to the state in December 1847, nearly doubling the number of paintings in the national collection. After 1883 the collection was no longer exhibited together at the National Gallery, and most of it is now part of the Tate collection (*ODNB*; Macleod, *Art and the Victorian Middle Class*, 484–485; Kathryn Moore Heleniak, "Victorian Collections and British Nationalism: Vernon, Sheepshanks and the National Gallery of British Art," *Journal of the History of Collections* 12, no. 1 [2000]: 91–94).

Geologist Charles LYELL (1797–1875) sought to make geology truly scientific and to "free the science from Moses" through writings such as his three-volume *Principles of Geology* (1830–1833). Like Charles Darwin, for whom he was a mentor, Lyell reached an audience well beyond the scientific community. In 1832 Lyell married Mary Horner (ca. 1809–1873), daughter of Whig reformer and geologist Leonard Horner. Mrs. Lyell was well educated, spoke French and German fluently, and helped her husband with translations. Lyell's exclusion of his wife from scientific discussions in social situations drew remarks from his contemporaries, including Darwin (*ODNB*).

The architect John Buonarotti Papworth (1775–1847) designed the interior of Mary Anne and James MORRISON'S townhouse at 57 Upper Harley Street and advised Morrison in his art collecting. Waagen catalogued Morrison's extensive collection, which included several paintings by Turner. Morrison also maintained important collections in his country estates, Fonthill and Basildon Park (*ODNB*; Macleod, *Art and the Victorian Middle Class*, 455–456; Caroline Dakers, "'A Casket to Enclose Pictorial Gems,'" *Apollo* 159 [Apr. 2004]: 29–35; Gustav Waagen, *Galleries and Cabinets of Art in Great Britain* [1854], 105–113).

The portrait artist Sir MARTIN ARCHER SHEE (1769–1850) had been president of the Royal Academy since 1830, the same year he was knighted, and he oversaw its move out of Somerset House to the National Gallery in 1837 (*ODNB*).

Charles Lock EASTLAKE (1793–1865), elected to the Royal Academy in 1830, favored Greek and Italian subjects in his paintings. He went on to become president of the Academy, as well as keeper of the National Gallery, and was responsible for the interior decoration of the new Palace of Westminster (*ODNB*).

CORDON-BLEU: A first-class or gourmet cook, so named for the blue sash worn by senior students at the Institut de Saint-Louis (*OED*; *Oxford Dictionary of Food and Nutrition* [2009], s.v. "cordon bleu," Oxford Reference Online).

Pianist, composer, and teacher Ignaz MOSCHELES (1794–1870) was born in Prague and studied piano in Vienna. After touring throughout Europe he settled in London in 1825. Moscheles was co-director of the Royal Philharmonic Society and conducted the first English performance of Beethoven's Mass in D. His "classical chamber concerts," or "historical soirées," were designed to introduce the public to the "best works of all periods," including "select compositions of the most ancient as well as the most modern masters," such as the music of Scarlatti and Bach performed on the harpsichord. An early teacher of Felix Mendelssohn, Moscheles left London at his invitation to become the principal professor of piano at the Leipzig Conservatory (*ODNB*; *Oxford Companion to Music* [2002], s.v. "Moscheles, Ignaz," by Henry Roche, Oxford Reference Online; *Times* [London], 15 Feb. 1839).

Monday. 18th March.

I spent friday evening with the Miss Berrys where I found Lady Charlotte Lindsay, Lady Anna Maria Donkin, Mr Temple, Mr Wilmot &c. The society at Miss Berrys' is always the best. These ladies receive habitually, & of course without effort. Every thing about the house is arranged accordingly, the servants well trained & the whole establishment monté for such a state of things. I should become one of the "habituées" if I remained in London, the Miss Berrys having been kind enough to give me a cordial, general invitation. The conversation in these "re-unions" is easy, light, versatile, touching on many subjects & resting only on such as promise entertainment. I cannot always join freely & fully, because I am not sufficiently <u>at home</u> on the topics often discussed, but a casual observation on my part is always kindly received, a question readily answered, and I am never made to feel myself out of place or "de trop."

Saturday March 16. was a day of great enjoyment to me. I called by appointment at Mr Morrison's and Mrs Morrison accompanied me to several places where she had the "entrée" and where I found much to interest and amuse me. First we went to Sir Francis Chauntrey's. I had been once through his studio in company with Mr Coolidge and Mr Ashburner, but now we were hospitably received & entertained in his house by Lady Chauntrey, whom I found on further acquaintance altogether more amiable & agreeable than her first address betokens. The English ^as a general rule^ certainly do gain by being better known. As individuals they should not be judged by first impressions. Second thoughts, as far as this people are concerned, are apt to be best. A few among them from natural disposition or the effect of foreign travel, have an ease of manner which is pleasant from the first, but usually they are stiff, or proud, or cold, or "gauche," or indifferent, or disagreeable after some one or other of the most approved patterns. This is the first-sight aspect of things, but it is surprising how much kindness & courtesy is often concealed under a forbidding exteriour. This is particularly the case with the classes of society immediately below the Aristocracy who, with a few exceptions, are more easy in their address than other persons; simply I presume, from that confidence in their own position which puts distrust out of the question.——There is on the second floor of Sir Francis Chauntrey's house, a suite of two large & two small rooms, the drawing-rooms being front. In the first & smallest room, I admired several pictures by Wilkie & Calcott. One of Wilkie's is the "Cut Finger" which has been engraved without doing justice to the original. In fact how can the best engraving approach a painting, and a painting by such an artist as Sir David Wilkie? This "Cut Finger" is one of his earlier pictures, done before the change in his style which took place after a visit to Italy. At least this is what I hear. I am told also that the early pictures are preferred by connoisseurs to the later ones, as having a unique character & style native, unborrowed & purely the artist's own. So that however highly esteemed he may be, his first productions are those most highly prized. I must acknowledge that the "Peep of day Boy" which I saw at Mr Vernon's, struck me as somewhat melo-dramatic in it's style.

Lady Chauntrey has another small Wilkie, a scotch christening, where the awkward father holds the red-faced baby to receive the sprinkling of cold water which is sure to make it squall, whilst the complacent mother, relieved of her charge, smiles placidly in her corner. The face of the boy in the "Cut Finger" is taken from Sir David's own, and he is said to have made faces in the glass in order to catch the puckers & wrinkles which he has transferred to his canvas. In the second drawing room is a picture by Edwin Landseer the history of which is interesting. Sir Walter Scott made Sir Francis Chauntrey a present of a favorite dog called Mustard, one of the breed to which such pungent & spicy names as Pepper, Mustard &c were always given. The dog was already fourteen years old and lived to the extreme age of nineteen, when he became so infirm, miserable, diseased & disgusting, that it was thought best to administer a dose of Prussic Acid for his relief & that of his masters. This was an unpleasant though neces-sary termination to a painful existence, & I was sorry that my too curious inquiries had put me in possession of it. As long as Sir Walter Scott lived, after giving his dog to his friend, he never came to the house without call-ing for & caressing (I think Lady Chauntrey said <u>kissing</u>) his old favorite. Of this dog so highly favored, Landseer made a portrait. He is represented lying on a table where are the modelling tools of Sir Francis, a snuff-box given him by his wife, which has been twirled between finger & thumb (a trick it seems of the artist) until it is evidently worn almost through, and a pair of woodcocks, important birds, killed by Sir Francis Chauntrey at one shot at Holkham, whilst on a visit to Lord Leicester. This exploit gained him great applause at Holkham, & the spot where it took place, a rising ground, has since been called Chauntrey's Hill. Sir Francis in return could not do less than carve the images of these Woodcocks in marble, so that dead as they are they still live by the chisel of Chauntrey & by the pencil of Landseer. The marble birds of which I saw a plaster cast in the studio, are I think, in alto relievo, and I am told that many Greek inscrip-tions have been written in their honour, or rather in honour of their death and of the hand by which they died. But Landseer in his picture has not confined himself to the Dog & the Woodcocks. His own Cat makes her appearance, half hid under the table cover, part of her head and one shining eye protruded as if watching an opportunity to seize the dead birds; whilst the Dog, aged & stiff but faithful to the last, is evidently quite as determined on the protection of his master's property as the Cat is on it's invasion. Both animals are admirably done, true to their several instincts & characters. Some one says that in the pre-existent state, the transmigration of souls, Landseer has evidently been a dog himself, and has thus acquired his intimate acquaintance with their nature. A Bust of Sir Walter Scott on the table close to his faithful Mustard, completes the picture.

From the second drawing room we passed into a small apartment furnished with Ottomans & adorned with looking glasses, the last display of the fantastic taste of Sir John Soane. A little of it as in this room, does well and produces a good effect, too much as in his own Museum, becomes fatiguing. Beyond is a small sculpture gallery containing however only plaster casts, large as life & no doubt good of their kind. Among these are the group of the Laocoon and single statues of Venus, Diana, Germanicus, Antinous, the fighting Gladiator & others. There were also ^several very^ small figures & groups in clay by Nollekens.

Having seen Lady Chauntrey's rooms, we went down stairs and walked through the Studio, where my previous impressions of Chauntrey's sort of talent were confirmed. He is certainly great in busts. He was at this time absent, at Buckingham House, where he is at work on a bust of the Queen. Mrs Morrison & myself after going through the sculpture rooms, returned to lunch with Lady Chauntrey. Before luncheon was over the bust of her Majesty arrived from the Palace and we were allowed the privilege of looking at it. The clay of course, being quite wet, there was a freshness & rawness about it which did not, however, injure the effect. The likeness is excellent; the air & expression more noble than in the original, but this is allowable. The hair is arranged in the modern fashion, plaited in front & carried down the cheeks and round the ears. The bust is fine, the throat almost too substantial; if the Queen lives & thrives she must inevitably become coarse; there is too much firm flesh already about the neck & chest for so young a person.

Whilst we were looking at the bust Allan Cunningham came in, Lady Chauntrey introduced him, (or presented him to us would I suppose, be the better expression,) and a request followed from Mrs Morrison, that he would shew me his relics of Burns. He accordingly brought into the drawing-room, whither we had returned, a box containing many autograph letters and poems of Robert Burns, with a small pair of pistols manufactured for him in Birmingham, and having the maker's name, Blair, upon them. Burns is said to have written to him in a bold, almost blasphemous style, that "he could say for the pistols what he could not say for many men, that they did credit to their maker."

The letters were written in a legible, coarse & decided hand, some of them signed with the name of Burns spelled with an e and a double ss, as the poet's father (& likewise himself) were for a long time in the habit of spelling it.—Burness—Among the poems were the "Cotter's Saturday Night" and others equally well known, written more fairly & in rather smaller characters than the letters were. Allan Cunningham has written a life of Burns, and spoke of his character & manners as strangely in contrast with his poetry. He describes him as dirty in his person, and coarse, almost brutal in his tastes & habits. Drunken we all know him to have been, and from this loathsome vice all the rest would follow. Latterly he was a soured & discontented man, having been as Allan Cunningham said, "sent back to his plough from the first circles in Edinburgh." He was taken up with too much warmth by these "first circles" and let fall again with too little consideraton. I observed that he had been at least very gently handled by his biographers, to which Mr Cunningham replied that he had been handled too ungently by the world not to excite the compassion of those who undertook to write his life.

Allan Cunningham began his own career as a stone-mason, a builder of stone walls. Having a taste for poetry, and falling in love with a lady's maid, he addressed verses to her which were seen & admired by her mistress. This brought him into some degree of notice & favour. He was patronised afterwards by Mrs Fletcher of Edinburgh, one of the benevolent of the earth, who introduced & recommended him to persons who had it in their power to advance his fortunes. He came to London, wrote more poems, cultivated literature, and finally found his right place in a Sculptor's Studio. He was taken up by Sir Francis Chauntrey, befriended & employed by him, and is now living in a small house communicating with Chauntrey's own, (or at least with the Sculpture rooms,) and in the enjoyment of an income sufficient for his wants. All these particulars I have (since I met him at Chauntrey's) heard from Mrs Carlyle, and also that in the midst of his success and his improving condition in life, he had not forgotten his early love but had returned and married his lady's-maid, who made him a very excellent wife—better than a woman of higher pretentions might have done.

This little history, I have said, was afterwards given me by Mrs Carlyle. But in this interview with Allan Cunningham he told me some particulers of Mrs Carlyle herself and of Carlyle also. Carlyle was the son of a small farmer, I think, in Dumfrieshire; of very humble origin he certainly was, his uncle being a stone-cutter. Mrs Carlyle the daughter of a laird, a person of some importance, had married her husband for love, her rank being far above his. They were both excellent in many ways. Mrs Carlyle a little given to sarcasm and "a hard way of speaking," for which says Allen Cunningham, "I like her none the worse. I am not fond of too much milk." "What," said I, "not when 'tis the milk of human kind-ness?" "No indeed, I do not object to a touch of bitterness. I do not think well enough of any body to believe that they never have bitter feelings, and if they have them it is better they should give some expression to them."

From Sir Francis Chauntrey's we went to Christie's Auction room, to see a piece of carving in wood by Grinling Gibbons. It represented the stoning of St Stephen but did not appear to me equal to the works of Gibbons which I had seen elsewhere, although of higher pretension. It is, however, in a bad state, and I saw it in a crowded room, where an auction sale was going on. Among other articles of real or conventional value exhibited at Christie's, was an old Buhl table much broken & defaced but undoubtedly of genuine antiquity, inlaid with various materials of brass, silver, mother-of-pearl, tortoise-shell, coloured ivories &c, in a most quaint & curious pattern with human figures intermixed. This rattle-trap, in it's delapidated state, brought eighty guineas. So much for fashion!

From the Auction room we proceeded to Mr Buchanan's rooms. He is a picture dealer and had on hand four paintings of old masters which Mrs Morrison wished me to see. A Madonna & Child by Guido purchased from the collection of Marshall Soult for 30.000 francs, & just sold to a gentleman in the country for £1400. A St. Jerome or perhaps, a St. Mark, having a Lion crouched at the feet of the principal figure, by Rubens, also from the collection of Marshall Soult. The Marshall, it is said, is very willing to part with his pictures for a con-sid-e-ra-tion, and nobody better understands their money value, nor how to set a price upon them. Mr Buchanan says however, that he gives the proceeds of these sales to his daughter; his son, the heir of his property, being a man of no taste. If this be true it is quite as well to part with the pictures to persons who have taste, and let the daughter have the benefit of the money. Both of these pictures I admired much. In Guido's there is a more pensive & thoughtful expression in the countenance of the Virgin Mother than one often sees, as if she felt the weight of her high destinies and understood the price which was to be paid. The attitude of the infant is charming although I thought the colour of the flesh somewhat milky. The other two of these old paintings were a Claude & a Gaspar Poussin. The Claude a beautiful back ground, probably the Bay of Naples & the Island of Capri, with high ground in front & a Grecian temple. The only thing that I did not like was a flock of Geese, not Swans, swimming in the stream on the bank of which stood the temple. The piece by Gaspar Poussin was a landscape with figures, the latter from the hand of Nicholas Poussin. Altogether a brighter & more smiling scene than ^in^ the other works which I have seen of this artist—Gaspar Poussin.

Our next visit was to Rainy's rooms, I think they were called, where are the models sent in by different persons for the Monument to be erected to Lord Nelson in Trafalgar Square. I thought I had never seen so many failures—so many ways of doing a thing badly. I gave a hasty glance at the columns, obelisks, Tritons, River Gods, horses with the tails of fish, & such like novelties, and came away. Two things I remarked, that the British Lion was, in these Monuments, as inevitable as a Phoenix after a fire, and that the model sent in by the Sculptor Bailly, though it did not please me as a whole, included some graceful and beautiful figures.

In the evening of Saturday Mr Coolidge & myself went to two parties— a small one at Miss Martineau's where we met the Carlyles, and a larger one at Mr Babbage's where I again saw Mrs Marcet. By the way I heard a few days since, that this lady who spends much of her time at Geneva, had been remonstrated with by the Select-men or Syndics, (or by whatever name may be called the guardians of public morals in the City of Calvin,) on the bad example which she set in having, when she went out, a foot-man to walk after her, instead of a little maid with her clogs. Thus Luxury advances with rapid strides, the strides of a long-legged footman, over the territory of the Republic, and the wealth and pride of England are con-taminating the purity of the ancient manners & modes of life in Geneva.

This evening I made acquaintance with Sir David Wilkie & his sister. This lady sat for Meg in her brother's picture of Duncan Gray. Meg is an improved likeness of Miss Wilkie, but still a likeness.

Among the guests at Mr Babbage's were the President of the Royal Society the Marquis of Northampton, Sir Francis & Lady Chauntrey, Lady Ogle, sublime in velvet & point lace, & M. & Mme Van de Weyer—she in a white muslin dress & a coiffure of velvet & blonde, a solecism in dress of which no frenchwoman could ever have been guilty. The Grammar of the French toilette has it's inviolable rules. Certain things go together, certain other things have no fitness of companionship. The subordinate parts of the dress must agree with the principals as the adjective agrees with it's noun, or the verb with it's nominative. Blond lace & velvet with

Muslin is against the Syntax of dress, shews an ignorance of Concord & Government. The English commit many of these faults of Grammar. I have received a great deal of valuable instruction in this branch of female education from my french maid Josephine, who is learned and a pedant in such matters. The charm of a french toilette consists first in the observance of these laws, which have their foundation in good taste, but also in it's fitness to time, place & season.

The distinctions of summer, autumn, winter & spring dress, (I have seen an Englishwoman driving in Hyde Park in July with a Fur Boa on her shoulders,) of morning & evening, (English ladies sometimes wear rich silks to breakfast) of full dress and half dress, of walking, carriage & parlour costumes, are observed with a precision which custom renders easy. Then in a french toilette, even as I have seen it in England, there is a harmony of colours which you do not always find in the dress of an English lady, and there is a neatness & freshness in all the minor articles, gloves, shoes, ribbons, handkerchiefs, which I am sorry to say does not exist universally among similar small items, as they are worn & used by the Anglo Saxons. "They order these things better in France" than in any other part of the world.

On Sunday 19th[1] we went at 3.P.M. to St Paul's, to hear the Revd Sidney Smith <u>preach</u>. He whose mouth, on week days, never opens but to give utterance to a bon mot, a repartee, an anecdote or some pleasant, sprightly sally, how can he speak solemn words, grave truths on Sunday? Yet he did speak them seriously and as if he felt what he was saying. At first I could scarcely compose my own thoughts, not knowing what might be coming to sound strangely in unaccustomed ears. But I soon found that the wit of the parlour was a clergyman in the pulpit. He preached & his sermon was on the due observance of the Sabbath, on the necessity of keeping holy the seventh day. It was sensible, discreet & not over zealous; no affectation of more warmth than was necessary; of course much more likely to be listened to by reasonable people. The unreasonable listen to nothing but their own prejudices & passions. The Church, St. Paul's, was as cold as a church and as dirty as a schoolhouse. It is a pity that a vast pile like this, too vast for the simplicity of Protestant-worship, should be left in such a state of uncleanness & desolation. There is too much waste room.

No long processions or gorgeous displays, such as are seen in Roman Catholic churches, ever sweep through St. Paul's.—In the noble Cathedrals of old Romish days, like those of York, Durham & Winchester, I have been often struck by the want of agreement between the place & the people. The forms of protestant worship seem out of place in buildings intended for the pomp & pride of Roman Catholic ceremonial. But these Cathedrals are relics, sacred from their association with the past, and it would be Vandalism to lay a finger upon them but for the purposes of preservation & repair. It is one of the things for which I greatly admire the English, the care they take of such time-hallowed monuments. But St. Paul's was built only a century & a half ago, when the days of Priests and Processions were over, built too not in the Gothic style which might create an illusion of the past—thus it seems to want a character of fitness for any time or purpose, and to be a sort of architectural anomaly.

We dined on Sunday at Mr Grote's with a pleasant party, Mr Babbage among others, and Charles Austin the lawyer, who talked with me a good deal, and in a style which I liked, though of late I have not been accustomed to ^any thing so grave.^ Conversation in general society is, or means to be, light & brilliant, touching on many subjects, arguing or discoursing on none. This amuses me, & I listen with pleasure, but want of practice makes it difficult for me to say much. It does not, (to excel in this kind of talk,) require so much wit as that you should have your wits about you. Ease of expression, readiness, presence of imagination, a propos, such are the chief ingredients and necessary components where many persons join in the same conversation, and keep up the ball which must be struck back to the principal player by whoever has the quickest hand. When it comes to conversation between two persons, the case changes and the requisites for success are very different.

A person like Charles Austin who is a practical man and talks like one who talks at all because he has something to say, and ideas to communicate,—and who has a clear & precise mode of expression because his ideas are clear & precise, is worth more, where there are but two persons than the most brilliant wit or bel esprit could possibly be.

Mr Austin is called, in politics, a Radical. His views struck me as grand and gloomy, enlarged in generals, desponding in particulars. He spoke of the state of things in England, the ignorance, vice and physical force of the lower classes who are kept under only by the combined influence of the wealth, education and moral supremacy of the middle & upper ranks of society. He deplored the thoughtlessness and want of knowledge of the true state of things in the very persons whose safety depends on the wisdom of their own measures. As he described their want of sympathy in the sufferings of the people, and of respect for their rights & claims, their selfish enjoyment of their own privileges, and careless indifference to the deplorable state of those beneath them, I could not help exclaiming, "Mr Austin, you are, from your own account, like the officers and crew of a slave ship, amusing yourselves on deck, whilst in the hold below, there is the lowest degree of wretchedness—existence in it's most loathsome and miserable form." "Just so;" he replied; "you must only add that the slaves have it in their power at any moment, to rise & overcome their masters, or throw a torch into the Magazine."——What different views I get from different people! Yet all agree that many evil elements are at work, & that volcanic materials ready to burst forth at any moment, are just beneath the social surface of this great country. Will they be satisfied to rumble & end in slight shocks or is a real earthquake at hand? Time the friend or the enemy must show.

From Mr Grote's we went to Mr Mansfield's where we passed an hour pleasantly, and I saw & talked with Mr Frederic Elliot, the brother of Lady Hislop. He has been to America & seems to like the country ^&^ particularly Boston.

———

Sir Francis Chantrey sent a letter to Landseer in April 1835 signed MUSTARD, commissioning the dog's portrait. Chantrey's painting was exhibited at the Royal Academy show the following year, and his widow presented it to Queen Victoria in 1842 (Richard Ormond, *Sir Edwin Landseer* [1981], 108–109).

Charles Sumner visited HOLKHAM Hall, Thomas Coke's Palladian estate, and saw Chantrey's marble tribute to the woodcocks: "A beautiful marble tablet adorns the library, on which are two woodcocks falling together,—the offering of the sportsman and the sculptor to his noble host. Inscriptions for this tablet came in from various quarters." Sumner declined offering a poem himself but passed along several from Cornelius Felton, Harvard professor of Greek. These and other inscriptions were compiled and edited by James Muirhead in *Winged Words on Chantrey's Woodcocks* (1857) (Edward L. Pierce, ed., *Memoir and Letters of Charles Sumner* [1893], 1:161, 376–378).

QUEEN Victoria chose Sir Francis Chantrey to fashion her likeness in marble, making her the fourth successive British sovereign the sculptor would portray during their lifetimes. Between 1 October 1838, when the bust was commissioned, and 1 May 1840, Victoria sat for Chantrey seven times, and hers was probably the last bust Chantrey himself ever sculpted. Chantrey worked by creating clay models that provided the form for a plaster cast, which the sculptor then used to transfer dimensions to the marble block. Chantrey displayed the plaster casts in his studio; however, the clay models were destroyed and the material reused. Chantrey's studio was only a few hundred yards from Buckingham Palace, making it possible for the clay model to arrive wet. The resulting sculpture (fig. 31) was regarded by Prince Albert as the best likeness of the queen. It became well known through its reproduction on coins and medals and is part of the Royal Collection. Victoria ordered two copies of the bust, one for her father-in-law Ernest I, Duke of Saxe-Coburg-Gotha (1784–1844), and another for Robert Peel, which is now in the National Portrait Gallery (*ODNB*, s.v. "Chantrey, Francis"; Jane Roberts, *Royal Treasures: A Golden Jubilee Celebration* [2002], 144-145; Dr. M. G. Sullivan, Chantrey Fellow, Ashmolean Museum, University of Oxford, to Ann Lucas Birle, 29 May 2008; Sir Francis Chantrey, *Queen Victoria* [1841], NPG.org).

ALLAN CUNNINGHAM (1784–1842) became the superintendent of Chantrey's studio and gallery in 1814, acted as his secretary, and was a favorite of the sculptor's clients and visitors. After working from 6 A.M. to 6 P.M. in the studio, Cunningham wrote in the evening to support his "wife and weans," contributing to *Blackwood's Magazine*, submitting a drama to Sir Walter Scott, whom he had befriended at the studio, and publishing several volumes of poems and songs. Cunningham is most well known for his six-volume *Lives of the Most Eminent British Painters, Sculptors, and Architects* (1829–1833) and his eight-volume *The Works and Life of Burns* (1834). Cunningham's marriage to Jean Walker (1791–1864) was a happy one, and together they had five sons and one daughter (*ODNB*; Allan Cunningham, *Lives of the Most Eminent British Painters, Sculptors, and Architects* [1829–1833], 1:xix).

Robert Burns wrote to Birmingham gunmaker David BLAIR (1755–1814) that "the defensive tools do more than half mankind do, they do honor to their maker; but I trust that with me they shall have the fate of a miser's gold—to be often admired, but never used." On his deathbed Burns gave a brace of pistols made by Blair to his friend and attending doctor William Maxwell (1760–1834). At the time of Maxwell's death he owned two pairs of pistols that Blair had made, but the set that Allan Cunningham purchased had no connection to Robert Burns, despite his belief to the contrary. The Burns pistols were acquired after Maxwell's death by Bishop James Gillis, who in 1859 gave them to the National Museum of Antiquities of Scotland, one of the constituents of the present National Museums of Scotland, in whose collection they remain today (*ODNB*, s.v. "Burns, Robert"; Frances Wilkins, *Lock, Stock and Barrel: Robert Burns, Dr William Maxwell and a Pair of Pistols* [2009]; Rev. Bishop [James] Gillis, "A Paper on the Subject of Burns's Pistols," *Proceedings of the Society of Antiquaries of Scotland* 3 [1857–1860]: 239–244; Allan Cunningham, *Works of Robert Burns; With His Life* [1834], 1:344–345, 4:vi; Robert Burns, *The Complete Works of Robert Burns* [1886], 3:246–247; John Burnett, Curator of Modern Scotland, National Museums of Scotland, to Ann Lucas Birle, 26 Mar. 2010).

CHRISTIE'S AUCTION ROOMS were first established in 1766 by James Christie, who auctioned everything from chamber pots to sedan chairs. By the turn of the nineteenth century Christie became known for his fine art sales, and at the time of Coolidge's visit the firm was in the present-day location of the company's headquarters at 8 King Street, near St. James's Square (*London Encyclopedia*, 157; *Old and New London*, 4:123–139, 191–206).

The Stoning of St. Stephen (ca. 1680–1710) is considered the most impressive figural relief made by the decorative woodcarver GRINLING GIBBONS (1648–1721). The work depicts the stoning to death of the first Christian martyr set against a backdrop of a grand Italianate building. Gibbons displayed it in his home, which suggests that he created the piece for his own pleasure. It was offered for sale at Christie's in 1839 and eventually became part of the Victoria and Albert collection (*ODNB*; Grinling Gibbons, *The Stoning of St. Stephen*, [ca. 1680–1710], Victoria and Albert Museum, accessed 11 July 2011, http://collections.vam.ac.uk).

The Morrisons first became acquainted with the brash speculative art dealer William **BUCHANAN** (1777–1864) in July 1838. On 30 January 1839 James Morrison agreed to purchase the entire collection of Edward Gray of Harringay House—exactly 134 pictures—from Buchanan for fifteen thousand pounds, with the intention of selling off the majority at a profit. Morrison retained 22 favorites, primarily Dutch, styling his collection after that of the Barings, rival bankers with whom Buchanan also dealt. Buchanan chronicled his life as a collector in *Memoirs of Painting* (1824). He was married to Elizabeth Ann Murray (d. 1846), with whom he had a daughter, Mary Clara (*Oxford Companion to Western Art* [2001], s.v. "London: Patronage and Collecting," by Hugh Brigstocke, Oxford Reference Online; Hugh Brigstocke, *William Buchanan and the Nineteenth-Century Art Trade* [1982], 31, 463; Caroline Dakers, "'A Casket to Enclose Pictorial Gems,'" *Apollo* 159 [Apr. 2004]: 29–35).

Marshal **SOULT** was among the French officers who amassed a collection of Spanish art through coercion and the abuse of power during the occupation of the Iberian Peninsula by Napoleonic forces. In all Soult sent 109 paintings to his Paris home, most notably works by Murillo, where visitors, including artists such as David Wilkie, admired the collection. In 1823 Soult began negotiations through Buchanan for the sale of his pictures to English collectors, and in June 1840 Buchanan arranged an exhibition of works from Soult's gallery at 49 Pall Mall, London (Brigstocke, "London: Patronage and Collecting"; Hugh Brigstocke, *William Buchanan* [1982], 474).

Sculptor, metalsmith, and designer Edward Hodges Baily [**BAILLY**] (1788–1867) was a student of John Flaxman and worked in the shop of the royal jewelers Rundell & Bridge. A member of the Royal Academy, his entry into the design competition for Lord Nelson's monument was one of 41 models and 118 drawings on display in Alexander Rainy's auction rooms at 14 Regent Street. William Railton's design for a monumental column topped by a statue of Nelson won first place; Baily's design came in second. Baily was selected to sculpt the figure of Nelson for Railton's design, and his statue was raised atop Railton's 170-foot column on 6 November 1843 (*ODNB*; Tallis, part 17; "The Nelson Memorial," *Mirror of Literature, Amusement, and Instruction* 34 [1839]: 1–3).

The Scottish painter **DAVID WILKIE** (1785–1841) began his training in Edinburgh and came to London in 1805, where he studied at the Royal Academy Schools and was elected an associate of the Academy in 1809. Wilkie favored genre scenes, such as views of village life, done in a style adopted from Dutch and Flemish artists Ostade and Teniers. In London Wilkie received commissions from aristocracy and royalty, the most well known being the Duke of

Wellington's request for a painting showing "a parcel of old soldiers." Wilkie composed a scene that showed the reception of the news of the victory at Waterloo by pensioners near Chelsea Hospital. *Chelsea Pensioners* was so popular at the 1822 Royal Academy exhibition that it had to be protected from the crowds by a rail. Wilkie found affinity as well with fellow Scots Sir Walter Scott and Robert Burns, and the latter's song "Duncan Gray" inspired Wilkie's painting *The Refusal* (1814), now at the Victoria and Albert Museum. Using Wilkie's friend and fellow-artist William Mulready as a model for Duncan, the painting shows Maggie's initial refusal of her suitor's affections. Wilkie's sister Helen arrived in London the year he was working on *The Refusal* and may well have been the model for Maggie (*ODNB*; *Oxford Companion to the Romantic Age* [2009] and *Oxford Dictionary of Art and Artists* [2009], s.v. "Wilkie, Sir David," Oxford Reference Online; David Wilkie, *The Refusal* [1814], Victoria and Albert Museum, accessed 20 Dec. 2010, http://www.vam.ac.uk).

Spencer Joshua Alwyne Compton, second Marquess of **NORTHAMPTON** (1790–1851), was president of the Royal Society of London from 1838 until 1848. He was a minor poet and had a particular interest in geology (*ODNB*).

LADY OGLE was Mary Anne Cary (d. 1842), the third wife of naval officer Charles Ogle (1775–1858), commander-in-chief in North America from 1827 to 1830 (*ODNB*; Gray, *Daniel Webster in England*, 73–74).

REVᴰ SIDNEY SMITH ended his career at St. Paul's in July 1844 with another sermon on the observance of the Sabbath, saying that "We are so absorbed . . . in the business and in the pleasures of this world, that the recollection of any other would, but for the institution of the Sabbath, be very soon obliterated. . . . [U]ntimely amusement on the Sabbath leads to ungodliness, by checking seriousness and holiness of thought; and it is impossible that any human being can make progress in godliness, without stated periods, in which they may fall into an holy and serious train of thought" (Sydney Smith, *Sermons Preached at St. Paul's Cathedral, The Foundling Hospital, and Several Churches in London* [1846], 172–181).

Thomas Frederick **ELLIOT** (1808–1880) served in Quebec from 1835 to 1837 as secretary to the Earl of Gosford's commission of inquiry into Canadian affairs. After his return to England he became chair of the colonial land and emigration commission, through which he influenced government-assisted emigration to Australia (*ODNB*).

1. Ellen here misdates a reference to 17 March.

Thursday 21. March.

It is well we decided to delay our departure till the early part of April, for there is even now more to do than we can accomplish within the time. We have satisfactory accounts from Geneva and have almost decided to send our sons thither.

Monday 18th March, Mr Coolidge dined with Mountstuart Elphinstone, and my little Jefferson & myself with Mrs Searle.

Tuesday 19th, I went to see Guildhall with Mr Coolidge, but first paid a
visit to the Herald's office in Doctor's Commons. It pleased me to look over
the musty volumes which contain the records of so many families. Here I
found my own name & arms, and the arms belonging to my grandfather
Jefferson of which I have a rude copy made by his own hand, attached to
the name of Jeffery. In the Book of Crests however, which I have, his name
of Jefferson is included with the very crest, a Talbot's head erased, which I
find in the Herald's books, and in the drawing made by himself. In these
books is the name of Coulridge belonging to the counties of Bucks & of
Lincoln. A certain Ursula Colleridge married Geoffrey Dormer, and from
her was descended a Sir William Dormer, married to Mary a daughter of
Sir William Sidney of Penshurst. Thus my sons Algernon & Sidney, are
not without a shadow of a shew of fitness in their names. There is also an
intermarriage between one of Mrs Ursula's descendents and a daughter
of Sir Easeby Isham of Northumberland. Bart. Now my great, great, great
grandfather, the first of the Randolphs who settled in Virginia, was married to a Miss Isham, the daughter of a Baronet, probably of the same

FIGURE 12. A sketch of the Jefferson Coat of Arms, by Thomas
Jefferson, n.d. Ellen owned this sketch, which carries the motto
"He who gives life gives liberty." *(Courtesy of Private Collection.)*

Northamptonshire family. Ursula Colleridge or Coulridge or Colerich, was the daughter of Bryan or Bartholemew Coulridge of a family settled in Bucks, from Lincoln. The name of Coulridge or Coolidge is found among the early settlers in New England who are known, many of them, to have come from Lincolnshire, thus the name of Boston is as it were, a family name, among the Pilgrims.

The Hall at Guildhall is an immense place and the two ancient & grim figures called Gog & Magog, raised high above the ground, look hideous in their respective corners. They are Giants with yellow faces and black beards. I could not learn how long they have been frowning at Guildhall, nor what tradition may be attached to them. In the Common Council Room are several pictures. One which covers some acres of canvas, by Copley,—subject taken from the siege of Gibraltar. Another by Opie, said to be his best work, the murder of Rizzio. I did not greatly admire either of them. But I do not pretend to be a judge. There are likewise portraits of George 3^d Queen Caroline & the Princess Charlotte—Lord Heathfield, Lord Cornwallis & others. At Guildhall, Mr Coolidge & myself parted, and I returned home alone, calling on Miss Martineau by the way. She lives in a small, steep street called Fludyer street in Westminster, where it is almost as much as your neck is worth to visit her. Her door opens just upon the pinch of the hill, & the horses have to hold up the whole weight of the carriage whilst you alight from it. We were told that on the evening of her party Lord Jefferey, whom she was, no doubt, anxiously expecting, made his appearance & his leave-taking bow within five minutes of each other, having left his wife & daughter in their carriage, at the entrance of the street, afraid to venture up, and preferring to wait where they were till Lord Jeffrey & his son-in-law could pay their compliments & return.

The house is small & of homely appearance; a narrow staircase and one small room at each side of the landing place above, which landing place is of course, the only means of communication between the rooms. At Miss Martineau's parties it needs must that the company is divided or suffocated, according as they occupy one room or two.

I found the lady just come in from her walk & still attired in her walking costume. She received me kindly and talked, as she always does, fluently & frankly. She spoke of the Queen, of the difficulties of her position, and the unreasonableness of the public in requiring & expecting more than could be performed, and in making no allowance for her youth, inexperience, the influence of flattery, the intoxication of Royalty &c &c &c. "We should," said Miss Martineau, "give her credit for all the good we can find in her, and wonder not that she is spoiled, but that she is not entirely spoiled." Miss M— believes her Majesty to be very bad-tempered, and considers that her conduct to her mother is both disrespectful and unkind. She mentioned the fact that three days after Sir James Clarke had been dismissed in disgrace from the service of the Duchess of Kent, in consequence of his ignorant aspersions of the character of poor Lady Flora Hastings, the Queen having or pretending to have a finger-ache, ostentatiously required his attendance upon herself. The tracasseries & the intrigues, the gossip & the scandal of the Palace, furnish of course, ample matter for small talk and for all sorts of rumours. The Queen, it is said, hates Sir John Conroy, who was the tyrant of her childhood, and she cannot become reconciled to her mother's obstinately retaining him in her own service. The cause of the Duchess of Kent's adherence to this unpopular servant is, by some persons, ascribed to the most scandalous motives of personal preference—By others, and Miss Martineau among the number, to an honest, courageous determination not to sacrifice an old friend, whose conduct may have been unwise, but never unfaithful, to an unjust prejudice.

Whilst speaking of the Queen I will mention some other particulars interesting as connected with one filling so exalted a station, and who as sovereign of the greatest nation in the world, may be considered, young girl as she is, not only the first among women, but as second in rank & conventional importance to none. She is described as having been, before her accession to the throne, a cheerful & even mirthful girl, brought up very strictly by her mother, but with a good fund of animal spirits: She was never allowed to be a moment alone, the Duchess of Kent, her governess the Duchess of Northumberland, or some appointed person being always at hand. On the first news of King William's death, she is said to have requested that she might be left to herself for some short time, whether for the purpose of solitary prayer, or to collect her thoughts unseen, it might be difficult to say. The first night after her accession the Duchess of Kent directed that certain medicines, restoratives, should be at hand in case of the Queen's finding herself overcome by the excitement & novelty of her situation, & perhaps experiencing some attack of a nervous description. But the lady whose duty it was to wait upon her through that night, perhaps to sleep in her chamber (I think it was the Baroness Lehzen,) reported next morning that her Majesty had slept & waked at the usual hours, having passed a night of uninterrupted repose. Her temperament is certainly not an irritable one however her temper may be. She does not appear to possess quick feelings, at least where others are concerned. The Revd Sidney Smith is reported to have said of her that "she was a long-headed, cold-hearted girl." I distrust cold-hearted people—The Queen is regular, punctual, methodical & exact, & requires the same qualities in those who approach her. When still a child it was one of her amusements to play Queen, whilst one of her companions acted the part of lady-in-waiting or maid of honour. On one occasion the game was reversed & the Princess Victoria took herself the subordinate character. She went through all the forms & observances with great precision & exactness, and then said to the young girl who had been playing Queen—"Now observe the way in which I have waited on you, for just so, when I am Queen in good earnest, and you are my maid of honour, I shall expect you to wait on me." Soon after her accession she wrote with her own hand to Lady Tavistock requesting her to become one of her personal attendants. The letter was cordial & friendly, beginning, "Dear Lady Tavistock, you are one of my oldest friends," and going on to express her wish that Lady Tavistock should accept the place offered to her. Queens do not ask in vain & Lady Tavistock was installed in office. Not being acquainted with her new duties she conceived them to be nearly or entirely nominal, & that as lady-in-waiting she would have little or nothing to do. On the day after her arrival at Windsor she was brought to a sense of her deficiencies. The Queen called for her cloak. Lady Tavistock looked confusedly round to see who was bringing it. She saw by the countenances of the bystanders that she had been guilty of some neglect & hastened to repair it. She got the cloak but when it was to be arranged on her majesty's shoulders the unlucky waiting maid was again ^somewhat^ at fault, and acquitted herself but awkwardly of the important duty. The Queen gave her a slight reprimand, saying "Tavistock you must make yourself acquainted with the duties you have undertaken to perform."—The result was that this lady of high birth & breeding one of the proud aristocracy of England, took lessons from her own maid in the art of putting on cloaks & waiting upon a mistress. The person to whom Lady Tavistock herself told the story, and who afterwards related it to me, laughed when she heard it. "You may laugh," said the lady-in-waiting, "and so can I now, but these things when they took place were no laughing matter to me."—I believe this story to be strictly true. "On dits" are by no means, as a general rule, to be relied on, though I think they give the character of things & persons, and might have happened even if they did not actually take place.

But leaving the Queen to return to Miss Martineau, she gave me several anecdotes of her false friend Lord Brougham. She is no longer in alliance with him but she speaks of him without rancour, or at least without the appearance of it. She describes him as a man always on the verge of insanity, his father having been insane, whilst one of his sisters is but lately recovered from a regular fit of madness. Lord Brougham, says his late ally, is violent in temper, coarse even gross in mind and manners, bitter in his resentments, profane in his language, ungovernable in his passions, but having warm affections and transcendent abilities. Towards those who he likes his feelings are kind, and where he loves it is almost passionately. His love for his brother James lately dead, shewed itself during his illness by the most frantic manifestations of grief. He walked about his room and, says Miss Martineau, absolutely howled, shewing such violence as to alarm his secretary, who almost feared to venture into his presence. This death of his brother brought him into pecuniary difficulties as he had been indiscreetly liberal in lending him his credit and incurring responsibilities for him. He borrowed from his friends before & since, and at this very time he actually owes & has been for some time owing, one hundred pounds to Miss Martineau herself, whose sole support is in her own exertions. [I hope she does not know that he swears at her for a d—d Ass. If she does she probably thinks that she deserved the epithet when she lent him the money.] He has latterly become so indecent in his conversation that ladies are sometimes shy in his company.

Miss Martineau saw Mrs Austin, who is a very handsome ~~pers~~ ^woman^ and much admired by Lord Brougham, turn pale at a dinner table from the agitation into which she was thrown by his questions and allusions to some portion of the domestic history of Schlegel said to be not at all a fit subject for dinner-table discussion. It is not true that Lord Brougham can be called a drunkard, a common report at one time. He drinks even less than English gentlemen are wont to do, although about the time of his brother's death, or after it, he indulged to a greater extent. As a young man he loved wine, and was once, after an illness, warned by his physicians, to abstain from stimulants, as there was in him a tendency to irritation of the brain. He was told that his general regimen should be of a cooling and quieting description. He disregarded the warning however, and continued to drink freely though not excessively until one evening, at a large dinner party, having taken a drop more than enough, he gathered from his plate the bones of a chicken upon which he had been feasting, and threw them across the table into the face of a gentleman sitting opposite. Great confusion ensued. Gentlemen rose from their chairs—there were exclamations of indignation. Brougham's friends gathered round him, some apologizing to the insulted man, others hurrying the offender away to bed, the fittest place for him, whilst he was protesting and declaring that he could not possibly refrain from throwing the chicken bones into the face opposite to him at table, seeing that this face was so villainous a face. The next morning he was penitent and ashamed, made all necessary apologies, and was so painfully impressed by the sense of his own misconduct that he was for a long time after, entirely abstemious, drinking little or no wine. Mr Sumner who has this winter seen a great deal of him, says that he never saw him take more than four glasses at one time, and when we consider that an English gentleman will sometimes drink two bottles of wine at one sitting, four glasses must be called the extremest modiration.

Miss Martineau says that Lord Brougham shews the greatest aversion for the unfortunate sister who has crossed the dividing line on which he stands himself between sanity & insanity. She has been positively mad and he hates her for having been what he may possibly become. She is worse to him than a memento mori. I have heard from others than Miss Martineau however, that the case of the sister is one of ideocy, yet this cannot be as she has recovered from the attack & there is no recovery from ideocy.

Lord Brougham visits freely at the house of Lady Blessington, the English Ninon de l'Enclos. Even her ears are too chaste for his stories, which in grossness occasionally exceed the limits of her forbearance, & call forth a reproof from the "femme galante." This still fair & fascinating courtezan receives the best company of the Metropolis that is of the male sex, at her elegant & recherché dwelling—gives dinners & petits-soupers at which wits & witlings, scholars & gentlemen, authors & artists, statesmen & generals, Lords & Commons assemble to enjoy her hospitalities and the society which she gathers round her. This account I receive from Mr Sumner who visited at her house. She was for a long time at feud with Lord Brougham but is lately reconciled to him.——

Miss Martineau talked politicks of course, how could it be otherwise? She is rather despondent about the state of things in England, deprecates any thing like revolution, thinks the people of England unfit for any form of republican government, deplores the folly of the Ministry whose course has been to yield to clamour what they denied to reason, to let the people see that they may gain by faction what is refused to justice, "just," said I in my rather commonplace reply, "as a foolish mother misgoverns her children, giving them what they cry for & only yielding to importunity what might have been granted from kindness." "You have it exactly," quoth Miss Martineau.

I have heard in other quarters some silly stories of Lord Melbourne's "paternal love for the Queen," that he frequently speaks of her with "tears in his eyes" from the excessive interest he takes in her—Mr C. asked if these tears were not shed <u>after dinner</u>,—not Crocodile but maudlin tears. Paternal love for the Queen! What twaddle! He is a hypocrite, Lord Melbourne; but some people like to be imposed upon. "He is so kind and affable," says good Lady Chauntrey,—"when we were staying at Holkham together, he would often give his arm to me, to lead me to dinner as if I had been a great lady, and when I said to him, 'Lord Melbourne, there is Lady So & So of high rank,' he would answer, 'of what consequence is that Lady Chauntrey, if I prefer you.'"

I parted from Miss Martineau with kinder feelings than those with which I met her. Whether she is improved by travelling & a longer use of good society, whether she is the better for having been occasionally snubbed, or that she does ^not^ feel entitled in England to the dogmatism she assumed in America, I do not know; but she is decidedly a pleasanter person at her own home than she was in mine. Her conversation is very lively, animated & entertaining, not at all disfigured by pedantry, nor offensive by the arbitrary tone she allowed herself in the United States.——

In 1771 Thomas **JEFFERSON** had a set of family arms in his possession, but he questioned their authority. He asked a friend in London to "search the Herald's office for the arms of my family. I have what I have been told were the family arms, but on what authority I know not. It is possible there may be none. If so I would with your assistance become a purchaser, having Sterne's word for it that a coat of arms may be purchased as cheap as any other coat." The results of this request are unknown. A second opportunity to clarify his family heraldry came in 1786, when Jefferson spent six weeks in London as a treaty commissioner. On 26 March 1786 he purchased a very expensive seal, and within a few weeks the wax impression of a seal with the Jefferson arms made its first known appearance on several treaties that Jefferson signed in London. Thomas Jefferson is not known to have purchased these arms nor is he recorded as being entitled to their use. Jefferson's descendants, however, considered this to be his coat of arms and had them illustrated in Henry Randall's 1858 biography, engraved on the Monticello coffee urn, and incorporated in the graveyard entrance gate.

The sketch that Jefferson made and Coolidge owned (fig. 12) shows the coat of arms granted by the College of Arms to the Jeaffersons of Dullingham House in Cambridgeshire in 1839; that family had evidently used the arms for generations. These arms are described by the college as "Azure a Fret Argent on a Chief of the last three Leopards' heads Gules. The crest: On a Wreath Azure and Argent a Talbot's Head erased Argent eared Gules." Coolidge noted that the coat of arms illustrated by Randall used a lion's head rather than that of a talbot for the crest. Also, the motto that appears in Jefferson's drawing is different from that employed by the English branch of the family, suggesting that he may have created his own. "Ab eo Libertas a quo Spiritus" has been translated as "the spirit (comes) from him from whom liberty comes," or more freely, "he who gives life gives liberty" (College of Arms, London, correspondence in the Jefferson Library Research Files, Thomas Jefferson Foundation, Inc.; *PTJ*, 1:62, 9:xxvii and facing page 418; *MB*, 1:615; engraving of Jefferson coat of arms as illustrated in Randall with Coolidge memorandum, ca. 1858 [private collection, N.Y.]; Thomas Jefferson, drawing of coat of arms, undated [private collection, N.Y.]).

The **BOOK OF CRESTS** that Coolidge owned was most likely the two-volume London edition of *The Book of Family Crests* (1838). This was among the titles that formed the West End branch of the Boston Public Library in 1896, to which Coolidge's son-in-law Edmund Dwight Coolidge donated 1,080 volumes. An 1838 London edition of H. Clark's *An Introduction to Heraldry* was also in that library's holdings (*Classified Finding List of the West End Branch of the Public Library of the City of Boston* [1896], 5; Boston Public Library, *Forty-Fourth Annual Report 1895* [1896], 158).

WILLIAM SIDNEY (ca. 1482–1554) was a courtier to King Henry VII and King Edward VI, from whom he received Penshurst in Kent in 1552 (*ODNB*).

Around 1675 William Randolph (1650–1711) married the widow Mary **ISHAM**, daughter of Henry Isham from Northamptonshire. Nine of their children survived to adulthood and formed the foundation of one of the most powerful dynasties in colonial Virginia (*ODNB*).

GOG & MAGOG were a pair of giants said to have been living in Cornwall when Brutus, legendary founder of Britain, first arrived there. According to Tudor legend, Brutus captured Gog and Magog alive, brought them to London, and chained them to the gate of his palace to serve as porters. Beginning in the fifteenth century, effigies of the giants were used on royal occasions and displayed in Guildhall as defenders of the city and the nation. Effigies of Gog and Magog have been carried in the Lord Mayor's Show (fig. 21) since the reign of Henry V, and the tradition continues to this day. The wooden statues Coolidge saw, carved in 1708 by Capt. Richard Saunders, had been restored in 1837 but were destroyed in World War II (Timbs, *Curiosities*, 331–333; *A Dictionary of English Folklore* [2000], s.v. "Gogmagog," Oxford Reference Online; the Lord Mayor's Show, accessed 11 July 2011, http://lordmayorsshow.org).

Harriet **MARTINEAU** lived with her mother at 17 Fludyer Street in a modest house near St. James's Park, within easy walking distance of Samuel Rogers's home. Martineau recalled that Rogers's gardener would leave the garden gate unlocked for her so that she could enter his home through the breakfast room. Martineau appreciated her own house's airiness, three sitting rooms, and location: "We were in the midst of the offices, people and books which it was most desirable for me to have at hand; and the house was exactly the right size for us; and of the right cost." She recalled, however, that "meddlers and mischief-makers" rendered her and her mother "discontented with the lowliness of our home. They

were for ever suggesting that I ought to live in some sort of style, — to have a larger
house in a better street, and lay out our mode of living for the society in which I
was moving. . . . To all remonstrances about my own dignity my reply was that if
my acquaintance cared for me, they would come and see me in a small house and
a narrow street: and all who objected to the smallness of either might stay away"
(Martineau, *Autobiography*, 196–197, 256).

Francis Jeffrey [**JEFFEREY**] (1773–1850), Scottish jurist and member of Parliament, was a founder and editor of the *Edinburgh Review*. Jeffrey first met Harriet
Martineau in 1832 in the company of Jane Marcet and Sarah Austin, and they
developed a friendship based on mutual respect. His wife was Charlotte Wilkes,
an American whom he met during her tour in Europe in 1810 and followed back
to America, where they were married in 1813. While in America Jeffrey traveled to
Washington and met with Pres. James Madison and Secretary of State James Mon-
roe before returning to Edinburgh. The couple's only child, Charlotte, married
the lawyer and *Edinburgh Review* contributor William Empson (1791–1852) in
1838. In 1847 Empson became the editor at the *Review* and remained so until
his death (*ODNB*, s.v. "Jeffrey, Francis" and "Empson, William"; Martineau, *Autobiography*, 242–243; N. T. Cockburn, *Life of Lord Jeffrey with a Selection from His
Correspondence* [1852], 325–326).

Three days after the death of King William IV, Victoria noted in her diary, "I wrote
a letter to the Marchioness of **TAVISTOCK** while Stockmar was here, asking her
to become one of my Ladies of the Bedchamber." Lady Tavistock accepted the
position the following day and within the week accompanied Victoria to pay
her respects to Queen Adelaide at Windsor Palace. The indignities and inconveniences suffered by Victoria's ladies of the bedchamber were frequent topics
of conversation and seen as evidence of the young queen's immature and self-
centered nature. Victoria did not like reprimanding those in her service but did so
on Melbourne's advice that otherwise they would come to take advantage of her
(Christopher Hibbert, *Queen Victoria: A Personal History* [2000], 62; Brett, *Girlhood
of Queen Victoria*, 1:202–203).

JAMES Brougham (1780–1833), lawyer and member of Parliament, benefited
from his brother's position as chancellor with appointments to office that generated criticism and scrutiny of Lord Brougham's administration. Little is known
about their only **SISTER**, Mary, other than Lord Brougham's description of her
having been the chronicler of the births, marriages, and deaths of the family
(*ODNB*, s.v. "Brougham, Henry Peter"; *Gentleman's Magazine*, n.s., 1 [1834]: 331–
332; *Gentleman's Magazine*, n.s., 1 [1868]: 121–122; "The Reform Ministry and the
Reformed Parliament," *Quarterly Review* [London] 50 [1834]: 239; *Legal Observer*
[London], 11 Jan. 1834).

NINON DE L'ENCLOS (1620–1705) was a French courtesan who advocated a form
of Epicureanism in her book *La Coquette vengée* (1659). Her fashionable salon attracted literary figures (*Oxford Dictionary of English*, rev. ed. [2005], s.v. "Lenclos,
Ninon de," Oxford Reference Online).

Sunday 24th March.

As my stay in England approaches it's close my engagements multiply, and I have less & less time to write. I have fallen now nearly a week in arrears in my account of things. I must, after premising that this 24th March is a beautiful spring day and that my table is covered with violets & primroses, begin by at least a list of the places I have been to, & the persons I have seen since thursday 19th when I called on Miss Martineau—The details I give in my letters, this journal being nothing more than an outline or the cord on which only part of my beads are strung.

Wednesday March 20t we visited a fine collection of pictures by modern artists, at Park Cottage, Blackheath, the house of Mr Sheepshanks, a friend of Mr Leslie the painter. This gentleman is a great lover of art & a patron of artists whom he treats with much liberality and by whom he is greatly esteemed. One visit to such a collection of paintings as these at Park Cottage only serves to whet one's appetite. We are to go again, for another feast.

Thursday March 21st we saw the East India Museum, the tiger of Tippoo Saib, an abundance of sanscrit MSS. & of jewels & pearls the ornaments of native princes; and we saw Professor Wilson whom some people consider a Lion far excelling all tigers, and a jewel of oriental learning far more precious than precious stones.

I have never seen a more melancholy-looking place than the East India House in Leadenhall St. Surely the glory of the illustrious Company is departing. Their Museum strikes me as unworthy of their great opportunities for making a better collection. It contains to be sure some barbaric pearl & gold, the spoils of native princes; stones genuine no doubt but badly polished and ill set, and inferiour in effect to imitations made by better workmen; and the pearls though large are often discoloured and misshapen. I presume however that articles of real value would not be displayed in a Museum. One large gold plate, enamelled in rich patterns of flowers & birds, a present from the Shah of Persia, was, as far as the enamelling went, of beautiful workmanship. Professor Wilson shewed us a collection of medals, principally of Bactrian Kings which are no doubt rare & curious; also cups of gold and silver taken from the topes found in India. These topes are masses of solid masonry, except for small cavities left for the purpose of enclosing relics. In these cavities are found cups, sometimes several one within the other, the innermost of all being often of gold. Here also are coins, and within the cups, substances not always easy to recognize—some of these when analysed appear to be animal matter. One of the most stupendous of these Topes was erected, says an inscription, to enshrine seven of Buddha's hairs. Mr Wilson shewed me a small cup, taken from a Tope, in which are some grains of musk still retaining their odour, and which, for more centuries than can be told, have gone on emitting these subtle particles without apparent diminution.

One of the most curious things (morally curious) that I saw was a machine constructed for the amusement of Tippoo Saib. It was a Barrel Organ in the form of a Tiger standing on the prostrate figure of a man in European dress. On turning the handle the man screams in a shrill plaintive voice, and the Tiger gives a sort of grunt denoting satisfaction. The sounds alternate as the instrument grinds, the man raises his hand and presses it to his mouth and cries out piteously; the Tiger whose claws are in his body & his teeth on his throat, responds with his grunt of enjoyment, and thus the childish tyrant, the Sultan, was entertained at once by the exhibition of ingenious machinery and the pleasant idea of revenge on his enemies.

The Library of the Museum contains many M.SS. in oriental languages which are no doubt curious & valuable. Some are in Sanscrit, others in Persian and illuminated like the old missals of the Roman Catholics. The Sanscrit, Mr Wilson tells me, is read from left to right, and not from right to left as ^are^ most oriental languages. We asked him if there was a literature locked up in this ancient tongue (which is still used by the Priests and the Learned as Latin is among the nations of the Franks) and which rewarded the labour of the Student. He thinks there is.——

There are in this Museum, fragments of Oriental sculpture, bas-reliefs taken from the Topes of the Buddhists, and these are by no means deficient in effect. There are bricks from Babylon with stamps upon them, and specimens on stone of those arrow-headed characters which have, I believe, so far, baffled all attempts to discover their meaning. They are there, but they leave their tale untold even more entirely than the foot-prints on stone of those gigantic birds whose existence has no other record.

As we were returning home from our visit to Leadenhall St. we met a discomfitted procession. The Lord Mayor in his State Coach, with his Aldermen (Charlemain and all his peerage,) coming home from their visit to Buckingham Palace and the Queen, after ill success in their petition in favour of their ancient, time-hallowed rights. Unquestionably this is not an age of reverence.

Thursday evening we went to a party at Miss Berry's, one of the very pleasantest houses that I know. One finds there the best society, a charming intermixture of rank and literature, high-breeding and intelligence.

We found on this evening a party whose names we sat down from memory as soon as we got home. Lord Jeffrey—Miss Burdett Coutts—Sir Wilmot Horton—Lady Horton—Lord & Lady Eliot—Lady Langdale—Lady Munroe—Lady Georgina Wortley—Honble Stuart Wortley—M^r & Mrs Frederic Elliot—Lady Hislop—Revd Sidney & Mrs Sidney Smith—Lady Stratford Canning—Lady Charlotte Lindsay—Henry Taylor—Mr Babbage—Mr Morier—Mr Standish—Mr Baring Wall—Honble Mr Ferguson—Moncton Mills—and others whose names escaped us. With Lord Jeffrey I had some plain, pleasant, perhaps common-place talk about America and his visit there in 1813, "too long ago," said his Lordship politely, "for you to have known much about the state of things then existing." Lord Jeffrey found Washington what every one else, before or since, has found it, a place of interminable streets & scattered houses, cold, dirty, dreary & comfortless. Boston he thought had a better society & that there was there more refinement and civilisation, Lord Jeffrey implied without expressing this last word, than in any other city in the United States.

He is a small, quiet looking Scot with a strong expression of good sense and a simple, unpretending manner. He looks as little as possible like a bloody-minded Reviewer who cuts people up alive, half hangs & quarters them, & tears from yet palpitating breasts the quivering hearts.

Lord Jeffrey is not what I expected to find him. He is more amiable and less brilliant than I anticipated. He said in my hearing no one distinguished thing, but expressed some kind thoughts & good feelings. He left me, in short, less impressed by his intellect and more by his pleasant temper than before I had seen & talked with him. There was certainly no great opportunity in our conversation for the display of intellect, but it has always seemed to me that very great cleverness shews itself involuntarily & even in small matters.

Miss Burdett Coutts, an heiress of £70.000 a year, is neither very young (I should judge,) nor very handsome, but she seems quiet & modest, has an intelligent countenance and something of the high-bred air which distinguishes her father in the caricature from Landsear's Dog, (see his picture of High Life & Low Life) Her dress was plain white muslin with no ornament but a comb adorned with magnificent pearls.

Lady Horton is said to be the original of Byron's "She walks in beauty—" I should not have supposed from her present appearance that she could ever have set for such a portrait. The "all that's best of dark and bright," certainly does not now "meet in her aspect and her eyes."

Lady Munroe is the widow of the late Sir Thomas Munroe.

Mr Stuart Wortley and Lady Georgina have travelled in America. She has an insolent expression of countenance, a disagreeable thing in a woman, but she may be mild & modest for any thing that I know to the contrary.

Of the Revd Sidney Smith & Mrs Sidney I saw but little—All that you do see of them however is worth seeing.

Lady Hislop, a sparkling and witty person, brought with her to Miss Berry's, her daughter Nina, a nymph who has seen but fourteen summers & is as tall as Mamma. She was on her way to her first ball at her great uncle Lord Minto's; not to be followed up, for the present at least, by other balls. Lady Hislop makes no secret, in a half-jest half-earnest tone, of her intention to secure a brilliant establishment, some day or other, for this pretty & distinguished-looking young daughter of hers.

Lady Charlotte Lindsay is appearing before the public in a very charming letter, written by her in answer to one from Lord Brougham, requesting some particulars of the private life of her father, Lord North; a sketch of whose character & history he was preparing for his "British Statesmen."

Henry Taylor, the author of Philip Van Artevelde. A clever man and a consummate puppy.

Of Lord & Lady Eliot I know nothing but that they are Lord & Lady Eliot, and that Lord Helliot's carriage stopped the way just before ours. Of M^r & Mrs Frederic Elliot I can say that they are very pleasant people who have been in America.

Lady Langdale is one of the few English women (or men) who do not improve upon acquaintance. I like her less as I see more of her.

Lady Stratford Canning looks very sentimental with long ends to her cap which descend gently to her shoulders.

Friday, March 22. I went with Mrs Stevenson to a ball at Lady Sligo's. Mr Coolidge declined going and I gave a seat in my carriage to Mr Rush the American Secretary of Legation. Mrs Stevenson's equipage led the way & we followed: Lady Sligo lives in Mansfield St. Her house is too small for a large party. There was no shew, except of servants & diamonds, which I have not seen equalled in my own country. Above stairs were four rooms, two large & two small on the same floor. Lady Sligo received in one large room, dancing went on in the other. The two smaller ones were fitted up with sofas & Ottomans for Chaperons & dowagers. Among the company were Lord & Lady Brougham. I was very glad of the opportunity to see the remarkable man. I found him very much what I had expected, and answering in person to Miss Martineau's description of his character. His head is long and the crown slightly bald, his features rough, coarse &

singularly flexible. His nose moves up & down like the trunk of an Elephant. Occasional twitchings of the mouth & a constant tremor in the muscles of the face indicate a nervous & irritable temperament, whilst coarseness, violence and power are stamped on the whole countenance and constitute the characteristic expression of the face.

Lady Brougham with her head covered with small flowers, looked sufficiently second-rate and insignificant.

In the course of the evening Mr Rush came up to propose that I should go into the adjoining room with him, that he might point out to me some young beauties who were to be the belles of the ensuing season, now close at hand. The most conspicuous of these were Miss Stewart the daughter of Lord Stewart de Rothesay, and two Ladies Campbell, daughters of the Earl of Cawdor and famed for their personal attractions.

Every people has a standard of beauty, differing somewhat even among the most civilized nations. The delicacy & grace, the very slightness and fragility of our fair young Americans indisposes me to admire the embonpoint of English girls, whilst the "universal propensity to scragginess" among American women of a certain age, enhances in my eyes the charm of full proportions in the Mammas, dowagers & old maids of England. Young women in the United States and old ones here excite my admiration. I quarreled with the broad shoulders and fat white backs of the Ladies Campbell. Their small, delicate features are almost lost in their plump cheeks & chins—one of them at least has straw-coloured, I suppose her adorers call them flaxen tresses, and altogether they, the sisters look much like well dressed Dolls. Miss Stewart is of a higher style of beauty, and is undoubtedly uncommonly handsome. Her face has character & intelligence and she is moreover "trés-distinguée" in her air & movements.

I went to the ball with Mrs Stevenson about half past eleven or a quarter before twelve and came away at ½ past one. We stopped for a few moments in the dining room below where an elegant supper of cold meats, salads, jellies, creams, ices, cake, fruit of various sorts and rich wines was prepared for the refreshment of the guests. The table was ornamented by two pieces of plate presented to the noble Marquis as the friend of Emancipation and of the oppressed Africans. Slavery is a hateful thing. Though born & brought up in a Slave State I was early taught to abhor an odious system. The Marquis of Sligo may be a genuine philanthropist & friend of the oppressed for aught that I know to the contrary, but as I looked at the plate I thought within myself how much there is of what the English call Humbug in such manifestations of gratitude & admiration.

How little there is, after all, I fear, of virtue or sincerity in many advocates of ^even^ a good cause. What is it that urges men on in the career of philanthropy as lovers of their kind and haters of oppression? What is it often but ambition, vanity, fanatacism, self-love, the desire of personal distinction or aggrandisement? Or perhaps hatred of one set of men assumes the form of love for another.—Yet what great works are often performed by most unworthy tools. Good works itself out of evil, and though we are expressly forbidden to do evil that good may come of it yet bad motives often accomplish good purposes. Fortunate it is for the world that as the Scotch say, "There is ain aboun a."

At this ball of Lady Sligo's, Mrs Stevenson presented me to Lady Cecilia Underwood, the married wife of the Duke of Sussex, (the Queen's uncle,) whose name she cannot take, neither share his honours, in consequence of her being a subject, and he a member of the Royal family. I found her very pleasant & amiable. She invited me to visit her at Kensington Palace and promised to present me to the Duke, who is liberal in politics and friendly to Americans. Lady Cecilia & himself have been always particularly kind and attentive to M^r & Mrs Stevenson, and on this occasion it was arranged that Mrs Stevenson should accompany me to Kensington next day.

Accordingly the next morning, Saturday March 23. we drove together to the Palace where we were received by a man dressed like a Highlander, and conducted to the apartments of Lady Cecilia. Her manner was cordial & kind and after a while, saying that she would go & inform the Duke of our arrival, she requested us, during her absence, to amuse ourselves by inspecting her apartments. We availed ourselves of the permission & walked through the rooms. Her dressing table I especially noticed & the tasteful arrangement of the toilette apparatus, due no doubt to her Ladyship's maid. On our return to the drawing-room we were joined by Lady Cecilia; and soon after his Royal Highness, a clumsy, pur-blind old gentleman, came stumbling & tumbling into the room. No one could be more awkward & ungainly then was this descendent of Kings. He reminded me of Mr Tupman the friend of the illustrious Mr Pickwick, being as old & as fat, and if not dressed exactly in the fancy costume to which Mr Pickwick objected, he was certainly attired in a manner very different from the one usually adopted by English gentlemen. He was however ~~very~~ gracious in manner and treated me very civilly, whilst with Mrs Stevenson he was almost affectionate. He talked principally with her whilst Lady Cecilia addressed herself to me. Presently however, my attention was attracted by something which the Duke was saying and which amused me not a little. His Royal Highness sometimes, like other people, forgets names, and blunders about facts. He was now in some little embarass-ment from which he desired, by Mrs Stevenson's aid, to be extricated. "You see, my dear Mrs Stevenson, a book was sent me by the author, one of your countrymen, and I wish to return my thanks. But I have forgotten his name and I want you to help me to it." "Will your Royal Highness tell me the name of the book?" "I have forgotten that too, & the book is mislaid." "What was the book about?" "I cannot say that I read it. I do not know what it was about." Mrs Stevenson looked somewhat puzzled as she well might be, when required to find from among American authors one to whom there seemed no possible clue. His name forgotten, his book never read, & the subject of it unknown.

The Duke gave Mrs Stevenson & myself an invitation to dine with Lady Cecilia & himself after his return to town from a short absence—the day to be named when he got back. I shall have sailed for the United States probably by that time, and shall miss what I should much like to have been present at—the dinner of a Royal Highness

After my return from Kensington Mrs Stevenson & myself made sev-eral calls & after dinner Mr C. & myself walked to Gower St. where we passed the evening with Mrs Wormeley.

John SHEEPSHANKS (1787–1863), the son of a wealthy cloth manufacturer, re-tired from his father's firm before the age of forty and turned his attention to promoting and collecting works by contemporary British artists. Unlike fellow collector Robert Vernon, Sheepshanks bought drawings and engravings as well as paintings and sculpture. He developed warm relationships with engravers and painters such as Landseer, Mulready, and Leslie, all of whom valued his enthusi-asm and generosity in accepting their prices without haggling. In 1857 Sheep-shanks offered 233 paintings in oil and 289 drawings as a gift to form the nucleus of a national gallery. Though Sheepshanks did not require that his collection be kept together or named after him, his donation nevertheless came to be known as the Sheepshanks Gift and it formed the foundation of the collection of British oil paintings at the Victoria and Albert Museum. See William Mulready's *Portrait of John Sheepshanks at His Residence in Old Bond Street*, figure 32 (*ODNB*; Macleod, *Art and the Victorian Middle Class*, 473–474; Kathryn Heleniak, "Victorian Collec-tions and British Nationalism: Vernon, Sheepshanks and the National Gallery of British Art," *Journal of the History of Collections* 12, no. 1 [2000]: 94–96; "The British Galleries 1500–1900" and "John Sheepshanks," Victoria and Albert Museum, ac-cessed 20 Dec. 2010, http://www.vam.ac.uk).

The EAST INDIA MUSEUM and Library each occupied a wing of the East India House, headquarters of the East India Company. The imposing, 190-foot-long, neoclassical building was remodeled between 1796 and 1799 by architect Richard

Jupp (1728–1799), who was the company's surveyor. The museum and library were established in 1801 to educate officers, scholars, and colonial administrators about the native cultures with which the company traded. There was no attempt to restrict accessions, which resulted in an eclectic collection containing precious gems, Roman tiles, birds from Java, and the spoils of military conquests, in addition to books and manuscripts. The artifact that was the most popular with the public—and remains so today—is a life-size mechanical **TIGER** made of carved and painted wood, shown in the act of attacking a man in European dress, his red coat evocative of the British military. The object was commissioned by Sultan Fateh Ali Tipu [**TIPPOO SAIB**], who adopted the tiger as his personal symbol, boasting "I would rather live two days as a tiger than two hundred years like a sheep." Tipu's tiger was among the objects that British soldiers took from his palace after the capture of Seringapatam. Placed on display in the East India Museum in 1808, it immediately became a London tourist attraction as well as a nuisance to readers in the adjacent library. It is now part of the collection of the Victoria and Albert Museum (fig. 33) (*ODNB*, s.v. "Jupp, Richard"; Maya Jasanoff, *Edge of Empire: Lives, Culture, and Conquest in the East, 1750–1850* [2005], 177–181; Ray Desmond, *The India Museum, 1801–1879* [1982], 1–37; Thomas H. Shepherd and James Elmes, *London and Its Environs in the Nineteenth Century* [1829; repr. 1968], 43–44; *London Encyclopedia*, 250; Veronica Murphy, "Tipu's Tiger," Victoria and Albert Museum, accessed 11 July 2011, http://www.vam.ac.uk).

Horace Hayman **WILSON** (1786–1860) was the librarian of the East India House for twenty-four years, taking up the post in 1836, after leaving Oxford, where he had held the first professorship in Sanskrit and written extensively on that subject. Wilson was the author of *Ariana Antiqua* (1841), a catalogue of the "antiquities and coins of Afghanistan" that included a "Memoir on the Buildings Called **TOPES**," by Charles Masson (1800–1853), the alias of archaeologist James Lewis. Lewis changed his name after deserting from the British army in 1827 and embarked on a decade-long investigation in Afghanistan, during which he collected over eighty thousand ancient coins and relics. In 1835 he became a reporter for the East India Company in exchange for a pardon for his desertion; he returned to London in 1838 and published his findings. The "stupendous" tope that Coolidge mentioned was what Wilson described as the "Shwe-da-gon pagoda near Rangoon. This is a mass of solid masonry, standing on an elevated platform; it is more than three hundred feet in height, and its circumference at the base is one thousand three hundred and fifty-five feet.... [U]nderneath its stupendous weight are deposited the relics of the four last Buddhas," including "eight hairs from the head of Gautama" (*ODNB*, s.v. "Masson, Charles" and "Wilson, Horace Hayman"; Horace Hayman Wilson, *Ariana Antiqua: A Descriptive Account of the Antiquities and Coins of Afghanistan* [1841], 46).

The **LORD MAYOR** and alderman had addressed the queen to ask her "aid and protection against a measure now pending in Parliament" that proposed to add the City of London to the jurisdiction of the Metropolitan Police Force, which had come into existence with the Metropolitan Police Act in 1829. It was the lord mayor's position that the city already had a police force that was equal, if not superior, to the Metropolitan Police. Ultimately the threat of the Metropolitan Police taking control over the nucleus of the city compelled the city corporation to form the City of London Police on 17 August 1839, a force of 543 officers patroling one square mile. Nonetheless, the 1839 Metropolitan Police Act extended the scope of its officers to include the city portion of the Thames River, thus absorbing the Thames police force (David Ascoli, *The Queen's Peace: The Origins and Development of the Metropolitan Police, 1829–1979* [1979], 103-114; *Encyclopedia Britannica* [1894], 19:352; *London Encyclopedia,* 607–608; *Morning Chronicle* [London], 23 Mar. 1839).

In 1837 Angela Georgina BURDETT COUTTS (1814–1906) was named heir to the £1.8 million estate of her grandfather, the banker Thomas Coutts, and became an instant celebrity. Charles Dickens guided her philanthropic work, and under his influence she supported causes ranging from aid for homeless women to projects in London's East End, where she funded the first model housing for workers. Burdett-Coutts also supported the Church of England, endowing churches in South Africa, Australia, and British Columbia. She became known as the "Queen of the Poor," and her philanthropy, estimated to have amounted to between £3 and £4 million during her lifetime, set a new standard for its breadth, practicality, and sincerity (*ODNB*).

Anne Beatrix HORTON (d. 1871), a renowned beauty, was the wife of Robert John Wilmot-Horton (1784–1841), with whom she had eight children. Wilmot-Horton was governor of Ceylon from 1831 to 1837 (*ODNB*).

Edward Granville ELIOT (1798–1877) was appointed lord of the treasury during Canning's administration and served in diplomatic legations in Madrid, Lisbon, and Spain, where he was envoy-extraordinary until his 1837 return to London. His wife was Jemima Cornwallis (1803–1856) (*ODNB*).

Jane Campbell Munro [MUNROE] (d. 1850) was the widow of Thomas Munro (1761–1827), a Glasgow native who had a distinguished career as an army officer in the East India Company (*ODNB*).

In April 1825 John Stuart-WORTLEY, second Baron Wharncliffe (1801–1855), visited Monticello and the newly opened University of Virginia in the company of John Evelyn Denison (1800–1873), Speaker of the House of Commons, and Henry Labouchere, Baron Taunton (1798–1869). After his return to England later that year, Stuart-Wortley married Georgiana Elizabeth Ryder (ca. 1804–1884), who was described in 1839 by Daniel Webster's sister-in-law Harriette Paige (1809–1863) as "very clever, and very attractive." Paige recalled that while in Washington Stuart-Wortley had won "the regard of all, by his simple, and unostentatious manners. He is like all other gentlemen of the highest rank here; they are conspicuous for their entire want of pretension and their simplicity in every respect" (*ODNB*; Gray, *Daniel Webster in England,* 75–76; Edmund Lodge, *The Peerage the British Empire* [1856], 578; Henry S. Randall, *The Life of Thomas Jefferson* [1858], 3:520; *Patriot* [Carlisle, Cumbria], 27 Oct. 1855).

Eliza Charlotte Alexander CANNING (d. 1882) married diplomat Stratford Canning (1786–1880) in 1825, after his return from the United States where he had served as Britain's minister plenipotentiary from 1820 to 1823. Coolidge met Canning in Washington in 1822 and reported to her grandfather, "I have met with a good many of your old friends here, who have been very particular in their inquiries after you, and their attentions to me on your account. Of the foreigners, M. de Neuville had been the most polite. I have reason to believe that the neglect I have experienced from Mr Canning has proceeded more from some absurd ideas of etiquette, then from any intentional disrespect. He is generally considered a man of amiable temper and manners, although possessed by hypochondria and constitutional melancholy. When we meet in society, we are always as sociable as he knows how to be." Canning's memoirs reveal that the slight may well have been intentional. He wrote that he "did not wish to see" Jefferson, who was in retirement at Monticello, and blamed him for introducing to diplomatic Washington a "loose tone, which differed so much from his illustrious predecessor's example." Canning continued, "his bearing appears to have been very much that of a political coxcomb. Among his competitors were some whom he could hardly have expected to surpass by genuine merit, and it is allowable to presume that he sought to give weight to his own scale by popular manners and revolutionary principles. It is reported of him that he received Mr. Merry, our first envoy to the independent States, in his dressing-gown, seated on a sofa and catching a slipper after tossing it up, on the point of his foot" (*ODNB*; Stanley Lane-Poole, *The Life of the Right Honourable Stratford Canning* [1888], 1:315–316; Coolidge to Thomas Jefferson, 22 Mar. 1822 [private collection, N.J.]).

MR. STANDISH was probably the art collector and author Frank Hall Standish (1799–1840) (*ODNB*).

Charles BARING WALL (1795–1853) was a Liberal member of Parliament and director of the British Institution. He was the grandson of Francis Baring, founder of Baring Brothers & Company and chairman of the East India Company. His mother, Harriet Wall (1768–1838), was the leader of an evangelical secession from the Church of England known as the Western Schism (*ODNB*, s.v. "Wall, Harriet"; *Gentleman's Magazine*, n.s., 40 [1853]: 643–644).

HON^{BLE} MR FERGUSON was most likely the physician and author Robert Ferguson (1799–1865), who gained entrée into London's literary world through Sir Walter Scott's son-in-law John Gibson Lockhart, also a physician, and the publisher John Murray. Ferguson was the first professor of midwifery at King's College Hospital and in 1840 served as Queen Victoria's physician accoucheur at the birth of her first child (*ODNB*).

Richard Monckton Milnes [MONCTON MILLS] (1809–1885), a Tory member of Parliament from 1806 until his retirement in 1818. He traveled extensively in the early 1830s, publishing poems and travel narratives, before returning to Parliament in 1837. He entertained lavishly, first in London and after 1836 at Fryston Hall, imitating the famous breakfasts of Samuel Rogers (*ODNB*).

Byron's poem "SHE WALKS IN BEAUTY," from which all the quotations in this paragraph are taken, was published in *Hebrew Melodies* in 1815.

NINA was Emma Eleanor Elizabeth Hislop (1824–1882), later Countess Minto, the only child of Emma Elliot, Lady Hislop, and Thomas Hislop (1764–1843), an army officer who served in India. In 1844 Nina married one of her "great Uncle Minto's" sons, her cousin William Hugh Elliot-Murray-Kynynmound (1814–1891), third Earl of Minto. She edited three volumes on the Elliot family, including the memoirs of her grandfather Hugh Elliot, governor of Madras, and the *Life and Letters of Sir Gilbert Elliot, First Earl of Minto* (1874) (*ODNB*, s.v. "Hislop, Thomas"; Frederic Boase, *Modern English Biography* [1897], 2:900; John Foster Kirk, *A Supplement to Allibone's Critical Dictionary of English Literature* [1899], 2:965; "The Earl of Minto, G. C. B.," *Gentleman's Magazine*, n.s., 7 [1859]: 306).

Lady Charlotte Lindsay's LETTER of 18 February 1839 to Henry Brougham was published in the appendix to his *Historical Sketches of Statesmen Who Flourished in the Time of George III* (1839–1843). Lindsay recounted her "impressions of my father's private life" including her family's rejoicing when North resigned as prime minister, which he had wanted to do for his last three years in office: "At length, the declining majorities in the House of Commons made it evident that there must be a change of ministry, and the King was obliged reluctantly to receive his resignation. This was a great relief to his mind; for, although I do not believe that my father ever entertained any doubt as to the justice of the American war, yet I am sure that he wished to have made peace three years before its termination." Lindsay's letter was praised by the London *Monthly Review* for revealing North's "equanimity, gaiety of spirit, and keen sarcasm" (Henry, Lord Brougham, *Historical Sketches of Statesmen Who Flourished in the Time of George III* [1840], 391–397; *Monthly Review* [London] 2 [1839]: 85).

Benjamin RUSH (1811–1877), secretary of the U.S. legation in London, was a grandson of Dr. Benjamin Rush and the son of Richard Rush, former American minister to Great Britain. Richard Rush had just spent two years in London negotiating the release of funds bequeathed to the United States by James Smithson, which were used to establish the Smithsonian Institution (*ANB*; *DAB*, s.v. "Rush, Richard"; *National Cyclopædia of American Biography* [1893], 3:333; Charles Francis Adams, ed., *Memoirs of John Quincy Adams* [1876], 10:317).

The four-story, brick terrace house at 16 MANSFIELD Street was designed by Robert Adam around 1770 and survives in modified form today (David King, *The Complete Works of Robert and James Adam* [2001], 82–89).

Miss Stuart [STEWART] was Louisa Anne Stuart Beresford, Marchioness of Waterford (1818–1891), daughter of Charles Stuart, Baron Stuart de Rothesay (1779–1845) (*ODNB*).

The two ladies CAMPBELL were Emily Caroline Campbell Duncombe (ca. 1821–1911) and Elizabeth Lucy Campbell Cuffe (1822–1898), the daughters of John Frederick Campbell, Earl of Cawdor (1790–1860), and his wife, Elizabeth Thynne

(b. 1795) (*ODNB*, s.v. "Cuffe, Hamilton"; *Debrett's Illustrated Peerage and Baronetage* [1865], 84–85).

The PIECES OF PLATE displayed by the Marquess [MARQUIS] OF SLIGO, governor of Jamaica from 1833 to 1836, were called *The Emancipated*. A deputation of eighteen men, including Lord Brougham and two "gentlemen of colour," formally presented the silver to Sligo on 16 March 1839, the week before the Coolidges' visit. The *Morning Chronicle* reported the speeches given at the presentation, and descriptions of the sculpture by George Scharf (1820–1895), executed by Green and Ward, appeared in American newspapers. The centerpiece was a three-and-a-half-foot silver candelabrum in the shape of an Arica Palm with a family of "West Indian negroes" at its foot: "On the left is seen a mother suckling her babe; and on the right her husband, with a book on his knee, and in the act of explaining what he had been reading—a broken whip is under his feet. The third figure is exhibited at the side, a grown boy playing with a goat." The candelabrum was inscribed to the marquess "by the negroes of Jamaica, in testimony ... for his unremitting efforts to alleviate their sufferings and to redress their wrongs." The fact that funding for the "testimonial" came from the former slaves themselves was reported throughout Great Britain and in America.

During his governorship the marquess oversaw Jamaica's transition from slavery to apprenticeship, which proceeded without the revolt or violence feared by planters and Parliament. The marquess became a "decided abolitionist," emancipating the apprentices on his own Jamaican plantations. Sligoville, a settlement for freed slaves established in 1835, was named in his honor. *The Emancipated* and another piece of silver by Papworth bearing the same title, but given to the marquess by his ancestral home of Westport, Ireland, were exhibited at the 1839 Royal Academy exhibition (Tim Barringer, Gillian Forrester, and Barbaro Martinez-Ruiz, *Art and Emancipation in Jamaica* [2007], 363–372; W. L. Burn, *Emancipation and Apprenticeship in the British West Indies* [1937], 146–153, 267–271; Algernon Graves, *Royal Academy of Arts: A Complete Dictionary of Contributors* [1906], 6:47; James Mursell Phillippo, *Jamaica: Its Past and Present State* [1843], 33, 135–140, 169–187, 222–223, 254–255; "Exhibition of the Royal Academy," *Literary Gazette* 23 [1839]: 379; "Obituary, The Marquess of Sligo, K. P.," *Gentleman's Magazine*, n.s., 23 [1845]: 423; *Morning Chronicle* [London], 18 Mar. 1839; *Emancipator* [New York], 13 Oct. 1836, 31 Oct. 1839; *Philadelphia Friend*, 7 Nov. 1835; "History," Westport House, accessed 20 Dec. 2010, http://westporthouse.ie./home/history/).

AIN ABOUN A: Coolidge likely meant to write "ane aboun a," one above all.

The 1831 marriage of the Duke of Sussex to LADY CECILIA UNDERWOOD (1793–1873) was outside the terms of the Royal Marriages Act, as was the duke's first marriage to Lady Augusta Murray (ca. 1761–1830), which George III declared void in 1794. Lady Cecilia was the daughter of the second Earl of Arran and widow of George Buggin. She took the name Underwood, her mother's maiden name, the year that she married the duke; she was created Duchess of Inverness in 1840. Her title and standing within the royal family prompted gossip and controversies, including an incident at a Guildhall dinner in 1838 when the Duchess of

Sutherland and Lady Mulgrave refused to dine with her. The duke's will directed that he be interred at the public cemetery Kensal Green rather than at Windsor, where his wife's burial would have been excluded. Queen Victoria was fond of Lady Cecilia, who resided happily at Kensington Palace until her death. She was buried alongside the duke at Kensal Green (*ODNB*, s.v. "Augustus Frederick, duke of Sussex"; Jane-Eliza Hasted, *Unsuccessful Ladies: An Intimate Account of the Aunts (Official and Unofficial) of the Late Queen Victoria* [1971], 212–221; Benson and Brett, *Letters of Queen Victoria*, 1:598–601; *Blackwood's Edinburgh Magazine* 43 [1838]: 80).

In Charles Dickens's *Posthumous Papers of the Pickwick Club* (1837), **MR. TUPMAN** wore an elaborate costume while Mr. Pickwick went in his own suit.

Monday. 25ʰ March.

I have come in tired from a long drive. The day is fine but as I am beginning now to make serious preparations for my departure, my movements must be regulated accordingly, and I am afraid there is an end to my sight-seeing. Yesterday Mr Coolidge and myself called on Mrs Marcet and received much satisfactory information on the subject of the schools at Geneva. I then went to see Miss Rogers and spent the evening with Mrs Searle.

Tuesday 26. March.

We dined yesterday with Mr Davis in Spanish Place with a set of old Indians. A yellow-faced General Somebody half deaf & half tipsy; A doctor, in shape and movement like a huge turtle; A Captain who seemed a cross between a Spaniel & a Donkey, fawning as the one, dull as the other. There were several others, men and women, all in some way connected with East India affairs, or with other persons so connected. What I have seen of these oriental occidentals does not impress me greatly in their favor. Their day is passing. The company at Mr Davis's dinner however, were not ^all^ of a piece with the General, the Captain & the Doctor, and I had the good fortune to have seated next to me a sensible, gentlemanly man. One subject discussed at table was the visit of the Lord Mayor and his satellites to Buckingham House and the Queen. After dinner the same subject was renewed among the ladies and the character and manners of the Queen very freely commented upon. The little Sovereign is losing her popularity. In every company I hear some new fault found with her, and the most absurd stories are afloat of her passionate & imperious temper. Such straws however, shew which way the wind blows. One day she is missed by her ladies and is at last found in her dressing room, on her knees, washing her Lap Dog. One of the ladies ventures on a respectful remonstrance and has the dog thrown at her head and her ears boxed by the Queen's soapy hands. This out-queen's Queen Bess! Another young lady is reproved by the little Victoria for a trick that she has of playing with her chain, and the influence of habit, stronger even than her fear of the Queen, causing her to repeat the offence she is peremptorily ordered off to her chamber. A friend intercedes in her behalf—"If your Majesty only knew how very unhappy poor Miss—is! She is crying dreadfully—" "Then you had better go and console her—" and the second lady is dismissed to share the disgrace of the first. All this is abundantly ridiculous but shews as I have said, that people take pleasure in hearing and repeating things that place the Queen in an unfavorable light.

What is not ridiculous however, but exceedingly disgraceful, is the history of Lady Flora Hastings published at length in the Morning Post of the 25th March. Sad doings and sayings for the Court of a Maiden Queen. Poor young girl! She seems surrounded by a wretched set. An impotent Ministry to dictate her public measures and shed their unpopularity upon her, and a knot of talking, meddling, indiscreet women to influence her in private. Her Court seems a perfect school for Scandal, with fewer Lady Teazles than Mrs Candours & Sir Benjamin Backbites.

I think we shall not sail before the 10th of April so that I have more time than I thought for. I think too that Josephine will go with me. There is however, notwithstanding this reprieve, a great deal to do in a short few days.—To-morrow we dine with Mr Sheepshanks & take another look at his beautiful pictures. On Good Friday—Mrs Searle's wedding day, we dine with her. On salt-fish I suppose, of course—with plenty of good things besides.

Queen Victoria's LAP DOG was a King Charles spaniel named Dash, a beloved childhood companion. The painter Charles Robert Leslie related an anecdote involving Dash in his description of how childlike Victoria appeared on the day of her coronation: "She is very fond of dogs, and has one very favourite little spaniel, who is always on the lookout for her return when she has been away from home. She had of course been separated from him on that day longer than usual, and when the state coach drove up to the steps of the palace, she heard him barking with joy in the hall, and exclaimed 'There's Dash!' and was in a hurry to lay aside the sceptre and ball she carried in her hands, and take off the crown and robes *to go and wash little Dash*" (*ODNB*; Charles Robert Leslie, *Autobiographical Recollections*, ed. Tom Taylor [1860], 2:329).

FLORA HASTINGS's uncle Hamilton Fitz Gerald detailed Hastings's own account of the events surrounding her illness in a 21 March 1839 letter to the editor
of the *Examiner*, which the *Morning Post* published on 25 March 1839: "Lady Flora
arrived some weeks since from Scotland, very unwell. She immediately consulted
Sir James Clark, the physician to both her Majesty and the Duchess of Kent. . . .
[O]n or about the 1st of March, Sir James Clark went to her room and announced
to her the conviction of the Ladies of the Palace that she was pregnant," and that
"'nothing but her submitting to a medical examination would ever satisfy them,
or remove the stigma from her name.' Lady Flora found that the subject had been
brought before the Queen's notice, and that all this had been discussed, arranged,
and denounced to her without one word having been said on the subject to her
own mistress, the Duchess of Kent. . . . [T]he Queen would not permit Lady Flora
to appear till the examination had taken place. Lady Portman (who with Lady
Tavistock are those whose names are mentioned as most active against Lady Flora)
expressed to the Duchess of Kent her conviction of Lady Flora's guilt."

Lady Flora "submitted herself to the most rigid examination, and now pos-
sesses a certificate, signed by Sir James Clark, and also by Sir Charles Clark, stat-
ing, as strongly as language can state it, that 'there are no grounds for believing
that pregnancy does exist, or ever has existed.' Lord Hastings . . . went to London
instantly, and demanded and obtained from Lord Melbourne a distinct disavowal
of his participation in the affair, and demanded and obtained an audience of her
Majesty, in which, while he disclaimed all idea that the Queen had any wish to
injure his sister, he plainly, though respectfully, stated his opinion of those who
had counselled her, and his resolution to find out the originator of the slander,
and bring him or her to punishment. Lady Flora is convinced that the Queen was
surprised into the order which was given, and that her Majesty did not understand what she was betrayed into—for ever since the horrid event her Majesty
has showed her regret by the most gracious kindness to Lady Flora, and 'expressed
it warmly with tears in her eyes.' The Duchess of Kent's conduct was perfect; 'a
mother could not have been kinder.'"

Benjamin Disraeli wrote to his sister of the unfolding scandal, "The truth I believe is that the Queen in a passion with the Duchess of Kent and her household,
with whom she is always quarrelling, bolted out that Lady Flora Hastings had
been once in that domestic situation, vulgarly called 'the family way'—and that,
of all people in the world Conroy was the cause. It turns out I believe to be *really*
vile slander" (Benjamin Disraeli to Sarah Disraeli, ca. 4 Mar. 1839, in *Benjamin
Disraeli Letters, 1838–1841*, ed. Melvin George Wiebe and John Alexander Wilson
Gunn [1987], 152–153; *Morning Post* [London], 25 Mar. 1839).

The gossip of Sir Benjamin Backbite and Mrs. Candour threatens to corrupt
Lady Teazle's morals in Richard Brinsley Sheridan's comedy, The SCHOOL FOR
SCANDAL (1777).

Anne Noble and Thomas SEARLE were married on 29 March 1834 (*Proceedings
of the American Academy of Arts and Sciences* 57 [1922]: 508; Francis H. Atkins,
Joseph Atkins: The Story of a Family [1891], 72).

Thursday. 28. March.

A fine, bright, cold, windy day—and now what have I been doing since my last date. Tuesday 26ʰ I went through Westminster Abbey for the purpose of seeing the Monuments. I have several times attended divine service there, but yesterday I attempted a task quite beyond my strength, that of going over the Abbey in two hours, when a week would be too little for such an object. I came away with a general impression, (which I hope to retain,) of the whole, but of the details my ideas are of course confused. Last summer, in July, I <u>went to church</u> in Henry 7ᵗʰˢ Chapel, was but little edified by the sermon I heard, but greatly impressed by the air of majesty & antiquity which pervaded the place, where the banners of the Knights of the Bath were waving from the walls. But one thinks more of the glory of man I fear than of the glory of God in a spot which seems consecrated to the remembrance of earthly distinctions. Yet Westminster Abbey is a grand, solemn sight, and whatever excites high thought must be religious in it's influence over the mind.

The number of illustrious men whose names are recorded in Westminster Abbey and whose monuments surround you, cannot but remind you what a glorious land England has been and is—What a mighty mother of mighty men! Heroes, Statesmen, Philosophers, Poets! Such men belong to mankind, to the world—they are the ornaments of humanity, and do honour to the name & race, which God has created little lower than the angels and to whom he has given dominion over all the works of his hands.

I felt while in this place of noble tombs as if the whole record of English history was unrolled before my eyes, not in it's details but in the grand outline of it's changes & revolutions from the old Saxon days of Edward the Confessor to the reign of the present young & girlish Queen. Here are remains of Roman Catholic & of Feudal times, records of change in religion & government, mute memorials of great events, the whole history of a nation advancing steadily from comparative barbarism & feebleness to that climax of power and civilization to which England has now attained. Hers is the great name among nations, and unkind as she has almost always been to us of the United States, her own blood, insolent & overbearing as she has shewed herself in her relations with us, we cannot but feel that the fact of having sprung from such a stock has made us what we are, and will make us what we are going to be. The Anglo-Saxon race are the guardians & constituted defenders of liberty upon earth and of the best hopes and sights of man. And this reminds me of the talk of war at this time between England & America! War for a boundary line, for a few acres more or less of land, when both parties have millions of acres, waste and uncultivated, which they cannot occupy. War for an imaginary point of honour!—the maintenance of a right in a question utterly unimportant! No—There is too much good sense & good feeling on both sides to render possible so wicked an absurdity!

The Chapel of Edward the Confessor is the oldest part of Westminster Abbey. The tessalated pavement is much worn. In Henry 7^{ths} Chapel, the most modern & richest part of the building, is found the monument of Mary Queen of Scots with a recumbent statue—also that of Queen Elizabeth. There are many Kings, Gorgeous dames & Barons bold, in all the amplitude of ruff & drapery, and Statesmen old in bearded majesty, whom I have neither time nor memory to enumerate.

The Poet's Corner is in the Southern Transept. The Northern contains many great names & the aisles on both sides of the Nave are studded with monuments. Few of these are in good taste and many are decidedly bad. There are works of Roubillac & Nollekens, Banks, Baillie, Westmacott, Chauntrey &c. &c. There is one monument by Roubillac which we hear often spoken of—that to Mrs Nightingale—Lady Nightingale as the guide called her & perhaps he is right. The conceit here struck me as absurd. The principal figure is a dying woman supported by a man who strives to ward off the dart of Death, represented as a hideous skeleton issuing from a tomb which serves as a pedestal for the other statues. The details of the sculpture are no doubt good, but the idea of grim Death springing on his prey, with his dry bones & ragged shroud cut in marble, is any thing but touching. It has a cast of the disgusting and even of the ludicrous. At the time of the Coronation when temporary seats & galleries were erected for the accommodation of the spectators, several of the monuments were mutilated by the workmen; among others grim Death got a rap and lost his dart which has since been replaced. I hope the omen may be a good one for her most gracious Majesty, Queen Victoria. The best thing that I have seen of Chauntrey's is, I think, the statue of Watt. The inscription upon it came from the pen of Lord Brougham. His statue of Channing is likewise in the Abbey.

There is on the North Aisle a monument to Sir Isaac Newton by Rysbrach. In the South Transept one to Handel, the last work of Roubillac. Shakespeare's has nothing so beautiful as his own lines inscribed upon it.

The cloud capped towers, the gorgeous palaces &c Goldsmith, Guy, Garrick, Thomson, Prior, Grey, Butler, Spencer, Ben Jonson, "O rare Ben Jonson," Old Chaucer, John Milton, who surely second only to Shakespeare, is enough in himself to glorify any burying place, Dryden, "Glorious John," and many other distinguished men & poets find their places in the Poet's Corner.

Yesterday, Wednesday 27. March, we spent most pleasantly, going at one o'clock to Blackheath, to see, for the second time, the fine collection of pictures by modern artists, [. . .] the property of Mr Sheepshanks. This queer name belongs to a respectable family in Yorkshire, who bear as their Crest a Sheep "passant," shewing his shanks to the best advantage. Mr John Sheepshanks is a man of handsome property, living in a pretty cottage surrounded by pleasant grounds, called Park Cottage, on Blackheath, not very far from Shooter's Hill of Highwayman memory. He is a most liberal friend and patron of English painters & engravers, often having the pictures which he purchases from the first engraved by the second—thus giving employment to artists of merit and disseminating abroad their works & their fame. He is a bachelor whose house is well-kept & well-ordered, with all the comforts and many of the elegancies of wealth, but nothing of it's ostentation or troublesome superfluities. We were hospitably & cordially received, found assembled to meet us (we had been invited to dine,) a pleasant party of artists & engravers, among the last Mr Robinson who stands at the head of the profession in England and a Mr Gibbon. They were all men of good manners and apparently well-informed minds, the conversation before and at dinner was interesting, turning generally on art & artists, & enlivened by anecdote. We dined early, at about four o'clock, and came away after coffee at eight, bringing with us a roll of several fine engravings presented to us by Mr Sheepshanks. They were taken from plates in his own possession.

The pictures which I remember with most pleasure were,

1.1. Landseer's "Jack in Office" which has furnished the subject of a biting caricature where Jacks in office & their beggars are treated as they should be. 2nd "Suspence," a Dog waiting at a door through which his wounded master has been carried. Drops of blood on the ground shew that the intense expression of sorrow in the Dog's countenance is not without cause.   3^d A Dog dressed in an old woman's cap with a pipe in his mouth. Another dog at his side. The principal figure is a portrait. The original was a pet dog of the late Countess-Duchess of Sutherland. 4th The Shepherd's Chief Mourner, a very touching picture. 5^h The "Two Dogs" done when Landseer was only about twenty years old. 6th "The Fire-side party." Mr Sheepshanks owns several other Landseers now absent at the engraver's, and many drawings & sketches of the same great artist, one done when he was only five years old, & others at six, seven, eight, nine, ten, shewing the growth & development of the boy's talent. Landseer's father lived opposite a Hackney Coach stand and the poor animals who drag these wretched machines furnished frequent subjects for the young artist's pencil. Besides the pictures I have enumerated was one representing sheep of the black-nosed Highland breed & several smaller paintings of dogs &c——

2. of <u>Leslie</u> Mr Sheepshanks has 1st Characters from Shakespeare—2nd & 3^d The Burgomaster's Daughter. 1st the girl walking with her father meets a lover, and 2nd receives a billet-doux. 4th Catherine & Petruchio, said to be one of his best. 5th & 6th Scenes from "a Winter's Tale," Autolycus & Florizel & Perdita—beautiful. 7th An English girl in boddice waist adjusting her hair. 8th Sancho before his physician. 9th Children in the Tower; these three last pictures small. 10th Uncle Toby & Widow Wadman.

3. <u>Mulready.</u> 1. The Seven Ages of Man. 2nd A Boy biting an apple. 3^d Mr Sheepshanks & his Housekeeper. 4th A child frightened at a black woman. 5^h Boy going reluctantly to school. 6th A girl with a child in her arms, her back partly turned.—Many other of Mulready's pictures were with the engraver.

4. <u>Wilkie's</u> Duncan Gray.

There is a Bassanio & Portia which I think is by Stewart Newton & to these must be added landscapes by Turner, Calcott & Stanfield, several pieces by Stothard, among them Tam o'Shanter's Escape from the Witches, two figures of children, perhaps Cupids, of which I got an indistinct view, by Etty, and various other charming pictures which I cannot now enumerate.

I passed as pleasant a day as possible. The dinner was easy & <u>went off</u> admirably though I was the only lady present. Mr Sheepshanks apologized for the absence of womankind but I cannot say I missed my own sex—I did wonderfully well without them. The gentlemen were too well-bred either to overwhelm me with attentions, or to make me feel that I was one alone of my kind. They talked to me as to an educated person, capable of understanding & appreciating what was said and of taking my part in conversation with men of talent and taste. I heard some anecdotes of Mr Sam Rogers the Poet, not very creditable to him and not surprising to me, for I have heard many things of late which shew him to be essentially <u>small</u> in some important particulars. Mr Sheepshanks told me that among Artists, Rogers is not esteemed a liberal man. He has frequent dealings with them and can drive a very hard bargain, beat them down in their demands, haggle for pounds instead of guineas, and do many little things to which perhaps the word meanness might not be too harsh in it's application. He does not own the original sketches made to illustrate his works, never having been able to prevail upon himself to pay the price asked for them.—A propos to the works of M[r] Rogers I saw a splendidly bound & elegantly illustrated copy of them which he presented I think as a wedding present, to Mme Van de Weyer, with some lines of poetry expressive of regard & good wishes written in his, the Poet's, own hand on the fly leaf of the book. M[r] Van de Weyer considers him as one of his best friends; M[r] Bates spoke of the almost <u>paternal affection</u> with which M[r] Rogers regarded M[r] Van de Weyer, yet of this very gentleman I, with my own ears, have heard the old traitor speak in a disparaging & sneering tone when with persons who, like M[rs] Stevenson for example, regarded the little Belgian with no great favour. So much for M[r] Samuel Rogers. M[r] Charles Sumner too thinks himself a prime favorite with the author of the Pleasures of Memory. I wish he could have heard the tone & seen the look with which his friend uttered the sneering words, a propos to M[r] Sumner's proposed departure, "So we are to lose <u>the great</u> M[r] Sumner."— The same vain, irritable man is said never to have forgiven M[rs] Jamieson for some allusion made, in one of her books, to his want of personal beauty. She speaks of meeting him in Italy & alludes to his well-known ugliness, for which offence he visits her with a most heavy dislike.

———————————————————————————————

Great Britain and the United States were engaged in the bloodless Aroostook **WAR**, a confrontation over the Maine boundary line.

The monument to Lady Elizabeth **NIGHTINGALE** (1704–1731) by sculptor Louis François Roubiliac (1702–1762) remains one of the most memorable works in Westminster Abbey. Nightingale was the eldest daughter of Washington Shirley, Earl Ferrers and Viscount Tamworth, and his wife, Mary. In 1725 she married Joseph Nightingale (1695–1752), with whom she had three children. Only their son Washington survived them both, and it was his will that directed the erection of this memorial, completed in 1761. John Wesley was among its early admirers, but by the time of Coolidge's visit the monument had its share of critics as well. Allan Cunningham deemed Roubiliac's sculpture "more generally praised than any of his works. Those who are not pleased with the natural pathos of one part, are captivated by the allegorical extravagance of another; and persons who care for none of these matters, find enough to admire in the difficult workmanship of the marble skeleton. . . . [T]he sculptor conceived a design, at once striking and strange—an ingenious conceit, which won the love of the public, and has kept it these eighty years" (*ODNB*, s.v. "Roubiliac, Louis François"; Whinney, *Sculpture in Britain*, 109–110; Allan Cunningham, *The Lives of the Most Eminent British Painters* [1880], 3:58; "The North Transept," Highlights of the Abbey, Westminster Abbey, accessed 20 Dec. 2010, http://www.westminster-abbey.org).

The painter John Callcott Horsley attended the weekly dinners that John SHEEP-
SHANKS hosted on Wednesdays at three o'clock in his "charming" Blackheath
Park house, surrounded by a beautiful garden that revealed its owner's devotion to
horticulture. Horsley recalled that "to a certain number of painters he gave a general invitation to put in an appearance at that hour. . . . His repasts were of the sim-
plest, but everything, eatables and drinkables, perfect of its kind. . . . Sheepshanks
had a wonderful servant who looked after everything, and was trained never to
take a sixpence offered her by any guest" (John Callcott Horsley, *Recollections of a
Royal Academician* [1903], 49–55).

BLACKHEATH lies southeast of London in the parishes of Greenwich and Lew-
isham along the Roman road leading to Canterbury and Dover. Travelers were
advised to avoid the heath and nearby Shooter's Hill for fear of highwaymen.
Lord Byron alludes to the area's reputation in canto XI of *Don Juan* (1823) when
his hero visits Shooter's Hill and, lost in reverie, is accosted by a gang of thieves
demanding "your money or your life!" (*London Encyclopedia*, 69-70, 784; *Old and
New London*, 6:224–236).

John Henry ROBINSON (1796–1871) established himself as an engraver with William Mulready's *The Wolf and the Lamb*, made to benefit the Artists' Benevolent
Fund in 1823. He supplied plates for Samuel Rogers's *Italy* (1830) and engraved
works by David Wilkie, Thomas Lawrence, and Edwin Landseer. In 1836 he was
among nine petitioners to the House of Commons calling for an investigation of
the state of engraving and the following year campaigning for full recognition
of the engraving profession by the Royal Academy, where he was not accepted as
a full member for another thirty years (*ODNB*; *Grove Art Online*, s.v. "Robinson,
John Henry," Oxford Art Online).

The engraver Benjamin Phelps GIBBON (1802–1851) was the sole pupil of John
Henry Robinson and produced animal and portrait engravings for print pub-
lishers, frequently after the works of Edwin Landseer (*ODNB*, s.v. "Gibbon, Benjamin Phelps" and "Robinson, John Henry").

Landseer's FATHER was the engraver and author John George Landseer (1763/9–
1852), who with his wife, Jane (1773/4–1840), had fourteen children, seven surviving to adulthood. All three of their sons, of whom Edwin was the youngest,
were artists. Thomas Landseer (1793/4–1880) was a printmaker, and Charles Landseer (1799/1800–1879) was a genre and history painter. Two of Landseer's sisters,
Jessica (1807–1880) and Emma (1809–1895), painted miniatures. The family lived
at 71 Queen Anne Street East and later 33 Foley Street (*ODNB*, s.v. "Landseer,
Edwin Henry" and "Landseer, John George").

In *Visits and Sketches at Home and Abroad* (1834) Anna Jameson [JAMIESON] recalled that "Samuel Rogers paid us a long visit this morning. He does not look
as if the suns of Italy had *revivified* him—but he is as *amiable* and amusing as
ever." Jameson went on to relate that while in Italy Rogers spent an hour every
day gazing at a statue of Venus, in whose fingers a young Englishman slipped a
poem addressed to Rogers in which the goddess asks him to stop his daily "*ogling.*"

Venus claims to know by his looks that Rogers "had come from the other side of the Styx" and she concludes by begging him to stop haunting her with his "*ghostly*" presence (Anna Jameson, *Visits and Sketches at Home and Abroad* [1834], 3:287–288).

Saturday. 30ᵗʰ March.

My dear daughter's birth-day. Heaven bless her! How well I remember the day of which this is the anniversary. It began a new era for me. No woman knows what her heart is made of until she becomes a mother.——

On thursday 28ᵗʰ I brought my boy from Highgate, having called to enquire after Miss Berry & to visit Mʳˢ & Miss Richards. Mʳˢ Richards is a second edition of Lady Edgermond, cold, dull, formal, with the stiffest habits of propriety, the most unamiable love of right, her very virtues are prejudices, her strongest feelings are of dislike, and her affections partake of the asperity and sour melancholy that form the colouring of her character. Her daughter is very much what Lucilla would have become had she remained unmarried. An amiable but angular old maid. The same day we dined with a pleasant party at Mʳˢ Stevenson's.

Friday—Good friday, I should have been at Church, but rather dreading the singsong service & dull sermon, I went instead, with Mʳˢ Morrison to a place called Haveringay, a very pretty country house within five miles of London, formerly occupied by a Mʳ Grey, but since his death, dismantled & for sale. Mʳ Grey had loved pictures and collected a good many even of the old masters. Of these Mʳ Morrison had bought many. One a Rubens, an original study, a sketch from which a larger picture was made & afterwards I believe, destroyed by fire. It represents people of a Dutch town doing homage to a monarch called by Mʳˢ Morrison Charles 5ᵗʰ. Among the crowd were many portraits and one of Rubens himself. They wear ruffs or collars & have short doublets & slashed sleeves. Mʳ Morrison had also secured a Gerard Dow, a Jan Stein, an Ostade, a Vandyke & several others.

The most curious picture that I saw was a very early Raphael. It represented various scenes in the garden of Eden. An Eve tempted by a serpent with a human head, the Saviour in conversation with Adam &c &c.

There was a good library and extensive Conservatories belonging to the establishment, and old servants who had been in Mʳ Grey's service for thirty or forty years. It made me sad to see such an ~~establishment~~ ^old place^ broken up and I almost wished for an <u>eldest son</u> to keep things together. There are only granddaughters among whom the property is to be divided. One of them a Miss Smith-Wright, we saw. She seemed just what the English would call a very nice person.—There is a fine collection of Camellias at Haveringay.——

This Friday being the anniversary of Mrs Searle's wedding day, we dined with her "en famille."

LADY EDGERMOND was the staid British stepmother to Corinne, the extroverted and brilliant Italian heroine of the novel *Corinne, ou l'Italie* (1807), by the French author Anne Louise Germaine Necker, baronne de Staël Holstein (1766–1817). Lady Edgermond's daughter Lucile [LUCILLA] is the model of the dutiful English bride and marries the Scottish nobleman Lord Nelvil, who had earlier fallen in love with her half-sister Corinne. The novel was an immediate success and inspired British authors including Felicia Hemans and Letitia E. Landon. Madame de Staël, as she is best known, was the daughter of Jacques Necker, the Swiss banker who was finance minister under Louis XVI. She witnessed the French Revolution and her father's triumphant re-entry into Paris after the fall of the Bastille. Her mother's Paris salon attracted Thomas Jefferson when he was minister plenipotentiary, from 1784 to 1789, and they corresponded after his return to the United States. In 1807 de Staël sent the president a copy of *Corinne* for which he thanked her, writing, "I shall read with great pleasure whatever comes from your pen, having known it's powers when I was in a situation to judge, nearer at hand, the talents which directed it" (*Oxford Companion to the Romantic Age* [2009], s.v. "Staël, [Anne-Louise] Germaine [Necker] de," Oxford Reference Online; Linda M. Lewis, *Germaine de Staël, George Sand, and the Victorian Woman Artist* [2003], 15–16, 24; Sowerby, 4353).

Harringay [HAVERINGAY] House was the Hornsey home of Edward Gray [GREY] (d. 1838), a linen-draper from London. Gray had one daughter, Lydia (d. 1820), who married John Smith Wright, with whom she had four children. It was Gray's granddaughter Lydia Rachael Smith Wright (b. ca. 1813) whom Coolidge met and described in a scene that bore striking similarities to the dispersal of Jefferson's estate and belongings at Monticello following his 1826 death.

Edward Gray began purchasing land north of London in 1789, eventually amassing 192 acres. From 1792 to 1796 he built a fourteen-bedroom brick house on a wooded knoll in the curve of the New River. There he displayed what William Buchanan called "one of the finest small collections of pictures in the country," which included works by Titian, Rubens, and Rembrandt. Gray ordered that his estate be sold at the time of his death, and Christie's auctioned Gray's library and prints, as well as his collection of silver, porcelain, and marble sculpture, at their St. James's Square rooms in May 1839. Buchanan negotiated the sale of Gray's paintings, many of which he had initially sold to Gray, to collectors such as the Morrisons. Harringay's gardens and grounds were as impressive as its art collection. The gardens were "elegantly diversified and filled with the choicest American plants and evergreens, standard and well trained magnolias of surpassing beauty and luxuriant growth." Harringay's ten steam-heated hothouses, magnolias, and "semi-double" red camellias earned mention in contemporary gardening publications, as did the estate's second-generation gardener, Thomas Press (William Buchanan, *Memoirs of Painting* [1824], 1:114, 189, 204, 208, 241, 2:152–153, 286–287, 318–336, 343–345, 392–397; J. C. Loudon, *Encyclopedia of Gardening* [1824], 327–328; George Don, *A General System of Gardening and Botany* [1831], 1:575; *Gardener's Magazine and Register of Rural and Domestic Improvement* 11 [1835]: 69–70; J. C. Loudon, *Arboretum et Fructicetum Britannicum; or, The Trees and Shrubs of Britain* [1838], 1:386; John Burke, *Burke's Genealogical and Heraldic Dictionary of the Landed Gentry* [1847], 2:1640; T. F. T. Baker and C. R. Elrington, eds., *A History of the County of Middlesex* [1980], 6:107–111, 146–149; Register of marriages, London Metropolitan Archives, Saint Mary, Hornsey, s.v. "Gray, Lydia," Ancestry.com; 1861 Census Returns of England and Wales, High Legh parish, s.v. "Leigh, Lydia Rachel," Ancestry.com; *Times* [London], 27 Oct. 1838, 2 Feb., 16 May, 1 June, 19 Sept. 1839).

Wednesday. 3ᵈ April.

Very busy with my preparations for departure. Saturday March 30th, we visited the two great Artists, Mulready & Landseer, than whom there cannot be two persons more unlike. Mulready is a large full-faced, middle-aged man, somewhat brusque and something of a humorist, complaining in a tone between jest & earnest, that he is called coarse, his pictures vulgar, full of fighting & the passions of low-life. Edwin Landseer young, about thirty four, courtly, not entirely free from affectation but gentle & civil. He has been much taken up by the higher classes and petted by the Aristocracy, being a favorite artist among people of fashion. He is the best living painter of animals, and perhaps as good as any who have preceded him. He is also eminently happy in his portraits of children. Mulready is more highly esteemed among artists than in general society, though his pictures command high prices. The only pieces he would allow us to see were such as had been expressly named by Mʳ Sheepshanks in his note of introduction, and it was evident that we were entirely indebted to this note for the courtesy with which we were treated. Mʳ Sheepshanks is so good a friend, and buys so many pictures, that his name goes a great way among painters, and I suspect that in the present instance, it was the sole charm. There is a certain something in the countenance & manner of Mulready which does not indicate much patience with intruders, especially such as pretend to no knowledge of art. Heaven knows I love it enough to be my excuse for unavoidable ignorance. Pictures are my passion—

I did not know how much so till since I have had the opportunity to see good ones.

The three Mulready's pictures which we saw were,

1st "The fight interrupted" — Two schoolboys, one evidently the aggressor & still full of fight, the other lubberly if not cowardly, are interrupted in their single combat, by a grave and reverend clergyman, who is hearing the merits of the case from other boys, bystanders, and is recommending to these witnesses truth & impartiality in their statements. The group is admirable, the sullen anger of one boy who has not had or given enough, the somewhat pusillanimous complaining of the other, the eagerness & animation of the partisans on both sides, the grave, reproving looks of the clergyman are all as true as possible to nature. I could not help thinking there might be something in a criticism which Mulready told us had been made upon his works, that none but a man who himself had been a pickle as a boy, could have executed such subjects so well.

2nd A girl reading a sonnet whilst the author, a young man, watches the expression of her countenance.

3^{d} A girl shutting her eyes and opening her mouth to receive a cherry, which a man, reclining on the turf, is bobbing at her lips. These two small & charming pictures belong to Mr Sheepshanks. Mulready is particularly good as a colorist, but his drawing and his conception of character seemed to my unlearned eyes equally as admirable as his colouring.

The pictures shewn us by Landseer were mostly unfinished but far enough advanced to produce a most charming effect. We were kept waiting in his parlour awhile, till he had finished with a sitter, who with a female attendant passed out soon after our arrival; a charming little girl, a daughter of Sir Robert Peel, whose portrait with her mother's dog, a small spaniel, in her arms, Landseer is now at work upon.

The other pictures that we saw were,

1st Princess Mary of Cambridge, a lovely child with a large Newfoundland Dog whom she is trying to tempt & teaze with a biscuit. The noble animal seems to understand and lend himself to the joke.

3. Two fair children, portraits, feeding rabbits.

4. A boy holding a horse at the door of a rustic inn — with two dogs.

5. A scene in an English Park with a group of deer.

6. 7. Two half lengths. Girls dressed as Summer & Winter

8. An unfinished sketch of the Queen on horseback. Landseer had influence enough to prevail on her Majesty to substitute a sort of Spanish

Hat & Feather for the unbecoming round Men's hat usually worn by ladys in riding.

9. Van Amburgh & his Lions. The man inferiour to the brutes. The old Lion is a noble animal, a monarch discrowned but not degraded — in captivity but right Royal still. He reminded me of Sir Joshua Reynold's "Banished Lord" in the National Gallery. Landseer says a sort of King Lear.

Edwin Landseer is good-looking & well-mannered. He lives in a small and somewhat humble house on the St. John's wood road, with his sister who has his affectation without his talent. She may be clever, she is certainly a "precieuse"

Mulready lives beyond Kensington, Leslie on the Edgeware road — all far enough from the idle part of the town to avoid ^escape^[1] too frequent intrusion.

———

William **MULREADY** (1786–1863) was born in Ireland, the son of a leather breeches maker named Michael Mulready and an unnamed mother. Mulready's family settled in London, and in 1800 he entered the Royal Academy Schools, where his success led to his election as a full member of the Academy in 1816. At seventeen he married the landscape artist Elizabeth Robinson Varley (1784–1864) and the couple had four sons who all became artists. After charges of infidelity and abuse caused the couple to separate, Mulready gained custody of their unruly sons, with whom he lived in a villa in Linden Grove off of Notting Hill Gate. The artist J. C. Horsley observed that "Mulready was in his own fashion an affectionate and excellent father, but after this painful break in the family circle the four high-spirited, wild Irish boys were of necessity much left to themselves; and as they were all of the same pugnacious nature, a good deal of their time seems to have gone in fighting each other and the Kensington *gamins*. Their house was cold and comfortless, as one would expect. . . . The figures in Mulready's inimitably painted and life-like picture, called 'The Fight Interrupted,' were painted from these boys." John Sheepshanks was Mulready's most loyal patron (*ODNB*; *Grove Art Online*, s.v. "Mulready, William," Oxford Art Online; John Callcott Horsley, *Recollections of a Royal Academician* [1903], 20).

The **THREE MULREADY'S PICTURES** that Coolidge saw, *The Fight Interrupted*, *The Sonnet*, and *Open Your Mouth and Shut Your Eyes* were all given by John Sheepshanks to the Victoria and Albert Museum (Victoria and Albert Museum, http://collections.vam.ac.uk).

ROBERT PEEL and his wife, Julia Floyd (1795–1859), had seven children in twelve years, the youngest of whom was Eliza Peel (b. 1832). Landseer exhibited *Miss Eliza Peel with Fido*, "a gem of a picture, yet nothing more than a pretty child fondling her pet-dog," at the Royal Academy show in 1839 (*ODNB*; James Dafforne, *Pictures by Sir Edwin Landseer, Royal Academician* [1873], 9–19).

Edwin Landseer's PICTURES *Princess Mary Adelaide of Cambridge with Nelson, a Newfoundland Dog* and *Queen Victoria on Horseback* are part of the Royal Collection. Landseer lived with his SISTER Jessica Landseer on a two-acre property west of Regent's Park. Harriet Martineau described him as a "friendly and agreeable companion, but holding his cheerfulness at the mercy of great folks' graciousness to him. To see him enter a room, curled and cravatted, and glancing round in anxiety about his reception, could not but make a woman wonder where among her own sex she could find a more palpable vanity; but then, all that was forgotten when one was sitting on a divan with him, seeing him play with the dog" (*ODNB*; Martineau, *Autobiography*, 268–269; Edwin Landseer, *Queen Victoria on Horseback* [ca. 1838] and *Princess Mary Adelaide of Cambridge with Nelson, a Newfoundland Dog* [ca. 1839], Royal Collection, http://www.royalcollection.org.uk/eGallery).

1. Word interlined in an unidentified hand.

Thursday 4ᵗʰ April.

Very busy packing and arranging matters for my departure. Have passed the evening with Mʳˢ Searle and brought Tom home from the Wormeleys.

Sunday 31. March, we went to the Royal Chapel at St. James' Palace where we saw the Queen. She was simply dressed with a pale, blue silk bonnet, entered her Gallery without parade, and was to receive the sacrament after the other services were over. The altar was in full dress with all it's bravery of gold plate, whether in honour of the day, Easter Sunday, or of the Queen, or whether this be it's usual costume on the occasion of the Communion, I do not know. I sat in the pew of the Bishop of London, to which my kind friend, Mʳˢ Stevenson had procured me admittance. No persons except the Queen's suite were permitted to remain during the ceremony of the Lord's supper.

After leaving church we called "pour dire adieu" on Miss Martineau and had some pleasant conversation with her. I asked where I could find ear-trumpets like those which she uses and she kindly allowed me to take two that she had to dispose of for the maker, the husband of her cook. We likewise went to say good bye to excellent Mʳˢ Marcet, and called at Miss Berry's to ask after her health. She has been "un peu souffrante." Miss Agnes Berry received us and we have met Lord & Lady Elliot, whose manners, particularly <u>his</u> are very pleasing. These leave-takings make me feel very heavy-hearted. A card left for Mʳˢ Mansfield completed our rounds.

The CHAPEL Royal at St. James's Palace was built by Henry VIII and is modest in size and ornament. The Royal Gallery abuts over the main entrance, opposite to the communion table on the eastern end of the oblong room. Two galleries supported by cast-iron pillars stretch the length of the chapel and on the floor are two pews on each side, placed longitudinally. It was here that Queen Victoria and Prince Albert of Saxe-Coburg-Gotha (1819–1861) were married in 1840, and the communion table was similarly covered with a "vast quantity of golden plate, including six salvers, one of gigantic dimensions, two ponderous and rich vases, four flagons, four communion-cups, and two lofty and magnificent candelabra." The Chapel Royal was open daily for public services, and Holy Communion was served twice every Sunday when the queen was in residence. Victoria typically took communion only twice a year, at Easter and Christmas (*ODNB*; Helen Rappaport, *Queen Victoria: A Biographical Companion* [2003], 312; "Table of Public Services in London," *Tracts for the Times* [1840], 5:43; "Marriage of Victoria the First, Sovereign of England, with Prince Albert, of Saxe Coburg and Gotha," *Mirror of Literature, Amusement, and Instruction* 38 [1840]: 115; "The Chapels Royal," The Official Website of the British Monarchy, accessed 20 Dec. 2010, http://www .royal.gov.uk/TheRoyalResidences/TheChapelsRoyal/History.aspx).

Charles James Blomfield (1786–1857) was **BISHOP OF LONDON** from 1828 to 1856 (*ODNB*).

The **EAR-TRUMPETS** Harriet Martineau used during this time were unlike the "caoutchouc tube" she employed during her travels in the United States, which Martineau described as having "a cup at one end for the speaker to speak into. It was a good exchange when I laid aside this in favour of a trumpet with which the speaker had no concern." Coolidge may have sought the trumpets on behalf of her nephew Thomas Jefferson Trist (1828–1890), the eldest son of Nicholas and Virginia Randolph Trist, who was born deaf. More likely, they were for her own son Joseph Randolph Coolidge, whose hearing was damaged by a childhood disease, possibly scarlet fever, the same illness that caused his sister Elizabeth's death in 1832. The Geneva surgeon Theodore Maunoir discovered that Joseph Randolph Coolidge suffered from "perforated" tympanums in both ears and treated his worsening condition with surgery in 1842 (Martineau, *Autobiography*, 240; Shackelford, *Descendants*, 2:125, 155–157; Coolidge to Jane Nicholas Randolph, 17 May 1843 [ViU: Ellen Wayles Randolph Coolidge Correspondence]).

Friday 5th April.

The weather has been gloomy and chilly for some time past, but to-day is a regular snow storm.

I am writing before breakfast & resume where I left off last night. Monday, All Fools Day, I did no foolish thing, but on tuesday I received news that my sisters Mrs Trist, Cornelia & Mary & Virginia's children are probably at this time in France!—whilst I am leaving England! They sailed from Havana. My dear sisters, friends of childhood, youth & advancing life—Tender, true, unchanging, it seems as if the same quarter of the world was not to hold us. You arrive in Europe as I return to America. and soon I shall be on my voyage to China, to the very Antipodes— leaving behind not only sisters but my children! My heart sinks & fails at the thought. Ours, my sisters & mine, seems a strange uncertain lot, with a settled home no where. We may well call ourselves "Tribe of the wandering foot and weary breast." Heaven knows how rejoiced I should be to find myself quietly seated with my family round me and to know that I might remain so, going no farther and no oftener away from my home than inclination prompted. I like my sisters' plan of a summer in France, or even a residence there of some years. They will have among other advantages, the opportunity of acquiring a habit of speaking French.

Tuesday & Wednesday were passed in shopping & thursday in packing. To-day I shall be very busy as the Quebec sails on Sunday, or rather leaves the dock, so that the luggage must be on board to-morrow, and there will be much trouble in accomplishing the task. We shall not ourselves leave London before tuesday 9th, as the vessel sails from Portsmouth on the 10th, and we shall have nothing to do but to go on board. This is no season for seeing the Isle of Wight, otherwise we should regret passing so near without the power of visiting this garden of England.

Coolidge's SISTERS Virginia Jefferson TRIST (1801–1882), CORNELIA Jefferson Randolph (1799–1871), and MARY Jefferson Randolph (1803–1876) accompanied two of the Trist's three children, Martha Jefferson Trist (1826–1915) and Hore Browse Trist (1832–1896), to France in 1839. Martha attended school first at St. Servan in Brittany and later in Paris, departing Europe in 1841. Her brother Browse joined the Coolidge brothers at school in Geneva, where he studied until 1845.

Virginia Trist, Coolidge's closest confidante, was married to Nicholas Philip Trist (1800–1882), the grandson of Jefferson's old friend Elizabeth Trist. The couple first met in 1817, when Nicholas and his brother accepted an invitation from Jefferson to come to Monticello. During a ten-month stay Nicholas fell in love with Virginia and began his lifelong friendship with Coolidge. After leaving Monticello in 1818 Nicholas pursued his studies at the U.S. Military Academy at West Point, but he returned in 1823 to study law with Jefferson. He and Virginia were married the following year and together had three children. Nicholas became Jefferson's private secretary and, after the latter's death in 1826, an executor of his estate. He then served as clerk in the U.S. Department of State from 1828 to 1831 and briefly as Andrew Jackson's private secretary. In 1834 the Trists relocated to Havana, Cuba, where Nicholas took up an appointment as consul. He returned to Washington in 1845 as chief clerk of the State Department and was sent to Mexico in 1847 to negotiate a peace treaty. While there Nicholas defied a presidential recall, an act that essentially ended his political career. The Trists later moved to Alexandria, Virginia, where Nicholas served as postmaster.

Coolidge's sister Cornelia Randolph had an aptitude for art and taught drawing, painting, and sculpture in the family's Edgehill School for Girls. She never married and lived alternately at Edgehill, the home of her older brother Thomas Jefferson Randolph; with the Coolidges in Boston; and in Cuba and France with the family of her sister Virginia J. Trist. Late in life, Cornelia translated and edited *The Parlor Gardener: A Treatise on the House Culture of Ornamental Plants. Translated from the French and Adapted to American Use* (1861).

Mary Randolph was born at Edgehill but spent much of her time at Monticello, relocating there with her family following her grandfather's retirement in 1809. Like her sister Cornelia, Mary never married but lived alternately with one sibling or another helping to raise her nieces and nephews. She taught at the Edgehill School for Girls and traveled variously to New England, Cuba, and France. After the Civil War, Mary moved to Alexandria, Virginia, to live with two of her sisters at the home of her niece Martha Jefferson Trist Burke (Betts and Bear, *Family Letters*, 394; *PTJRS*, 3:635n; Shackelford, *Descendants*, 1:108–109, 147–153, 253, 2:151–159; Cornelia Randolph, commonplace book [DLC: Randolph Family Manuscripts]).

TRIBE OF THE WANDERING FOOT is from Lord Byron's poem "Oh! Weep for Those," published in *Hebrew Melodies* (1815).

The packet ship **QUEBEC** was put into service in 1837 as part of the London line of Fish & Grinnell, later Grinnell, Minturn & Company (Joseph Alfred Scoville, *The Old Merchants of New York City* [1885], 2:261–262; Ship's Manifest for the *Quebec*, 15 May 1839, Ancestry.com).

Tuesday 9ᵗʰ April.

Sunday 7ᵗʰ April Mʳ Coolidge & myself went to say good bye to the Carlyles. He was out but Madame received us kindly. She conversed with much spirit but shewed more of the caustic temper alluded to by Allan Cunningham than I had yet perceived. She spoke of Miss Martineau, her madness on the subject of abolitionism & her arguments with Mʳ Carlyle whom she cannot get to sympathise with her, to the full extent of her wishes, in the cause of those "interesting critters the niggers." Carlyle has his own prejudices and one, whether well or ill-founded, against the natural equality of the black & white races. He looks upon the negro as constitutionally inferior—capable of improvement no doubt, but still a lower race than the white man. Mʳˢ Carlyle speaks also of Miss Martineau's exaggerated tone both of commendation and blame—her ultra praise of Dr Follen, (too good a man to require it,) her absurd eulogiums of Mʳˢ Chapman &c &c. She alluded to the misrepresentations contained in Miss Martineau's article in the Westminster Review on what she calls the "Martyr Age in America," the extravagance of her assertions & the almost ludicrous excess of her exaggerations & tragic declamations.

I asked Mrs Carlyle for an autograph of Mr Carlyle. "What" said she, in a tone slightly sarcastic, "are you a collector of autographs?" "By no means," I replied, "but I have a few, accidentally obtained, and I wish to add Mr Carlyle's to the number." She gave me some pages of the French Revolution, and quietly went on to say that whilst she lived in Scotland and heard much of celebrated men, she had made a collection of their autographs. "But" she continued, "when I came to know the men themselves, I burnt almost all the autographs."

Having said goodbye to the clever, honest & caustic Scotch woman, we went to pay a leave-taking visit to Lady Charlotte Lyndsay, a most intelligent, animated, spirited & amiable person, whose acquaintance I value as highly as any I have made in England. I have read her letter to Lord Brougham, published in his public characters, with great pleasure and approbation. From her we learned that the Miss Berrys were out of town, nor have I seen them since though I have received a kind note from the elder sister.

From Green St. we drove to Upper Grosvenor to say adieu to the Mansfields from whom we have received many kindnesses. We had previously shaken hands with Mrs Frederick Elliot and after our return home, Mr Elliot himself came in and sat with us a pleasant half hour.

The evening came and we again went out to leave last words with our friends the Wormeleys & Searles, to take leave of pretty Mrs Cryder, and to sit for the last time at the hospitable tea-table of Mrs Stevenson, whose conduct to me since my arrival in England, but especially during the last months of my stay, has been so cordial, warm-hearted and in the true spirit of old friendship and old neighbourhood, that I can never think of it without gratitude and affectionate acknowledgement. In Portland Place we met Mr Rush & Mr Duer. Mr Duer is a lawyer of high standing in New York who has been well received in English society, and seems to be just the right sort of American, manly, intelligent yet strongly marked by the national characteristics. He neither merges into the Englishman on one side, nor fawns nor swaggers the Yankee on the other.

Monday April 8th, we dined with M^r & Mrs Bates in their new house on Portland Place, M. & Mme de Weyer being of the party & Mr Heard with us. Mr Bates has taken a much larger & finer house in consequence of the marriage of his daughter who is to live with him, & of course requires a good deal of room in her new quality of Ambassadress. She bears her honours as if she had been born to them, not meekly but calmly. She is ambitious & I should say cold-blooded & cold-hearted. Prudent & worldly, "tant soit peu" inclined to be insolent where the indulgence of such a humour is perfectly safe. M^r & Mrs Bates will themselves now take a much higher position in the social scale seeing that their son-in-law M. Van der Weyer is the envoy of King Leopold, the Queen's uncle, & is himself somewhat in favour with her Majesty. Mr Bates will be always cool, calm & self-respectful—of Mrs Bates least said is soonest mended, but no rank that could be conferred by Courts or Princes would make a lady of Mrs Bates.

I had passed the morning of monday leaving p.p.c. cards.——

To-day, tuesday, I have been to take leave of Mrs Searle whom I have found from first to last most hospitable, amiable & kind. Then having a spare hour I have devoted it to visiting the exhibition of Miss Linwood's Needle work in Leicester Square. From a child I have heard of the wonders accomplished by Miss Linwood. As a young girl, being somewhat awkward in the use of my needle, and seeing many of my friends excelling & surpassing me greatly in the management of that small, sharp, bright & admirable weapon, I often thought of Miss Linwood whom I considered as a sort of rival of Minerva, the patroness of female industry. As might be expected I had expected too much. In presence of these tapestry pictures I was disappointed in their effect. Where the subjects are rural & domestic they do very well. The copies from Gainsborough & the representations of animals I thought better than more grave & ambitious subjects. The head of Christ, however, is I believe considered the best, and Miss Linwood is said to have refused 3000 guineas for it. One of these embroideries, a copy from Mrs Cosway, attracted my attention. It is the Nymph Lodona dissolving into the stream of the Loddon. It looks cold & watery—you see the transition from the solid to the liquid, the streaming of the fingers, the flowing away of the hair, the drapery winding along the limbs & falling over the bank on which the nymph reclines, her face concealed, her whole figure sinking, having lost as yet nothing of it's proportions, but evidently just about to undergo the change which has already commenced in the garments & in the long streaming tresses.

Coolidge compiled an impressive **AUTOGRAPH** collection, including signatures from four U.S. presidents, John Adams, James Madison, Martin Van Buren, and Jefferson; politicians Charles Sumner, Harrison Gray Otis, and Josiah Quincy; and authors Ralph Waldo Emerson, Washington Irving, Henry Wadsworth Longfellow, and Henry David Thoreau. She encouraged her grandson Thomas Jefferson

Coolidge to collect autographs as well, presenting him with a "very modern" autograph book in 1876 for his thirteenth birthday (Autograph Collection of Ellen Wayles Coolidge [private collection, N.J.]; Coolidge to Thomas Jefferson Coolidge, 16 Mar. 1876 [private collection, Mass.]).

John DUER (1782–1858), lawyer and publisher of *The Revised Statutes of the State of New York* (1827–1836), was the London correspondent for the *New York American*, which published a letter from Andrew Stevenson to Duer regarding the Bank of the United States that caused some to demand Stevenson's recall from London. Duer was among Sally Coles Stevenson's admirers when she dressed for her audience with the queen, and he looked to the Stevensons for comfort after suffering the tragic loss of his sister Henrietta Elizabeth (Minnie) Robinson, who died of cholera during her 1839 visit to London with her husband and two daughters. Duer returned to the United States where he continued to publish legal works and became chief justice of the superior court of the City of New York (*DAB*; Boykin, *Mrs. Stevenson*, 53, 229–230; Wayland, *Andrew Stevenson*, 181–182; Ship's Manifest for the *Great Western*, 7 Mar. 1840, Ancestry.com).

LEOPOLD I (1790–1865), king of Belgium, was a valued mentor and father figure to Queen Victoria. From the time she turned fourteen, Leopold advised Victoria on matters of state and politics, but his most enduring influence was the introduction of his nephew, her future husband, Prince Albert of Saxe-Coburg-Gotha (*ODNB*).

Mary LINWOOD (1755–1845) began exhibiting her needlework in 1776 at the Society of Artists in London alongside works by her mother, Hannah Linwood (d. 1804), who operated a boarding school. Linwood's skill was in using unconventional techniques and a wide range of stitches to achieve a painterly effect. Newspapers celebrated her work, she was introduced to Queen Charlotte, and one of her needlework landscapes was sent to Catherine the Great of Russia. After several temporary and traveling exhibitions Linwood established a permanent gallery in Leicester Square in 1809, where her work remained on exhibit for forty years. Harriette Story Paige, who also visited the gallery in 1839, called the exhibition one of the "'Lions' of this wonderful city" and found it a "very interesting monument of taste, and industry." Of the needlework itself, which was displayed in frames, she remarked that "the deception is perfect at a short distance" (*ODNB*; Gray, *Daniel Webster in England*, 109–110; *Miss Linwood's Gallery of Pictures, in Worsted, Leicester Square* [1822]).

Ship Quebec.
Wednesday 1st May.

Off the Banks of Newfoundland. Three weeks at sea. Dismal weeks of incessant sickness & suffering. Let no one talk of sea-sickness who has not felt it in it's horrors—it's weakness, it's helplessness, it's utter prostration of all power bodily and mental. O long days & weeks of giddiness & nausea, wretched days, followed by wretched nights! Restlessness, feverishness, low-spirits, overwhelming debility, broken sleep, perturbed dreams, unwillingness to go to a bed where there is no rest, and disability to rise when you have once laid down. Once at least my situation has not been exempt from danger. Fierce cramps brought on by long continued vomitings. Agonizing pain, contraction of limbs, my hands clenched so that no force could open them—no relief but from opium in considerable quantities & hot brandy. I believe I should have died but for an English surgeon or physician who was on board, and who immediately came, at near midnight, from his bed, to my relief. Now I am somewhat better, able to move but very wretched & uncomfortable. Still I can read, I can write, I can crawl to the deck and see what is going on in our ship.

We are in all respects badly off. The ship is dirty, crowded, uncomfortable—full of disgusting sights and more digusting odours. A hundred & sixty unfortunate creatures in a close fetid, noisome steerage; men, women & children literally packed above, below & around. I have not visited the scene of horrors, but those who have give a sickening account of it. These unfortunate emigrants seem to me to be the victims of sordid ship-masters & agents. Is there no one whose business it is to prevent such abuses?

In the cabin are twenty eight ill-assorted passengers of different sexes, ages, rank ^in society^ habits, manners, dispositions, degrees of education, yet <u>getting</u> <u>along</u>, upon the whole, decently & quietly, with a certain respect for each others wishes, rights & necessities. There are no altercations and some attempts not altogether abortive, at friendly intercourse. Things might be worse in this respect. There are no individuals outrageously selfish; one lady childishly so, chuses to leave her state room and sleep on the sofa in the ladies cabin, and for fear of taking cold, insists upon keeping the sky-light closed all night, thus depriving us all of fresh air & ventilation. I wonder there is no open rebellion against this petty tyranny. We are certainly a good-natured set. Even the sick woman is simply thoughtless. She is young, silly, newly-married & "enceinté"—uncomfortable & obstinately determined to continue so, as she will make no effort to rally her powers or rouse herself from the torpour of nausea, indolence & feebleness of body & mind. She is a Jewess with an old husband who tries in a clumsy way to be kind to her, and succeeds by pawing & scrambling to shew his good-will at least in his efforts to adjust her couch & arrange her pillows, whilst he hangs over her with uncouth fondness & snores or dozes away his own heavy hours at her side. We have another new-married couple on board, very loving & the man very devoted. He is a canny Scot from Aberdeen, married to a girl from Devon who likes to be waited on, and is waited on by her young husband. I wonder how it will be some years hence. — Next comes a patient, American mother waiting on her child, a little girl of two years old, and not waited on herself or assisted in any way by her English husband, who seems good-natured enough but has probably taken up Miss Martineau's idea, that American women are spoiled by too much attention from the men. One of our most useful shipmates is the young English doctor, going out on speculation. He is a little bit of a cockney & misplaces the letter h now & then, but he has been active in his efforts to afford relief to all sufferers both in cabin & steerage. I am certainly indebted to his seasonable assistance when in the horrors of cramp. Luckily Mr Coolidge has not become a convert to Miss Martineau's doctrine that the weaker vessel is strengthened by neglect, (what an old maid's idea!) and takes very excellent care of me. Then I must say for myself that I have no desire to make bad worse and therefore do what I can to get well & keep well, but the weather has been most unpropitious, a succession of calms & gales — the vessel now lying idly on the water with little or no motion, and then reeling, tossing, bounding corvetting, throwing every thing and every body about, so that just as we begin to get better of our sea-sickness, and more accustomed to sea-life, we are all cast back again by the throes & agonies of the sea-tortured vessel.

Harriet Martineau, who delighted in nearly every aspect of her 1834 passage by packet ship to America, noted that SEA-SICKNESS was "an annoyance scarcely to be exaggerated while it lasts." She found relief from her own sea-sickness by going on deck during a storm, where she lashed herself to the post of the binnacle and observed what the captain later recorded as a hurricane (Stephen Fox, *Transatlantic: Samuel Cunard, Isambard Brunel, and the Great Atlantic Steamships* [2003], 6; Harriet Martineau, *Retrospect of Western Travel* [1838], 1:22, 28–30).

The ENGLISH SURGEON was twenty-four-year-old Charles Griffing. Coolidge was fortunate that he chanced to be on board; as Charles Dickens advised the author Martin Tupper, "few packet ships carry Surgeons. Take a Medicine chest." The pregnant SICK WOMAN was probably Martha Jonas (b. ca. 1807), who traveled with the merchant Joseph Jonas (b. ca. 1793). The NEW-MARRIED COUPLE may have been Thomas Thurin (b. ca. 1815) and Mary Thurin (b. ca. 1814), and the AMERICAN MOTHER is Matilda C. Lister (b. ca. 1815), who traveled with Elizabeth Lister (b. ca. 1837), the only CHILD in the cabin besides eight-year-old Thomas Jefferson Coolidge (Madeline House, Graham Storey, and Kathleen Tillotson, eds., *The Letters of Charles Dickens, 1850–1852* [1988], 6:68; Ship's Manifest for the *Quebec*, 15 May 1839, Ancestry.com).

Thursday. 2nd May.

As I approach America the thought of my children, from whom I am again so soon to part, saddens rather than cheers me.

Tuesday 9th April was my last evening in England. I passed part of it with my friend Mrs Stevenson. On my return to my lodgings, after bidding her a sad farewell, I found Mr Coolidge hard at work settling accounts and making preparations for departure, assisted by his kind and excellent friends, Mr Sindry & Mr Bowman. I sat up till one o'clock and Mr Heard aided me in the examination of my last household accounts, which being completed I sought my solitary bed, for Mr Coolidge was kept up all night by the necessity of making various arrangements before leaving London. Mr Bowman staid with him until three o'clock and returned in the morning to an early breakfast. Finally, on Wednesday 10th April 1839, all being ready for our departure, we took our seats at 8. A.M. Mr Coolidge, Mr Heard, Josephine, Jefferson & myself, in the Portsmouth Coach called the Rocket. I drove in my own comfortable carriage to the starting point. Mr Bowman & Capt. Wormeley walked with Mr C. & Mr H. to the same place, and here taking leave of these good friends, we were soon whirled away, passed rapidly down Piccadilly by Hyde Park Corner & turned our backs on the great Metropolis. I was thinking too intensely of all that happened since last I passed the same road to pay much attention to it now. We had one inside passenger, a lady from the Isle of Wight, the rest of the coach being occupied by Jefferson, Josephine & myself. She was a pleasant person, who talked enough and not too much, was courteous without being intrusive, and helped to make my last impressions of England & the English favorable, as so many previous impressions have been.

We reached Portsmouth by four o'clock & found the ship, which was not to arrive before night, already there & waiting for us. We left the Rocket Coach to enter the boat which conveyed us to the Quebec. Her anchor was up and all ready for sailing. I was somewhat dismayed, on being hoisted on board, to see the vessel so crowded & so dirty. It was a foretaste of the excessive discomfort of the voyage—but a fresh easterly wind was filling the sails, and we soon found ourselves borne rapidly onward and bade a long adieu to beautiful England.

Sunday. 5th May.

Twenty five days at sea. An incompetent, lazy Captain, without authority & utterly indifferent. Contrary winds—losing one day what we had made the day before—rough sea—rolling vessel—or rather the Ship rears, plunges, backs, kicks, dashes forward, sidles, starts, shies, tosses, prances—every thing that the most vicious horse could do—Vile smells of bilge water and other abominations—Women all sick—Men all cross—passengers beginning to quarrel—They are, with few exceptions, a very so-so set.—I am constantly suffering from giddiness, nausea, oppression, pains in back & limbs, unwillingness to exertion which I do not indulge, taking as much exercise as the weather will permit, walking on deck whenever I am able, with the aid of two good arms, Mr Coolidge's & Mr Heard's. Thank heaven my boy continues well & active. I read whenever I am well enough and have got through the four last volumes of Lockhart's Scott, having read the three first some time ago. This book amuses without satisfying me. It is, as Carlyle says of it, mere materials for biography, and those in a crude state, brought together in chronological order for some better man than Lockhart to work upon.

I heard both in Scotland & England, that his daughter Sophie's choice of a husband was distasteful to Sir Walter Scott, and that Lockhart himself had found ample evidence of this fact under Scott's own hand-writing, among the letters & papers which he had collected as materials for his biography. Some letters addressed to friends were given to Lockhart, perhaps inadvertently, containing such expressions as these, "that coxcomb Lockhart"—"Lockhart whom nobody likes but my daughter Sophia" &c &c. Sir Walter is said to have yielded only to the conviction that Sophia had set her heart too entirely on the "coxcomb" to give him up without a greater sacrifice than her kind father was willing to require of her. Every now & then, in reading this book, I come across expressions relating to persons or places with whom & which I have become more or less familiar during my stay in England, and this adds greatly to the interest. My pleasure has been diminished by the necessity of reading an ugly Philadelphia re-print instead of the English edition of these memoirs—four volumes being squeezed into one.

Allan Cunningham whom I saw & liked at Sir Francis Chauntrey's, was a friend of Sir Walter Scott. Lockhart calls him in one place "the manly and amiable author of Sir Marmaduke Maxwell" (a romantic drama)—and again, "the high spirited & independent author"—Scott says in his Diary, 14. November. 1826—"We breakfasted at honest Allan

Cunningham's—honest Allan—a leal & true Scotsman of the old cast—
a man of genius besides." Sir Walter afterwards exerted his influence to
obtain cadetships in India for two of Allan Cunningham's sons. He, Sir
Walter, criticises Cunningham's style as sometimes "obscure," and says
that he "overlays his meaning."

In the Diary, Aug. 10. 1826, I see this mention of Lady Anna Maria
Donkin, whose maiden name was Elliot, she being a sister of Lord
Minto and a very clever, amiable & agreeable person. "Went with Anne
to Minto. I like Lady M. particularly, but missed my facetious and lively
friend, Lady Anna Maria. It is the fashion with some silly women and
silly men to abuse her as a blue stocking. If to have good sense & good
humour mixed with a strong power of observing, and an equally strong
one of expressing—if of this the result must be blue, she shall be as blue
as they will. Such cant is the refuge of fools who fear those who can turn
them into ridicule, it is a common trick to revenge supposed raillery with
good substantial calumny."

The **CAPTAIN** of the *Quebec* was Frederick Hovey Hebard (or Hibbard) (1799–
1856), and at the time of the Coolidges' voyage he had twelve years of experience
commanding packet ships. He was commended for his 1830 rescue of a crew
member of the U.S. frigate *Brandywine* and went on to have one of the longest
careers as a captain of ocean packets, working for thirty-five years for Grinnell,
Minturn & Company. He commanded the *Hannibal* and the *London* as well as
the *Quebec*. Hebard worked his way up through the company from the "humblest
position to the command and ownership of one of their London packets" and
became one of Brooklyn's leading men, his wealth valued at $35,000 in 1847. He
bequeathed $20,000 to the Brooklyn Hospital and contributed to the building
of facilities to house the Society for the Relief of Destitute Children of Seamen,
where he was a member of the board. Hebard lived at 118 Columbia Street in
Brooklyn, New York, and was married to Margaret F. Hebard (b. ca. 1809–1865)
(Daniel Hovey Association, *The Hovey Book* [1913], 161; Henry Wysham Lanier,
A Century of Banking in New York: 1822–1922 [1922], 142, 145; Charles W. Leng
and William T. Davis, *Staten Island and Its People* [1930], 1:594; Robert Greenhalgh
Albion, *Square-riggers on Schedule: The New York Sailing Packets to England, France,
and the Cotton Ports* [1938], 336; *New-York Spectator*, 23 Mar. 1830; *New York Times*,
12 July 1852, 21 Jan. 1856, 24 June 1865; Ship's Manifest for the *Quebec*, 15 May
1839, Ancestry.com).

All quotations in this entry come from John Gibson **LOCKHART'S** seven-volume
Memoirs of the Life of Sir Walter Scott (1837–1838).

In 1828 Scott obtained cadetships in the Indian service for **ALLAN CUNNING-
HAM'S SONS** Alexander Cunningham and Joseph Davey Cunningham (*ODNB*).

Monday 6th May.

A fine bright day—sat two hours on the rail where Mr C. & Mr H. made me a sort of "chaise longue" out of ropes & cushions—feeling sick & headachy—there is no such thing as comfort at sea. I go on with the life of Sir Walter Scott. I thought I perceived in London, in my conversations with Miss Rogers, that she was not particularly well affected towards him, (Sir Walter,) and as she takes her impressions very much from her brother, I came to the conclusion that the very irritable vanity of the author of the Pleasures of Memory had been, in some way or other, wounded by the author of Marmion: Miss Rogers alluded to a passage in the Diary where Scott speaks of a dull dinner with Rogers, and expressed her opinion that London society was too refined for the Scotch lawyer and country gentleman, who liked more of conviviality & good fellowship than he found at a London dinner party—preferred whisky punch to Champagne, and broad mirth and the roaring out of a good catch to the quiet subdued tone of fashionable society at the West End. The passage in the Diary runs as follows. "April 17th 1828. Dined with Rogers with all my own family and met Sharp, Lord John Russell, Jekyll & others. The conversation flagged as usual, and jokes were fired like minute guns, producing an effect not much less melancholy. A wit should always have an atmosphere congenial to him, otherwise he will not shine." This I dare say was wormwood to Rogers, not much sweetened by the friendly rather than flattering tone of another entry of somewhat later date. "May 25. 1828 . . . at parting Rogers gave me a gold mounted pair of spectacles, which I will not part with in a hurry. I really like S. R. and have always found him most friendly."— "I have always found him most friendly" is stinted praise to one who claims so much as the aforesaid S. R. Rogers prides himself on his conversational powers and is called one of the best talkers in England. He would be offended at Scott's estimate of this sort of talent. He, Sir Walter, says, "the worst of this talent is that it seems to lack sincerity. You never know what are the real sentiments of a good converser, or at least it is very difficult to discover in what extent he entertains them. His politeness is inconsistent with energy. For forming a good converser good taste and extensive information and accomplishment are the principal requisites, to which must be added an easy and elegant delivery, and a well-toned voice. I think the higher order of genius is not favorable to this talent."—Now this is not a propos to any thing which Sir Walter has said of Rogers, which may be an aggravation of the offence, for he has been mentioning the names of some good conversers among whom he does <u>not</u> mention Rogers. He says "George Ellis was the first converser I ever knew ... Richard Sharp is so celebrated for this peculiar gift as to be generally called Conversation Sharp." Another more general remark of Sir Walter's applies to the style of conversation in the three sister kingdoms. "The art of quiet, easy, entertaining conversation, is, I think, chiefly known in England. In Scotland we are pedantic & wrangle, or we run away with the harrows on some topic we chance to be discursive upon. In Ireland they have too much vivacity, and are too desirous to make a shew, to preserve the golden mean." There is under date of 1826, two years before the dinner party of Mr Rogers where he talks of "jokes being fired like minute guns."

Whilst on the subject of Rogers. I will mention some other anecdotes that I heard of him not long before I left London and which confirm my impression of his vanity & hollow-heartedness.

At one of his own breakfasts a party had assembled one morning. Hayward the translater of Faust was expected but did not appear. Rogers may have been a little nettled by his voluntary absence. The company round the table began to talk of his peculiarities. Soon all joined in ridicule of the unlucky absentee, Rogers among the first. He began to repeat a ludicrous poem written by some wag expressly in mockery of Hayward, & having a chorus which brought in his name at the termination of every verse. The door opened the missing man was announced. Rogers rose & advanced to meet him, holding out both hands to grasp his, and exclaiming in a tone of the most frank cordiality, "My dear Hayward we were just talking about you!!"——Another time in the course of a morning visit to a lady of his acquaintance he spoke of another lady in terms of high praise, and having concluded his panegyric, made his bow and retired. The mistress of the house observed to some other guests, that she had never before heard Mr Rogers give any one <u>unqualified</u> <u>praise</u>. At the instant the door opened and Mr Rogers re-appeared, hat in hand—"But," said he, "my good lady, you must remember that even the Sun has spots!"—and with a second bow he again retired. He seemed to have repented, on the staircase of speaking too well of any body, and returned to utter at least one qualifying sentence. These stories I heard from Mr Kenyon who is really friendly to Mr Rogers and admires his talents, although he acknowledges his habits of "médisance."

Sir Walter Scott's partiality for lawyers is often observable in his Diary. He says April 30. 1826—"We have Mr Adolphus, (author of the Letters to Richard Heber) and his father the celebrated lawyer to breakfast, and

I was greatly delighted with the information of the latter. A barrister of extended practice, if he has any talents at all, is the best companion in the world"—and again, April 26—"Dined at Richardson's with the two chief Barons of England & Scotland . . . far the pleasantest day we have had. I suppose I am partial, but I think the lawyers beat the Bishops, and the Bishops beat the wits."——

I have been much struck during my visit to England, at the omnipotence of this profession, (the Law.) The lawyers seem, in almost all cases, the leading men. Law is the road to wealth, honour, power & place. All other professions are limited in their range; Law only aspires to all things. A clergyman may become a Bishop and be called my Lord, a successful physician gets a large income and the title of Sir—a merchant may in some very rare cases, as in Lord Ashburton's, even buy his way into the peerage; but what are these hard-earned distinctions in comparison with the rewards which await a first class lawyer? Even in fashionable society they predominate in a great degree above the members of all other professions. Merchants are hardly considered gentlemen (though peers are often glad to marry their daughters,) The Clergy and the Faculty count not much in what is called the world. I believe that one great secret of Charles Sumner's success here was his being a lawyer; a clever, well-read lawyer, bringing letters from a man learned in the law, Judge Story, to other distinguished lawyers who took him up as one of the craft.

The politician Richard SHARP (1759–1835) was known for his eloquence and kindness, which made him popular and influential both in Parliament and in society (ODNB).

Joseph JEKYLL (1754–1837), lawyer and politician (ODNB).

The writer GEORGE ELLIS (1753–1815) became friends with Sir Walter Scott in 1801 and often hosted him at his home near Ascot. Much of their correspondence is reproduced in John Gibson Lockhart's Memoirs of the Life of Sir Walter Scott (ODNB).

Abraham HAYWARD (1801–1884) translated Goethe's Faust, earning him acclaim and entrée into salons in Germany, England, and Great Britain (ODNB).

John KENYON (1784–1856), poet, was a lion of London society and a particular friend to Americans such as Daniel Webster and George Ticknor (ODNB).

John Leycester ADOLPHUS (ca. 1794–1862) was the author of the anonymously published Letters to Richard Heber, Esq., containing critical remarks on the series of novels beginning with 'Waverley,' and an attempt to ascertain their authorship (1821), in which he demonstrated with wit Sir Walter Scott's then unacknowledged authorship of the Waverley novels. His FATHER was John Adolphus (1768–1845), barrister and historian (*ODNB*).

John RICHARDSON (1780–1864) was a lawyer and a friend of Scott's (*ODNB*).

JUDGE STORY was the Massachusetts native Joseph Story (1779–1845), a justice of the Supreme Court of the United States (*DAB*).

Tuesday. 7th May.

Bright, cold and with a contrary wind. Small chance of seeing New York by the 10th. We are crossing the Atlantic as the snail crawled up the wall, every day ascending four feet, and every night slipping back three. Patience. Time and the hour wear through the roughest day.

To return to Scott. He seems to have accomplished more in less time than ever man did before. Lockhart says "the grand secret was his perpetual practice of his own grand maxim, never to be doing nothing." He had no "unconsidered trifles of time." Scott was no reader of newspapers—(What an immense saving of time in this one thing only!) nor of Reviews & Magazines. Many people fritter away their whole leisure over the periodical press—a diet by no means strengthening, and well calculated to make intellectual dyspeptics. Scott was habitually an early riser and thought the morning hours best adapted for work. He found his powers of mind & even of body in their fullest vigour before breakfast. He thought the half hour between waking & rising the most fertile in ideas ^the most propitious for^ invention and for memory. He considered the first hour of the morning "most favorable to bodily strength"—He could perform feats before breakfast which he could accomplish at no other time.

I have somewhere else noted down that all Mrs Somerville's scientific studies & labours occupy the four hours between four & eight o'clock. A.M. From eight o'clock A. M. she gives her time to family affairs, society, literature &c &c.

Sir Walter Scott says Oct. 24. 1826. "Dined with Mr Wilmot Horton & his beautiful wife, the original of the "She walks in beauty" of poor Byron." I saw Sir Wilmot & Lady Horton at a party at Miss Berry's. Her beauty has walked away. She forms an exception to the general rule that English women retain their good looks in losing their youth.

I find Nov. 16 th this compliment to Rogers—a mere morsel for such an appetite as his. "Breakfasted with Rogers—Rogers was exceedingly entertaining in his dry, quiet, sarcastic manner."

I did not know until I find the fact mentioned by Lockhart, that Carlyle was the translator of Goethe's Wilhelm Meister which I read thirteen years ago. Goethe wrote to Scott 12th Jan. 1827. Scott answered his letter, & this answer is described by Goethe, "in writing to his friend, Mr Thomas Carlyle as cheering and warm hearted."——

In 1827, Sir Walter Scott was invited by Lord & Lady Ravensworth to meet the Duke of Wellington at their castle near Durham. I remember the appearance of the Castle on the road between Durham and Newcastle, and a queer story which I heard of one of the Ravensworth family. I was walking in the streets of Newcastle on Tyne, with two friends, Mr & Mrs Chevalier of Durham, when they were accosted by a stout, vulgar-looking woman in a homely dress, having something the air of a bustling charwoman. They answered respectfully but seemed willing to abridge the conference and pass on. They told me afterwards that this person was the sister of Lord Ravensworth, once the Honble Miss Liddell, now Mrs Richmond, but parted from her husband. She had been in former days celebrated as a bold rider, a great foxhunter, and was in the habit of galloping over the country dressed in a pair of <u>buckskin breeches</u> under her riding habit. On one occasion she visited a farmer's house on a distant estate, arrived at night, found the farmer from home & determined to remain till morning. There being no spare bed in the house it became necessary that she should share the couch of the good-woman in the husband's absence. In the dead of night the farmer returned. Upon entering his bed-room he found on one of the chairs a round hat, a riding whip and a pair of buckskin breeches, whilst a dark, close-shorn head rested on his own pillow. The first impulse was to drag the Epicene incognito from his sleeping place and bestow upon him a severe dressing with his own whip, which was in part accomplished before the mingled screams of two female voices, and the name of the Honble Miss Liddell shrieked in the most piteous accents of pain & terror, convinced the good man of his mistake.

——How now Cammer, how now, quoth he,
How comes a man here without the leave of me.

On the 3d October, Sir Walter dined with the then Bishop of Durham (Van Mildert) with the Duke of Wellington and

"I know not who besides—Lords and Dukes, and noble Princes,
All the pride and flower (not) of Spain" —but of a far nobler land, England. About one hundred & fifty persons in the old Baronial Hall of Durham Castle. This was before the passage of the Reform Bill, before the Bishopric of Durham had been shorn of it's honours, and the

Bishop cut down from his fair proportions, made a Razee of. When I passed part of a day at Bishop Auchland with the present incumbent, the excellent & learned Bishop Maltby, so much of former state was gone as to make me regret that the loss should have fallen on so good a head. The income reduced from £20.000 to £8000, the dignity of Count Palatine, rank & title, passed away,—Then the stately old castle, so long in possession of the Counts Palatine & Bishops of Durham, now become an appurtenance of the College, it's old chambers & corridors cut up and partitioned off into parlours & sleeping rooms for young men. The Baronial Hall is, I think, the eating room for the Students. How these changes would have grieved the loyal heart of Sir Walter! Even I, who had never known the Bishopric under other circumstances, grieved ^mourned^ over the downfall of time-hallowed abuses I suppose the Radicals would call them

The better sort of people in Durham seemed to me all Tory and they appeared to derive a spiteful sort of pleasure from the fact that Maltby, a Whig and advocate for reform, should be the first sufferer by the new state of things. "He finds his income too small for his rank & for the demands made upon him—calls himself the poor Bishop of Durham—Verily he has his reward."

In a letter to Terry of April 15. 1828. Sir Walter Scott advises his friend who has fallen into difficulties, not to come to Scotland, for, says he, "My countrymen taken in their general capacity, are not people to have recourse to in adverse circumstances. John Bull is a better beast in misfortune."

I am sorry to hear this of my friends the Scotts whom in their own country I admired so much. I remember telling Lady Elizabeth Hope Vere, who asked me how I liked Great Britain, that I liked England & the Scotch. The beautiful country of the first, and the frank, cordial, hospitable manners of the second. It is true that at this time, when I spoke with Lady Elizabeth, I knew less of the English and liked them less than afterwards. There are no people who improve so much on acquaintance.

Lord and Lady RAVENSWORTH were Thomas Henry Liddell (1775–1855) and Maria Susannah Simpson Liddell. Ravensworth Castle was rebuilt in 1808 to architect John Nash's designs (*ODNB*, s.v. "Liddell, Henry Thomas").

Temple Chevallier [CHEVALIER] (1794–1873) was a Church of England clergyman and professor of mathematics at the University of Durham; his wife was Catharine Wheelwright Chevallier (d. 1858). Chevallier's lasting legacy is the Durham Observatory, completed in 1841, for which he began raising a public subscription in 1839. The observatory continues to operate and has the second-longest unbroken series of meteorological observations for any university in the United Kingdom (*ODNB*; "Durham Weather," Department of Geography, Weather Data, Durham University, accessed 13 July 2011, http://www.dur.ac.uk/geography/).

MRS RICHMOND was the daughter of Henry George Liddell (1749–1791) and Elizabeth Steele Liddell, and she lived with her brother Thomas Henry Liddell, Baron Ravensworth (1775-1855), at Ravensworth Castle. Her niece Georgiana Liddell Bloomfield described her as "a singular character, and many are the funny stories told of her. As a young woman she was a splendid rider." In his novel *Tremaine, or the Man of Refinement* (1825), Robert Plumer Ward offered a version of the story that the Chevalliers related to Coolidge. One of Mrs. Richmond's contemporaries noted that "Mrs. Richmond was the heroine of the queer story in Mr. Ward's Tremaine, and she actually did wear the breeches" (L. G. Pine, *The New Extinct Peerage, 1884–1971* [1972], 227; Georgiana Liddell Bloomfield, *Reminiscences of Court and Diplomatic Life* [1883], 8; Elizabeth Grant Smith, *Memoirs of a Highland Lady* [1899], 283; Robert Plumer Ward, *Tremaine, or the Man of Refinement* [1825], 2:64–66).

HOW NOW CAMMER . . . is an adaptation of the Scotch ballad "Our Goodman," which was translated into German and spread into Scandinavia, Hungary, France, and the United States. The ballad tells the humorous tale of a cuckolded husband arriving home to find evidence such as a horse, boots, breeches, and finally a man in his bed, whom the wife explains away as a milkmaid sent by her mother (Francis James Child, *English and Scottish Popular Ballads* [1956], 5:88–95).

William Van Mildert (1765–1836) was the last BISHOP OF DURHAM before the 1832 Reform Act stripped the bishopric of its palatine status and what remained of its ancient secular powers. He was instrumental in the founding of Durham University in 1833 (*ODNB*).

RAZEE: A warship or other vessel reduced in height by the removal of her upper deck or decks (*OED*).

Edward MALTBY (1770–1859), then bishop of Durham (*ODNB*).

Wednesday 8th May.

Wind still ahead with a bright, <u>cold</u> Sun. We are tangled in the Gulph Stream which sweeps us back at something more than the retrograde motion of the Snail. When we are to see New York is a problem to be solved by the winds. Life at Sea, in a crowded packet ship, is weary & dreary enough. I am too uncomfortable to settle into any thing like regular employment. A little reading, some writing, a few stitches of coarse rug-work or knitting, with a rubber of Whist at night—voila tout—To-day I have helped Tom to study his lessons which he says in the morning (not with my good will) to Mr Adam. I have also walked on deck between Mr Heard & Mr Coolidge. This day completes the fourth week since we left London. I find the Life of Sir Walter Scott my great resource. The interest is immensely increased by my having been myself in Scotland & having staid so long in England.

Sir Walter seems to have been much distressed at the death of Sir William Forbes of Pitsligo which took place in 1828. This gentleman had been Scott's successful rival and married the object of his early love. The marriage does not seem to have been a happy one. Sir William had great domestic afflictions of some sort, which are alluded to in Scott's letter of condolence to Sir Alexander Wood the brother-in-law of Sir William Forbes. He also refers to the friendship which had subsisted between Sir William & himself. Nothing could be more generous than the conduct of Sir William Forbes at the time and after the misfortunes of Sir Walter Scott. Scott says "in the whole course of life our friendship has been uninterrupted as his kindness has been unwearied." And farther on, "It is most melancholy to reflect that the life of a man whose principles were so excellent, and his heart so affectionate, should have, in the midst of external prosperity, been darkened, and I fear I may say, shortened, by domestic affliction."

There is something which I cannot understand in the manner in which Sir Walter Scott speaks of his wife. His language is most affectionate. He appears to have deplored her loss long & truly, yet I have heard it said by such persons as Mrs Fletcher of Edinburgh, and I think, Lady E. Hope Vere, that her habits were those of disgraceful intoxication, that she has been seen at the theatre, in Edinburgh, absolutely drunk. Lockhart in summing up the domestic virtues of Sir W. Scott, says, "He was a patient, dutiful, reverent son; a generous, compassionate, tender husband; an honest, careful & most affectionate father." Now this word compassionate is a singular one in such an application. It is also observable that Sir Walter never introduced his wife into one of his poems or novels. His early love afforded him one or two very happy models. The Matilda of Rokeby for example. His daughter Anne is the Alice Lee of Woodstock. His father figures in Redgauntlet. His mother has given some of her features to the Mrs Bethune Baliol of the Chronicles of the Canongate, although this character is taken, in general, from that of Mrs Murray Keith. No where do you find that he borrows any thing from his own Charlotte—his companion of thirty years.

There are at the close of Lockhart's book, some interesting extracts from a Family Journal kept by Mrs John Davy, resident in Malta at the time of

Sir Walter Scott's visit there in 1831. (November.) This lady whose husband was brother to Sir Humphrey, is herself the daughter of Mrs Fletcher of Edinburgh. — Sir Walter Scott died Sept. 21st 1832, at Abbotsford, surrounded by his children. Before he was too far gone to understand what was going on around him, Lockhart was in the habit of reading aloud to him. When very low & retaining his mind only in uncertain glimmerings, he one day asked his son-in-law to read to him — "From what book?" "Need you ask? There is but one." "I chose the 14th Chapter of St. John's Gospel. He listened with mild devotion and said when I had done, Well this is a great comfort — I have followed you distinctly, and I feel as if I were yet to be myself again." During this painful interval between life & death, the books which Scott desired to hear read aloud were the New Testament and the poems of Crabbe. Lockhart read to him passages from the Borough and the tale of Phoebe Dawson which last, "as is known to every one had formed the last solace of Mr Foxes death-bed" — Sir Walter & Lady Scott were buried at Dryburgh. I visited their tombs. His daughters Mrs Lockhart and Anne Scott, & his grandson John Hugh Lockhart (Hugh Little John) lie in the New Cemetery on the Harrow Road, near London.

Coolidge's son TOM recalled his trip "to New York in the old packet 'Quebec'" as a "tempestuous passage of over sixty days." Mr. Adam likely tutored him alone, but Harriet Martineau noted that on her packet ship voyage a New England cleric taught children on the ship's deck: "He took his seat behind the roundhouse, with a row of children from the steerage before him to do their lessons. I wondered at first how he would teach them without books, slates, or any other visible implements of instruction; but when I saw him get a potato, and cut it into two and four parts, to show the children what halves and quarters were, I was assured he would prosper with them" (Coolidge, *Autobiography*, 2; Harriet Martineau, *Retrospect of Western Travel* [1838], 1:19).

Scott's LETTER OF CONDOLENCE TO SIR ALEXANDER WOOD was written from Abbotsford on 28 October 1828 (John Gibson Lockhart, *Memoirs of the Life of Sir Walter Scott* [1837-1838], 4:184).

Scott's WIFE was the Frenchwoman Margaret Charlotte Charpentier (1770–1826), to whom Scott proposed three weeks after they met in 1797. Though Scott was still mourning his rejection by Williamina Forbes, his marriage to Charlotte was apparently loving. Charlotte was ill toward the end of her life and likely became addicted to the laudanum she took to ease her pain. After his wife's death Scott wrote to their daughter Sophia that "whatever were her failings they hurt only herself and arose out of bodily illness" (*ODNB*; Sir Walter Scott, *The Letters of Sir Walter Scott*, ed. Herbert Grierson et al. [1971], 10:39).

MRS MURRAY KEITH was Anne Murray Keith (d. ca. 1831), a Scottish woman to whom Scott professed to be indebted "for the *substratum* of his Scottish fictions" (Sir Walter Scott, *Waverley Novels: Chronicles of the Canongate*, vol. 39, 1st ser. [Boston, 1833], 1:xix).

George CRABBE (1754–1832), poet and clergyman, included the story of Phoebe Dawson in his 1807 poem *The Parish Register* (*ODNB*; *Oxford Companion to English Literature*, rev. ed. [2009], s.v. "Parish Register, The," Oxford Reference Online).

Sir Walter Scott and his wife, Charlotte, were buried at DRYBURGH Abbey, a twelfth-century ruin on the River Tweed in Scotland. John Gibson Lockhart was buried there in 1854, according to his wishes, at the feet of Scott. Sophia Lockhart and John and Sophia's son, John Hugh Lockhart (1821–1831), the HUGH LITTLE JOHN from *The Tales of a Grandfather* (1827–1830), were buried in Kensal Green Cemetery, as is Scott's other daughter, Anne (*ODNB*, s.v. "Scott, Walter" and "Lockhart, John Gibson"; Curl, *Kensal Green Cemetery*, 102).

Friday. 10th May.

Just a month at sea. A weary month — unpleasant & unprofitable. We are still between two and three hundred miles from New York, with light winds, contrary winds or no winds at all. The Captain plays Whist & Hop Scotch, the Mate or first Officer puffs his cigar on the <u>Quarter deck</u> almost in the Captain's face — Mr Adam preaches socialism & encourages the steerage passengers to invade the same aristocratic precincts. Every one seems out of humour. Some of the gentlemen can scarcely devour their disgust at the want of neatness, want of order, want of discipline, want of every thing which should be in a first class packet ship. "Paciencia" as the Spaniards say — the longest lane has a turning.

The night before the last I saw, for the first time in two voyages, something like beauty & variety in the Ocean. Generally speaking, nothing can exceed the monotony of the world of waters as seen from a vessel floating lazily over it's surface, or even tossed by an ordinary swell. The horizon is apparently so limited as to destroy all character of vastness or grandeur. It is unbroken & it's circular, even edge gives you no idea but of a deep, round dish in the midst of which a child's toy-boat has been set afloat. Heaven forbid however, that we should be called on to exchange our uncomfortable & inglorious safety for the fearful greatness of a storm! Let us be content in our pudding dish.

About one o'clock the night of the 8th, or I should say the morning of the 9th, Mr Coolidge who had remained on deck, came down and begged me to rise & take a look at the waters as they then were. Cloaked

& shawled I ventured up and was well rewarded for the effort. There was a fresh wind blowing, the vessel no longer rolling like a lazy tub, moved gallantly forward, the waves were running comparatively high & the spray thrown far above the bows. But the whole surface of the Sea was blazing with phosphoric light, every wave rose capped with silver, inumberable stars sparkled from below rivalling in brightness those which shone above, and the waters as they rolled astern, divided by the passage of the ship, shone with a radiance so intense as to dazzle our eyes. This phosphoric light is white and cold, unlike that of either day or night, of the Sun or of the moon—round the whole horizon, broad, pale flashes illuminated the waters as they rose & fell & the Quebec moved on in a path of liquid flame which bathed her sides, broke over ^her^ bows and flowed broad & free to her wake.

Saturday 11th May.

A bright and rather pleasant day but little or no wind—the passengers wandering about idly and listlessly—the ladies lying about on sofas & benches, the gentlemen yawning, smoking & playing whist. They are, take them altogether, what in slang, which a lady never should use, may be called a rum set. I have been walking on deck, helping Tom with his lessons—(I wish Mr Adam had never volunteered to teach him—he manages him theoretically, and mis-manages him shockingly—yet what beautiful reports he writes about education for the Indians!) I have knit a few rows on my scarf and read some of Lord Brougham's "Characters." But this is not a book to read regularly. It should be taken up a propos to something else—to a history of the times, or a description on the merits of the men whom it pourtrays. It is a Gallery of portraits and only interesting to those already acquainted with the originals. There are few anecdotes or biographical details, but when these do occur they are so well given that one regrets that there should not be more. But this would have been trenching on the province of the historian or writer of Lives, whereas the "Characters" are mere abstractions, judgments upon facts, not facts themselves.

Yesterday I wrote a few lines to Mrs Lyde Goodwin, (the sister-in-law of Mrs Greenwood) in Baltimore, to recommend to her patronage one of the steerage passengers, a poor Irishwoman going out to her husband, from whom she has not heard these six months, and craving no aid in a strange land, but liberty to work and earn her bread in the sweat of her brow. I hope that Mrs Goodwin, who is very kind hearted, may find some employment for her. Take women as you will, gentle & simple, in all ranks, ages & conditions, their lives are full of uncertainty, perplexity, and too often of sorrow. I have at this moment before my eyes, on the printed cover of a pamphlet, two lines from Byron, which somebody has taken as an epigraph for a book he is advertising.——

> Woman,
> Poor thing of usages! co-erced, compelled,
> Victim when wrong and martyr oft when right.

What an unpleasant voyage this has been! How many painful or disagreeable impressions it will leave on more minds than one! Very different from my last, which, except for ^my^ terrible sufferings from sea-sickness, I might think of with gratitude & satisfaction.——

Coolidge is referencing Henry Peter **BROUGHAM'S** *Historical Sketches of Statesmen who Flourished in the Time of George III* (1839–1843).

In 1813 Elizabeth Augusta Campbell (d. 1853) married Lionel **LYDE GOODWIN** (1762–1845), the brother of Maria Goodwin Greenwood (1792–1878). Coolidge received an invitation to stay with Mrs. Goodwin in 1822, when she was consulting a dentist in Baltimore. Maria Greenwood, a girlhood friend of Coolidge, and her future husband, Rev. Francis William Pitt Greenwood (1797–1843), visited Monticello in June 1819 with a letter of introduction from John Adams. Reverend Greenwood baptized the Coolidge children at King's Chapel in Boston, and Mrs. Greenwood was a friend and frequent companion to Coolidge (William B. Sprague, *Annals of the American Unitarian Pulpit* [1865], 485–492; Maryland Marriages, 1655–1850, s.v. "Goodwin, Lyde," Ancestry.com; Malcolm H. Stern, *First American Jewish Families: 600 Genealogies, 1654-1988*, 3rd ed. [1991], s.v. "Campbell, Elizabeth Augusta," Jacob Rader Marcus Center of the American Jewish Archives, accessed 20 Dec. 2010, http://americanjewisharchives.org/FAJF/; Coolidge to Martha Jefferson Randolph, 13 Jan. 1822, Coolidge to Virginia Randolph Trist, 9 May 1826 [ViU: Ellen Wayles Randolph Coolidge Correspondence]).

WOMAN, POOR THING is paraphrased from canto XIV of Lord Byron's *Don Juan* (1823).

Monday 13. May.

During my stay in England I was not always satisfied with the <u>specimens</u> sent out from the United States. I had sometimes to blush for my countrymen & country women. Of Charles Sumner I say nothing. He suited the English better than he did the Americans, but of this we had no right to complain. Of Mr Duer I have already spoken. Of Mr Stevenson I am sorry to say that, a part from his good looks, (he is a handsome portly man,) there is not much to say in his favor. He is under-bred & under-educated, conceited & provincial, speaks bad English & not always good sense. John Van Buren, the son of our President, and according to English ideas, the man of the highest rank among the Americans, except the Minister Plenipotentiary & Envoy Extraordinary, is very superiour to Mr Stevenson in intellect, being acute, clever & quick-wittted, but I believe him to be false, mean & malignant. What in fact may be called a shabby fellow, always doing small things.

At the time of the Queen's coronation almost all the foreign powers sent special representatives to do honour to the young Sovereign & the British nation. Nothing could be more splendid than the dress & equipages not only of the new-comers but of the whole diplomatic corps. Their carriages on the procession to Westminster Abbey, formed a striking part of the pageant. No display of this kind could be expected from the American Minister. Neither his public salary nor his private fortune permitted it, nor, perhaps, would it have been in character with our institutions. But Mr Stevenson had a handsome Coupé & good horses. To do honour to the occasion his equipage had been brushed up & his servants put into new liveries. He being a handsome man and Mrs Stevenson handsomely dressed, they would, if left to themselves, have made a good and creditable appearance. But it was not so ordained. John Van Buren who was notoriously mean in money matters, determined to form part of the shew without expence to himself. He chose to be present in the ceremony of the Coronation, but instead of hiring for himself a proper equipage, a thing most easily done had he not grudged the outlay, and following as the American attachés did, in the train of the American Minister, he chose to squeeze himself in between M^r & Mrs Stevenson to their great inconvenience—and thereby violating a standing law of English etiquette, which forbids that, even on ordinary occasions, more than two persons should sit on the same seat of a carriage—and most especially if the carriage be a Coupé. And thus in the Royal procession, in the train of foreign Ambassadors, the American Minister & his lady made their appearance with the President's son stuck in riding bodkin between them! A sight most ludicrous if not mean. Mr Stevenson was greatly to blame for permitting it. But he had not moral courage to say no, standing in awe as he did of the higher powers at home. He dared not run the risk of affronting Prince John and through him, perhaps, his august father. Mrs Stevenson understood & felt severely, the ridicule of the whole affair. This same distinguished individual, Mr John Van Buren, in his anxiety to save his purse, was accused of getting to the parties no one knew how, and then, when it was time to get away, complaining of want of punctuality in his coachman, and <u>gratefully</u> accepting the civility of a seat in the carriage ^of any individual^ who took pity on his awkward situation, left in the lurch by a mythical charioteer.

Amiable Prince John, whose veracity seemed on a par with his liberality, returned my kindness in taking him home one evening, from a party where, as usual, his coachman had been unpunctual, by trying to make mischief between the Stevensons & myself. But in this he failed. Mrs Stevenson was not a person to let a thing rankle. She called me to account for indiscretion in repeating things which she had told me in implied if not in bespoken confidence. I was able to refute the charge, to justify myself completely, and to retort upon the tell-tale his own accusation.

The Secretary of Legation, Mr Rush, was a well-mannered, sensible & kind person, gentlemanly in his conduct & bearing. Mrs Stevenson told me more than one little anecdote of his pleasant & obliging disposition. Poor woman, she is very fond of an unamiable husband, who is infinitely her inferiour, morally & intellectually.—But for her his position socially considered in England, would be scarcely tenable. She is much liked, he greatly disliked, but of this state of things neither of them seems at all aware.

Mrs. Stevenson wrote to her sister of the inconvenience posed by **JOHN VAN BUREN** that day: "we took him in our Carriage, which was a great annoyance to me, as it prevented my seeing, and forced me to sit back in a corner, so that my friends complained I would not notice them altho they waved their hankercheifs, & threw flowers at our Carriage and sought in every way to attract our attention as we passed them in the procession" (Boykin, *Mrs. Stevenson*, 146).

Tuesday. 14. May.

At length we are in sight of land! The American shore is visible, but the day is damp, lowering, gloomy & cold. What wind there is, ahead. We took in our Pilot between eight and nine this morning and are now doing what I believe is called "beating up"—hoping to get in to-night. I stood looking on the first that I saw of American ground with mixed sensations in which melancholy prevailed over all others. Here are my children but I can hardly say my home. Home I have none. My family are all dispersed. My sisters, who during Mr Coolidge's absence in China, have been with me so much, I have left behind me in France. My daughter I hope to find in Staten Island, but my sons are scattered, Joseph in Virginia, Algernon

& Sidney in the neighbourhood of Boston, one only, Jefferson, at my side. There is no spot where I can collect my darlings around me and call it home. We must visit them at their different places of sojourn, & during the short time that we remain in America, we have no abiding place but a Hotel. A caravanserai where wanderers & strangers find a temporary dwelling from which is banished every thought of home. Soon we are to recommence our pilgrimage; another long, long and longer voyage lies before us. We again bid adieu to our children. Time and Space are now to be measured by years & by degrees, not by months and miles. We shall reckon in distance half the circumference of the earth, in absence so many of it's revolutions round the Sun. Be it so! Let me feel that I am following the path of duty, obeying it's call, and it shall lead me no matter how long—no matter how far!

Boston. June 1839.

We landed at the Quarantine Ground, Staten Island, the afternoon of tuesday 14. May—We found our dear daughter well under the kind care of her and my good Aunt M[rs] Hackley. We remained two days and continued our course into Virginia. Here, at Edgehill with my excellent brother & sister, true & dearly loved friends, was our eldest son,—Three days passed rapidly away. Our daughter was with us, and taking leave of my poor boy, with a sad, sad heart, I returned to Staten Island and went from thence to Boston, where my Twins awaited us in fine health & spirits. They had not learned much at M[r] Green's school, but they were well & happy. But in our absence we had lost one of our best & dearest friends. Aunt Storer died just before our arrival in America. How well I remember the last time that I saw her. It was the 18th June of last year. I was to sail from N.Y. on the 20th and to leave Boston the afternoon of the 18th. I meant to visit Aunt Storer who was not very well at her own lodgings, but she anticipated me by coming herself to say good bye. This little thing shews what she was. Ever thoughtful, ever loving, in small matters as in great, considerate, kind & judicious. From the first time of my arrival in Boston a stranger, to the last hour when we parted not to meet again, Aunt Storer was my wisest, best, most affectionate, most valuable friend.——

We have, after long deliberation & consultation, determined to send all four of our sons to Geneva, to the school of Mess[rs] Briquet & Humbert, to remain certainly during our absence in the East. Ellen continues with Aunt Hackley until the autumn, when she may perhaps join my sisters at

St. Servan. May He who is a Father to the fatherless protect and bless these orphans whose parents, still living, are about to bid them what may be a long Farewell.

Anna Bulfinch STORER (1772–1839) was the daughter of physician Thomas Bulfinch and Susan Apthorp. Her sister Elizabeth Bulfinch was Joseph Coolidge's mother, and their brother was the renowned architect Charles Bulfinch, designer of the Massachusetts State House. Her husband, George Storer (1764–1838), whom she married in 1795, was the son of Boston merchant Ebenezer Storer, treasurer of Harvard. From 1811 until 1830 the Storers maintained a summer residence at Fresh Pond in Cambridge, where they kept cows and grew fruits and vegetables. They frequently invited family members and friends to visit or stay at the house, where they could boat on the pond and bask in country life. Mrs. Storer was a favorite among the Randolphs, who came to know her when Martha Jefferson Randolph boarded in Cambridge. Cornelia Randolph sent a "collection of trees" from Monticello to Fresh Pond as replacements for those that Coolidge had "carried & lost," presumably on her return to Boston from a visit to Monticello in 1826. Cornelia's collection, which she chose "according to my own taste," included her favorite snowberry, a pyracantha, a yellow currant, and the *Halesia*, or snowdrop tree, which "is so beautiful that I send it though I am afraid it will not bear the winter at fresh pond but it is worth trying" (*DAB*, s.v. "Bulfinch, Charles"; Jill Sinclair, *Fresh Pond: The History of a Cambridge Landscape* [2009], 17–18; Harold Kirker and James Kirker, *Bulfinch's Boston* [1964], 78; Boston Church Records, s.v. "Storer, Anna" and "Storer, George," American Ancestors; Cornelia Jefferson Randolph to Coolidge, 12 Nov. 1826, Coolidge to Martha Jefferson Randolph, 6 May 1828 [ViU: Ellen Wayles Randolph Coolidge Correspondence]).

ACKNOWLEDGMENTS

This volume is the culmination of a decade-long collaboration between the Thomas Jefferson Foundation and the Massachusetts Historical Society. The editors first wish to thank Daniel P. Jordan and Leslie Greene Bowman, former and current presidents respectively of the Foundation, and Dennis A. Fiori, president of the Society, for recognizing the value of Ellen Coolidge's words and sharing our commitment to make them available to a wider audience. We owe a special thanks to Peter Drummey, the Society's Stephen T. Riley Librarian, who has nurtured the project from beginning to end. Andrew J. O'Shaughnessy, Saunders Director of the Foundation's Robert H. Smith International Center for Jefferson Studies, and J. Jefferson Looney, editor of *The Papers of Thomas Jefferson: Retirement Series,* have given their encouragement and shared their wisdom as scholars, colleagues, and friends. Doug Wilson and Jim Horn, both former directors of the Robert H. Smith International Center for Jefferson Studies at Monticello, were instrumental in the project's founding.

The editors also wish to thank the many other individuals and institutions who provided assistance in the preparation of this manuscript, including our colleagues at the Foundation, especially Anna Berkes, Jack Robertson, Martin Perdue, and Leah Stearns of the Jefferson Library; Richard Gilder Senior Curator Susan Stein, Elizabeth Chew, Diane Ehrenpreis, Justin Sarafin, and Carrie Taylor of the Curatorial Department; Director of Gardens and Grounds Peter Hatch, Director of Restoration William L. Beiswanger, Shannon Senior Research Historian Lucia C. Stanton, Mary Scott Fleming, Leni Ashmore Sorenson, and Gaye Wilson of the International Center. Ellen C. Hickman and Susan Holbrook Perdue, current and former editors respectively of *The Papers of Thomas Jefferson: Retirement Series,* lent their expertise to reviewing the transcription and annotation, and Heidi Hackford, also a former editor, assisted in the early stages of transcription.

The editors are especially grateful for the work of Christopher Oliver, who took time away from his doctoral studies in art history at the University of Virginia to research and compile the art appendix, a subset of which appears here as the appendix "Visits to Art Collections and Galleries." Ready assistance came from many individuals at the Massachusetts Historical Society, including Curator of Art Anne Bentley, Digital Projects Coordinator Nancy Heywood, and Digital Projects Production Specialist Laura Wulf, all of whom helped with arranging for the photography of private works of art and made accessible works within the Society's collection; and Jeremy Dibbell, former assistant reference librarian and resident bibliophile, offered welcome advice on a wide range of topics. Suzanne Carroll, associate editor in the Society's Publications Department and coincidentally a former Monticello guide, turned her keen eye to the original manuscript to clarify several troublesome items, and Director of Publications Ondine E. Le Blanc provided her knowledge and expertise as we considered some of the ways in which to treat the manuscript. The editors give particular thanks to Ondine, Suzanne, and Sarah Allaback, the Thomas Jefferson Foundation's publications manager, for guiding the manuscript through the publication process to this finished volume.

Our colleague and friend Rick Britton crafted the maps of Great Britain and London with his usual energy and creativity. For the other illustrations that appear in this volume we are grateful to Revinder Chahal, Victoria and Albert Museum; Katherine Chaison, Ipswich Museum; Jean Collier, Bayly Art Museum, University of Virginia; Jamison D. Davis, Virginia Historical Society; Karen Lawson, The Royal Collection, Great Britain; Chris Linnane, Harvard University; Amelia Morgan, Tate Images, Tate Museum; Fulvio Rubesa, Dulwich Picture Gallery; John Benicewicz and Liam Schaefer, Art Resource, Inc., New York; Jeremy Smith, City of London; Cathy Wood, Norman B. Leventhal Map Center, Boston Public Library; and Wendy Zieger, Bridgeman Archive, New York.

The editors also thank John Burnett, Curator of Modern Scotland, National Museums of Scotland, for his knowledge of Robert Burns; Kate Dalton, curatorial assistant, Worcester Art Museum, for her assistance with James and Nancy Dunlop; John Dorsey, Rare Books Department, Boston Public Library, for his assistance unraveling the collection of books given by Coolidge's son-in-law Edmund Dwight; Dr. Katharine B. Patterson, director, Art Studies in Research and Writing, University of British Columbia, for her expertise on George Grote; Dr. M. G. Sullivan, Chantrey Fellow, Ashmolean Museum, University of Oxford, for his understanding of the life and work of Francis Leggatt Chantrey; Will Rieley of Rieley and Associates, Charlottesville, Virginia, for his knowledge of the Coles family; Alan Walker, Special Collections, Toronto Reference Library, for help in locating Anna Jameson's sketches of Canada; and Kate Wilson at the Parliamentary Archives, House of Parliament, for bringing to our attention the engraving of the 1839 opening, in which Coolidge herself may well be depicted.

The Coolidge family's patronage of art and the printed word is perhaps one of Joseph and Ellen Wayles Coolidge's greatest legacies. Several members of the family deserve particular recognition for their leadership in supporting the project and for advancing our scholarship by sharing their knowledge and collections. Gerald and Mary Morgan were among the diary's earliest proponents. The editors are deeply grateful for Mr. Morgan's assistance in promoting the diary project among his extended family, the members of the Monticello Association. Frank and M. L. Coolidge's enthusiastic embrace of the project and their warm hospitality would have made Ellen proud. John Lastavica and Dr. Katherine Lastavica, whose ancestor Thomas Jefferson Coolidge appears as a young boy in the diary's pages, provided the initial funding to launch this endeavor and graciously shared their Coolidge Point home. J. Linzee Coolidge took time to seek out the original diary at the Society, and we thank him and his wife, Elizabeth, for their support and encouragement. To Jack Taylor and Rick Hinton, past and current presidents of the Monticello Association, we express our deepest thanks, and to those individuals who believed enough in the merit of the project to commit their own resources our gratitude is boundless.

Ann Lucas Birle would like to particularly thank former Foundation colleagues Zanne Macdonald, Susanne M. Olson, Ann Macon Smith, Louise M. Lowe, and Kris Onuf, whose transcription of Ellen Coolidge's letterbook is an invaluable resource. My work greatly benefited from the scholarly community at the Robert H. Smith International Center for Jefferson Studies, and especially from conversations with Carol Cullen, who explored Ellen Coolidge's life during her 1999 fellowship. Early advice and encouragement also came from members of the Foundation's several advisory boards, including David McCullough and Merrill Peterson, as well as Richard Wilson, Dell Upton, and Jan Lewis. David Seaman offered early guidance, and his wife, Kelly Sundberg Seaman, shared her knowledge of Monticello as well as her writer's wisdom. Jan Karon's advice kept me on task, and her wisdom is manifest in this volume.

Preparing Ellen's diary for publication unexpectedly led Endrina Tay and I to Washington University in St. Louis, where in early 2011 we discovered Ellen and Joseph Coolidge's library, along with over eighty volumes that had belonged to Jefferson. I would like to thank Endrina, the associate librarian for technical services at Monticello's Jefferson Library, for her skillful collaboration in piecing together the puzzle of the Coolidge and Jefferson libraries. The library staff at Washington University embraced the challenge of reassembling the three-thousand-volume Coolidge library, and I am grateful for the assistance of Shirley K. Baker, Dean of University Libraries; Anne Posega, head of special collections at Olin Library; and Erin Davis, curator of rare books at Olin Library.

To Cinder Stanton, my mentor at Monticello, I owe a tremendous debt for guiding my work from the very start. Cinder's sensitivity as an author, researcher, and artist are only surpassed by her friendship. Likewise, Susan Kern, former acting director of archaeology at Monticello and now at the College of William and Mary, seamlessly combines the traits of friend and colleague, and her brilliant work on the Jeffersons at Shadwell is a defining prologue for the diary. Of all the acknowledgments, however, the thanks to my family cannot be surpassed. To my parents, Jane and Hugh Lucas, I owe my own curiosity and love of the past, and to my siblings Martha Bar, Thomas Lucas, and Susan Cockrell my understanding of what it means to grow up in the Virginia countryside. Hans and Gertrud Birle shared with me their son—a greater gift I cannot fathom. It was Roger Birle who introduced me to the city of Boston and in whose company I continue to learn and love. Finally, I dedicate my work on this volume to my three beautiful children, Eleanor Lucas Birle, Thomas Lothar Birle, and Susannah Lockridge Birle. They are a constant source of inspiration, wonder, and support.

Lisa Francavilla, whose work on the diary filled thousands of her off-work hours, wishes to thank first and foremost her supportive and endlessly patient husband, Patrick Carmichael, and her always cheerful daughter, Stephanie. She is also grateful for the continuous encouragement of her mother, Marcia Francavilla, and deeply regrets that she will not see the completion of the project, the details of which filled many a late-night telephone conversation.

Sincere thanks also go to her fellow editors and friends at *The Papers of Thomas Jefferson: Retirement Series*, Catherine C. Crittenden, Andrea R. Gray, Robert F. Haggard, Ellen C. Hickman, Julie Lautenschlager, J. Jefferson Looney, Christine Patrick, Susan Spengler, Paula Viterbo, and former editor Susan Holbrook Perdue, who have always been ready with advice or a joke, depending on the need. Finally, she wishes to thank her many other colleagues in the history profession, especially Jane Turner Censer, Myra Glen, Annette Gordon-Reed, Cynthia Kierner, Gloria Main, Kelly Schrum, and Rosemary Zagarri, all of whom gave generously of their friendship and their expertise, not only with regard to this project, but toward her larger objective of becoming a historian of the family, of women, and of antebellum American society.

APPENDIX

Visits to Art Collections and Galleries

This list is organized by the date of the diary entry in which Ellen Coolidge recorded a visit to a gallery or to view a private collection. The text in quotation marks replicates her term for the place she visited, followed by a clarification in square brackets if necessary. Each item also notes anyone known to have accompanied her, the date of the actual visit, and the guidebook she consulted. The editors have also prepared a complete database listing individual works of art viewed at each location, which will be made available separately.

27 July 1838: "Chauntrey's Studio" [studio of Francis Leggatt Chantrey, 13 Eccleston Square], visited with Joseph Coolidge and George Ashburner, 25 July 1838.

31 July 1838: "Exhibition of Pictures by modern artists, at the National Gallery" [Exhibition of the Royal Academy at the National Gallery], visited with Susan Searle, 28 July 1838, in consultation with *Exhibition of the Royal Academy* (1838).

31 August 1838: "British Museum," 31 August 1838, including "the Natural History rooms," "the noble Library," "the Egyptian Saloon," and "the Phigalian Saloon." See *Synopsis of the Contents of the British Museum* (1838) and Waagen, *Works of Art,* volume 1.

13 November 1838: "British Museum" [second visit], with John James Dixwell, 13 November 1838. See *Synopsis of the Contents of the British Museum* (1838) and Waagen, *Works of Art,* volume 1.

8 December 1838: "Adelaide Gallery" [National Gallery of Practical Science], visited with Augustine Heard, 8 December 1838.

13 December 1838: James Deville's "Museum of casts" [workshop of James Deville, 367 The Strand], visited with Joseph Coolidge, 13 December 1838.

15 December 1838: "Leslie's house in Pine Apple Row" [studio of Charles Robert Leslie, 12 Pineapple Place], visited with Joseph Coolidge?, 15 December 1838.

18 December 1838: "Dulwich Gallery" [Dulwich Picture Gallery], visited 18 December 1838. See Waagen, *Works of Art*, volume 2.

18 December 1838: "Hamilton Palace," visited between 4 October and 13 November 1838

21 December 1838: "Bath House to see Lord Ashburton's pictures," visited with Joseph Coolidge, Augustine Heard, and Mr. Higginson, 20 December 1838. See Waagen, *Works of Art*, volume 2.

27 December 1838: "Bridgewater Gallery" [Bridgewater House on Cleveland Row, residence of Francis Egerton], visited with Joseph Coolidge?, 27 December 1838, in consultation with unidentified catalogue. See Waagen, *Works of Art*, volume 2, and Jameson, *Private Galleries*.

27 December 1838: "Mr Wells' collection at Redleaf" [estate of William Wells, Penshurst, Kent] visited with Joseph Coolidge and Joseph Di Ribera, between 1 and 15 September 1838.

27 and 30 December 1838: "Rundell & Bridge" [jewelers, 32 Ludgate Hill], visited with Joseph Coolidge?, 27 and 30 December 1838.

28 December 1838: "Mr Hope's collection of vases & pictures in Duchess St." [residence of Thomas Hope, Duchess Street], visited with Joseph Coolidge, 28 December 1838. See Waagen, *Works of Art*, volume 2.

5 January 1839: "Dean St. . . . Angus Fletcher" [studio of Angus Fletcher, 91 Dean Street], visited 3 January 1839.

5 January 1839: "Chiswick" [residence of William Cavendish, sixth Duke of Devonshire], visited with Joseph Coolidge, 4 January 1839.

11 January 1839: "National Gallery" [second visit], visited 10 January 1839, in consultation with Waagen, *Works of Art*, volume 1.

11 January 1839: "Knowle Park" [Knole House, residence of the Duke of Dorset], visited with Joseph Coolidge and Joseph Di Ribera, between 1 and 15 September 1838, with assistance from housekeeper.

15 January 1839: "house of a Mr Lane" [residence of Richard Lane, Regent's Canal], visited with Joseph Coolidge, 14 January 1839.

15 January 1839: "Mitchell's" [shop of John Mitchell, 33 Old Bond Street], visited with Joseph Coolidge, 14 January 1839.

16 January 1839: "National Gallery" [third visit], visited 16 January 1839, in consultation with Waagen, *Works of Art*, volume 1.

19 January 1839: "Elgin Saloon" [British Museum, third visit], visited 18 January 1839, in consultation with *Synopsis of the Contents of the British Museum* (1838). See also Waagen, *Works of Art*, volume 1.

27 January 1839: "Mr & Mrs Leslie" [Leslie residence, second visit], visited with Joseph Coolidge?, 23 January 1839

27 January 1839: "Albert Chalons rooms" [residence of Alfred Chalon, 42 Great Marlborough Street], visited 24 January 1839.

27 January 1839: "National Gallery" [fourth visit], visited 24 January 1839, in consultation with Waagen, *Works of Art*, volume 1.

31 January 1839: "Egyptian Saloon" [British Museum, fourth visit], visited 30 January 1839, in consultation with *Synopsis of the Contents of the British Museum* (1838) and John Gardner Wilkinson, *Manners and Customs of the Ancient Egyptians* (1837). See also Waagen, *Works of Art*, volume 1.

2 February 1839: "house of Mr Rogers the poet" [residence of Samuel Rogers, 22 St. James's Place], visited with Joseph Coolidge?, 1 February 1839, in consultation with Waagen, *Works of Art*, volume 2. See also Jameson, *Private Galleries*.

10 February 1839: "Etruscan room" [British Museum, fifth visit], visited 8 February 1839, in consultation with *Synopsis of the Contents of the British Museum* (1838). See also Waagen, *Works of Art*, volume 1.

14 February 1839: "British Institute" [British Institution for Promoting the Fine Arts in the United Kingdom], visited with Augustine Heard, 14 February 1839.

14 February 1839: "National Gallery" [fifth visit], visited with [Augustine Heard], 14 February 1839.

17 February 1839: "Mr Rogers" [Samuel Rogers residence, second visit], visited with Joseph Coolidge, 16 February 1839, in consultation with Waagen, *Works of Art*, volume 2. See also Jameson, *Private Galleries*.

21 February 1839: "Miss Rogers" [residence of Sarah Rogers, 5 Hanover Terrace], visited 19 February 1839. See Jameson, *Private Galleries*.

23 February 1839: "Miss Rogers" [Sarah Rogers residence, second visit], visited 21 February 1839. See Jameson, *Private Galleries*.

26 February 1839: "house of a Mr Windus" [residence of Benjamin Godfrey Windus, Tottenham Green], visited with Joseph Coolidge?, 25 February 1839.

27 February 1839: "National Gallery" [sixth visit], visited with Sarah Rogers, 26 February 1839, in consultation with Waagen, *Works of Art*, volume 1.

5 March 1839: "Sir John Soane's Museum," visited with Joseph Coolidge?, 5 March 1839, in consultation with Waagen, *Works of Art*, volume 2, and with assistance from George Bailey, curator.

7 March 1839: "house of Mr Windus" [Windus residence, second visit], visited with Sarah Rogers, 4 March 1839.

8 March 1839: "rooms of the Asiatic Society" [Royal Asiatic Society], visited with Mr. Bowman, 7 March 1839.

15 March 1839: "house of a Mr Vernon" [residence of Robert Vernon, 50 Pall Mall], visited with Joseph Coolidge?, 12 March 1839

18 March 1839: "Sir Francis Chauntrey's" [Chantrey residence, second visit to studio], visited with Mary Anne Morrison, 16 March 1839, and received by Lady Mary Anne Wale Chantrey and Allan Cunningham.

18 March 1839: "Christie's Auction room," visited with Mary Anne Morrison, 16 March 1839.

18 March 1839: "Mr Buchanan's rooms" [probably Marshall Soult's Gallery, 49 Pall Mall], with Mary Anne Morrison, 16 March 1839.

18 March 1839: "Rainy's rooms" [auction rooms of Alexander Rainy, 14 Regent Street], visited with Mary Anne Morrison, 16 March 1839.

21 March 1839: "Guildhall," visited with Joseph Coolidge, 19 March 1839.

24 March 1839: "Park Cottage, Blackheath, the house of Mr Sheepshanks" [residence of John Sheepshanks, Blackheath Park], visited with Joseph Coolidge?, 20 March 1839.

24 March 1839: "East India Museum" [in East India House, Leadenhall Street], visited with Joseph Coolidge?, 21 March 1839.

28 March 1839: "Westminster Abbey," visited 26 March 1839.

28 March 1839: "Mr Sheepshanks" [Sheepshanks residence, second visit], visited with Joseph Coolidge, 27 March 1839.

30 March 1839: "a place called Haveringay" [Harringay House, former residence of Edward Gray], visited with Mary Anne Morrison, 29 March 1839.

3 April 1839: "Mulready" [residence of William Mulready, 1 Linden Grove, Bayswater], visited with Joseph Coolidge?, 30 March 1839.

3 April 1839: "Landseer" [residence of Edwin Landseer, 1 St. John's Wood Road], 30 March 1839, visited with Joseph Coolidge?, 30 March 1839.

9 April 1839: "exhibition of Miss Linwood's Needle work" [Miss Linwood's Gallery of Pictures, Leicester Square], visited 9 April 1839.

INDEX

Richmond and Lennox, Charles Gordon-Lennox, fifth Duke of, 109, 112

Riego y Nuñez, Miguel del (Canon Riego), 5, 133, 136

Riego y Nuñez, Rafael del, 133, 136

Rippingille, Edward Villiers: works in Vernon's collection, 299

Robert Menzies and Son, 32

Robertson, Miss, 92–93, 96

Robertson, Mr., 92–93

Robinson, Ellen Jane, 42, 45

Robinson, Ellen Jane (mother), 45

Robinson, John Henry, 341, 344

Robinson, Marianne, 42, 45

Robinson, William, 45

Robinson Crusoe (Defoe), 246, 287

Rogers, Samuel, 4, 6, 8, 9, 170, 233, 255; collection and residence of, 205–209, 210, 211, 240 (fig. 9), 244, 385; Coolidges at breakfast of, xxviii, 7, 234, 240–242; Coolidges dine with, 100–101; correspondents of, 242, 244; EWC on, 240–241, 249–250, 296–297, 299, 363; EWC quotes, 252; identified, 101; invitations from, 203–204, 234; Jameson on, 344–345; *Pleasures of Memory*, 100–101, 266; Scott on, 362–363, 365; Sheepshanks on, 342–343

Rogers, Sarah, 7, 9, 233, 244, 276; collection and residence of, 248–249, 252–253, 254, 385; Coolidges dine with, 8, 100–101, 248–250, 299; EWC calls on, 267, 336; EWC on, 245; identified, 101; outings with EWC, 254–256, 286–287; on Scott, 255, 362–363

Roland, Madame, 199, 200, 296

Romilly, Charles, 297, 301

Romilly, Edward, 295

Romilly, Samuel, 294, 295

Romilly, Sophia Marcet, 294, 295

Root, George Gabriel, 79

Root, Maria Glass, 79

Rosa, Salvator: EWC reads about, 184, 209; works at Bridgewater Gallery, 116; works at Chiswick House, 141; works at National Gallery, 174; works in Hope's collection, 123

Rosetta Stone. *See* British Museum—Egyptian Saloon

Roslin Castle: Coolidges see on Scottish tour, xlviii (map), 75

Rossini, Gioachino: *Il Barbiere di Siviglia*, 92; *La Gazza Ladra*, 56, 57; *Guillaume Tell*, 87–88

Rotherhithe, 58, 59, 60, 61

Roubiliac, Louis François: works at Westminster Abbey, 340, 343

Rowe, Nicholas: *Tragedy of Jane Shore*, 115, 120

Royal Academy of Art: EWC attends show at National Gallery, 47–49; EWC dines with president of, xxix, 300; exhibitions of, 173, 217, 266, 301, 314, 335, 349; and Soane's collection, 281

Royal Asiatic Society, 7, 288–289, 291, 386

Royal George (ship), 52, 55

Royal Saxon Military Institute (Dresden), 16, 17

Royal Vauxhall (balloon), 25, 27

Rubens, Peter Paul: works at Bath House, 103, 104; works at Dulwich Gallery, 99; works at Hamilton Palace, 99, 103; works at Harringay House, 345, 346; works at National Gallery, 163, 234–235, 267; works in Hope's collection, 124; works in Samuel Rogers's collection, 208; works in Sarah Rogers's collection, 248

Rubini, Giovanni Battista, 43–44, 46, 56

rugwork, 106, 152

ruins, 13, 63, 74, 75, 147, 371. *See also* antiquities

Ruisdael, Jacob van: works at Bridgewater Gallery, 116; works at Redleaf, 116; works in Hope's collection, 124

Rundell, Philip, 121

Rundell & Bridge (jewelers), 5, 117–120, 121, 122, 130, 384

Rush, Benjamin (1746–1813, physician), 178, 255, 257–258

Rush, Benjamin (1811–1877, secretary of American legation), 327, 328, 334, 354, 375

Russell, Lord John, 362

Russell, Rachel Wriothesley: EWC reads life of, 283, 285

Russell, William Russell, Lord: execution of, 283, 285